COLOR
CORRECTION
HANDBOOK

PROFESSIONAL TECHNIQUES FOR VIDEO AND CINEMA, 2ND EDITION

ALEXIS VAN HURKMAN

COLOR CORRECTION HANDBOOK:
Professional Techniques for Video and Cinema, Second Edition

Alexis Van Hurkman

Peachpit Press
www.peachpit.com

To report errors, please send a note to errata@peachpit.com
Peachpit Press is a division of Pearson Education

Copyright © 2014 by Alexis Van Hurkman

Senior Editor: Karyn Johnson
Development Editor: Stephen Nathans-Kelly
Production Editor: David Van Ness
Copyeditor: Kim Wimpsett
Compositor: WolfsonDesign
Proofreader: Liz Welch
Indexer: Valerie Haynes Perry
Interior Design: Kathleen Cunningham
Cover Design: Aren Howell Straiger
Cover photo: Kaylynn Raschke
Cover models: Gal Friday

ISBN-13: 978-0-321-92966-2
ISBN-10: 0-321-92966-7

9 8 7 6 5 4 3

Printed and bound in the United States of America

DEDICATION

To my wife and companion, Kaylynn.

I merely create the appearance of beauty.
You make the world beautiful wherever you go...

TABLE OF CONTENTS

PREVIEW: COLOR CORRECTION LOOK BOOK

FOREWORD

This is the book I've been waiting for: the definitive book on grading for colorists and aspiring colorists alike.

I've been involved in postproduction since 1983. Over the years I have color corrected more than 3,000 music videos, countless commercials, and numerous television shows and features. I've worked with some of the most talented directors, actors, and singers in the world. I can't imagine any other job where I could have had such an impact on pop culture. I love what I do, and I'm so happy that this book will lead more people to a fulfilling career in grading.

I started my color correction career in Toronto, Canada, at a post house called The Magnetic North Corporation. Color correction was still relatively new. We had a Rank Cintel flying spot scanner and an Amigo Color Corrector with primary color control, no secondaries, and not much else. How times have changed! Today's colorists have a massive amount of control over the look of the image and can choose from a variety of color correctors to help them achieve their goals.

Back in the 1980s, the only way you could become a colorist was to work at a post house, or possibly a television station. You started as a tape assistant and learned all the basics of video, such as lining up a tape for the online editor and understanding what acceptable video levels were for broadcast. It often took years before you got the opportunity to sit in "the chair."

Back in those days, we mostly color corrected film, and clients were still nervous about letting us put their precious negative on a machine that could possibly scratch it or worse. Because of our limited color control of the images, we colorists were considered a necessary evil (at best) in the film-to-tape process.

Luckily for us, in 1984, the DaVinci color correction system came out and gave us much more latitude in how we manipulated the images. Suddenly, talented telecine colorists became a more important part of the post process, much sought after, and constantly booked. Most of our work came from doing commercials, music videos, and television shows; films were still color corrected only photochemically.

During the 1980s, many people who worked at post houses had come from a television background, so when we colorists starting experimenting with crushing blacks and manipulating color, there were many technicians staring at their scopes and scratching their heads worrying that the networks might reject these looks. Looking back, it's funny to think about how many times I was told I had crushed the blacks and lost all the detail. What was I thinking?

In the 1990s we transitioned from analog into digital. In the analog world there were all kinds of issues that could make a colorist prematurely gray. The telecine itself often had some color drift; to get around that, after we colored a take, we would immediately record it to tape. Even when the telecine itself was stable, the still store's color could drift, throwing off all of your color matching. I still get a knot in my stomach just thinking about it. With the arrival of the digital era, many of these issues went away, and we could usually count on a more stable color correction environment.

At that time, the best colorists became the rock stars of postproduction. Directors and DPs had to have their favorite colorists working on their projects. We had more color control than ever, and when music videos directed by David Fincher, Mark Romanek, and Michael Bay debuted on MTV, the world took notice. What's more, when the commercial world saw how much attention music videos were attracting for their "look," advertising agencies demanded the top coloring talent as well.

But the coloring world remained mostly closed off to anyone who thought they might want to do color grading as a career. You still had to come up through the post house system, and you had to be talented, lucky, and patient enough to slowly build a clientele.

There were no books to help you learn your craft back then. Learning color grading was trial and error and a good deal of frustration. Back then, a grading suite could cost more than a million dollars and needed a lot of tech support. Today, as we know, it's a much different story. It still takes technical knowledge and artistic skill to build a client following, but the opportunities to do so are much more accessible than before.

As the millennium came upon us, digital colorists began to realize the possibility of grading feature films, but barriers persisted. Among other things, the amount of storage needed seemed almost inconceivable. Finally, in 2004, Company 3 built a feature-film DI suite, and I got to grade my first feature; it was *Constantine,* starring Keanu Reeves and directed by Francis Lawrence, for whom I had graded more than 50 music videos. I can't say how thrilling it was after all those years to color for the big screen.

Over the past seven years, much of the film and broadcast world has been transitioning away from film cameras to digital. Digital cinematography has affected the way we as colorists do things as well. Now that we have the capability to color correct raw footage in cut order, we can be much more accurate and detailed in how we grade a project. We can take advantage of all the improvements in color correction systems such as advanced secondary control, windowing, LUTs, and more.

It's an exciting time in our profession. Things are changing quickly, and color correction is finally getting the notice and respect it deserves after all these years. I can think of no more opportune time for the arrival of this new edition of Alexis Van Hurkman's *Color Correction Handbook.*

I'm a huge fan of Alexis's book. This is a great tool for anyone who has ever wondered, "How did they get it to look like that?" Whether you're an aspiring colorist or a seasoned pro, you'll find it an amazing learning tool or a great book of reference. For the novice, it's organized in a way to make even fairly advanced ideas easy to understand and to emulate. For an experienced professional like me, some of the techniques discussed here inspired me to try things in a different way than I might have. I can't think of any major color correction issue that this book does not cover.

And it's all presented in a concise, easy-to-understand format. Reading this book is like taking a master class in color correction. Years of experience fill its pages, and it's there for your reference whenever you need it.

—David Hussey, colorist and cofounder, C03 LA

INTRODUCTION

Color is life, for a world without colors appears to us as dead. Colors are primordial ideas, children of the aboriginal colorless light and its counterpart, colorless darkness. As flame begets light, so light engenders colors. Colors are the children of light, and light is their mother. Light, that first phenomenon of the world, reveals to us the spirit and living soul of the world through colors.
—Johannes Itten (1888–1967)

This book is intended for developing colorists who aspire to master the art and engineering of serious color grading. It incorporates information and techniques that I've found useful during my career as a colorist of narrative and documentary projects. It has also provided me with an excellent excuse to delve more deeply into not just *how* to create the adjustments we make in the most efficient way possible but *why* we make them in the first place and how they interact with the viewer's visual perceptions so that we can exert more direct and informed control over the process.

Although this book generally assumes you're a paid professional who's working in client-driven situations, the information is accessible to anyone with an interest in giving their programs a creative polish, from the do-it-yourself (DIY) filmmaker to the creative editor who's looking to enhance her skill set.

It used to be that the ranks of color timers, telecine operators, and colorists for broadcast were an exclusive and high-priced club. Because professional color grading required half-million-dollar suites filled with dedicated hardware, there were few such suites. Learning to operate such systems typically involved an apprenticeship (starting out as a tape operator) where you had the opportunity to learn at the elbow of the senior colorist before eventually graduating to junior colorist, grading dailies and doing night-shift work, and eventually proving your mettle and getting involved with more serious sessions.

This is changing. With the proliferation of high-quality, dedicated color grading systems on desktop hardware, the half-million-dollar investment has dropped precipitously, opening up the field to an ever-increasing number of boutique post houses that can offer truly professional services, not to mention individual filmmakers and production facilities that are daring to go "in-house" with their color grading.

As a result, editors and compositing artists alike are gravitating toward adding color correction to their already wide skill set. This is natural, and one of many reasons I think this book is an important offering to the postproduction community. There are no longer as many opportunities for apprenticeship with a seasoned professional, and the need for talent in this arena is growing as more and more producers that once would never have considered putting their programs through a color correction pass are coming to the realization that if the program isn't graded, it's not finished.

However, even though color correction is becoming increasingly absorbed into the postproduction process, I make a passionate argument for the role of the dedicated colorist working within a specifically configured suite or grading theater. I don't have a problem with color correction being done in a home-office environment, but no matter where you park your gear, it's essential (as I discuss in Chapter 2) to monitor your image in a proper environment on an appropriate display if you want professional results. I liken grading rooms to audio mixing stages: For both audio and video, the best decisions are made by an experienced artist working in a carefully focused environment that allows a fine degree of control over the process.

Although it's arguable that colorists are perhaps the smallest subcommunity in postproduction, a *lot* of applications are currently available that are dedicated to the task of grading. At the time of this writing, some of the more notable of these include DaVinci Resolve, FilmLight Baselight, Assimilate Scratch, Adobe SpeedGrade, SGO Mistika, Digital Vision Film Master, Autodesk Lustre, and Marquise Technologies RAIN.

Each of these applications differs widely in their real-time capabilities and their overall approach to the grading user interface (UI), yet they all share a largely common toolset so that once you learn the basics of three-way color balancing, curves, lift/gamma/gain contrast adjustment, HSL Qualification, and the use of shapes, video scopes, and grade management, you'll have a very good idea of how to go about getting the job done in any one of these applications.

Furthermore, I've deliberately chosen to focus on applications that are compatible with dedicated control surfaces, on the premise that serious-minded practitioners will come to appreciate the comfort and efficiency that these surfaces offer during long grading sessions.

In terms of the specific applications that I mention in this book, it's impossible to do a comprehensive survey of functionality for every single application. Instead, I've tried to include information that's applicable to the most widely used of the color grading applications with which I'm familiar and to call out notable functions within specific applications where appropriate. For obvious reasons, I created most of the examples using one of four applications that I personally have had installed during the development of this book: DaVinci Resolve, FilmLight Baselight Editions, Assimilate Scratch, and Adobe SpeedGrade. But I've worked hard to make sure that the majority of the examples apply equally well to other grading applications.

This is not to say that the techniques explored within this book are useful only to operators of dedicated grading applications. As the postproduction software industry has matured, advanced color correction tools have snuck into a wide variety of applications, ranging from ambitious combination editorial/compositing/finishing apps such as Autodesk Smoke and Avid Symphony, to more focused nonlinear editors (NLEs) including Avid Media Composer, Apple Final Cut Pro X, Adobe Premiere Pro, and Sony Vegas Pro. Furthermore, if an NLE's built-in tools don't float your boat, additional third-party color correction plug-ins such as Red Giant's Colorista II, Magic Bullet Looks, and Synthetic Aperture's Color Finesse let you significantly extend your editing software's capabilities.

Last, but certainly not least, compositing applications such as Adobe After Effects and The Foundry's Nuke have color correction capabilities built in, primarily for plate matching and effects work, but there are hardy souls who use these applications for full-bore grading work. If you're among that group, I salute you for your moxie.

For all of these applications, if you have access to the basic tools I mentioned earlier, then you'll be able to adapt the techniques found here. I've found that it's almost more important to see the idea behind general approaches to solving a particular problem or creating a unique grade than it is to get a specific step-by-step list of instructions. Once you've got an idea of what would be interesting to do, figuring out how to do it in your particular application is simply a detail. For that reason, I've deliberately chosen to put creativity first and to generalize application functionality as much as possible so that the techniques are applicable on the widest possible array of applications.

COLOR CORRECTION VS. GRADING

At one time (not so very long ago) *color correction* was the description given to color work on video, while *grading* was the term applied to the process of color timing motion-picture film.

As the tools for both film and video have merged, times have changed, and now the terms have become suspiciously interchangeable. However, I would argue that color correction refers to a process that is more technical in nature, of making adjustments to correct clear qualitative problems in an image, bringing it to a fairly neutral state, whereas grading refers to a more intensive process of developing an appropriate overall *style* for the image, relative to the narrative and artistic needs of a program.

Practically speaking, you'll find me referring to corrections and grades in different contexts. When describing the process of actually working on a shot, a correction is an individual adjustment, whereas a grade is a collection of multiple adjustments that together create the overall look you're developing for a shot.

Colorist Joe Owens, who was the technical editor for this book, said it best in a note he sent me for the first edition, which I paraphrase here: "Correction is a sword-fight, while grading is the war." Well said.

THE SIX LABORS OF THE COLORIST

This section is an updated version of material I wrote, originally, for the documentation of another, now-defunct, grading application, but knowing how many people actually *read* user manuals, I felt it was important enough to include here, where it might actually be seen.

In any postproduction workflow, grading is typically one of the last steps taken to finish an edited program, although on-set grading, digital dailies correction, and ongoing grading in sync with rolling project re-conforms are increasingly bringing the colorist into the production and postproduction process at earlier and earlier stages.

Regardless, in the end, every program you work on requires some combination of the following steps.

CORRECTING ERRORS OF COLOR AND EXPOSURE

Images acquired digitally almost never have optimal exposure or color balance to begin with. Just one example of this is that digital cameras deliberately record blacks that aren't quite at 0 percent in order to avoid inadvertent crushing of valuable shadow detail.

Furthermore, accidents happen. For example, someone may have used incorrect white balance settings when shooting an interview in an office lit with fluorescent lights, resulting in footage with a greenish tinge. Unless your client is a big fan of the Wachowski siblings' *The Matrix,* this is probably something you'll need to do something about.

MAKING KEY ELEMENTS LOOK RIGHT

Every scene has key elements that should be the focus of the viewer. In a narrative or documentary video, this is probably the people in each shot. In a commercial, this is undoubtedly the product being sold (the color of packaging or the glossiness of a vehicle). Whatever these key elements are, your audience will likely have certain expectations of their appearance (referred to in this book as *audience preference*), and it's your job to navigate the difference between the uncorrected shot and the preferred image characteristics that correspond to the key subjects within.

A common example is one of the guiding principles of color correction: All things being equal, the skin tones of people in a scene should look as good as (or better than) those in real life.

BALANCING SHOTS IN A SCENE TO MATCH

Most programs, narrative or documentary, incorporate footage from a variety of sources, shot in multiple locations over the course of days, weeks, or months of production. Even with skilled lighting and camera crews, differences in color and exposure are inevitable, even in shots being combined within a single scene.

When viewed together in an edited sequence, these inconsistencies of color and contrast cause individual shots to stick out, making the editing appear uneven and throwing the audience out of the scene.

With careful color correction, all the different shots that make up a scene can be balanced to match one another so that they all look as if they're happening at the same time and in the same place, with the same lighting. Although this has traditionally been referred to as scene-to-scene color correction, I refer to it in this book as a process of shot-matching and scene-balancing.

CREATING STYLE

Color correction isn't just about making every shot in your program match some objective model of color balance and exposure. Color and contrast, like sound, provide another level of dramatic control over your program when subtly mixed and adjusted.

With imaginative grading, you can control whether the image is rich and saturated or muted and subdued. You can make shots warmer or cooler and extract detail from shadows or crush it, all with a few turns of a dial or trackball. Such alterations change the audience's perception of a scene, setting the mood.

CREATING DEPTH

As Vittorio Storaro says in the 1992 documentary *Visions of Light,* one of the cinematographer's jobs is to create depth in an essentially two-dimensional medium. With the tools available in modern grading applications, this task also falls to you to implement where improvements to the original image are possible. This has nothing to do with stereoscopic imaging and has everything to do with simple, two-dimensional principles of how color and contrast affect our depth perception in various scenes.

ADHERING TO QUALITY CONTROL STANDARDS

Programs destined for broadcast usually need to adhere to quality control (QC) guidelines specifying the "legal" limits for the signal—things like minimum black levels, maximum white levels, and minimum and maximum chroma and composite RGB limits. Adherence to these guidelines is important to ensure that your program is accepted for broadcast, since "illegal" values may cause problems when the program is encoded for transmission. QC standards vary, so it's important to check what these guidelines are in advance.

THE COLORIST'S RELATIONSHIP WITH THE CINEMATOGRAPHER

Many, many people involve themselves in the postproduction process. As a colorist, you'll find yourself working with the producer, director, and cinematographer in different proportions that are unique to every project.

The cinematographer's job during the shoot is to work with the director to plan for and implement the look of the program while it's shot. Choosing specific digital formats or film stocks, camera equipment, and lenses, as well as determining the quality of lighting, are all decisions within the cinematographer's domain of responsibility, as is the ultimate quality of the recorded image. For that reason, the cinematographer has a vested interest in your activities.

It's worth emphasizing that if a good range of color and contrast isn't shot during the production, you won't have the data necessary to do a good job—you can't really add anything that wasn't there to begin with. In this regard, the cinematographer isn't working alone; you should also consider that the art department (set design/dressing, props, wardrobe) exerts direct control over the actual range of colors that appear in each and every shot. Visually, the filmmaking process is a symphony of artists working with paint, fabric, light, and optics to create the image that is ultimately entrusted to your care.

Although the producer or director usually has the final say over the creative aspect of your work, the cinematographer should be involved in the color correction process as well. This is usually dependent on the size and budget of the project, as well as the creative relationship of the principals. Typically, the higher the budget, the more involved the cinematographer will be.

DIFFERENT WAYS OF WORKING WITH THE CINEMATOGRAPHER

Another factor in the cinematographer's involvement is the image pipeline that was decided upon in preproduction. Traditionally, a program's overall look was primarily determined *in camera,* through careful choice of film stock, lens filtration, white balance manipulation (in video), and lighting setups.

Although the notion of deliberately exposing the image for later grading is seeping into the field of cinematography, there's still plenty of room, and need, for a traditional adherence to careful photography on the set. When contrast and color is adjusted to taste in the initial exposure, according to the latitude of the recording format, and care is taken to balance each lighting setup for maximum compatibility with the other angles of coverage within the same scene, the need for later color correction isn't simply minimized so much as the potential for creating even more spectacular images is increased.

On the other hand, with digital grading becoming an increasingly affordable and flexible process, some cinematographers are beginning to expose film and digital media in such a way as to sacrifice the immediate projectability of the dailies in favor of preserving maximum image data for the color correction process in post. Methods include slightly (and it should be *only* slightly) overexposing the shadows and underexposing the highlights in order to minimize the loss of detail due to digital clipping and crushing (telecine operators may also do the same thing when transferring film to video for a *safety transfer*). During color correction, the contrast is then easily readjusted to emphasize whichever portion of the image is necessary for the desired look.

When a program's look has been decided in camera, your job is to balance and correct according to the originally intended lighting scheme. If the image was exposed intentionally to maximize image data for later digital manipulation, the creative possibilities are considerably more open-ended and subject to reinterpretation. In either case, the cinematographer's involvement will be invaluable in guiding you through how everything was originally intended to look, freeing you from having to make assumptions (with the inevitable later revisions) and saving you time to focus on the truly important creative issues.

In turn, your job also includes making options available in circumstances where the cinematographer is considering alternatives based on changes during editing, problems with the originally recorded image, or a producer's and director's ambivalence with the originally rendered lighting scheme. You will also find yourself assuming the role of negotiator when conflicts between producers, directors, and cinematographers occur over the look of a particular sequence.

Lastly, issues of quality control must be resolved in programs destined for terrestrial or satellite broadcast, and that is where you need to be mindful of when a requested adjustment needs to be subdued in order to maintain a legal signal. You should always discuss the QC standard that a program should adhere to in advance and be prepared to tactfully find alternatives for or overrule adjustments that violate those standards.

LEARN TO COMMUNICATE

One of the best ways you can improve your rapport with both cinematographers and directors, as well as generally improve your skills as a colorist, is to take the time to learn more about the art and craft of lighting for film and digital media. The more you know about how color and contrast is manipulated on location through all of the tools of the cinematographer's craft, the better you'll be able to analyze and manipulate each clip. Furthermore, the more you know about how a film crew works, the better you'll be able to conduct the detective work necessary to figuring out why one clip isn't matching another. (Was there a wind blowing the gel in front of the key light? During what time of day was that insert clip shot? Did one of your lighting fixtures become unavailable in the reverse shot?)

Cinematography, like every discipline, has its own language. The more familiar you become with terms like *low-key* and *high-key*, different lighting setups, film stocks, digital media formats, and color temperatures, the easier it will be to discuss and understand the cinematographer's goals and suggestions.

SPECIAL THANKS

I want to first extend a deep, heartfelt thanks to the filmmakers who have graciously allowed me to abuse their work in public within this volume. All of these projects are programs that I've personally graded, and they represent a fair spectrum of what you'll see in the real world. All were terrific clients to work with, and I sincerely appreciate their contributions to this book.

- Josh and Jason Diamond (directors) for excerpts from their *Jackson Harris* music video and their narrative short *Nana*.

- Matt Pellowski (director) for excerpts from *Dead Rising*.

- Sam Feder (director) for excerpts from his documentary feature *Kate Bornstein: A Queer and Pleasant Danger*.

- An excerpt from my own narrative short, *The Place Where You Live* (me, director), is featured as well, and I'd be neglectful if I didn't thank Marc Hamaker and Steve Vasko at Autodesk, who sponsored the project.

- Gianluca Bertone (DP), Rocco Ceselin (director), and Dimitrios Papagiannis for their brilliant "Keys Ranch" F65 footage.

- Yan Vizinberg (director), Abigail Honor (producer), and Chris Cooper (producer) for excerpts from Persona Films' feature *Cargo*.

- Jake Cashill (director) for excerpts from his feature-length thriller *Oral Fixation*.

- Bill Kirstein (director) and David Kongstvedt (writer) for excerpts from their feature *Osiris Ford*.

- Lauren Wolkstein (director) for excerpts from her award-winning short *Cigarette Candy*.

- Michael Hill (director) for excerpts from his 16mm short *La Juerga*.

- Kelvin Rush (director) for excerpts from his Super 16mm short *Urn*.

- Rob Tsao (director) for excerpts from his comedic short *Mum's the Word*.

- Paul Darrigo (producer) for excerpts from the television pilot *FBI Guys*.

I must extend additional thanks for the use of clips from programs I didn't work on but that provide unique qualities that are valuable to the examples I needed to show.

- The nice folks at *Crumplepop* including Gabe Cheifetz, Jed Smentek, and Sara Abdelaal (who shot the material) for a wealth of stock videography they provided me with, as well as other materials from Crumplepop's scanned film grain library and film LUT analyses

- Warren Eagles (colorist) for clips of film and video distress from his Scratch FX library (available from *fxphd*)

- Suzann Beck (portraitist) for images from her personal collection of work

- Peter Getzels (producer/director), Dr. Robert Lawrence Kuhn (executive producer), and Robbie Carman (colorist) for a clip from the documentary series *Closer to Truth*

- John Dames (director, Crime of the Century) for clips from *Branded Content for Maserati Quattroporte*

I also want to give thanks to Kaylynn Raschke, a talented photographer (and my lovely wife) who is responsible for the images gracing the covers of both the previous and current editions of this book and for many additional images that appear within numerous examples. She has also gamely put up with my triple-shifts as I've brought this and many other works to light this year.

Thanks are also due to photographer Sasha Nialla, who assembled the models and executed the photo shoot for the skin tone study that appears in Chapter 8. It was an invaluable and last-minute effort that I couldn't have done myself.

Additionally, I could not have written this book without the help of many, many individuals at companies that include true titans of the grading industry (presented in no particular order).

- Grant Petty, CEO of Blackmagic Design; Peter Chamberlain, product manager for DaVinci Resolve; and Rohit Gupta, director of DaVinci software engineering, all of with whom I've been fortunate enough to work with over the years, for sharing as much as they have in both the previous edition and the current one.

- Bram Desmet, general manager of Flanders Scientific, who humored my endless questions during a week spent at BIRTV in Beijing, China, and continued to provide an inexhaustible supply of technical information over the months, along with an invaluable peek behind the curtain of professional display manufacturing.

- At FilmLight, Martin Tlaskal, lead developer of Baselight; Mark Burton, head of marketing; and Jo Gilliver, technical writer, for providing so much great information and so many screenshots for Baselight.

- Special thanks also to Richard Kirk, colour scientist at FilmLight, for providing detailed information about LUT calibration and management, as well as deep, ongoing information about the *colour* science behind film emulation procedures and processes.

- At SGO, Sam Sheppard, colorist, for providing great information, demo time, and screenshots of Mistika.

- Steve Shaw, owner of Light Illusion, for in-depth information about LUT calibration and color management and for film simulation LUTs that I was able to use as examples in Chapter 2.

- Luhr Jensen, CEO, and Jenny Agidius, at Klein Instruments, for providing loaner hardware and extensive information about their Klein K10 spectrometer's interoperability.

- At Autodesk, Marc-André Ferguson, user experience designer; Ken LaRue, lead trainer; and Marc Hamaker, senior product marketing manager, for variously fielding all of my questions about Autodesk Smoke and Lustre.

- At Quantel, Lee Turvey, sales manager (New York); Brad Wensley, senior product specialist; and David Throup, R&D group leader, for providing excellent information, screenshots, and demonstrations of Quantel's Rio and Pablo grading workstations.

- Sherif Sadek, "assimilator," at, you guessed it, Assimilate, for providing demo licenses of Scratch, screenshots, and answers to numerous questions as I integrated Scratch examples into this book.

- Patrick Palmer and Eric Philpott at Adobe for their ongoing support and information about Adobe SpeedGrade.

- At X-Rite, Tom Lianza, director of R&D (Digital Imaging), and Chris Halford, senior product manager (Pantone), for providing crucial details about color calibration. Tom also went the extra mile in doing the mathematical conversions that appear in Chapter 8.

- Andy Knox, operations director, and Chris Rose, technical director at Tangent Designs, for providing control surfaces for evaluation and for fascinating and ongoing discussions about control surface design.

- Steve Bayes, product manager at Apple, Inc., for being a generally great guy and making the occasional introduction when necessary.

- Mike Ruffolo at RTI Film Group for providing images of the Filmlab Systems International Colormaster color analyzer, the Hazeltine color analyzer, and the BHP wet/dry film printer seen in Chapter 9.

- Ronald Shung, product marketing manager at Tektronix, for providing screen-shots of the patented Tektronix gamut scopes in Chapter 10.

- Rob Lingelbach, colorist, and the fine community on the TIG (TKcolorist Internet Group) for their support and for the general wealth of information that's been shared over the years.

- Mike Most, colorist, effects artist, technologist, and all around digital wizard, for the most detailed conversation about the ins and outs of log grading that I've had, which added immeasurably to this book.

- Warren Eagles, freelance colorist without borders, for numerous discussions over the months and for sharing his knowledge so freely with all of us in the color grading community.

- Giles Livesey, freelance colorist and international man of mystery, for sharing some of his key tricks of the trade with me and for insights into the history of commercial looks in the UK post industry.

- Michael Sandness, senior colorist at Splice Here and my good friend and colleague in the Twin Cities, who was a great sounding board during discussions too numerous to mention and who provided much-needed human conversation (albeit about color grading) during my many weeks in authorial seclusion. I'll take a weekend off yet, Michael....

A big thank-you to my technical reviewers for this second edition, starting with digital imaging authority and author Charles Poynton, who graciously reviewed Chapters 2 and 10, challenging my assertions, correcting my math, and giving generously of his expertise. Thanks also to Dave Hussey, senior colorist at Company 3, a veteran artist and true giant of the industry who agreed to review all other chapters despite his incredibly busy schedule. His encouragement, kind words about the content, and additional insights have been invaluable, and I deeply appreciate his foreword to this book.

My thanks remain to the reviewer of the original edition, Joe Owens—colorist (Presto!Digital), defender of the video engineering faith, and generous contributor to numerous online forums on the topic of grading—for reviewing my original chapters and providing terrific feedback.

To all of my reviewers, I owe more beers than are brewable; there was a lot to read, and I put this book forth in confidence having had some of the leading lights of our industry weigh in on my material.

I also want to personally thank Karyn Johnson (senior editor, Peachpit Press), who initially championed the first edition of this book, who went on to encourage a second edition when the time was right, and who continued to give me all the rope I needed to hang myself ever higher as I went ahead and created two books worth of information. Karyn, every colorist who buys this book owes you a debt.

Last, but very certainly not least, I want to thank Stephen Nathans-Kelly (editor), who in *both* editions has gamely reviewed each increasingly enormous chapter, for treating my prose and technical content with delicacy; this stuff ain't easy to edit. With Karyn, Stephen, and Peachpit Press's support, I've continued to create exactly the books that I wanted to, with no compromises. I hope you enjoy them.

A NOTE ABOUT IMAGE FIDELITY

In all instances, I took great care to present realistic grades within this book, and yet it's often the case that certain adjustments required exaggeration to be notice-able in print. Unfortunately, knowing that a digital edition was going to be made available, I've been in the unfortunate position of having to serve two masters with a single set of images.

I feel that the results serve the purpose of illustrating the topics admirably, although I cannot guarantee what certain images will look like on every possible digital device to come. To those of you who are reading this on your tablets, phones, smartwatches, augmented reality devices, or VR goggles, I hope you like what you see.

A NOTE ABOUT THE DOWNLOADABLE CONTENT

NOTE

If updates to this book are posted, those updates will also appear in your Account page at www.peachpit.com.

Throughout this book, you'll see examples of scenes in commercially produced shows that are used to demonstrate various concepts and techniques. The down-loadable content includes a wide variety of corresponding QuickTime clips that you can use as a playground for experimenting with the techniques discussed. These clips are the raw, uncorrected source material for each example and can be imported into any grading application that's compatible with Apple ProRes media. For more information about the media on the disc, please see the Read Me file that accompanies the download.

At the back of this book is a card with an access code. To access the files, please do the following:

1. On a Mac or Windows computer, go to www.peachpit.com/redeem and enter the code at the back of your book.

2. If you do not have a Peachpit.com account, you will be prompted to create one.

3. The download files will be listed in the Lesson & Update Files tab on your Account page.

4. Click the file links to download them to your computer.

This process may take some time to complete, depending on the speed of your com-puter and Internet connection.

COLOR CORRECTION WORKFLOWS

In order to start grading, you need to get the project you've been hired to work on into the application you're going to be working with. As unexciting a topic as this may seem, understanding how it works is vital, so this is where we shall begin. This chapter isn't meant to provide an exhaustive overview of postproduction work-flows, nor is it intended to cover every format you can expect to have to deal with as a colorist. Instead, it's meant to give you a better window into how the colorist fits into the postproduction process and what decisions get made that will affect your well-being.

This chapter has been written with the medium-sized boutique facility in mind. Colorist/finishers working in smaller outfits will undoubtedly have much more on their plate, while colorists at top-level facilities get to ignore a lot of this and focus on the art of the grade. I'm guessing you're probably somewhere in the middle, so if you have any influence at all over how the footage you'll grade will be shot, or how the workflow that the post supervisor organizes will go down, read on.

ARE YOU GRADING FOR CINEMA, BROADCAST, OR THE WEB?

This is a trick question, because it doesn't matter. Whether you're working on a movie that's going to 300 theaters, a network or cable television episode that's going to broadcast, or a science-fiction web series that's going to YouTube or Vimeo, your program needs to be graded. If you're treating your project in a professional manner, then the workflows are similar if not *identical*. This goes double if your client says, "I think my program actually looks fine as it is, I don't know what really needs grading...."

It's a misconception that color correction or color grading (whichever you want to call it) is primarily about fixing problems and dealing with broadcast-safe issues. The notion that the colorist's job is curative-only assumes that if your video is well-shot and headed straight to video/late-night cable/wherever-on-the-Web, then color grading doesn't matter much and you can skip it. The truth is, while fixing problems is a meaningful part of what the color correction process is all about, that's not actually the main reason you want to incorporate color grading into your workflow.

You grade projects because *you want them to look as good as they can.* You grade them because you want to emphasize and preserve image detail that's important and to lend a sense of style and occasion when necessary to finesse the project's look. And this is something you need to do whether your program was shot on a RED Dragon, an ARRI Alexa, a 5D Mark III DSLR, or a GoPro taped to someone's crash helmet.

WHERE COLORISTS FIT IN

Color correction, as I'm fond of saying, ideally starts in preproduction. It doesn't have to wait until the very end of the postproduction process (although it all too frequently does). You, as the colorist, can meaningfully contribute to the overall process of preproduction, production, and postproduction in a variety of ways.

- **Preproduction:** At this stage, you can recommend shooting formats based on the postproduction needs for a particular project, work with the cinematographer and director during camera tests to evaluate how differently graded looks hold up with different cameras and shooting conditions, and turn these looks into evaluation lookup tables (LUTs) that can be loaded into on-set production displays and used by the digital imaging technician (DIT) during the creation of dailies.

- **Production:** DITs incorporate many skills of the colorist into their job description as they help the cinematographer to evaluate the images being shot, manage the monitored image in video village, create on-set grades, and generate digital dailies for use in postproduction. On union shoots, colorists who aren't in the camera union cannot participate directly in this process on-set, but communication between a DIT and the colorist is often essential, especially in situations where grading data, whether LUTs, CDL, or other presaved grading formats, is being exchanged along with the recorded media.

- **Editing:** Prior to editing, productions using raw camera formats or highly compressed long-GOP or H.264-compressed media must have this potentially unwieldy camera original media turned into a set of easily editable QuickTime or MXF media files. This process is usually referred to as creating "digital dailies" and may involve syncing audio and applying or creating grades for the media so the editor and director aren't stuck looking at low-contrast, ungraded media for the duration of postproduction. Sometimes this work is done on-set by a DIT; sometimes it's done by a colorist back at the suite. As an edit nears completion, colorists are sometimes called upon to do a quick "offline color" pass for projects that will be undergoing test screenings. Sometimes this color pass is the beginning of the final grade, sometimes not.

- **Visual Effects (VFX):** During the process of creating visual effects, colorists are often called upon to help grade and match greenscreen elements and to grade (and regrade, and regrade again) finished VFX being incorporated back into the edit. There's usually a lot of back and forth between color and VFX when a program is undergoing final finish.

- **Grading:** For the colorist, this is the main event; once the edit has been locked (one hopes) with all final media and VFX elements (good luck with that), the edited timeline using the digital dailies is *reconformed* to use the camera original media instead. This is done within the grading application being used, usually by an assistant at a large facility or by the colorist at a tiny one. At that point, the colorist takes control of the timeline to adjust the color, contrast, look, and feel of every clip in the project.

- **Finishing:** Sometimes, some or all of the finishing process—finalizing titles; adding header elements such as the slate, bars, and tone; making last-minute edits; laying in the audio mix; taking care of VFX-like tasks such as light digital paint, compositing, or simple blurring to remove unlicensed materials from the image—falls to the colorist, depending on the size of your facility and on the skill set of the other folks you work with. Top-level colorists usually focus *only* on the grade, while colorists at smaller boutiques are often invited to a broader level of participation in these sorts of activities.

- **Mastering:** Increasingly, the tools for final mastering of a finished project are being incorporated into the very grading software that colorists use, whether the program is being output to tape, rendered and copied to SSD as a digital master, or exported as a Digital Cinema Package (DCP) for cinema distribution. Again, dedicated colorists aren't usually involved with this process, but colorists at smaller facilities may very well be.

These are all the aspects of preproduction and postproduction you may be expected to weigh in on, depending on the budget and the workflow of the project you're participating in. Of course, on most projects the post supervisor will simply wait until they're almost finished with the edit and then give you a call, in which case you get what you get.

Ideally, they call you early enough in the editing process so that you can talk them through what will be necessary to conform the project they're editing in their NLE of choice to your grading application of choice. Oftentimes, small decisions made early on can make all the difference between a five-minute conform and days of tedious work.

BEFORE THE SHOOT: CHOOSING A RECORDING FORMAT

If anyone actually asks you, the colorist, what format would be best to shoot for the best possible experience in post, then you're a lucky, lucky person. Unfortunately, the answer is not as simple as "the highest-quality format you can afford," although that is certainly a rational first response. In truth, there are a variety of ways to obtain high-quality media that's suitable for grading, and the right one depends on the budget, the schedule, and the style of shooting a production will employ.

I'm making the deliberate decision not to talk about specific cameras in this section. For you as the colorist, the data format of the recorded media is much more important than the particular camera being used, although one would hope the cinematographer chooses good glass (lenses) to shoot with. Moreover, digital cameras are such a moving target that it's pointless to discuss them in print; new models that have surpassed or succeeded any that I'd recommend would already be available by the time you read this. However, the media formats these cameras record to don't change nearly as quickly, and there are certain characteristics that distinguish one format from another that you should be familiar with.

FILM

If anyone ever asks you whether they should shoot 35mm film and their budget is sufficient to the task, you should probably just say yes. While this book is primarily occupied with the process of digital grading workflows and techniques, film is easily (if not cheaply) made into digital media through the use of a film scanner, which ingests each reel of negative or reversal film frame by frame and produces 2K or 4K DPX image sequences with reel information and timecode based on the frame numbers that were scanned. Scanned film DPX sequences have lots of latitude for later adjustment, can be converted into more easily edited offline or online-quality formats using the same techniques discussed in this chapter, and can be either graded and finished via online-quality transcodes or matched back to the finally edited sequence for grading and finishing at maximum quality.

Film scanning workflows will continue to be with us long after film is no longer used as a regular acquisition format because of the necessity of digitally converting material from film archives around the world, either to remaster older programs or to incorporate archival media into contemporary projects. If you're interested in digital intermediate film workflows, consider reading Jack James' *Digital Intermediates for Film and Video* (Elsevier, 2006) to get started.

RAW VS. "MASTERING-QUALITY" CODECS

When shooting digitally, one of the most basic decisions any production needs to make is whether to record to a raw format such as RED raw, ARRI raw, or CinemaDNG, or to a more highly compressed "mastering quality" format such as QuickTime or MXF (discussed in the next section). Most digital cinema cameras have the ability to do both, and increasingly smaller cameras are being made to record raw video data as well, such as those made by Blackmagic Design, and others thanks to third-party camera modifications available via the open source Magic Lantern project.

Raw camera formats record linear light data directly from the sensor to a file. Some use compression to make these potentially huge files more manageable in post (RED raw is a notable example); others don't. Since digital cinema cameras are so named because they use a single large-format image sensor—typically the equivalent of a super 35mm or super 16mm film aperture—the main thing you need to understand about raw media is that it must be *debayered* or *demosaiced* in order to produce an image that you can work with and watch.

The advantage of media in a raw format is that, since raw format records everything the camera sensor sees, it provides the colorist with the maximum amount of image data to work with in postproduction. Typically, any ISO or aperture settings you make with a camera shooting raw affect only how that image is monitored on the set and what default camera metadata is written to each raw file, rather than modifying the image data that's being recorded. Changes made to the image being monitored from the camera will certainly change how the cinematographer is lighting the set, but the fact remains that you can change this metadata after the fact as you begin grading raw clips. This is a fantastic amount of flexibility.

One other advantage is that raw media formats that are also compressed (meaning that the color space of the media is raw even if the data format is not) can be quite small, easing storage space and bandwidth requirements necessary for working on a project.

However, raw formats have disadvantages, depending on your point of view. They are usually difficult or impossible to edit directly, necessitating conversion to a different format in a second step and possibly a reconform later when the time comes for grading, adding time and complexity to the postproduction process. Furthermore, recording in raw formats produces large amounts of data that need storage and backup. Perhaps the biggest liability of raw formats is that they require a certain amount of postproduction know-how to incorporate smoothly into a given workflow, and the benefits may not seem immediately worthwhile. For all of these reasons, cameras usually provide the option to record to other formats.

QUICKTIME OR MXF MEDIA

Alternately, most digital cinema cameras have the ability to record either QuickTime ProRes (usually either ProRes 422 [HQ] or ProRes 4444) or MXF (typically using DNxHD) video media. Furthermore, even if your particular camera is constrained in the media formats it supports, many productions elect to output uncompressed video data from a camera's HD-SDI or HDMI connection to an external digital recorder of some kind, which in turn records QuickTime or MXF media.

Either way, the advantage of recording to one of these formats, instead of raw, is that it dramatically simplifies your postproduction pipeline since you can copy the QuickTime or MXF media straight from the camera into your editor's system, and they can start cutting immediately. Furthermore, when they're finished, they can easily hand the resulting project and its media off to grading and finishing without the need to reconform to media in another format.

These workflow advantages are significant, but there is an additional consideration. When recording to QuickTime or MXF, you usually have the option (depending on the camera) to shoot either log-encoded media or Rec.709 (BT.709) media. Log-encoding is explained in more detail later in this chapter, but to simplify for now, the main difference is in how the contrast of the image is recorded, which is important.

NOTE

While camera menus typically present this option as Rec.709 (as we'll refer to it in the next paragraph as we discuss menu options), this book adheres to the naming convention of BT.709.

Log-encoded media compresses the contrast of the image captured by the sensor in order to preserve the greatest amount of latitude for adjustment within the available bit-depth of these formats (either 10-bit or 12-bit depending on the codec you use). This gives the colorist the greatest amount of image data to work with when it comes time to do the grade. Even though log-encoded media looks strange when uncorrected, this is a good thing, although it means that the editor is going to have to apply either a correction or a filter, or they will have to enable a monitoring setting if they want to see what the media actually looks like straight out of the camera (as opposed to working with a duplicate set of normalized dailies that have cloned timecode and reel information). This isn't really a big deal but needs to be factored in. Friends don't let friends edit log-encoded media without correction.

The other option—recording QuickTime or DNxHD media as normal-looking Rec.709 video—is guaranteed to make your colorist cranky. While Rec.709 is drop-dead simple to monitor, simple to work with (no corrections necessary), and simple to conceptualize in terms of workflow, the reduction in available latitude for adjustment between log-encoded and normalized Rec.709 media is *significant*. If you're shooting magazine show segments that need to be rushed to air, then the advantages of recording Rec.709 video probably outweigh the disadvantages. However, if you're shooting a music video or narrative production that would benefit from detailed grading, then shooting straight to Rec.709 would be doing the project, and the colorist, a disservice. And if you're a shooter and you do this without asking anyone, it just might get you fired.

H.264 MEDIA

On the opposite end of the scale from digital cinema cameras are ENG-style cameras, DSLRs, and crash-cams that record highly compressed H.264 media. However, be aware that not all H.264 formats are created equally. The H.264 standard can use any one of a variety of standardized *profiles*, each of which uses a higher or lower level of compression and ratio of chroma subsampling. This affects the data rate of the files that are recorded, resulting either in higher-quality files that are larger or in lower-quality files that are smaller. Furthermore, each profile can be encoded at one of a number of *levels*, meaning that any given profile can be throttled up or down to fine-tune the ratio of quality to size used to encode your media.

Practically speaking, different cameras record video using different profiles at different levels. The combination used by your camera will affect the quality of the media that's recorded in addition to the quality of that camera's lens system, digital sensor, and image processor. Taking this into consideration, your selection of camera has a big impact on your final visual result, as well as how much latitude for grading the recorded media will have.

Colorists in general tend to have a really bad attitude about H.264 video, and for good reason. The deadly combination of high compression and limited chroma subsampling (explained in the next section) usually means that the latitude for adjustment of DSLR media is significantly more limited than that of cameras shooting raw, QuickTime, or MXF media. And woe to the client who asks a colorist to match GoPro footage to their camera raw ARRI Alexa media (and they will). There's only so much you can do.

However, the prudent colorist will bear in mind that a job is a job, and while these media formats may be abominable from an imaging purist's point of view, the cameras that shoot these formats tend to be small, light, inexpensive, documentary- and low budget-friendly, and in some cases they are useful for situations in which no other camera would possibly work, such as the aforementioned GoPro cameras attached to every crazy place you can imagine. There are a lot of projects that simply wouldn't exist were it not for these cameras, and that's worth keeping in mind.

To provide a gentle attitude adjustment, I'll share some personal history. I came up as a colorist during the transition from analog Beta SP to DigiBeta, in the time when the industry first embraced DV-25 digital video as a production format. I did the vast majority of my early grading work for clients shooting DV-25, with latitude that was positively abysmal when compared even to today's H.264 media formats. And grade it I did, as hard and as detailed as I could. Sure, you can't do miracles, and any significant adjustment you make to the image will likely introduce more noise than you'd wish, but there's a lot you can still do if you stop complaining about it and use the tools. Tough love, my friends.

Of course, if anyone asks you, tell them to shoot raw.

> **NOTE**
>
> As mentioned earlier, the Magic Lantern project is an open source software hack for modifying various DSLR cameras to shoot raw. While I neither advocate nor discourage its use, it's worth pointing out that raw media recording is expanding to ever smaller cameras.

UNDERSTANDING CHROMA SUBSAMPLING

To enable recording to ever-smaller storage devices, different video formats discard varying proportions of chroma information from the signal, and this also affects how much you can stretch contrast before introducing noise. As with the difference between log-encoded and Rec.709 media, you *want* media that's recorded with the most chroma you can get, but what you get depends on the camera's capabilities and the media format being recorded.

To put things into perspective, 4:4:4 chroma-sampled media stores 100 percent of the chroma information and thus has an impressive amount of latitude for exposure correction. This allows the colorist to lighten dark shots aggressively before artifacts such as excessive noise become a problem. Digital cinema cameras shooting raw typically shoot 4:4:4 data, as do cameras that shoot ProRes 4444 and DNxHD 444. Most low-cost cameras do not (unless they're tethered to an external recorder).

The next step down is the 4:2:2 chroma-sampled media that's typical of high-end HD camcorders. Media encoded at 4:2:2 chroma subsampling has a fair amount of latitude within which a colorist can adjust contrast by a decent amount before noise becomes a problem. ProRes 422 and most other DNxHD formats are both 4:2:2 chroma-subsampled formats, which are considered suitable for broadcast. It's also worth mentioning that while there is an H.264 profile that utilizes 4:2:2 chroma-subsampling, few devices use it.

The majority of consumer-level and DSLR cameras that record to H.264-based video formats encode 4:2:0 chroma-sampled media. This discards three-quarters of the chroma data in a manner considered to be perceptually indistinguishable from the original, in an effort to shrink file sizes to create media that's more manageable in low-cost workflows. While in many cases 4:2:0-subsampled source media is considered suitable for professional work, the discarded color information makes it difficult to make significant adjustments to contrast without introducing noise. This type of chroma subsampling can also make various types of visual effects work, such as greenscreen compositing, more challenging to accomplish.

However, for many types of programs, the advantages in cost and ease of use far outweigh the disadvantages, and it is to your DP's advantage to shoot such highly compressed formats with the best lighting and exposure possible in order to make the most of the format's limited bandwidth and to minimize the necessity of the colorist having to make difficult decisions later.

PREEMPTIVELY UPCONVERTING 4:2:0 MEDIA IS OFTEN A WASTE OF TIME

If your video was originally recorded with 4:2:0 chroma sampling, preemptively convert-ing it to a 4:2:2 or 4:4:4-subsampled format before you conform the media for grading can make these clips easier to work with in terms of real-time decoding performance, but it won't, by itself, improve image quality. Keep in mind that a 4:2:0 to 4:4:4 conver-sion is automatically performed as the first step of the internal image processing pipeline by nearly all grading applications, which typically work in 32-bit floating-point 4:4:4 color space internally as a matter of course. So, doing this conversion prior to grading as a sepa-rate step is unnecessary unless you need to convert the media from a format that's not supported by your grading software to one that is.

On the other hand, you *do* want to render your final color-corrected output out of your grading application to a 4:2:2 or 4:4:4 subsampled format in order to retain the higher-quality image processing that your grading software produces. One tip, though: It's tempting to render projects using media acquired with a 4:2:2 or 4:2:0 chroma subsam-pling ratio out to a 4:4:4 chroma-sampled format for mastering. This is fine, but given what you started out with, this will generate huge files that will likely have no appreciable increase in quality over mastering to a less storage-intensive 4:2:2 chroma-subsampled format. However, if your source media was originally acquired in a 4:4:4 sampled format, then mastering to a 4:4:4 format is obviously ideal if you want to retain all the quality of the original.

COMPRESSION AND BIT DEPTH

Different cameras let you choose among formats using differing amounts of com-pression. It goes without saying that less compression is better than more. For DSLR cameras recording H.264 video, common data rates range from 17–42 megabits per second (Mbps), depending on the frame size, frame rate, and level you choose (if these qualities are user selectable). This is an important consideration that differen-tiates more expensive professional camcorders, which typically offer more choices for recording less compressed video that can range from 145–440 Mbps (although the differing compression technology means this is not an apples-to-apples com-parison). Additionally, most low-cost video acquisition formats are nearly always 8-bit, while 10- and 12-bit video capture is available for more expensive camcorders and digital cinema cameras.

H.264 compression is designed to be as visually imperceptible as possible; however, it's processor intensive to decode and can exacerbate the kinds of artifacts you get from chroma subsampling in situations where you need to make dramatic adjust-ments. In the editorial process, it's common to transcode H.264 media to another, more editing-friendly codec to reduce the processing overhead (freeing resources for real-time effects performance), and usually you end up transcoding to a 4:2:2

subsampled format when you do this, but the advantage of this workflow at this particular stage of postproduction is to improve real-time performance, not to improve image quality (as discussed previously).

As with chroma subsampling, promoting your video from a highly compressed 8-bit format to a less-compressed 10- or 12-bits-per-channel format does nothing to immediately improve the image. Keep in mind that image data that was discarded by compression and chroma subsampling while recording is lost forever, and most modern grading applications automatically promote any clip to 32-bit floating-point within the image processing pipeline regardless. However, rendering your final color-corrected output to a 10- or 12-bit format preserves any higher-quality image processing or compositing done by your grading application and is highly recommended.

LOG VS. NORMALIZED MEDIA

Most digital cinema cameras offer the option of recording either *logarithmically encoded* ProRes or DNxHD media. Furthermore, you usually have the option of debayering raw media to *logarithmic-encoded* formats in your grading software. In both cases, creating log-encoded media lets you preserve the greatest latitude for adjustments in grading.

While each camera has a differing method of log-encoding that is customized to take maximum advantage of its particular sensor, many are based on the Cineon log curve that was originally developed by Kodak for scanning the 13 stops of latitude that film is said to record into the Cineon and DPX image sequence formats, in an effort to preserve as much detail as possible within the 10 bits per channel of data these formats use.

Log-encoded media should be considered as a sort of "digital negative," and while the initial appearance of log-encoded media is unpleasant, being deliberately low-contrast and desaturated, the recorded image preserves an abundance of image data that can be extracted for maximum flexibility in the grading process.

When debayering raw media, these log standards are usually available as a gamma setting of some kind. As of this writing, these standards include the following:

- **Log C:** Media recorded by ARRI Alexa cameras can be recorded or debayered using Log-C gamma and color processing, which is similar to the standard Cineon Log gamma curve.

- **REDLog Film:** Media recorded by RED cameras can be recorded or debayered using this logarithmic gamma setting that's designed to remap the original 12-bit R3D data similarly to the standard Cineon gamma curve, and this media is compatible with most log workflows, including those intended for film output.

- **S-Log** and **S-Log2:** Sony's proprietary S-Log gamma settings for its digital cinema line of cameras are very different from the Cineon curve, owing to their wide dynamic range. The original S-Log was introduced with the Sony F3 camera. S-Log2 was introduced with the Sony F65 and F55 cameras, owing to the even greater dynamic range those cameras offer. There are two methods that Sony recommends for normalizing this media using LUTs. A 1D LUT can be used to transform S-Log and S-Log2 clips into a standard Cineon (or Log-C) curve first, if that suits your workflow. Or, you can use a dedicated LUT to normalize S-Log and S-Log2 media directly. For more information on these formats, search the Web for Sony's document "S-Log: A new LUT for digital production mastering and interchange applications."

- **BMD Film:** Blackmagic Design's logarithmically encoded gamma setting is a modified version of the standard Log-C curve. This modifications is designed to emphasize the strengths of the sensors used by the Blackmagic Design cameras.

Despite the differences among each camera manufacturer's brand of log-encoding, the process of *normalizing* log-encoded data to match the appearance of the original scene is essentially a careful contrast adjustment, and there are several ways you can accomplish it, depending on the capabilities of your grading system. The process of normalizing and grading log-encoded media is covered in both Chapter 3 and Chapter 4.

PRESERVING QUALITY BY "SHOOTING FLAT"

A common strategy for preserving image quality when shooting with DSLRs that lack log-encoding is to instead use the in-camera menu settings to create an image recording profile with "flat" contrast in order to preserve highlights and shadows at the extreme ends of signal bandwidth. The idea is that by not "precorrecting" your image in-camera to boost its contrast, risking clipping of highlight or shadow detail that you might want to keep, you improve your ability to make more careful exposure decisions later, during the color correction process.

It's important to point out that "shooting flat" really means "recording image data flatly." In other words, it is neither necessary nor desirable to deliberately light your scene in a low-contrast manner. Instead, light the scene however you like—low key, high key, whatever—and instead use the settings of your camera to record a low-contrast signal that will preserve as much as the image data as is possible.

Similar to log-encoded media, clips recorded using flat data result in lackluster images when you first see them. However, that's just because they haven't been color corrected yet. Such "flat" imagery can result in superior shadow and highlight detail when you readjust contrast during the color correction process, but there are a couple of things you might want to keep in mind.

First, even though you're adjusting your camera settings to shoot low-contrast data in order to avoid clipping the bottom and top of the signal, you don't want to shoot *too* low contrast, or you won't be using enough of the range of the 8 bits per channel that you have available to you to preserve artifact-free midtone detail. Second, in choosing to shoot low-contrast data, you're forcing the need for color correction later. While obviously the purpose of this book is to encourage the grading of every project, if you're working on a project that will be constrained for time, this is a consideration.

If you're considering recommending a DSLR shoot flat, there are three widely publicized profiles for doing so.

- **Prolost Flat (www.prolost.com/flat):** Filmmaker and photographer Stu Maschwitz has long advocated these camera settings for shooting DSLR media that's easier to grade, and he gives a lengthy explanation at this page.

- **Technicolor Cinestyle (www.technicolorcinestyle.com/download/):** Grading powerhouse Technicolor released a downloadable camera profile for recording low-contrast media with wider latitude. The profile and user guide are downloadable at this page.

- **Canon EOS Gamma Curves (www.lightillusion.com/canon_curves.html):** Created by Steve Shaw's Light Illusion, these in-camera curve profiles can be used to maximize the image data stored in the limited bandwidth these cameras record to.

- **Flaat Picture Controls for Nikon DSLRs (www.similaar.com/foto/flaat-picture-controls/index.html):** Available from Similarly, this set of picture styles for both Canon and Nikon cameras also aims to give you a low-contrast, latitude-increasing starting point, but also claims to handle skin tones well.

DIGITAL DAILIES: THE START OF POSTPRODUCTION

NOTE
The consolidation of film labs into fewer and fewer markets makes the notion of same-day film dailies unlikely anymore, although scanned digital deliverables can speed up the return trip.

In the classic film studio workflow, when production stopped for the day, the camera negative would be rushed to the lab for developing, and then workprints would be made and synced with production audio. The workprints would then be assembled into a set of *dailies* that the film crew would watch either that evening or the next morning to evaluate the day's performances, check that there's enough coverage for the scene, and make sure there are no technical problems. The dailies would then be handed off to the editing team, which would begin cutting.

Unless you're shooting a camera with tethered audio that's recording ProRes or DNxHD media directly and handing that media directly off to the editor to begin work, chances are that some kind of digital dailies workflow will be necessary, since raw and log-encoded media still has to be adjusted and processed, and separately recorded audio still has to be synced. On a professional set, the day's work should still be evaluated.

As mentioned, digital dailies are created either during production by the DIT or later in more controlled conditions by a colorist at a post facility. The process of generating dailies for a production generally has three components, though there may be other creative workflow innovations pursued by specific facilities.

SYNCING DAILIES

If the production tethered audio to the camera during the shoot, then you already have high-quality production audio incorporated into the camera media, and there's no other syncing work to do.

On the other hand, productions recording dual-system sound, where the audio is recorded separately from the visuals, are going to require that the audio and video be synced when you create the dailies. If you're lucky and the production recordist and assistant camera operator (AC) were on the ball, this process can be automated in a couple of ways. If not, then you (or your assistant) get to rock it like it's 1985 and sync each pair of video and audio clips manually by lining up the closing of the clapstick of a clapperboard slate in the video (now possibly a tablet running a clapperboard app) to the audible clap on the audio track that's visible as a spike in the waveform. Clip by clip. Good times, but hey, at least you don't have to line up mag tracks on a Steenbeck.

Preferably, the production will be using timecode-synced dual-system sound, where time-of-day timecode is synced between the digital cinema camera and the audio recorder and periodically jam synced over the course of the day to keep the sync relationship frame-accurate. While the equipment and expertise are generally more expensive for other methods of syncing dual-system sound, with careful file management of the video and audio media, the matching timecode on each pair of video and audio files makes syncing the audio fast and nearly flawless. I've synced three days' worth of production media in seconds using this method, with no problems. Needless to say I'm a fan of productions that work this way. Applications including DaVinci Resolve, FilmLight Baselight, and Assimilate Scratch (and Scratch Lab) are able to facilitate timecode sync.

If timecode sync wasn't in the budget, you can still get good automated audio/video syncing using the technique of waveform synchronization. Using this method, an on-camera microphone records lackluster audio along with the video. The on-camera audio can then be used, when syncing to superior audio recorded elsewhere, to line up the matching waveforms of each pair of on-camera and dual-system audio files. Applications such as Red Giant PluralEyes are dedicated to this task and are capable of processing batches of files all at once for linking inside of other NLEs. However, editing applications such as Final Cut Pro X have also jumped into the fray, providing similar functionality that's built in.

GRADING DAILIES

Another task awaiting the DIT or colorist who is creating the digital dailies is the grading of the dailies, if necessary. When it comes to on-set grading and dailies workflows, there are all manner of ways to proceed, depending on the type of production, the budget, and the schedule. I'll restrict myself to a very high-level overview here; bear in mind that this only scratches the surface of the workflows that are possible.

ON-SET VS. IN THE SUITE

Once, most dailies were done by film labs, and later by postproduction facilities, where junior colorists would often cut their teeth doing unsupervised evening-shift work, while senior colorists would work on the supervised daytime projects. Increasingly, digital workflows using more affordably priced and portable grading workstations are enabling this work to be done on-set by the DIT.

If a DIT is involved, on-set color is typically restricted to setting primary grades so that the cinematographer can see how the scene is shaping up via the live camera display in video village; this is especially critical in workflows where log-encoded data is being recorded, which looks terrible unless monitored with an appropriate correction. As grading applications reach farther back in the pipeline toward production, there are increasingly sophisticated workflows becoming available that enable more intricate grading work to be done, if desired.

On the other hand, grading software developers are increasingly facilitating a bi-directional workflow, where the facility colorist and cinematographer is able to set looks in advance based on footage from test shoots, which can be made available to the DIT for reference and as a starting point for the on-set work.

GRADING DATA INTERCHANGE

The grades created by the DIT may be "baked" into the digital dailies being created for the benefit of the editor and director, but these grades may also be handed off to the colorist who's doing the final finish as a starting point for the final grade. Granted, they won't always be used, but at least they'll provide valuable insight into what the cinematographer was thinking on the set. There are a variety of ways these grades can be preserved and handed off for later use.

- **Camera metadata:** Digital cinema cameras usually store the ISO, exposure, and other metadata inside each recorded media file. Grading applications that are compatible with a particular raw camera format will be able to both read and manipulate this image adjustment metadata, which affects how that media is debayered for use within the image processing pipeline.

- **Lookup tables:** Used extensively in commercial shoots with limited locations, LUTs are saved image-processing operations that can be created to set looks for how the scene should appear when viewed by the on-set display. LUTs are advantageous since they can be loaded directly onto a variety of production displays, and they can also be handed off to the colorist in post for use within a grading application, either for reference or to use as a starting point for ongoing work.

- **Color Decision Lists (CDLs):** CDLs are an industry-standard file format originally developed by the American Society of Cinematographers' technology committee. CDL files are formatted similarly to EDLs, with SOP (Slope/Offset/Power) and SAT (Saturation) values embedded as metadata in much the same way as comments are in a more typical EDL. CDLs are used in television and long-form programming to organize on-set color data. Using a CDL, primary grade adjustments can be organized for a collection of shots in different locations and retrieved by the colorist later for reference or as a starting point for ongoing work.

USING GRADING APPLICATIONS ON THE SET

Although there are dedicated applications for facilitating on-set color and digital dailies workflows, since this book focuses on dedicated grading applications, I'll focus on three studio grading applications covered elsewhere in this book that also facilitate on-set workflows as a subset of their functionality. Of course, if you have the infrastructure, you can use pretty much any grading application on the set, but some applications are more carefully designed for this than others.

- *Scratch Lab* is a version of Assimilate Scratch that is specifically set up for doing on-set work and that can be run on a variety of very portable Windows and OS X computers. Primary grading, import and export of LUTs, CDL support, grade matching, and other features for processing dailies is built in, and once you're done, either you can either export LUTs and CDLs for use in other applications or you can move your on-set project into the full version of Scratch and begin working that way.

- FilmLight has developed a self-contained "Baselight in a box" called the *Flip*, which essentially puts a full Baselight product in a form factor that's easily equipped on the DIT's cart. The Flip can ingest live output from the camera so that the DIT can set looks as the crew works, as well as record video, but it also has all of the dailies synching, LUT and CDL exchange, and media processing features of Baselight. If you're using Baselight from end to end, the Flip can save Baselight Grade (BLG) files that contain the full Baselight grade, LUTs that were used, and keyframes that were set, along with two reference stills (one graded, one ungraded) and timecode metadata. These BLG files can be shared among all versions of Baselight including Baselight editions for Avid, Final Cut Pro, and Nuke, as well as the Baselight studio software used for the final finish, so that grades generated on the set can be carried through and refined during editorial and VFX and then used as a starting point during the grade.

- DaVinci Resolve (either the Full or Lite version), which can run on your choice of Linux, Windows, or OS X computers, has a feature called *Resolve Live* that lets you monitor and grade the live image coming from the camera from within Resolve, while simultaneously monitoring live HD-SDI output, creating and saving full-blown Resolve grades while the crew works, along with an image still and timecode metadata that enables easy syncing to the camera original media when ingested later. Since it's DaVinci Resolve, you also have all of the LUT and CDL compatibility workflows, dailies synching, and media processing capabilities you'd have in the studio.

Other applications are available, but these provide a good look at how the on-set and facility grading experiences are becoming increasingly connected.

NOTE
If you're going to do on-set color, it's crucial that you have a high-quality, color-critical display as described in Chapter 2 and that you do your best to shield it from ambient light reflecting on the front of it so that you can judge the contrast of the image reasonably well. Otherwise, the resulting grading information that is handed off will not truly reflect an accurate transformation of the image data as it will be viewed in studio conditions. Granted, you can do only so much in the hectic conditions of video village, but the closer you get to studio monitoring conditions on the set, the better and more useful the grades you'll be handing off.

ONE LIGHT VS. BEST LIGHT

When generating digital dailies, there two approaches. If the on-set look or saved camera metadata applies equally to all media from a given reel, then a "one-light" grade, where a single adjustment is applied to an entire collection of similarly shot media, should be sufficient to create decent-looking media for editorial to start with. If it's not perfect, that's not a problem since the offline media will be replaced with online media during the reconform process, just prior to final grading.

On the other hand, if the director is especially picky or if the camera original media is being transcoded to an online-quality format that will be used for final finishing, then it might be preferable to apply more detailed grades to each clip to bring out the best the media has to offer. This is typically referred to as a "best light" grade and is more typically carried out by a colorist back at the grading suite.

CAMERA RAW TRANSCODING WORKFLOWS

When shooting raw media, another aspect of digital dailies creation is the decision concerning how to go about transcoding a set of useful offline or online media. Although nonlinear editing applications are beginning to get fast enough to allow direct editing of camera raw media, in my opinion doing so is inadvisable, at least as things stand at the time of this writing. The performance requirements for real-time debayering are significant, and the trend of editors using more affordable and portable equipment to work is at odds with having to go back to using a high-powered desktop system just to accommodate a camera format (although don't let me stop anyone who wants to do this).

Also, the storage requirements even of compressed raw formats, while smaller than uncompressed mastering formats, are still far larger than the low-bandwidth offline codecs that are available for editing. Consequently, using offline-quality media with smaller file sizes and lower bandwidth requirements can significantly accelerate the performance of one's editing software, as well as lowering your storage requirements by an order of magnitude.

This means that the creation of an alternate set of matching digital dailies is typical in raw workflows. If shooting raw and creating digital dailies is the preferred workflow, there are three ways of dealing with this.

- Debayer and transcode the raw media to an offline format that's lower quality, that's lower bandwidth, that has smaller file sizes, and that is overall easier to edit, but that will require reconforming to the camera original raw media when grading and finishing. While the reconform is an extra step, raw media gives the colorist maximum flexibility for making adjustments, assuming their grading software supports this workflow.

- Debayer to DPX image sequences (typically log-encoded) to create uncompressed, mastering-quality media that you can use for finishing if you're in a workflow where raw files are inconvenient but you need top-quality media, such as for VFX-heavy programs. DPX clips are huge and will require significant storage capacity for longer projects, and they aren't typically NLE-friendly, so you'll need to also generate a set of edit-friendly offline media with matching time-code and reel information to facilitate reconform to the DPX sequences during finishing. You lose the flexibility of raw media, but log-encoded DPX files will have all the image data you need if the media was competently shot with appropriate metadata settings from the camera.

- Debayer and transcode the raw media to a mastering-quality yet NLE-friendly format (QuickTime ProRes or MXF) at the resolution you'll be finishing the project at, ideally as log-encoded media if you want to preserve the maximum latitude for later adjustment. This generates media that won't need to be reconformed to another format later but that will be compressed (depending on the codec) and will likely have higher storage requirements if you choose a high-quality codec like ProRes 422 (HQ), ProRes 4444, DNxHD 220Mbit/s, or DNxHD 444. However, since storage is pretty cheap these days, this may not be an issue depending on the type of project you're editing. The advantage of filling up your storage system with mastering-quality media is that you don't have to reconform to the camera original raw media when you finish, sacrificing the flexibility of raw (which you may or may not need) in order to save yourself the potential hassle of an extra step.

While there are vocal advocates for all of these workflows, I do not prefer one over the other. All have their merits depending on the nature of the project at hand, and I've done all three—raw to offline with a reconform, raw to DPX to offline with a reconform, and transcoding to and finishing with mastering quality media—with satisfying results relative to each project.

The key, if you're planning on debayering and transcoding to a mastering-quality format, is to do so using a high-quality codec, to check your metadata settings and perhaps make some simple adjustments (if necessary) to make sure you're debayering files with appropriate ISO and exposure settings, and to preferably debayer log-encoded media (discussed next) that preserves the greatest latitude for adjustment later, during the grade.

ROUND-TRIP WORKFLOWS

While there are some exceptions, grading applications are generally designed to import an EDL, XML, or AAF file that's been exported from an NLE after the edit has been completed and then to export a corresponding EDL, XML, or AAF file of the finished project to send back to the original NLE. This process is referred to as a *round-trip*, and this section illustrates a generic round-trip workflow to help you understand what is involved, overall, and where grading fits in.

An outline of the average round-trip workflow is as follows:

1 Lock the edit (you hope).

2 Prep your timeline for handoff.

3 Export the edit, and organize its accompanying media.

4 Grade the project.

5 Reconform last-minute VFX changes and stock footage buys.

6 Render the final graded media.

7 Export the graded timeline, and reimport it into your NLE or finishing application.

Every application does this differently. For example, Adobe SpeedGrade has the enviable ability to import a Premiere Pro file directly, rather than relying on XML or AAF interchange formats. However, if you're going to be organized (something I strongly suggest), variations of these steps apply no matter what combination of postproduction applications you plan on using.

BEFORE YOU BEGIN: LOCKING THE EDIT

Much has been said about the benefits of applications that allow more flexible workflows in terms of passing timelines back and forth between the editorial and finishing departments. Ultimately, the desire is to eliminate the notion of "locking" changes made to an edit altogether, to enable any little alteration to be implemented at any time right up until the program is output.

While this sounds great on paper and this kind of flexibility is certainly welcome in terms of application interoperability, many key advantages to locking an edit remain, not the least of which is cost savings. At the risk of editorializing, locking the edit should not be looked at as a technological limitation but as a *scheduling milestone*.

Sooner or later, the director and producer will have to make up their minds, be done with the edit, and allow the project to go through finishing. The longer this is put off, extending reedits into the finishing stage, the more time the grading team will have to spend reconforming these last-minute changes, with their attendant alterations to grades within each updated scene, and the more hours of work will end up on the bill (or so the finishing facility hopes). If the project is a tentpole summer blockbuster with a $200 million budget, this may not be an issue, but if the project is a $500,000 indie feature or $100,000 documentary, those hours add up fast, and not just because of the grade.

Typically, audio is mixed at the same time that the visuals are being graded, and any changes made to the edit will affect the audio timeline just as much as the grading timeline. For the lower-budgeted project, locking the edit to avoid such last-minute changes reaps all kinds of efficiencies when it comes to the finishing process, and that will save you cash.

None of this is to say that you shouldn't expect updates to titles, visual effects shots, last-minute stock footage purchases, or other media substitutions; these sorts of one-to-one clip replacements are inevitable, and modern grading applications make these sorts of changes relatively easy to handle. What becomes problematic are more sweeping changes made to the program that alter the total run time by rearranging clip position and duration for multiple scenes, which can become very complicated very quickly without careful organization.

Bottom line, if the edit can be locked, it should. If it can't, someone should ask why not. All things must end.

PREPARING YOUR EDIT FOR GRADING

It's always a good idea to do some prep work to your edited sequence before handing it off for grading. Every grading application is compatible with a different collection of effects beyond edits and dissolves, but there are invariably going to be some effects and media types that won't be supported. While often these effects are either ignored or preserved and sent back to the original NLE after grading has finished, these sorts of things can cause unwanted complications, so a bit of timeline reorganization will always help keep things on the rails. In general, I always recommend making the following organizational changes to a duplicate of your edited sequence.

MOVE CLIPS TO TRACK 1

It's best to move all noncomposited clips to track V1. Many editors use superimposed series of clips not to create layered effects but to edit a scene together. While this works well within a given NLE, color correcting a program with hundreds of clips spread across several video tracks can be a pain in the neck for the colorist to manage. It's much easier to keep track of what you're doing and to copy grades across multiple shots when they're all on the same video track.

On the other hand, superimposed clips that are part of a compositing or transparency operation should be left alone. Many grading applications have incorporated the ability to do basic compositing, so there is a good chance your application can import these effects, or at the very least re-create them.

ISOLATE UNSUPPORTED EFFECTS

Checking ahead to see which timeline effects a grading application does and does not support is a great time-saver for the person doing the reconform at the finishing facility. One way to do this is to move all unsupported clips to a superimposed video track. For example, many grading applications don't support long-duration still image files, freeze frames created by the NLE, generators specific to a particular NLE, or exotic compositing operations. When you export a project from an NLE to a grading application using XML or AAF, either these types of clips will usually not appear or they'll appear as offline or disconnected clips. Sometimes these unsupported effects are preserved internally in order to let them be sent back to the original NLE on the return trip, but sometimes not.

If you have these types of clips in your project and you don't need to grade them, you can simply ignore them. For example, you typically don't bother color correcting clips such as titles, lower-thirds, or other computer graphics that have been created specifically for the program, on the premise that they've been created specifically with the limits of broadcast or film output in mind.

On the other hand, if there are freeze frames or composited effects that you do need to grade, a good workflow is to do the following:

1 Move the unsupported clip to a superimposed track.

2 Render it as a self-contained media file using a mastering-quality codec.

3 Reimport the media file movie you just rendered back into your project, and edit it back into the sequence on track V1.

At this point, you can delete the original, superimposed clip in track V2, but leaving it there makes it easier to locate and rework it should you decide you ever need to make a change to the original effect. Now that the effect has been turned into a plain old media file, it can be graded like any other clip.

FIGURE OUT WHAT TO DO WITH SPEED EFFECTS

Grading applications all have varying support for speed effects, *especially* variable speed effects, so check ahead to see whether your grading application will work properly with imported speed effects coming from the NLE in question. If not, there are plenty of ways you can use plug-ins, built-in NLE functionality, or dedicated compositing effects applications to preprocess high-quality speed effects using optical flow processing in order to create a high-quality self-contained media file with which to replace the original speed-affected clip, all *before* you move the media into your grading application of choice (similar to the workflow presented in the previous section).

SORT OUT AN EDIT'S EFFECTS PLUG-INS

Grading applications don't typically support the same effects plug-ins that are used by NLEs—at least not in the same format. If there are plug-in effects that you want permanently applied to a clip prior to grading, you'll need to render out and reimport "baked" versions of these clips as described previously. However, you should consider just what kind of effect it is. If it's a grading plug-in or an effect or look that your colorist might be able to do better, you should strip it out of the edit prior to handoff.

However, before you start stripping out an editor's grades and looks, it's often useful for the colorist to refer to such offline corrections and effects during the grade so they know what the client has gotten used to. Consider rendering a self-contained "reference" file of the entire sequence in QuickTime or DNxHD form to hand off along with the actual project and source media. Such a reference movie serves several purposes. It provides a reference of how the edits in the timeline are supposed to line up, in case something goes wrong during import. It gives a reference of which clips are supposed to go where, in case something goes wrong with the conform. And it provides a visual reference of what kinds of sizing changes, temp grades, and other effects have been applied to the project that you may need to re-create (or outdo).

PREPARING YOUR MEDIA, IF NECESSARY

As with any finishing workflow, it's essential to use media that has been ingested and/or transcoded at the highest possible quality. In general, there are two ways to do this, depending on what kind of media was used for editing.

PROGRAMS EDITED USING HIGH-QUALITY MEDIA

For example, if you're working on a program that was edited using mastering-quality media from the beginning such as ProRes 422 (HQ), ProRes 4444, DNxHD 220, or DNxHD 444 (or whatever codec the production decided was suitable for mastering), then probably all you have to do is to export an XML, AAF, or EDL of your edited sequence, media manage the accompanying media onto a portable hard drive, and hand those things over to the grading facility for them to be able to quickly reconform the project on their workstation.

TIP

Dave Hussey, senior colorist at Company 3, refers to the phenomenon of "temp love," where the clients have fallen so in love with temp music or a temporary grade during the edit that it's difficult for them to fairly evaluate the original work it is being replaced with. It's a genuine challenge you'll face time and time again, and it will test both your salesmanship and your patience.

PROGRAMS EDITED USING OFFLINE MEDIA

If you're working on a project that, for convenience, was edited using an offline-quality format such as ProRes 422 (Proxy) or DNxHD 36, then you're going to want to conform the exported XML, AAF, or EDL of the edited sequence either to the high-quality camera original media that was originally recorded or to a set of online-quality transcoded media that was generated for that project, from which the offline clips were generated. Doing this kind of *reconform*, where you substitute the offline-quality clips with the camera original or online media, is a core feature of most grading applications.

Reconforming typically uses a combination of media filenames, unique identifier metadata (UUID), timecode, and reel name information to match each offline-quality clip to its corresponding online-quality clip in order to replace each low-quality clip in a timeline with its high-quality equivalent, ready for grading. For this reason, it's essential to manage the metadata of your media with care from production through postproduction.

If the offline-quality media was output by the same grading application that will be used for the final finish, then the easiest thing to do is usually to conform the edited project to the original database of media created to output the dailies. If this is the case, things should go quickly and easily. Otherwise, it's usually not that difficult to copy the camera original data to the facilities storage system in preparation for project reconform from scratch.

AUTOMATIC EDIT DETECTION

Every once in a while, you'll end up needing to grade a program for which there's only a single rendered master media file that's available. If this is the case, you can sometimes use a grading application's ability to "notch," or cut up a single media file to match the edits specified by an EDL. If you don't even have an EDL, however, then some grading applications (including but not limited to DaVinci Resolve, FilmLight Baselight, and Adobe SpeedGrade) have the ability to automatically detect edit points in a movie file (based on changes to color and contrast) and build an edit list that you can then verify and use to cut the file into individual clips for easy grading. This is particularly useful for archival workflows from film or tape, where only the final master remains.

IMPORTING THE PROJECT FOR GRADING

Nearly every grading application is capable of importing a variety of project inter-change formats, including XML, AAF, and EDL files. None of these files is an actual format saved by a nonlinear editing application; they're file formats that are specifically exported by NLEs for the express purpose of converting a sequence of clips and effects in one application to a matching sequence of clips and effects in another. Again, importing one or more of these formats is a core feature of grading applications; you need only determine which format is best for your particular combination of editing and grading application.

RENDERING THE FINAL GRADED MEDIA

For most workflows, it is necessary to render a completely new set of graded media files from your grading application before sending the edit to the originating NLE or on to a finishing application. There are two ways you can do this.

RENDERING INDIVIDUAL CLIPS

If the client is concerned about last-minute changes being made to the program, they may ask for individually rendered clips such that the edited timeline can be completely reconstructed, only with graded shots. This is a workflow that every credible grading application can support. In general, you'll end up with one new color-corrected media file for every shot in the edited sequence that's been graded, and it is these new media files that will be linked to when you send the finished XML, AAF, or EDL file from the grading application back to the NLE or finishing application where the application will be completed.

RENDERING A GRADED MASTER MEDIA FILE

Alternately, if the project is well and truly finished, you may be asked to simply output the entire timeline as a single digital master file. Typically this will be a text-less master that can be loaded back into an NLE or finishing application for the final application of titles, end credits, and anything else that needs to be added prior to final output and delivery.

SEND THE EDIT OR MASTER RENDER FILE BACK FOR FINAL FINISH

After you've rendered the graded project, either as individual clips or as one great big one, you need to move the resulting media back into an NLE or finishing application in preparation for whatever else needs to be done (titling, format conversions, last-minute VFX, marrying the soundtrack, and so on). In particular, if you rendered individual media files to preserve the structure of the edit to facilitate truly eleventh-hour changes, then you'll send an XML, AAF, or EDL back to your NLE or finishing application—which is why it's called "round-trip."

Once the project is in the finishing application (assuming this is even necessary), the rest of the team can add whatever is necessary for final mastering and delivery.

WHERE DOES GRADING END AND FINISHING BEGIN?

Where once there was a hard dividing wall between grading applications and "finishing" applications, with the evolution of the main grading applications used by the industry, there is increasingly a gray area between grading and finishing applications that gets grayer every year. The definition of finishing depends on who you talk to, but in general it includes editorial changes, titling, clip resizing, multiple-format support and format conversion, effects such as digital paint to remove previously unnoticed flaws and trackable blurs to eliminate onscreen elements the producers don't have rights to, and the ability to output to tape, digital formats, and master other sorts of digital deliverables such as digital cinema masters (DCMs) for projects requiring digital cinema distribution.

Over time, more of these features have creeping into the toolkits of various grading applications, such that in some instances a full round-trip may be unnecessary assuming you can output directly from the grading application. Realistically, however, most workflows involve a return-trip to the editing application of origin.

CHAPTER 2

SETTING UP A COLOR CORRECTION ENVIRONMENT

Before you can cook, you need a kitchen. Successful color correction requires you to use a display that accurately shows the image you need to adjust and to work in an environment that's been carefully set up for the critical evaluation of the program you're working on.

This means the display you select and the room you view it in need to adhere carefully to some time-honored best practices. In this respect, color correction is more exacting than editing, compositing, or even broadcast design tend to be, although those disciplines also benefit from the same attention to monitoring and environment.

This chapter suggests criteria by which to choose a reference display and ways to set up your room so that you can work quickly, comfortably, and accurately.

Best practices for room setup can be accomplished in many ways, and it's important to understand how careful display selection and placement, wall color, and lighting affect your perception of a video or film image. Once you appreciate the impact all these elements have, you then can decide how far to go to set up your color correction environment to meet your needs.

Although the advice in this chapter is most applicable to dedicated professionals who are willing to spend the time and money to convert existing edit suites into color correction rooms, many of the suggestions are feasible even for individual operators with smaller rooms or for editors who are setting up rooms in which to do color correction as one part of the finishing process.

UNDERSTANDING DISPLAY-REFERRED COLOR MANAGEMENT

The key to understanding color management for video, as it's practiced today, is that it's *display-referred*, as opposed to being scene-referred as with stills that have been scanned or shot with a camera. Display-referred means that color fidelity is judged based on the appearance of the image on the display—there's no inherent color profiling within the video file.

NOTE

Some of you may be asking, "What about ACES color management?" At the time of this writing, ACES is not yet in wide use, and most workflows are still largely display-referred. Still, ACES is an important new development, and those wishing to read more about it should consult www.oscars.org/science-technology/council/projects/aces.html. Additionally, check out colorist Mike Most's article, "All About ACES," at www.mikemost.com.

This is all a long way of saying that, in video workflows, the quality and calibration of your display are very important. Whether you consider yourself to be a finishing editor or a colorist, the adjustments you make to the color and contrast of your video clips based on *how they look on your display* is going to determine the color of the final product.

VIEWERS DON'T HAVE COLOR MANAGEMENT

It gets worse when you consider what happens once you output a video program for distribution. Once people start watching it on the Web, on their televisions via cable or terrestrial broadcast, or on disc, you have no control over how the final image will look.

Indeed, a selling point of many consumer televisions is that they have multiple color settings that can be used to make the image more or less colorful, cooler or warmer, or brighter or darker, depending on the whims of the viewer. When digital video streams go to air or are delivered via cable, no color profile information is distributed within them. Likewise, no color profile information goes out with streaming video on the Web.

However, the same assumptions that govern color management from camera to postproduction also govern color management from postproduction to audience: Televisions will be generally the BT. 709 specification for color, and display gamma will be set to somewhere between 2.2 and 2.4. In the case of web video, it's more likely that users will have their computer displays set to use sRGB color, with a gamma of 2.2.

COLOR MANAGEMENT FOR VIDEO IS IMPORTANT

Lest the previous sections make you despair that there's no point in trying to maintain accurate color in video workflows, here's why it's still important.

MULTIPLE-FACILITY WORKFLOWS

Many video projects involve multiple postproduction professionals, at multiple locations, using multiple displays. If everyone doesn't work to a common display standard, your program risks becoming a hodge-podge of varying video levels once you reassemble all of the pieces together into a single timeline.

BROADCAST AND DIGITAL DISC DELIVERY

Broadcasters and digital disc distributors both assume you're delivering video in the BT.709 color space for distribution to an audience that will be watching on displays using the same standard. If you don't also color correct and master your program to adhere to that standard, you risk delivering something that won't look like you intend it.

SOME OF THE AUDIENCE CARES PASSIONATELY

Thanks to home-theater enthusiasts, color calibrators, and the efforts of the consumer division of THX, awareness of the importance of television color fidelity to home-viewing enjoyment continues to grow. These days, it's easy to purchase a big-screen television with a THX setting, which more or less guarantees the gamut will be BT.709, with appropriate gamma (more on that later), which means that the built-in menu settings exist to calibrate the display to be BT. 709-compliant (more or less) with factory settings that should be close. If you don't work to this shared standard, then enthusiasts will have no hope of seeing your project as you intend them to see it.

DISPLAY-REFERRED COLOR MANAGEMENT IN ACTION

It's important to use standards-compliant displays throughout the postproduction process precisely *because* consumer televisions, projectors, and computer displays vary so unpredictably. From manufacturer to manufacturer and from model to model, the same image will invariably look ten different ways on ten different televisions. You'll never be able to control that, but what you *can* control is the baseline reference that you, other postproduction facilities, television networks, and cable broadcasters all use to evaluate your images.

Here's an example to illustrate this point:

1 You color correct a commercial, making specific adjustments to color and lightness according to how it appears on your carefully calibrated display.

2 You hand off the program for finishing in another suite (or another facility), where other changes are made to the program: graphics are added, the format is converted from HD to SD, the signal is legalized prior to tape out, and so forth. The post facility needs to make sure the image doesn't get altered. To do so, they need to view it on a display set up identically to yours.

3 Finally, the finished commercial is handed off to the broadcaster, who sends it to air. The broadcaster needs to make sure it adheres to their quality control standards, which means they need to view it on yet another display, and if it's not set up identically to yours, they might think there's a problem when in fact there is none.

In other words, your display must match the post facility's display, which must match the broadcaster's display, to prevent someone from making an incorrect adjustment that would erroneously alter the image you adjusted in the first place (**Figure 2.1**).

Figure 2.1 This diagram simulates an ideal signal chain with the image surviving two handoffs in post.

Grading suite   Finishing suite   Audience

Video Signal

This is possible only if everyone involved in the process is using a standards-compliant display that's been calibrated accurately to adhere to the same standard.

Now, if you, the post facility, and the broadcaster were all using displays with mismatched calibrations, it's possible that other adjustments might be made to "correct" the image relative to an erroneously calibrated display, which would inadvertently alter the image that was intended for the public to see (**Figure 2.2**).

Figure 2.2 The finishing suite is using a display that's miscalibrated (too dark), so an adjustment is made to "recorrect" the image. The result is that the master that's handed off ends up brighter than the colorist intended.

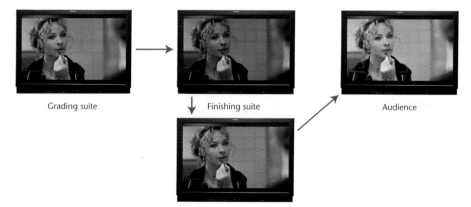

Grading suite   Finishing suite   Audience

As long as there's consistency among all the parties responsible for evaluating and adjusting a work in progress, it ultimately doesn't matter that the final, broadcast image will look different on different consumers' televisions. It's up to them to decide whether they want to take the time to adjust their TVs to show the image as it was meant to be seen. As long as the broadcasted image is faithful to the mastered program (another story entirely), consumers still have the potential to see the true image as long as they're the last step in the "signal adjustment" chain.

However, if there's no consistency prior to broadcast, it's anybody's guess what kind of image will be broadcast, and the viewer will never have any guarantee of seeing the program as it was meant to be seen.

CHOOSING A DISPLAY

Which display to choose is one of my least favorite questions to answer, because there is no single best answer. Numerous different display technologies are employed for color critical monitoring, and each has its own strengths and weaknesses. Since the broadcast display is your primary tool for evaluating the images in your program, this is probably the single most important piece of equipment you'll own, and quite possibly the most expensive.

Ultimately, display selection is going to require you to do a bit of research and get some demonstrations in order to make a decision you'll be comfortable with. Depending on the size of your operation, your budget is going to dictate, in large part, what kind of display you'll be able to install. However, the type of work you do is a much more important factor in choosing which type of display to use.

THE TYPES OF DISPLAYS

Five types of professional display technologies (including several varieties of LCD panels and two varieties of projectors) are commercially available at the time of this writing.

LCD

Liquid crystal displays (LCDs) have the great advantage of accurate and stable color, making them trouble-free choices for a wide variety of programming. These days, color-critical LCD panels can be found in a variety of sizes, from 17" displays good for on-set evaluation to 50" displays suitable for multiclient suites. The black level and contrast of LCD displays for broadcast continue to improve year after year, at last becoming competitive with plasma for producing images that are not only accurate but client-pleasing. Today's LCD models are widely used for color-critical monitoring at a variety of facilities worldwide.

Furthermore, 10-bit LCD panels are much more common now than they once were, making high-bit-depth monitoring easily available with this technology. In terms of price, LCD panels can be more expensive than comparable plasma displays but in all cases are cheaper than OLED offerings at the time of writing this book.

Models that are suitable for broadcast work have menu settings for appropriate color standards, some have built-in calibration software compatible with external display probes, and most have some facility for loading 3D lookup tables (LUTs) generated by color management software such as LightSpace CMS for externally calibrating these displays when necessary.

NOTE
Because of how ND filtration works, if a display is in a darkened environment with no ambient light, there will be no glare or reflections to filter, and the ND filter will have little effect.

In some models, neutral density (ND) filters placed over the entire panel improve black representation and enhance contrast by reducing unwanted reflection and glare from the ambient environment. This works because the ND glass filters emitted light coming out of the display only once, but it filters reflective light coming from the room twice. However, improvements to LCD panel contrast and black levels mean that newer generations of displays aren't typically paired with ND filtration.

For displays without an ND filter, glossy panels provide a perceptible improvement in contrast by eliminating the extremely slight veiling glare that antiglare coatings introduce as a function of how they work. However, the debate between antiglare and glossy monitors should really be settled based on your ambient environment. If you're a colorist in a room with controlled lighting (as you should be), glossy monitors shouldn't pose any problems because reflections should be minimal. However, if you're forced to work in an environment with more ambient lighting, antiglare screens have value, and in any case the overall effect on the image being output is so minor as to make this largely a case of individual preference.

LCD displays are also differentiated by the type of backlighting they employ. Three schemes are currently in use: CCFL fluorescent backlighting, white LED, and RGB LED.

- Wide-gamut CCFL fluorescent backlighting was once the most common type of panel in use and is still widely available. Because of the nature of the CCFL bulbs used, high-quality CCFL backlit panels typically provide a wider gamut than do white-LED panels, often reaching up to 97 percent of the P3 gamut for DCI monitoring (maximally saturated green is what gets omitted in that last 3 percent). For rooms using multiple displays, the spectral output of CCFL backlighting also makes for a better calibrated match with plasma displays and with cinema projectors using Xenon bulbs. On the other hand, CFL backlights require 30 minutes to warm up when you first power them on before stabilizing for color critical use. In terms of calibrated stability, 24/7 use will probably necessitate recalibration every six months, while more intermittent use may extend the necessary time between recalibrations by as much as a year.

- White LED backlighting has only recently seen use in color-critical displays, owing to improvements to the quality and consistency of white LED manufacturing. Unlike CCFL backlighting, white LED requires no warm-up period and is color critical and ready to go pretty much as soon as you turn on the display. On the other hand, white LED backlit panels have a narrower gamut than CFL backlit panels (typically 74 percent of P3 for DCI monitoring). However, for BT. 709 video, this isn't a problem as the gamut is more than wide enough for broadcast video. For rooms with multiple displays, the spectral output of white LED panels make for a better calibrated match to digital projectors using Mercury Vapor bulbs and to the majority of newer consumer LCD displays, most of which now use white LED backlighting. In terms of calibrated stability, LED backlighting can allow for remarkably long times between recalibrations; I'm told that high-quality edge-lit panels can potentially go up to two years without an appreciable drift in color accuracy.

- RGB LED backlighting is a more complex backlighting scheme used by a handful of higher-end LCD broadcast displays, most significantly the Dolby PRM-4220. With this technology, small groups of pixels in the LCD panel are backlit by "triads" of variably controllable red/green/blue LEDs on a second LED panel, an approach Dolby refers to as *dual modulation*. This both expands the display's gamut and increases bit-depth, as well as providing deep black levels and precisely detailed shadows by controlling backlight output in specific regions of the picture. Consequently, the Dolby display has a wide enough gamut to cover both BT. 709 *and* 100 percent of DCI P3, with appropriately adjustable color temperature and reference luminance. RGB LED backlighting does require a warm-up period and, similarly to CCFL backlit LCD 24-7 use, may require recalibration every six months. Of the three display technologies described here, those using RGB LED backlighting are also typically the most expensive.

PLASMA

Top-of-the-line plasma displays have been used in color correction suites for several years now, both as hero displays and as less critical client displays. Their main advantages are deep black levels, excellent contrast representation, and relatively low cost at client-pleasingly large sizes. For broadcast work and commercial spots, plasma displays have a lot going for them in terms of how they look in light-controlled environments.

High-end models accommodate accurate calibration via internal menu settings, although plasmas are often calibrated via outboard calibration hardware, as described in the "Calibration" section later in this chapter. By the nature of the technology, plasma displays require more regular calibration than most LCD displays, as well as requiring 30 minutes to warm up before stabilizing for color-critical use.

The advantages these displays in price and large size are partially offset by two less useful aspects of plasma technology. First, imaging detail in the very darkest shadows is not as good as LCD or OLED displays, owing to the subtle noise pattern that's inherent in plasma technology. This isn't the worst problem in the world, but it's something to be aware of. Additionally, plasma displays all have an auto brightness limiter (ABL) circuit, which is designed to reduce plasma power consumption by automatically dimming the display whenever image brightness exceeds a particular threshold. This can be readily exposed via test patterns and can be a problem if you work on graphics-heavy programs. However, most conventionally shot live-action video isn't going to trigger this circuit in an appreciable way, and in any event these limitations have not stopped plasmas from seeing professional use.

OLED

Organic Light Emitting Diode (OLED) displays, once small and experimental, are slowly becoming more widely available from a variety of high-end display vendors. Self-illuminating OLED displays don't require backlighting and exhibit stunning black levels and incredibly high-contrast ratios owing to their ability to turn pixels "off" to display absolute black, with no backlight bleeding through. Having vivid color and exceptional contrast, working with an OLED display can be like looking through a stained-glass window at Notre Dame—they're *gorgeous* and give you a terrific view of the video signal.

As of this writing, OLEDs are expensive and for practical purposes are limited to 24" displays and smaller. Both of these issues can be attributed to how difficult OLED is to manufacture; panel yields from factories are low, with the result being a constrained supply. This combination of small size and high price relative to other technologies limits their appeal for the living room, which means that the amazing image you see in your suite won't necessarily be seen by television audiences out in the world. There is some debate over whether grading an image that's not representative of what the audience will be looking at is a problem; in truth there is no right answer.

Early OLED displays had poor off-axis viewing, although subsequent generations of displays have improved upon this significantly. Another issue with OLED displays, as of the time of this writing, is that they can be difficult to match to other displays in multimonitor suites. Furthermore, the perceived hue by which OLED displays don't match other displays may be experienced differently by different people. Anecdotal reports have been made that people of different ages may experience faint green versus faint magenta casts in comparison to other displays side-by-side. These perceptions of a color cast largely disappear when OLED displays are the only monitor in the room, but it's something to be aware of when you design your suite.

That said, OLED is an important emerging technology. Similar to plasma and CCFL backlit LCD, OLED displays require 30 minutes to warm up before stabilizing for color-critical use.

WHY DON'T MY DISPLAYS MATCH? METAMERISM FAILURE IN A NUTSHELL

This is a long and complicated topic that I'll attempt to summarize quickly, to free you from the anxiety of wondering why two calibrated displays might perceptually differ from one another and to encourage you not to have multiple "hero" displays for image evaluation in color-critical client environments. Here are four points to remember.

- Different display illumination methods employ very different light-emitting technologies, with the result being that the spectral distribution of each display's light output is subtly different.

- The CIE 1931 standard observer model for color measurement allows different spectral distributions of red, green, and blue primaries to produce identically measured color, as long as each spectral distribution results in the same light absorbency by the cones of our eyes that are sensitive to long (blue), medium (green), and short (red) wavelengths of light. These measured matches are called *metamers*.

- When comparing multiple displays that use different spectral distributions of light output side by side, our eyes are capable of perceiving these spectral differences, even when measurement devices show an exact chromaticity match. *Metamerism failure* occurs when perceived differences persist despite the use of measured metamers.

- The narrower the bandwidth of the primary light sources used to illuminate a display, the more that individual biological variation between different people can cause viewers to see subtly different "tints" when comparing displays. This is the reason for reports of perceived differences between different people looking at the same OLED display, as OLED panels use much more spectrally pure primaries to illuminate the display. This is also a challenge for experimental laser projectors.

Bottom line, a display's method of illumination has an effect on your perception of the image, *mainly* when two displays with different backlighting methods are sitting side by side, giving your eyes the opportunity to employ simultaneous contrast to compare the radiometric difference between light sources. When you go back to viewing any type of display by itself in the proper environment, these perceived differences largely disappear. A more in-depth video about this topic is available on the Flanders Scientific technical resources page (www.flandersscientific.com/index/tech_resources.php).

CHAPTER 2

VIDEO PROJECTION

Programs graded for theatrical presentation benefit from being viewed on a digital projector. All digital projectors work by focusing light through some mechanism to produce an image on a front projection screen. Digital projectors employ several technologies, but the ones most suitable for color-critical work use Liquid Crystal On Silicon (LCOS) and Digital Light Processing (DLP). One could make the following generalizations:

- Professional DLP projectors are ideal for high-end digital cinema grading; however, be aware that projectors capable of displaying the DCI P3 gamut are relatively expensive and require more infrastructure in terms of theater size, noise isolation, and cooling.

- DLP and LCoS projectors designed for the upper end of the home-theater market are useful for suites offering BT. 709 workflows with projection monitoring for lower-budgeted work, such as independent films destined for the film-festival circuit or home viewing.

In addition to employing different projection technologies, projectors use one of four methods of illumination: Xenon bulbs, Mercury Vapor bulbs, LEDs, and lasers (largely experimental at the time of this writing). While any professional projector can be calibrated, some illumination technologies are more representative of theatrical exhibition in a particular market than others, making this an additional topic of research for you to consider. I'll discuss projection suites in greater detail later in this chapter.

WHAT'S IMPORTANT IN A DISPLAY?

Display technologies are advancing at a furious pace, and just like computers, the display models available from each company update year after year, so it's difficult to recommend specific models that will still be valid six months later.

However, no matter what technology you're interested in, you should keep the following criteria in mind when you evaluate different monitoring solutions.

BROADCAST AND DISTRIBUTION STANDARDS COMPLIANCE

Whichever display you choose should be capable of supporting the exact gamut (range of colors) and gamma (luma reproduction) required for the standard of video you're going to be working on.

Currently, three standards govern the color and lightness-reproducing character-istics of electronic display devices for the broadcast and film industry, plus one additional consumer standard that's emerging (**Figure 2.3**).

- **BT. 601 RP 145 (ITU-R Recommendation BT.601)** governs standard-definition video and assumes a gamut defined by SMPTE RP 145 primary colors (the SMPTE-C phosphors used by previous generations of professional CRT displays).

- **BT. 601 EBU** governs a differently defined set of chromaticity targets for PAL and SECAM that's slightly different gamut (matching the EBU phosphors of other professional CRT displays).

- **BT. 709 (ITU-Recommendation BT.709)** governs high-definition video, specifying the gamut and gamma of HD devices.

- **DCI P3** is the gamut defined by the Digital Cinema Distribution Master (DCDM) specification that governs digital distribution and projection.

Different display technologies handle the challenges of gamut and gamma repro-duction differently, so it's important to have assurance from the manufacturer that your display conforms to the required standards. Professional displays usually have precalibrated settings available from a menu.

High-end consumer devices, however, may have no such guarantees. On some high-end televisions, a mode identified as "Cinema" may be somewhat close to the broadcast standard, but the gamut may still be too large, while the gamma may not be altogether accurate. Although manufacturers are increasingly including industry-standard calibration presets that approximate BT. 709 (true for displays with a THX rating for video), it's still important to either get a display with onboard calibration options suitable for both gamut and gamma adjustment or use an out-board hardware calibration device capable of 3D LUT processing to bring the display into standards compliance.

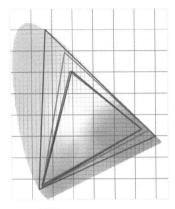

BT. 709
DCI-P3
Rec. 2020
SMPTE-C (NTSC)
EBU (PAL)

Figure 2.3 This chart compares the variations in gamut for each display standard currently in use, when plotted against the standard CIE chromaticity graph (a visualization of color space in two dimensions approximated by the colored gra-dient in the background). The corners of each triangular gamut represent the assignment of each gamut's primaries.

CHAPTER 2

WHAT ABOUT RECOMMENDATION ITU-R BT. 2020?

In an effort to get ahead of the curve on wide-gamut broadcast (in other words, televisions capable of displaying more colors than today's TVs can), the ITU has put forth a recom-mendation on how to standardize high-resolution (up to 7,680x4,320), high-frame-rate (up to 120fps), wide-gamut video signals. But the truth is that no display currently in use is capable of encompassing this gamut, which I'm told corresponds to chromaticity coordi-nates that are reachable only by laser light, a highly experimental technology as of the time of this writing.

More than once I've heard colorists quip that Rec. 2020 won't actually be possible to implement until the year 2020, and if you're reading this in the future, you can laugh at either the hopeless optimism or pessimism of this sentiment as you power on whatever dis-play you happen to be using.

BIT DEPTH OF THE DISPLAY TECHNOLOGY

In general, video signals use 8, 10, or 12 bits per channel (signals to cinema projectors in DCP workflows are 12-bit). Higher bit depths than this are not used for connecting video displays. Consumer displays are often 8 bits per channel, while digital displays capable of 10 bits per channel are becoming more widely available for professional use. Depending on the type of work you do, it's important to check whether the display you're considering supports 10 bits per channel. Never assume that a display is capable of 10-bit support.

10 bits per channel support is not, strictly speaking, necessary for a display to be useful for *color* critical evaluation, although it doesn't hurt. Colors should appear the same on either 8- or 10-bit panels. However, a 10-bit per channel display lets you accurately monitor and evaluate the smoothness of *gradients* within a 10-bit signal. One problem that can occur is that 8-bit-per-channel displays may exhibit banding in shallow ramps such as light blue skies or dark shadows that aren't actually in the signal you're adjusting, causing you to add corrections that may not actually be necessary.

On a side note, some manufacturers talk about displays having "32-bit processing." This is *not* a description of the actual display panel's capabilities but is instead a measurement of the accuracy of the internal image processing for images being color calibrated via LUT support or otherwise processed via resizing or deinterlacing.

BROADCAST STANDARD COLOR TEMPERATURE

Simply put, color temperature is the "color of white" on a given display device. The image on a display set to a lower color temperature appears "warmer," or more orange, while the same image on a display set to a higher color temperature appears "cooler," or more bluish. This is most apparent when you view a field of pure white while switching between two different color temperatures.

Here are the standard color temperatures used in professional projectors and video displays (expressed in Kelvins, or K, the industry-standard unit of color temperature measurement):

- **5400K (D54):** SMPTE Standard 196M specifies 5400K as the color temperature of projected film. Although this is not relevant for digital displays or projectors, it's useful to be aware of this time-honored standard for film presentation.

- **6300K:** According to the DCI specification, 6300K is the correlated color temperature for a reference projector for digital cinema applications.

- **6500K (D65):** The standard for SD and HD broadcast video in North and South America and Europe is 6500K.

- **9300K (D93):** According to Sony, 9300K is the broadcast standard color temperature for video in Japan, Korea, China, and other Asian countries. Adjustability of color temperature is another key difference between consumer and professional displays. Although these standards are the recommended best practice for "reference viewing" during color correction, the reality of how the audience at large will view the image can be quite different.

Paradoxically, although high-end consumer displays are increasingly equipped with color temperature settings closer to the broadcast standard, the color temperature of the average consumer television is usually quite a bit cooler than the broadcast standard, ranging potentially from 7200K to 9300K. Unfortunately for professionals, a "bluer" white appears to be a brighter white, and the average viewer comparing televisions at an electronics store will likely respond more favorably to a higher color temperature than to a set right next to it that's employing the standard D65.

Movie theaters have their own variances as well, differing based on the age of the Xenon bulb in a given theater's projector. The older the bulb gets, the lower the color temperature becomes, and the warmer the projected image will be.

Although it's interesting to keep these factors in mind when grading your program, it's imperative that you work with a display employing the appropriate color temperature standard for the program's intended venue and region in order to maintain consistency and predictability among post houses and broadcast facilities.

HIGH CONTRAST RATIO, REASONABLY DEEP BLACKS

For many, contrast ratio is one of the most visible and important characteristics of any display technology for color correction work. If your display won't display a wide range of contrast, including deep blacks and clear whites, you won't be able to make a proper evaluation of the images you correct. In particular, displays with muddy blacks (blacks that appear dark gray) may tempt you (or your client) to crush your blacks unnecessarily to compensate for the appearance of the image in your suite.

The prior dominance of CRT displays for grading was partially because of the high contrast ratios they were capable of, which translated into deep, rich blacks (in a proper viewing environment) and bright, pure whites.

Now that there are a wide variety of display technologies vying for a place in your video suite, you need to pick a display that gives you similar contrast performance. If you're evaluating a properly calibrated display for purchase and the blacks appear gray to you, you should probably look elsewhere.

The only published standard that covers black level at the time of this writing is from the EBU (search the Web for *EBU Guidelines for Consumer Flat Panel Displays*), which recommends a measured black level of below 1 cd/m^2. Based on manufacturers I've spoken with, these days just about every monitor can do that.

That said, different display technologies have different black levels, with commensurately different contrast ratios. When it comes to measuring contrast, perhaps the most useful benchmark to consider when comparing displays is *concurrent contrast* (sometimes referred to as *simultaneous contrast*), which is a measurement of the white and black elements of a checkerboard pattern that display peak white and minimum black at the same time, reflecting your most important concerns as a colorist (the real-world difference between the lightest and darkest areas of a picture).

The following simultaneous contrast ratios are considered excellent for their category as of this writing, although undoubtedly these specifications should improve year over year with subsequent new generations of equipment.

- LCD continues to improve significantly year over year, with high-quality glossy-panel models with white LED or CCFL backlighting being measured with a real-world simultaneous contrast ratio of 1400:1 or better. Matte displays with an antiglare coating typically exhibit slightly less contrast of around 1100:1 or better.

- Plasma displays continue to have a modest edge over LCD panels in terms of deep blacks, with a higher (if noisier in the deepest blacks) contrast ratio of 1800:1.

- OLED displays offer stunningly deep blacks with incredible contrast. While Sony literature often publishes a contrast ratio of 1,000,000:1, a more real-world simultaneous contrast ratio for this technology is 5000:1 or better. Even this number is vastly wider than either of the other technologies available; it's pretty clear that images displayed on OLED monitors are going to be portrayed differently than those on LCD or plasma. Whether this is better for purposes of HD mastering or merely different is a matter of some debate.

BROADCAST STANDARD GAMMA

Gamma refers to the nonlinear representation of luminance on a broadcast or computer display, technically referred to as the electro-optical transfer function (EOTF). However, different displays may interpret gamma differently, which significantly impacts how your video appears. It's important to make sure your display's gamma setting is set appropriately.

In the section on picture rendering in Charles Poynton's *Digital Video and HD Algorithms and Interfaces* (Morgan Kaufmann, 2012)—which I largely paraphrase in this section—Poynton explains that the luminance that's reproduced by a video display is far lower than the luminance of the original scene that was recorded. The Hunt effect dictates that colorfulness decreases as luminance decreases. Therefore, the result is that if we linearly reproduced the UC values that were recorded from the original scene on a display, we would perceive the displayed image as less colorful and lower-contrast. This would make us sad.

It turns out that our vision systems (eyes and specialized areas of the brain) exhibit a nonlinear perceptual response to luminance, wherein lightness is approximately the 0.42 power function of the relative luminance of a scene. Meanwhile, the luminance output by a CRT was a nonlinear function of the input voltage, and this

NOTE

While consumer devices from different manufacturers seem to be settling on a gamma of 2.2, be aware that different television and projector settings may apply varying gamma adjustments, allowing for maladjustment of the displayed gamma, causing headaches for colorists and filmmakers alike.

gamma response of studio reference CRTs has been averaged at 2.4, which just happens to be nearly the inverse of our vision's luminance-to-lightness function.

With all of this in mind, video imaging specialists decided that as we move to digital displays, a strictly linear representation of the luminance of a scene is inappropriate, and CRT-like gamma continues to be applied to obtain the best perceptual representation of recorded (and color-graded) scenes.

This, in conjunction with the Bartleston-Breneman effect—which states that the perceived contrast of an image increases with an increase in the surround luminance around it (discussed later in this chapter)—means that it's important to match the reference luma and gamma settings of your display to the luminance of your surround lighting. This is the reason there are different gamma settings to choose from.

Although the standard for broadcast displays is well-defined, it's easy to be confused when evaluating displays that can be used for both web playback and broadcast. Here are the current standards:

- **2.6**: This is the gamma standard for digital cinema projection in a blackened theater environment with no ambient lighting.

- **2.4**: This is the recommended gamma setting for HD video displays as described by BT. 1886. A gamma of 2.4 replicates the average measured gamma of CRT displays, which once defined the standard for color-critical monitoring and is intended for use in a viewing environment with 1–10 percent surround illumination, with 1% seeming to be the current level used in higher-end mastering suites.

- **2.35**: This has been adopted by the EBU (search the Web for *EBU Guidelines for Consumer Flat Panel Displays*) for displays in a "dim surround" environment.

- **2.2**: This is a common setting for consumer televisions, meant for a viewing environment with a 5 percent surround (dim living room) to 20 percent surround (office environment).

- **sRGB 2.2**: Differing from the 2.2 standard used for consumer televisions, sRGB uses a gamma setting that's defined by IEC 61966-2-1:1999. This is the default gamma setting used by all displays connected to computers running Windows and Mac OS X. It is also intended for a viewing environment with a 5 percent surround (dim living room) to 20 percent surround (office environment).

NOTE

Because of all this, a strictly linear representation of the luminance in a recorded image wouldn't make the best use of the available bandwidth or bit-depth for a given video system. Consequently, devices that record BT. 601 or 709 video do so with an inverted adjustment immediately applied within the device, both for suitable display and to retain more image detail. Broadcast and computer displays then apply a matching, but inverted, gamma correction, with the result being a more or less true representation of the image.

LEARN MORE ABOUT GAMMA FROM THE EXPERT

I've presented the briefest summary of the subject of gamma for studio work here. For a more rigorously technical and wide-ranging explanation of gamma for broadcast, computer, and film applications, see the Gamma FAQ at www.poynton.com. The technically minded should also consult Charles Poynton's *Digital Video and HD Algorithms and Interfaces* (Morgan Kaufmann, 2012).

SETUP

After all these years of primarily digital signal usage, the *setup* (sometimes referred to as *pedestal*) or black level that a display should use continues to be a source of confusion. If you read only this first paragraph, keep this in mind: *All digital signals have a black level of 0 percent/IRE/mV.* If there are pixels of absolute black in the image, they should sit on the 0 line of your video scope's Waveform Monitor, Parade Scope, or histogram. It's as simple as that.

Now, on to the full story, which is relevant to those of you dealing with analog tapes and decks (such as Beta SP) in archives around the world. Most professional displays give you a choice of either 7.5 IRE or 0 IRE. Here are the rules for when it's appropriate to use a setting other than 0:

- Use a setup of 7.5 IRE only for standard-definition NTSC video being output to or played from analog Beta SP decks via analog component $Y'P_BP_R$. For most video interfaces, this is an analog issue that the video output interface takes care of when the driver software is properly configured, usually via a menu item or preference panel.

- Use a setup of 0 IRE for all other situations, including standard-definition NTSC in Japan, PAL in all countries, any standard-definition digital signal output via SDI (serial digital interface), and all standards of HD video output via both analog and digital interfaces.

Again, if you're not using analog Beta SP decks for input or output, then using a setup of 7.5 is *incorrect*. All digital and HD signals have a setup/black level of 0.

LIGHT OUTPUT

To correctly judge the quality of an image, it's also important that the peak, or reference, luminance output by a display be adjustable to account for different standards in place at different institutions and facilities. A standard governing peak light output is important, since the same image will appear to be more highly saturated and perceptually higher-contrast with higher light output and will appear less saturated and lower-contrast with lower light output (the Hunt/Stevens effect). As a result, the luminance output by your display has a huge impact on your grading decisions.

The reference luminance setting dictates what a display will output when fed a video signal that's set to 100 percent white (or 100 IRE/700 mV depending on how you're measuring the signal) and analyzed by a probe measuring the light output.

Surprisingly, there is no current SMPTE guidance specifying reference white luminance for HD displays. In practice, the reference white levels employed by past generations of CRT displays are used as an informal standard. Display manufacturer recommendations vary, but the principal recommendations are as follows:

- **80–100 cd/m²**: LCD/OLED/plasma in a darker light-controlled environment with bias lighting for the display surround. A survey conducted to measure CRT displays in color-critical use revealed that the practical output of these displays ranged between 80 and 100 "nits." Some imaging professionals I've talked to believe there is room for personal preference, depending on the relative strength of the ambient client lighting you may have in the suite. Charles Poynton recommends 100 cd/m².

- **120 cd/m²**: LCD/OLED/plasma, light-controlled environment with bias lighting for the display surround. This is the traditional recommendation for digital postproduction displays, based on the now-retired SMPTE Recommended Practice document RP 166-1995 (which, as of the time of this writing, hasn't been replaced). This light output is still appropriate for grading suites with brighter client lighting.

When selecting your display's gamma and light output, the display environment matters a lot, and these recommendations assume a professional display in a room with careful light control.

Consumer displays are typically much brighter, with light output from 150–250 cd/m² and higher; in fact, the EBU recommendation for consumer displays up to 50 inches diagonally is at least 200 cd/m². (For reference, 48 cd/m² is the DCI-recommended light output for a digital projector in a blackened theater environment with no ambient lighting.)

However, there are also proponents of even brighter reference white settings. For example, the Dolby 4220 boasts adjustable backlighting capable of up to 600 cd/m² output with no change to the black level of the display. In its PRM-4200 white paper, Dolby states, "The extended luminance ceiling of the DYN mode allows images to be clearly viewed even under elevated and challenging ambient light" related to the on-set monitoring conditions of a production's video village.

NOTE

When properly calibrated, the measured output of the white square at the bottom left of SD or HD color bars displayed onscreen should equal the current reference white setting.

NITS VS. FOOT-LAMBERTS

In the United States, the light output from displays and projectors has traditionally been measured in *foot-lamberts* (ft-L). However, the industry is slowly moving toward using *candelas/meter squared* (cd/m²), otherwise referred to as *nits* (nt) as a standardized unit of measurement. When converting between these values, 1 foot-lambert (ft-L) = 3.4262590996323 candela/meter² (cd/m²).

ADJUSTABILITY

Display adjustability is not just for accuracy. Your display, just like your video scope, is intended to be an instrument you can use to carefully examine any aspect of your picture. There are times when you may want to manually raise or lower the brightness, contrast, or chroma of the image from unity (the default calibrated levels) in order to see how your signal holds up in different situations.

At the very least, a display should have the following:

- **Under scan**, for evaluating outer action safe areas.

- **Bright/Chroma/Phase/Contrast** adjustments for deliberately misadjusting in order to spot check how your corrections hold up on miscalibrated displays.

- **Monochrome only** button, for evaluating image contrast and for turning off the color of a second in-suite display so that it's not distracting to you or to clients.

RESOLUTION

NOTE

Incidentally, if you're used to multiformat CRT displays, you'll remember that resolution was represented differently because of the way the electron beam painted the image onto the surface of the cathode ray tube. Most professional CRT monitors advertised 800–1000 lines of resolution, which was acceptable for color correction work but is well below the native resolution of modern digital displays.

For quality-control purposes, it's important you have a display capable of showing the full resolution of whatever video standard you're working on. Most digital display technologies have a fixed native resolution based on the construction of the screen or the imaging chips being used to create the picture, although just about any professional display is capable of switching resolutions depending on the signal being fed to the display.

A display capable of standard definition (SD) should be able to handle both NTSC and PAL resolutions. Also, although SD video ordinarily has a 4:3 (1.33) aspect ratio, a professional display should have an anamorphic mode (usually a button or menu option) to accommodate widescreen SD using a 16:9 (1.78) aspect ratio by squeezing the image down vertically. The resolutions are as follows:

- 720×486 for NTSC

- 720×576 for PAL

To accommodate the wide range of high-definition (HD) acquisition formats, an HD display should be capable of displaying both of the standard full-raster HD frame sizes at their native 16:9 (1.78) aspect ratio.

- 1280×720

- 1920×1080

Some newer displays are also able to accommodate digital cinema resolutions as defined by the DCI specification. Technically, projectors using these resolutions should also be capable of displaying the P3 DCI gamut. These resolutions also need to be displayable at either 1.85 (Academy) or 2.39 (Cinemascope/anamorphic) aspect ratios (**Figure 2.4**).

- 2048×1080 is the digital projection standard for 2K resolution

- 4096×2160 is the digital projection standard for 4K resolution

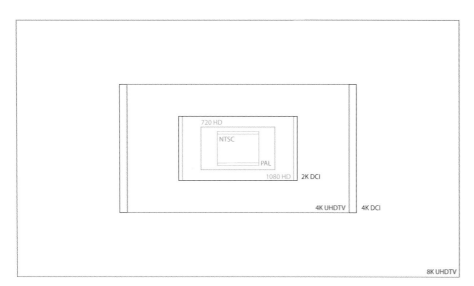

Figure 2.4 The frame sizes of various acquisition and mastering formats, compared. Note that there are only 128 pixels of horizontal difference between 2K and 1080p.

A newer generation of consumer televisions is now being produced with different, more broadcast-friendly resolutions referred to as *ultra-high-definition* television, ultra HD, or UHDTV. They're broadcast-friendly because of being multiples of the 1920x1080 HD standard, making downconversion easier for backward compatibility. Notably, the ITU has included these resolutions in the BT. 2020 standard currently being recommended. These resolutions are to be displayed with a native 16:9 (1.78) aspect ratio:

- 3840×2160 is the standard for 4K UHDTV.

- 7680×4320 is the resolution of 8K UHDTV, identified by the NHK in Japan as the Super Hi-Vision format.

At the time of this writing, the only color-critical displays capable of 4K are high-end projectors, although this will doubtless change over time.

WHY IS A DISPLAY'S NATIVE RESOLUTION IMPORTANT?

Keep in mind that, for any digital display, the sharpest resolution will be its *native* resolution; all other resolutions need to be scaled up or down to fit the full area of the display, which can result in a softening of the image if the processing isn't done well.

However, some displays have a 1:1 mode that disables such scaling, enabling you to see a smaller image at its native resolution, albeit at a smaller size relative to the screen.

CHAPTER 2

ASPECT RATIO

Professional displays capable of HD resolutions have an aspect ratio of 16:9 (1.78). If you work on other types of video but are using an HD display, the other formats of video should fit within the frame as follows:

- **SD video displayed on an HD display** should be *pillarboxed*, with vertical black bars to the left and right of the image on the screen, preserving the size and shape of the 1.33 image.

- **The wider aspect ratios of the DCDM resolutions** should appear *letterboxed* on an HD display, with horizontal black bars above and below to preserve the shape of either 1.85 or 2.39 images (**Figure 2.5**).

Figure 2.5 At left, pillarboxing resulting from fitting an SD image into an HD display. At right, the letterboxing that results from fitting a 16:9 HD image into an SD display.

Pillarboxed

Letterboxed

INTERLACING

One other consideration for any digital display is how it handles *interlacing*, in which two fields, one containing the odd-numbered horizontal lines in an image and the other containing the even-numbered horizontal lines in the image, are combined to form each "frame" of video. Digital display devices are inherently *progressive frame*, displaying full frames for each image. This is great for finishing 24p programs. However, many programs destined for broadcast continue to be shot and finished using an interlaced SD or HD format because of broadcaster requirements (and bandwidth limitations).

NOTE

If you're still using a CRT display, this is not a problem because CRTs have always been designed for interlaced signals.

A professional display should be able to handle interlacing in a predictable and visible manner, ideally with a mode that lets you evaluate whether the fields are being played in the proper order (accidentally reversed field order is a *big* quality control problem that you want to be able to spot). Some displays do this by simulating field-by-field playback, whereas others simply show a deinterlaced signal during playback and reveal both fields together when the video is paused.

IMAGE SIZE

This is one of the biggest factors affecting the price of your display. Ideally, you'll want a display that's large enough for both you and your client to be able to sit back and watch the picture from a comfortable distance, but color-critical displays larger than 24" can be expensive.

Also, it's important to keep in mind the size of your room and the type of clients you work with. Larger displays make it easier to evaluate a grade's impact as it will be seen in an ideal home-theater situation. A large image also makes it easy to see whether grain and noise are unpleasantly exaggerated after large corrections.

However, it's entirely possible to get a display that's too big for your space. Ideally, you want the image to be small enough so you can take in the entire image at a glance. This will help you make quick decisions when you're matching one shot to another, and it'll keep you from getting a crick in your neck from turning it back and forth just to see the image.

- **Color-critical LCD displays** now range in size from 17" (suitable for on-set use) and 24" (good for small suites) up to 32", 42", and 50" from some vendors.

- **Plasma displays** can go larger—commonly 42" to 65" diagonal or larger—and can be a good choice as a client display for larger video suites with a dedicated client area (assuming you calibrate the displays properly).

- **Video projectors** are suitable only for large video suites and grading theaters, projecting images from 80" to 142" in a large suite and much larger in a proper grading theater.

More information on display placement and on setting up video projectors is presented later in this chapter.

CRT RIP

High-end CRT displays were long the only choice for color correction work. However, aggressive European Union regulation on lead content in electronic equipment spelled the death-knell of CRT manufacturing. As a result, most facilities have retired their aging CRT displays because of the limited lifespan of the tubes and have moved on to using digital displays for color-critical evaluation work instead, leaving CRT as a historical footnote in the industry.

CHAPTER 2

WHO MAKES DISPLAYS?

Several companies are developing high-end displays for color-critical use. At the time of this writing, Flanders Scientific, Sony, Dolby, FrontNICHE, Hewlett-Packard, Panasonic, Penta Studiotechnik, and TV Logic offer products worth investigating.

When it comes to professional plasma displays suitable for color-critical work, at the time of this writing Panasonic is the leading choice for professional post houses.

VIDEO INTERFACES FOR PROFESSIONAL MONITORING

You'll want to make sure that, as you color correct your project, you're looking at the highest-quality image possible. Also keep in mind that the accuracy of your display is only as good as the weakest link in your video signal chain. Whatever type of display you decide to use in your video suite, you need to make sure it's capable of supporting (or being upgraded to) the highest-quality video signal output supported by your color correction system or your editing computer's video interface.

Here are some quick recommendations:

- **If you're working on a standard-definition program in an aging suite**, either $Y'P_BP_R$ or SDI would be a good choice for connecting your computer's video output to a reference broadcast display.

- **If you're working on a high-definition project**, you should be monitoring using HD-SDI.

- **Dual-Link HD-SDI and 3G SDI** are necessary only if your video format or device requires a higher-bandwidth signal with 4:4:4 chroma sampling.

- **Quad-Link HD-SDI and 6G SDI** are necessary only if you need to monitor a 4K signal on a 4K display or projector.

- **HDMI** is often the only connection option for high-end home-theater equipment. Although this is a high-quality standard, you may need HD-SDI-to-HDMI conversion hardware to incorporate this equipment into your system.

The following sections present more detailed information about each video interface standard used for high-quality video output, as well as additional suggestions regarding which one might be appropriate for your application and the maximum recommended cable lengths for each interface.

$Y'P_BP_R$

$Y'P_BP_R$ (it's not an acronym) is a three-cable professional *analog* component video interface. It outputs each video component (one for luma and two for the color difference components) over three separate signal wires, connected using Bayonet Neill-Concelman (BNC) connectors that fasten securely when properly connected.

While no longer typically used in modern digital postproduction suites, $Y'P_BP_R$ is nonetheless suitable for monitoring both SD and HD video signals and is the highest-quality *analog* signal path used for professional video monitoring applications.

$Y'P_BP_R$'s maximum cable length is generally 100' (30 m) and possibly up to 200' (60 m), depending on the quality of your cable.

SDI

Serial digital interface (SDI) is typically used for digital, uncompressed, standard-definition video input and output. SDI is the highest-quality digital signal you can use for monitoring standard-definition video. All three signal components, Luma (Y') and the two color-difference channels (CB and CR), are multiplexed onto a single BNC cable.

SDI's maximum cable length is approximately 300' (90 m) using a high-quality cable. SMPTE 259M contains more guidance for calculating SDI cable transmission lengths.

HD-SDI, DUAL-LINK SDI, 3G SDI, AND 6G SDI

High-definition serial digital interface (HD-SDI) is the high-definition version of SDI, capable of carrying 4:2:2 digital video signals.

Dual-Link SDI (using two BNC cables) and 3G-SDI (a higher-bandwidth signal that uses a single BNC cable) are designed as the interface for the output and input of high-definition uncompressed 4:4:4 video signals (such as those recorded and played by Sony's HDCAM SR equipment).

Quad-Link SDI is used to transmit 4K signals, requiring four BNC cables. The newest 6G SDI standard allows for 4K to be transmitted over a single cable.

HD-SDI's maximum cable length is approximately 300' (90 m), depending on the quality of cable you're using. SMPTE 292M contains more guidance for calculating HD-SDI cable transmission lengths.

HDMI

High-definition multimedia interface (HDMI) is an "all-in-one" standard capable of transporting both audio and video, in a wide variety of formats, over a single multiconductor cable. Although designed with simplicity in mind for consumer devices, HDMI can be useful in smaller video postproduction suites depending on your mix of equipment.

NOTE

$Y'P_BP_R$, which is an analog video standard, should not be confused with $Y'C_BC_R$, which is the standard for digital component video signals and is conducted via one of several digital interfaces.

CHAPTER 2

An evolving standard, subsequent versions of HDMI continue to introduce enhanced capabilities. To guarantee the correct signal path, both the output device and the display device must use the same version of HDMI. The versions of HDMI currently available are as follows:

- **HDMI 1.2** supports SD and HD $Y'C_BC_R$ at 8 bits per channel.

- **HDMI 1.3** adds support for 2K resolutions up to 2560×1600, along with "Deep Color" support for 10, 12, and 16 bit-per-channel color, and adds support for $Y'C_BC_R$ using either 4:2:2 or 4:4:4 and for RGB using 4:4:4.

- **HDMI 1.4** adds support for the Ultra HD 4K resolution of 3840×2160 (at 24, 25, and 30 fps) along with support for the DCI 4K resolution of 4096×2160 (at 24 fps). There's also support for various stereoscopic 3D formats including field alternative (interlaced) and frame packing (full-resolution frames stacked top and bottom), with additional stereoscopic formats introduced in HDMI 1.4a and 1.4b (which support stereo 1080p at 60 fps).

- **HDMI 2.0** added 60fps playback at 4K resolution, $Y'C_BC_R$ 4:2:0 chroma sub-sampling in order to support higher compression for larger resolutions, 25 fps stereoscopic 3D formats, multiple video and audio stream support, support for a 21:9 aspect ratio, and support for up to 32 channels of audio (including 1536 kHz audio).

NOTE

For more information about HDMI, you can obtain the HDMI specification at www. HDMI.org.

It's important to understand that just because a particular version of HDMI supports a particular bit-depth, resolution, or gamut, it doesn't mean that the device you're either outputting from or connecting to supports it. For example, even though most newer versions of HDMI support 10-bit color, many devices continue to output only 8-bit color over HDMI. If you're planning on using HDMI for signal routing, check your equipment to make sure you're actually able to output and display the signal you want to be using.

HDMI's maximum cable length is 50' (15 m) using a high-quality shielded cable. When you are running 1080p video at the maximum length, it's recommended to use Category 2-certified HDMI (sometimes called *high-speed*) cables to guarantee quality.

DISPLAYPORT

DisplayPort was designed as a next-generation interface for computer displays and not necessarily for broadcast. However, DisplayPort is capable of carrying 6, 8, 10, 12, and 16 bit-per-channel RGB and Y'CBCB signals (accommodating both BT. 601 and 709 video standards) with 4:2:2 chroma subsampling, and it supports a variety of resolutions including 1920×1080 and higher.

Interestingly, DisplayPort is backward-compatible with HDMI signals (although the date of your DisplayPort device's manufacture will dictate *which* version of HDMI). This means that specifically designed converter cables can easily change one format into the other on supported devices. Furthermore, because DisplayPort is such a versatile interface, manufacturers are creating video signal converters that can turn an HD-SDI signal into a DisplayPort signal. See the next section for more information on signal conversion.

DisplayPort's maximum cable length is 9' (3 m) at full resolution (2560×1600, 70 Hz) or 49' (15 m) at 1920×1080 (1080p60).

CONVERTING ONE VIDEO SIGNAL TO ANOTHER

Newer models of displays sometimes require the use of signal conversion hardware to turn the HD-SDI output from a color correction system into HDMI or DisplayPort. Available solutions include the following (in alphabetical order):

- AJA's HI5 and HI5 3G
- Ensemble Designs' BrightEye 72 and 72-F 3G/HD/SD converter
- Gefen's HD-SDI and 3G-SDI to HDMI Scaler Boxes
- Miranda's Kaleido-Solo 3Gbps/HD/SD-to-HDMI converter
- FujiFilm's IS-Mini
- Pandora's Pluto
- SpectraCal DVC-3GRX
- Blackmagic Design's HDLink Pro

BUT WHAT ABOUT DVI?

Even though many early high-definition devices supported digital visual interface (DVI), single-link DVI supports only 8 bit-per-channel output. Dual-link DVI supports 12 bit-per-channel output, but it is less common on video devices and virtually never used in professional video applications.

For video equipment, DVI has been superseded by HDMI. For computer applications, DisplayPort is the emerging standard, going forward.

SHOULD MY SUITE HAVE TWO DISPLAYS?

While I recommend having no more than one "hero" display in a room to which everyone can refer, many suites employ dual-display setups, with a smaller, more rigorously standards-compliant display for color-critical viewing by the colorist and a larger display (often plasma) for more impressive and comfortable client viewing.

The key to making this work is to make sure that the spectral output of the backlighting technologies used by both displays are relatively compatible with one

NOTE
Projector/LCD or OLED combos
are the most challenging dual-
display combinations. Projectors
need a darkened theater environment to look their best,
whereas self-illuminated displays
require backlighting to "tone
down" the eye's perception of
their abundant light output and
the high apparent saturation
that results. A self-illuminated
display in a darkened room next
to a projector will always look
brighter and more saturated
than the projected image; this
leads to client confusion if you
aren't careful to explain the
difference.

another, that they're calibrated as precisely as feasible, and that accurate calibration is maintained. Unfortunately, if the two monitoring devices you have use different display technologies, visible differences between the two may be unavoidable no matter *how* carefully you calibrated them.

The peril of this situation is having your client give you the most aggravating bit of feedback I can think of: "Could you make the image on *that* display look like the one on *the other*?" For this reason, it's generally best to try to encourage your client to restrict their feedback to the output of only one display.

DISPLAY SANITY-CHECKING

Another option is to have some type of "cheap" consumer television available (that's usually wheeled in for a dedicated evaluation session) so that you can check how your programs hold up on an average TV. Another option is to have a display capable of storing multiple LUTs. If you load one or two LUTs that are characterizations of lesser displays, you can simply switch your beautifully color-critical display to "rubbish mode" so you can see how the monitored image will degrade on inferior televisions.

Some colorists also like to have a small, dedicated monochrome display, either a little display on the desk, a monochrome video preview on a video scope, or a second display with the chroma set to 0. This can be helpful for evaluating just the contrast of the image, and since there's no color in the picture, clients are unlikely to pay much attention to it.

DISPLAY CALIBRATION

For professional digital displays, the design of a given display's panel, image processing, and backlighting (if necessary) must be tailored to comply with the BT. 709 or P3 DCI standards for gamut and gamma discussed previously, and many displays can be switched among a variety of precalibrated standards via a simple menu selection.

However, although a display may advertise that it's standards-compliant, that doesn't mean it leaves the factory with exact accuracy. For this reason, it's also important to invest in a display that can be calibrated to match the standards you require as exactly as possible. Even if your display leaves the factory with precisely calibrated color, eventually your display will drift due to aging of the backlight system or other components. There are three main strategies for maintaining standards compliance.

GET A PRECALIBRATED DISPLAY

A variety of professional displays come precalibrated from the factory. While many modern displays have extremely stable color, eventually every display will need to be recalibrated. If you're on a budget, research the manufacturer of the display you're looking to purchase to see whether it offers factory recalibration. If available, this frees you from the expense of either hiring a calibrator to come on-site or investing in expensive calibration probes and software (and the learning curve that accompanies them).

One example of a company that offers factory recalibration is Flanders Scientific. For the price of shipping your monitor to its service center, the company will recalibrate the display using a level of equipment and hardware that is far beyond the means of most freelancers. For more expensive displays on the other end of the spectrum, Dolby offers a yearly service program you can subscribe to for its PRM-4220 that gets you calibrator flown to your facility for periodic recalibration (their displays are a little large to ship). Other manufacturers have their own policies; check ahead to see what makes sense for you.

GET A DISPLAY THAT CAN BE CALIBRATED BY A SPECIALIST

Another approach—especially useful if your reference display is a prosumer display intended for the home-theater market—is to have it calibrated on-site by a professional. THX compliance requires display and projector manufacturers to provide the built-in controls necessary to calibrate a given display for BT. 709 adherence. To do this, you'll likely want to hire a qualified calibration specialist to make sure your monitor is within spec. Older displays could require dedicated hardware to adjust the output, but the current generation of display hardware shouldn't require any extra calibration hardware.

What you spend on the calibrator's fee, you'll end up saving on the highly accurate *colorimeter* or *spectroradiometer* (more simply referred to as a *probe*) that they'll use to measure the output from your monitor or front-projected screen. Professional models range in price from $12,000 to in excess of $26,000, which would pay for a lot of calibration sessions over the years if you're a small shop with only a periodic need for calibration.

Additionally, calibrators have an investment in other hardware and software necessary to do the job; test pattern generators output a variety of test color fields in succession for the spectrophotometer to measure, and a color-management application collates the readings and controls the process. The resulting data is used to adjust your display's gamma and gamut parameters using the display's built-in controls or outboard hardware if necessary.

Increasingly, specialists are also available who do LUT-based calibration as described in the next section.

BUY CALIBRATION SOFTWARE AND A PROBE

This approach is also accomplished using a monitor probe, but instead of collating automated measurements into a series of individual adjustments, the software taking the measurements mathematically generates a LUT file that is used to calculate how to convert the gamma and gamut of the display device into a standards-compliant gamut of your choosing, taking into account the display's unique characteristics.

This LUT file can be loaded into compatible outboard calibration hardware (connected between your computer's video output interface and the display) to process the signal being sent to the display, it can be loaded directly into the control software of a display with built-in LUT calibration, or it can be loaded as a display LUT for NLEs or color correction software that offers this as an option.

Good probes and calibration software can be expensive, but it gives you the freedom to recalibrate whenever necessary and can ultimately save you money if you need to regularly recalibrate a facility full of monitors.

CHECKING YOUR DISPLAY'S ALIGNMENT

Even if you decide to use factory recalibration or calibration specialists to keep your display up to snuff, it's still useful to periodically check your display's alignment to verify whether calibration is necessary. Two application vendors have solutions that let you run a test to check whether your display is running accurately. Such tests typically use inexpensive probes and software to verify whether the calibration of your display is up to specifications. This lets you track drift and alerts you to any kind of failure that would affect your display's accuracy so you can send it in for service.

* LightSpace DPS is free software for Windows that lets you use any compatible probe (including the inexpensive X-Rite i1d3 probe) to verify your display's calibration, in conjunction with either a pattern generator or an AJA T-Tap for outputting patterns from the computer running LightSpace DPS (http://www.lightillusion.com/lightspace_dps.html).

* CalMAN ColorChecker works similarly to test the calibration of your display in conjunction with compatible probes and pattern generators (www.studio.spectracal.com).

HOW LUT CALIBRATION WORKS

Monitor calibration is an obscure corner of the already obscure profession of color correction. However, once you know how things work, automated calibration is really a simple and straightforward procedure. Essentially, you use color management software to control both a color probe and a pattern generator (which can be either stand-alone hardware or software running on a computer and outputting via a video interface of some kind) that work together to measure your display (**Figure 2.6**). The color management software controls the pattern generator, directing it to output a series of color patches to the display you're calibrating; the color probe measures each patch; and the software saves the resulting measurements.

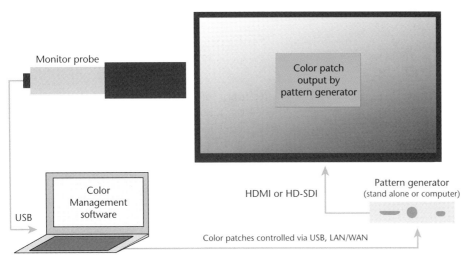

CHAPTER 2

Figure 2.6 A typical color management software setup.

The process of measuring hundreds or even thousands of patches of different colors *characterizes* your display, providing data about what your display is capable of showing. This lets you see how much and where your display deviates from an ideal colorspace, such as the BT. 709 standard for high-definition video. Once your display has been characterized, the difference between an ideal calibration and your actual display can then be used to mathematically generate a LUT that you'll use to transform whatever signal is sent to your display into how it should look on an *ideal* display.

Before you get too excited about the promise of automated, LUT-based calibration, it's important to know what it *can't* do. LUT calibration works well only when your display is already capable of meeting or exceeding the full gamut, or range of colors, of the calibration standard you require. For example, if you're calibrating a high-end plasma display that's capable of BT. 709 to precisely meet the BT. 709 standard, then you're in good shape. However, if you're trying to calibrate it to meet the DCI standard of digital cinema calibration, which has a much larger gamut, then you're probably out of luck.

LUTs, specifically 3D LUT cubes, are mathematical tables that automatically calculate what RGB value to output based on each RGB value that's input. When used for calibration, 3D LUTs are capable of transforming larger gamuts to match smaller gamuts, but there's no way you can make a display with a smaller gamut properly display a larger gamut. Physics denies you.

LUT calibration doesn't let you off the hook as far as getting a good display; you still need to do the research and purchase the best display technology you can afford. LUT calibration is *not* about making poor displays good; it's about making good displays accurate.

A DEEPER LOOK AT CALIBRATION—HOW LIGHTSPACE CMS WORKS

To give you a better idea of what color management software actually does behind the scenes, I thought it would be useful to take a closer look at one particular application in a more detailed way. Different calibration apps have different methods of working, but since I've worked with LightSpace for some time, its process is familiar for me to describe (with help from Steve Shaw, principal at Light Illusion, the company that develops it).

LightSpace CMS is a professional, LUT-based color management application that's compatible with a wide range of display probes and pattern-generation methods and is used by grading facilities worldwide. LightSpace works by decoupling the process of monitor characterization from that of LUT generation. After first doing some basic display setup using initial test patterns to ensure the display is correctly configured, the first step of calibrating a display using LightSpace is to run a series of test patches, measuring the displayed result and collating the resulting data about how your monitor is currently outputting color at every level of RGB.

Once a display has been characterized in total, the resulting data can be analyzed by LightSpace in a second step in the process: identifying and addressing any *cross-coupling* of the red, green, and blue color components, such as when a color change that should affect only the blue channel also contaminates the red and green channels, causing miscalibration. Additionally, probe measurements that can be mathematically determined to be errors in the data set (often in the shadows where many types of probes can have problems) can be corrected prior to further use of the data.

An actual calibration LUT is then generated in a third step. In this process, you simply choose which viewing standard you want LightSpace to calibrate your monitor to (for example BT. 601, BT. 709, DCI P3), and LightSpace mathematically calculates an accurate calibration transform for that display. You can use this same process to match multiple displays to one another in multidisplay suites.

With that accomplished, you can choose to export the resulting calibration LUT to a wide variety of LUT formats. This enables you to export LUTs that are supported by a display's internal hardware, by dedicated LUT calibration hardware, or by grading applications that are capable of applying LUTs internally. LightSpace also gives you additional options for concatenating, or combining, multiple LUTs—for example combining a display LUT with a film emulation LUT for digital intermediate workflows where you need to grade in context to how the project will look after film printing on a particular stock. Other tools let you apply offsets, manual adjustments, and other tweaks for power users who need to address specific workflow needs.

In addition to the accuracy that's gained through the mathematical analysis made possible by characterizing your display first and generating LUTs later, the overall process can be sped up considerably. As an added bonus, you have the ability to measure the display once and then generate a variety of LUTs for different monitoring standards or simulation applications without further measurement.

COLOR MANAGEMENT SYSTEMS

As of this writing, there are three software suites for display measurement and LUT generation.

- FilmLight's Truelight film color management system (www.filmlight.ltd.uk) is a complete solution, comprising FilmLight's own Truelight projector and display probes and software.

- Light Illusion's LightSpace color management system (www.lightillusion.com) is another suite of software utilities for display measurement, LUT generation, and LUT conversion and reprocessing, along with many other useful features, such as probe matching.

- SpectraCal CalMAN video calibration software (www.spectracal.com) provides a third option for calibrating displays and LUT conversion.

DISPLAY PROBES

This is an extremely big topic, and honestly there are so many opinions about what probes are appropriate for which applications that I'm going to refer you to the documentation of whatever color management software you're planning on using for more information and to recommendations about which probes are compatible and appropriate. Overall, there are two categories of display probes: spectroradiometers and colorimeters. Both have advantages and disadvantages.

- *Spectroradiometers* are, by far, the most expensive of the two. They work by measuring the absolute spectral power distribution of light, taking many readings and producing tristimulus values that can be converted into chromaticity coordinates, useful for calculating transformations. Spectroradiometers are the last word in accuracy but can be slow to take readings, especially in low-light conditions.

- *Colorimeters* are considerably less expensive and work by using three filters that are matched to CIE tristimulus values to take a more limited set of spectral energy readings using three discrete detectors, producing the resulting measured chromaticity coordinates. For colorimeters to work properly, the illuminant needs to be known to calculate the readings.

Because of their low cost, colorimeters are much more common for individual use than spectroradiometers, which are generally found in the hands of professional calibrators and at large facilities. Colorimeters aren't as general-purpose or intensively accurate as spectroradiometers, but for the specific purpose of taking monitor measurements, they're completely suitable; in fact, colorimeters can be much faster, and the right models can be better at taking low-light readings.

However, because of possible variations in the manufacturing of the filters, the aging of the filters, and the susceptibility of some filters in less expensive colorimeters to change because of humidity, it's important to calibrate your colorimeter using a spectroradiometer first (this can be done by the manufacturer or via your calibration software) and to make sure your colorimeter is correctly set up for measuring the type of display you're calibrating.

The following are some monitor probes in common use. Do your research and check with the developer of the color management software you plan on using before making a decision. Depending on your display, your clientele, and your application (calibration or sanity checking), it doesn't make sense to buy more probe than you need, or less. Here is a sampling of probes that are supported both by LightSpace CMS and CalMAN:

- X-Rite i1 Display Pro, i1 Pro 2 colorimeters (www.xrite.com)
- Basiccolor Discus colorimeter (www.basiccolor.de)
- Klein K-10A colorimeter (www.kleininstruments.com)
- Jeti 1211 spectroradiometer (www.jeti.com)
- Photo Research PR-655, PR-670 spectroradiometer (www.photoresearch.com)
- Konica Minolta CA-310, CS-200 spectroradiometer (www.sensing.konicaminolta.asia/products/)

PATTERN GENERATORS

For a color management application to measure a display, a precise test color signal needs to be output for the probe to measure. Pattern generation can be handled in one of a variety of ways.

- Traditionally, pattern generators have been dedicated hardware boxes that can be controlled by the color management software and that have a video output that is connected to the display being calibrated. Dedicated pattern generators from companies like Accupel (www.chromapure.com) are a good example of this.

- A handful of multipurpose signal convertors and LUT calibration boxes, such as the FujiFilm IS-Mini (described in a moment), can also be used as controllable pattern generators, which is convenient since you'll also need them to apply the LUT for calibration.

- Pattern generation can also be done via software. For example, LightSpace CMS can act as its own pattern generator by outputting color patches via an AJA T-TAP connected to the Windows computer running LightSpace. Or, if you're using a grading application with a LightSpace plug-in such as DaVinci Resolve (including the free Lite version), Assimilate Scratch, or SGO Mistika, the grading software can be used as a pattern generator with no additional setup. Users of CalMAN have the option of using SpectraCal's VirtualForge pattern generator running on a computer using OS X.

APPLYING LUTS USING HARDWARE

Many displays are capable of using LUTs via their own integrated hardware. Furthermore, most grading applications are capable of applying calibration LUTs for display purposes in software as part of the grading process.

However, if neither your software nor your display is capable of loading a LUT, then you can use a LUT via outboard calibration hardware that you insert into the signal chain between the video output of your color correction hardware and your display device for the purposes of calibration (**Figure 2.7**). You usually load a LUT onto such a device using USB from your computer.

NOTE

Using outboard LUT hardware for calibration is also the best way to calibrate your monitor if you're using outboard video scopes.

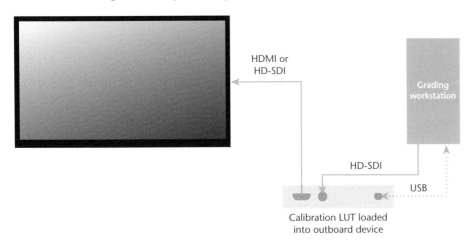

HDMI or
HD-SDI

Grading
workstation

HD-SDI

USB

Calibration LUT loaded
into outboard device

Figure 2.7 An outboard calibration LUT box that sits between your grading workstation's output and your display's input, modifying the signal to be perfectly calibrated.

Here are the options available as of this writing:

- **FilmLight's Truelight SDI** (www.filmlight.ltd.uk) is a multifunction device that can apply one of 15 preloaded 1D LUT + 16×16×16 point LUT cube combinations. It works as a hardware legalizer with soft clipping, and it can also function as a test pattern generator. It's designed to work with FilmLight's Truelight software.

- **Pandora Pluto** (www.pandora-int.com) does both signal conversion and LUT calibration, offering conversion from Dual Link to Single Link and from HD-SDI to HDMI. LUT calibration supports 16, 17, 32, and 33×33×33 cubes. It's compatible with FilmLight Truelight, LightSpace CMS, and CalMAN Studio.

- **eeColor processor** (www.eecolor.com) is another inexpensive signal processing device with HDMI input and output, to which you can load a 64×64×64 LUT cube for monitor calibration. It's compatible with LightSpace CMS and CalMAN Studio.

- **FujiFilm's IS-Mini** (www.fujifilm.com/products/motion_picture/image_processing/is_mini/) is a multipurpose device designed for on-set camera previews and 26×26×26 LUT-based monitor calibration, signal conversion from HD-SDI to HDMI, and pattern generation. It's compatible with LightSpace CMS and CalMAN Studio.

CHAPTER 2

- **Lumagen Radiance** (www.lumagen.com) is a line of calibration boxes designed for high-end home-theater calibration, multisignal switching, and signal conversion. The Radiance 20XX series model has added support for 1D LUT + 9x9x9 LUT cube calibration, while other models support 5x5x5 LUT cube support. It's compatible with LightSpace CMS and CalMAN Studio.

- **Blackmagic Design's HDLink Pro** (www.blackmagicdesign.com) is an inexpensive signal conversion device that can also apply a 16×16×16-point LUT cube for the purposes of signal processing or calibration. It's compatible with LightSpace CMS and CalMAN Studio.

- **Cine-tal's Davio** is another multifunction device that can be expanded with software add-ons. It can apply one of multiple 64×64×64-point LUT cubes for calibration, can merge two LUTs to combine calibration and simulation profiles, and can work as a frame store and stereo image processor. While Davio is no longer manufactured, there are many units still in use. It's compatible with LightSpace CMS and CalMAN Studio.

These hardware devices are designed to take a single or dual-link HD-SDI input, process the video signal with a LUT, and output an HD-SDI, HDMI, or DisplayPort signal to your video display. Each device differs in the size of the LUT cube it supports. For color-critical monitoring, it's generally accepted that a 16×16×16-point LUT is sufficient, while 32×32×32-point and 64×64×64-point LUT cubes are often used for processing image data in digital cinema and digital intermediate workflows.

NOTE
Much more detailed information about LUT calibration and the digital intermediate process can be found at Steve Shaw's Light Illusion website. Visit www.lightillusion.com and see the pages on working with LUTs.

When asked about the minimum required precision for color-critical LUT-based display calibration, colorist and LightSpace developer Steve Shaw says, "Anything above 17 points is overkill, assuming the interpolation used within the color system is good. If not, a higher-point cube will help, but most systems have good interpolation."

Furthermore, Richard Kirk, color scientist at FilmLight in the UK, points out that the Truelight's color management system combines a 1D LUT with a 16×16×16 3D LUT for the purposes of display calibration. "I cannot speak for all our customers," he told me, "but 1D + 16×16×16 3D has always worked for me, and I have never had a complaint that didn't turn out to be some measurement or computation error and not a lack of cube precision."

LUT CALIBRATION AND FILM OUTPUT SIMULATION

If you're setting up a workflow to accommodate film output, there's one other thing to keep in mind. LUT calibration can serve two purposes. The first is to display characterization and calibration to bring it into spec. The second is to profile a film printer and film stock to simulate how an image on your particular display will look after it's been printed to film so that it can help you make informed decisions about how to grade the picture.

To better understand how this works, let's take a quick look at the process of LUT transformation. The basis for LUT transformations is the extrusion of RGB values into 3D space. In other words, the maximum tristimulus values defining the total possible range of red, green, and blue color in digital images are plotted as a 3D cube (**Figure 2.8**).

The gamut for a particular image or video standard is represented by a polygon within this cube, with its shape dictated by the range of colors it encompasses. Every imaging standard can be represented by a different shape (**Figure 2.9**).

A LUT, therefore, is simply a table of input values (representing the image being processed) with corresponding output values (representing how that image is to be displayed) that defines how one gamut's shape can be matched to another to achieve the most reasonably faithful representation of an image no matter what device it appears on.

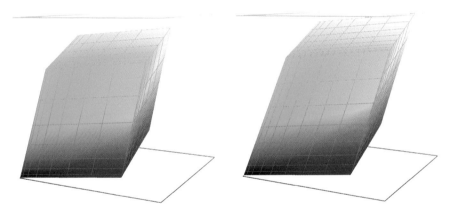

In **Figure 2.10**, you can see how a LUT can be used to transform an image output to a video projector to show how it will look after it's been printed to film.

Based on this visualization, you can make appropriate adjustments to optimize the image for film printing, before disabling this "simulation LUT," prior to rendering the final images to deliver to the lab.

Figure 2.8 The standard LUT cube representation for the RGB color space.

Figure 2.9 To the right, the LUT cube representation for the P3 gamut used for digital cinema; to the left, the LUT cube representation for BT. 709 HD video, as generated by Apple's ColorSync Utility.

CHAPTER 2

Figure 2.10 On the left is the BT. 709–monitored image, and on the right is the same image with a film-simulation LUT applied. This enables the colorist to grade within the context of the effect of the film printer and stock on the final print. *LUT courtesy of Steve Shaw, Light Illusion.*

The creation of a film-profiling LUT for a given combination of film printer and film stock is accomplished by the following procedure:

1   The vendor of your LUT measurement and generation software provides you with a set of full-frame test images. Give this test image to the facility or lab that you'll be hiring to do the film output.

2   The facility prints the test image to film using the combination of film printer and film stock you've agreed upon.

3   The resulting film print is sent back to the color management software vendor, who scans and measures each test patch, using the resulting analysis to generate a characterization LUT that you can use to simulate how your work will look *after* it's been printed to film.

4   The last step can be taken either by your calibration software or by you. Merge the calibration LUT that is being used to bring your display device into perfect standards compliance with the film simulation LUT created in step 3. This can be done in one of three ways:

  • By using a utility that uses the first two LUTs to create a third

  • By loading the calibration LUT into your display or outboard calibration hardware and the simulation LUT into your color correction software

  • By loading both LUTs into an outboard hardware calibration device designed to combine the two

SETTING UP A COLOR CORRECTION SUITE

NOTE
Much of the information in this section comes from the SMPTE Recommended Practice document "Critical Viewing Conditions for Evaluation of Color Television Pictures" (document RP 166-1995) and Sony's booklet, "Sony Monitor Basics." Information about DCDM standards for monitoring is drawn from the Digital Cinema System Specification Version 1.2, from Digital Cinema Initiatives, LLC, and from Glenn Kennel's *Color and Mastering for Digital Cinema* (Focal Press, 2006). All are important references to have.

The environment in which viewers watch your program has almost as big an effect on how the picture is perceived as the display at which you're looking. Conversely, the type of display you'll be using dictates how you'll need to set up your room.

If you're making critical color evaluations of video, it's vital that your viewing environment is suited to your particular display.

VIDEO SUITES VS. GRADING THEATERS

Generally speaking, a video suite is a smaller room employing a medium-sized display (probably LCD or plasma) to monitor the image being adjusted. There's usually subdued light, with surround lighting behind the reference display. Video suites are ideal for color correcting programs destined for broadcast, as well as for long-form programs operating on a low budget.

A grading theater is a considerably larger room using a video projector (or digital cinema projector) to monitor the image. Because of the projector, grading is done in "black box" conditions, with no ambient light other than some limited lighting for work desk areas. Grading theaters are most appropriate for programs destined for theatrical presentation.

THE AREA SURROUNDING YOUR DISPLAY

If you're setting up a display of some kind, the décor of the room in which you're working should be generally subdued and desaturated. Most critically, the visible area behind the display, referred to as the *surround wall*, should be a neutral (achromatic) gray.

You can achieve neutral gray by painting the wall or by covering it with drapery or fabric. Whichever method you choose, the ideal shade of the wall covering is somewhere around 18 percent gray and uses a paint or material that remains neutral when illuminated by appropriate surround lighting (see the next section). What's important is that the material is neutral, so make sure your paint or fabric is not slightly bluish or reddish. The exact lightness may vary so long as it's neither white nor black (digital projection rooms being set up according to DCDM specifications are another story). Sony recommends that the gray surround wall be greater than eight times the display's screen area, but it's basically a good idea to paint or cover enough of the wall to fill your field of view while you're looking directly at the display.

Establishing such a surround does two things. First, by making sure that the wall isn't any particular hue, you'll be able to evaluate the colors of the image on the display without outside influence. Because our eyes judge color relative to surrounding colors, having an orange wall behind your evaluation display would influence your color perception, potentially causing you to overcompensate and make inaccurate corrections to the video, delivering images with an incorrect cast when viewed in standard conditions.

Second, the contrast of images on your reference display is going to be influenced by the brightness of the wall surrounding it. When grading television programs, if the wall is either bright white or deep black, you risk misjudging the lightness or darkness of the image on your display as a result.

Incidentally, don't illuminate the surround too evenly. SMPTE Recommended Practice document RP 166-1995, section 5.4 states, "Practice has shown that a uniform field is not optimum but that a gradation of intensity from top to bottom, or bottom to top, is more pleasing."

You can accomplish this by avoiding overly even lighting on the surround wall and allowing falloff. However, another anecdotal strategy is to cover the display surround wall with a neutral, *textured* surface, such as appropriate cloth with a coarse weave or draping that is gathered. In general, the idea is to reduce eye fatigue by providing variation in the surfaces within your field of view so you're not spending all day "staring into infinity."

CHAPTER 2

HOW DO I FIND NEUTRAL GRAY PAINT OR FABRIC?

If you're painting the surround, scouring the Web will reveal various formulas for neutral paints from a range of vendors that will likely work well for you. However, if you're a stickler for absolute accuracy, you can also find spectrally accurate gray paints that are based on the Munsell color system. GTI Graphic Technology manufactures two neutral gray paints based on the Munsell N7 and N8 standards of gray (N8 is a lighter gray, and N7 is darker). eCinema also sells a spectrally flat gray paint it calls SP-50. Other paint and fabric manufacturers also sell products that conform to the Munsell scale, on which N0 represents solid black and N10 is the lightest white.

If you want to mix your own, Flanders Scientific has published a paint formula at www.flandersscientific.com/index/tech_resources.php.

DISPLAY SURROUND LIGHTING

The luminance of the surround lighting in your video suite is hugely important to the critical evaluation of monitored images. This is partially because of the Bartleston-Breneman effect, which states that the perceived contrast of an image increases with an increase in the surround luminance around it. (See Mahdi Nezambadi's *The Effect of Image Size on the Color Appearance of Image Reproductions* [Biblio LabsII, 2008].)

For this reason, it's important to match the luminance of your surround lighting to the reference luma and gamma setting you're planning on using for monitoring. For precision, the luminance of your surround lighting can be measured with a spot photometer, capable of measuring intensity and luminance in foot-lamberts (ft-L) and lux.

Here are the recommended guidelines:

- **100 cd/m² with gamma of 2.4**: A more permissive range, accounting for the tremendous amount of debate and personal preference around monitoring settings, would be 80–120 cd/m² with gamma of 2.2–2.4. When you're complying with the BT. 1886 standard for gamma and the currently recommended monitor reference luminance of 100 cd/m², current practice for broadcast mastering is that surround lighting be no more than 12 cd/m². In other words, the ambient lighting reflected from the wall surrounding the display should be 1–10 percent of the illumination from a 100 IRE white signal shown on your display. While it seems dim, I am told that many professional facilities are operating at 1 percent surround lighting for HD mastering.

- **200–320 cd/m² with gamma of 2.2**: Intended for living room conditions and office environments with controlled lighting and perhaps descriptive of a more pleasingly lit editing (not mastering) suite, surround lighting for the display is appropriate here as well, at a suggested 20 percent of the illumination from a 100 IRE white signal shown on your display.

SURROUND LIGHTING COLOR TEMPERATURE

In most North and South American and European countries, surround lighting should have a color temperature of 6500K (standardized as D65). This matches the color temperature for noon daylight and is also the color temperature to which your broadcast display and computer displays should be set.

One of the easiest ways to make sure your lighting is exact is to use color-balanced fluorescent lighting. You can easily obtain D65-rated tubes, and the newer electronic ballasts turn on instantly. Electronic ballasts also eliminate the unpleasant flicker of older fluorescent lighting fixtures.

In some Asian countries including China, Japan, and Korea, the standard color temperature for broadcast displays is 9300K (standardized as D93), which is a "bluer" white.

SURROUND LIGHTING COLOR ACCURACY

The *color rendering index* (CRI) of a light is a measurement of the faithfulness of the color of a set of color test object reflectances illuminated by that light. With a high CRI (90 and greater), if a certain brand of red soda label is placed in the light of a particular fixture, the measured color of that label is likely to be reasonably accurate.

The CRI scale ranges from 0 to 100, where 65 represents typical commercial lighting fixtures that output light unevenly at different wavelengths, and 100 represents spectrally perfect light that outputs equally at every wavelength of the spectrum.

Practically, what you're looking for are fixtures that have a CRI of 90 or greater. If you're installing fluorescent lighting, you can easily find fluorescent tubes with appropriate CRI values that are electronically dimmable.

> **NOTE**
>
> When selecting lighting fixtures for surround lighting, be extremely careful of any LED-based lighting solutions. While this technology is improving yearly, low-cost LED fixtures have been notorious for low CRI and terrible color temperature accuracy. Fluorescent lighting is still the most common.

CHAPTER 2

RECOMMENDED SURROUND LIGHTING

There are many options for color-balanced lighting fixtures, depending on how you're configuring your room. Here are a few quick recommendations:

- An easy solution is CinemaQuest's line of Ideal-Lume home-theater lighting fixtures, designed specifically for providing accurate surround lighting for large mounted flat-panel displays.
- If you're a do-it-yourselfer, consider Sylvania's line of Octron 900 T8 electronic-ballast fluorescent tubes with a 90 CRI rating. These bulbs can also be effective as cove lighting for ambient lighting in larger suites.

WORKSPACE LIGHTING AND SETUP

The lighting throughout the rest of your color correction room should be tightly controlled as well. You do *not* want too much ambient light in your room, so if you have an outside window, it's best to completely block it using a light-blocking material. Duvetyne or other blackout drapery fabrics work well, but whatever material you select, make sure it blocks *all* the light; otherwise, you risk allowing a bit of light into the room that's filtered by the fabric, which is potentially even worse!

Once you've blocked all outside light, the interior lighting of your room should be set up very specifically, according to the guidelines described in the sections that follow.

LIGHTING LOCATION

All lighting in the room should be *indirect*, meaning there should be no light source directly within your field of view. It's common for lighting fixtures to be hidden behind your desk, beside your console, or in some kind of alcove and bounced off of the wall or ceiling.

There should be no light reflecting off the front of your broadcast display. Any light that spills onto the face of a broadcast display will result in a *veiling reflection*, a translucent reflection that obscures the image and lowers its apparent contrast on the display. Veiling reflections make it difficult to critically evaluate black levels, shadow detail, and overall contrast ratios. This is another reason for indirect lighting. If you're using lighting from above, you can use egg-crate louvres in front of the fixture to direct the light downward, toward work surfaces, while eliminating spill-off to the sides.

LIGHTING INTENSITY

There are specific recommendations in the now-retired SMPTE RP 166-1995 document for lighting intensity that provide still-relevant guidance for directing light in the places you and your clients need it most to see what you're doing.

- **Colorist workspace lighting**: The recommended practice is for the colorist's working area to be illuminated by 3–4 ft-L (10–13 cd/m^2), which should be just enough to see your controls. No light should spill on the display. The color temperature of the colorist workspace should definitely match that of the display surround.

- **Client workspace lighting**: Your clients need to be able to see their notes so they can tell you what to do, and the SMPTE-recommended lighting level of the client desk is 2–10 ft-L (6–34 cd/m^2). The illumination should fall directly on the client's desk or sitting area and must not spill onto the wall facing the display (which could cause unwanted reflections) or directly onto the display itself.

Since the ambient lighting in the room has a significant effect on the perceived contrast of the image, a good rule of thumb is that your room's ambient lighting should match the ambient lighting of the intended audience's environment. In other words, if you're color correcting a program that will be watched in an average living room, then brighter ambient lighting is appropriate. If you're color correcting a program intended for an audience in a darkened theater and you're not using a projector, then you should lower the amount of surround and ambient light.

AMBIENT LIGHTING FIXTURES

If you're planning on using halogen fixtures for client and work lighting, Ushio offers a line of Whitestar halogen bulbs that are available at 5300K and 6500K balanced color temperatures. In conjunction with miniature egg-crate louvres covering the bulb, this can be an effective and accurate source of work lighting.

MORE ABOUT AMBIENT ROOM LIGHTING

In a smaller room, sufficient ambient room lighting may be obtained simply by careful illumination of the display surround area, the colorist's work desk, and the client's work desk. Larger rooms may require additional ambient lighting, often achieved via cove fixtures or recessed lighting running along the sidewalls. A topic of some debate is what color temperature is desirable for ambient client lighting in your suite.

One point of view is that *all* additional ambient lighting should match the color temperature of the display and surround lighting in order to keep the room neutral. Variation between the color temperature of the colorist workspace and the client area may be bothersome as the colorist swivels between the image being evaluated and the client in conversation. If you're intent on absolute accuracy, you can't go wrong with this approach.

On the other hand, some colorists believe that D65 lighting in the client area can be cold and unpleasant over a long day in a dark room, and since they want clients to come back for the next job, they have instead opted to install "warmer" lighting such as 5500K or 4100K fixtures. So long as such lighting is *behind the colorist* and not in their field of view or spilling onto the display, I can't argue too vigorously with this.

Lastly, whatever you do, remember to avoid veiling reflections on the monitor through careful placement and treatment of any ambient lighting you install. This includes avoiding illumination of the wall directly behind the display.

Obviously, these are ideals, all of which may or may not be practical for you to implement in your room. However, ignore these recommendations at your peril. Room lighting that's clearly too warm and too bright can have a visible effect on

TIP

Some colorists set up a "white spot" in their room, which is a pure, desaturated area of white on the wall, illuminated with D65 temperature lighting. Think of it as a videographer's white card for your eye. As you work, your eye fatigues, and your sense of white may drift. Glancing at the white spot lets you regain a sense of neutral white. The same thing can also be accomplished with a white still frame output to your display.

CHAPTER 2

the perceived color and contrast of the picture on your display, which in turn will have a definite impact on the grading decisions you make. You don't want to be crushing the blacks overzealously because there's too much light spilling on your display to see the true black level of the image you're working on.

COMFORTABLE, NEUTRAL FURNITURE

You want to set up your working surface to be as comfortable as possible, with the height of your seating, typing/mousing surface, and displays ergonomically adjusted to avoid neck and back pain or wrist fatigue. You're going to be sitting there a lot, so you'd better be physically relaxed in order to focus on the work.

Your chair should be durable, comfortable, and adjustable (you really can't spend too much on a good chair). And make sure that the clients have comfortable chairs, too; it improves their attitudes immensely.

To go along with the need for a neutral environment, you should avoid bright colors and reflective surfaces. Matte black is good for the desktops, and your desk surface should be nonreflective to prevent light spill on your displays.

DECOR

As far as the environment goes, it's not necessary to work in a gray room, to sit on gray furniture, and to wear a gray jumpsuit to do color-critical work. A bit of tasteful, muted color is fine so long as it's not within the colorist's field of view while working, and it isn't lit to reflect on the front of your display.

While most grading suites I see these days tend to use varying shades of gray and just off-gray colors in nonsurround parts of their color suites, it may amuse you to know that SMPTE RP 166-1995 recommends, "For other areas, the use of pastel colors is preferred if a change from neutral is desired. The Munsell color system defines acceptable color choices by a category called 'nearly neutral.'" If you want to see what these "nearly neutral" colors look like, X-Rite/Munsell publishes the "Munsell Nearly Neutrals Book of Color."

Aside from the technical requirements for creating a mastering suite, you should remember that clients are going to come to you not just for your technical and creative expertise but to spend this necessary time somewhere they'll like being. It's easy to laugh at leather couches and exotic coffee table books, but it's important to design your room with some client amenities in mind, geared for the clientele you'll be working with. Having a comfortable, stylishly decorated, and practical client work area with WiFi and places to lean back and relax will make folks feel at home, which is important if you want them to come back.

DISPLAY PLACEMENT

Unlike an editing suite, in which the broadcast display may be more for the client than for you, the reference broadcast display in a color correction room should be placed for the comfortable, ongoing viewing of both you and your client, because you're both going to be staring at it throughout every session.

For your own sanity, it's best to have a single color display to which both you and the client refer during the session. Although there are situations in which multiple displays are advantageous (for example, an extremely high-quality video projector and a smaller reference display for you), there should be only *one* display that the client refers to when describing desired changes.

If you have a small room and a small display, placing it to one side of your computer display is a perfectly reasonable setup, but it's a good idea to create some space at your work desk for the client, as they'll likely need to be sitting at your side in order to participate in the process.

If the size of your room (and your budget) permits, it's preferable to get a larger reference display and place it above and behind your computer's displays (**Figure 2.11**). This makes it easier for your clients to sit back in their designated area, and it also helps to prevent the light from the computer displays from creating glare on the broadcast display.

> **NOTE**
>
> It's not unusual for a client to point at an image within the user interface of the grading software on your computer display and say, "Can't you make the image look more like that?" Although this is a perfectly reasonable request, it can be maddening, and it's often difficult to explain to clients why they shouldn't be looking at your computer's display in the first place.

Figure 2.11 My current suite in St. Paul, Minnesota.

CHAPTER 2

Ideally placed, an HD reference display should enable easy viewing by both you and the client and also be located behind the computer displays to prevent light spill from unwanted glare. The distance from the reference display to you (the colorist) should be *3.3 times the vertical height* (picture height) of the image. You want to make sure that your reference display is positioned such that you're not constantly turning your head left and right and up and down every time you switch between looking at the broadcast display and your computer's display.

Depending on your room size and display, you may find yourself a bit closer to the display than these guidelines recommend, with your client at the outer boundary of the recommended distance for the corresponding display size. Bear in mind that the closer you sit to your display, the greater the likelihood that you'll start to see the pixel pattern of your display, which is not desirable. Sitting at the appropriate distance guarantees that the pixels of the image will merge together into the unified whole that you need to be seeing for proper evaluation.

- **24" diagonal displays**: The suggested ideal seating is 1 meter (3.5') away.

- **32" diagonal displays**: The suggested ideal seating is 1.3 meters (4') away.

- **42" diagonal displays**: The suggested ideal seating is 1.7 meters (5.5') away.

- **50" diagonal displays**: The suggested ideal seating is 2 meters (6') away.

Furthermore, Sony recommends placing a display 2–6' away from the wall in order to accommodate backlighting the display surround area.

Obviously, the practical realities of the space available to you will dictate how closely to these recommendations you adhere, but keep them in mind when you decide how large a display to obtain. If you're going for a large display, it's ideal to be able to take in the entire image at a glance as you work. If your display is too big or if it's too close to you, it'll be difficult to see the forest for the trees, so to speak.

NOTE

Front-projection screens have different distance requirements, presented later in this chapter.

Also, don't forget about your clients. They need to see the reference display just as much as you do. Ideally, you'll have a display that's big enough for them to view accurately from a comfortable client area behind you (replete with comfy leather furniture, a working desk, wireless Internet access, magazines, candy, and Legos to distract them when things get boring).

If your budget doesn't allow for either a huge display or an expansive client area, then you'll need to create room for your client somewhere beside you, so you can both sit and evaluate the image together.

CONFIGURING A GRADING THEATER

The purpose of a grading theater is to create an ideal reference environment to match, as closely as possible, how an audience in a movie theater will see the program you're working on. Unlike the average video suite employing a backlit display and subdued ambient lighting, the grading theater requires total light control, and work is done in a darkened environment. If the only programs you color correct are for broadcast, then setting up even a small grading theater probably doesn't make sense. However, if you work on programming destined for the big screen, doing color correction in a miniature theater environment is an incredible experience for both the colorist and the client.

There are two ways of approaching the creation of a grading theater (**Figure 2.12**). The low-budget approach is to create a "mini-theater" that's suitable for mastering 1080p HD using BT. 709 specifications. This can be effective for small productions destined for the film-festival circuit or a limited three-city release, especially since BT. 709 programs can be easily remastered to DCP using software such as easyDCP from Frauenhofer. The only limitation to this workflow is that you can neither monitor nor master the most saturated values that the P3 gamut for digital cinema is capable of displaying. However, if you're working on a small project that's destined, ultimately, for home distribution as the main venue for distribution via Blu-ray, Netflix, pay-per-view, or broadcast, this may not really be a drawback.

NOTE

The information in this section is drawn from a number of documents: the SMPTE Recommended Practice document RP 431-2-2007, "D-Cinema Quality–Reference Projector and Environment"; Thomas O. Maier's article "Color Processing for Digital Cinema 4: Measurements and Tolerances" (published in the Nov/Dec 2007 *SMPTE Motion Imaging Journal*); and Glenn Kennel's *Color and Mastering for Digital Cinema* (Focal Press, 2006).

Figure 2.12 The grading theater at Company 3 in Santa Monica.

CHAPTER 2

The second approach is to obtain a full-blown DCI P3–capable reference projector, building an environment to work at 2K or 4K resolution, at considerably greater expense. However, if you're working on big-budget projects that will have significant theatrical runs, this is the only way to properly master for the full digital cinema experience.

The guidelines presented in the following sections are suitable for whichever approach you decide to implement. Keep in mind that the size of the room, the size of the screen, and the type of projector you use are all interconnected decisions that determine how you'll be laying out your room.

DIGITAL PROJECTION FOR POSTPRODUCTION

Obviously, the entire reason for configuring a grading theater is to make your grading decisions using a projector. The display characteristics of front projection are different enough from most self-illuminated displays such as LCD, plasma, and OLED to make it desirable to grade your program's images within the context of the projected image, guaranteeing the best match between your corrections and what the audience will see.

ADVANTAGES OF VIDEO PROJECTION

Aside from being generally impressive to watch, video projectors have several advantages.

- **Projectors employing LCoS or DLP technology** are at the top of the heap (at the time of this writing), being capable of very high-contrast ratios with deep and accurate blacks when used with the right projection screen.

- **With proper installation and an appropriate screen**, projected images have negligible color and brightness shifts over a wide viewing angle.

- **They're capable of producing a huge image for viewing**, assuming your room has the space for the throw that's necessary given your projector's light output. This provides a critical sanity check for how programs destined for theatrical projection hold up on a larger screen.

This last point is important. As you'll learn in later chapters, the colorfulness of an image is significantly influenced by its size. If you don't work on a screen that's representative of the theatrical experience, you'll make very different grading decisions.

When I grade projects via a projector, it's usually the first time the client sees their program that big. This gives them a great opportunity to discover visual effects shots that don't work or unexpectedly soft-focus shots that seemed fine on a 24" display but now look considerably worse while there's possibly time to do something about it.

It's also an excellent way to meaningfully evaluate image grain and noise for a given shot or correction. Again, noise that seems fine on a smaller display shows its true nature when it's blown up on the big screen.

DISADVANTAGES OF VIDEO PROJECTION

The biggest disadvantage of video projectors for smaller facilities is cost; keep in mind that this includes the additional expense of a suitably high-quality screen and the inevitable need for qualified calibration and bulb changes (which aren't cheap). The minimum acceptable HD projectors for color correction work tend to fall at the very highest end of the scale of home-theater equipment, while full-blown 2K-capable projectors usually start around $30,000 and can easily go much higher.

Another significant disadvantage is that video projectors require total light control. *Any* ambient light in the room degrades the displayed image, so you must take care to eliminate any light spill on the screen, and you must carefully design and shield workspace and client lighting. Projectors are suitable only for the blackout conditions that grading for a darkened theater requires. If you primarily color correct programming for television, video projection is probably not an ideal solution.

Lastly, video projectors require careful installation, and you'll definitely need a larger room than other types of displays require. The *throw*, defined as the distance between the projector lens and the screen, must be planned in advance, and the height at which the projector is installed must suit the size and location of the screen. The type of screen you choose affects the brightness of the image. There are many types of screens from which to choose, depending on your situation.

CHOOSING A VIDEO PROJECTOR

The criteria for choosing a video projector are identical to those for choosing other types of displays. However, it's important to keep in mind the following list of things to specifically avoid in a video projector intended for postproduction use:

- **Avoid projectors with less-than-full HD resolutions.** Many projectors intended for conference rooms and presentation theaters don't actually support the native resolutions of 1920×1080 or 2048×1080 that are necessary for video and digital cinema use.

- **Avoid projectors that rely on "advanced iris" or "dynamic iris" mechanisms to improve contrast.** These mechanisms work by doing a series of uncontrollable automatic contrast adjustments whenever the lightness of the video signal changes abruptly (to account for scene changes). These adjustments make it impossible to objectively evaluate the image. You want a projector with a high "native" contrast ratio that's consistent and unchanging.

- **Watch out for projectors that don't have built-in calibration controls for either the BT. 709 or DCI P3 standards.** Many home-theater projectors have a wider gamut or primaries that don't line up with the proper color coordinates. This can result in oversaturated colors, or color variations such as reds that are "too orange." Such projectors can be calibrated using outboard hardware, but calibrations that use this equipment will incur an additional expense.

- **Avoid projectors that are too bright or too dim for your room.** A properly calibrated projector in a reference environment should output 48 cd/m² of light when displaying a flat reference white field. If the image is too bright, it will fatigue your eyes over long grading sessions. If the image is too dim, the colors will appear to be less vivid, inviting incorrect adjustments to image saturation.

- **Always evaluate a given projector's output in advance to make sure it doesn't exhibit "screen door" artifacts or "rainbow" artifacts.** *Screen door artifacts* are visible lines separating the pixels of an image, and *rainbow* artifacts are seen as brief colored undertones in high-contrast, fast-moving scenes.

CHARACTERISTICS OF COLOR-CRITICAL PROJECTORS FOR DIGITAL CINEMA MASTERING

To be useful for digital cinema mastering, video projectors should exhibit the following characteristics, according to Glenn Kennel's *Color and Mastering for Digital Cinema* (Focal Press, 2006):

- A reference projector should output peak white at 48 cd/m².

- The gamma of a projector should be 2.6, with a tolerance of ± 2%.

- The color temperature should be 5400K (D55).

- Most digital cinema projectors use Xenon lamps.

- Ambient light level reflected from the screen should be less than 0.01 cd/m².

- The projector should be capable of 1.85:1 and 2.39:1 aspect ratios.

- For true digital cinema mastering, the projector should be capable of encompassing the DCI P3 gamut, with a calibrated accuracy of ± 4 delta Eab*, where Eab* represents the magnitude of error in a* b* color coordinates. SMPTE RP 431.2 on Reference Projector provides information on calibration.

VIDEO PROJECTOR VENDORS

> **NOTE**
> Keep in mind that the HD resolution of 1920×1080 is only 128 pixels shorter than the DCDM standard 2K resolution of 2048×1080.

At the lower end of the scale is JVC's line of D-ILA home cinema projectors, all of which are suitable for small projection suites working to the BT. 709 standard for gamut and gamma. D-ILA technology is JVC's variation on LCoS; it provides deep blacks and good light output, with native 1920×1080 resolution, and is suitable for screens up to 9.75 meters (16') wide. It's a good idea to call a calibration professional in advance to see which of the current lineup of models can be most accurately calibrated for your needs.

Another high-end home-theater projector company making HD-resolution projectors worth investigating is Sim2, with a line of SUPER PureLED illuminated DLP projectors.

If you're considering a full-blown digital cinema projector, be aware that there's a significant difference in both price and performance between projectors available for the home video enthusiast and those that are intended for digital cinema–viewing applications. Digital cinema projectors also have more light output and require a larger theater space in order to function properly.

At the higher end of the scale are three vendors that use DLP technology (favored for digital cinema applications), with 2K resolutions of 2048×1080, that meet the DCI P3 standards for gamut and gamma.

- **Barco** has a line of video projectors that have been specifically designed with postproduction facilities in mind, suitable for screens up to 10 meters (32') wide.

- **Christie** also makes a compact digital cinema projector, suitable for screens up to 10.5 meters (35') wide.

- **NEC** makes a smaller professional digital cinema projector suitable for post-production use, appropriate for screens up to 8.5 meters (28') wide.

CHOOSING AND INSTALLING THE SCREEN

Once you've decided on a projector that's appropriate for your needs, the second most important decision you can make is to choose a screen.

As for the type of screen you should choose, you should pick one that reflects spectral energy equally across all viewing angles without changing the color (referred to as *Lambertian*). Perforated screens are not recommended in order to avoid aliasing of the image.

The recommendation is for a flat matte screen with 1.0 gain. The *gain* of a screen refers to how well it reflects light. Some projection screens are actually gray, with a gain of 0.8 (or lower), in order to lower the black point of projected images in rooms where the projector is too bright or to improve contrast in less-than-ideal lighting conditions. Other screens have more highly reflective coatings, resulting in screen gains of 1.5 times the projected light level (or more), which is useful for projectors that lack sufficient light output for the room but can result in visible hot spots within the image. What you want is the simplest screen of all—flat matte—with as close to a 1.0 gain as you can get.

CHAPTER 2

The size of the screen is going to be dictated by the size of your room, the capabilities of your projector, and how far away from the screen you want to sit. The SMPTE-recommended viewing distance for critical evaluation is 1.5–3.5 times the screen height, with 2.0 times the screen height being the "sweet spot" (which, ideally, is where you'll be sitting). With that said, screening rooms typically fall into two categories.

- For serious digital cinema mastering using a high-end projector, a 15' screen is a good minimum size, while larger facilities employ up to a 20–30' wide screen, to replicate the scale of commercial cinemas.

- Budget projection mastering in smaller rooms with smaller projectors can range anywhere from 5–10 ft. wide. The larger, the better, although the ability of your projector, after calibration, to achieve 48 cd/m^2 will dictate the practical size of your screen.

Another important recommendation is for a screen frame that has a sharp, nonreflective matte black border. Many vendors make wide-border fixed-screen frames covered in light-absorbing black velvet, which is ideal. Having a crisp black border improves the perceived contrast of the image, and it eliminates any possible light spill around the edge of the screen.

Lastly, if you plan to work on programs with varying aspect ratios, you'll need some sort of matte black masking system for the top and bottom or the sides of the screen to black out the unused letterboxed or pillarboxed area. If you have the budget, there are motorized systems for this purpose.

Vendors to research for front projection screens include (in alphabetical order) Carada, Da-Lite, GrayHawk, Screen Innovations, and Stewart.

PROJECTOR INSTALLATION

Once you have the screen size worked out, you can figure out the ideal placement of your projector.

Generally, there are three ways of installing a projector. Smaller home-theater projectors can be either mounted at the rear of the room on a shelf against the back wall or attached to the ceiling via a heavy-duty mount. Professional digital cinema projectors are generally much heavier and louder, and as a result, they must be installed in a projector booth behind the rear wall, with a glass projection window letting the light through.

However you decide to install your projector, its distance from the screen is based on the amount of light the projector puts out (which can usually be adjusted), the width of the screen you want to project onto, and the *throw ratio* of the projector's lens, which is the distance from the screen required for a projector to create an image of a specific size.

Most projectors suitable for color correction work have either a zoom lens with variable throw (for instance, JVC D-ILA projectors have throw ratios of 1x–2x) or a selection of prime lenses from which you can choose the throw most appropriate for your room.

SETTING YOUR PROJECTOR-TO-SCREEN DISTANCE

You can calculate your ideal projector-to-screen distance by multiplying the width of your screen by the throw ratio of your lens. The goal is to ensure that the reference white-level output by the projector is as close to 48 cd/m^2 as you can make it.

Once you've figured out the distance of the projector from the screen, you need to mount it so that the projector is centered on the width of the screen, with the lens fully within the vertical height of the screen. Even though most projectors have keystone controls that allow geometric adjustment of the projected image if the projector is off-center, it's a better idea to simply mount your projector correctly in the first place.

STRICTLY CONTROLLED LIGHTING

Critical viewing using a digital projector requires blackout conditions within the reference room. This means total light control—absolutely no windows without blackout shades, no kidding.

Matte black paint, drapery, carpeting, furniture, and décor are encouraged, although dark grays are also fine (and potentially a necessary step toward making the room a more pleasant place to be). The essential reason is to eliminate, as much as possible, ambient reflected light that might bounce off any surface within the room.

Of course, you need to be able to see the controls of your workstation, but any workspace lighting must be tightly controlled. While neither the SMPTE recommendation for a D-Cinema reference environment nor the DCDM specification provides specific guidance with regard to acceptable colorist and client area lighting levels, no spill whatsoever is allowable on the projection screen. This necessitates highly directional lighting of minimal strength, although from my experience, running sessions in a completely darkened environment has never been a problem, and in fact it focuses the clients on the work at hand.

For more information on reference projector and environment setup, consult Glenn Kennel's excellent *Color and Mastering for Digital Cinema* (Focal Press, 2006).

CHAPTER 2

OTHER HARDWARE FOR COLOR CORRECTION

Color correction platforms can be divided into two categories: turnkey color correction systems with specific software running on specific hardware using specific drive storage systems and do-it-yourself software-based color correction applications (such as DaVinci Resolve) for which you assemble your own system with third-party hardware.

It's impossible to cover every detail of every color correction system in an ever-changing market, but here are a few additional items to consider when you are putting together a room for color correction. Overall, it's important to be careful about the equipment you select. Because you are the last word in the quality of the video program, you need to have the cleanest, highest-quality video interface and reference display you can afford, as well as the most accurate monitoring and test instruments available to you.

HARD DRIVE STORAGE

No matter what system you use or what kind of media you're working with, you're going to need a whole lot of really fast storage in order to work efficiently. Uncompressed HD, 2K, 4K, and 6K RAW formats and image sequences can easily consume terabytes of storage space for a single project, and if you're busy, you'll want to have room to store multiple projects at once.

If you're using a turnkey color correction system, drive storage is likely part of the package, and you'll be using what the vendor recommends. However, if you're assembling your own hardware to run a software-driven color correction application, you'll need to do some research to figure out what will work best for you.

The ideal storage technology for you to use really depends on what kind of facility you're working in (or if you're working in your own, private video suite). For high-bandwidth color correction and finishing work, your choices are either direct-connected drive arrays using one of a variety of technologies or networked storage systems, probably using Fiber Channel.

The advantage of direct connect storage is price; you can generally get more terabytes for the money spent. The advantage of more expensive Fiber Channel–networked storage systems is multiroom flexibility, as several editing, compositing, and color correction workstations can access shared media on one storage volume, eliminating the need to copy data or move hard drives around.

One last thing: If you're working on time-critical client projects, it behooves you to consider getting a storage system that employs some level of redundancy, to protect you in the event of drive failure. RAID 5 is a commonly used protection scheme that strikes an acceptable balance between high performance and drive safety. Should one drive in the array fail, it can be replaced and the entire volume can be rebuilt without loss.

TAPE BACKUP

In today's world of tapeless acquisition and postproduction, the new rule is that if you create it, you should have a way to back it up safely. Hard drive storage is good for the short term, but over the long term, tape-based storage is the only proven technology rated to last up to 30 years.

While there have been several tape backup technologies of varying popularity over the years, Linear Tape-Open (LTO) has emerged as a dominant standard in tape-based backup, owing partially to it being an open standard developed by the LTO Consortium, which includes Seagate, Hewlett-Packard, and IBM.

As of this writing, the LTO Consortium has released four versions of LTO, with LTO-6 being the highest-capacity version of this format. Each successive version of LTO has doubled the storage capacity, while remaining backward-compatible with previous versions of LTO. Several vendors offer LTO backup solutions, and you owe it to yourself and your clients to investigate this as a way to safeguard your projects and media.

YOUR VIDEO OUTPUT INTERFACE

If you're assembling your own computer system, keep in mind that to successfully display the picture, the video interface connected to your computer *and* the video display must have the same interface. Most professional video displays are expandable so that you can purchase the appropriate interface cards for whichever format you intend to display.

OUTBOARD SCOPES VS. BUILT-IN SCOPES

Anyone needing to do broadcast-legal color correction is advised to have an outboard scope to make a comprehensive evaluation of the video signal. Even though many software color correction environments and non-linear editing (NLE) systems have software scopes built in with which to analyze the internal, digital state of the image data you're working on, outboard scopes still have abundant uses. In particular, they're terrific diagnostic tools for determining the state and quality of your video at specific points in the signal chain *after* the video has been output by your system.

Even in regular use, many outboard scopes have higher resolution, additional options such as zooming into a scope's graph or superimposing a freeze-frame graph from one shot onto the live graph from another shot, and additional scope views for gamut-checking out-of-range Composite and RGB excursions.

Furthermore, when it comes time to do a quality-control (QC) check of your program, many outboard scopes have the ability to log QC violations, along with the timecode identifying the frame of the problem, in an automated fashion as you play the program through.

Bottom line, it's a very good idea to have an outboard scope available to you in your room.

CONTROL SURFACES

Control surfaces for color correction usually consist of Ethernet or USB-connected devices sporting three trackballs (corresponding to the black, midtone, and white color adjustment controls of the software), three contrast rings (corresponding to lift or black point, gamma or midtones, and gain or white point), and a variety of other buttons and knobs that let you manipulate the controls of your color correction software directly (**Figure 2.13**).

Figure 2.13 The FilmLight Blackboard 2, designed for Baselight, is a highly evolved control surface with all the trimmings: adaptive buttons capable of displaying images and video, push-for-detente optical rotary controls with LED feedback, high-resolution screens for software feedback, and finely engineered trackballs, rings, and jog/shuttle controls, as well as a built-in tablet and keyboard.

Controls surfaces also often have controls for program playback and navigation and for grade copy/paste and management. Typically, control surfaces for color correction have a system allowing the same physical controls to be used for different software operations via some kind of modal change.

High-end color correction platforms such as Blackmagic Design's DaVinci Resolve, Quantel's Pablo, and FilmLight's Baselight have dedicated control surfaces manufactured specifically for them (**Figure 2.14**).

Figure 2.14 While Resolve is compatible with many other control surfaces, the DaVinci Resolve control surface is manufactured by Blackmagic Design specifically for DaVinci Resolve software. More controls provide faster access to Resolve functions at any one time.

Other color correction software such as Assimilate Scratch, Autodesk Lustre, and Adobe SpeedGrade use third-party color correction control surfaces from companies such as JLCooper, Tangent Devices, and Euphonix.

Aside from making your color correction suite look like the control room of a rocket ship, there are many important advantages to using a control surface.

- Using physical controls instead of mousing around with software controls lets you keep your eyes on the video display while you work.

- Once you get used to a particular control surface, the muscle memory you gain from repetition enables you to work faster, and as an added bonus, you'll have fewer keyboard shortcuts to remember.

- Control surfaces let you adjust multiple parameters simultaneously, which is fantastic when you want to stretch contrast with the black and white point rings at the same time.

- Using a control surface eliminates the wrist strain that excessive mousing can cause when you're color correcting 600 shots in one day. **Figure 2.15** shows the Tangent Element control surface.

Figure 2.15 The Tangent Devices Element control surface panels are compatible with a wide variety of professional color correction applications.

Using a control surface is like playing an instrument. It takes practice, but the more you work with a specific physical interface, the faster and better you get.

CHAPTER 2

OTHER INPUT OPTIONS BESIDES CONTROL SURFACES

NLEs such as Avid, Final Cut Pro, and Premiere Pro are not compatible with any of the third-party color correction interfaces available for other color correction applications; neither are the majority of compositing applications such as After Effects.

However, if you're doing color correction in these environments, there are a handful of input devices you can use to make your job easier.

NOTE
Some dedicated color correction control surfaces, such as Quantel's Neo and FilmLight's Blackboard control panels, include a built-in graphics tablet.

- **A mouse with a scroll wheel and multiple buttons** is an absolute must. Many applications let you use the scroll wheel to make fine adjustments to onscreen controls simply by rolling the wheel. Additionally, you can map a grading application's keyboard shortcuts to the multiple buttons on a mouse (some gaming mice have several mappable buttons) in order to perform multiple tasks whenever your hand happens to be on the mouse.

- **Graphics tablets** are incredibly useful if you do work that requires creating a lot of secondary corrections using *masks* or *mattes* (also called *vignettes*, *user shapes*, or Power Windows). They make it more comfortable to draw and modify complex shapes, instead of the "drawing with a brick" experience that using a mouse provides.

- **Touchscreen accessories** are also starting to appear; some programmers have been experimenting with using an iPad as a control surface, either to control custom plug-ins or to control a full-blown color correction application via that application's control APIs. At the time of this writing, these experiments are few and far between, but I anticipate this idea may catch on more widely as time goes on and hardware progresses.

VIDEO LEGALIZER

Video legalizers are hardware video processors that clamp or compress parts of an incoming video signal that fall outside of user-programmable limits (in other words, luma or chroma that's too high or too low) before sending the video signal out to a video deck during print-to-tape or edit-to-tape operations. Companies including Ensemble Designs, Eyeheight Designs, and Harris/Videotek make stand-alone legalizers that are designed to sit between the video output of your workstation and the video input of your VTR.

These are not intended to replace the color correction process, because it's usually better to adjust an out-of-range signal manually in order to retrieve valuable image detail than it is to simply clip it off. Instead, these are meant to be a final wall of defense against broadcast illegality, protecting you from the occasional stray pixel, and freeing you to focus on the creative aspects of your color correction adjustments.

This is by no means a required item, but if you don't have one, you'll need to be incredibly careful about legalizing your programs. For more information about quality control and broadcast legalization, see Chapter 10.

CHAPTER 3

PRIMARY CONTRAST ADJUSTMENTS

In the color correction process, all digital images can be broken into *luma* (video signal lightness and darkness) and *chroma* (color) components. In this chapter, we'll examine how adjustments to an image's luma component let us control image contrast.

Contrast is the foundation of an image, representing an image's underlying tonality from absolute black through the dark gray of shadows, the light gray of midtones, and the whites of the brightest highlights, as shown in **Figure 3.1**.

Figure 3.1 The original image on the left appears with the color removed in the version on the right, making it easier to spot the highlights, shadows, and midtones that comprise its overall tonality.

HOW WE SEE COLOR

The human visual system processes luminance separately from color, and in fact the visual cues we get from image *luminance* or *tonality* have a profound effect on how we perceive the sharpness, depth, and organization of subjects within a scene.

In Margaret Livingstone's *Vision and Art: The Biology of Seeing* (Harry N. Abrams, 2008), the human visual system is described in detail to show how luminance and color are processed by entirely separate regions of our brains. To summarize, the rods (which are sensitive only to luminance in dimly lit conditions) and the three types of cone cells in the retina (that are sensitive to red, green, and blue wavelengths of light in well-illuminated conditions) all connect to two types of retinal ganglion cells, as shown in **Figure 3.2**. Smaller *midget* (or simply *M*) ganglion cells encode color opponent information that is passed along to what Livingstone refers to as the "what" part of the brain, which is responsible for object and facial recognition, hue perception, and the perception of very fine detail (more on that in Chapter 4).

Figure 3.2 The interior cell structure of the eye, showing a simplified version of the connections among the rod and cone cells that gather light, the bipolar cells that collate their signals, and the M and P cells that assemble the dual channels of color and luminance information that are sent onward to the occipital lobe.

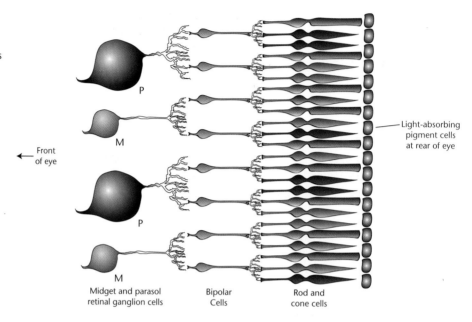

← Front of eye

Light-absorbing pigment cells at rear of eye

Midget and parasol retinal ganglion cells

Bipolar Cells

Rod and cone cells

The second type of retinal ganglion cells that the rods and cones connect to are the larger *parasol* (or *P*) ganglion cells, which encode luminance information that is processed specifically by what Livingstone calls the "where" part of the brain, which is color-blind and responsible for the perception of motion, spatial organization, depth, and overall scenic organization.

Because of this neurological organization, the adjustments described in this chapter have very real and specific effects on audience perception of a program's visuals. Learning the perceptual effects of specific changes to image tonality—as well as how to capitalize on them as a colorist—is essential.

LUMINANCE AND LUMA

There is an important distinction between *luminance*, which is a measurement of the eye's perception of light intensity, and *luma*, which is the nonlinearly weighted measurement of light intensity used in video.

Luminance is a description of *perceived*, rather than measured, image lightness. The standard method for determining the scale of luminance is to have human observers arrange a series of gray chips so that the entire arrangement of chips appears to be an even and linear progression from black through gray to white. According to Maureen C. Stone in *A Field Guide to Digital Color* (A.K. Peters, Ltd., 2003), people are consistent about how they arrange chip lightness and consistently choose around 100 chips for the final scale.

Luma, on the other hand, refers specifically to the component of a video signal or digital image that carries the monochrome portion of the image that determines image lightness. In video applications, luma is often independent of the *chroma* (or color) of the image, although the method of image processing used by the application you're working in determines to what degree you can adjust luma without affecting chroma.

DERIVING LUMINANCE FROM WHAT WE SEE

The human eye has varying sensitivity to each portion of the visible spectrum, which is represented by the *luminous efficiency function*. This function is approximated in the curve shown in **Figure 3.3**, superimposed over the wavelengths of the visible spectrum.

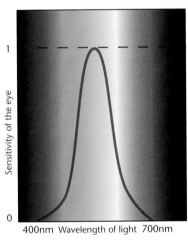

Approximation of the luminous efficiency function

Figure 3.3 The curve represents the portion of the visible spectrum to which the human eye is most sensitive, referred to as the *luminous efficiency function*.

As you can see, the eye is most sensitive to the green/yellow portion of the spectrum. Luminance, therefore, is a linear representation of the intensity of light, calculated by weighted sums of red, green, and blue according to a standardized model of the eye's sensitivities, as defined by the Commission de L'Eclairage, or CIE color system. According to Charles Poynton in *Digital Video and HD Algorithms and Interfaces* (Morgan Kaufmann, 2012), luminance is calculated approximately 21 percent from red, 72 percent from green, and 7 percent from blue (interestingly, only 1 percent of our cones are blue-sensitive).

This distribution of color can be seen in **Figure 3.4**, where the Waveform Monitor's measurement of the luma corresponding to the pure red, green, and blue bars in the image is unequal, even though the B value (brightness) of the HSB (hue, saturation, brightness) color picker used to create each bar was identical.

Figure 3.4 A Waveform Monitor set to display luma analyzes a test pattern with pure red, green, and blue bars. The Waveform Monitor's graph shows the portion of each color channel that contributes to the luma component of video.

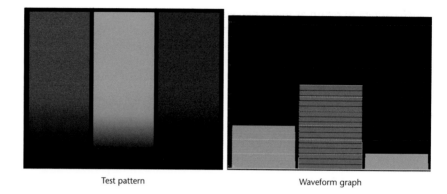

Test pattern   Waveform graph

LUMA IS LUMINANCE MODIFIED BY GAMMA

Because the eye's perception of brightness is nonlinear, a *gamma adjustment* is applied by video recording and display equipment by making a nonlinear adjustment (a power function) to the luminance calculation described previously. Gamma-corrected luminance is called *luma*, designated by the Y' in $Y'C_BC_R$. The ' (prime symbol) indicates the nonlinear transformation taking place.

There's an easy way to see why the standard gamma adjustment of video systems accounts for our eyes' nonlinear sensitivities to lighter and darker image tonality. Look at the two gradients in **Figure 3.5**, and see whether you can pick the one that seems to have the most even distribution of white to black across the entire bar.

Figure 3.5 Can you pick which of these two graphs is a true linear distribution of tonality?

If you picked the top gradient, you might be surprised to learn that the bottom gradient is the image that is actually a mathematically linear progression of white to black. The top image has had a gamma adjustment applied to it to make it *perceptually* more even.

The human visual system is far more sensitive to differences in lightness than in color, a physiological trait that informs many decisions on video standards. Partially because of this, video imaging specialists decided long ago that a strictly linear representation of the luminance in an image wouldn't make the best use of the available bandwidth or bit-depth for a given analog or digital video system. As a result, images are recorded with a gamma adjustment immediately applied within the video camera to retain as much perceptible detail as possible. Broadcast and computer monitors then apply a matching, but inverted, gamma correction, resulting in a more or less true representation of the image (**Figure 3.6**).

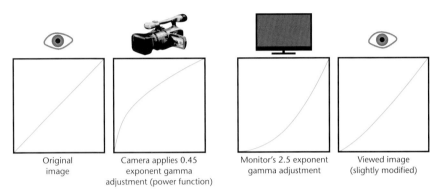

Original image

Camera applies 0.45 exponent gamma adjustment (power function)

Monitor's 2.5 exponent gamma adjustment

Viewed image (slightly modified)

Figure 3.6 How gamma adjustments are made when shooting video and reversed during video playback on a broadcast display.

The standard for video gamma is specified by BT.1886, which defines a gamma of 2.4 to be used by video displays in broadcast postproduction work. The ideal gamma setting for your application goes hand-in-hand with corresponding surround lighting, as discussed in Chapter 2.

Despite this well-known and published standard, computers using different monitors, cameras, codecs, and applications may interpret this gamma correction differently, which can have a visible effect on how an image appears (**Figure 3.7**). If this seems complicated, it is, but understanding what gamma means and how it's applied is essential to avoiding inconsistencies in your video, especially when you exchange media with other video editing, compositing, and color correction applications.

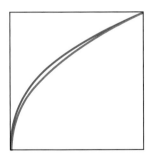

BT.1886 (HD) gamma (2.4)
sRGB gamma used by Windows/OS X (2.2)

Figure 3.7 BT.1886 gamma—compared to the gamma used by computer displays.

LUMA IN Y'C$_B$C$_R$

The Y'C$_B$C$_R$ color model was originally devised to ensure compatibility between color and monochrome television sets (monochrome TVs would simply filter out the chroma component, displaying the luma component by itself).

NOTE

The notation for component video varies depending on whether it's digital or analog. Y'C$_B$C$_R$ denotes digital component video, whereas Y'P$_B$P$_R$ denotes analog component video.

In component Y'C$_B$C$_R$-encoded video, luma is carried in the Y' channel of the video signal. Since the eye is more sensitive to changes in luma than to changes in color, the two color difference channels are usually encoded with less information than the luma channel, and various image formats are bandwidth limited, employing chroma subsampling to encode more or less color information (you've seen this described as 4:2:2, 4:2:0, or 4:1:1 video). However, all video formats, regardless of the chroma sampling scheme they employ, encode the full amount of luma.

LUMA IN RGB

The RGB color model is used by the DPX image sequence format, which is used for both film scanning and digital cinema camera acquisition. RGB is also used by the Sony HDCAM SR video format (with the dual-link or 3G options), as well as by an increasing number of RAW image recording RAWdigital cinema cameras such as those made by RED, ARRI, Sony, and Blackmagic Design.

NOTE

For a more rigorous and techni-cal explanation of gamma for broadcast, computer, and film applications, see the Gamma FAQ at www.poynton.com/ GammaFAQ.html. The techni-cally minded should also consult Charles Poynton's *Digital Video and HDTV: Algorithms and Interfaces* (Morgan Kaufmann Publishers, 2002). For more information about human vision and digital systems, see Maureen C. Stone's excellent *A Field Guide to Digital Color* (AK Peters, Ltd., 2003).

RGB image formats encode discrete color component channels for red, green, and blue image data. These formats typically encode the full sampled amount of each color, with no chroma subsampling, although various acquisition or distribution formats may employ spatial or temporal data compression.

When working with component RGB-encoded media formats, luma-specific opera-tions can still be performed, as luma is derived mathematically—21 percent from red, 72 percent from green, and 7 percent from blue, as mentioned earlier.

LOG-ENCODED AND NORMALIZED GAMMA

As discussed in Chapter 1, digital cinema cameras not only record RGB color but offer the option of either recording *logarithmically encoded* ProRes or DNxHD media or debayering RAW media to logarithmic-encoded images in your grading software. They provide this flexibility in order to preserve the greatest *latitude*, or range of image data from the shadows to the highlights of the original scene, for use while you grade.

Log-encoded media must be *normalized* in order to convert a log-encoded image to how it would look in linear light, a requirement for you to be able make the neces-sary adjustments to achieve the final result that the audience will see (**Figure 3.8**). Compositing applications often refer to this as *linearizing* and provide a function called *log-to-lin* to deal with decoding log-encoded media. However, grading appli-cations typically call this *normalizing*.

Figure 3.8 Log-encoded frame shown at left, normalized version at right.

The bottom line is that log-encoded media needs to be normalized as part of the grading process, which is a contrast adjustment.

You can choose to normalize log-encoded media by making manual adjustments with the controls described in this chapter (typically a Curve control), or you can use a lookup table (LUT) to perform a perfect mathematical inversion of the original log encoding, which you can then customize by making your own adjustments either before or after the LUT, depending on your needs. I'll explain both methods later in this chapter.

WHAT IS CONTRAST?

When most people talk about *contrast*, they're usually trying to describe the relative difference between the light and dark portions of an image. Images with shadows that aren't very dark and highlights that aren't very bright are generally considered not to have very much contrast (**Figure 3.9**).

Figure 3.9 This night shot has low contrast; the highlights aren't particularly bright, and the darkest shadows are a bit lighter than absolute black.

CHAPTER 3

When photographers and videographers discuss contrast, they often refer to the tonal range of a photograph or video image. If you plot the entire range of image tonality within the luma component of the Figure 3.9 image, from black to white, you'll find it's not using the entire possible range of black and white values. Instead, the tonality of the entire image lies in the middle of the scale, which gives the image its subdued appearance (**Figure 3.10**).

Figure 3.10 In this illustration, the actual black and white points from the previous image are shown in grayscale, relative to the full range of luma that's possible. As you can see, the image does not occupy the full tonal range available.

Images combining deep, dark shadows and bright highlights are considered to be high contrast (**Figure 3.11**).

Figure 3.11 This image, while also an evening shot, has high contrast. The highlights of the man's face are as bright as they can be, and the darkest shadows are deep black.

Plotting the range of tones in the luma channel of this image reveals that it's occupying the fullest tonal range possible. The presence of 0 percent blacks and 100 percent whites makes this image more vivid (**Figure 3.12**).

Figure 3.12 In this illustration, the actual black and white points from the previous image are shown to occupy almost the full tonal range that's available.

In short, contrast (also referred to as *contrast ratio*) as described in this book is the difference between the lightest and darkest values in an image. If there's a large difference between these, then we consider it high contrast. If there's a small difference between the lightest and darkest parts of an image, then it's low contrast.

WHY IS CONTRAST IMPORTANT?

Adjusting a clip's luma component changes its perceived contrast and also exerts an indirect effect on the color of an image. For this reason, it's important to exercise careful control over the contrast of your clips to maximize image quality, keep your video signals broadcast legal, optimize the effectiveness of any other color adjustments you want to make, and create the desired look of your program.

Typically, you'll want to maximize the contrast found in your clips to make the images look more vivid. At other times, you'll find it necessary to lower the contrast of an image to match one clip to another that was shot at a different location or to create the impression of a particular time of day or night.

One fundamental way you can alter and improve video images is by manipulating the contrast between the darkest and brightest areas of the picture. Even well-exposed images benefit greatly from minor tweaks to maximize the contrast ratio, readjust the midtones, and balance different angles of coverage within a scene.

In other cases, film and digital video may be shot and/or processed with deliberately compressed contrast. This means that the blacks may be well above the minimum of 0 percent/IRE/millivolts (mV) and the whites may be below the maximum broadcast legal value of 100 percent/IRE (or 700 mV). This is done to guarantee maximum flexibility during color grading by avoiding accidental overexposure and underexposure that would remove detail from the image.

By making simple adjustments using a color correction application's three primary contrast controls, you can quickly do the following:

- Make the highlights legal for broadcast
- Make muddy shadows deeper and darker
- Lighten underexposed clips
- Change the apparent time of day
- Improve overall image definition

CONTRAST ALSO AFFECTS COLOR CONTROL RESPONSE

The distribution of the luma component of a clip influences which portions of the image are affected by the Lift, Gamma, and Gain color balance controls. For example, if no areas of the image are greater than 60 percent in the Waveform Monitor or Histogram, then the Whites color balance control won't have much of an effect. For this reason, it's often useful to adjust a clip's contrast first, *before* correcting its color. Otherwise, you may find yourself wasting time going back and forth, making constant readjustments.

For more information on both of these effects, see Chapter 4.

EVALUATING CONTRAST USING VIDEO SCOPES

Luma is generally measured as a digital percentage from 0 to 100, where 0 represents absolute black and 100 represents absolute white. Professional color correction applications also support super-white levels (from 101 to 110 percent, as shown in **Figure 3.13**) if they exist in the source media (most typical for $Y'C_BC_R$ material). While super-white video levels are not considered to be safe for broadcast, most camcorders record video with super-white excursions anyway in an effort to protect you from the inevitable overshoots that come from unexpected highlights.

Figure 3.13 Correspondence of
0 to 100 percent luma, with the
110 percent overshoot called
super white.

Of course, we evaluate luma based on the contrast we perceive on our monitors. However, because the apparent contrast on your display is subject to so many variables—not to mention the toll that eye fatigue takes over long sessions—it's important to have a more objective guide as you make contrast adjustments. Your three primary tools for evaluating contrast are Waveform Monitors, image Histograms, and your broadcast monitor.

> **NOTE**
>
> Unadjusted super-white levels will be clamped by whatever broadcast-safe settings exist in your color correction application (if they're enabled) so that pixels in the image with luma greater than 100 percent will be set to 100 percent.

Y'C$_B$C$_R$ AND RGB NUMERIC ENCODING

Even though most video scopes and color correction tools deal in either percentages or image processing values of 0–1, it's a good idea to understand the encoding standards used for 8-bit, 10-bit, and RGB encoded video. For example, the DaVinci Resolve video scopes display the numeric encoding values for a direct evaluation of the digital signal levels in your media.

For more information, see Chapter 10.

When learning to evaluate contrast using video scopes, it's important to learn how to spot three characteristics of video:

- The *black point*, representing the very darkest part of the shadows
- The *white point*, representing the very lightest part of the highlights
- The *average distribution of midtones*, representing the overall perceived lightness of the image

THE HISTOGRAM

An image Histogram set to display luma is an ideal tool for evaluating the contrast ratio of an image very simply. It displays a graph where the brightness of every single pixel in the image is plotted against a vertical digital scale from 0 to 110 percent (with 101 to 110 percent being the super-white portion of the scale).

An image's contrast ratio, then, can be determined by the width of the Histogram's graph. The position and height of individual bulges in the graph make it easy to see how dense the shadows, midtones, and highlights are.

CHAPTER 3

The black point is represented by the leftmost part of the graph. The white point is represented by the rightmost part of the graph. The average distribution of midtones is a bit more ambiguous but likely corresponds to the fattest bulge within the graph.

Figure 3.14 has a wide contrast ratio, with deep shadows and blown-out windows and lots of midtones in between.

Figure 3.14 A high-contrast image, with bright highlights and deep shadows.

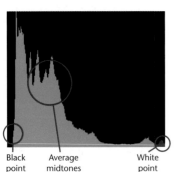

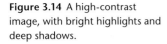

Black point | Average midtones | White point

Figure 3.15 The luma Histogram that corresponds to Figure 3.14, with callouts showing the black point, white point, and average distribution of midtones.

In the corresponding Histogram (**Figure 3.15**), the huge spikes at the left indicate the depth and solidity of the shadows (although you should notice that there are relatively few 0 percent blacks right at the bottom of the scale). The part of the graph in the middle shows that there is a good range of values in the midtones, which taper off toward the top of the scale toward the highlights. One last pair of lumps at the right of the scale represents the highlights in the picture that correspond to the blown-out windows. This is one example of a high contrast-ratio histograph.

Next, let's take a look at a lower-contrast image: an interior scene with no direct light sources or hard highlights of any kind (**Figure 3.16**).

Examining the corresponding Histogram, by comparison, we can see that the width of the graph is restricted to a far narrower portion of the scale (**Figure 3.17**). There's a sharp spike in the blacks corresponding to the abundance of shadows in the image. In other low-contrast images, the graph might be restricted to a narrow portion of the midtones instead, but in any case it's easy to see that the Histogram's graph does not extend across the full tonal range, tapering off sharply above 30 percent, with no values whatsoever greater than 54 percent or so.

Figure 3.16 A low-contrast image.

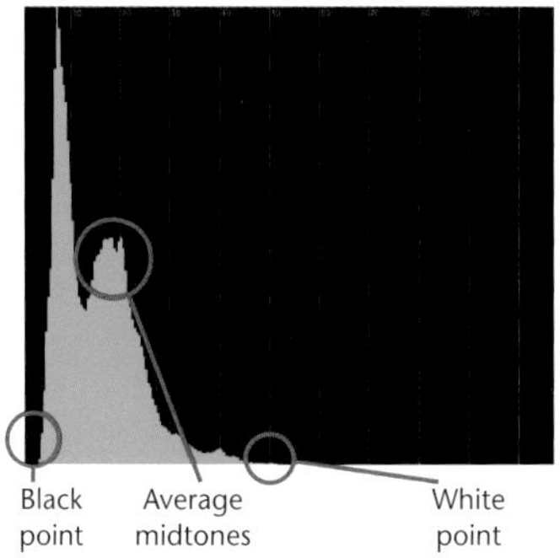

Black point   Average midtones   White point

Figure 3.17 The luma Histogram corresponding to Figure 3.16, with callouts for the black point, white point, and average distribution of midtones.

A WAVEFORM MONITOR SHOWING LUMA

You can also evaluate contrast using a Waveform Monitor (sometimes called a WFM), which has the added advantage of making it easier to associate the features of the Waveform graph with those in the original image, so you can get a sense of which portions of the image are sitting at the bottom or top of the scale. Waveform Monitors can often be set to analyze different components of a video signal, but in this section we're focused on a Waveform Monitor set to evaluate luma.

When a Waveform Monitor is set to luma, the height of the overall graph indicates the contrast ratio of the clip.

The black point is represented by the very bottom of the graph. The white point is represented by the top of the graph. The average distribution of midtones is usually fairly easy to see as the densest cluster of traces within the middle of the graph, although if it's an image with a lot of midtone values, the traces may be somewhat spread out.

Different video scopes use different scales. Software scopes often rely on a digital scale of 0 to 100 digital percent, while outboard scopes commonly use either an IRE scale of 1 to 100 IRE or a millivolts scale of 0 to 700 mV.

CHAPTER 3

IRE AND MILLIVOLTS

IRE (which stands for Institute of Radio Engineers, the organization that established the standard) is the unit of measurement typically used for NTSC test equipment. On a Waveform Monitor with a graticule set to display IRE, the full range of a theoretical broadcast signal (including both the visible signal area and the sync portion of the video signal) is 1 volt, which corresponds to the range of –40 to +100 IRE. One IRE, then, is equal to 1/140 volts.

Traditionally, reference white and reference black in analog and digital video have been measured in millivolts (mV). In case you're looking to impress a video engineer at a dinner party, 1 IRE is equal to 7.14 mV.

When examining a video signal using an outboard hardware waveform, you'll notice two parts of the signal. The portion of the video signal from the black level through 100 IRE (714, usually rounded to 700 mV) is the picture itself. The portion of the signal extending below 0 through –40 IRE (–285 or –300 mV) is the footroom of the signal, which contains the

sync portion of the video signal, which provides timing information crucial to the proper display of video. The exact levels, in millivolts, depend on the black level (setup) employed by your video capture/output interface, as you can see comparing the left and right ranges in Figure 3.18.

The IRE and millivolt units of measurement are typically relevant *only* when evaluating *outboard* video scopes that are analyzing the video output of your color correction workstation. The software scopes within most color correction applications measure the digital video signal of your media on disk in digital percentages, or sometimes by the digital encoding values used by your particular media.

When monitoring a video signal that extends from reference black to reference white using internal software scopes, the usable range of contrast is usually from 0 percent/IRE/mV at the bottom of the scale to 100 percent/IRE (or 700 mV) at the top of the scale.

In **Figure 3.18**, the Waveform graph to the left corresponds to Figure 3.14. Notice that the high spikes of the white point at 100–110 percent/IRE correspond to the blown-out windows, while the dips in the graph between 5–10 percent/IRE correspond horizontally to the deepest shadows within the image.

Figure 3.18 Two graphs of a Waveform Monitor set to luma, analyzing a high-contrast image at the left and a low-contrast image at the right.

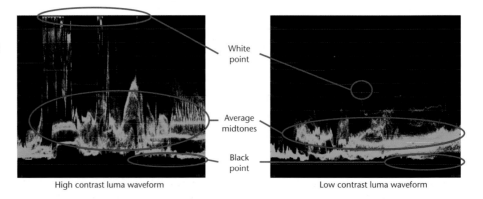

White point

Average midtones

Black point

High contrast luma waveform

Low contrast luma waveform

The image to the right is the graph for Figure 3.16, and you can see by the shortness of the graph that the contrast ratio is much lower. The highest part of the graph peaks at about 55 percent/IRE, and the densest cluster of midtones is between 10 and 28 percent/IRE, with dense shadows between 5 and 10 percent/IRE.

YOUR ENVIRONMENT MATTERS FOR CONTRAST EVALUATION

No matter what your video scopes are telling you (so long as the signal is broadcast legal), the bottom line is that the image should look right on your display, so make sure that it's properly calibrated and that your room is set up for you to evaluate contrast as accurately as possible.

The apparent contrast you perceive when looking at a monitor is highly dependent on the amount of light being reflected off your monitor (ideally, there should be no reflected light on the monitor), so you must strictly control the light in your room. Also, the use of a back-lit gradated or textured surround lighting behind the display helps establish a consistent contrast ratio, as well as provide relief for eye strain.

While you're controlling the light level in the room, you should also match the ambient light level of your intended audience. If you're judging contrast to be seen by an audience in a darkened theater, work in a similarly darkened environment. If you're working on a television program intended for the living room, brighter indirect ambient lighting will help you better judge the contrast ratios that your viewers are perceiving.

For more information on these and other environmental concerns, see Chapter 2.

CONTROLS TO ADJUST CONTRAST

In any given color correction system, there are usually at least three sets of controls that are available for making contrast adjustments: Lift, Gamma, and Gain controls; an Offset or Exposure control; and a Luma Curve.

LIFT, GAMMA, AND GAIN CONTROLS

Every single color correction application on the market provides a set of primary contrast controls that have been designed for manipulating *normalized* full-range or video-range digital images that occupy the BT.709 color space and BT.1886 gamma profile.

The names of these controls vary, and they're sometimes called *master* controls since they adjust the RGB components all together, but their function is usually similar from application to application. Used collectively, these controls let you make many kinds of contrast adjustments by altering the black point, distribution of midtones, and white point of an image.

In the following sections, we'll see how each contrast control affects the composite image in **Figure 3.19**. The top part of the test image shows the real-world effect of each contrast adjustment. The bottom of the test image consists of a linear gradient that shows specifically how each adjustment affects the overall range of image tonality, as shown by the corresponding straight diagonal line in the Waveform graph.

Figure 3.19 In the screenshot on the left, the top of the image creates a typical Waveform graph, while the ramp gradient at the bottom creates a straight diagonal line running from the bottom left (0 percent) to the upper right (100 percent) of the Waveform Monitor.

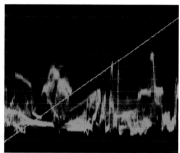

LIFT

The *Lift* control (sometimes incorrectly called Shadows) raises and lowers the *black point*—the darkest part of the picture. This corresponds to the left side of the Histogram's graph or the bottom of the Waveform Monitor's graph, as shown in **Figure 3.20**.

Figure 3.20 Raising the Lift control lightens the darkest parts of the image (circled in red) while keeping the highlights pinned in place (circled in gray). All midtones are compressed between the new black point and the unchanged white point.

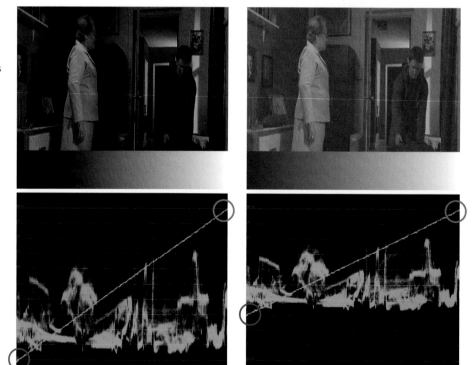

MASTER OFFSET OR EXPOSURE

In some applications, a control named *Master Offset* or *Exposure* works differently from controls typically referred to as Lift. Strictly speaking, in this instance, a Master Offset control raises or lowers the overall signal, whereas a Lift control raises the black point of the image relative to the current highlights, which aren't changed, while the midtones are stretched or compressed depending on the adjustment (**Figure 3.21**). Some applications provide both Lift and Master Offset controls together.

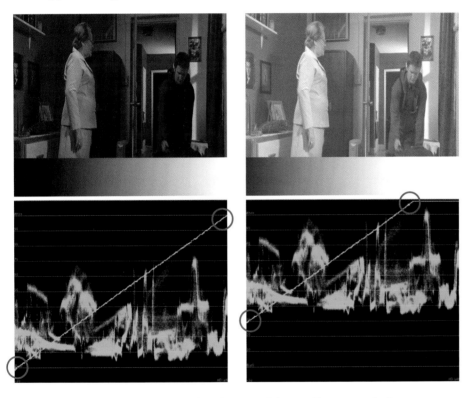

Figure 3.21 When raising the values in a true Master Offset operation, the entire image is lightened by a uniform amount. The shadows, midtones, and highlights all get brighter, with the lightest highlights being clipped at the edge of the scale.

These controls are often associated with Log or Film grading controls, but even when used with normalized images, Exposure can be useful for dropping the overall signal down when you need to park the black point at a particular level.

NOTE

On older equipment and software, this might be called Setup when controlling a digital percentage or Pedestal when controlling IRE.

CHAPTER 3

GAMMA

The *Gamma* control lets you change the distribution of midtones, darkening or lightening the portions of the image that fall between the black and white points. Ideally, the black and white points of the image remain relatively unchanged by a midtone adjustment, but large midtone adjustments may affect the highlights and shadows of the image (**Figure 3.22**).

Figure 3.22 Raising a Gamma/Midtone control lightens the midtones of the image (highlighted in red), while leaving both the black point and white points pinned in place (highlighted in gray). The curved line corresponding to the grayscale ramp shows this is a non-linear adjustment.

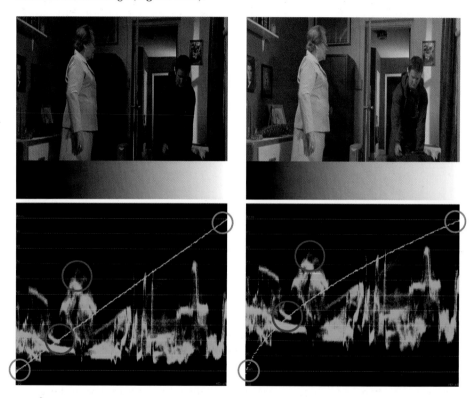

GAIN

The *Gain* control (sometimes incorrectly called Highlights) raises and lowers the white level—the brightest part of the picture—relative to the black level. Usually, the black level is relatively unchanged by a highlights adjustment, but large highlights adjustments can drag the black point of the image up, lightening the shadows.

Highlights adjustments correspond to the right side of the Histogram's graph or the top of the Waveform Monitor's graph (**Figure 3.23**).

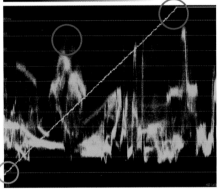

Figure 3.23 Raising the highlights lightens the brightest parts of the image (circled in red) while pinning the black point in place (highlighted in gray). All midtones in between are stretched up, while the darkest shadows remain relatively unchanged.

INTERACTION AMONG LIFT, GAMMA, AND GAIN CONTROLS

The adjustments shown in the previous sections are ideals. In reality, keep in mind that each of these three controls usually interact with one another when you adjust image contrast.

For example, changes to a Lift control will also affect the mids/gamma and may affect the highlights/whites if you're making a large adjustment (**Figure 3.24**). For this reason, it's often ideal to make any necessary blacks adjustments first.

CHAPTER 3

Figure 3.24 A Histogram with callouts showing the general influence that various contrast controls have over one another.

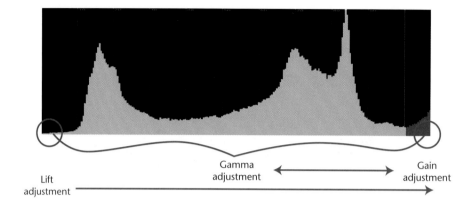

HOW TO MANIPULATE LIFT, GAMMA, AND GAIN CONTROLS

Manipulating these three controls lets you expand, compress, and redistribute the luma component of an image in different ways. Every professional color correction application has a set of onscreen contrast controls that correspond to a set of rings or knobs on a compatible control surface. Ordinarily, you'd use the control surface to make your adjustments, but the onscreen controls can also be used directly should you either lack a control surface or need to use some special feature of the onscreen interface.

Each onscreen interface for contrast adjustment is different (**Figure 3.25**). Some applications use vertical sliders; others are horizontal. Some curve each slider around the corresponding color balance control, while others simply present a parameter control set up as a virtual knob or mouse-adjustable number field.

In an effort to make the examples in this book as universally applicable as possible, onscreen contrast controls are illustrated simply as a set of three vertically oriented sliders, with the détente (default) position at the middle (**Figure 3.26**). This is a fairly typical arrangement, and similar to many such interfaces. Lowering a particular slider's handle reduces that value, while raising it increases the value.

With few exceptions, the control surfaces for most applications use a set of three rings surrounding the color balance trackballs to correspond to these contrast controls (**Figure 3.27**).

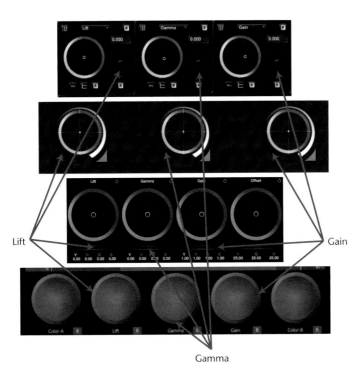

Lift

Gain

Gamma

Figure 3.25 Onscreen contrast controls from different applications compared. From top to bottom: FilmLight Baselight, Adobe SpeedGrade, DaVinci Resolve, ASSIMILATE SCRATCH.

Lift

Gamma

Gain

Figure 3.26 A generic user interface similar to nearly every color correction application currently in use. The sliders to the left of each color balance control adjust contrast.

Figure 3.27 On the Tangent Devices Element control panel, contrast is controlled via three rings surrounding the color balance trackballs.

CHAPTER 3

Turning a ring to the right raises that control's value, while turning it to the left lowers it. For purposes of illustration, that's what's presented in this book (**Figure 3.28**).

Figure 3.28 An illustration of the type of physical control surface commonly used by color correction applications. The center trackballs control color balance, while the outer rings control contrast, similar to using the sliders in the onscreen user interface.

Shadows/Lift   Midtones/Gamma   Highlights/Gain

However, if your particular control surface uses a set of dials instead (the Tangent Devices CP100 and Wave control surfaces are two examples), know that the adjustments shown by the arrows in each example are the same. **Figure 3.29** shows the two kinds of control surface, dial and ring.

Figure 3.29 Control Surface Contrast controls compared. The Tangent Devices Wave, on the left, uses separate dials, while the DaVinci Resolve control surface uses rings.

In every example presented in this book, the onscreen controls are shown above the same adjustment made with the control surface (adjustments are indicated by arrows indicating the direction to turn the control, with the amount indicated by each arrow's length). Since each application uses different values and has varying sensitivity for the controls, all examples are presented as relative instructions. You'll want to experiment with your particular application to see how to best implement the examples in this book.

HOW TO MANIPULATE OFFSET, GAMMA, AND GAIN CONTROLS

Grading applications often provide Lift, Gamma, and Gain controls with an additional Master Offset control. However, Adobe SpeedGrade uses a different scheme, providing Offset, Gamma, and Gain controls as your primary method of contrast adjustment (**Figure 3.30**).

The difference is subtle but significant. When using Lift/Gamma/Gain, since Lift is an adjustment that is relative to the white point of the signal set by the Gain control, you can make a Lift adjustment any time you like without overly altering the current Gain—though there usually is some interactivity (**Figure 3.31**).

Figure 3.30 The Offset, Gamma, and Gain controls found in Adobe SpeedGrade.

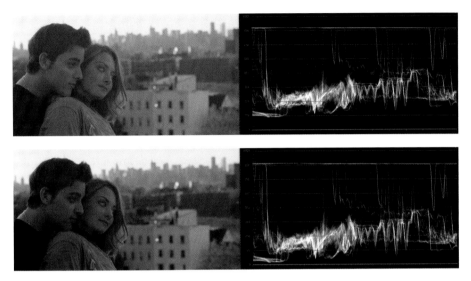

Figure 3.31 Lowering Lift so the black point is at zero doesn't affect the white point of the image.

However, since Offset controls are an absolute adjustment to raise or lower the level of the entire signal, you typically want to set your Offset first, before you do anything else. All other adjustments you make to Gain and Gamma will be relative to your Offset adjustment, and later adjustments to Offset will make a far larger change (**Figure 3.32**).

Mathematically, this method of contrast control is neither better nor worse than Lift/Gamma/Gain. It's simply a different method of adjusting the signal.

Figure 3.32 Lowering Offset so the black point is at zero also lowers the white point by the same amount. A corresponding Gain adjustment will then set your overall contrast ratio however you want.

LUMA CURVE CONTROLS

Curve controls let you make specific adjustments to individual image components by adding control points to bend a diagonal or vertical line. At the very least, most color correction applications typically have one Curve control for each color channel (red, green, and blue) and a fourth that controls luma (**Figure 3.33**).

Figure 3.33 Onscreen Curve controls compared. Top to bottom: SGO Mistika, DaVinci Resolve, FilmLight Baselight.

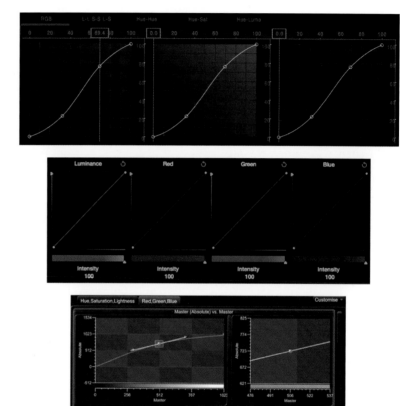

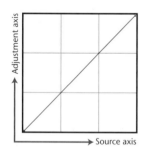

Figure 3.34 A Curve control at its most neutral position, with all source values along the curve equal to the adjustment values, with the result of no change to the image.

Curve controls are two-dimensional graphs. One dimension is the source axis (the x-axis), while the other is the adjustment axis (the y-axis).

Different applications handle the curve interface in various ways. Sometimes curves appear within a perfectly square box (**Figure 3.34**); other times they're rectangular.

However curves are set up in your software, you may consider the line of the curve to represent the actual values in the image.

Typically, the leftmost part of the curve represents the darkest pixels in the image, while the rightmost part of the curve represents the lightest pixels in the image.

While this white line is a straight diagonal from left to right (the default position), the source axis equals the adjustment axis, and the result is that *no change* is made to the image. A grid in the background of many Curve controls helps you verify this, since at its most neutral position the line of the Curve control intersects each horizontal and vertical pair of grid lines through the middle diagonal, as you can see in **Figure 3.35**.

Curves get interesting when you add a control point with which to make adjustments. **Figure 3.36** shows a control point dragged up, increasing the values along the middle section of the curve.

In the resulting image adjustment, the values within the middle of the image (the midtones) are raised. The curve is higher along the adjustment axis than the source axis, so the midtone image values in that channel are consequently raised, lightening the image. The result is similar to the gamma adjustment shown in Figure 3.22. If instead you dragged this control point down, then the same parts of the image would be lowered, darkening the image.

In most applications, each curve begins with two control points that pin the left and right of the curve to the bottom and top corners. These can be also be adjusted to manipulate the darkest and lightest values in that channel, but most of the time you'll be adding one or more control points along the middle of the curve to make your adjustments.

HOW DIFFERENT APPLICATIONS LET YOU ADJUST CURVES

While Curve controls are implemented in various ways by different color correction applications, they all generally work by letting you click the surface of the curve to add a control point and then dragging it around to reshape the curve. The more control points you add, the more complicated a shape you can create, and the more complex an adjustment you can make.

You can usually drag a point off the surface of a curve to remove it, and there's also usually a reset button of some kind for restoring the curve to its default neutral shape.

Where curves vary is in *how* they let you manipulate the shape, as shown in Figure 3.33. DaVinci Resolve control points are directly attached to the curve, influencing it in a different way, but without the need for handles. FilmLight's Baselight, on the other hand, uses Bezier handles similar to those found in many illustration applications to create different curve shapes. Consult the documentation for your particular color correction application to learn the details of how its curves implementation works.

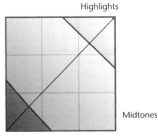

Figure 3.35 Approximate regions of image tonality affected by each portion of the curve interface. In reality, these regions overlap widely.

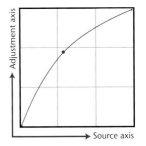

Figure 3.36 A Curve control with one control point making an adjustment in the middle of the midtones. The curve representing the color or luma values in the image is moved up along the adjustment axis.

NOTE

Quantel Pablo allows curve adjustments using its Fettle control. For more information, see Chapter 4.

CHAPTER 3

CONTRAST AND PIVOT CONTROLS

In addition to Lift/Gamma/Gain/Offset and Curves, many applications have Contrast and Pivot controls that provide another way of expanding and compressing image contrast. Used most simply, the Contrast control can, with a single adjustment, alter both the white and black points while linearly scaling all image values falling in between (**Figure 3.37**). Some pivot controls, such as the one found in Baselight, can also be unganged so as to be used to adjust the contrast of individual color channels.

Figure 3.37 Contrast and Pivot controls shown in Adobe SpeedGrade, DaVinci Resolve, and FilmLight Baselight. Baselight's Pivot control is a slider in the LUT graph below.

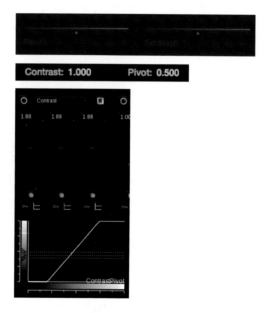

The Pivot control lets you adjust the center value around which the black and white point are adjusted, effectively weighing more of your contrast adjustment toward the shadows or toward the highlights as necessary given the starting point of your image. In **Figure 3.38**, all three versions of the image have Contrast increased to 1.48 in DaVinci Resolve, but the Pivot control has been set to .5, then .350, and then .232, respectively.

As you can see, lowering the pivot point weighted more of the contrast adjustment up, toward the highlights. Raising the pivot point would weigh more of the contrast adjustment down, toward the shadows.

One important thing to learn about your particular application, however, is whether expanding contrast beyond the lower and upper limits of the signal will clip or compress the shadows and highlights. In **Figure 3.39**, an image with a superimposed ramp shows that in DaVinci Resolve, expanding contrast *compresses* the highlights and shadows of the signal in order to prevent clipping, resulting in an S curve where the highlights and shadows fall off the closer you come to these outer limits.

Figure 3.38 The same Contrast adjustment used to widen image contrast, but with three different Pivot settings defining the level of image brightness about which contrast expansion occurs.

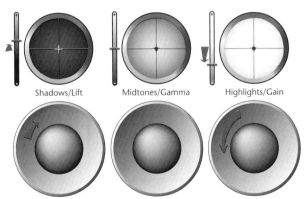

Shadows/Lift Midtones/Gamma Highlights/Gain

Figure 3.39 Before and after using the Contrast control in DaVinci Resolve to stretch image contrast. The higher you set Contrast, the more the highlights and shadows of the signal will be compressed to avoid clipping, which can be seen by the bend in the grayscale ramp trace.

Other applications clip the highlights and shadows of the signal, requiring you to be more careful when you stretch image contrast to fill the full tonal range. Once you learn how to use these controls, Contrast and Pivot can provide a fast shortcut for all kinds of contrast adjustments.

EXPANDING CONTRAST

Within the boundaries of broadcast legality, one of the most general guidelines for adjusting contrast is that the audience should be able to readily distinguish the most important subjects within the frame.

Aside from that, increases or decreases to the contrast ratio in your clips will be dictated by the content of your program and by the look the cinematographer, director, and you are trying to achieve. Whatever your goals, keep in mind that maximizing the contrast of your images, whenever appropriate, gives them more "punch" (exciting descriptors vary from client to client), resulting in a more vivid image for reasons described later in this chapter.

In some images, it's appropriate to park an expanse of highlights at 90 to 100 percent and all of the shadows down around 0 percent. In other images, a few pixels of highlights at the top of the range and a few pixels of shadows at or near 0 are all it takes to give a bit more life to your image.

In general, contrast is *expanded* by lowering the shadows, raising the highlights, and adjusting the midtones to taste, according to the mood of the scene and the time of day you want to convey. In the following example, we'll adjust the contrast of a typical on-location clip to enhance its look:

1 Take a casual look at the image in **Figure 3.40** on a broadcast monitor. Doing so reveals a generally well-exposed image with a relatively full range of tonality. However, the Waveform graph indicates that both the highlights and the shadows are well shy of the outer boundaries of what's permissible.

Figure 3.40 An image with initially compressed contrast.

In this particular clip, there are no pixels under 23 percent, which accounts for the muddy shadows. At the other end of the scale, there are no pixels above 87 percent, resulting in muted highlights in the sky. This clip was clearly either exposed or transferred to protect highlights and shadows from being clipped, and there's ample room to lower the black point and raise the white point in order to expand the image into the full 0 to 100 percent range.

2 By dragging the Lift contrast control until the bottom of the graph in the Waveform Monitor comes to around 5, you can darken the shadows, giving them solidity or density (**Figure 3.41**).

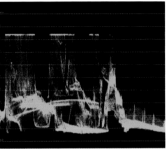

Figure 3.41 Lowering the Lift control stretches the Waveform graph down toward 0 percent/IRE.

Watch the image on your broadcast monitor as you make this type of adjustment to make sure the dark portions of the picture aren't becoming too dark. In this example, the darkest part of the image corresponds to the soldier's dark blue jacket, so it's inappropriate to lower the shadows all the way to 0, as that would eliminate much-needed detail in that part of the image.

3 Raising the Gain contrast control until the very top of the graph in the Waveform Monitor touches 100 gives the highlights a little more energy. At the same time, you might also elect to raise the Gamma control a bit in order to lighten the overall image (**Figure 3.42**).

This might result in your needing to drag the shadows back up a bit too much, so lowering the Lift control to compensate would be your last adjustment.

NOTE

No matter what the scopes tell you, you should limit your adjustments to what looks appropriate on a calibrated monitor within a suitable viewing environment.

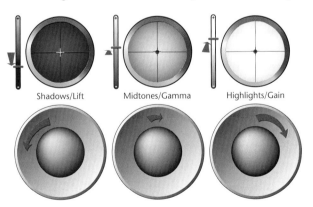

Shadows/Lift   Midtones/Gamma   Highlights/Gain

Figure 3.42 Adjustments to lower the shadows and raise the highlights and midtones are shown on both the onscreen interface and by using the rings of the control surface.

CHAPTER 3

Again, take a look at this image on a broadcast display. You can see that this seemingly small change makes a significant difference to the quality of the image, analogous to wiping a film of dust off the image. That's the magic of contrast expansion. The result should be a more vivid image, with good definition, strong shadow detail, and healthy highlights resulting from the image using the maximum broadcast legal dynamic range (**Figure 3.43**).

Figure 3.43 Adjustments to widen the contrast have resulted in denser shadows and more energetic highlights.

NOTE

Contrast adjustments are often subtle, especially when you're working with an experienced cinematographer's carefully exposed footage. Whenever possible, avoid making assumptions; ask the cinematographer what the intended look for the footage is supposed to be. In some cases, on-set grades will be available in the form of LUTs providing a direct representation of the cinematographer's intent.

The corresponding luma Waveform should now show that the image is occupying the widest reasonable expanse of tonality, with shadows within the 0–10 percent/IRE range and with highlights just under 100 percent/IRE.

Most clips look perfectly fine with limited contrast expansions, but major contrast expansions might create problems because of a lack of image data. In any event, don't worry about these gaps; the image on your monitor is what's really important.

WHAT DO GAPS IN MY VIDEO SCOPES MEAN?

Depending on what kind of software-based video scopes you're using, you may notice gaps that form in the graphs of images where you've stretched the contrast (**Figure 3.44**).

Figure 3.44 Gaps in software scopes indicate that you've stretched a limited amount of image data into a wider range of tonality and are perfectly normal.

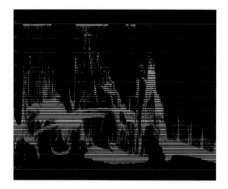

These gaps appear because we took a limited amount of image data and stretched it out to fit a greater tonal range and because the source media uses 4:2:0 chroma sub-sampling. The gaps serve as a reminder that you can't get something for nothing. Different media using different chroma sampling (for example, 4:4:4, 4:2:2) will have fewer gaps corresponding to the increased amount of chroma information that's available. These gaps will also appear in vectorscopes.

COMPRESSING CONTRAST

If you're trying to match clips shot and balanced for dusk, nighttime, or any location with faded blacks and weak highlights or if you're creating a deliberately low-contrast look, you can also *compress* the contrast.

You can compress contrast in several ways. You can lower the white level while raising the mids to reduce contrast in the highlights. If you're really going for it, you can also opt to raise the black level, although you should do this with care, as the result will be milky blacks, which you may or may not want.

In this example, we'll compress the contrast of an interior shot to make the lighting conditions look much dimmer.

1   Examine the Waveform Monitor. This clip has a fairly wide contrast ratio to begin with for an interior scene, with highlights extending to nearly 93 percent/IRE and with blacks that extend down to 5 percent/IRE (**Figure 3.45**).

 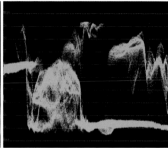

Figure 3.45 The original image before compressing the contrast.

2   Create the desired look by compressing the overall contrast ratio of the clip; begin by lowering the Gain control to mute the highlights.

At the same time, raise the Lift contrast control to lighten the darkest areas of the picture to keep the shadows from being too inky, but not so much that they're visibly faded relative to the rest of the picture (**Figure 3.46**).

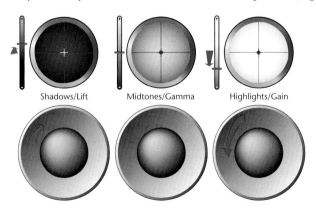

Shadows/Lift   Midtones/Gamma   Highlights/Gain

Figure 3.46 The onscreen control adjustments used to compress contrast and the corresponding control surface adjustments.

CHAPTER 3

Figure 3.47 The final result of compressing the contrast of the image.

When you're finished, you'll have shortened the graph in the Waveform Monitor—in this example, you squeeze it between 75 and 80 percent/IRE (**Figure 3.47**).

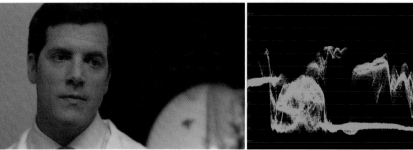

The result is a muted image, with fewer vibrant highlights indicating dimmer lighting in the room.

Remember that the perceived brightness of the lightest tone in an image is relative to its darkest tone, and vice versa. Even though we've reduced the overall contrast ratio, we're not draining all the contrast from the image, so long as there is enough of a spread between the darkest and lightest values in the picture.

TAKE CARE WHEN RAISING THE BLACK LEVEL

Raising the black level of an image works best when the blacks aren't crushed to begin with and have a lot of image detail that will emerge from such an adjustment. If there were large areas of solid black in the original image, raising the black level creates flat gray areas that won't look particularly good.

Raising the black point can also result in unexpected color appearing in the shadows of the image, which may creep in from a Gamma contrast adjustment. Such problems may not be apparent until you see the video on a display that's inappropriately bright, at which point it may be too late. If you do catch a problem like this, you might try desaturating the shadows (using either your application's Shadow Saturation control or an HSL Qualifier to isolate the shadows and then using the regular Saturation control).

Y'C$_B$C$_R$ LUMA ADJUSTMENTS VS. RGB LUMA ADJUSTMENTS

While we're talking about contrast adjustment, it's important to understand the relationship between contrast and color in different applications.

The primary contrast controls of most color correction applications make RGB image processing adjustments, where image lightness is adjusted via equal and simultaneous adjustments to all three color components. The resulting adjustment has a measurable and perceptible impact on *image saturation*, or the intensity of colors throughout the image.

Figure 3.48 shows an example of an image with low initial contrast.

Figure 3.48 The original low-contrast image.

In a low-contrast image like one in Figure 3.48, increasing contrast by raising gain and lowering lift results in increased saturation, intensifying the colors of the image (**Figure 3.49**).

Figure 3.49 Expanding contrast using a master RGB control raises image saturation.

CHAPTER 3

TIP

Y'-only contrast-adjustment controls are great for selectively altering shadow density to get punchier blacks without changing the color too much or for fixing specific broadcast legalization issues.

Figure 3.50 Expanding contrast via a Y'-specific adjustment perceptually lowers image saturation.

Some applications have separate controls for controlling image luminosity in a very specific way via $Y'C_BC_R$ image processing—by manipulating the Y' channel independently of the two color difference channels (Cb and Cr). In this way, changes to contrast have no measurable effect on image saturation (the vectorscope graph remains unchanged). However, the *perceived* image saturation does in fact change.

In this case, stretching the contrast of an image results in perceptually diminished saturation and seemingly lackluster colors, even though the numeric saturation as measured by the vectorscope hasn't actually changed (**Figure 3.50**).

In this situation, simultaneously raising image saturation compensates for this effect, providing you with the image you want.

The important thing to consider in both instances is that one approach is not necessarily "better" than the other. They're simply two different methods of adjusting contrast, with plusses and minuses depending on what you need to accomplish. In most instances, the RGB processing method is used, so it's best to get used to that approach.

MULTIPLE LUMA CONTROLS VIA A CONTROL SURFACE

DaVinci Resolve is one example of an application that provides both types of contrast adjustment, with RGB and Y'-only controls. The typical three-ring control surface interface makes RGB-style adjustments. However, there are three more control surface knobs for Y'-only luminosity adjustments.

Other applications expose additional Luma adjustment controls in the onscreen interface. See your color correction application's documentation for more information.

REDISTRIBUTING MIDTONE CONTRAST

You've seen how to manipulate highlights and shadows using contrast controls to affect the overall contrast ratio of clips. Now let's take a look at making adjustments to the midtones of an image.

To use a nonvegetarian metaphor, if highlights are the salt and shadows are the pepper, then midtones are the steak. Overall image contrast ratio is important, but it takes only a few highlights and a reasonable number of shadows to give a shot the flavor it needs. Overall, midtones comprise the majority of most images. In particular, it's a good bet that the main subject of any given shot—whether it's an actor, a car, or key features of a location—is sitting squarely within the midtones of the image.

The average level of an image's midtones reflects whether the location is interior or exterior. The midtone levels reflect the time of day, whether it's morning, noon, late afternoon, or evening. Midtones also convey mood: Whether a shot is low key or high key is influenced by how much light appears upon the subjects in the shot. The following example involves a shot being adjusted a few different ways to illustrate how important midtones adjustments are to the look of the environment.

The image in **Figure 3.51** is well-exposed, with a good distribution of tonality from strong shadows to healthy highlights. It isn't particularly dark, but it's not particularly bright, either. It's very middle of the road.

NOTE

Sometimes you'll need to lower the Gain control to keep the highlights from getting pushed above 100 percent/IRE when you're raising the midtones a significant amount, but in this image it's not necessary.

 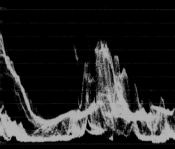

Figure 3.51 The original image, before midtone adjustments.

1   First try to give the image a more midday look. You can raise the Gamma contrast control to lighten the image while lowering the Lift contrast to keep the shadows deep (**Figure 3.52**).

CHAPTER 3

Figure 3.52 Applying contrast control adjustments to raise the midtones.

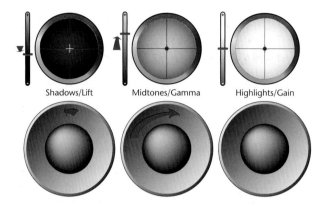

The result is a brighter image, yet one that retains the deep shadows that keep the contrast ratio high (**Figure 3.53**).

Figure 3.53 The image with raised midtones, giving it a brighter, midday look.

2 Now, let's make the same image look like it was shot much later in the afternoon, possibly toward dusk. Lowering the Gamma control darkens the image, while raising both the Lift and Gain controls keeps this adjustment from lowering the overall image contrast and crushing the shadows too abruptly (**Figure 3.54**).

Figure 3.54 Contrast control adjustments to lower the midtones.

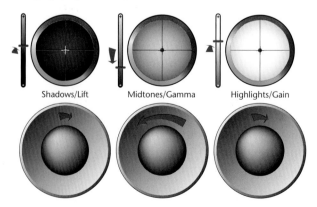

The result is an image that's much darker, overall, and yet it retains highlights that make the shadows seem that much darker. Raising the Lift control in turn retains as much detail in the darkest parts of the image as possible, as shown in **Figure 3.55** (although such dark details are difficult to reproduce in print).

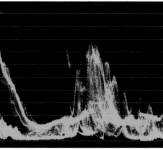

Figure 3.55 The image with lowered midtones gives the impression of having been shot later in the day.

As you can see, you can make some simple adjustments to redistribute the midtones of an image; doing so has a large effect on the audience's perception of the scene, and you don't even need to change the black or white points of the image.

ADJUSTING MIDTONES USING CURVES

Using a Curve control, you can make incredibly specific contrast adjustments to the midtones of an image that would be impossible to perform using just the three regular contrast controls, which we'll see in the following example.

1 Let's start by examining the image, shown in **Figure 3.56** in its original, unaltered form. It's an interior shot with wide contrast and generally soft shadows. However, the movie is a thriller, and the client expressed a desire for a more threatening feeling to the scene, with sharper shadows.

Figure 3.56 The original image— good but not edgy enough for the client.

If it were necessary to expand the overall contrast ratio of the image (to adjust the white and black points of the image to maximize the available contrast), then this would be the first thing you'd do.

You'll usually want to make changes to an image's overall contrast by adjusting the primary contrast controls to the right of each of the color balance controls. Since Luma Curve controls are often pinned at both the highest and lowest parts of the Curve control graph, you can't raise the brightest highlights or lower the deepest shadows using just curves. For this reason, you might consider the luma curve to be an extremely detailed midtones control.

The image in Figure 3.56 already has wide contrast, so these changes aren't necessary, and you can move on to the adjustments we want to make using the luma curve.

2 We want to deepen the shadows on the woman's face. To figure out where to add a control point to the curve, you should know that there's a rough correspondence between the height of portions of the graph shown in the Waveform Monitor and the height of the control points you add to a Curve control (**Figure 3.57**).

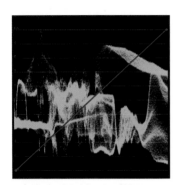

Figure 3.57 A Curve control superimposed over the Waveform graph from Figure 3.56. Placing a control point on a curve allows you to adjust the luma represented by the Waveform at the same height as that point.

Before beginning your curve adjustment, you first need to decide whether you want to make an RGB adjustment or a Y'-only adjustment. Many grading applications let you gang the red, green, and blue curves together (or the YRGB curves together) so that an adjustment made to one curve is made to all. In this case, stretching contrast using the RGB curves also increases image saturation, as you saw earlier in this chapter. However, if you ungang the curves from one another or use a specific Y'-only Curve control, then an increase in image contrast appears to desaturate the image, resulting in a starker look.

3 To begin adjusting the shadows, open your application's Y'-only Curve control; then add a control point corresponding to the lower portion of the midtones in the graph and drag it down to deepen the lighter shadows in the image (**Figure 3.58**).

The resulting adjustment darkens the overall image (**Figure 3.59**).

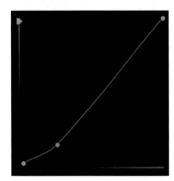

Figure 3.58 Lowering the darker midtones by dragging a control point down.

Figure 3.59 The curve adjustment in Figure 3.58 darkened the image.

4 Next, add a second control point to the curve, corresponding to the lighter midtones on the woman's face, and then drag it upward (**Figure 3.60**).

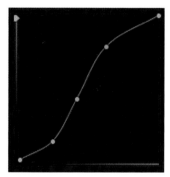

This type of adjustment is sometimes referred to as an *S curve*, as it bends the Curve control to resemble the letter *S*. The practical result is to stretch contrast within an extremely localized portion of image tonality. The shadows are darker, and the highlights are nearly as bright as they were before (**Figure 3.61**).

 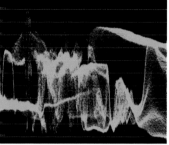

Figure 3.60 Using two control points to create an "S" curve, stretching contrast within a narrow range of image tonality.

Figure 3.61 The result caused by the curve adjustment in Figure 3.60.

5 To make the image just a little bit edgier, bump up the highlights on the woman's face by adding one last control point near the top of the curve, and then drag it upward (**Figure 3.62**).

This adjustment has the desired effect of adding a bit of gloss to the woman's skin, without changing the high-contrast shadows you've added to the rest of her (**Figure 3.63**).

 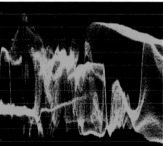

Figure 3.62 Adding a control point to the top of the curve in order to lighten the brightest high-lights on the woman's face, neck, and shoulders.

Figure 3.63 The final image after stretching midtone contrast using the luma curve.

CHAPTER 3

As you can see, you can use curves to exert much finer control over contrast within an image. However, here's one last word of advice: With most Curve controls, a little bit of adjustment goes a long way.

In particular, aggressive curve adjustments can magnify the shortcomings of source media with "thin" image data. Also, Curve controls tend to be pretty sensitive, although the onscreen interfaces of some applications allow you to counter this by zooming into the curve itself in order to make finer adjustments. To see whether your application has this capability, check your documentation.

ADJUSTING LOG-ENCODED CONTRAST

The Lift, Gamma, and Gain controls described in this chapter originated with equipment designed for telecine (video transfer from film) and tape-to-tape color correction. In both cases, you're generally working with normalized media, which is what these controls are designed to manipulate.

However, the introduction of wide-latitude log-encoded media to postproduction workflows has necessitated additional controls over image contrast in order to take advantage of this extra latitude and to make it easy to normalize log-encoded media to provide the quickest and best starting point for the rest of your grade.

Log controls are unusual in that they've been designed specifically with the compressed contrast of Cineon and Log-C in mind, and yet they work best when you're normalizing the image via another adjustment. Since expanding low-contrast log-encoded media into the full tonal range necessary for the final image is your first priority, that will be the focus of this section. Chapter 4 has more information about grading color using Log controls.

DEBAYERING RAW MEDIA TO LOG FOR GRADING

As discussed in Chapter 1, you can debayer most RAW formats to a log-encoded image in order to extract the maximum amount of image data and adjustable latitude from that source, should you decide this is both necessary and worth the extra time to deal with while grading. If you go this route, then the resulting image needs to be normalized in order to create your starting point for the final grade, just like any other log-encoded format.

NORMALIZING LOG MEDIA

When you're grading a project that originates with log-encoded media, your first order of business is to normalize it, using a contrast adjustment of some kind, to take the first step in your grade and to be able to see what you're working on. Your first adjustment to normalize log-encoded media is *not* intended to achieve perfect contrast; its purpose is to provide an ideal starting point for moving the wide-latitude log data into the 32-bit floating-point precision of your grading application's image processing pipeline, in preparation for more work.

In other words, *first* you normalize and *then* you fine-tune.

There are two ways of normalizing a log-encoded image so you can start working with it in more depth: using a lookup table and manually.

NORMALIZING LOG MEDIA WITH A LUT

Lookup tables (LUTs) provide a way of mathematically transforming an image using a precomputed table of data that describes, for each input value in the table, what the output should be. Since this reduces the math of an image transformation into a simple lookup operation, LUTs are computationally cheap. They're also versatile, and LUTs are used for all kinds of image transformations, from monitor calibration (described in Chapter 2) to log normalization, printer emulation, and even look generation.

LUTs are categorized by how many dimensions they have, and there are two kinds: 1D and 3D LUTs. A 1D LUT is suitable for a normalizing contrast adjustment, but sometimes a particular application will require a 3D LUT, simply because of the way it's been designed. In these cases, you can use a suitable utility to convert a 1D LUT into a 3D LUT that does the same thing.

To use a LUT in this way, you need to first obtain a LUT that's an inverse transformation of the log encoding used by the camera that shot the media you're grading. Since cameras are updated all the time, this is a moving target, so it may take a bit of research. Additionally, some camera manufacturers provide a 3D LUT that adjusts both the color and the contrast of the log-encoded signal in order to account for the camera's color matrix, which may also require some adjustment.

Once you've obtained the correct LUT for your application, you need to use the node or layer organization of your application to apply the LUT transformation somewhere after an initial set of as-yet-unused contrast adjustments (**Figure 3.64**). This is because LUTs will clip any image data that goes outside the boundaries they define, so you want to be able to apply a contrast adjustment *prior to* the LUT in order to bring all the available image data into the grade.

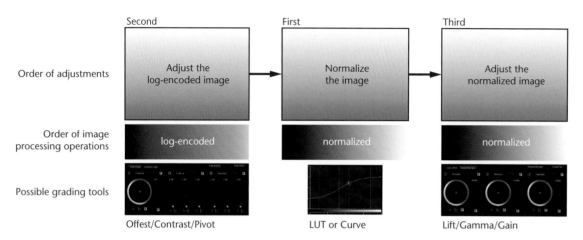

Figure 3.64 Log grading works best when you add adjustments in a specific order, while exercising careful control of how each adjustment is organized in your grading application's image processing pipeline.

As Figure 3.64 illustrates, one of the potentially confusing things about setting up a series of corrections when grading log-encoded media is that the order in which you work is different from the order in which adjustments are applied by your application. In particular, you need to add the LUT *first*, even though it's the *second* operation in the image processing stack of your application.

Here are three examples of how this can be done in three widely available grading applications:

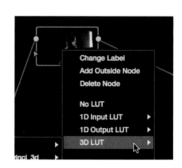

Figure 3.65 Applying a LUT to a node within a grade in DaVinci Resolve.

Figure 3.66 Applying a LUT as a layer within a grade in Adobe SpeedGrade.

- **DaVinci Resolve:** You can add a Resolve-formatted .cube LUT to any node in the node tree (**Figure 3.65**). 3D LUTs that are assigned to a node act as the last image processing operation within that node, so you can add a LUT to a node and still use the log-grading controls within that node to process the pre-LUT transformed image data.

- **Adobe SpeedGrade:** You can add the LUT custom look layer to the Layers list in order to insert a LUT operation (**Figure 3.66**), with which you can either apply one of the pre-installed LUTs (such as log_to_lin.lut) or load a LUT from disk.

- **FilmLight Baselight:** Any layer in Baselight can be set to work as a "Truelight" operator, enabling you to apply a LUT transform to the image using any FilmLight-formatted LUT at that layer (**Figure 3.67**).

Bearing in mind that most professional grading applications provide a method of applying multiple operations one after another, you'll find it useful to organize your image processing operations in order to make adjustments both before and after the LUT. You make adjustments before the LUT to access the original log-encoded image data; adjustments made afterward enable you to work with the normalized image data the LUT provides.

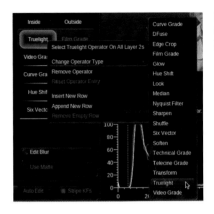

Figure 3.67 Applying a LUT by assigning a Truelight operator within a layer in FilmLight Baselight.

WHERE DO I GET A LUT FOR A PARTICULAR CAMERA'S MEDIA?

This is a very good question, and I bring it up only to mention how difficult this can be. Often, grading applications provide a set of LUTs for normalizing clips; however, you don't always get a complete set, and not all LUTs are created equal. ARRI does everyone a huge service via its LUT generator (www.arri.com/camera/digital_cameras/tools/lut_generator/lut_generator.html), which makes it easy to export 3D LUTs designed for their Alexa and D-21 cameras, as well as to export 1D LUTs suitable for any log-encoded format that's similar to Log-C. If you need to work with media from Sony's digital cinema cameras, LUTs for the F55 and F65 can be found at http://community.sony.com.

NORMALIZING LOG MEDIA USING YOUR GRADING APPLICATION'S COLOR SCIENCE

Increasingly, developers of color grading applications are acknowledging the wide range of source and destination color spaces we must work with by implementing built-in color management schemes. This enables applications to provide a variety of image transforms (such as normalizing log media) without the need to hunt down LUTs, but it also enables you to more easily work in one color space, display the results within a second color space, and output your final media to yet a third color space.

For example, in addition to LUT support, FilmLight Baselight provides integrated color management options in the Scene Settings window and Cursor menu. Within the scene settings, you can choose a "working color space" based on your workflow, either normalizing media on input or keeping it logged and specifying the particular camera and format you're working with. These selections are not LUTs; they're 3D mathematical functions to convert the source image data from one color space to another as cleanly as possible.

CHAPTER 3

NOTE

For more information on the integrated color management provided by Baselight, check out the highly informative movie at www.filmlight.ltd.uk/ resources/video/baselight/FLT-BL-0027-Baselight-13.php.

You also choose a "display rendering transform" that defines the transformation from the working color space to the display device that you're using to evaluate and grade the image. Ideally, this should be a device capable of displaying exactly what the audience will see—for example, a P3-capable projector for digital cinema projects or a BT.709-capable LCD/OLED/Plasma display for broadcast projects.

Furthermore, Baselight also has a Viewing Format option in the Cursor menu that lets you choose the color space of the view on your computer's display to ensure that the image you're working on is shown properly on every display in your suite.

While Baselight currently possesses one of the best examples of this kind of integrated color management, other grading applications are beginning to incorporate similar features, especially those with support for ACES (Academy Color Encoding Specification, covered briefly in Chapter 2), which is a similar scheme that attempts to standardize the management of different source media formats and the handling of image transformations from input through output.

NORMALIZING LOG MEDIA MANUALLY

The other method of normalizing log-encoded media is to make a manual adjustment. To this end, it may interest you to know that LUTs can be visualized as *curves*, and in fact you might consider a 1D LUT to simply be, say, a 21-point curve.

This is useful to know because the other way of normalizing log-encoded media is to make a very careful curve adjustment within a second layer or node, to stretch the contrast of the log-encoded image to obtain the kind of contrast you want. By making this adjustment as a second operation, you make room for additional contrast adjustments made using other controls prior to the normalization adjustment.

I've always had the best luck doing manual normalization in two stages: first by using some manner of contrast expansion to stretch the log-encoded signal to fit the desired tonal range, basically assigning the white and black point, and then by building an S curve in a second operation to create pleasing contrast by adding density to the shadows and increasing highlight brightness. It can take quite a few control points to get a curve that makes the image look smooth and nice (**Figure 3.68**), as this is a far more specific adjustment than a simple S curve to make an already-normalized image pop.

There's nothing inherently better or worse about this approach over using a LUT, and in fact the math involved is very similar, conceptually speaking. In general, the advantages of grading log media by building a curve manually is that you get to create exactly the kind of contrast curve you want for the image at hand. If you have experience with curve grading, this can give you incredible control over the image, considering how much latitude log-encoded media gives you to play with.

However, there are two potential disadvantages. First, normalizing clips by hand using curves can be considerably more time-consuming than using a LUT and applying adjustments before and after it. What you gain in control you lose in schedule, so you want to make sure you've arranged your day accordingly.

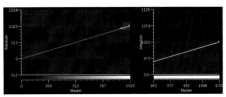

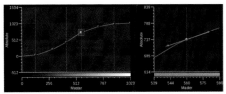

Figure 3.68 Before and after normalizing a log-encoded image using the Master RGB curve in FilmLight Baselight.

Second, this degree of manual contrast adjustment using curves requires a *really* good eye for smooth gradations of image tonality. This is one reason why it can require so many more points to get the results you want when using curves to normalize than you may be used to; since you're building up image contrast from such a flat starting point, you need to manually adjust each and every zone of the image to achieve the results you want. When you're using a lot of points on a curve, it can be really easy to stretch one segment of a curve so that it doesn't make a smooth transition from the previous point to the next, and the result can be unwanted sharp contouring in the image (**Figure 3.69**).

Figure 3.69 Three manual curve adjustments: A nice smooth transition between regions of highlight and shadow on the woman's face and shirt (left). Too much contrast creates unpleasantly sharp contouring (middle). Too little contrast causes flat-looking areas in the picture (right).

This isn't a problem with curves; it's the result of how much flexibility they give you. Thus, it's incumbent upon you to be careful and keep an eye on the tonality of your image when using this approach. This is also the reason why applications including FilmLight provide a zoomed-in view of your curve adjustments, and it is the reason for the "large mode" curves, shown in DaVinci Resolve, that make it easier to make small adjustments.

CHAPTER 3

Once you've built up a manual curve adjustment for a particular scene, you can usually save it for use throughout the rest of that scene, making whatever small alterations are necessary to match shots in your second, fine-tuning pass using other controls.

NORMALIZATION AND SATURATION

In addition to having low contrast, log-encoded media is also typically low in saturation as well. Fortunately, the same operations that stretch RGB contrast also stretch saturation, effectively taking care of two components with one adjustment. This phenomenon is explained further in Chapter 4.

However, if you find that, after normalizing the image, you still have too little saturation, all you need to do is to use whatever saturation controls are provided by your application to increase saturation, either overall or in more targeted fashion.

FINE-TUNING CONTRAST WITH LOG CONTROLS

However you've done it, once you've normalized log-encoded media, you will of course need to make whatever adjustments are necessary to get the look you want. It must be stressed that, ordinarily, normalization is only a starting point. Assuming you're using an application that lets you apply operations *before* and *after* your normalizing LUT or curve operation, you have some choices about how to proceed.

USING OFFSET/EXPOSURE AND CONTRAST CONTROLS

Let's assume you've normalized the image using a LUT. Now that the image appears close to the way you expect, it's easier to pinpoint what other adjustments need to be made to achieve the final result. A fast set of controls to use for doing this are the Offset and/or Exposure controls, which let you set the overall level of the signal by setting the black point, and the Contrast and Pivot controls, which let you stretch or compress overall image contrast (**Figure 3.70**).

Using these controls within an operation that takes place *before* the LUT lets you control contrast *and* retrieve any image detail that the LUT might clip.

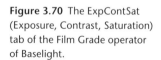

Figure 3.70 The ExpContSat (Exposure, Contrast, Saturation) tab of the Film Grade operator of Baselight.

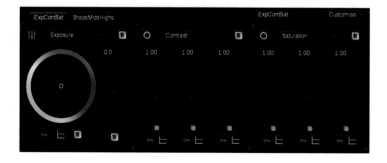

SHADOW, MIDTONE, AND HIGHLIGHT CONTROLS

Applications that have Film or Log controls provide an additional set of contrast adjustments via the *Shadow*, *Midtone*, and *Highlight* controls, which are specifically mapped to log-encoded data ranges (**Figure 3.71**). For this reason, they must be applied prior to a normalizing adjustment to work as they're designed to.

Figure 3.71 The ShadsMidsHighs (Shadows, Midtones, Highlights) tab of the Film Grade operator of Baselight.

Compared to Lift/Gamma/Gain controls, the Shadow/Midtone/Highlight controls are much more specific by default, as shown in **Figure 3.72**.

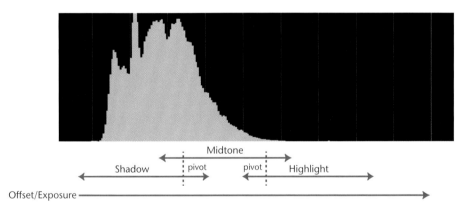

Figure 3.72 An approximation of the tonal zones of a log-encoded image as it's affected by the Shadow/Midtone/Highlight controls.

Here's the important thing. The effect these controls have on your image depends entirely on how much contrast there is in the image. In particular, the Shadow/Midtone/Highlight controls were specifically designed for *low-contrast* images. While each of these controls affects a narrower range of image tonality, they will overlap widely with one another to provide a smooth transition between adjusted regions of the image *as long as they're applied to the log-encoded state of the image*.

If you use Shadow/Midtone/Highlight controls on normalized media, you'll find that the overlap among each tonal zone is more minimal and not quite as useful. This is the reason you want to use these controls within an adjustment that comes before the LUT.

In general, here's what the log contrast controls are meant to adjust:

- The *Shadow* control affects the bottom third of the image, just the lowest shadows.

- The *Midtone* control affects a broad range of midtone values, not quite reaching into the brightest highlights. Interestingly, the midtone control will most likely affect the diffuse highlights in your image, omitting the peak whites and providing you with an easy way of stretching or narrowing the difference between these two tonal regions of the picture.

- The *Highlight* control affects the peak highlights at the top third of the image, focused mainly on the "sparkly bits" in the image.

Figure 3.73 shows the difference between making a shadow adjustment to the log-encoded state of an image and to the normalized state of an image. You should be able to clearly see via the red box that the log-encoded adjustment extends farther into the midtones, resulting in broader overlap and a smoother transition between the shadow and midtone controls, while the normalized adjustment is much more restricted to the bottom of the signal, which can result in more visible contouring at the transition from shadow to midtone.

Figure 3.73 A comparison of a shadow adjustment made to raise the darkest part of an image when applied to the pre-LUT log-encoded image and when applied to the post-LUT normalized image. The log-encoded adjustment has broader and smoother overlap.

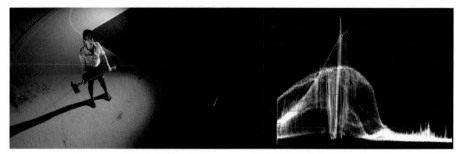

Before

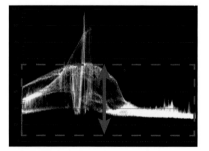

Affected range when raising shadow of log image

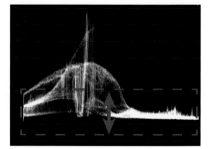

Affected range when raising shadow of normalized image

Another difference of the Shadow/Midtone/Highlight controls is that, unlike Lift/Gamma/Gain, the boundary where the shadows end and midtones begin and where the midtones end and the highlights begin are adjustable using *pivot*, *range*, or *band* parameters (the names vary with the application) to change the center point of image tonality at which each adjacent pair of controls overlaps. This enables you to make contrast adjustments with great specificity.

In general, you'll probably find that adjustments made with the Offset/Exposure and Contrast controls regulate the log-encoded image very nicely to create an overall adjustment, while the Shadow, Midtone, and Highlight controls allow you to fix much more specific issues.

POSTNORMALIZED CONTRAST ADJUSTMENTS

Of course, you always have the option of making additional contrast adjustments, using all the other controls described in this chapter. All you have to do is to add another layer or node after the normalized state of the image and grade away.

SHADOW/MIDTONE/HIGHLIGHT CONTROLS AND NORMALIZED MEDIA

While Log controls are more specific even when used on the log-encoded state of the image, they become even more specific when used on the normalized image. While this can be an advantage with the color balance controls (as you'll see in Chapter 4), this makes the Log contrast controls less useful for practical adjustment, since they'll introduce quite sharp contouring into the image.

SETTING APPROPRIATE HIGHLIGHTS AND SHADOWS

Now that you've learned how to make contrast adjustments, let's consider how to go about deciding where to park your levels.

WHAT SHOULD MY WHITE LEVEL BE?

To make a huge generalization, an image's highlights usually occupy the upper-third of the currently utilized image tonality when viewed on a Waveform Monitor. The white point is the lightest pixel found within the highlights, appearing at the very top of the Histogram or Waveform Monitor graphs.

Where, exactly, the white level in your video should lie is partially a matter of preference, dictated by the look you're going for and the nature of the highlights in the image. If you're going for a high-key, high-contrast image, parking your highlights

NOTE

For reference, the white bar to the left of the yellow bar on a standard color bars test pattern is 82 percent/IRE (585 mV), and most people feel that it's plenty "white."

close to 100 percent/IRE is probably a good bet. On the other hand, if you're adjusting for a low-key, low-contrast look, there's no reason not to keep your highlights down at 80, 70, or even 60 percent, depending on the image and what looks good to you.

The *type* of highlights in the scene has a lot to do with where you'll park them. Peak whites correspond to the "sparkly bits" in an image. These include sun glints, chrome reflections, lit candles, sparks, or the sun itself, and they should probably sit at or near the top end of the scale; otherwise, you risk having these highly exposed features look dingy. For example, in **Figure 3.74**, the highlights reflecting off the car, as well as those on the man's shirt, are uniformly bright and partially overexposed, and they should probably remain at the maximum exposure level.

Figure 3.74 Isolated highlights with low midtones.

However, there are other highlights that correspond to diffuse white, which include tablecloths, white clouds, light bouncing off a white wall, and other bright highlights on clothing or other features in the picture that may well belong to the midtones of the image, even if there aren't any brighter highlights to be found. Consider the late-afternoon image in **Figure 3.75**: The highlights on the actor's skin are well within the midtones, as is the highlight on the man's undershirt.

Figure 3.75 Muted highlights within a brighter scene.

These highlights, though lighter than the rest of the picture, typically contain some kinds of image detail. Simply lowering the shadows helped to maintain healthy contrast without any adjustment to the highlights. Furthermore, notice that the blue sky sits comfortably just at 70 percent/IRE (500 mV).

PERCEIVED HIGHLIGHT BRIGHTNESS IS RELATIVE TO SHADOW DEPTH

It's extremely important to remember that, because of the way our eyes work, the audience's perceptions of your highlights are always going to be relative to the depth of the shadows in the image. Sometimes, you'll get better results from lowering the shadows and leaving the highlights alone than you will from raising the highlights. *The contrast in an image is entirely relative.*

It's important to distinguish between the average highlights in an image and the *peak highli*ghts in the image. With the very brightest peak highlights sitting at the maximum level, the average highlights can and should be lower, unless you're going for a deliberately overexposed look. In **Figure 3.76**, the sun's reflection in the car window is typically overexposed (shown by the bunching near the top of the Waveform graph). The peaks extend far above the average brightness of the rest of the highlights that correspond to the clouds in the sky, which have detail coming from the contours of their shadows.

 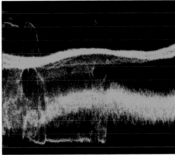

Figure 3.76 Clipped highlights, with white clouds within the upper midtones.

CHOOSING A MAXIMUM WHITE LEVEL

Even the maximum white level you choose can vary. Technically, you should never output whites brighter than the maximum allowable signal strength, typically 100 percent/IRE (700 mV) for broadcast. However, some broadcasters have QC guidelines that are so strict you may want to employ a self-imposed maximum white level of 98 percent just to be on the safe side (and to allow 2 percent/IRE for inevitable small overshoots). If your application has broadcast-safe controls or hardware to clip offending highlights, then this won't be an issue, but if you're having to manually adjust to keep things legal, using a conservative maximum white level gives you that much more protection from transient levels that could result in getting your program bounced by a zealously conservative broadcaster. For more information on broadcast-safe guidelines, see Chapter 10.

Besides, letting your application's broadcast-safe controls clip the highlights can result in the loss of valuable highlight detail, which may or may not be important.

MAINTAINING MIDTONES WHEN LEGALIZING WHITES

You'll find yourself constantly lowering the whites of clips to legalize the inevitable super-white values that cameras capture. Keep in mind that if you do this simply by lowering the Gain contrast control, you're going to subtly darken the midtones, as well. A more precise correction is to boost the mids a few points while pulling down the whites to compensate for this effect. If you don't have a control surface, you may have to push and pull the onscreen controls for Lift and Gain until they're where you want them.

While you're at it, don't let the midtones of your clips be held hostage by such specular highlights as sun glints, direct light sources, and reflections. Highlights will pop up in the tiniest details and can sometimes appear as a 2-pixel twinkle in an actor's eye. Although it's important to legalize these errant pixels, it shouldn't stop you from making other adjustments to otherwise brighten and improve your image.

In this example, you'll adjust the highlights and the midtones together to brighten the image while still legalizing the whites:

1 Examine the Waveform Monitor or Histogram; you'll see that **Figure 3.77** is a dark shot that nonetheless has numerous super-white highlights (the streetlamps). You need to bring these highlights down to less than 100 percent/IRE (700 mV).

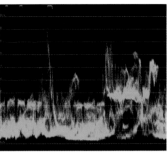

Figure 3.77 The original image. Note the streetlights cause spikes greater than 100 percent/IRE that need to be legalized.

2   Adjust the highlights control to bring the top of the Waveform or Histogram down to 100 percent/IRE (700 mV) as shown in the video scopes (**Figure** 3.78).

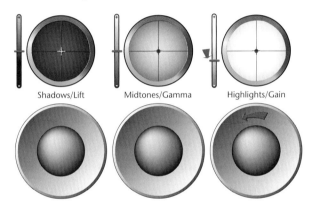

Shadows/Lift   Midtones/Gamma   Highlights/Gain

Figure 3.78 The correction needed to legalize the highlights.

You immediately see that the highlights have been legalized, but the overall image has been darkened (**Figure** 3.79). This is not what you wanted to happen.

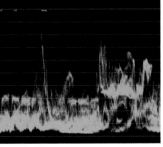

Figure 3.79 The resulting adjustment legalized the highlights but also darkened the midtones, which we didn't really want to happen.

3   Raise the Gamma control to push the middle of the Waveform or Histogram up, lightening the image to compensate for the unwanted darkened areas.

Depending on your color correction application, the resulting adjustment might also lighten the shadows and boost the highlights up a little bit, in which case you simply lower the Gain control until the super-white values fall back under 100 percent/IRE, and you lower the Lift control until the darkest shadows are as black as you want them (**Figure 3.80**).

Figure 3.80 The three adjustments you need to make to boost the midtones back up to compensate for the highlights reduction, along with corresponding reductions to the highlights and shadows to maintain contrast and keep the highlights legal.

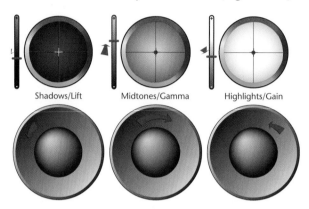

Shadows/Lift   Midtones/Gamma   Highlights/Gain

Since you're lowering the brightest highlights, it may also be a good idea to lower the lift a bit more to maintain the wide contrast. This, in turn, might lower the midtones a bit, so one more Gamma boost may be necessary. However, the client wants to retain the dark look of night, so you need to stop the correction before it becomes too bright (**Figure 3.81**).

Figure 3.81 The final image. The highlights are legal, the midtones match the original shot, and the shadows are a little bit darker.

It's times like this when having a control surface really pays off. The ability to adjust highlights, shadows, and midtones simultaneously when making such adjustments is a real time-saver. The resulting image now has appropriately brighter contrast and a broadcast-legal white level.

DON'T BE AFRAID TO CLIP PEAK HIGHLIGHTS

Peak highlights, the sparkly bits of an image, are typically either direct light sources or reflections off mirrored surfaces that might as well be direct light sources. In either case, these highlights are off the scale in terms of brightness and have little actual detail that's worth preserving. For this reason, don't be afraid to let peak white features of the image clip as a trade-off for setting the average whites of your image where you want them to be. As long as you have a good clipper, you have nothing to lose.

WHAT SHOULD MY BLACK LEVEL BE?

Unlike the white level, which is open to interpretation, the lowest black level you can set is simple: 0 percent/IRE/mV.

Deep shadows usually fall into the bottom 15 percent of the digital scale, with lighter shadows creeping further up into the bottom half of the mids. As always, how dark the shadows appear to be is entirely relative to the lightness of the brightest highlights in the picture, but generally speaking, deepening the darkest shadows tends to have more of a visual impact.

One of the biggest things you can do to impress almost any client is to lower the Lift or Master Offset controls to deepen the shadows in an image. Even lowering the shadows by a few percentage points can give an image additional snap that it didn't previously have, and viewers love it.

This being the case, you might ask why so many images, and even well-exposed footage, start out with a slightly elevated black level. It turns out that many video cameras record a black level that's not quite at 0 percent digital. **Figure 3.82** shows the Waveform of a segment of pure black video, recorded with the lens cap on.

NOTE

For those of you who have been in the industry for a while, all digital signals use 0 IRE/mV/% as absolute black. The setup of 7.5 IRE is no longer in use. As far as you're concerned as a colorist, the lowest level of absolute black on the scale is 0, period.

CHAPTER 3

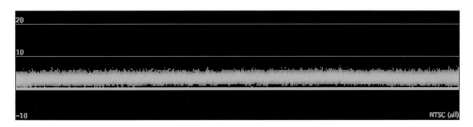

Figure 3.82 Isolated camera noise displayed on a Waveform Monitor.

This reveals two things: First, it illustrates that the average black level is centered at approximately 3 percent/IRE. Second, it shows just how much random noise the recorded signal contains. As you can see, even prerecorded black can benefit from being deepened.

HOW LOW SHOULD I MAKE MY BLACK LEVEL?

How much you adjust the shadows depends entirely on how dark they are in the original image. Well-exposed images may not have blacks that extend all the way to the bottom of the scale. This gives you room to deepen them, or not, as the look you're trying to achieve dictates.

If an image already has deep shadows, there may be no need to adjust them. **Figure 3.83** shows an image that has extremely healthy shadows, with the black level itself sitting squarely at 0 percent.

Figure 3.83 Dark shadows with no need for adjustment.

Figure 3.84, on the other hand, has a black level hovering somewhere around 5 percent, allowing some detail to remain in the shadows of the man's dark trousers. If our objective is to portray a typically over lit office environment, it would be appropriate to leave the other shadows in the scene higher, for a softer look.

Figure 3.84 Appropriately lighter shadows in a scene. Bright highlights maintain healthy contrast despite the elevated levels of the shadows.

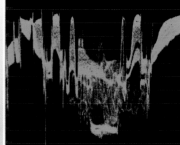

CRUSHING AND COMPRESSING BLACKS

Once you've lowered the darkest parts of your picture to 0 percent/IRE/mV, they're pitch black, as dark as the shadows can go. But that doesn't stop you from continuing to lower the Blacks control to move more of the shadows in the image down toward 0. Moving lighter areas of shadow down to 0 percent/IRE/mV is referred to as *crushing* the blacks. Crushing is most easily seen in the Waveform Monitor graph in **Figure 3.85** as the pixels corresponding to the shadows at the bottom of the graph start clumping up at the 0 percent line.

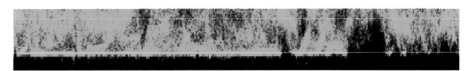

Figure 3.85 Crushed blacks appear as a bunched-up Waveform sitting at the 0 percent/IRE line.

Crushing the blacks is an easy way to jack up the perceived contrast ratio, and, depending on the image, it can make it seem even "snappier" but at the expense of shadow detail (**Figure 3.86**). Because 0 is the lowest luma level there is, all of the pixels at 0 percent assume a uniform flat blackness. Although it's arguable whether the detail lost when crushing the blacks just a little is noticeable, if you crush the blacks too much, the shadow regions of your image will become progressively harsher, flatter, and potentially more aliased in areas of the image that make the transition from shadows to midtones.

Figure 3.86 shows the effects of crushing blacks in a more discernable way.

Figure 3.86 The original test image, showing shadow detail as a series of titles.

1 To begin, examine the image in the Waveform Monitor or Histogram. This example is an image generated for testing purposes where the black background is at 0 percent and each word of the text is a couple of percent darker than the one beneath it. Because the levels used in this image are so low, the full image is visible only on a properly calibrated external broadcast display—a computer display might not show all the words.

2 Lower the Lift control gradually; this results in the words disappearing one by one, as they merge with the black background (**Figure 3.87**).

Figure 3.87 The test image after lowering the Shadows control to "crush" the blacks. The darkest words have merged with the surrounding black.

This also shows off the sensitivity of a color correction application's contrast controls. Continuing to lower the blacks eventually causes all of the text to disappear. This image detail is completely lost, replaced by an expanse of flat black.

BROADCAST COMPRESSION VS. CRUSHED BLACKS

Aside from a loss of detail, one other risk of crushing the blacks of an image too much reveals itself later, when the image is compressed digitally for broadcast. Overly crushed blacks sometimes respond poorly to the MPEG-2 or H.264 compression used for digital broadcast or cable delivery. The results can be visible macro-blocking in the darkest shadows of the image that looks like an unsightly blocky banding. Less crushing leaves more detail in the shadows that will minimize this sort of artifacting.

TRY LOWERING THE MIDS INSTEAD

Not every image needs to have lots of shadows down at 0 percent. For example, a scene with abundant fill light causing diffuse shadows is one instance where leaving deliberately deep shadows would be inappropriate. For example, **Figure 3.88** already has a few reasonably dark shadows.

Figure 3.88 A light image with diffuse fill light and a naturally low black point.

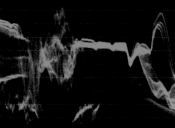

With these kinds of shots, lowering the mids, as in **Figure 3.89**, is a much more appropriate adjustment when you want to darken them to change the perceived time of day, whether the image looks like an interior or exterior shot or whether the feeling of the image is bright and happy or dark and gloomy.

 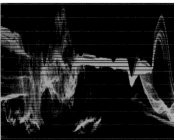

Figure 3.89 To darken the image, lowering the midtones is a better strategy than lowering the black point and risking unnaturally dark shadows.

Although the boundaries of acceptable shadow and highlight adjustments are very much guided by the video scopes, mids adjustments are typically eyeballed (unless you're precisely matching one clip to another). There are no really firm guidelines for adjusting the mids, other than to try to make the image look right for the location and time of day and to make sure the clip matches the others in the scene in which it appears.

WORKING WITH HIGH DYNAMIC RANGE (HDR) MEDIA

A new generation of digital cinema cameras produce high dynamic range (HDR) video, which means they're capable of recording an incredibly wide range of exposure within a single signal without clipping. A typical video camera has about five to ten stops of latitude (depending on what ISO or gain setting you're using), in terms of how much usable image detail there is from the darkest shadows to the lightest highlights before clipping. Cameras capable of HDR recording are able to record a greater range of exposed image data, promising fewer blown-out windows and more detail in shadows.

At the moment, there are two approaches to HDR video.

RED HDRX MEDIA

Ordinarily, RED cameras at this writing have a claimed latitude of 13 stops of image detail. Using their proprietary HDRx format, additional latitude can be recorded, up to a claimed 18+ stops.

This is done by simultaneously recording two "bracketed" exposures within a single R3D media file when in HDRx mode, the normally exposed "A" channel, and an underexposed "X" channel designed to preserve highlights. How much the X channel is underexposed is user-selectable, depending on one's shooting conditions. How you later use these separate exposures depends on the capabilities of your grading application.

In the example in **Figure 3.90**, you can use the Blend Type and Blend Bias controls that RED exposes to your grading application to automatically blend the two exposures together into a single image with a smooth tone mapping transition from one to the other. Blend Type picks one of two different ways in which the A and X channels are merged, and Blend Bias is a numeric parameter that lets you weigh how much of the A and X channels contribute to the final image. The simplicity of this approach is useful for images with a lot of motion or for images in which there's a lot of overlap between the brightest and darkest regions.

Figure 3.90 The A and X channels shown here can be combined into a single image with wider latitude using controls provided by RED or by blending both channels using your grading application's tools.

Normally exposed "A" channel

Underexposed "X" channel

Combining both channels into a single range of tonality

Another possibility is to split the A and X exposures into separate image streams using whatever controls your application exposes in order to use shapes or qualifiers to layer one over the other (**Figure 3.91**). This can be a useful approach when trying to retrieve detail from an easily isolated feature such as a window or sky. The example in Figure 3.91 shows this set up using a window in DaVinci Resolve.

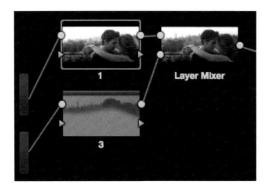

Figure 3.91 The A and B channels can be individually adjusted via two inputs in the node editor of DaVinci Resolve. Using a window, overexposed highlights from the X channel can be layered back onto the A channel.

While extremely useful, RED HDRx shooting is storage-intensive because of the need to record two full-image streams, so productions shooting with RED cameras tend to use this feature only when they think it will be necessary.

WIDE-LATITUDE CAMERAS SHOOTING RAW

The other way that high dynamic range media is being acquired is through newer generations of cameras capable of recording ever-greater stops of latitude within RAW formats. As discussed in Chapter 1, RAW media formats record image data straight off the camera sensor, with no transformation applied. If a given sensor has a wide dynamic range, then all of that image data gets written to the RAW file and is available when you debayer the media later.

At this writing, cameras shooting what one would consider to be wide-latitude RAW media include the RED Epic, Arri Alexa, Sony F55 and F65, and the Blackmagic Design Cinema Camera, all of which advertise 13 to 14 stops of usable latitude when shooting RAW. How true that is depends on how you're exposing the image; a stop of latitude is not useful if it's too noisy for viewing. Furthermore, different cameras emphasize low noise in different parts of the signal. Some have more retrievable detail in the highlights, while others offer better shadow rendition with lower noise.

All of these cameras require you to record RAW to reap these benefits. If you record ProRes or DNxHD media instead, even if you're recording log-encoded media, you won't have as many stops of retrievable image detail available to you.

CHAPTER 3

The funny thing about wide-latitude RAW media is that upon first debayering it, images often look blown out. However, these highlights are retrievable, as you can see in **Figure 3.92**.

Figure 3.92 A RAW clip shot with a Sony F65 camera, before and after grading. The extreme latitude makes the image initially appear to be overexposed; careful grading retrieves all of the available detail from the sky. Image courtesy Gianluca Bertone.

HOW TO GRADE WIDE-LATITUDE MEDIA

Sadly, BT.709-compatible displays simply cannot show the wide range of image detail that cameras can shoot. In fact, the equivalent latitude of a BT.709 signal being limited to the 0-100 IRE/percent (700 mV) range turns out to be about five stops. In other words, there's just not enough room in the signal to show both the stunning highlights and the noise-free shadows that have been captured during the shoot.

This means that one of the challenges of grading is finding the most aesthetically pleasing way of selectively fitting portions of a wide-latitude signal into a viewable range for distribution. In general, there are three strategies you can pursue.

COMPRESS HIGHLIGHTS AND SHADOWS

One of the simplest things you can do is to bring as much of the signal as you want back into the image and then use curves to shape the midtone image contrast to achieve the most pleasing balance of shadows and highlights (**Figure 3.93**).

Original

Figure 3.93 Retrieving highlight detail in two steps: first compressing overall contrast and then using curves to selectively widen contrast and lighten the image without clipping highlight or shadow detail.

Contrast compressed to retrieve detail

Curve used to add lightness and contrast back while compressing highlights and shadows

The challenge when doing this is to compress the least visually important parts of the image (depending on the scene) in order to *hide* the parts of the image that are being squeezed, while keeping gradations of fine detail in the midtones nice and smooth. If you're not careful about preserving the smooth tonality of the key subject of the shot, you can end up creating a chunky image with unpleasantly sharp contouring.

USE SHAPES/WINDOWS TO SEGMENT THE IMAGE

Another strategy for fitting the most available image data into the picture is particularly useful when the image is easily *segmented*, or divided into discrete regions. For example, the views out a window, through a doorway, or of the sky above a field are all examples of easily isolated regions that tend to be blown out as a function of exposing for the most important subject in the scene. When shooting with a wide-latitude format, you have the option of retrieving this data, but you can do a better job of combining the highlights you want with the shadows and midtones that look best by splitting the image into segments using a shape or window.

CHAPTER 3

In **Figure 3.94**, a shape/mask/window isolates the sky from the rest of the shot, so you can apply separate adjustments to each region of the image. In this way, you can use aggressive adjustments to retrieve detail and color from the sky, while using a completely different set of less intense corrections to make the field and the actor look their best.

Figure 3.94 The four nodes used to grade this image in DaVinci Resolve. Nodes 2, 3, and 4 use windows to isolate adjustments made to bring sky detail back, separately adjust the grassy field, and independently adjust just the plane along which the woman walks.

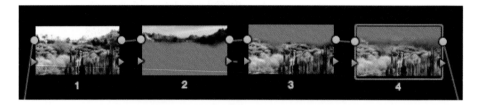

This gives you the best of both worlds but can be tricky to set up, depending on how the scene is composed, and it will certainly be a bit more time-consuming. For more information on image segmentation, secondary color correction, and isolating corrections using qualifiers and shapes, see Chapters 5 and 6.

CLIP UNNEEDED IMAGE DETAIL

The last strategy is probably the least desirable, and that is to simply clip out highlight or shadow detail that you don't think you need. If you have some manner of soft-clip operation that you can use to "roll off" the portion of the image being clipped for a softer result, there's an abundance of image detail in the out-of-bounds region of the image that can make for a nicely soft result. This isn't the best way of dealing with wide latitude, but it's fast when you're in a pinch.

CONTRAST AND PERCEPTION

A number of phenomena affect how people "see" contrast. You can exploit these perceptual tricks to your advantage to maximize the perceived quality of your images. One of the most demonstrable examples is the surround effect.

NOTE

Relative contrast is why you don't typically want to position your broadcast display in front of a large expanse of white or black.

As you'll learn in Chapter 4, the human visual system evaluates image contrast relative to all the tones within a scene. The lightness or darkness of surrounding colors affects the apparent brightness of a subject in the middle. In **Figure 3.95**, the two stars at the center of each box have the same levels of gray but appear darker against white and lighter against black.

Figure 3.95 The two stars within each box have identical lightness, but the surround makes them appear lighter or darker.

USING THE SURROUND EFFECT

With digital video, the overall scale of available image tonality is fixed. Especially if you're adhering to broadcast video standards, the overall range available for the darkest shadows to the lightest highlights is from 0 to 100 percent/IRE, or 0 to 700 mV, depending on the scale you're using.

Despite this seemingly limited range, it's possible to exaggerate the apparent brightness of image highlights by making the shadows darker. Similarly, it's possible to make shadows seem darker by raising the highlights, creating (you guessed it) more contrast between the two.

The example image in **Figure 3.96** is a bit dark, shot at the end of the day. The client is worried that the shadows might be a bit washed out, but the man's dark hair and the shadows in his shirt are already really low, and lowering the black point any further might eliminate detail.

We're going to take advantage of the surround effect to make the shadows seem darker by lightening the highlights, while doing our best to avoid making the average midtones seem brighter than they are.

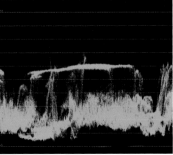

Figure 3.96 The original image. The client wants darker blacks, but it's not possible to lower them any more without losing detail.

Let's take a look at how such an adjustment would be made during a color correction session.

1 First, raise the Gain control (**Figure 3.97**).

Figure 3.97 Raising the highlights.

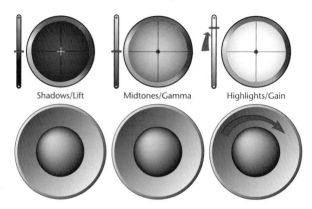

Shadows/Lift   Midtones/Gamma   Highlights/Gain

This lightens the highlights, as shown in **Figure 3.98**, but results in a much brighter image, which isn't what you want. To get back to the "end of the day" look, you need to make a few more adjustments.

Figure 3.98 Simply raising the highlights brightened the entire image, so we need to make further adjustments.

2 To reduce the perceived lightness of the image, lower the Gamma control. This reduces the highlights a bit, but you raised them so much in step 1 that a little lowering won't hurt.

Reducing the midtones also lowers the shadows a little too much, resulting in overly solid blacks and a loss of detail in the man's hair, so compensate by making a corresponding increase to the Lift control (**Figure 3.99**).

The result brings the shadows and average midtones close to where they were before you increased the highlights (**Figure 3.100**).

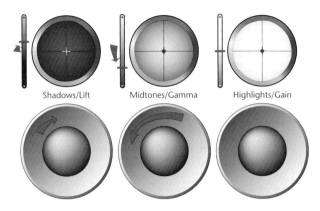

Figure 3.99 Further adjustments to lower the midtones and raise the Lift to bring the perceived average lightness of the image close to what it was originally, despite the increased highlights.

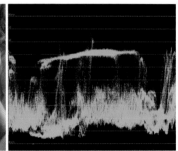

Figure 3.100 The final result. Lighter highlights make the existing shadows seem darker.

The end result is a more dynamic image, with brighter highlights in the main character's arms, in his face, and in the sky. The shadows throughout the image seem darker, even though they haven't changed at all. At this point, you would ordinarily move on to make any necessary color adjustments.

INCREASING PERCEIVED SHARPNESS

One other effect of contrast manipulation is that increased contrast ratios can give the appearance of sharper detail. Consider the two images in **Figure 3.101**.

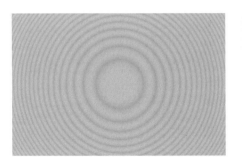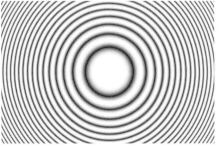

Figure 3.101 Low- and high-contrast versions of the same image. The high-contrast version to the right appears sharper than the low-contrast version to the left.

Anyone would say that the image on the right is sharper than the image on the left. However, both images have the same resolution and are identical except for a simple adjustment to expand contrast by lowering the darker portion of the image and raising the highlights.

Let's evaluate a more real-world example. **Figure 3.102** shows a muted interior, meant to be an emotionally somber scene. However, it's just a bit too low-contrast, and the details sort of fade into one another.

Figure 3.102 The original image.

By stretching out the contrast ratio—in this case, lowering the shadows 10 percent and raising the highlights by another 10 percent—you're increasing the difference between the darker and lighter pixels that define the edges within the image. The result is enhanced detail. In particular, the sitting man pops out from the background a little better because of the contrast between the rim lighting on his arm and shoulder and the shadows against the walls (**Figure 3.103**).

Figure 3.103 The image after the contrast has been stretched a bit. Notice how details appear sharper after this adjustment.

More contrast at the edges gives the appearance of greater sharpness; in fact, this is similar to how sharpen filters work in many popular image-editing applications. Dedicated sharpen filters are usually more targeted, detecting and adjusting contrast only in edge regions, but the general idea is the same.

It's important to realize that this is only for appearance. You're not actually adding any detail to the image; in fact, you may be eliminating individual pixels of detail if you need to crush the blacks of your image significantly enough to achieve this effect.

CONTRAST DURING EXHIBITION

There's one last important detail to consider when dealing with black levels. Because there are so many manufacturers of camcorders, VTRs, DVD and Blu-ray Disc players, televisions, video projectors, and other playback and display devices, there is often confusion about the black level that any given device is set to either output or display.

Playback devices outputting analog video with one black setup level that are connected to display devices with a different black setup level can cause no end of grief, either washing out or crushing the blacks unintentionally. If you're a filmmaker at a festival and this happens, it can be an excruciating experience.

Furthermore, most people's televisions are likely uncalibrated. If the brightness isn't adjusted correctly, the blacks may appear washed out or crushed. If the contrast isn't adjusted correctly, the overall image may be too bright or too dark.

And, if all that wasn't scary enough, many digital display devices (such as video projectors) have customizable gamma settings. Although the right gamma setting, properly matched to the environment, can maximize image quality, the wrong setting can be disastrous.

Unfortunately, the best that you, the colorist, can do in this exhibition minefield is to trust your calibrated display, give the program a test viewing on a friend's uncalibrated consumer television, and have a sit-down viewing with the client in whatever environment their audience is most likely to view the result. In this way, you're likely to catch any corrections that don't play well in those environments before wrapping up the job. It's also a good idea to warn a filmmaker who's about to march out on the film festival circuit about what can go wrong and recommend that they get some time before the screening to check the projection quality and make any necessary adjustments (if possible).

DEALING WITH UNDEREXPOSURE

The process of maximizing image contrast isn't always beer and skittles. Not everyone is going to be shooting HDR media, and underexposed clips are the ultimate examples of images in which you desperately *need* to maximize contrast but where trade-offs in image quality become inevitable.

Underexposure is one of the most common problems colorists face. While underexposure is easily avoided by doing careful lighting and keeping an eye on the sun during available-light shoots, the truth is that many reality TV shows, documentaries, and independent films don't have the luxury of time or large lighting crews and have to get the shot whenever and however they can.

However, it's important to understand what the necessary compromises are going to be in these situations. Also, it's valuable to know what factors can improve your chances of making a suitable correction and when the format of media that was recorded makes an ideal correction completely impossible.

NOTE TO SHOOTERS: PLEASE BRING A BOUNCE CARD!

At the risk of sounding like a nag, one of the most frequent corrections I run into in reality TV shows, documentaries, and low-budget productions of all kinds is underexposed faces. One of the key things separating people in the frame from the background in a shot is a bit more light on their faces. While we can lighten faces in post, sometimes the format of the media and the extent of the necessary correction mean that noise is introduced as a result. When the choice is between brighter actors and a bit of noise and not seeing the talent, most clients choose the noise.

You can avoid this problem by having a spare person holding a bounce card on the set. Just reflecting a bit more of the available light onto the subject's face makes a world of difference; even if a correction still needs to be made, it provides more image data, which improves the quality of any correction.

CHROMA SAMPLING AFFECTS THE QUALITY OF UNDEREXPOSURE ADJUSTMENTS

When you're color correcting underexposed clips, the chroma sampling of your source media (whether it's 4:4:4, 4:2:2, 4:1:1, or 4:2:0) has a significant effect on the extent to which contrast adjustments can be made without problems occurring.

For example, 4:4:4 chroma-sampled media, such as film scanned image sequences, digital cinema camera output, or video recorded to HDCAM SR (with the dual-link or 3G option), have a considerably wide amount of latitude for exposure correction. Dark shots can be lightened very aggressively before artifacts such as excessive noise become a problem.

The 4:2:2 chroma-sampled media that's typical of high-end HD and SD videocameras, or telecine'd film that's been recorded to video formats such as HDCAM, D5, or Digital Betacam, has a fair amount of latitude and can be adjusted by a moderate amount before noise becomes a problem.

More consumer-level and HDSLR cameras record to AVCHD, HDV, DV-25, and a variety of other MPEG-2 and H.264-based video formats that use 4:1:1 or 4:2:0 chroma-sampled media. These formats discard three-quarters of chroma data in a manner considered to be perceptually indistinguishable from the original (remember, the human vision system is more sensitive to luminance than it is to color), in an effort to shrink file sizes to create media that's more manageable for casual shooters and editors.

The problem with 4:1:1 and 4:2:0 media is that in many cases the images are considered suitable for more professional work, but the discarded color information makes it difficult, or even impossible, to make significant adjustments to stretch contrast without introducing noise. Also, such limited-bandwidth media formats make various types of visual effects work, such as greenscreen, considerably more difficult.

In these situations, you're going to have to work with what you've got. This doesn't mean you won't be able to correct your footage; it just means you're going to have to be a little more careful about how large a contrast correction you make to underexposed clips. Noise is going to be a fact of life, and strategies for minimizing noise in situations where you need to increase the exposure no matter what will be important.

> **NOTE**
> The wisest piece of advice to give to shooters using highly compressed formats is that it's even more important to light the scene and expose the image properly than ever. The better exposed the source image is, the more flexibility there will be later for color correction.

UNDEREXPOSED ADJUSTMENTS COMPARED

The following clip is very dark. As you can see in the Waveform Monitor in **Figure 3.104**, the majority of the pixels in the image are less than 10 percent, the midtones stretch from 10 to 35 percent, and what few highlights there are stretch in *very* small clumps all the way up to 48 percent.

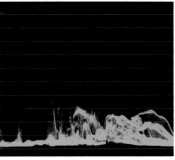

Figure 3.104 The original, underexposed image.

If you wanted to brighten the actors' faces, the easy fix would be to raise the Gain and Gamma contrast controls. Making a fairly aggressive adjustment to a clip with 4:2:2 color sampling does the trick, and the results are quite clean (**Figure 3.105**).

Figure 3.105 Stretching the contrast of underexposed 4:2:2 chroma-subsampled media.

Making an identical adjustment to a version of the same clip that's been down-converted to 4:2:0 chroma sampling (similar to what's used for HDV and H.264-compressed source media) results in a much noisier clip, with more compression artifacts visible than before (**Figure 3.106**).

Figure 3.106 Stretching the contrast of underexposed 4:2:0 chroma-subsampled media.

This is difficult to see in print, but comparing close-ups of the man's head in **Figure 3.107** should reveal the problems clearly.

Figure 3.107 The close-up on the left shows the lightened 4:2:2subsampled clip, relatively free from noise. The close-up on the right shows the lightened 4:2:0 subsampled clip, with visible noise and macroblocking.

The separations in the Waveform indicate that the image is being stretched beyond the available image data, which results in more visible noise in the image. The right image in Figure 3.107 has more visible banding than the one on the left because the lower amount of image data is being stretched further, causing artifacts.

OTHER FACTORS AFFECTING IMAGE NOISE

Aside from the format of the source media discussed earlier, some video cameras are simply noisier than others and respond to varying light levels differently. You'll find that every scene you work on will have different tolerances for how much contrast expansion you can get away with, so it's important to be aware of this issue and always play a bit of the clip you're adjusting before you move on—otherwise, you might miss spotting a potential noise problem.

HOW TO HANDLE UNDEREXPOSED CLIPS

Underexposed clips usually suffer from three simultaneous problems when you try to correct them to add some brightness to the midtones:

- Excessive noise

- Oversaturation (or undersaturation, depending on the type of image processing being used)

- Inadequate shadow detail

These issues might not seem like much, but they can cause you headaches, especially if you're working with highly compressed source media.

1   Examine the image in **Figure 3.108**. The clip is pretty underexposed, but the color is rich, and we need to match this to a scene shot much earlier in the day. Take a look at the Waveform to get a good idea of what to do to lighten the shot.

 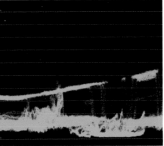

Figure 3.108 The original underexposed image.

NOTE

The smaller a display you're looking at, the harder it is to see noise manifesting itself in your corrections. This is a good reason to invest in a larger display for color correction work. Also, it can be difficult to see emerging noise without playing the clip to see how jittery the noise is during playback.

CHAPTER 3

NOTE

Sometimes, boosting midtones can be a better bet for trying to avoid noise than adjusting the whites, and it's generally more effective with severely underexposed clips. It depends on the shot.

2 To make the subjects more visible and increase contrast, make a few simple adjustments with the contrast controls to raise the highlights and midtones and lower the blacks.

However, when you do this, the image becomes noisy (this is easier to see when the clip is playing), and the lower shadows seem washed out, even though the black point is as low as reasonably possible for this image (**Figure 3.109**).

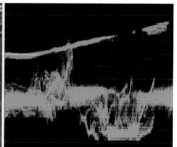

Figure 3.109 Stretching the contrast results in muddy shadows, even though the black point is low.

3 To fix this, use the Curve control to stretch the lower midtones down, while keeping the upper midtones where they are (**Figure 3.110**).

Figure 3.110 Using a curve adjustment to deepen the shadows while leaving the midtones and highlights alone. Some call this an S curve. Colorist Joe Owens calls this a "hockey stick," which I rather like. He's Canadian.

This fix provides denser shadows without lowering the midtones you just boosted. Also, this serves to push the most objectionable shadow noise back down closer to black, making it less visible (**Figure 3.111**).

Figure 3.111 The final image.

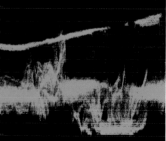

With some underexposed images, you may also notice that the very darkest shadows of the image start to look "chunky" if you stretch the contrast too much. This is because any image data appearing at or below the noise floor of the camera recording the image was irretrievably crushed while recording—typically there is no image data below 0 other than subzero excursions because of random image sensor noise.

Any attempt to raise the level of the blacks to retrieve more image data exposes this crushed expanse of uniform black as a large, dark gray area, likely with harsh macro-blocking creating chunky-looking banding where there aren't enough levels of image data to render a smooth image. Unfortunately, these are the unavoidable consequences of pushing underexposed clips.

Interestingly, a similar phenomenon occurs when you ask a film lab to push a roll of exposed film during development. *Pushing* film means having the lab develop the film for a longer period of time, raising its exposure at the expense of additional film grain and muddier shadows, very similar to what happens when you expand the contrast of underexposed video (**Figure 3.112**).

NOTE

If your video was originally recorded with 4:1:1 or 4:2:0 chroma sampling (common for highly compressed formats), converting it to a 4:2:2 or 4:4:4 subsampled format won't help. Incidentally, this step is already done internally as part of the image-processing pipeline of most color correction applications, so doing it as a separate step is unnecessary.

Figure 3.112 An underexposed shot of film pushed during development, and further lightened with digital color correction, exposes enhanced grain in the image.

I mention this as reassurance that you're not doing anything wrong and that, when comparing a telecine'd video transfer to an originally recorded video clip with equal chroma-sampling ratios, film doesn't have any advantage over video when it comes to dealing with underexposure. In fact, you may find that underexposed digital images have a bit more shadow detail than underexposed film (although film wins out when it comes to retrievable detail in overexposed highlights).

Although this is a small consolation in post, the best solution is to make sure that the clips are properly exposed to begin with and to let your client know in advance that there are limits to what is correctable.

TIP

Underexposed images typically are lacking in saturation. Depending on the color correction application you're using, you may or may not need to boost saturation even further once you've made your corrections to lighten the image.

CHAPTER 3

Ideally, when you're in a situation where you're correcting a severely underexposed clip, the client will be so overjoyed at being able to see any detail at all that these problems will be forgiven, and you'll be showered with praise for saving the show. Unfortunately, excessive noise may require a careful explanation of the limitations of technology and then some additional work.

HOW TO DEAL WITH NOISE

When confronted with exaggerated noise, you can address the problem in several ways. Many color correction applications have built-in noise reduction tools you can try. For example, DaVinci Resolve includes an optical flow-based noise reduction tool (**Figure 3.113**), Baselight includes a degrainer/denoiser operation that can be added to any clip, Lustre has a noise plug-in that's included as part of its Sparks plug-in architecture, and SGO Mistika has built-in noise reduction tools that can be used along with its integrated compositing to address a variety of issues. Other color correction applications have other specialized tools that you can employ; consult your software's user manual for more information.

Figure 3.113 Zoomed-in detail of a noisy, underexposed HD clip before and after noise reduction using DaVinci Resolve.

Often, built-in noise reduction tools have the option to be limited using qualifiers, windows/shapes, or any other tool in order to restrict their effect to one region of the image. For instance, if the shadows are noisy but the highlights are clean, you can isolate the shadows and apply noise reduction where it's needed most.

Alternately, if you're unhappy with your application's built-in tools, there are dedicated plug-ins for noise reduction that are compatible with most of the popular editing and compositing applications currently in use. In a round-trip workflow, you may elect to hold off on noise reduction until you send the clips back to the nonlinear editor (NLE). If you're finishing the program within your color correction application, then you may want to process individual clips with noise issues in a compositing application before completing the project.

In either case, examples of noise reduction plug-ins and applications commonly used include the following:

- **Neat Video**, from Neat Video, which is an acclaimed noise reduction plug-in available for Premiere Pro, After Effects, Final Cut Pro X and 7, Media Composer, Nuke, Scratch, Vegas Pro—well, just about every piece of software that processes video

- **Dark Energy**, from Cinnafilm, which is an After Effects plug-in (with plans to support other applications) offering extensive controls for noise reduction

- **GenArts' Monsters**, which includes a pair of plug-ins called **RemGrain**

- **The Foundry's Furnace** plug-ins, which include the plugins **DeNoise** and **DeGrain** and which have a pair of **DeFlicker** plug-ins

- **RE:Vision Effects'** noise reduction plug-in, **DE:Noise**

- **The Pixel Farm's PFClean**, a dedicated film restoration application with noise and grain removal built in

If you're unsatisfied with the default noise reduction tools in your application and you don't have the time or inclination to send the offending shots to an external application, you can also try to create your own noise-reducing adjustments.

However, there are simpler ways you can go about trying to minimize the problem. For example, if you made the adjustment by boosting the whites, you might try lowering the whites and boosting the mids a bit more to make the same correction.

Video noise is often most excessive in the darkest shadows of the image. If this is true for your image, you should notice a low, fuzzy trace running along the bottom of the graph in the Waveform Monitor, as in **Figure 3.114**.

Figure 3.114 The jagged bottom of the Waveform reveals noise in the shadows.

In this case, it might also help to crush the darkest shadows of the shot you're adjusting, flattening the noise floor of the image into a 0 percent/IRE/mV expanse of solid black.

More often than not, you'll split the difference between the corrected and uncorrected contrast ratios in an effort to find a reasonable middle ground between the too-dark source material and a reasonably lightened final version with a minimum of added noise. If you're trying to match a handful of underexposed shots to an otherwise well-exposed scene, one effective—though heartbreaking—strategy is to add noise to the other clips in the scene to even out the overall look (see Chapter 9).

Noise is a tough problem. However, there's another exposure issue that can prove even more of a hassle.

DEALING WITH OVEREXPOSURE

Overexposure is one of the most incurable problems that afflict digital media. However, there's a difference between clips that are slightly overexposed, which can be corrected, and those that are dramatically overexposed, which may be beyond repair.

The highlights of clips suffering from slight overexposure, such as those between 101 and 110 percent/IRE (or 701 and 770 mV), are typically retrievable. This is the super-white part of the signal, intentionally set aside to provide a bit of extra headroom for blown-out highlights. In fact, there may be an extra 5 percent of overshoot available for highlight detail beyond what shows up on your video scopes, depending on the signal source and the color correction system you're using (**Figure 3.115**).

Figure 3.115 An overexposed image with highlights in the super-white range. Notice how the window is blown out.

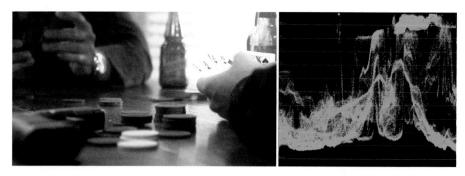

This highlight detail can usually be reclaimed by simply lowering the Gain contrast control until the top of the Waveform Monitor's graph drops below 100 percent/ IRE (700 mV), as shown in **Figure 3.116**.

Figure 3.116 Lowering the high- lights brings more of the detail from the blinds in front of the windows back into the shot.

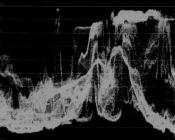

Dramatically overexposed media poses a much more difficult problem, as illustrated in **Figure 3.117**. When camera imaging sensors are overexposed to the point of maxing out the red, green, and blue channels of video data, any highlight detail corresponding to these higher values is simply clipped. The result is a flattened area of uniform white that contains *no image detail whatsoever.*

Figure 3.117 An image with more harshly overexposed highlights.

In this case, lowering the Gain control doesn't bring back any more detail in the image. Instead, it simply makes this uniform pool of white into a uniform pool of gray (**Figure 3.118**).

Figure 3.118 Lowering the highlights of a more harshly over-exposed image retrieves some additional detail along the front of the buildings (upper left), but most of the other blown-out detail of the image remains lost.

In the case of excessive overexposure, there's nothing you can do to bring back the lost image detail other than to reshoot the scene (admittedly, this is not likely for the majority of programs that are at the finishing stage).

CHAPTER 3

WHEN ARE HIGHLIGHTS IMPORTANT ENOUGH TO KEEP?

Before we discuss how to go about minimizing the damage within excessively over-exposed clips, it's worth discussing when it's necessary to preserve highlight detail and when it's not.

Not all highlights are important enough to save. To illustrate this fact, let's take a bit of a detour into how light output is measured when considering brightness. The international standard unit of luminance is the candela per square meter (cd/m^2), colloquially called a *nit*. Here are a few measured light sources for reference:

- Sun at noon = 1,600,000,000 nits

- Sun at horizon = 600,000 nits

- T8 White Fluorescent Bulb = 11,000 nits

- White on an LCD television = 400–500 nits

- White on a plasma television = 50–136 nits

Each one of the cited light sources could easily take its place as the brightest element within a recorded scene, with a white point of 100 percent/IRE (700 mV). However, the actual measurable brightness of the originating light sources is clearly much, much brighter. In fact, it's hopelessly brighter than anything else within the scene that you'd consider to be the primary subject.

For example, a sun glint shining off a vintage car's chrome bumper is going to be off the charts by any scale of measurement. That's not a highlight worth preserving, because chances are the camera that shot the scene recorded next to no discernible image data within that highlight. This is a highlight you should have no problem sacrificing to the broadcast-safe clipper of your color correction application in order to lighten more important parts of the image.

On the other hand, the highlights on the side of an interview subject's face are not likely to be nearly so bright and definitely contain image detail that's worth preserving.

When evaluating a scene that has severe highlights, be discriminating about what you go out of your way to save. The sun, point light sources such as bulbs, direct light sources reflected in mirrors, sun glints, signal flares, and other similar phenomena likely have no detail recorded to preserve, and aside from making sure that you've appropriately legalized the image for broadcast, clipping these parts of the image won't do you any harm.

On the other hand, *significant highlights* such as those on faces, reflected light off buildings, and generally any highlights where you have an opportunity to retrieve some detail from the image are worth spending some time on, sculpting the exposure with contrast controls and curves to maintain the contrast of the image while maintaining valuable image detail.

DEALING WITH WINDOWS

One of the biggest challenges facing colorists is what to do about a blown-out window. If the exterior image detail was really important to the scene, the cinematographer should have arranged to fit a neutral density gel in front of it to cut down the amount of light to match the overall exposure of the scene. If that wasn't done, you'll have to decide whether to lighten the subject and let the window become overexposed or try to correct the window separately using an HSL qualification or shape mask. The two images in **Figure 3.119** illustrate two different ways of dealing with the effect of windows on a shot.

Figure 3.119 The windows in the shot on the left have had the outside detail preserved as much as possible, where the windows in the image on the right have been intentionally blown out to eliminate detail. Both sets of highlights are similarly set to peak at just under 99 percent/IRE.

There is no right or wrong answer to what to do with overexposed windows. Some filmmakers, such as Stephen Soderbergh, have no problem blowing out windows to focus the viewer's attention on the interior subjects (see *The Girlfriend Experience*, *Bubble*, and *Full Frontal* for a few examples that were shot digitally). Other filmmakers jump through flaming hoops to preserve as much image detail as possible, outside and in. It's an aesthetic choice, not a technical one, assuming there is any image detail in the window highlights that's possible to retrieve.

POSSIBLE BAND-AIDS FOR OVEREXPOSURE

In this section I'll present some useful techniques for "patching" overexposed areas. Keep in mind that there's no universal panacea. Every shot you encounter is different, and a technique that works well for one shot may look awful when used with another—your mileage *will* vary.

OVEREXPOSURE OPTIONS FOR FILM TRANSFERRED TO VIDEO

If you're working on media that was transferred from film via a telecine session, you can request that the shots at fault be retransferred. Film often contains much more retrievable detail in the highlights than is available on video, but this detail can only be gotten back by making adjustments to the telecine that's putting light through the film (assuming the camera negative wasn't irretrievably overexposed in the first place).

If the budget allows, create a pull list for shots that should be retransferred with more attention paid to the highlights and afterward reedit this new media back into your project to replace the originally overexposed clips.

NOTE

Some of the methods presented in this section use techniques not yet covered. If you have questions, read through the cited chapters of the book and come back when you understand all of the functionality that's necessary for each technique.

CHAPTER 3

OVEREXPOSURE OPTIONS FOR RAW FORMATS

If you're grading media in some kind of RAW format, such as the RED camera's R3D media, you can change the exposure with which the RAW media is decoded using the native media controls provided by your color correction application.

The interesting thing about these decoding controls is that the ISO set during the shoot for monitoring purposes is merely recorded as user-adjustable metadata; the actual RAW, linear-light image data that was recorded by the camera potentially has much more latitude available if you raise or lower the ISO metadata parameter.

For example, the RED media image shown in **Figure 3.120** uses the settings that were selected in-camera during the shoot as the starting point for the grade.

Figure 3.120 The original overexposed image.

At the original ISO setting of 400, there's good exposure and detail in the interior of the vehicle, but the window is blown out.

Figure 3.121 The RED camera metadata controls as seen inside the Camera RAW palette. Other color correction applications have similar controls.

1 One way to solve this, if the client wants to see more detail outside of the window, is to lower the ISO value to 160 (**Figure 3.121**).

   This results in the exterior being well exposed, with a lot more visible detail, at the expense of the interior, which becomes underexposed.

2 Using a custom user shape or power window, you can now isolate the interior portion of the shot in order to lighten it using a secondary operation, as shown in **Figure 3.122** (for more information, see Chapter 5).

3 Since the R3D media has 4:4:4 chroma sampling, you can raise the Gain and Gamma contrast controls to lighten the interior without introducing much noise (**Figure 3.123**).

Because you've lightened the interior as a secondary operation, the contrast change has no effect on the now perfectly exposed exterior highlights, so you've been able to split the difference to good effect.

Figure 3.122 A custom user shape used to isolate the woman and the interior of the van for separate correction.

Figure 3.123 The final correction, balancing a well-exposed exterior with a nicely rendered interior.

ADD A BIT OF COLOR TO THE OVEREXPOSED AREA

If you don't have the advantage of working with a RAW color space format, the following is an easy fix that you might be able to get away with if the overexposed area isn't too large. This sometimes helps make blown-out highlights on people's faces less objectionable.

1 You can legalize overexposed highlights by lowering the Gain contrast control. Since we're adding color to "fill the hole," we need to bring the highlights well under 100 percent/IRE (700 mV) so that we can put some saturation in without running into the "no saturation at 100 percent" rule (see Chapter 10 for more information). Lowering the highlights to 90–95 percent/IRE should do the trick.

CHAPTER 3

2 If necessary, raise the midtones using the Gamma control to compensate for any darkening of the image caused by reducing highlight brightness (**Figure 3.124**).

Figure 3.124 The legalized image, with a spot of mild overexposure on the woman's forehead.

3 Next, isolate the blown-out highlights using the luma control of the HSL Qualification controls (**Figure 3.125**).

Figure 3.125 The mask created with the luma control of the HSL qualifiers, used to isolate the overexposed highlight on the woman's forehead for targeted adjustment.

4 Then drag the Gain color balance control toward a color that's analogous to the subject you're "patching" in order to tint the overexposed area to match. **Figure 3.126** shows the final corrected image.

Figure 3.126 The fixed image.

You may need to lower the highlight and adjust the saturation of the isolated "patch" in order to make it blend in better with the surrounding skin, but you should be able to achieve good results with a minimum of work. This is an effective quick fix.

ADD SOME GLOW TO THE HIGHLIGHTS

This next technique isn't really a fix so much as a way of trying to make a virtue out of a vice when overexposed highlights can't be hidden in other ways.

Interestingly, different types of media handle overexposure more or less gracefully. For example, most conventional SD and HD camcorders recording highly compressed media tend to clip overexposed levels harshly, resulting in aliased edges and an unflattering look (**Figure 3.127**). Such harsh areas of overexposure in an image are sometimes referred to as *cigarette burns*.

NOTE

For more information on using HSL Qualification, see Chapter 5. For more information on using the color balance controls, see Chapter 4.

Figure 3.127 An example of over-exposed harsh camcorder video.

Film, on the other hand, overexposes more flatteringly. Light bounces between the different dye layers and the emulsion, diffusing and causing *halation* that appears as a light glow surrounding the overexposed highlights of the image.

A similar phenomenon affects some digital cinema cameras with higher-end imaging sensors. The surplus charge of overexposed photosites on the camera sensor (each of which is converted into a pixel in the final image) bleeds into adjacent photosites, causing a similar glowing effect, referred to as *blooming*. This effect can be seen in overexposed clips recorded by the RED One camera (**Figure 3.128**).

CHAPTER 3

Figure 3.128 An example of an overexposed image with slight halation or blooming at the edges of overexposure.

When dramatic overexposure is inevitable, halation and blooming can render it more pleasing by softening the edges of the overexposed areas. When shooting film or a predictably responsive digital cinema camera, some filmmakers and cinematographers actually welcome halation and blooming as a dramatic effect.

Here's how to add some glow to your image's highlights using any color correction application that has HSL Qualification:

1 First, legalize the overexposed highlights by lowering the Gain contrast control so that the top of the Waveform Monitor's graph falls somewhere around 95 percent/IRE (700 mV).

   If necessary, raise the midtones using the Gamma control to compensate for any darkening of the image caused by reducing highlight brightness.

2 Next, key or isolate just the blown-out highlights using the luma control of the HSL Qualifier (**Figure 3.129**).

Figure 3.129 Using the HSL qualifier to isolate the over-exposed highlights.

3 Using the Blur or Soften controls of the HSL Qualifier, blur the key you just pulled so that it ends up being larger and softer than the overexposed area you originally isolated (**Figure 3.130**).

Figure 3.130 The highlight mask after being softened.

4 Now, raise either the Lift or Gamma master contrast controls (whichever ends up giving you a more pleasing effect) in order to lighten the area you just keyed. The result should start to glow softly, similar to the way it would if halation or blooming were taking place (**Figure 3.131**).

Figure 3.131 The final image with simulated blooming.

These are the simplest quick fixes with which you can attempt to remedy overexposure. There are more intensive techniques available for applications that have more integrated compositing features built-in.

NOTE

For more information on using HSL Qualification, see Chapter 5.

CHAPTER 3

REBUILD THE CLIPPED CHANNEL USING A CHANNEL MIXER

The following technique is one of the most time-consuming operations in this section. However, it may be a good solution for shots with significant overexposure that affects one channel disproportionately to the others, causing a flattening of the image in the highlights that's unflattering. A common example of this is overblown red channels corresponding to overexposed faces.

An easy way to tell whether this technique will be useful is to examine the RGB parade mode of your Waveform Monitor or the RGB Histogram. If one channel is extending well above 110 percent/IRE (770 mV) but the other channels aren't, then the shot may be a candidate for this type of fix.

However, this technique is more of a compositing operation than it is a traditional color correction procedure. While the latest versions of color correction applications increasingly include more compositing features, this functionality is implemented in many different ways—using layer-based compositing, node-based compositing, operation-based compositing in a stack, and so on.

For the purposes of illustration, I'll show a technique using the RGB Mixer in DaVinci Resolve. The workflow should translate easily to other applications offering similar functionality, no matter how the interface is exposed.

One last caveat is that this is a last-ditch technique, and the purpose is more to give you something usable than to give you something beautiful. You can't discard this much image data without consequences, and while this technique can help you salvage a scene in an emergency situation, a filmmaker is better off looking for a different take or reshooting the scene to achieve a truly superior result.

1 Check the RGB parade scope to see which of the color channels is overly clipped. In **Figure 3.132**, the red channel is clipped.

Figure 3.132 The red channel is irretrievably clipped. This shot is an emergency overexposure requiring extreme measures.

2 Use the Color and Contrast controls of your application to achieve the best possible color balance. Don't worry about the clipped bit; you just want to make an overall correction. In this case, the Offset color balance control (covered in Chapter 4) realigns the three color channels to be less red-balanced, and the Master Offset control lowers the signal to bring more shadow density into the image. In **Figure 1.133**, the problem is even easier to see, which is the point of this adjustment.

Figure 3.133 The image after making the best basic correction you can.

3 Create a new layer or node within which to fix the blown-out channel. Ultimately, the correction you make in this adjustment is going to be overlaid on top of the previous correction. In this example, a final combination of nodes is shown in **Figure 3.134** DaVinci Resolve, with two nodes feeding a Layer Mixer that combines them such that the adjustment made in node 4 is laid on top of the original adjustment, propagated to node 2.

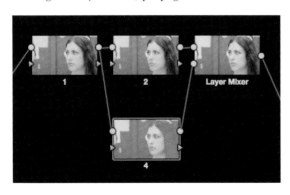

Figure 3.134 Creating a node structure in DaVinci Resolve with which to overlay a channel-mixing fix with your initial correction. The same thing can be done in other applications using layers.

4 Now, select the new layer or node, and examine the blue and green channels on the parade scope to see which has more image detail within the area that's clipped in the red channel for separation. In this example, both the green and blue channels have the necessary image data we need to fill in the gaps of the red channel (**Figure 3.135**).

Figure 3.135 Examining the blue and green highlights of the signal for detail that can be mixed into the clipped red channel.

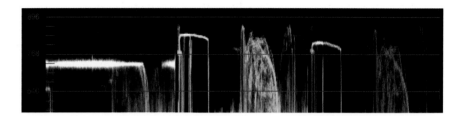

5 Use whatever RGB Mixer, Channel Blending, or channel isolation and blend mode operations your application provides to mix a bit of both the green and blue channels into the red channel. If this is working, you should see some peaks in that channel of the scope start to emerge from the previously flattened waveform (**Figure 3.136**). If this adjustment ends up boosting the red channel too much, you can use whatever individual RGB Lift/Gamma/ Gain parameters you're provided to lower the Red Gain to bring that channel into line.

Figure 3.136 RGB Mixer and RGB Gain operations used to build detail back into the red channel.

As you make this adjustment, your goal should be to have a seamless blend between the patch you're creating and the rest of the image. If you know there's a red color cast in the image, then you want the red channel to be as proportionally stronger to the green channel as the green channel is to the blue channel. The result should be additional detail in the blown-out area, although at this stage the color still won't look quite right (Figure 3.136).

In an added optional step, since the problem was originally in the highlights and there was detail in the shadows of the original image that looked just fine, you can preserve the original shadow color while adding this fix just to the highlights using a Qualifier (covered in Chapter 5).

6 Using the luma controls of an HSL Qualifier, isolate the blown-out highlights of the image, making sure to soften the edges well, and use that isolation to limit the RGB remixing you did (**Figure 3.137**).

Figure 3.137 Isolating only the clipped highlights in order to preserve the original color in areas of the image that weren't clipped.

At this point, the image is looking pretty much as good as it's going to get, in terms of adding detail back to the blown-out areas (**Figure 3.138**).

Figure 3.138 The patched image, ready for further correction.

CHAPTER 3

Lastly, you'll want to add additional corrections after this fix, treating the entire image as a whole again (**Figure 3.139**). It'll likely take a lot of pushing and pulling to get a naturalistic result, and you may never quite get the perfect image you would have liked, but this is the compromise when you get an image that's this degraded. Ultimately, you have to be happy you have any kind of image at all. In this example, four additional adjustments were made including a selective boost to saturation in the most desaturated parts of the image, curve adjustments to improve contrast, RGB Lift/Gamma/Gain to improve color balance, and other small tweaks.

Figure 3.139 The final result after considerable tweaking.

CHAPTER 4

PRIMARY COLOR ADJUSTMENTS

In this chapter we'll examine the common methods you can use to make primary color adjustments to affect an overall image.

As discussed at the beginning of Chapter 3, the human visual system processes color signals separately from luminance, and as a result, color conveys a completely different set of information. Color is used by what Margaret Livingstone refers to as the "what" system of the brain to identify objects and faces. Other studies support the idea that color plays an important part in speeding object identification and in enhancing memory recall.

For example, in their article "Revisiting Snodgrass and Vanderwart's Object Databank: Color and Texture Improve Object Recognition" (*Perception Volume 33*, 2004), Bruno Rossion and Gilles Pourtois used a set of standardized images first assembled by J.G. Snodgrass and M. Vanderwart to determine whether the presence of color sped subjects' reaction times for object identification. The study sorted 240 students into separate groups and asked them to identify one of three sets of test images: black and white, grayscale, and color (such as those images shown in **Figure 4.1**). The resulting data showed a clear increase in the speed of object recognition by nearly 100 milliseconds with the addition of color.

Figure 4.1 One of a set of 260 line drawings used to test the differences in object identification speed for black and white, grayscale, and color images.

Similarly, in "The Contributions of Color to Recognition Memory for Natural Scenes" (Wichmann, Sharpe, and Gegenfurtner, *Journal of Experimental Psychology Learning Memory and Cognition,* 2002), subjects were reported to have performed 5–10 percent better at memory retention tests that used colored images than they did with grayscale images.

> **NOTE**
>
> In an interesting aside, this research dovetails with other research on so-called memory colors (a topic covered in more detail in Chapter 8), in that the memory-enhancing effect is dependent on a subject's conceptual knowledge of the object being remembered (in other words, knowing in advance that bananas are yellow). Memory retention improvements diminished when subjects were tested with false-color versions of the same images.

Beyond these purely functional benefits to color, artists, critics, and researchers over the centuries have called attention to the emotional signifiers of various colors and the importance that color exerts on our creative interpretation of visual scenes.

For example, not many people would dispute that orange/red tones are high-energy colors and that an abundance of warmth in the art direction of a scene will lend a certain intensity to what's happening, as shown in **Figure 4.2**.

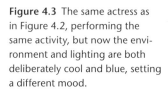

Figure 4.2 An actress in an environment with predominantly warm tones and warm, golden lighting.

Similarly, blue has an innate coolness, and bluish lighting will give an entirely different impression to an audience (**Figure 4.3**).

Figure 4.3 The same actress as in Figure 4.2, performing the same activity, but now the environment and lighting are both deliberately cool and blue, setting a different mood.

In her book, *If It's Purple, Someone's Gonna Die* (Elsevier, 2005), designer, author, and professor Patti Bellantoni cites numerous color experiments with her art students, whom she separated into groups, asking each to create an environment based on a specific color. The resulting color-dominated rooms not only drew a clear emotional response from the students, but over a number of years, successive classes of students exhibited strikingly similar interpretations for identical colors.

In the "backstory" chapter of her book, Bellantoni says, "[M]y research suggests it is not we who decide what color can be. After two decades of investigation into how color affects behavior, I am convinced, whether we want it to or not, that it is *color* that can determine how we think and what we feel."

Simple primary corrections won't unrecognizably alter the art direction and costumes within a scene. However, by correcting, shifting, and deliberately controlling the overall color tone of the lighting, you can create distinct audience impressions about the emotional atmosphere of a scene, the health and attractiveness of your characters, the tastiness of food, the time of day, and the kind of weather, no matter what the lighting of the shot originally was. **Figure 4.4** shows two contrasting versions of the same scene.

NOTE

This chapter is not concerned with specific color changes to isolated objects, which is the purpose of the secondary color corrections covered in Chapters 5 and 6.

Figure 4.4 Which room would you rather wake up in?

CHAPTER 4

To master these kinds of adjustments, we'll examine the role that color temperature, manipulation of the chroma component, additive color math, and an understanding of color contrast all play in the use of the color balance and RGB Curve controls present in nearly every professional color correction application.

COLOR TEMPERATURE

All color in a scene interacts with the dominant light source, or *illuminant*, of that location. Each type of illuminant, whether it's the sun, practical tungsten or halogen light fixtures, or stage and cinema lighting instruments, has a particular *color temperature* that dictates the color quality of the light and how it interacts with subjects in a scene.

Nearly every lighting effect dealt with in this book is a result of differing color temperature, or color of light, in various circumstances. Every time you correct or introduce a color cast in an image, you're effectively manipulating the color temperature of the light source.

Color temperature is one of the most important concepts for a colorist to understand because the color temperature of the lighting in any scene changes the viewer's perception of the colors and highlights found within. Despite the human eye's adaptive nature, when the color temperature of the dominant lighting is not taken into account through the use of film stocks, filtration, or white balance, a color cast will be recorded. Sometimes a color cast is desirable, as in the case of "magic hour" lighting or sunset photography. Sometimes it's not desirable, such as when you're shooting interior scenes with incorrectly balanced or spectrally varied light sources.

Each type of light source used to illuminate subjects recorded by film or digitally has its own particular color temperature, which in many cases corresponds to how hot that light source must be to emit light. Light emitters can be modeled in physics as black-body radiators, which are idealized light sources that output pure color corresponding to their temperature. For example, the heating elements in some toaster ovens are approximate black-body radiators. The hotter they get, the brighter they glow: first dark orange and then progressively lighter. The carbon rods used for arc welding are so hot that they glow a bright blue-white.

Candles, light bulbs, and sunlight operate at very different temperatures, and as a result, they emit more or less radiation at different wavelengths of the visible spectrum. Thus, comparing two different light sources (such as a household lamp next to a window on a clear morning) reveals differently colored light. Consider **Figure 4.5**, color-balanced for tungsten, which accounts for the white quality of the interior lighting. This reveals how cool the sunlight coming in through the window is, which by comparison is a vivid blue.

Figure 4.5 Mixed lighting reveals strikingly different color temperatures.

The color temperature of a light source is measured in Kelvin (**Figure 4.6**), named after William Thompson (aka Lord Kelvin), a Scottish physicist who first proposed a scale for absolute temperature measurement. While named for Kelvin, Max Planck was the physicist who developed the principle (called Planck's law) that, as Wikipedia explains, "describes the spectral radiance of electromagnetic radiation at all wavelengths emitted in the normal direction from a black body in a cavity in thermodynamic equilibrium."

The math is complex, but for our purposes the general idea is that the hotter an emission source, the "bluer" the light. The cooler the emission source, the "redder" the light. Consider how the scale in Figure 4.6 matches to light sources and other illuminant standards.

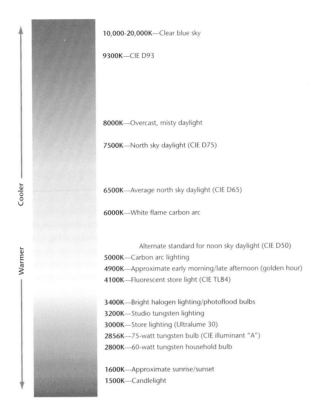

10,000-20,000K—Clear blue sky

9300K—CIE D93

8000K—Overcast, misty daylight

7500K—North sky daylight (CIE D75)

6500K—Average north sky daylight (CIE D65)

6000K—White flame carbon arc

Alternate standard for noon sky daylight (CIE D50)
5000K—Carbon arc lighting
4900K—Approximate early morning/late afternoon (golden hour)
4100K—Fluorescent store light (CIE TL84)

3400K—Bright halogen lighting/photoflood bulbs
3200K—Studio tungsten lighting
3000K—Store lighting (Ultralume 30)
2856K—75-watt tungsten bulb (CIE illuminant "A")
2800K—60-watt tungsten household bulb

1600K—Approximate sunrise/sunset
1500K—Candlelight

Cooler

Warmer

Figure 4.6 Approximate colors corresponding to popular known color temperatures.

CHAPTER 4

It's not a coincidence that the color gradient from 1600K to 10000K matches the progression in the quality of sunlight from sunrise to bright, noon sunlight.

"D" ILLUMINANTS AND D65

A second color temperature standard you may hear mentioned describes the so-called "D" illuminants (also listed in Figure 4.6), which are defined by the Commission Internationale de l'Eclairage (CIE). The CIE defined standard illuminant graphs to describe the spectral distribution of different types of lighting. The "D" illuminants are all intended to describe daylight color temperatures so that manufacturers of lighting fixtures can standardize their products.

Each of the CIE illuminants was developed for a specific purpose. Some illuminants are intended for use as lighting for critical color evaluation; others are meant for use in commercial lighting fixtures.

One illuminant you should memorize is D65 (corresponding to 6500K), which is the North American and European standard for noon daylight. This is also the standard setting for white that broadcast video monitors use in the United States and in Europe, and it is the type of ambient lighting you should employ in your

NOTE
The native white point used by computer displays typically defaults to D65.

color correction suite. Inconsistent lighting in your environment will cause your eyes to adapt incorrectly to the colors on your monitor, resulting in bad color decisions.

Broadcast monitors in China, Japan, and Korea are balanced to D93, or 9300K, which is a significantly bluer white. This should ideally be paired with matching D93 ambient lighting.

SPECTRALLY VARIED LIGHT SOURCES

The simple color temperature measurements shown in Figure 4.6 are good for describing light quality in general terms, as well as for standardizing film stocks, optical filters, and HDSLR, camcorder, and digital cinema camera white balance controls. However, the spectral distribution of real-world light sources isn't always so perfect. Different light sources have unique spectral distributions that may include numerous spikes and dips at specific wavelengths of light.

A good example of a spectrally varied light source is fluorescent lighting, which has spikes in its spectral distribution that can illuminate other colors differently than you might expect. An average office fluorescent tube has small but significant spikes in the green and indigo-blue portions of the spectrum that, while appearing perfectly white to the human eye, may lend a greenish/blue cast to unfiltered film and improperly white-balanced video. For example, the image on the left in **Figure 4.7** is incorrectly balanced for tungsten, and the fluorescent lighting lends a greenish cast to the image (especially visible in the gray doors). The image on the right is properly white balanced.

Figure 4.7 The image to the left exhibits the greenish tint of fluorescent lighting shot with an incorrect white balance. The image to the right is shot using the correct white balance.

Generalizing about the light given off by fluorescent tubes is difficult because there are many different designs, all of which have been formulated to give off different qualities of light. Some fluorescent tubes have been specially designed to eliminate these spectral inconsistencies and produce light with nearly equal amounts of radiation at all frequencies of the visible spectrum.

Other spectrally varied light sources are the sodium vapor lamps used in municipal street lights, which give a severe yellow/orange cast to an image, as shown in **Figure 4.8**.

Figure 4.8 The spectrally mono-chromatic light put out by sodium vapor lamps produces a harsh, orange light that's difficult to compensate for.

Other spectrally varied light sources include mercury vapor lamps, which lend an intense off-red tint to shots, and metal halide lamps, which can give off either magenta or blue/green casts.

With a shot that has one of these intensely red/orange light sources as the primary source of illumination, you'll be surprised at how much of a correction you can make, assuming that the main subjects of the shot are people. Because these light sources have a strong red component, you can generally bring back relatively normal-looking skin tones. Unfortunately, other colors won't fare as well, so cars, buildings, and other colorful exterior objects may prove troublesome.

WHAT IS CHROMA?

Once the illuminant within a scene has bounced off a subject and has been captured by the optical/digital components of a camera, the reflected color information is stored via the chroma component of video. *Chroma* is that portion of an analog or digital video signal that carries color information, and in many video applications it can be adjusted independently of the luma of the image. In component $Y'C_BC_R$-encoded video, the chroma is carried in the Cb and Cr color difference channels of the video signal.

This scheme was originally devised to ensure backward compatibility between color and monochrome television sets (back when there were such things as monochrome television sets). Monochrome TVs were able to filter out the chroma component, displaying the luma component by itself. However, this scheme of color encoding also proved valuable for video signal compression, since the chroma component can be subsampled for consumer video formats, lowering the quality in a virtually imperceptible way, while shrinking the bandwidth necessary for storing initially analog, and later digital files, allowing more video to be recorded using less storage media.

The color of any recorded subject with an encoded chroma component has two characteristics: *hue* and *saturation*.

NOTE

The notation for composite video varies depending on whether it's digital or analog. $Y'C_BC_R$ denotes digital component video, whereas $Y'P_BP_R$ denotes analog component video.

WHAT IS HUE?

Hue simply describes the wavelength of the color, whether it's red (a long wavelength), green (a medium wavelength that's shorter than red), or blue (the shortest visible wavelength of all). Each color we consider to be unique from any other (orange, cyan, purple) is a different hue.

Hue is represented on any color wheel as an angle about the center (**Figure 4.9**).

Figure 4.9 How hue is represented by a color wheel.

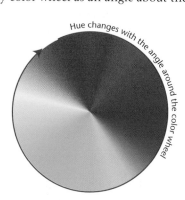

When hue is assigned a control in a color correction application, it's typically as a slider or parameter in degrees. Increasing or decreasing the degree of hue shifts the colors of the entire image in the direction of adjustment.

WHAT IS SATURATION?

Saturation describes the intensity of a color, such as whether it's a vivid or deep blue or a pale and pastel blue. A desaturated image has no color at all—it's a grayscale, monochrome image.

Saturation is also represented on the color wheel used in onscreen color correction interfaces in some applications, seen as completely desaturated (0 percent) at the center of the wheel and completely saturated (100 percent) at the wheel's edge (**Figure 4.10**).

Figure 4.10 This shows 100 percent and 0 percent saturation on a standard color wheel, corresponding to the saturated and desaturated regions of a vectorscope.

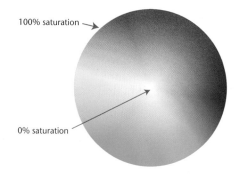

Increasing saturation intensifies the colors of an image. Decreasing saturation reduces the vividness of colors in an image, making it paler and paler until all color disappears, leaving only the monochrome luma component.

PRIMARY COLORS

Video uses an additive color system, wherein red, green, and blue are the three *primary colors* that, added together in different proportions, are able to produce any other color that's reproducible on a particular display (**Figure 4.11**).

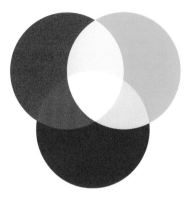

Figure 4.11 Three primary colors combining. Any two result in a secondary color; all three produce pure white.

Red, green, and blue are the three purest colors that a display can represent, by setting a single color channel to 100 percent and the other two color channels to 0 percent. Adding 100 percent of red, green, and blue results in white, while 0 percent of red, green, and blue results in black.

Interestingly, this scheme matches our visual system's sensitivities. As mentioned previously, our sensitivity to color comes from approximately 5 million cone cells found within our retinas, distributed into three types of cells:

- Red-sensitive (long-wavelength, also called *L cells*)
- Green-sensitive (medium-wavelength, or *M cells*)
- Blue-sensitive (short-wavelength, or *S cells*)

The relative distribution of these is 40:20:1, with our lowest sensitivity corresponding to blue (the chief penalty of which is limited sharpness perception for predominantly blue scenes).

These are arranged in various combinations that, as we'll see later, convey different color encodings to the image-processing part of our brains, depending on what proportions of each type of cone receive stimulus.

You may have noticed that some stage lighting fixtures (and increasingly, LED-based lighting panels for the film and video industry) consist of clusters of red, green, and blue lights. When all three lights are turned on, our naked eyes see a bright, clear white. Similarly, the red, green, and blue components within each physical pixel of a video or computer display combine as white to our eyes when all three channels are at 100 percent.

RGB CHANNEL LEVELS FOR MONOCHROME IMAGES

Another important ramification of the additive color model is that identical levels in all three color channels, no matter what the actual amounts are, result in a neutral gray image. For example, the monochrome image in **Figure 4.12** is shown side by side with an RGB parade scope displaying each color channel. Because there's no color, every channel is exactly equal to the others.

Figure 4.12 The three color channels of a completely monochrome image are equal.

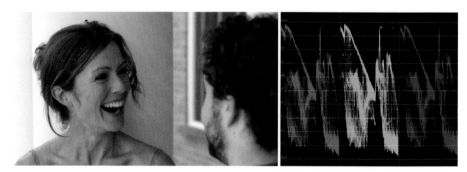

Because of this, spotting improper color using an RGB or YRGB parade scope is easy, assuming you're able to spot a feature that's supposed to be completely desaturated or gray. If the gray feature does not have three perfectly equal waveforms in the RGB parade scope, then there's a tint to the image.

For example, the white pillar in the image corresponds to the leftmost high spikes in the red, green, and blue waveforms of the parade scope (**Figure 4.13**). Since they're nearly equal (actually, there's a bit of a blue cast, but that makes sense since they're outside in daylight), we can conclude that the highlights of the image are fairly neutral.

Figure 4.13 Even though the red waveform is generally strongest and the blue waveform is weakest, the close alignment of the tops and bottom of the waveforms lets us know that the highlights and shadows are fairly neutral.

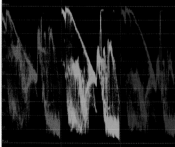

WHAT ABOUT FILM?

Color negative film uses a subtractive model. Three sets of layers that contain light-sensitive silver halide crystals are separated by a color filtering layer to restrict what colors are exposed by each layer record color information and absorb different dyes when developed:

- Blue-sensitive layers on top absorb yellow dye when they are developed.
- Green-sensitive layers in the middle absorb magenta dye when they are developed.
- Red-sensitive layers at the bottom absorb cyan dye when they are developed.

Since cyan absorbs red, magenta absorbs green, and yellow absorbs blue, all three layers added together at their maximum result in black, while all three layers at their minimum pass all light, creating white.

This book discusses digital color correction procedures that require film to be either telecine'd or scanned into a digital medium, to be operated upon within the additive color system of the computer. Even if you're working on a digital intermediate, you'll be using the additive color principles described in this section to perform your work.

SECONDARY COLORS

Secondary colors are the combination of any two color channels at 100 percent, with the third at 0 percent:

- Red + green = yellow
- Green + blue = cyan
- Blue + red = magenta

Because the primary and secondary colors are the easiest colors to mathematically create using the RGB additive color model, they are used to comprise the different bars of the standard color bars test pattern used to calibrate different video equipment (**Figure 4.14**).

As discussed later in "Using the Vectorscope," each bar corresponds to a color target on the vectorscope graticule. These color targets provide a much-needed frame of reference, showing which traces of a vectorscope graph correspond to which colors.

NOTE

Please note that secondary colors as described in this section have nothing to do with secondary corrections, which are target corrections that are focused on a specific subject within the frame. Secondary corrections are covered in detail in Chapters 4 and 5.

Figure 4.14 Full-frame color bars used by the test pattern common for PAL video. Each bar of this test pattern corresponds to a color target on a standard vectorscope graticule.

COMPLEMENTARY COLORS

There's one more aspect of the additive color model that's crucial to understanding how nearly every color adjustment we make works: the way that complementary colors neutralize one another.

Simply put, complementary colors are any two colors that sit directly opposite one another on the color wheel, as shown in **Figure 4.15**.

Figure 4.15 Two complementary colors sit directly opposite one another on the color wheel.

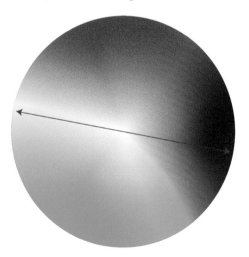

Whenever two perfectly complementary colors are combined, the result is complete desaturation. As the hues fall off to either angle of being complementary, this cancelling effect also falls off, until the hues are far enough apart for the colors to simply combine in another additive way (**Figure 4.16**).

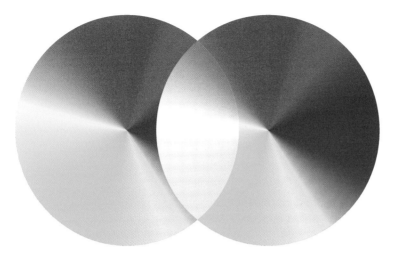

Figure 4.16 Where the hues are perfectly complementary to one another, the colors are completely cancelled out. As the angle of hue falls off from being complementary, so does this desaturating effect.

To understand why this works, it's useful to delve deeper into the mechanics of human vision. As discussed in Margaret Livingstone's *Vision and Art: The Biology of Seeing* (Harry N. Abrams, 2008), the dominant theory for how bipolar and M retinal ganglion nerve cells encode color information for processing in the thalamus of the brain is the *color-opponent* model.

The cones described earlier connect in groups to bipolar cells that compare the cone inputs to one another. For example, in one type of bipolar cell, (L)ong-wavelength (red-sensitive) cone inputs inhibit the nerve, while (M)edium-wavelength (green-sensitive) and (S)hort-wavelength (blue-sensitive) cone inputs excite it (**Figure 4.17**). In other words, for that cell, each red input is a positive influence, and each green or blue input is a negative influence.

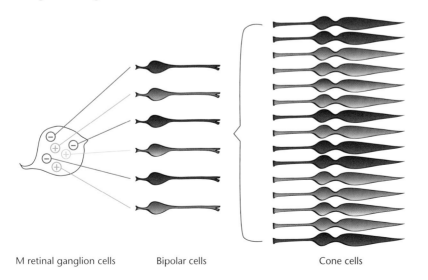

M retinal ganglion cells   Bipolar cells   Cone cells

Figure 4.17 This is an approximation of opponent model cell organization. Groups of cone cells are organized so that multiple cell inputs influence the retinal ganglion cells, which encode cell stimulus for further processing by the brain. Some cells excite (+) the ganglion, while other cells inhibit (–) the ganglion. Thus, all color signals are based on a comparison of colors within the scene.

In Maureen C. Stone's *A Field Guide to Digital Color* (A K Peters, 2003), the first level of encoding for this color-opponent model is described as conveying three signals corresponding to three different cone combinations:

- *Luminance* = L-cones + M-cones + S-cones

- *Red – Green* = L-cones – M-cones + S-cones

- *Yellow – Blue* = L-cones + M-cones – S-cones

Color-opponent cells, in turn, connect to double-opponent cells, which further refine the comparative color encoding that's used to pass information on to the thalamus, the vision-processing region of our brains.

Two important byproducts of double-opponency are the cancellation of complementary colors discussed previously and the effect of simultaneous color contrast, where gray patches are seen to assume the complementary hue of a dominant surround color (**Figure 4.18**).

Figure 4.18 The gray patches at the center of each colored square appear as if they're tinted with the complementary color of each surrounding area of color. The patch inside the green square appears reddish, and the patch inside the red square appears greenish. This effect becomes more pronounced the longer you look at one or the other of the squares.

Perhaps the simplest way of summing up the opponent model of vision is that cone cells don't output specific wavelength information—they simply indicate whether long-, medium-, or short-wavelength light is present, according to each cell's sensitivities. It's the *comparison* of multiple combinations of triggered and untriggered cone cells that our visual system and brain interpret as various colors in a scene.

In short, we evaluate the color of a subject relative to the other colors surrounding it. The benefit of this method of seeing is that it makes us capable of distinguishing the unique color of an object regardless of the color temperature of the dominant light source. An orange still looks orange whether we're holding it outside in daylight or inside by the light of a 40-watt bulb, even though both light sources output dramatically different wavelengths of light that interact with the pigments of the orange's skin.

We'll see later how to use complementary color to adjust images and neutralize unwanted color casts in a scene.

COLOR MODELS AND COLOR SPACES

A *color model* is a specific mathematical method of defining colors using a specific set of variables. A *color space* is effectively a predefined range of colors (or gamut) that exists within a particular color model. For example, RGB is a color model. sRGB is a color space that defines a gamut within the RGB color model.

The print standard of CMYK is a color model, as is the CIE XYZ method of representing color in three dimensions that's often used to represent the overall gamut of colors that can be reproduced on a particular display.

There are even more esoteric color models, such as the IPT color model, a perceptually weighted color model designed to represent a more uniform distribution of values that accounts for our eyes' diminished sensitivity to various hues.

COLOR MODELS IN 3D

Another interesting thing about color models is that you can use them to visualize a range of color via a three-dimensional shape. Each color model, when extruded into three dimensions, assumes a different shape. For example, a good pair of color model extrusions to compare is RGB and HSL:

- **The RGB color model appears as a cube**, with black and white at two opposite diagonal corners of the cube (the center of the diagonal being the desaturated range of neutral black to white). The three primary colors—red, green, and blue—lie at the three corners that are connected to black, while the three secondary colors—yellow, cyan, and magenta—lie at the three corners connected to white (**Figure 4.19**, left).

- **The HSL color model appears as a two-pointed cone**, with black and white at the top and bottom opposite points. The 100 percent saturated primary and secondary colors are distributed around the outside of the middle, fattest part of this shape. The center line of the shape connecting the black and white points is the desaturated range of gray (**Figure 4.19**, right).

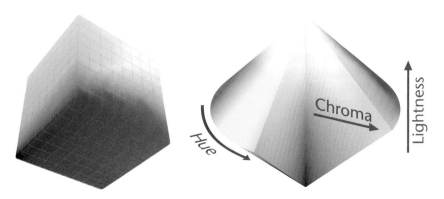

Figure 4.19 Three-dimensional RGB and HSL color space models compared.

These color models sometimes appear as the representation of a range of color in a video analysis tool, such as the 3D Histogram in Autodesk Smoke (**Figure 4.20**). Three-dimensional color space representations also appear in the onscreen interfaces of applications that use 3D keyers.

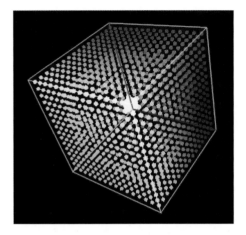

Figure 4.20 A three-dimensional Y'C$_B$C$_R$ graph found in Autodesk Smoke. The value of each pixel in the image is extruded into 3D space according to the Y'C$_B$C$_R$ color model.

Outside of the practical use of 3D color space shapes in application interfaces, these representations also are useful in giving us a framework for visualizing ranges of color and contrast in different ways.

RGB VS. Y'C$_B$C$_R$ COLOR MODELS

In general, the digital media you'll be color correcting will be delivered as either RGB- or Y'C$_B$C$_R$-encoded files. Consequently, color correction applications all work with both RGB and Y'C$_B$C$_R$ color models. Components of each can be mathematically converted into those corresponding to the other, which is why even though you may be working with Y'C$_B$C$_R$ source media shot using video equipment, you can examine the data using RGB parade scopes and make adjustments using RGB curves and RGB lift/gamma/gain parameters.

Similarly, RGB source media ingested via a film scanner or captured using a digital cinema camera can be examined using the Y'C$_B$C$_R$ analysis of Waveform Monitors and vectorscopes and adjusted using the same luma and color balance controls that have been traditionally used for video color correction.

Converting one color space into the other is a mathematical exercise. For example, to convert RGB components into Y'C$_B$C$_R$ components, you'd use the following general math:

- **Y'** (for BT.709 video) = (0.2126 × R') + (0.7152 × G') + (0.0722 B')

- **Cb** = B' − L'

- **Cr** = R' − L'

NOTE

This simplified math is excerpted from Charles Poynton's *Digital Video and HD Algorithms and Interfaces* (Morgan Kaufmann, 2012). The full math required for this conversion is a matrix equation that is beyond the scope of this book.

THE HSL (HSB) COLOR MODEL

HSL stands for Hue, Saturation, and Luminance. It's also referred to sometimes as HSB (Hue, Saturation, and Black). HSL is a color model, a way of representing and describing color using discrete values.

Even though digital media is not actually encoded using HSL, it's an important color model to understand because it appears within the onscreen interfaces of numerous color correction and compositing applications. HSL is convenient because the three parameters—hue, saturation, and luminance—are easily understood and manipulated without the need for mind-bending math.

For example, if you had the R, G, and B controls shown in **Figure 4.21**, how would you change a color from greenish to bluish?

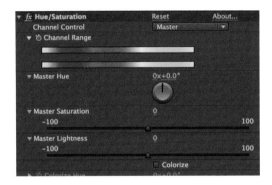

Figure 4.21 RGB Gamma, Pedestal, and Gain controls in an Adobe After Effects filter.

If you instead examined a set of H, S, and L sliders, it's probably a lot more obvious that the thing to do is manipulate the H(ue) dial. To provide a more concrete example, **Figure 4.22** shows the HSL qualification controls used to isolate a range of color and contrast for targeted correction.

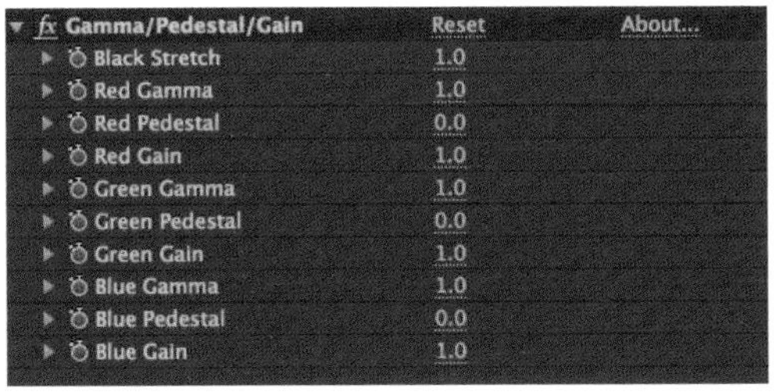

Figure 4.22 HSL controls found in the Adobe After Effects hue/saturation filter.

Once you understand the HSL color model, the purpose of each control in Figure 4.22 should at least suggest itself to you, even if you don't immediately understand the details.

ANALYZING COLOR BALANCE

Most of the time, you'll be able to spot inaccurate color balance visually, simply by looking at your calibrated display. For example, a tungsten-lit scene will look orange when you're using film stock that is balanced for daylight or a video camera with its white balance set to daylight.

Aside from the obvious color cast, orange light from incandescent fixtures may lend an inadvertently theatrical look because of the viewer's association with artificial lighting. For example, the image on the left in **Figure 4.23** is incorrectly balanced for daylight, and the tungsten lighting lends a warm, orange cast to it. The image on the right is properly white balanced, with whiter highlights and truer colors throughout the scene (note the blue sunlight spill in the foreground).

Figure 4.23 On the left, a tungsten-lit scene with incorrect color balance; on the right, the same scene with correct color balance.

Similarly, a daylight scene shot using tungsten-balanced film stock or a video camera with its white balance set to tungsten/indoors will look bluish (**Figure 4.24**).

Figure 4.24 On the left, a daylight-lit scene with incorrect color balance; on the right, the same scene white-balanced correctly.

If the filmmaker was not intending to portray a cold winter day, this is clearly a shot that would benefit from correction. Compare the image on the left in Figure 4.24, which is incorrectly balanced for tungsten, to the properly white-balanced image on the right.

USING THE VECTORSCOPE

The vectorscope measures the overall range of hue and saturation within an image. Measurements are relative to a *graticule* that's overlaid on the scope, which provides a frame of reference via crosshairs, diagonal I and Q bars, and labeled color targets corresponding to 75 percent saturated primary and secondary hues. **Figure 4.25** shows all of these indicators relative to the color wheel that represents the reproducible range of color and saturation.

Figure 4.25 should clearly illustrate that hue is indicated by the location of a graph trace's angle *around* the center, and saturation is indicated by a trace's distance *from* the center.

In reality, the graticules of most software vectorscopes are considerably simpler. At the least, a vectorscope should have the following graticule elements:

- Primary and secondary color targets that correspond to the top row of bars on the SMPTE color bars test pattern (**Figure 4.26**).

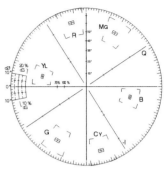

Figure 4.25 An idealized NTSC vectorscope graticule, showing all the crosshairs and targets you might expect to use to measure a displayed graph, superimposed over a color wheel showing their approximate correspondence to hue and saturation. Typically HD vectorscopes don't have as many reference items.

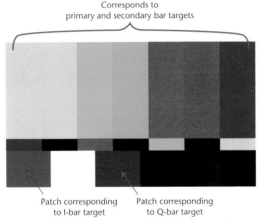

Corresponds to primary and secondary bar targets

Patch corresponding to I-bar target

Patch corresponding to Q-bar target

Figure 4.26 Portions of the SMPTE test pattern that correspond to vectorscope graticule elements are called out.

- Crosshairs that indicate the desaturated center of the vectorscope graph.

- I and Q diagonal crosshairs (and their –I and –Q counterparts). These stand for In-phase and Quadrature (an amplitude modulated phase 90 degrees relative to In-phase), which correspond to the purple and cyan/blue patches at the bottom of the color bars signal.

- Tic marks along the I- and Q-bars correspond to the voltage waveform that would be traced by the discrete I and Q components, while tic marks running along the outside border note 10-degree increments.

CHAPTER 4

When it comes to graticules, most vectorscopes have some manner of centered crosshairs at the center, which are critical for providing a reference of neutral black, gray, and white in the signal. The "I-bar" (as I've come to call it) is optional, and opinions vary as to whether it truly belongs on an HD scope. I happen to think it's still a useful reference, as I discuss in Chapter 8.

Different software scopes display different graticule elements and also draw the vectorscope graphs differently. Some software scopes represent the analyzed data as a discrete point of data on the graph, while others emulate the CRT method of drawing *traces* corresponding to each line of video that connect these points together. These traces aren't necessarily adding any actual data to the graph, but they make it easier to see the different points, and so they can be easier to read. **Figure 4.27** illustrates the differences in three commonly used vectorscopes.

Figure 4.27 Three excellent examples of different software vectorscopes compared (left to right): DaVinci Resolve, Autodesk Smoke, and Divergent Media ScopeBox (showing the optional Hue Vectors graticule that I designed).

 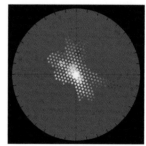 

DaVinci Resolve has a traditional vectorscope, the graph of which emulates a trace-drawn graph, with 75 percent color bar targets and an In-phase reference line. Autodesk Smoke has a unique vectorscope graph option that averages analyzed color as a scatter graph that consists of differently sized dots representing the amount of color at that position, which makes it really easy to read and calls attention to the outer boundary of signal that light traces might not make apparent. Smoke draws both crosshairs and 75 percent targets.

The third vectorscope shown, Divergent Media's ScopeBox, has a more traditional graticule available, with a trace-drawn graph, but it's also a forward-looking application that was the first software scope to incorporate the Hue Vector graticule I designed, which presents lines that are aligned with each of the primary and secondary colors to help give colorists reference points for comparison, a center crosshair that's aligned with the warm/cool axis of naturalistic color temperature for lighting, an In-phase positioned reference line, a user-customizable reference line, and both 75 percent and 100 percent tic marks for color intensity. ScopeBox also has a *peak* option for the vectorscope, which shows an absolute representation of the outer boundaries of the signal, making it easy to spot signal excursions that can be hard to see with faint traces. In fact, you may notice that the peak outline shape matches the scatter graph of the Smoke vectorscope.

CHAPTER 4

TRACES VS. SCATTER GRAPHS

Older CRT-based hardware scopes used an electron beam to sweep over the phosphores-cent coating on the screen from one point of data to the next in order to draw an analysis of each sequential line of video in the image, thus creating the overall graph. The result-ing series of overlapping *traces* served to "connect the dots" and produce the graph that's characteristic of CRT video scopes.

Software scopes, on the other hand, don't need to draw this trace from point to point and sometimes draw a more direct plot of all the values in the image, similar to a scatter graph. This plot bears more resemblance to a series of individual points than overlapping lines. This is most apparent in the optional Smoke 2D vectorscope.

As a result, individual points of data represented by software scopes won't necessarily look the same as they do on older video scopes. However, some dedicated outboard digital scopes from such companies as Videotek and Tektronix have hybrid displays that integrate both types of graphs: plot and vector.

JUDGING COLOR BALANCE USING A VECTORSCOPE

Since the center of the vectorscope graph represents all desaturated, neutral values, it follows that if a graph is uncentered and the image is supposed to have neutral tones in it, a color cast is present.

In **Figure 4.28**, the vectorscope graph to the left is suspiciously lopsided, leaning heavily toward yellow-green. This may not necessarily be wrong, but it should at least cause you to look at the source image a bit more closely to make sure this makes sense.

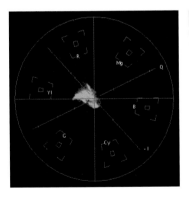 

Figure 4.28 Comparing an off-center graph (left) and an image with a centered graph and image (right).

The vectorscope graph to the right corresponds to a neutral version of the same image. Notice how this graph is much more evenly balanced relative to the center crosshairs of the graticule, with arms stretching more prominently toward several different hues. Again, this is no guarantee that the color balance is correct, but it's a pretty good indication that you're in the right ballpark if the image on your broad-cast display looks right.

TEKTRONIX LUMA-QUALIFIED VECTOR (LQV) DISPLAY

Tektronix' video scope models feature a luma-qualified vector display that can make it easier to judge color balance within specific tonal zones. Essentially, it's a regular vectorscope with additional controls to limit its analysis to a specific range of luma. The range of tonality that's analyzed is customizable, and if you like, you can display multiple vectorscopes, each set to analyze chroma within a different range of video luma.

For more information, see the Tektronix How-To Guide, LQV (Luminance Qualified Vector) Measurements with the WFM8200/8300, available from www.tek.com.

JUDGING SATURATION USING THE VECTORSCOPE

Judging the relative amount of saturation of an image is easy, since more saturated values extend farther away from the center of the scope than do less saturated values. In the following low-saturation image, the vectorscope graph is small, hugging the very center of the vectorscope graticule (**Figure 4.29**).

Figure 4.29 A low-saturation image with a correspondingly small vectorscope graph.

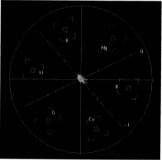

Take a close look at the graph. There are in fact excursions (parts of the graph that extend in various directions) that stretch toward the R(ed) and B(lue) targets, but they're small, indicating that while there is color within the image, there's not very much.

Most vectorscopes have the option to zoom into the graph, allowing you to see the shape of the graph with more clarity, even if the image is relatively desaturated (**Figure 4.30**).

The high-saturation image in **Figure 4.31** yields a much larger vectorscope graph, with arms stretching out toward the various color targets that correspond to each hue.

In the more highly saturated image in Figure 4.31, notice how the abundance of red reads as an arm of the graph that extends toward the R(ed) target, while the blues in the man's clothing appear as another arm of the graph that extends toward the B(lue) target. An abundance of yellow and orange creates a cloud in the vectorscope

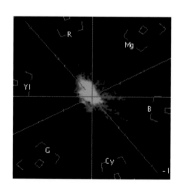

Figure 4.30 Zooming into the vectorscope graph from Figure 4.29 makes it easier to see more detail in the graph of an image with low saturation.

graph stretching toward the Yl (yellow) target. Finally, two conspicuous gaps in the graph, in the direction of the G(reen) and Mg (magenta) targets, tell us that there's very little of either of these two hues present in the image.

 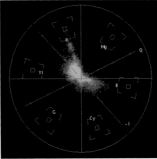

Figure 4.31 A highly saturated image with a correspondingly large vectorscope graph stretching farther out toward the edge of the graticule.

USING THE RGB PARADE SCOPE

The parade scope shows separate waveforms analyzing the strength of the R, G, and B components of the video signal. This is a composite representation, even if the original video is Y'C_BC_R-encoded. By showing a comparison of the intensity of the red, green, and blue components of the image, the parade scope makes it so you can detect and compare imbalances in the highlights (the top of the graph), shadows (the bottom of the graph), and midtones for the purposes of identifying color casts and performing scene-by-scene correction.

Recall that the whitest highlights and darkest blacks of an image are nearly always desaturated. With that in mind, red, green, and blue waveforms with tops at or near 100 percent/IRE and bottoms at or near 0 percent/IRE should typically align very closely.

In **Figure 4.32**, we can see that the lighting outside the window is a cool blue, the lighting on the wall behind the woman is fairly neutral, and the shadows are deep and black.

Figure 4.32 An evening scene for analysis.

Each feature can be seen within the parade scope, and the relative height of the corresponding graphs indicates the color balance within that zone of image tonality. For example, the blue window can be seen in the elevated spike at the left of the blue waveform (**Figure 4.33**). The woman's face corresponds to the elevated spike in the middle of the red waveform. And the neutral wall can be confirmed by the equally level shape of all three color channels at the right of all three waveforms.

By learning to identify features within the parade scope graphs, you can quickly spot where unwanted color casts appear and get guidance as to where within the image you need to make corrections.

Figure 4.33 The parade scope analysis for Figure 4.32.

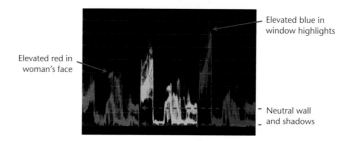

Elevated red in woman's face

Elevated blue in window highlights

Neutral wall and shadows

LEARNING TO READ PARADE SCOPE GRAPHS

The RGB parade scope is essentially a Waveform Monitor that displays separate graphs for the red, green, and blue channels of an image. To understand the parade scope's analysis, you need to learn how to compare the shape and height of the three Waveform graphs to one another.

Similar to the Waveform Monitor, each of the parade scope's graphs presents a left-to-right analysis of the tonality in the scene. The difference is that while the Waveform Monitor measures the luma component, each graph in the parade scope represents the individual strengths of the red, green, and blue color channels.

Figure 4.34 An image with an RGB parade scope analysis showing evenly balanced highlights and shadows.

In **Figure 4.34**, the generally accurate and neutral color balance of the scene is evidenced by the relative equality of the heights of the red, green, and blue channels, especially at the top and bottom of each waveform.

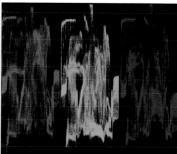

Even though the graphs look similar, closer inspection reveals that the peaks and valleys of the parade scope's three graphs correspond to various features in the picture. While strong highlights, shadows, and desaturated elements often have components of equal height in each graph, saturated subjects will certainly vary.

For example, splitting apart the red, green, and blue channels of the image in **Figure 4.35** and superimposing the red, green, and blue parade scope waveforms shows the correspondence between individual features within the image and the strength of each parade scope waveform. Keep in mind that each individual color channel is merely a grayscale image and that the corresponding waveform is simply an amplitude measurement of that channel.

Original image

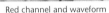

Red channel and waveform   Green channel and waveform   Blue channel and waveform

Figure 4.35 In this image, the red channel is significantly stronger (elevated) all the way through the graph, while the green channel is the next strongest. This indicates a strong yellow/orange (the secondary combination of red and green) color cast throughout the shadows, midtones, and highlights of the image.

Looking closely at each waveform reveals that, while the highlights corresponding to the pillar and window sill are of equal height, the portion of the red waveform corresponding to the faces is stronger than in the green and blue channels, which we'd expect. There's also a spike in the red channel that lines up with the brick wall, which we'd also expect.

By identifying a particular feature within the graph, you can check its color balance. Generally speaking, color casts are the result of one or two of the color channels being either too strong or too weak. Whatever the problem, it's easy to see which color channels are at fault using the parade scope. In **Figure 4.36**, a bit of detective work might reveal that the white balance setting of the video camera was incorrectly set relative to the lighting of the environment. If you're dealing with a film image, a film stock may have been used that was inappropriate for the lighting.

Figure 4.36 In this image, the red channel is significantly stronger (elevated) all the way through the graph, while the green channel is the next strongest. This indicates a strong yellow/orange (the secondary combination of red and green) color cast throughout the shadows, midtones, and highlights of the image.

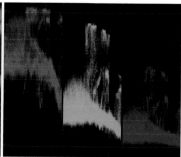

Whatever the reason for the color cast, simply knowing that one of the channels is inappropriately strong is a starting point. A closer examination of the parade scope's graph will also tell you exactly what you can do about it.

In **Figure 4.37**, the bottom of the blue channel's graph is significantly lower than those of the red and green, even though the top of the blue channel is higher (providing the strong bluish highlights for this night scene). This is your cue that the deepest shadows (blacks) of the image are imbalanced, which lends an odd, washed-out look to the image.

Figure 4.37 A low-light image with a color imbalance in the shadows.

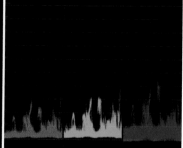

Keep in mind that balancing shadows using the Lift control can be a tricky operation that, if not done precisely, can cause more problems than it solves if you inadvertently add a different color imbalance to the blackest parts of your image.

Most scopes have an option to zoom into the graph so you can get a closer look at how closely the shadows of the parade scope waveforms are aligned, making it a lot easier to do this critical black balancing.

In **Figure 4.38**, we can clearly see after zooming into the parade scope that the blue channel is weaker in the shadows than the red and green channels.

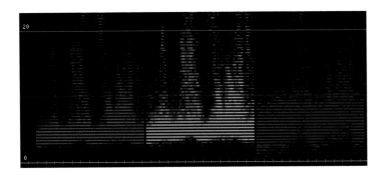

Figure 4.38 Zooming into the bottom of the parade scope makes it easier to align the blacks of the image.

RGB PARADE VS. RGB OVERLAY

An RGB parade scope and an RGB overlay scope both display the same information, but they differ in their presentation. As we've seen previously, parade scopes display discrete waveforms of information side by side so that you can see each waveform independently and in its entirety. Overlay scopes, on the other hand, superimpose all three waveforms over one another so that you can see how they align more interactively.

Which is better is completely a matter of preference, but here's a hint on how to spot where the red, green, and blue waveforms line up, and where they don't, on an overlay scope: Modern overlay scopes usually have the option of displaying each of the three color-channel waveforms with the color they represent and the three graphs combined additively (**Figure 4.39**). This means that, where the three waveforms align perfectly, the resulting traces in the graph turn white (since equal red + green + blue = white).

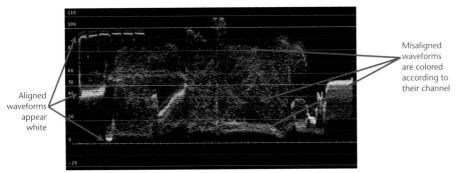

Figure 4.39 RGB overlay scopes.

Aligned waveforms appear white

Misaligned waveforms are colored according to their channel

Many software scopes provide the option to turn color on and off, on the premise that the colors can be a distraction in a darkened suite. While parade scopes can still be read with the graph colors turned off, color is essential to being able to make sense of an RGB overlay scope, so make sure it's turned on.

Where the waveforms don't line up, the discrete colors of each waveform are more or less clearly visible in the region of image tonality where the incongruity occurs, making offsets more visible.

RGB HISTOGRAMS

Different applications also present individual histograms for the red, green, and blue channels. Similar to a luma histogram, each color channel histogram shows a statistical analysis of the number of pixels at each level of image tonality. The results are somewhat similar to the RGB parade scope in terms of seeing the comparative strength of each color channel in the highlights, midtones, and shadows of an image.

Unlike the RGB parade scope, there is no way to correlate an individual feature or subject within the frame to the rises or dips on any of the color channel histograms. Large rises indicate a lot of color channel pixels at that range of image tonality, while dips indicate fewer color channel pixels.

Depending on the application, RGB histograms can be either presented in parade mode or overlaid over one another. Sometimes histograms are oriented vertically, as in FilmLight Baselight (**Figure 4.40**, left), while other applications present them horizontally (Figure 4.40, right).

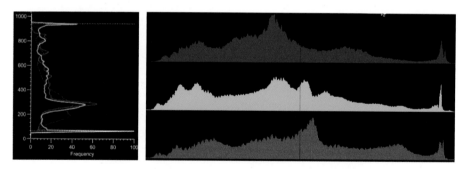

Figure 4.40 Two RGB histogram graphs compared. FilmLight Baselight is on the left; SpeedGrade is on the right.

RGB histograms are very good, however, at allowing you to compare the overall strengths of each color channel within each zone of image tonality.

USING COLOR BALANCE CONTROLS

Whatever your intention, there are two ways you can manipulate the overall color within an image using the primary color correction interface of most applications. You can use color balance controls, or you can use curves (covered later in this chapter).

Color balance controls are a vital means of making adjustments. Once you master how they work, you can quickly solve a wide range of common issues relating to color temperature, white balance, and unexpected hues within your images.

As you'll see in the following sections, color balance operations rely on the fact that complementary colors cancel one another out. This phenomenon is what makes it possible to selectively eliminate an unwanted color cast from an image by dragging or rolling a color balance control toward the color that's complementary to it. It also allows us to introduce warmth or coldness that wasn't in the shot to begin with, for creative purposes.

Depending on the application you're using, color balance controls can be manipulated in several ways. The more you understand how color balance controls affect the image, the better you'll be able to control your corrections, targeting them to the specific areas of the image that need adjustment.

ONSCREEN INTERFACES FOR COLOR BALANCE

Nearly every color correction application prominently features a set of color balance controls (you can see four of them in **Figure 4.41**). Most feature three or four controls, usually presented as a set of onscreen color wheels, that provide a graphical interface for rebalancing the red, green, and blue color components of a video clip to remove or introduce color casts in specific portions of the image.

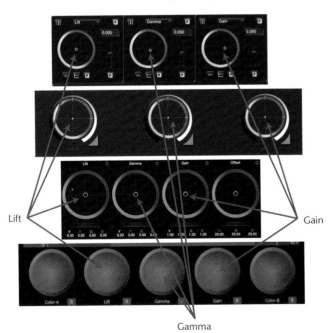

Lift

Gain

Gamma

Figure 4.41 Color balance controls for different applications, compared. Top to bottom: FilmLight Baselight, Assimilate Scratch, DaVinci Resolve, Adobe SpeedGrade.

Other grading applications may feature five onscreen color wheels (**Figure 4.42**), or they may allow you to assign the three onscreen color wheels to three different ranges of image lightness or tonality, for a total of nine color wheel assignments.

Figure 4.42 Five-way color balance controls featured in SGO Mistika and the Shadow, Midtone, and Highlight buttons that let you make adjustments to nine different zones of image tonality shown in SpeedGrade.

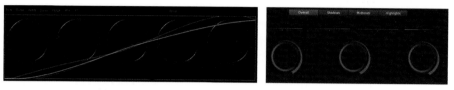

The procedure for making an adjustment using a color balance control is pretty much the same no matter what application you're using: Click anywhere inside the color wheel that is the outer boundary of each control (you usually don't have to click right on the handle or indicator that shows what the balance is) and drag.

The color balance handle or indicator moves from the center détente position that indicates no correction is taking place, into the direction you drag, toward one color and away from its complement on the outside of the color wheel. Professional color correction applications let you see the correction while you're making it on your broadcast display and within the video scopes.

Interestingly, most current color correction applications feature color balance controls that distribute the angle of hue correction in the same way as the vectorscope. With time, this distribution of hues will become second nature to you as you grade more and more shots so that your ability to both read the vectorscope and manipulate the color balance controls will become a matter of instinct and muscle memory.

OTHER ONSCREEN COLOR BALANCE CONTROLS

There are usually other ways of manipulating color balance besides the color wheels. Many, but not all, onscreen interfaces provide numeric controls for making specific adjustments. Keep in mind that many color correction interfaces express numeric controls as floating-point numbers to many decimal places of precision.

If you're making a creative adjustment, you're probably better off using an onscreen slider while watching your broadcast display. However, if you're trying to match one parameter of an adjustment specifically to another parameter, numeric entry can be a benefit for copying and pasting values from one correction to another.

Another method for making specific color balance adjustments is to use either keyboard modifiers (press a key while dragging a color balance control) or dedicated onscreen sliders to alter only a single parameter of color balance. Common options include the following:

- **Hue Balance Only:** Lets you keep the current distance of the handle/indicator locked while you rotate the handle/indicator around the center of the control to change the hue of the correction

- **Color Temperature:** Locks the angle of hue to the orange/cyan vector while allowing you to drag the handle/indicator closer to or farther from the center détente position

- **Adjustment Amount:** Locks the angle of hue to whatever the current angle happens to be, while allowing you to drag the handle/indicator closer to or farther from the center détente position

Methods for making these adjustments vary by application, so be sure to check your documentation for how to perform these operations.

COLOR BALANCE CONTROLS IN DAVINCI RESOLVE

Notable exceptions to the typical color balance wheel interface are the *level indicators* used in the Primaries palette of DaVinci Resolve (**Figure 4.43**). Three sets of four vertical sliders show adjustments to the YRGB channel controls corresponding to Lift, Gamma, and Gain. These are intended primarily as visual indicators for adjustments made using the trackballs and contrast wheels of a control surface.

When altered, the colored interior "handles" show each control's offset from the center détente position, with the height of each handle showing the magnitude of the adjustment (above the center is positive, below is negative). To accommodate large adjustments, the overall framing of the interior handles relative to the slider border changes dynamically to fit the numeric adjustments being shown.

These controls can be manipulated using the mouse, allowing individual YRGB channel adjustment for Lift, Gamma, and Gain. Drag any of these sliders up to increase or down to decrease the corresponding contrast or color channel.

Double-click the numeric value appearing beneath a slider to reset it to the détente value.

Center-clicking and dragging the Lift, Gamma, and Gain controls is identical to using the control surface master ring to adjust all three values simultaneously by the same amount.

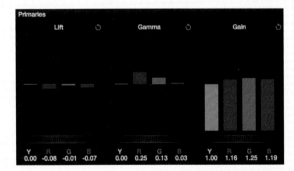

Figure 4.43 The alternate color balance control sliders used by DaVinci Resolve.

ADJUSTING COLOR BALANCE USING A CONTROL SURFACE

It's mentioned frequently in this book, but the advantages control surfaces provide for color balance cannot be overstated. The ability to quickly adjust one control relative to another lets you implement many of the interactions covered later in this chapter to make very detailed corrections.

Also, the ergonomic benefits, in terms of operator comfort, are a big deal. It's not that you can't work using a mouse-based interface alone, but the "mouse-claw" you'll develop after hundreds of click-and-drag adjustments will make the price of a dedicated control surface seem pretty reasonable after a while.

The three color balance controls typically correspond to the three trackballs found on most control surfaces. For example, the JLCooper Eclipse at the left of **Figure 4.44** has three trackballs that correspond to the Shadow, Midtone, and Highlight controls.

Figure 4.44 Control surface trackballs that correspond to the onscreen color balance controls. On the left is the JLCooper Eclipse; on the right is the DaVinci Resolve.

Some control surfaces have more trackballs. The DaVinci Resolve control surface, shown on the right in Figure 4.44, has a fourth trackball that can be used for Log grading controls, moving windows, adjusting control points on curves, and other things.

AUTOMATIC COLOR BALANCING

Before going into manual color balancing, it's worth mentioning that most color correction applications provide one of two methods for performing automatic color balancing. Automatic color balancing can be quick to use in instances where you're having a difficult time identifying the exact nature of a color cast, and auto color balance controls are usually designed to give you a solid neutral starting point for further manual adjustments to a particular color balance control.

AN AUTO-BALANCE BUTTON

The first method usually involves nothing more than clicking an appropriately named button. With this method of automatic color correction, the application automatically samples the three darkest and lightest parts of each color channel, on the premise that these correspond to black and white in the image. If they're misaligned, an automatic calculation is made using the equivalent of the Shadows and Highlights color balance controls, and the correction is applied to the image.

In many cases, the contrast of the image is also stretched or compressed automatically to fit into the maximum and minimum allowable range from reference black at 0 percent/IRE/mV to reference white at 100 percent/IRE (700 mV). The results are usually fine, but you can sometimes run into problems if the sampled parts of the waveform don't actually correspond to true black and white values, in which case you'll get unexpected results.

MANUAL SAMPLING FOR AUTOMATIC CORRECTION

The second method of automatic balancing is more hands-on, but the results are usually more predictable. Once you have identified which part of the image's tonal range a color cast belongs to, you usually click the equivalent of an eyedropper for the Shadows, Midtones, or Highlights controls and then click a feature that's supposed to be a clean, neutral white, black, or gray in your picture to make an automatic adjustment to that tonal region of the image.

> **NOTE**
> Truly neutral grays are the most difficult features to find in a typical clip, so you'll want to be careful. If you don't click a feature of the midtones that's truly gray, you will introduce a completely different kind of color cast to the image.

THERE'S NO SUBSTITUTE FOR MANUAL COLOR BALANCING

The manual method, which is ultimately more flexible (especially if you're not planning on making a completely neutral correction), is to adjust the color balance controls for the Gain, Lift, and Gamma by hand, usually by dragging the color balance control in the direction of the color that's complementary to that of the unwanted color cast.

This book focuses mainly on the manual method of making adjustments. The beauty of manual color balancing is that you can correct an overzealous color cast as aggressively or as gently as possible, making a deliberate choice about whether to neutralize it completely, preserve part of it, or introduce a completely different color balance of your own.

Also, as we've seen in numerous examples, our perception of color within a scene is often at odds with the strict numerical hue and saturation of the image components. Computer applications generally can't take such perceptual quirks into account, which makes your eyeball the best judge of what "looks right."

COLOR BALANCE EXPLAINED

When you manipulate a color balance control, you're simultaneously raising or lowering all three color channels. Every time you adjust a color balance control, you're either boosting one color channel at the expense of lowering the other two channels or raising two channels while lowering the third. It's simply not possible to boost all three color channels, nor would you want to, because simultaneously boosting all three channels is the same as brightening the image with a Master Offset control.

To see this effect in action, try this exercise:

1   Examine the parade scope. You see a trio of flat graphs at 50 percent/IRE (**Figure 4.45**). Any time you see three equal graphs in the parade scope, you know the image is completely desaturated.

Figure 4.45 The original gray test image, with three equal color channels.

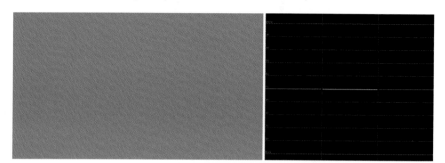

2   Drag the Gamma color balance control away from the center détente position toward red, which causes the reds graph to shoot up toward the top and the green and blue graphs to move down together (**Figure 4.46**).

Figure 4.46 The adjustment described in step 2.

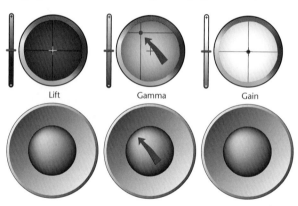

Lift   Gamma   Gain

The gray field turns red (**Figure 4.47**).

Figure 4.47 The results of the adjustment in step 2.

3 Now, drag the color balance control toward a hue that's between cyan and blue to lower the red channel while boosting both the green and blue channels simultaneously, if unevenly (**Figure 4.48**).

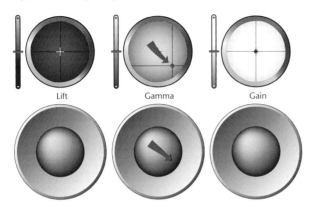

Lift   Gamma   Gain

Figure 4.48 The adjustment described in step 3.

As you move the control, the three color channels redistribute themselves based on this new direction, turning the field bluish (**Figure 4.49**).

Figure 4.49 The results of the adjustment in step 3.

As you can see, dragging a color balance control into a particular direction simultaneously rebalances all three color channels based on the direction of hue in which you move the control.

COLOR BALANCE CONTROL OVERLAP

The power of three-way color balance controls is that they let you make individual adjustments to the portions of an image that fall into the shadows, midtones, and highlights tonal zones.

These tonal zones are based on the luma component of the image. In other words:

- The Lift color balance control affects all portions of the image that correspond to a specific range of the lowest luma values in that image.

- The Gamma control affects all portions of the image that correspond to a range of middle luma values in the image.

- The Gain color balance control affects all portions of the image corresponding to high luma values above a specific range in the image.

Figure 4.50 shows this relationship visually using a false color representation to show how the luma channel corresponds to the lightest highlights (blue), the darkest shadows (green), and the range of midtones (red).

Figure 4.50 It can be difficult to discern the three zones of image tonality that correspond to shadows, midtones, and highlights with the color still in the image. Stripping away the color reveals the lightness of everything within the frame, and a false color representation shows the extremes of each tonal zone.

Chroma+Luma

Luma only (used to define tonal zones)

■ Highlights

■ Midtones

■ Shadows

False color approximation of tonal zones

> **NOTE**
>
> Color balance controls in RGB processing operations will have an effect on image saturation as well. For example, eliminating an extreme color cast in an image typically results in lower average levels in all three color channels, which reduces saturation. This is easily fixed by boosting overall saturation, covered later in this chapter.

The regions of the image that each of the three color balance controls affect are so dependent on the luma channel that any adjustments to the luma channel correspondingly affect how the color balance controls work. For this reason, it's a good idea to make any dramatic contrast adjustments that are necessary first, before moving on to the color of your image.

Naturally, there will be a certain amount of interactivity between color and contrast adjustments, with one set of adjustments affecting the other. This is yet another reason why control surfaces are a time-saver, as they allow rapid and often simultaneous adjustment of multiple color and contrast parameters.

Figure 4.51 is an oversimplification, however. In most professional color correction applications, the three tonal zones overlap broadly and fall off very smoothly, so you can make large adjustments without incurring artifacts such as aliased edges or solarized color that can be the result of a hard transition (or shelf) at the boundaries of affected tonality.

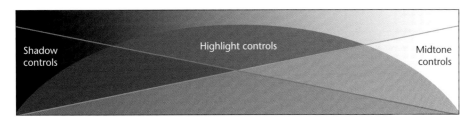

Figure 4.51 The overlapping regions of influence for each color balance control. The height of the Shadow, Midtone, and Highlight graphs corresponds to the amount of influence each control has on the overlapping luma levels.

Furthermore, these broad overlapping zones guarantee interactions among adjustments made with each of the three color balance controls. While at first these interactions may seem like an inconvenience, they're actually essential to exercising fine color control.

Exactly how the color balance of each control overlaps differs from application to application (**Figure 4.52** shows how the overlaps look in FilmLight Baselight's Region Graph). Some applications even allow you to customize these overlaps, setting them to whatever your working preferences happen to be.

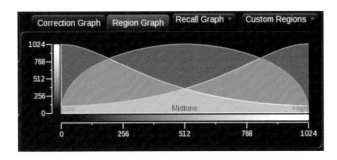

Figure 4.52 The Region Graph in FilmLight Baselight that shows the overlap among the three color balance controls. This interface allows these regions to be customized.

These differences in tonal overlap often account for the differences in "feel" between different color correction applications and plug-ins. If you're used to working using one application's approach, switching to another may throw you off a bit until you get used to the new default overlaps.

THE OFFSET CONTROL AND PRINTER POINTS

The Offset color balance control (sometimes called Master or Global) is so named because it rebalances color by *offsetting* each color channel up or down, basically adding or subtracting an adjustment value to move each channel. In the following example, an Offset adjustment is used to correct a color cast due to incorrect white balance (**Figure 4.53**).

Figure 4.53 The RGB channels before and after a simple Offset adjustment, which raises and lowers each channel in its entirety to correct the image.

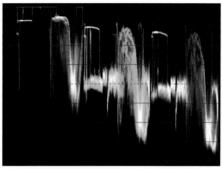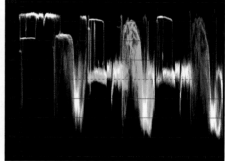

All of the techniques described later for balancing colors apply equally to the Offset control. Keep in mind that Offset rebalances the entire range of image tonality all at once. Because offset adjusts the entirety of each color channel, it's a time-saving and useful control for images where there's a huge color cast running from the shadows all the way through the highlights. Furthermore, with color casts that are this severe, the linear way in which this technique rebalances the signal may give you a more natural-looking result than separate adjustments to lift, gamma, and gain, depending on the image and on what you're trying to achieve.

Offset is related to *printer points* controls because both do the same thing: offset each color component of the image (**Figure 4.54**). However, the Offset color balance control adjusts all three color channels at once, allowing you to rebalance the color throughout an image with a single control or track ball. By contrast, printer points provide either sliders or plus and minus buttons (a more classic configuration) that let you adjust each color channel independently, one at a time.

Printer points controls are valuable for colorists and cinematographers who are used to working with the printer points system employed for color timing film (described in more detail in Chapter 9). As originally used by color analyzers such as the Hazeltine, the printer points dials of a color analyzer adjust the individual levels of the Red, Green, and Blue channels in discrete increments called *printer points*. Each point is a fraction of one *f*-stop (a doubling of light in the scale used to measure and adjust exposure).

Figure 4.54 Offset controls in DaVinci Resolve provide functionality similar to printer points controls.

Various applications use different fractions, and each printer point can be anywhere from 1/7 to 1/12 of an *f*-stop, depending on how the analyzer is configured. Most systems use a range of 50 printer points for each color component and for density, with 25 being the neutral détente for each control.

Working digitally, printer points controls make a uniform adjustment to the entire color channel, irrespective of image tonality, by adding or subtracting the adjustment value. Some applications even emulate the nature of the optical filtration used by color analyzers so that raising the Red printer points control doesn't actually boost the red; instead, it removes red, causing the image to shift to cyan (which is the secondary of green and blue). In this case, to increase red you actually need to *decrease* the Red printer points control.

FIVE-WAY AND NINE-WAY COLOR CONTROL OVERLAP

Some applications go beyond the lift/gamma/gain model of color balance control to provide five and even nine sets of controls, for even greater specificity in the adjustments you make.

For example, SGO Mistka provides an option for five-way color balance controls, with separate adjustments for Black, Shadows, Midtones, Highlights, and White.

These five color balance controls work together to enable targeted adjustments to the image in various zones of exposure, just like other variations on these controls. However, they overlap in a very different way.

Other applications, such as Lustre and SpeedGrade, use the same set of three-way controls provided for lift, gamma, and gain adjustments, but give you an additional three sets of controls over shadows, midtones, and highlights so you can divide each of the main tonal regions of an image into three subregions, allowing you to make very fine color balance and contrast adjustments to nine different tonal regions. In other words, you can adjust the offset, gamma, and gain of lift independently of the offset, gamma, and gain of gamma and gain, as shown in **Figure 4.55**.

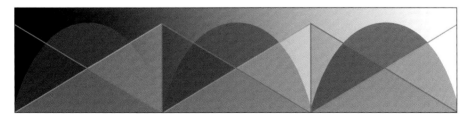

Figure 4.55 An approximation of the specific control that lift/gamma/gain for each zone of lift, gamma, and gain image tonality gives you. Different programs employ differing tonal zone overlaps, so this illustration is not specific to any application.

These types of overlapping multizone controls let you bend the video signal in ways that are similar to the kinds of adjustments you can make using curves but have the advantage of being operated by the rings and trackballs of a conventional control surface.

For example, using the Midtone color balance control to add a bit of blue to the shadows results in a wide portion of image tonality being affected (**Figure 4.56**).

Figure 4.56 Using the Gamma control to add blue to the image adds blue indiscriminately across a wide portion of image tonality.

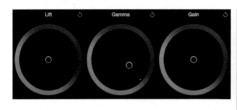 

Using SpeedGrade's ability to adjust the Gain color balance control of the Shadows zone, on the other hand, lets you make a much more subtle change. This control targets a much narrower zone of image tonality, such that you can add a bit of blue just to the lighter shadows (**Figure 4.57**).

Figure 4.57 Using the Gamma color balance control within the Midtone zone in Adobe SpeedGrade to add selective blue to the light shadows of the image.

If you're making large adjustments for bolder changes, you may find that a few control points on a curve control work faster. Also, if you want to insert color or make a correction to a narrow zone of image tonality, you can also use the Luma qualifier of a secondary operation (covered in Chapters 5 and 11) to isolate a custom tonal zone for correction using the nearest corresponding Lift/Gamma/Gain color balance control.

COLOR DECISION LISTS (CDLs)

In an effort to rein in the operational differences between various color correction applications, the American Society of Cinematographers (ASC) has spearheaded an effort to standardize primary color and contrast adjustments. The ASC Technology Committee responsible for drafting the Color Decision List (CDL) combines the expertise of leading cinematographers and film/video engineers in an effort to define and extend the CDL for use by the production and postproduction communities alike.

The reason this is important to know is that some applications provide a "CDL-compliant" mode that sets the color and contrast controls to act as the CDL specification dictates. Understanding this specification helps you to understand how to work in this mode.

The dual purposes of the CDL are to encourage predictability of operation from application to application and to facilitate project exchange among different color correction applications.

Currently, the CDL governs the following grading parameters, assuming an RGB rendering application:

- **Slope** (for contrast this is similar to gain; for color this is a multiply operation)
- **Offset** (for contrast this is similar to lift; for color this is an add operation)
- **Power** (for contrast this is similar to *gamma*; for color this is an *equal power* operation)
  Using these three parameters (sometimes referred to as SOP), a contrast and color balancing operation applied to a particular shot is governed by the following equation:

Output = (Input * Slope + Offset)

If this seems limited, it is. The CDL doesn't account for customizable color balance zones, or more exotic controls like RGB or luma curves, contrast or color temperature sliders, or highlight and shadow saturation controls. Nor does the CDL have a means for describing secondary color correction operations such as hue curves, HSL qualification, power windows or vignettes, or blending modes.

However, the current purpose of the CDL is to govern primary corrections, for which it is well suited. Furthermore, the CDL is a work in progress and will certainly evolve over time to take more parameters into consideration. For example, additional math has also been defined as of version 1.2 of the CDL specification to account for control over SAT, or a commonly agreed upon definition of RGB saturation (SOPS).

COLOR BALANCE OVERLAP IN ACTION

Despite the overlap described in the previous section, you'd be surprised at how targeted your changes can be. To examine how these controls overlap, we'll make adjustments using a simple grayscale ramp test pattern.

The following example demonstrates how the Lift, Gamma, and Gain controls' areas of influence overlap while you make corrections.

1 Adjust the Gain color balance control to push it toward blue and then adjust the Lift control to push it toward red; you'll get something like the result shown in **Figure 4.58**.

Figure 4.58 A grayscale ramp with the shadows pushed toward red and the highlights pushed toward blue.

When adjusting a grayscale ramp using any one of the color balance controls, you'll see the corresponding region become tinted.

2 Next, adjust the Gamma color balance control, pushing it toward green, in order to examine the resulting overlap in **Figure 4.59**.

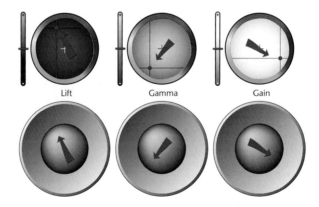

Figure 4.59 The adjustments made in steps 1 and 2. All three color balance controls are set to strongly different hues in order to examine their overlapping effects on a grayscale test image.

This new green adjustment smoothly blends into the red and blue zones, pushing them back to the extremes of shadow and highlight within the image (**Figure 4.60**).

Figure 4.60 The result of pushing the midtones toward green. The overlap of each of the three color balance adjustments can be seen clearly.

If you look carefully at the area of overlap, you may start to notice a stripe of cyan falling between the green and blue adjustments. This stripe makes sense when you remember that cyan is an additive mix of green and blue.

This is clearly an artificial example; with real-world images and subtle corrections, you won't often notice this effect. However, when you make large adjustments involving two color balance controls, you may see some unexpected interactions of this sort, so keep a sharp eye out.

MAKING A SIMPLE COLOR BALANCE CORRECTION

Now that we've gone over how color balance controls work, let's look at a simple example of how you would use these controls to make a relatively simple correction.

The shot in the following example exhibits a clear warm/orange color cast. This could be because of an incorrect white balance of the camera or simply a creative decision made during the shoot. The client has expressed a desire to ease off the warmth, so that's the correction you'll be making.

1 Take a look at the Waveform Monitor. Your first order of business is to adjust the contrast to fit within the acceptable limits of 0–100 percent/IRE (**Figure 4.61**).

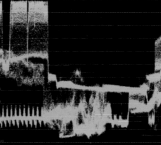

Figure 4.61 The original image, with a warm/orange color cast.

2 Additionally, look at the vectorscope in Figure 4.61. You'll see the truly mono-chromatic nature of the image. The overly warm lighting of the room serves to exaggerate the already orange tones of the brown jacket and the flesh tone of the actor. There are no spikes of color stretching toward any other hue in the vectorscope.

That's not necessarily a problem, but what does look a bit odd is the extent to which the entire graph is off center. Judging from the amount of white in the frame (the lampshade and lamp base), there ought to be at least some part of the vectorscope graph that sits directly on the center of the crosshairs, but the graph is almost entirely to the upper left of the crosshairs, as shown in **Figure 4.62**.

Figure 4.62 The lopsided nature of the vectorscope graph confirms that the color cast is fairly severe. Very little of the graph touches the center, and the entire wave-form stretches toward orange (the additive combination of red and yellow).

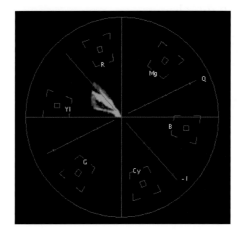

3 Examine the RGB parade scope. It's easy to see that the top of each waveform (corresponding to the blown-out window) is clipped off and thus relatively equal. The bottoms of the waveform are fairly level with one another (at least, level enough).

The biggest visible inequality here is right within the middle. The segments of the waveforms that are called out in **Figure 4.63** correspond to the wall.

Figure 4.63 The circled waveform sections correspond to the color of the wall.

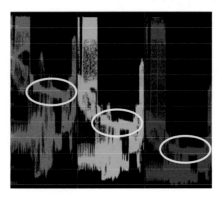

Even though the wall isn't pure white (a question put to the client revealed that the wall is actually a warmish/yellowish "antique" white), this is a fairly extreme inequality of nearly 30 percent, far more than at either the top or the bottom of the parade scope waveforms.

Having spotted the changes you need to make, it's time to do the correction. The fact that the color channel inequality lies in the middle of the RGB parade scope graph is a good clue that the best way to correct for it is to adjust the Gamma color balance control. The fact that you can see the imbalance in the vectorscope as being toward orange tells you that the best correction to make is to pull the midtones *away* from orange—or *toward* the complementary color to orange, which is a hue between cyan and blue.

4 Correct the contrast by lowering the Gain control until the top of the luma waveform touches 100 percent, while raising the Gamma control to keep the lightness of the midtones where it was to begin with. Lightening the midtones makes it necessary to lower the Lift control to restore some density to the shadows, thus keeping the appearance of a high contrast ratio even though you've compressed the highlights a bit.

5 Next, act upon the analysis you made in step 3, and drag the Gamma color balance control toward a cyan/blue split (in other words, between these two hues), as shown in **Figure 4.64**.

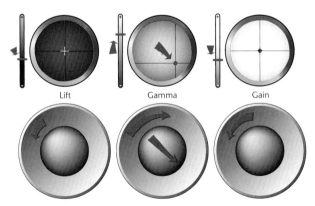

Lift   Gamma   Gain

Figure 4.64 The corrections made in steps 4 and 5.

While you drag the Gamma color balance control toward cyan/blue, keep one eye on the RGB parade scope. What you're trying to do is to balance the middle of the red, green, and blue channels so that they're closer together.

Also pay close attention to the image; you want to make sure you don't overcompensate. Keep in mind that although the lamp base and trim around the window are white, the wall color is not. So if you try to overcompensate, the image will start to look odd. In this case, the correction the client likes the best brings the middle of the red, green, and blue waveforms much closer to one another (**Figure 4.65**).

Figure 4.65 The image after our first set of corrections to the contrast and midtone color balance.

6   Examine the results of these corrections. The image is generally improved; however, there's something funny about it, particularly in the shadows and in the dark regions of the man's beard and hair. Look at the bottom of the waveforms in the parade scope; you can see that the extreme correction you made to the midtones has affected the shadows, and the bottoms of the three waveforms are now very unequal, with exaggerated blue shadows that you don't want.

You can also see that making this adjustment to balance the midtones has reduced the lightness of the image. This is because the correction dropped the levels of red channel to closer match that of the green and blue channels, and the results lowered the luma component, darkening the image.

7   To compensate, you need to raise the Gamma contrast control until the image is as light as it was before and then push the Lift color balance control back toward orange (since you're eliminating a blue/cyan cast in the shadows), as shown in **Figure 4.66**.

Figure 4.66 Adjustments in step 7 to correct the shadows.

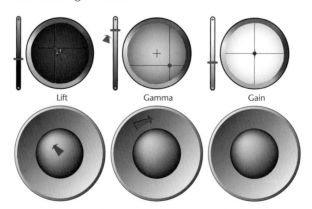

As you make this last adjustment to the color balance of the shadows, keep an eye on the bottoms of the RGB parade scope graphs. You'll know you made a successful adjustment when the bottoms of the red, green, and blue waveforms align as evenly as possible (**Figure 4.67**).

8 Lastly, the process of neutralizing the excessive color cast from the image resulted in a loss of saturation (you dropped the level of all three color channels when you leveled the highlights out), so turn up the overall saturation to compensate for this effect.

When making changes like this, it's easy for you (and the client) to forget what the original "problem" image looked like, since the eye is constantly adapting to the updated state of the image. This is the reason why most color correction applications have some sort of "disable grade" command, so you can get a before and after look at the image, to demonstrate that your correction is a tangible improvement over the original.

CHAPTER 4

Figure 4.67 Top, the original image. Below is the final corrected image, with legalized luma, rebalanced midtones, and corrected shadows.

The image is still warm, but it no longer has all that orange in it. Take a look at the vectorscope in the final correction; you can see that it's much more centered than before, and the overall level of orange saturation has decreased, creating a finer distinction between the colors in the wall, the actor's jacket, and the skin tone of his face and hands (**Figure 4.68**).

Figure 4.68 The vectorscope analysis of the final image. The graph is now more centered and isn't as widely stretched toward orange as it was originally.

This example showed several common strategies of using the video scopes in conjunction with color adjustment controls, not just for *spotting* a color cast but to help you figure out where a particular color cast is most pronounced in order to quickly use the most appropriate control for making a specific correction.

REDUCING THE OVERLAP OF HIGHLIGHT, MIDTONE, AND SHADOW COLOR CORRECTIONS

The previous example demonstrated quite clearly that a correction made in one tonal zone can inadvertently affect portions of the image you'd rather leave alone. In these cases, you will often find yourself making an opposite adjustment to an adjacent color balance control. This may seem counterintuitive, so if you're wondering how this works, take a look at **Figure 4.69**, which uses a simple ramp gradient, so that you can see this effect clearly.

Figure 4.69 The original test image, a ramp gradient with values from 0 to 100 percent.

1 Make a bold correction by dragging the Gain color balance control toward blue (**Figure 4.70**).

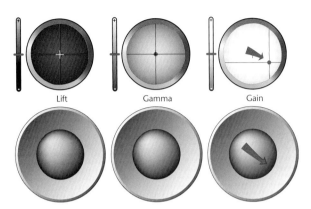

Figure 4.70 The adjustment described in step 1.

As you can see, the blue correction extends well past the midtones and a bit into the shadows (**Figure 4.71**).

Figure 4.71 The result of the adjustment you made in step 1.

There will be plenty of times when you'd want to ease off this correction in the lower midtones of a real-world image.

2 To compensate for this overly wide correction, adjust the Gamma color balance control, dragging it toward yellow, which is the complement of blue, to reduce the blue cast at the lower midtones (**Figure 4.72**).

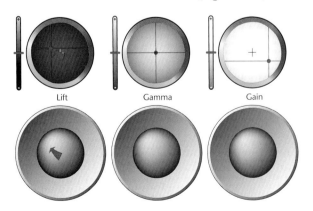

Figure 4.72 The adjustment described in step 2.

As you make this adjustment, you'll see more and more of the darker midtones become a neutral gray once again, while the upper range of the highlights continues to exhibit the original blue correction (**Figure 4.73**).

Figure 4.73 The resulting correction has neutralized the amount of blue in the darker portion of the midtones.

While the typical overlap of color balance controls may initially seem a bit overenthusiastic when it comes to affecting the image, this type of interaction is part of what makes these controls so powerful and quick to use. These kinds of opposing corrections are actually an extremely common way of further targeting corrections in exactly the tonal portion of the image where you need them.

CREATING A DELIBERATE COLOR CAST FOR EFFECT

You're not always going to want to create corrections to eliminate color casts. Deliberate color temperature adjustments can be also added as an audience cue for conveying the time of day or the environment in which the subjects find themselves. For example, audiences fully expect a candlelit scene to be extremely warm, like the image in **Figure 4.74**.

Figure 4.74 An example of a scene with exaggerated warmth in the midtones and highlights reflecting a candlelit scene. Notice that even though there's a deliberate color cast in the image, the shadows remain neutral, providing valuable contrast between the colorfulness of the main character and the cool neutrality of the background.

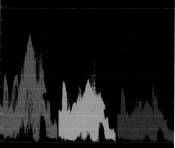

You can play off the audience's expectation of color temperature and change the perceived time of day, or the type of location, by throwing off the white balance and introducing a deliberate color cast.

As you saw in Figure 4.3 at the beginning of this chapter, color casts are also used to introduce mood to a scene. How many times have you heard lighting referred to as "cool" or "warm"? In general, this is the easiest way to discuss the quality of light because it embodies the entire range of lighting we experience in our everyday lives, from the extreme warmth of tungsten bulbs to the extreme cool of overcast sunlight. It's not surprising that these descriptions also tend to dramatize light quality, with warm lighting tending toward the romantic (sunsets, candlelight), and cold lighting signifying discomfort (rainy, overcast days have *literally* cold lighting).

These are huge generalizations, of course, and it's also fun to play lighting against type (cool lighting quality for a hot exterior shot), but it's good to develop a conscious rationale for your use of color temperature as you develop the visual vocabulary of your program.

In the following example, you'll look at three different corrections made to push a scene in three completely different directions:

1 First, examine the RGB parade scope for the original, unaltered shot (**Figure 4.75**).

   It's a well-lit scene. There's good color contrast in the actors clothing and within the background of the scene, and there's good separation between the actors in the foreground and the rest of the background. You can clearly see that the top of the red waveform is a bit taller than that of the green and blue waveforms—enough to let you know that the lighting in the environment is deliberately warm, which is most likely the original intent for the scene.

   When you examine the rest of the RGB waveforms, you'll find that the bottom of all three waveforms align well, so there's no color cast in the shadows. Likewise, the midtones line up, as you'd expect given the warmer highlights, so there's no overt color cast that adversely affects the actors.

   Bottom line, any adjustments you make to this shot are for creativity and not necessity.

 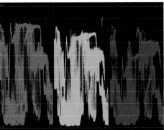

Figure 4.75 The original, unaltered shot.

2 Make the corrections shown in **Figure 4.76** to exaggerate this warmth and give more of a "golden-hour" look to the scene, mimicking the warm,

flattering quality of daylight that is seen in the hour preceding sunset. Because you're affecting the lighting, make the main change to the image using the Gain control.

Figure 4.76 Adjustments made to add warmth to the highlights of the scene, without exaggerating the color of the actors and background.

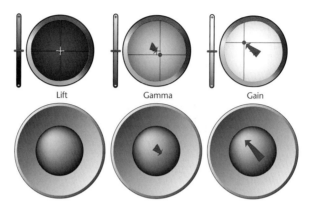

By pushing the Gain color control toward orange and making a small adjustment to the Gamma color control to push it toward the complementary cyan/blue, you can boost the warmth in the highlights without overdoing the orange of the actors' skin tone within the midtones (you don't want them to look like they have a bad spray-on tan).

The result is a warmer, more inviting look (**Figure 4.77**).

Figure 4.77 The visual result of warming up the highlights. Notice the elevated top of the red channel in the RGB parade scope relative to the tops of the green and blue waveforms. Notice also that the middle and bottom of the graphs still align. Notice also that the top of the red waveform remains well within the 100 percent/IRE limit.

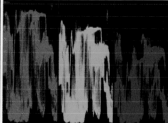

3   Next, make the corrections shown in **Figure 4.78** to cool off the scene, subtly boosting the blue in the highlights.

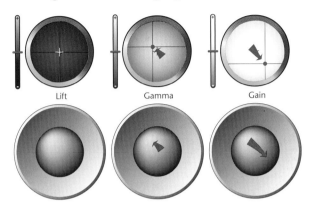

Lift   Gamma   Gain

Figure 4.78 Adjustments made to cool off the highlights of the scene, while trying to keep the actors from turning blue.

Similarly to the previous adjustment, you pushed the Gain color control toward a blue/magenta split in order to boost the blue channel within the highlights. This can be a tricky adjustment, as it's easy to add either too much green or too much red, which would end up adding magenta to the scene.

Since the blue you've added to the highlights can end up making the skin tones of the actors look a bit too pasty, the compensating adjustment of pushing the Gamma color control back toward a complementary orange backs this correction off within the midtones, where the actors are exposed.

The result is more of an overcast noon-time lighting—the scene becomes more sterile and clinical, as shown in **Figure 4.79**. As a side note, neutralizing the color in the highlights has also reduced the white point a bit, which might require a boost to the Gain contrast control.

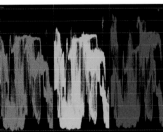

Figure 4.79 The now-cool scene. Notice the depressed red channel and the elevated top of the blue channel in the parade scope.

4 Lastly, make the adjustment shown in **Figure 4.80** to push the color temperature toward the kind of greenish hue you'd see if there were fluorescent fixtures in the scene.

Figure 4.80 Adjustments to add an unpleasant green "fluorescent" cast to the image. You need to apply a complementary adjustment to the midtones to keep the actors from looking nauseated.

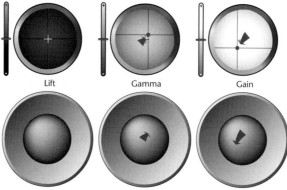

Pushing the Gain just a little (a little goes a long way when you're adding green) toward green elevates the green channel. In this case, it's really necessary to compensate by pushing the Gamma toward magenta (the complementary of green) to minimize the effect of this green tint on the actors' skin tone within the midtones (**Figure 4.81**).

Figure 4.81 The resulting green tint.

The result is a deliberately unflattering, "unaltered" office environment lighting that's guaranteed to put the audience on edge.

BUT WHAT ABOUT MAGENTA?

Despite the wide latitude you have for altering a scene's color temperature for creative intent, there's one direction of the color wheel you'll almost never move into—magenta (unless you're correcting for fluorescent lighting). Not only is magenta not a light source that's found in nature (although sodium vapor lighting comes unflatteringly close), it's a color that most people find immediately disconcerting and unpleasant, as illustrated in **Figure 4.82**, which shows the shot from the previous exercises adjusted toward magenta.

 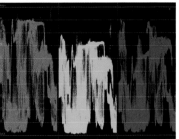

Figure 4.82 Almost nobody likes a magenta color cast in an image, so keep a sharp eye out for any hint of magenta creeping into the picture, especially within the skin tones of people within the scene.

This is particularly tricky as a magenta correction in the highlights is usually the solution to an unwanted greenish cast from fluorescent lighting that was recorded with improper color balance. It's easy, when correcting for the green spike in fluorescent lighting, to overcompensate a tiny bit and end up with too much magenta in someone's face.

Don't worry about this getting by you. Your client will likely be the first to say, "Does she look a little purple to you?"

NOTE

Greenish lighting is mainly a problem for scenes shot with practical fluorescent fixtures that are installed in the shooting location. When you have more time for the shoot, you can employ stage gel sleeves to correct this for existing fluorescent fixtures, or you can use special lighting instruments with electronic ballasts using color temperature-calibrated tubes instead.

USING LOG COLOR CONTROLS

The color balance control functionality described earlier for adjusting lift, gamma, and gain is a classic set of controls for manipulating normalized video images in a video grading environment. The origins of these controls lay in telecine and online tape-to-tape color correction, with the assumption of a BT.709 color space and BT. 1886 gamma profile. In this environment, these controls provide a lot of specific control over the image.

However, as digital intermediate film grading workflows emerged, they were accompanied by the need to grade logarithmically (log) encoded digital film scans, typically in the Cineon and DPX formats, in such a way as to fulfill two distinct requirements:

- First, it was necessary to map a set of image adjustment controls to the mathematical requirements of log-encoded media formats, with their compressed distribution of color and contrast image data.

- Second, it was necessary to limit the colorist to using only image-adjustment operations that matched what could be done by optical film printers. Imposing this restriction ensured that the digital colorist couldn't make adjustments that weren't compatible with those made by the color timer in projects that mixed digital grading with the photochemical process of color timing.

One of the pioneers of log grading is Lustre, itself originally a product named Colossus, developed by Colorfront and later acquired by Autodesk; it was used extensively on *The Lord of the Rings* trilogy, among many other films. Lustre has a dedicated Log grading mode that sets the Lustre interface to use these controls exclusively.

Another pioneer of grading using Log controls is FilmLight's Baselight, which has two different types of grading layers available: video and film. The Video layer exposes the lift/gamma/gain-style controls expected by the telecine professional. However, the Film layer exposes the Log grading controls of Exposure, Contrast, and Shadow/Midtone/Highlight (**Figure 4.83**). These film-style controls were first developed as part of an in-house compositing and finishing tool at the Computer Film Company, developers of which went on to found FilmLight and create Grader2, an early version of Baselight, to support work on *Chicken Run* in 2000.

Figure 4.83 Primary controls found in the Film Grade operator of FilmLight Baselight. The basic Exposure/Contrast/Saturation controls are shown, but log-oriented Shadow/Midtone/Highlight controls are also available on a second tab.

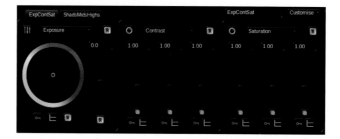

The original point of Log-style grading was to emulate, with digital tools, the color timing process in such a way as to enable digital colorists to create grades that wouldn't stray too far from a color-timed result. Even as digital intermediate grading went from being the exception to the rule, Log controls capable of working with native log-encoded media remained valuable for workflows where film output was expected.

Now, of course, many other grading applications including DaVinci Resolve and SGO Mistika support Log-style grading, though it's tempting to wonder why, given that film acquisition has become less and less common and true digital intermediate workflows for film print distribution are going the way of the dinosaurs.

The reason Log grading controls are still relevant is the increasing number of log-encoded camera acquisition formats, including camera raw formats that are debayered to a log-encoded result. It turns out that logarithmic encoding is still quite useful for efficiently moving a wide latitude of image data into a grading application's image processing pipeline in order to achieve a reasonable balance between image quality and data throughput/processor performance.

Additionally, when used in conjunction with true log-encoded media, Log controls encourage a very specific grading workflow that, while limiting in one sense, enable a creative aesthetic that's tied to the history of cinema.

SETTING UP A LOG GRADE

As discussed in Chapter 3, Log controls are designed to work with the peculiarly compressed mathematical distribution of log-encoded image data. To work in this way, it's important you use the log-style Shadow/Midtone/Highlight color balance controls to adjust the prenormalized state of the image, *before* the normalizing LUT or adjustment that you're applying in a second operation. Otherwise, your Log control adjustments won't work the way they should. For more information, see Chapter 3.

ADJUSTING OFFSET COLOR BALANCE

As always, you want to make sure you adjust the contrast of an image prior to adjusting its color, and this is even more true of Log controls. Then, the foundation of your log grade as far as color goes is a simple Offset adjustment. This may seem too good to be true, given everything you've learned about making color balance adjustments within specific zones of image tonality, but when working on competently shot images, a simple offset adjustment can give you a good, clean result that cures color imbalance from the shadows through the highlights.

Another reason to start with Offset first is that it's more creative in nature. Veteran colorist Mike Most, who's written of the advantages of log grading online and who was generous enough to discuss Log grading with me at great length, suggests that beginning your grade on a foundation of log-style controls may yield more inherently cinematic results. The reason given for this is simple: You can create nonlinear signal adjustments with Lift/Gamma/Gain controls that would never happen to a traditionally color-timed film, which is a visual cue the audience can spot.

The reason for this difference is that the principal controls of Offset (master color balance), Exposure (master offset), and Contrast/Pivot make *linear* adjustments that affect all three color channels evenly throughout the entire tonal range of the signal. This reflects the relatively straightforward adjustments that are made using a color analyzer's red, green, blue, and density controls but still gives you more control then any color timer ever had via Contrast and Pivot.

The following example shows this workflow in the context of a moodily lit and shot image of a woman contemplating the choices she's made. The client would like a naturalistic treatment in keeping with the project's "70s independent film" aesthetic, which you might take to mean no crushed blacks, no harsh whites, and a fairly linear color balance throughout the tonal range, where possible.

CHAPTER 4

1 As usual, you'll normalize the log-encoded clip using a LUT, or manually, in order to get the desired starting point for your grade (**Figure 4.84**). You'll want to do this in a layer or node after or on top of one or two initial adjustments you'll use for grading, depending on how your application is set up.

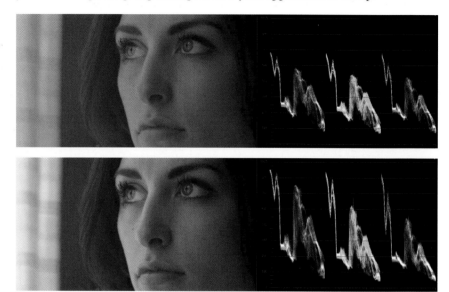

Figure 4.84 A CinemaDNG clip shot with the BMD Cinema Camera debayered as log-encoded media and after normalizing with a corresponding LUT from Blackmagic Design.

2 Make any necessary contrast adjustments as an operation *before* the normalization operation, in this case lowering Master Offset to the desired black point and using the Contrast and Pivot controls to expand contrast to push up the highlights of the signal to indicate sunlight streaming in through the window (**Figure 4.85**). On some control surfaces, such as the DaVinci Control Surface used for Resolve, Master Offset is mapped to a ring control around a fourth trackball.

Figure 4.85 The image after making master Offset and contrast adjustments to a correction inserted prior to the LUT operation.

3 In this case, stretching contrast has made the image extremely warm, but this is supposed to be a noon-day image. Consequently, the client would like a more neutral treatment, with natural skin tones. This can be achieved by

making an adjustment to the Offset color balance control (using a remapping of one of the existing trackballs, a fourth trackball, or an onscreen control). When making this kind of adjustment, a tip is to make your adjustment so that the dominant subject of the scene—a person's skin tone, the blue of a sky, or the green of foliage—looks the way you want it to look (**Figure 4.86**).

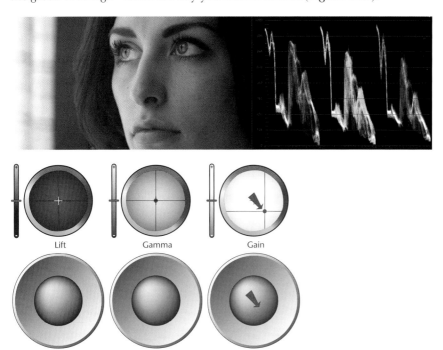

Figure 4.86 The image after a simple color balance correction pulling the Offset control toward blue to neutralize the extreme warmth.

Because the Offset control simply raises or lowers each of the three color channels in their entirety to rebalance the image, the theory is that once you correct a known feature, such as skin tone, the rest of the image will likely fall right into line (**Figure 4.87**).

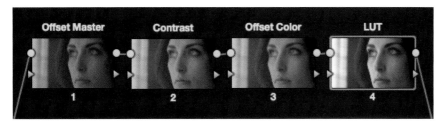

Figure 4.87 A set of nodes explicitly organized and labeled to show you one possible way of grading log media to exercise exact control over the image, in a deliberately restrained manner.

This order of operations is illustrated via a series of individually labeled nodes in DaVinci Resolve. Keep in mind that you don't need to create separate nodes or layers for each operation (unless you like being insanely organized). In particular, since in DaVinci Resolve the LUT is *last* inside of a node's internal order of operations, you can apply a LUT and make the Offset Master, Contrast, and Offset Color adjustments all within a single node. Figure 4.87, however, shows the node's internal order of operation artificially externalized.

The result, assuming you want a naturalistic grade, can be a simple color balance that lacks the kind of oversaturation in shadows and highlights that can give away a video image where you've independently adjusted the shadows and highlights. Again, Offset is similar to the printer points adjustments that color timers used for decades to balance films, and if you're careful and grading competently shot material, the results can be remarkably cinematic in their simplicity.

USING SHADOW/MIDTONE/HIGHLIGHT CONTROLS

Of course, sometimes you'll end up contaminating the color of the highlights and shadows when making an Offset adjustment, especially when you deviate from a natural treatment of the image as it was, to create an exaggerated color balance. For example, if you're grading an actress with very pale skin tone and you decide to add some life and saturation to her skin, you can end up exaggerating color throughout the rest of the image as well.

In the following example, rather than giving life to the skin tone, the client wants more of a deathly pallor to the lighting scheme illuminating the zombie attack (**Figure 4.88**). The media is log-encoded, and following the workflow of the previous section, you use the Offset color balance control to put some green into the lighting.

Figure 4.88 Before and after adding green via the Offset color balance control. The shadows are contaminated with green as a result.

As a result, there's green in the shadows as well. However, in these cases, your grading application's Shadow/Midtone/Highlight color balance controls are there to help you by allowing more specific adjustments that take into account the unique tonal characteristics of log-encoded media. **Figure 4.89** shows an approximation of how the default ranges of the Shadow, Midtone, and Highlight controls divide the tonal range of a log-encoded image.

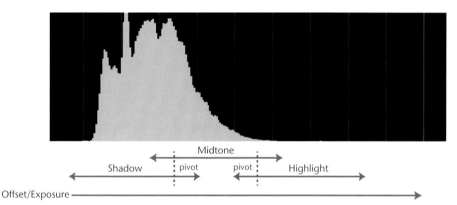

Figure 4.89 An approximation of how the Shadow, Midtone, and Highlight controls affect tonal zones based on the original log-encoded contrast for the purposes of color balancing.

As you can see, when used with a log-encoded image, the color interactions between each adjustment overlap softly. However, the changes you make are much more specific than those made using the Lift/Gamma/Gain controls, on the premise that you'll want to be making narrow corrections to fix color contamination, while leaving the rest of the signal adjustment you've made as linear as possible (**Figure 4.90**).

Figure 4.90 The final grade, after pushing the Shadow color balance control toward magenta to neutralize the green in the darkest parts of the image.

Furthermore, as with Log contrast controls, the boundaries of color adjustment where the shadows end and midtones begin, and where the midtones end and the highlights begin, are adjustable using *pivot*, *range*, or *band* parameters (names vary by application) to change the center point of image tonality at which each adjacent pair of color balance controls overlap (**Figure 4.91**). This gives you added flexibility to apply more specific contrast and color adjustments.

Figure 4.91 The Shadows, Contrast, and Highlights pivot parameters, with their accompanying graphical controls that show the center point of each pivot as a dotted blue line on the LUT graph, which shows a graphical representation of the adjustments being applied.

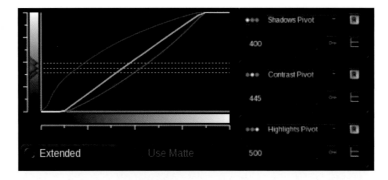

Obviously, the Shadow/Midtone/Highlight controls are nonlinear in nature, since they allow differing color adjustments to the highlights and shadows independently of one another. As a result, this is still cheating if you're looking to grade like the color timers do. Pragmatically speaking, since these controls *are* calibrated for log-encoded media, such targeted adjustments let you combine the best of both worlds, providing a cinematic base grade with digital refinements for fixing specific issues that need solving.

CONTINUING AFTER A LOG GRADE

Once you've made an adjustment using Log mode controls along with a normalizing LUT or curve adjustment, you can always apply additional operations to the normalized image, using lift/gamma/gain, curves, and any other controls you like to make further alterations to the now normalized image.

In fact, you can also use the Log color balance controls on normalized images, but the results will be slightly different. Because the Log controls are calibrated to work on a very narrow tonal range, their effect on normalized pictures will be more highly specific than with log-encoded pictures. In **Figure 4.92**, you can see an image that's already been normalized, with a wide range of image tonality from dark shadows to light highlights.

Figure 4.92 A normalized image with wide contrast.

Figure 4.93 shows the result of pushing the Highlights color balance control toward yellow on a normalized image. The resulting adjustment made to warm up the highlights of the image affects only the very brightest parts of the image (Figure 4.93).

Figure 4.93 Using the Highlight color balance control of the Log controls to add yellow results in a very specific adjustment when applied to a normalized image. While not necessarily suitable for general correction, this can be very useful for stylization.

Used in this way, the Log controls are very effective for inserting stylized color adjustments into very narrow zones of image tonality, especially when you take into account that most log controls can be altered using pivot or low/high range parameters, so you can customize the tonal range of the image you're affecting.

COLOR TEMPERATURE CONTROLS

Some applications, including Adobe SpeedGrade, provide an alternate set of color sliders specifically to address color temperature shifts and magenta/green corrections (**Figure 4.94**). Additionally, some formats encoded using a RAW color space, such as RED R3D files, expose similar controls.

In general, there's nothing you can do with these that you can't do with a typical set of color balance controls, but they are a convenience for specific operations.

Figure 4.94 Another way of adjusting color balance using the Temperature and Magenta controls found in SpeedGrade.

These are essentially color balance controls controlling the highlights zone of tonality, except that that each slider is locked to a specific angle of hue for the correction. In SpeedGrade, Temperature balances the red channel against the blue channel, while Magenta balances the red and blue channels against the green channels.

Like the color balance controls, these sliders aren't just useful for corrections. You can also use them to introduce color imbalances to stylize the image.

USING COLOR CURVES

Those of you who work with Adobe Photoshop and other image editing applications are probably already familiar with curves. Meanwhile, colorists and color timers who've been working in other applications specific to video correction and film grading may ask, "Why should I use curves when I'm already used to using color balance controls?"

The simple answer is that while the color balance controls shown previously let you adjust the red, green, and blue components of an image *simultaneously*, the red, green, and blue curves let you adjust the corresponding color components of the image *individually*. This opens up additional creative and utilitarian vistas with a specificity that the color balance controls simply aren't capable of.

In most color correction applications, the red, green, and blue color adjustment curves are located alongside the luma curve we saw in the previous chapter (**Figure 4.95**).

Figure 4.95 RGB curves lie next to the luma curve in most applications.

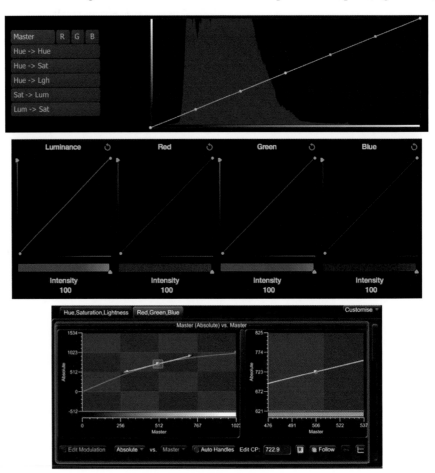

CHAPTER 4

CURVE ADJUSTMENTS IN QUANTEL PABLO

Quantel Pablo has a full set of curve controls that are arranged within a unique interface called *Fettle* that provides multimode RGB, HSL, and YUV channel manipulation using curves. A subset of this interface provides the equivalent to the RGB curves described here, as well as the luma curve (in YUV mode) and the hue curves (in HSL mode) described in Chapter 5.

In fact, Quantel's Fettle interface is one of the original curve control implementations, and colorists once referred to this style of adjustment as *fettling*. To save you a dictionary search, the noun fettle means "repair," as in "the bicycle is in fine fettle."

Each color curve controls the intensity of a single primary color component of the image. In some applications, these curves are locked together by default, enabling RGB contrast adjustment using the curves, as you saw in Chapter 3.

However, if you uncouple the curves from one another, you can make changes to specific color channels within as broad or as narrow a range of image tonality as you like. In fact, with a single curve, you can make as many specific adjustments to narrow portions of image tonality, from the shadows through the midtones through the highlights, as you can place control points onto the curve. **Figure 4.96** shows a rough breakdown of which parts of the default slope of the curve's interface correspond to which tonal areas of the image. Bear in mind that since the practical definitions of shadows, midtones, and highlights overlap considerably, this is only an approximation.

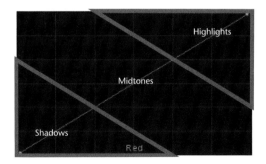

Figure 4.96 This image shows which parts of the curve adjust which tonal regions of the image, approximately.

In most color correction applications, adjustments to the color channels work identically to those made using a Luma curve, as covered in Chapter 3. Click a curve to add as many control points as you need to modify its shape, dragging each control point up or down to change the level of that color channel to different values at the corresponding region of image tonality.

In **Figure 4.97**, you can see that four control points have been added to the curve, raising the amount of red at the top of the midtones while simultaneously lowering the amount of red at the bottom of the midtones. This is a far more specific adjustment than can be made using the color balance controls.

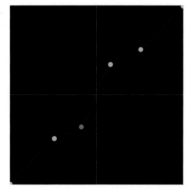

Figure 4.97 Adjusting the red channel within two different areas of image tonality.

The following section demonstrates this principle in greater detail.

MAKING TONALLY SPECIFIC COLOR ADJUSTMENTS WITH CURVES

Let's take a look at how we can affect tonally specific regions of an image using curves. **Figure 4.98** shows a low-key night shot with a cool blue cast in the highlights (the top of the blue waveform in the parade scope is taller than the red and green). Otherwise, it exhibits fairly neutral color throughout the midtones, with deep, neutral shadows (evidenced by the relatively equal bottoms of the three waveforms in the parade scope).

The client has expressed a desire for a bit more zest in the highlights, particularly in the lighting that can be seen though the doorway. One way we could accomplish this is using the color curves.

Figure 4.98 A neutral image with balanced graphs in the parade scope.

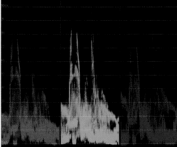

1 To simply add more red to this image using the curves, click the middle of the
   Red curve to add a single control point, and then drag it up to raise the amount
   of red, as shown in **Figure 4.99**.

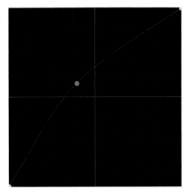

Figure 4.99 Raising the Gamma of
the red channel, along with most
of the shadows and highlights.

As you can see in **Figure 4.100**, this adjustment boosts the amount of red
throughout the image.

 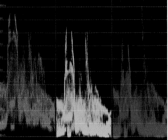

Figure 4.100 The result of the
correction shown in Figure 4.99.
Notice that the red channel is
elevated in its entirety.

When you make an adjustment with only one control point, it results in a
fairly extreme overall adjustment to the image, since it pulls nearly every part
of the curve upward. This creates a reddish color cast over the entire scene.

You should note that the initial two control points that the curve starts out
with at the bottom left and upper right partially pin the darkest and lightest
parts of the red channel in place. With ordinary adjustments of modest scale,
these two original control points at their default position help preserve the
neutrality of the darkest shadows and the brightest highlights in the image.

Figure 4.101 compares the unadjusted and adjusted red graphs of the parade scope from the previous image. If you look closely at the top and bottom, you can see that the highlights and midtones of the red channel have been stretched by a greater amount than the shadows.

Figure 4.101 Comparing the unadjusted red channel at the left to the curve-adjusted red channel at the right.

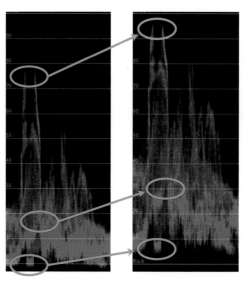

2 If you add a second control point to the Red curve (**Figure 4.102**), you can return the shadows of the red channel to their original state by dragging the new control point down until the bottom of the curve intersects the diagonal grid.

Figure 4.102 Adding a second control point to keep the shadows and darker midtones neutral, indicated by the proximity of the bottom of the curve to the intersection of the horizontal and vertical gridlines.

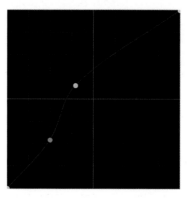

The diagonal of this grid indicates the neutral state of each curve. Wherever a curve intersects this diagonal, the values of the image at that zone of tonality are as they were in the original image (**Figure 4.103**).

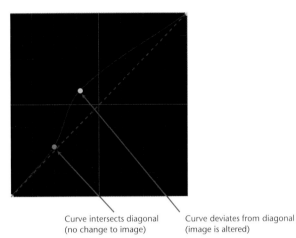

Curve intersects diagonal
(no change to image)

Curve deviates from diagonal
(image is altered)

Figure 4.103 Our modified curve, compared to the diagonal intersection of gridlines that represents the neutral détente position of the curve, along which the image remains unaltered.

With this last adjustment, the control point to the upper right continues to boost the highlights of the red channel. Meanwhile, the new control point you've added to the lower left pins the Red curve at a more neutral diagonal in the highlights. The curve from one control point to the other keeps this transition very smooth, producing a gradual transition from the unaffected shadows through the affected highlights, as shown in **Figure 4.8104**.

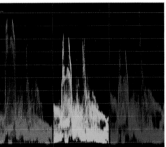

Figure 4.104 Boosting red in the highlights (especially as seen through the doorway) while keeping the darker midtones and shadows neutral.

The result is that the shadows of the room and the darker midtones of the woman and man remain neutral, but the brighter highlights, especially the highlight seen through the doorway, have the new insidious red cast you've introduced.

This is the power of curves. They give you specific, customizable control over the color in different tonal regions of an image that can sometimes border on secondary color correction.

MAKING CONTROLLED CURVE CORRECTIONS TO AN IMAGE USING THE PARADE SCOPE

If you want to use curves as a corrective tool to neutralize color casts, one of the best ways to spot which curves need to be adjusted is to use the RGB parade scope.

As you've already seen in the previous example, the graphs for each of the three color channels in the parade scope correspond perfectly to the three available color curve controls. Since color casts generally reveal themselves in the parade scope as an elevated or depressed graph corresponding to the channel that's at fault, these waveforms provide an instant guide to show you which curves you need to adjust and where to place the control points you need to use to make the adjustment.

The following example was originally shot with an extremely warm cast. As is so often the case, the director decided to ease off this bold decision in post. Large color casts like this are often ideal candidates for curve correction, since you can easily make very targeted corrections to the specific color channels that are at fault.

1 Examine the RGB parade scope for the image in **Figure 4.105**. This shows an image with a red channel that is obviously too high relative to the rest of the picture, and it's throwing off the highlights of the shot.

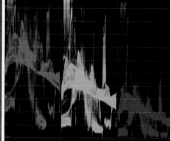

Figure 4.105 The original, unaltered image. The parade scope reveals that the red channel is too high and the blue channel is too low.

Correspondence between color channel and curve point placement

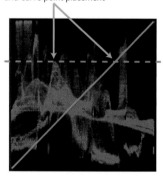

Figure 4.106 To affect the spike in the red channel waveform that just touches the dotted line, put a control point where the dotted line intersects the curve.

The parade scope indicates that your first adjustment should be to lower the midtones of the red channel relative to the green and blue channels. To figure out where to put a control point to do what you want, you need only compare the height of the waveform you want to adjust to the height of the curve (**Figure 4.106**).

2 Now, place a control point at the top third of the curve, and drag it down to lower the red channel midtones until the middle of the red channel (which is the portion of the waveform that corresponds to the wall) is only just a little higher than the middle of the green channel (**Figure 4.107**).

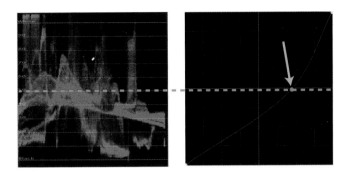

Figure 4.107 The red channel curve adjustment described in step 2.

This neutralizes the highlights, but now you've traded an orange color cast for a greenish-yellow one (**Figure 4.108**). Next, you need to raise the blue color channel.

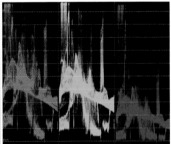

Figure 4.108 The result of the adjustment made in Figure 4.107.

3   Now, place a control point at the bottom third of the blue color curve, at a height that corresponds to the top of the blue midtones, and drag it up until the blue midtones are closer to the same height as the green curve. You'll know when to stop by keeping your eye on the monitor. Once the image looks neutral, you're done.

The resulting correction works well for the midtones, but the shadows now look a little weak. To fix this, add another control point near the bottom of the curve and drag it down to lower the bottom of the blue waveform (**Figure 4.109**).

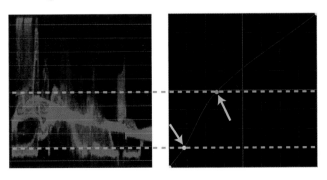

Figure 4.109 The blue channel curve adjustment described in step 3.

This last adjustment brings the image to a more neutral state (**Figure 4.110**).

Figure 4.110 The final result, after adjusting both the red and blue curves.

At this point, it's easier to introduce a more subtle warmth using the color balance controls that will complement rather than compete with the image.

As you can see, there is a fairly direct correspondence between the values displayed in the three graphs of the parade scope and the three color curve controls.

MAKING CORRECTIONS WITH RGB LIFT/GAMMA/GAIN

Most applications also have a set of Lift/Gamma/Gain controls that allow specific adjustment of the red, green, and blue color channels. These controls hearken back to older hardware and software color correction methods, and they allow very specific adjustment of wildly imbalanced images. In a sense, you might even consider these controls to be three-point curves, because their effect and use are similar to the procedure described in this section. Furthermore, using RGB Lift/Gamma/Gain controls with your parade scope is another great way to correct some really thorny problems or to make adjustments when you know exactly which part of the signal you need to boost or attenuate and by how much.

WHICH ARE FASTER, COLOR BALANCE CONTROLS OR CURVES?

Unlike the color balance controls, which simultaneously adjust the mix of red, green, and blue in the image, each of the color curves adjusts just one color component at a time. This means that sometimes you have to adjust two curves to make the same kind of correction that you could achieve with a single adjustment of the appropriate color balance control.

For example, in **Figure 4.111**, the parade scope indicates a color cast in the shadows of the image, via a blue channel that's too high and a red channel that's too low.

Figure 4.111 A fluorescent green color cast.

To correct this using the curves controls, you'd have to make three adjustments, to the red, green, and blue channels. However, to make the same adjustment using the color balance controls, you would only need to drag up the Gain control toward magenta (**Figure 4.112**). Both adjustments result in nearly the same correction.

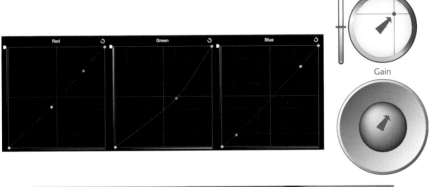

Figure 4.112 Two ways of neutralizing the green—one using curves, the other using a single Gain color balance operation—produce nearly identical results.

Which way is better? Well, that's really a matter of personal preference. The best answer is whichever way lets you work faster. In a client-driven color correction session, time is money, and the faster you work, the happier your client will be.

Both controls have their place, and my recommendation is that if you're coming to color grading from a Photoshop background, take some time to get up to speed with the color balance controls; you may be surprised at how quickly they work. And for colorists from a video background who haven't used curves that much before, it's worth taking the time to learn how to make curve adjustments efficiently, as it may open up some quick fixes and custom looks that you may have wrestled with before.

DAVINCI RESOLVE CURVES AND LUM MIX

One of the interesting differences between DaVinci Resolve and other applications is the YRGB image processing Resolve uses in order to maintain image luminance while you make adjustments to individual color channels. This feature is most noticeable when you unlink curves in order to make the kinds of adjustments shown in the previous few sections. In DaVinci, lowering one color channel using either curves or individual RGB Lift/Gamma/Gain controls automatically raises the other two color channels in such a way as to preserve the overall lightness of the image. In this scheme, raising one color channel also lowers the other two, maintaining a kind of symmetry.

This type of image processing can take some getting used to if you come from an application where each channel is totally independent, but Resolve lets you modify this behavior using the often misunderstood *Lum Mix* parameter. When set to 100 (the default), Lum Mix maintains this symmetrical relationship between all color channels, as shown in **Figure 4.113**.

Figure 4.113 With Lum Mix set to 100, lowering the green channel in DaVinci Resolve results in the red and blue channels being raised to maintain image lightness.

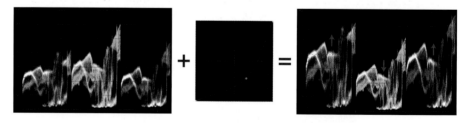

To disable this behavior, all you need to do is to lower Lum Mix to 0, and all per-channel operations within that node will have no effect on the other channels of the image.

SATURATION ADJUSTMENTS

As discussed earlier, image saturation is a measurement of the intensity of its color. Most images contain many different levels of saturation, which you can measure using the vectorscope.

Even though saturation is usually modified whenever you adjust color balance or contrast (so long as you're using an application that processes these adjustments in RGB space), there are frequently times when you'll want to adjust saturation all by itself. You may do this to create different looks, correct for broadcast legality, or perform scene-to-scene color correction.

Most color correction applications provide you with several controls for saturation adjustment, depending on whether you want to adjust saturation throughout the entire image or just the saturation within a narrow tonal range.

ANALYZING SATURATION USING THE WAVEFORM MONITOR SET TO FLAT (FLT)

To help you control saturation at specific tonal ranges, it's helpful to be able to analyze image saturation more specifically. The vectorscope shows you the overall saturation for the entire image, which is helpful, and shows you how strong the saturation is for specific hues, which is essential.

However, you can also configure most Waveform Monitors to display saturation as an overlay over luma, usually referred to as FLAT (FLT) or something similar. This way, you can see how saturated an image is at different tonal zones. This mode is principally useful for checking to see how much saturation exists in the highlights and shadows of an image. In this mode, the Waveform scope can't show you information about specific colors (that's what the vectorscope is for); it shows you only the amplitude of the chroma component corresponding to each level of the luma component.

Let's take a look at how this works. **Figure 4.114** comprises two halves. The bottom half is completely desaturated and shows the luma level that stretches across the entire frame from left (black) to right (white). The top half has saturated color added to this base luma level.

Figure 4.114 A split-screen test pattern. The top half is highly saturated, the bottom half has no saturation.

Examining this image in the Waveform Monitor confirms that the luma of the overall image is a simple ramp gradient (**Figure 4.115**).

Figure 4.115 The test pattern's overall luma is a simple ramp gradient.

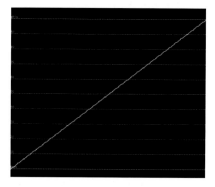

However, turning the Waveform Monitor's saturation option on shows a different picture. The shadow and highlight portions of the top half of the gradient are highly saturated, with excursions in the Waveform graph well below 0 and above 100 percent, which can be seen as the thick parts of the Waveform graph in **Figure 4.116**. This image makes it easy to examine the many different controls you're given to adjust saturation levels throughout the picture.

Figure 4.116 The thickness of the Waveform graph indicates high saturation from the shadows through the highlights when the Waveform Monitor is set to display FLAT (FLT).

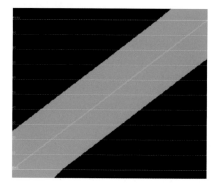

THE SATURATION CONTROL

Every color correction application and filter has at least one saturation control that simply raises the saturation throughout the image, creating a more vivid look, or lowers it for a muted result. Sometimes this control takes the form of a single slider or parameter, such as in DaVinci Resolve (**Figure 4.117**).

Saturation: 50.000	Hue: 50.000	Lum Mix: 100.000

Figure 4.117 The saturation slider in the primary color correction display of DaVinci Resolve.

The saturation controls in FilmLight Baselight let you control overall saturation, but they also allow independent adjustments to the saturation of the red, green, and blue hues within the image (**Figure 4.118**).

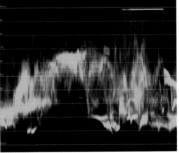

Figure 4.118 The saturation controls in the video grading panel of FilmLight Baselight.

However the saturation controls are set up, increasing saturation intensifies the colors of the image, as shown in **Figure 4.119**.

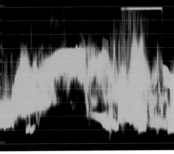

Figure 4.119 A clip with saturation raised throughout the image. Notice how the waveform displaying saturation is thick throughout the graph.

Decreasing saturation mutes the entire image, as shown in **Figure 4.120**.

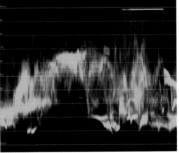

Figure 4.120 A clip with saturation lowered throughout the image. Notice how the waveform displaying saturation has thinned.

While simple control over saturation is often exactly what you need, there will be situations where you'll need to exert more selective control over the saturation in an image, boosting it in specific areas while lowering it in others.

TARGETED SATURATION CONTROLS

Many professional color correction applications also provide specific control over saturation within specific tonal regions of the image. In particular, you'll frequently be concerned with controlling saturation within the darkest shadows and brightest highlights of your image. Sometimes, these controls are fixed and defined by the same shadows/midtones/highlights tonal ranges used by an application's five-way and nine-way color controls, because the intention is to make quick saturation adjustments at the extremes of image tonality. When available, these controls make it really fast to perform the following operations:

- Desaturating shadows to make them seem more natural and to create an image with deeper blacks, creating the illusion of greater contrast

- Desaturating highlights that have troublesome color casts to make them instantly white (for example, shots with a bit too much red or blue at 0 percent/ IRE have off-color blacks that are easily fixed with this control)

- Boosting saturation within a specific region of midtones in order to avoid saturating the entire image

- Eliminating unwanted color artifacts in shadows and highlights that result from extreme color corrections made to the rest of the image (for example, making big corrections in shots with snow often adds color to the brightest highlights, and this control is a fast fix)

- Legalizing image saturation in the shadows and highlights (see Chapter 10 for more information)

Currently, the most common type of saturation control is a single saturation control that can be set to affect different tonal ranges via buttons that change the tonal range it affects, whether the overall image or just the highlights, midtones, or shadows (**Figure 4.121**).

Figure 4.121 Buttons in SpeedGrade and Smoke that change whether the primary controls affect the overall image or a specific tonal zone.

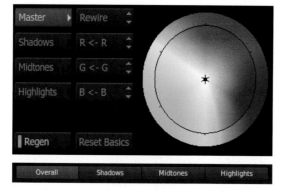

Let's take a look at how Highlights and Shadows controls work to limit a saturation control's effect, using them to affect the test pattern in **Figure 4.122**.

- **Highlights saturation controls** affect the brightest parts of the image. These controls often have the most effect where the luma component is above approximately 75 percent, with a gentle falloff toward the midtones.

- **Shadows saturation controls** affect the darkest parts of the image. These controls often have the most effect where the luma component is below approximately 25 percent, again with a gentle falloff toward the midtones.

Figure 4.122 shows the effect of setting both Highlights and Shadows saturation controls to 0, desaturating the brightest and darkest areas of the top strip of the test pattern.

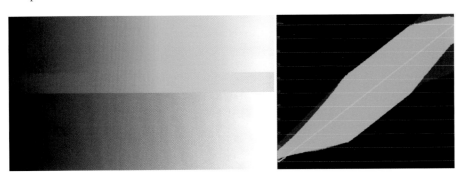

Figure 4.122 Highlights and Shadows saturation controls desaturating the opposite extremes of the image. This effect can be seen to the left and right edges of the uppermost strip of the test pattern (the middle blue strip shows the original saturation).

The Waveform Monitor to the right, which is set to FLAT (FLT), shows the desaturation that's occurring in the highlights and shadows through the tapering off of the thick part of the waveform.

Other applications, such as DaVinci Resolve and SGO Mistika, provide Curve controls that affect luma versus saturation, providing nearly unlimited fine-tuning of saturation throughout an image (**Figure 4.123**).

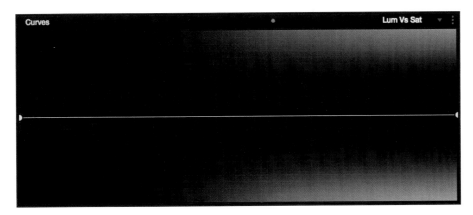

Figure 4.123 The advantage of Curve controls is that they enable you to quickly make custom adjustments over user-selectable ranges of image tonality. However, Highlight/Midtone/Shadow-style saturation controls can be easier to adjust for common operations owing to how they're mapped to your control surface, making fixing a shadow as easy as punching a button and twisting a knob.

ENRICHING SATURATION WITHOUT CHEAPENING AN IMAGE

If you're trying to create a super-saturated look, you don't want to just crank up the Saturation parameter and leave it at that. You'll get lots of color, but you risk losing detail due to color bleed, reduced color contrast, artifacts, aliasing in video formats with low chroma sampling, edge ringing, and, of course, broadcast illegality.

Saturation works hand-in-hand with contrast in shaping the look of your clips. Controlling saturation in the shadows and highlights of your images is the key to creating a sophisticated look when increasing the saturation of your images, not to mention maintaining broadcast legality with more stringent broadcasters.

You'll also find that excessive saturation is a bit more successful in darker images, where the distribution of midtones is weighted more toward the lower end of the digital scale, from about 10 to 60 percent. When the difference is described in terms used by the HSB color model, colors with a lower brightness value appear richer than those with a higher brightness value, which can easily appear artificial and excessive when in abundance.

When you increase the saturation of images, it's even more important than usual to make sure that neutral areas of the image don't have an incorrect color cast. If you're deliberately warming or cooling the image, you may need to ease off the correction.

In the following example, you'll safely boost the color intensity in **Figure 4.124** for an even more richly saturated look.

Figure 4.124 The original, unaltered image.

1 Examine the image using a vectorscope. You can see there's already plenty of saturation in the picture, which extends well out from the center of the center crosshairs (**Figure 4.125**).

Figure 4.125 Vectorscope analysis of the original saturation level.

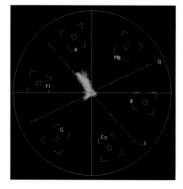

2 If you turn up the saturation, the image certainly becomes more colorful, but the color is added indiscriminately throughout the image, even in the deepest shadows. The result is a somewhat gaudy, overcolorful look, which is not what you want (**Figure 4.126**).

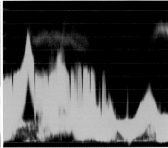

Figure 4.126 After increasing image saturation, the FLAT (FLT) analysis in the Waveform Monitor has grown thicker.

3 Examine the bottom of the Waveform Monitor with FLAT (FLT) turned on. You can also see that the thickness of the waveform that indicates increased saturation is extending down below 0 percent/IRE (**Figure 4.127**). This can also be apparent in *gamut* scopes that show a composite transformation of the image data with special markers for the upper and lower limits of acceptable saturation, as discussed in Chapter 10.

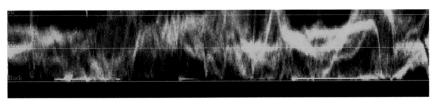

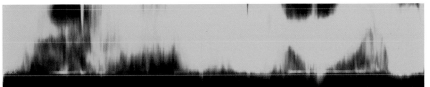

Figure 4.127 In the top image, the Waveform Monitor is set to luma. At the bottom, the Waveform Monitor is set to FLAT (FLT). Notice how the fuzzy part of the right waveform stretches below the bottom line corresponding to 0 percent/IRE.

Excessive saturation in the shadows is what makes the last adjustment look unflattering. You don't expect to see increased saturation in shadows; you expect saturation to diminish with the light level.

4 To correct this, you can use whichever controls your application provides to reduce shadow saturation, either lowering the shadows using the Shadows controls, or using a luma versus saturation curve to roll off the saturation in the darkest part of the picture (**Figure 4.128**).

Figure 4.128 Adding two control points to a luma versus saturation curve to reduce image saturation in the deepest shadows, with a smooth transition to the more highly saturated midtones.

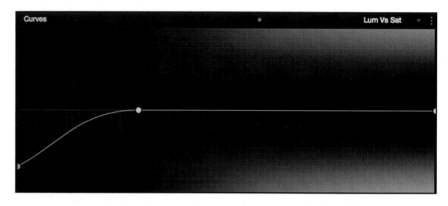

You don't want to desaturate the shadows all the way to 0, or the image might pick up a gritty, unpleasant look (unless, of course, that's what you're going for). You can see the result in **Figure 4.129**.

Figure 4.129 The high-saturation version of the image with both Highlights and Shadows saturation controls reduced to 20 percent.

A close-up of the bald man's head and the plant's shadow on the wall makes it easier to see the difference (**Figure 4.130**).

When boosting saturation, it's easy to play with fire. Reducing shadow saturation in the face of increased midtone saturation is a good way to keep the perceived contrast of your images higher and to keep the shadows of your image looking deep and clean. Alternately, you could use your controls to instead be more selective about how you boost saturation, raising it only in the midtones while leaving the highlights and shadows alone.

By keeping an eye on the saturation in the highlights and shadows of your images, you can more easily create more vivid looks without making your images look like a bad TV signal.

Oversaturated

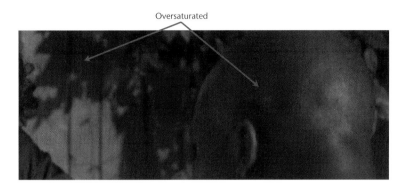

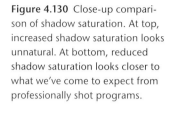

Figure 4.130 Close-up comparison of shadow saturation. At top, increased shadow saturation looks unnatural. At bottom, reduced shadow saturation looks closer to what we've come to expect from professionally shot programs.

Properly saturated

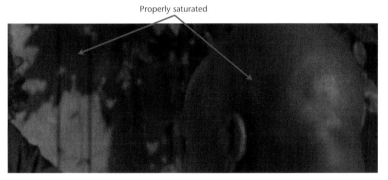

CONTROLLING "COLORFULNESS"

In Edward Giorgianni and Thomas Madden's *Digital Color Management: Encoding Solutions* (Wiley, 2009), colorfulness is defined as the "attribute of a visual sensation according to which an area appears to exhibit more or less of its hue." This is the definition I'm using for purposes of discussing the concept that a subject may appear more or less colorful *despite its actual level of saturation*.

This is an important concept, because it describes various perceptual foibles by which clients and audience members may perceive what's onscreen differently from what the video scopes show. In short, you may have highly saturated images that don't appear to be very colorful, and you may have relatively *desaturated* images that appear to be more colorful than you would think based on their saturation.

So, if saturation isn't the absolute determinant of colorfulness, then what other qualities affect one's perception of how much color is in an image?

BRIGHTNESS AND COLORFULNESS DURING ACQUISITION

In human vision and image recording, the more brightly illuminated a subject is, the more colorful it is perceived to be, even though the color of the subject is identical no matter what the lighting conditions. This is known as the Hunt effect: Reduced illumination results in reduced colorfulness (**Figure 4.131**).

Figure 4.131 The same set of colorful objects with both dim and bright practical lighting. While the dim version certainly has rich color, the brighter items such as the flowers seem more colorful still.

For the colorist, the Hunt effect relates directly to the perceived colorfulness of displays set to different peak white settings; given the same display surround, a higher peak white output results in a more colorful-looking image, whereas a lower peak white output appears less colorful. This is one of many reasons to maintain careful control over the calibration of your display.

CONTRAST AND COLORFULNESS WHILE GRADING

Interestingly, the relationship between saturation and image contrast when adjusted by master RGB controls as described in Chapter 3 is analogous to the Hunt effect. Expanding contrast increases saturation, which is usually a desirable result (**Figure 4.132**).

As has been discussed previously, things get more complicated when you exercise independent control over contrast of the luma component, separate from the chroma of the signal. In this case, given the mathematics of digital image processing, stretching the contrast of images to make them brighter offers *less* perceived colorfulness than would a darker image (**Figure 4.133**).

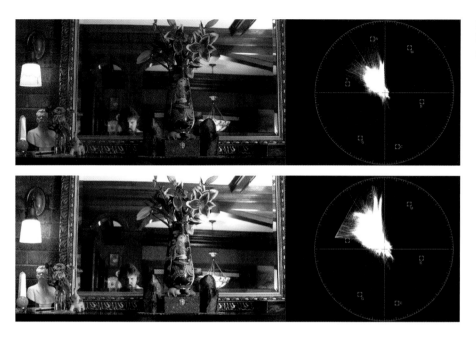

Figure 4.132 Our test image before and after contrast expansion.

Figure 4.133 Stretching contrast of just the Y' component diminishes colorfulness.

In both examples, image saturation is clearly intensified, but the quality of the graded images is quite different. This is the reason why clients often substitute the words *bright* and *saturated* with one another, because often the quality they're trying to describe is not so easy to isolate.

SIZE AND COLORFULNESS

The size of a feature has a direct relationship to its perceived colorfulness. In an example cited by Mahdi Nezamabadi ("The Effect of Image Size on the Color Appearance of Image Reproductions," Ph.D. dissertation, Rochester Institute of Technology, 2008), viewer observations of small paint patches were compared to their observations of the finally painted four walls of a room. Even though the color of the patch and the walls were demonstrably identical through spectroradiometric measurement, viewers reported an increase in lightness and chroma in the painted walls.

In other words, larger objects that have the same color as smaller objects are perceived as being more colorful. This is shown in the following two images, where the same vase, red box, gold frame stained glass lamp, and bottom of the vase appear in both images. However, when filling more of the frame in the image at the right, the objects being zoomed in on will *appear* to most observers to be more colorful, even though there's no actual change in saturation (**Figure 4.134**).

Figure 4.134 When pushing into a colorful object, the increased size can give an impression of greater colorfulness, even though saturation is the same.

This is a valuable phenomenon to be aware of when dealing with situations where you're trying to match one shot to another and you're wondering why the client keeps saying that one seems to be brighter or more colorful than the other, even though your video scopes show that the colors match exactly. In such a situation, you have a choice. You can "fudge it" by slightly lowering the saturation of the red box where larger or boosting the saturation of the red box where smaller in order to make the cut between the two less jarring. Or, you can explain the phenomenon to the client and point out how this can have a useful impact on the viewer for the right program, giving close-ups and push-ins more pop for the right cut.

This correlation between size and colorfulness also applies to the overall size of the image, which relates directly to how big of a display you're working with. In **Figure 4.135**, the same image is shown larger and smaller. Again, to most observers, the larger image appears to be more colorful, even though they're identical.

Figure 4.135 When viewing an image on a larger display, it's easy to get an impression of greater colorfulness than the same image on a smaller display, even though both images have identical saturation.

Now, one of the reasons for the careful monitoring practices described in Chapter 2 is to attempt to compensate for this effect via careful surround lighting and appropriate seating distance. For projection, this is also compensated for by the fact that images are projected with less illumination than from self-illuminated displays such as LCD, OLED, and Plasma.

However, it's inarguable that grading on a 20' projection screen is a far different experience than grading on even a 40" display which, perceptually speaking, is significantly different from grading on a 15" display. Having graded on projection screens and video displays both large and small, I can comfortably say that I make different decisions about certain adjustments based on the overall size of the image, which is a good bias to be aware of.

However, another approach to this issue is to grade while keeping in mind the size of the display viewers will watch your program on. Ideally, matching your grading suite's primary display, whether a monitor or projector, to the audience's experience (living room or theatrical) will enable the best decision making on your part as you make color adjustments.

COLOR CONTRAST AND COLORFULNESS

Finally, another aspect of the image that affects perceived colorfulness is color contrast, or how much of a difference there is between individual hues within an image. Described in much more detail in the following section, *contrast of hue* is one aspect of color contrast that makes a big difference between the perceived colorfulness of an image as your client sees it and the level of measured saturation.

Despite whatever measurable similarity in saturation there is, any client will tell you that an image with a greater range of hues in it will appear to be more colorful than one with fewer. On that note, let's take a closer look at color contrast, the different ways it can be expressed, and how you can control it.

UNDERSTANDING AND CONTROLLING COLOR CONTRAST

In Chapter 3, we saw how luma contrast contributes to the punchiness, sharpness, and overall appeal of an image. Within the domain of the chroma component, *color contrast* plays a similar role, though perhaps a more nebulous one, in shaping what the audience sees and how it responds to the various subjects within a scene.

Simply put, color contrast is the amount of differentiation among the various colors found within an image. The more varied the colors of different elements of the scene are from one another, the more color contrast there is.

When there is too little color contrast, the result can appear monochromatic, as if there's a tint washed over the entire scene. If there's a high degree of color contrast, then the variously colored elements of the scene will likely pop out at the audience with greater distinction.

The significance of color contrast is also supported by research into the contribution of color to object segmentation—the separation of specific subjects from textures found in the background and surround of a scene. To quote from "The Contributions of Color to Recognition Memory for Natural Scenes," "A possible evolutionary advantage for color over luminance-based vision may lie, however, in superior segmentation of objects from textured backgrounds." One would imagine that there'd be a significant advantage to being able to spot a colorful ripe fruit (or a dangerous predator) among the dense foliage of the forest or jungle where one might have lived 150,000 years ago.

NOTE

The examples shown in the following pages all refer to secondary correction techniques such as HSL Qualification and hue curves, which are covered in the next chapter.

One last note: I often run into situations where clients ask me to raise the saturation even though I feel things are probably as saturated as they ought to be. In these situations, what usually fixes the problem is finding a way to increase the color contrast in the image by selectively boosting the saturation of a specific hue, rather than increasing the saturation of the entire image. The following section covers a variety of different strategies for doing just this.

TYPES OF COLOR CONTRAST

From a creative perspective, Johannes Itten, in his landmark *The Art of Color* (John Wiley & Sons, 1961), identified several types of color contrast that are useful to us as colorists. I highly recommend Itten's book, which focuses on fine-art examples from numerous old masters. However, the following sections summarize the primary categories of color contrast Itten describes with examples that I've adapted to the problems and issues I encounter in real-world scenes in film and video.

It's worth reflecting that all of these color contrast effects are effective because of the opponent model of the human visual system described at the beginning of this chapter. Every color in an image is evaluated relative to the other colors that surround it. Whether you're adjusting the entire scene at once with a primary color correction or a specific element within the scene via a secondary color correction, these principles will help you to understand why certain seemingly small adjustments can "bring the shot alive."

In the following sections, you'll also see how you can use the vectorscope to evaluate color contrast of different kinds.

CONTRAST OF HUE

This is the most fundamental type of color contrast you can control. The tough thing about hue contrast is that its successful appearance requires deliberate color decisions and placement by both the wardrobe and production design departments.

In the following example, the art direction and lighting were deliberately monochromatic, to create the atmosphere of a dark, lush nightclub. The result is highly saturated, but it has low color contrast, since all the hues are within a very narrow range, as seen in the vectorscope (**Figure 4.136**).

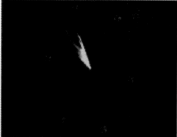

Figure 4.136 An image with high saturation but low color contrast.

In the next example, you'll see an image that's actually a bit less saturated than the previous example, but it displays considerably greater color contrast, as seen by the multiple arms of the vectorscope graph extending in multiple directions from the center (**Figure 4.137**).

Figure 4.137 An image with wide color contrast, showing a variety of hues.

I'm fond of saying during a session that if a range of different colors isn't in an image to begin with, I can't really put them there. That said, there's often ample opportunity to tease faint colors that aren't immediately obvious out of an otherwise dull-looking shot by doing some, or all, of the following:

- **Eliminating an excessive color cast from the image** to center the shadows and highlights within the vectorscope and redistribute the various other color spikes of the vectorscope graph about this center at as many different angles as possible.

- **Turning up the saturation of an otherwise desaturated image**, pushing all of the hues within the vectorscope farther out toward the edges, increasing the distance between each different hue cluster and increasing the color contrast.

- **Increasing saturation selectively**, bringing as many different colors out of the background as possible, while perhaps slightly desaturating the dominant hue. This requires secondary color correction operations covered in subsequent chapters.

Figure 4.138 has a slight orange color cast (or is it the sunset?), as well as low saturation overall, which gives the impression of low color contrast.

Figure 4.138 Low color contrast as a result of a color cast and reduced saturation.

Taking a different tack with this shot to increase the color contrast, you can neutralize the color cast, turn up the saturation, and use a hue curve operation to tease some of the already existent reds and oranges out of the newly revealed greens of the forest in the background. The same hue curve operation lets you tease more blue out of the sky and the water reflections, all of which gives you a lot of color contrast and a more polychromatic image (**Figure 4.139**).

Figure 4.139 Expanding color contrast by neutralizing the color cast and selectively increasing saturation to boost a variety of different hues.

Looking at the vectorscope, you can see that the graph in Figure 4.139 has become more centered, has stretched out further, and extends in more directions.

COLD-WARM CONTRAST

Another type of color contrast is the narrower combination of warm and cool tones, as opposed to a hodgepodge of different hues. Cold-warm contrast is subtle, realistic as far as naturally occurring color temperature is concerned, and it frequently occurs naturally in shots utilizing mixed-light sources. Of course, it doesn't hurt if the art directors went out of their way to keep the production colors cool and warm to reinforce the lighting scheme.

In particular, cold-warm contrast tends to be expressed as the interplay between the warm hues of human skin tone and background lighting or art direction choices.

In **Figure 4.140**, the interior of the van is deliberately bluish, with the result that it plays against the complexion of the actor to create this kind of contrast.

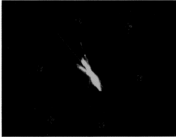

Figure 4.140 Cold-warm contrast as a result of art direction.

If you want to add cold-warm contrast to an image that's otherwise lacking it, you can try the strategy of making opposing adjustments to the highlights and midtones of an image using the color balance controls, adding warmth to the highlights, and cooling off the darker midtones and shadows (**Figure 4.141**).

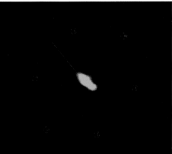

Figure 4.141 Cold-warm contrast as a result of lighting.

NOTE

You'll also see an example
of cold-warm contrast later,
when we examine how to
hold out naturalistic skin
tones against dramatically
graded backgrounds. This is
not an endorsement, simply
an observation.

Notice how the warmth of the woman's highlights makes her stand out from the
bluish background. Meanwhile, the man's face is still getting its color from the
background illuminant, so he blends in a bit more with the background.

COMPLEMENTARY CONTRAST

It's well known among painters and designers that placing highly complementary
colors adjacent to one another results in a high-energy interplay between the
two hues.

This type of color contrast is a much more aggressive choice and may require a
correction to eliminate it if the effect is too distracting. On the other hand, you
may go out of your way to create this particular color combination if it's to the
benefit of the scene; it could go either way.

In **Figure 4.142**, the baby blue/cyan of the woman's sweater is in almost perfect
complement to the beige/tans of the surrounding couch (with a little help from a
hue curve operation). The result is that the sweater adds significant color contrast
to the image, even though it's not really that saturated.

Figure 4.142 Complementary
contrast: The blue sweater is complementary to the beige/warm
couch surrounding it.

 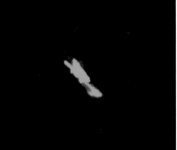

You know you're dealing with complementary contrast when there are two distinct
arms of the vectorscope graph that stretch out in almost opposite directions, as
shown in Figure 4.142.

In Joseph Krakora's documentary *Vermeer: Master of Light* (Microcinema, 2009), the
painter's rendering of blue fabric with yellow highlights is observed to have this
effect. Similarly, Vermeer's use of colors for shadows that are complementary to
those of the subject casting them has a similar, if more subtle, effect.

In the following example, the yellows in the glass of liquor have been emphasized
to play off the man's blue shirt, adding visual interest to the shot (**Figure 4.143**).

 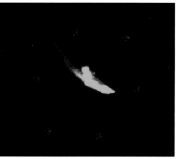

Figure 4.143 Complementary contrast. The yellow highlights of the drink contrast with the blue of the shirt.

Unfortunately, if excess complementary contrast is in a shot by mistake, the result can be distracting, so measures may be needed to reduce the amount of contrast by either selectively shifting the hue or reducing the saturation, of the offending subject, typically via a secondary color correction of some kind.

In **Figure 4.144**, the orange basketball in the background just happens to be the complement of the blue-painted wall. The result is that it sticks out like a sore thumb.

 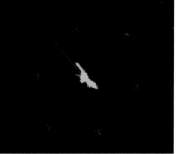

Figure 4.144 Unwanted complementary contrast: The orange basketball calls attention to itself when surrounded by the blue wall.

This is an example of a detail you'd probably want to suppress using a secondary color correction of some kind, either using a hue versus saturation curve to reduce the oranges in the scene, an HSL Qualification to key the basketball to create a matte with which to make the adjustment, or a mask/power-window shape to isolate the basketball if it's too close to the man's skin tone to key cleanly.

NOTE

On a related note, this is also an example of a feature that confuses the depth plane of the shot. Even though the perspective and placement of the basketball clearly positions it behind the actor, warm colors tend to project forward, while cool colors recede. This reinforces the impression that the basketball is sticking out. This concept will be covered in greater detail in Chapter 6.

SIMULTANEOUS CONTRAST

This type of contrast refers to the effect that a dominant surround or background color has on an interior subject. More often than not, simultaneous contrast is the source of problems, rather than the solution.

It's a difficult phenomenon to show in real-world shots, but the following example should illustrate. In the following three images (**Figure 4.145**), the shot has been modified so that the wall hue is different. Look back and forth among all of the shots. You may notice that the background color subtly affects the look of the woman.

Figure 4.145 Our perception of the woman's face is subtly altered by the color that surrounds her.

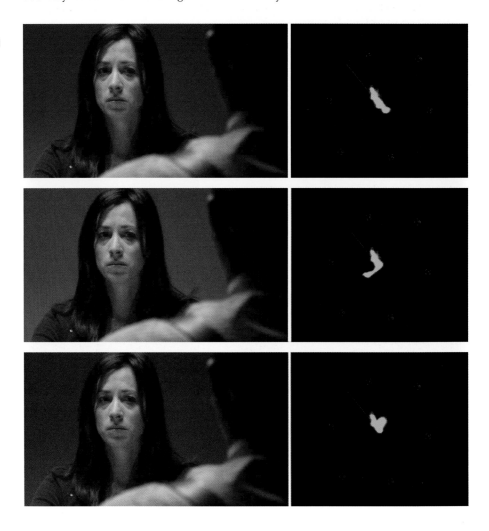

Now consider that the hue of the woman's face is identical in each of these three shots, and you can see how simultaneous contrast can often work against you when you're trying to match two shots with different backgrounds together. If the reverse angle in a scene happens to have a dominant color in the background when the primary angle doesn't, a face in the foreground may not seem to match the face in the previous shot, even though they may actually match quite closely!

In these cases, you may actually obtain a better *perceptual* result by making an adjustment to correct for the illusion of a color cast, as if it were real (and in fact it is, to your eye). This is a great example of when numeric accuracy isn't as important as the perception of accuracy.

CONTRAST OF SATURATION

Even within a more or less monochromatic shot (an abundance of earth tones, for example), if nothing else, ideally you can at least extract some contrast between highly saturated and less saturated subjects. This can be a good strategy for helping differentiate a foreground subject from a background when they're otherwise muddled together because of a similarity of hue.

In **Figure 4.146**, the vectorscope shows that the hue of the man and the wall are virtually identical. However, the man stands out from the background not just because his complexion is darker but because he's actually a bit less saturated than the wall. This contributes to the distinction between the foreground and background elements.

NOTE

Colorist Joe Owens points out another common example of simultaneous contrast getting in the way of a grade. In a shot with fluffy white clouds against a saturated blue sky, the blue can create the perceptual impression of yellowish clouds, even though your scopes clearly show them to be numerically neutral. The solution is to throw the clouds a bit toward blue, introducing a color cast to eliminate one that doesn't actually exist!

CHAPTER 4

 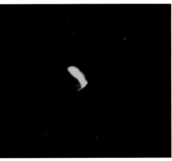

Figure 4.146 Even though the man's face is the same hue as the wall paneling, the differences in saturation and lightness make him stand out.

Figure 4.147 is similarly monochromatic, with a warm color tone across the entire frame. The vectorscope graph appears to be an indistinct blob of oranges.

Figure 4.147 In this image with low saturation contrast, the illuminant of the scene and woman are in the same range of hue.

To create a bit of distance between the woman in the foreground and the background, you can make a secondary correction to slightly desaturate the background (but not totally, you want to retain the warmth of the overall lighting), while increasing the saturation of the woman's face (just a bit, you don't want her to look like she's got a spray-on tan). You can see the results in **Figure 4.148**.

Figure 4.148 Reducing saturation in the surrounding scene and increasing saturation in the woman's face increases saturation contrast in this scene, bringing the woman more to the foreground.

 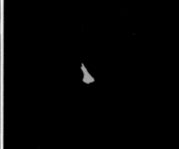

Just to make a point, no hues were altered in Figure 4.148. The resulting change is subtle but helps the woman in the foreground stand out a bit more, which adds some depth to the image and focuses viewer attention on her, both of which are distinct improvements. Also, notice how the vectorscope graph in Figure 4.148 has changed from an indistinct blob to a more defined shape pointing in two distinct directions: reddish/orange and a warm yellow.

CONTRAST OF EXTENSION

This final aspect of color contrast can be a lifesaver when you have only a little bit of differentiating color in an otherwise monochromatic scene. For example, **Figure 4.149** is awash in tans, browns, beiges, and orange, with warm lighting throughout. The one thing that keeps this image from being chromatically flat is the reflections of the vivid green lampshades.

Figure 4.149 The green lamp reflections, though small, add color and interest to an otherwise monochromatic scene.

It's just a small dash of green, but the fact that it's completely distinct from the general range of hues in the rest of the environment means that little bit of green matters *a lot*. This is the principle of contrast of extension that matters to us as colorists.

Notice that the difference between contrast of extension and complementary contrast is that contrast of extension can utilize hues that more closely neighbor the dominant hues within a scene, when viewed on a color wheel. Also, contrast of extension relies on increased saturation to allow the smaller feature to play off of the larger scene. Simply having an element of a suitably different hue isn't enough; it needs to be vivid enough to catch the viewer's eye.

With this in mind, there are often seemingly monochromatic scenes where, at second glance, you find that you're able to pull a little bit of color out of someone's shirt, or tie, or a bowl of fruit on a table. Anything that happens to have a bit of color that you can stretch out, when viewed in the vectorscope, can provide a way for you to introduce a bit more color contrast to an image that otherwise may seem flat.

The following shot is suffused with warm lighting that plays off the wood doors and the beige medical wallpaper. It's saturated, but there's not much pop (**Figure 4.150**).

Figure 4.150 Another scene with low color contrast.

By selectively boosting the color of the man's tie as much as we can, this little bit of shimmering blue brings just enough additional color to the image to make it look more interesting. It also serves to call a little more attention to the man in the foreground (**Figure 4.151**).

Figure 4.151 Boosting the color of the tie, even though it's a small element, creates contrast of extension because it stands out from the dominant hues in the scene.

Adjustments to extend the contrast of a specific element may be as simple as raising overall saturation. Other times, it's possible to tease a little more color out of an element in the frame by using a hue versus saturation curve or by using HSL Qualification to isolate and saturate a specific feature within the image.

Whatever method you use, remember that a little splash of color can go a long way.

CHAPTER 5

HSL QUALIFICATION AND HUE CURVES

There are many instances where, instead of making a *primary* color correction to an overall image, you need to adjust a specific object or subject within the frame, leaving everything else alone. For example, you may want to make the sky more blue, make the grass a bit darker, or tone down an actor's aggressively loud shirt.

These kinds of adjustments are referred to as *secondary* color corrections, since they're generally made after the primary color correction that you made to fix any issues with the overall color or contrast of the shot. Secondary color corrections are an essential part of any colorist's toolkit, and every professional color correction application provides a variety of ways to accomplish this important task.

This chapter, in particular, covers two of the principle ways of creating such targeted corrections. Most of the chapter is dedicated to how you use *HSL Qualification* to isolate regions of the image for secondary correction. At the end of the chapter, you'll also see how to use *hue curves* (and the slightly different user interface [UI] of *vectors*) to accomplish similarly targeted corrections in a different way entirely.

Many of the techniques in this book rely upon secondary color correction to make adjustments to very specific regions of the picture, but it's a mistake to rely on secondary corrections to deal with simple issues. It's good to get in the habit of checking whether you can make the same correction through careful manipulation of your primary color correction controls, instead of wasting time using qualifiers for operations that might be just as effective using the tonally specific Lift, Gamma, and Gain color balance controls.

However, with time you'll start to get the knack of when you can accomplish what's necessary via primary correction and when it's fastest to throw on a secondary correction to make that special tweak.

HSL QUALIFICATION IN THEORY

Before we launch into how to use these controls, let's first look at how HSL Qualification works. Essentially, what you're doing is pulling a *chroma key* to isolate part of the image based on a specific range of color or pulling a *luma key* to isolate part of the image based only on a specific range of lightness. Those of you who are familiar with compositing software know that keys are usually used to define areas of transparency—for example, making a greenscreen background transparent so that an actor appears to be floating in space.

However, when doing color correction, the key you're pulling creates a matte that is used to limit which part of the image is being affected by the color balance, contrast, or other controls, and which part is not (**Figure 5.1**).

Figure 5.1 The original image, an HSL Qualification matte, and the resulting secondary color correction. This is an example of why the costume department sometimes hates colorists (this is a deliberately extreme example for illustration).

Once you've defined a matte using your qualifier's color sampling controls and refined it using the individual H, S, and L color component controls (along with any blur or edge manipulation parameters), you can then choose whether you want to correct the region of the picture inside the matte (in white) or the region of the picture that's outside the matte (in black).

Once all this has been set up, it's a simple matter of adjusting the controls to manipulate the image.

ONSCREEN INTERFACES FOR HSL QUALIFICATION

In most color correction applications, the onscreen interface for HSL Qualification looks pretty much the same, although the programs may differ in how much they rely on the handles of graphical hue, saturation, and luma controls or whether they rely on sliders and numeric parameters.

Also, your results will vary because of the differences between various applications' under-the-hood image processing and the different algorithms used for each keyer's implementation (**Figure 5.2**). Still, the fundamental principles of use remain largely the same across many different applications, so if you learn one, you'll know how to use them all.

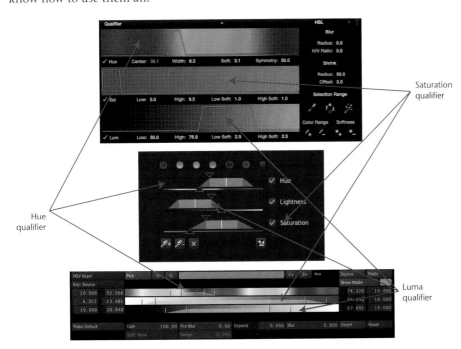

Figure 5.2 HSL controls compared; from top to bottom: DaVinci Resolve, Adobe SpeedGrade, Assimilate Scratch.

Saturation qualifier

Hue qualifier

Luma qualifier

Some brave UI designers have sought to develop this interface using a more graphical UI, a process I applaud when the result provides more obvious functionality in mouse-driven interfaces. For example, the Hue Angle keyer in FilmLight Baselight, while essentially an HSL keyer like those shown in Figure 5.2, presents a hue-wheel GUI for simultaneously adjusting hue and saturation in an intuitive way (**Figure 5.3**).

Figure 5.3 FilmLight Baselight's Hue Angle keyer is essentially an HSL keyer but with an integrated Hue/Saturation control for adjusting and customizing the key.

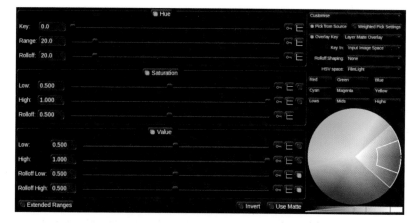

Another example of an application with a forward-looking approach to keying UI is Magic Bullet Colorista II, a color correction plug-in for nonlinear editors (NLEs) and compositing applications, shown in **Figure 5.4**.

Figure 5.4 The graphical interface of the keyer in Colorista II departs from the traditional HSL interface in order to make the process of pulling keys more approachable.

Though a departure from conventional HSL keying UIs, Colorista II retains the individual hue, saturation, and luma controls of the traditional HSL keyer in the form of the cube interface at the upper-right side of the UI and luma selection at the lower right. Most users will likely begin their key adjustments using the wedge/vectorscope interface underneath.

Keep in mind that most professional color correction applications map the HSL Qualifier parameters to knobs on a compatible control surface, so the onscreen UI may be incidental to their use. Indeed, many colorists prefer "dialing in" modifications to a keyed matte to tighten it up.

However, if you're working with a system that has a solid onscreen UI and you find yourself to be a mouse-oriented user, many onscreen UIs present options that aren't available via a control surface. At the end of the day, the best method to use is the one you find fastest.

WHAT ABOUT OTHER KEYERS?

Despite the availability of more advanced tools for keying, I focus on HSL keyers in this chapter because, in my experience, they're among the most useful tools for conventional grading tasks. They're also ubiquitous; nearly every grading application uses one, even applications with more advanced tools. Additionally, HSL Qualifiers tend to be processor-efficient, they're flexible to use, and the parameters are easy to understand, are easy to manipulate, are predictable, and provide a good baseline for understanding how to pull a good key.

However, the main advantage of the HSL keyer is that each color component can be individually isolated, which opens the door for a great many utilitarian and creative techniques that aren't necessarily available with more sophisticated keyers.

Later in this chapter, the "Advanced Keyers" section discusses other tools that are available for making color isolations.

INDIVIDUAL QUALIFIER CONTROLS

This section presents the typical onscreen controls you'll find in most HSL Qualifiers. When used together, each control contributes to a highly selective chroma key, letting you quickly sample a range of colors and refine the resulting key for the best possible effect. When used separately, these controls allow you to perform single-qualifier secondary color correction, isolating portions of an image based on individual characteristics of your image as interpreted using the HSL color model.

CHAPTER 5

Figure 5.5 The eyedropper in DaVinci Resolve.

Figure 5.6 The Color Picker options presented by DaVinci Resolve. From left to right: add to matte, subtract from matte, add softness, and remove softness.

EYEDROPPERS AND COLOR PICKERS

Most HSL keyers have an eyedropper tool (**Figure 5.5**) with which you can click on or drag an image to choose an initial value or range of values to begin creating your key. It's a great way to start if you're unsure exactly which range of values you need to select (which can be tricky with subtle ranges of color), even if you plan on immediately switching to manual adjustment of the qualifiers after you've found your starting point.

Some applications have just one color sampling tool, with keyboard modifiers enabling you to use the same tool to add to or subtract from the key by scrubbing different pixels of the image. Nucoda Film Master and Colorista II both use bounding-box sampling. Draw a box over the region of picture you want to sample, and the matte is started.

Other applications, such as DaVinci Resolve, have separate onscreen controls for explicitly sampling a primary value, expanding and subtracting from the range of values, and expanding or narrowing the range of softness (tolerance) of the matte (**Figure 5.6**).

However your controls are set up, once you click or drag with your application's eyedropper/color sampling tool, you should see the Hue, Saturation, and Luma qualifiers expand or contract to reflect the color vales of the pixels you're sampling.

Choosing an initial value or range of values with which to begin your key can be a tricky business. The noise, grain, and variation in detail inherent to any image will produce a range of color, even from pixel to pixel. This means that even if you think you've just clicked a light part of the image, you might have inadvertently clicked the one dark pixel of noise in that area, giving you a disappointing result. Don't worry, this is bound to happen; just sample other pixels until you find one that gives you the best initial result.

Here are two general tips for choosing a good initial value:

• Choose a color value that's right in between the lightest and darkest values you're trying to key, starting at the middle and working your way outward.

• If the subject you're trying to key has an uneven border with another subject— for example, the sky against the horizon—and you're trying to key the sky, choosing a value that's near the border at the horizon is a good way to start building the best part of your key where it's most important.

VIEWING THE MASK WHILE YOU WORK

Most color correction applications provide you with three or four different ways of viewing the key you're creating as you work. This is essential to creating high-quality keys. If you view only the final result, it can be difficult to see problem areas such as unwanted holes in the matte, excessive noise, or chattering edges. These three modes are as follows:

- A high-contrast grayscale matte-only view (**Figure 5.7**). I find this to be the most useful preview of the matte I'm creating, as it's drop-dead obvious to see the quality of the white areas that represent the keyed area (the *inside* of the correction) and the black areas that represent the unkeyed area (the *outside* of the correction).

Figure 5.7 A high-contrast matte, as seen in nearly any color correction application capable of HSL Qualification.

- The keyed area in color against the unkeyed area in grayscale or solid color (**Figure 5.8**). This can be a useful view for seeing how your key is shaping up, while also seeing which parts of the inside or outside of a key correspond to shadows or highlights in the subject you're isolating that you may or may not want to include in your key. The high-contrast mode can make these kinds of judgments difficult if you don't remember the image's details.

TIP

When using video scopes, the saturated/matte mode has the added benefit of flat-lining everything in the picture that isn't being keyed, effectively "soloing" the region you're keying in the Waveform Monitor. This can be extremely useful when you're trying to selectively isolate values of the image within a particular zone of image tonality.

Figure 5.8 A saturated vs. matte mode, as seen in the Matte Invert Overlay option in FilmLight Baselight, that shows you exactly which parts of the image are being included in the key. Other applications show the unkeyed area as simple grayscale, rather than a flat matte.

CHAPTER 5

- A reverse variation can often be found, where the keyed subject appears with a false-color overlay (**Figure 5.9**), while the unkeyed area remains in full color.

Figure 5.9 A false-color overlay, as seen in the Matte Overlay option in FilmLight Baselight, showing the element being keyed.

- The final effect. For some applications this mode is redundant, as the matte and final effect are viewed simultaneously on different onscreen portions of the UI. However, if you're viewing the key matte on your output display, you'll need to switch to this viewing mode to go back to making the correction once you've finished refining the key.

Ideally, it's good to create and adjust your key while simultaneously viewing the matte you're creating in your application's canvas or preview window, or you can even output it to your broadcast monitor to view it. Surprisingly, I've found that clients love watching these mattes being made, so monitor output isn't a bad thing.

THE INDIVIDUAL QUALIFIERS

Once you've sampled an initial range of values to get your key's starting point, the next step in the process is to fine-tune the matte using the qualifier controls. As seen previously, these controls typically follow some common conventions across different applications. In general, each color component has a set of handles and parameters that allow you to adjust one of two sets of values:

- **Range** handles let you enclose a base set of values that contribute to the hardest, whitest part of the key.

- **Tolerance** (or softening) handles let you include an additional set of values that add a gradual falloff around the edge of the key, which appears as a range of gradually diminishing grayscale values surrounding the hardest part of the key. Widening the tolerance yields softer edges and a more inclusive key, and narrowing them yields harder edges and a more restrictive key. If the edges of the key are gentle enough because of the softening that tolerance provides, you may not need to blur the resulting matte.

TIP

If you're using DaVinci Resolve, the "Mattes display high contrast black and white" check box in the Settings tab of the Config page determines how mattes are displayed when you turn on the Highlight button within the qualifier controls. Other applications may have more explicit buttons for choosing among available options.

Finally, Enable/Disable checkboxes let you manually decide which qualifiers you want to use for a particular keying operation (**Figure 5.10**).

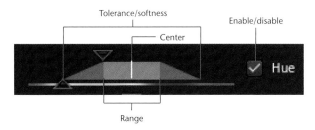

Figure 5.10 The GUI of a typical qualifier control (as seen in Adobe SpeedGrade), which ordinarily corresponds to either three or four control panel knobs.

Additionally, there are two general methods used for manipulating controls. The methods used depend primarily on how these controls are mapped to the rotary knobs on a control surface.

- **Centered** controls work using three knobs per color component. The first knob moves the center point of both pairs of range and tolerance handles all together to the left or right, a second knob expands and contracts the range and tolerance relative to the center, and a third knob expands and contracts the tolerance relative to the current position of the range handles.

- **Asymmetrical** controls use four knobs to move the left and right sets of controls of each qualifier separately. Two knobs for Low and Low Soft adjust the left range and tolerance, while two more for High and High Soft adjust the right range and tolerance separately.

If you're using a GUI rather than a control surface, you might actually be able to manipulate the qualifiers in either of these ways, using keyboard modifiers while dragging the appropriate handles.

HUE CONTROL

The Hue qualifier lets you select a portion of the color spectrum to isolate a range of color within an image. The spectrum is continuous, wrapping seamlessly from the left of the control to the right of the control (**Figure 5.11**).

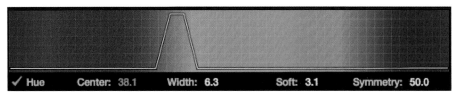

Figure 5.11 The Hue qualifier graph in DaVinci Resolve.

If you turn on the Hue control without turning on the Saturation control, you'll select all color values within a particular range of hues without regard to intensity or lightness.

SATURATION CONTROL

The Saturation qualifier lets you select a range of saturation, or color intensity, within the image. The black or colored end of the ramp represents 100 percent saturation; the white or gray portion of the ramp indicates 0 percent saturation (**Figure 5.12**).

Figure 5.12 The Saturation qualifier graph in DaVinci Resolve.

If you turn on the Saturation control without turning on the Hue control, you'll select all color values within a particular range of saturation without regard for the actual colors.

LUMA CONTROL

In a keyer, this qualifier lets you isolate a range of luma, the lightness component of an image (the Y' in $Y'C_BC_R$). The black end of the ramp represents 0 percent luma; the white end of the ramp indicates 100 percent luma. In some implementations, there's an additional region of this control that represents the super-white range from 100 to 110 percent (**Figure 5.13**).

Figure 5.13 The Luma qualifier graph in DaVinci Resolve.

If you turn on the Luma control without turning on the Hue or Saturation controls, you'll select all areas of an image within a particular range of lightness, without regard to the color. The result is that you will be creating a luma key. This frequently yields the greatest amount of edge detail with highly compressed media, and it is a commonly used technique for segmenting an image that we'll see later in this chapter.

LUMA KEYS MAKE SHARPER MATTES IN COMPRESSED MEDIA

Because the luma component, unlike chroma, is always sampled in its entirety, you'll get better results from luma keys than you will from chroma keys when working with 4:1:1 or 4:2:0 footage (although you'll still see some subtle aliased edges with 4:2:2-encoded video).

POSTKEY MASK UTILITIES—BLUR AND EDGE MANIPULATION

Once a key has been pulled using the eyedropper/color sampling and qualifier controls, the result is a grayscale image. Most HSL keyers provide additional filtering operations that you can use to manipulate this image to make it more usable in situations where a key was difficult to pull or when the key has noise, chatter, or other undesirable artifacts that would give the resulting correction away.

Although these operations lend themselves to quick fixes, make sure you've exhausted the possibilities of the qualifier controls to pull the best possible key, and be careful not to use settings that are too aggressive. If you overdo these types of operations, you may wind up with halos or other problems that might actually be worse than the artifacts you're trying to avoid.

BLUR/SOFTENING/FEATHERING

Softening simply blurs the keyed matte. This function is useful for eliminating spurious areas of keyed detail that you don't want affecting the final correction, as well as for minimizing the visible effect of animated buzz and noise in the matte (**Figure 5.14**).

Figure 5.14 A matte, before and after adding blur to soften the edges and minimize marginal portions of the key.

Oversoftening the matte and then creating a correction could result in the same correction being applied to an area surrounding the intended subject, producing an unwanted glow where the correction spills onto the over-feathered area (unless you're intentionally using a secondary to create a glow operation.

To help avoid this, FilmLight Baselight has an interesting function for not just blurring the matte but controlling whether the matte is blurred outward or inward. Using this tool, you can apply a negative amount of blur, which adds softness from the current edge of the matte inward, extending toward the interior of the matte (**Figure 5.15**).

Figure 5.15 "Negative" blurring in FilmLight Baselight to feather into the interior of a matte, rather than blurring outward. The resulting modification can avoid haloing around the subject.

Regardless of the sophistication of your tools, the best way to avoid haloing and edge artifacts is to rely on the softness or tolerance controls of each individual qualifier to create soft matte edges that accurately adhere to the contours of the subject you're keying. However, what's possible depends entirely on the image at hand, and there are plusses and minuses to both approaches.

For example, in **Figure 5.16**, you can see a key to isolate the skin tone of the performers that's reached the limits of what can be done via an adjustment of the inner range of the key.

Figure 5.16 A key to isolate skin tone near the limits of effective isolation.

Figure 5.17 shows two different approaches to feathering the edge of this too-hard matte. At left, blur is applied to the matte to soften the edges, and while it's softer and the blur has also filled in some of the noise of the matte, you can also see that the resulting feathered edges extend past the edges of the two people. An indiscriminate adjustment could result in haloing. However, at right you can see the result of extending the tolerance or softness controls of the qualifier in order to feather the edge. The result follows the area being isolated much more accurately, but now you've introduced spill into the background. You'll need to deal with that as well.

Figure 5.17 At left, feathering the edge of the matte using blur. At right, feathering the edge of the matte by increasing the softness/tolerance of the qualifiers to achieve a smoother falloff.

This situation illustrates the kinds of issues you'll be balancing in most shots. In truth, the best approach to this dilemma is probably to combine a little bit of HSL tolerance expansion with a little bit of blur to find the best combination of both.

SHRINK/ERODE

Some applications also have a Shrink parameter (or Erode or whatever the corresponding control in your application is named). This is usually an averaging control similar to the matte choke function found in compositing applications (**Figure 5.18**).

Figure 5.18 Left, the original mask; center, the matte after using the Shrink parameter to expand it, filling out holes; right, the matte after using the Shrink parameter to contract it, eliminating unwanted marginal areas of the matte. These mattes were created in DaVinci Resolve.

As shown in Figure 5.18, this control expands or contracts the edges of the matte.

- Expanding the edges of a matte is useful for filling in small holes appearing in a troublesome matte.

- Contracting the edges of a matte is useful for eliminating spurious pixels and unwanted details in the matte, as well as for shrinking the overall matte.

Using shrink all by itself can sometimes result in blockier edges, which is seldom desirable. In these cases, adding some blur will smooth out the result (**Figure 5.19**).

Figure 5.19 A shrunken matte that's been blurred to address the blocky edges.

CONTRAST ADJUSTMENT AND CURVES CONTROL

Applications including SGO Mistika include the ability to actually grade a key using Lift/Gamma/Gain controls. Mistika and Baselight both have a Matte curve that can also be used to shape the contrast of the matte being output in order to optimize it for the need at hand (**Figure 5.20**).

Figure 5.20 In Baselight, clicking the Edit Matte Tool button on the Matte tab reveals a series of matte postprocessing tools, which include a matte curve you can use to shape a matte's contrast.

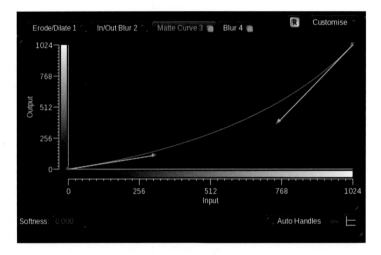

This can be exceptionally handy for manipulating the soft fringes of a matte in order to turn a dodgy key into a much more useful one. **Figure 5.21** shows a scene in which the client would like some minor adjustments to the environment, excluding the skin tone of the performers, in order to separate them from the background a bit more.

Figure 5.21 The original scene, before applying secondary adjustment.

In **Figure 5.22**, an attempt to isolate the skin tones of the two performers has resulted in fringing in the matte on the wall and print in the background, owing to the warm tones of the art direction. The fringe is light, so rather than continue worrying the HSL controls, you can use a Curve control to adjust the contrast of the matte to crush the fringing while retaining the strength of the best part of the matte, within the faces.

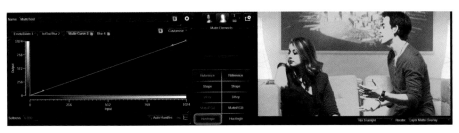

Figure 5.22 Fringing in the matte on the arms of the woman's shirt is easily eliminated by adjusting the contrast of the matte using a dedicated curve control in FilmLight Baselight.

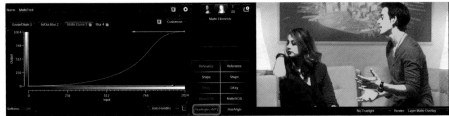

This is an extreme example, and the result could probably benefit from a touch of blur to soften the rough edges that can result, but it's a fast solution to the problem. Contrast adjustment is one of the most powerful and successful tools you can use to turn a matte that you were barely able to pull into something useful for the task at hand.

LIMIT THE KEY USING A SHAPE

There will be plenty of times when, no matter how hard you try, you'll simply find it impossible to isolate the one feature you're targeting using just the qualifier controls. There are going to be plenty of times when colors in the background are just too close to what you're trying to key (wood, sand, and skin tones are combinations designed to drive a colorist mad) for you to be able to create a clean isolation without some extra help.

Fortunately, that extra help can come in the form of overlapping a shape or window (covered in the next chapter) with the key you're pulling. For example, the skin tone that's being isolated is very close, in the golden-hour light of the city, to brownstone buildings and autumnal foliage in the background. As a result, a relatively decent key on the people's faces produces a lot of fringe in the background.

However, nearly all grading applications provide the ability to draw a shape around the area you're trying to key (identical to a garbage matte when compositing) to eliminate any unwanted keying elsewhere in the picture (Figure 5.23).

Figure 5.23 Using a shape in Baselight to omit parts of the performers' skin tone matte fringing in the background.

A skill that comes from experience is to know when you're just driving yourself crazy overworking the HSL controls and when to call it quits and use an overlapping shape.

INVERTING THE KEY

Color correction applications deal with whether corrections apply to the white portion (inside) or black portion (outside) of a matte in one of three different ways:

- Applications such as DaVinci Resolve and Assimilate Scratch let you invert the keyed matte, switching which part of the image a correction affects.

- Applications including Autodesk Lustre and FilmLight Baselight let you explicitly set whether a correction affects the "inside" or "outside" portion of the matte.

- DaVinci Resolve's node-based correction interface also lets you create an "outside node" that you can use to grade the opposite portion of a key relative to the original node you created.

Inverting a key is an ideal approach if the subject to be excluded from a color correction operation is uniform enough in color and lightness to be selected with an application's Limit Effect controls and you want to apply the secondary color correction to everything else.

For example, if we wanted to adjust everything within the frame *except* for the dress, we can still pull our key off of the dress since it's the easiest thing to do (**Figure 5.24**).

Figure 5.24 At left, the original key pulled off of the woman's dress. At right, the inverted matte, useful for adjusting everything *except* for the dress.

Then, using whatever control inverts the matte, you can reverse the black and white regions, so now the dress becomes the area that won't be affected by the secondary correction, while the rest of the image is set up for the correction you want to make.

A BASIC HSL QUALIFICATION WORKFLOW

This section shows you the basic procedure you'll use for doing HSL Qualification using nearly any color correction application. The exact UI may differ, but these general steps remain the same.

FIRST, DEFINE THE BASIC KEY

There are two ways to begin creating a secondary key.

In the first method, you click the Select Color button and then click somewhere in the Canvas with the eyedropper to select a primary Hue, Saturation, and Luma value. Depending on the HSB value of the pixel you clicked, Final Cut Pro 7, for example, turns on (checks) one or more of the qualifiers and sets them to the values found within that pixel. If you click a white pixel, the program may turn on the Luma qualifier only. If you click a red pixel, on the other hand, all three qualifiers are likely to turn on.

The second way to begin a key is simply to start adjusting one of the qualifier controls directly, manually dialing in the ranges of values you want to isolate.

Either method is appropriate, although with practice you'll find that single-component keys tend to be faster to pull if you know exactly which color component you want to isolate, whereas keys on subjects that naturally combine all components can be tricky. For example, the shadows and highlights of the skin tones on someone's face are always a mix of a variety of hues, luma levels, and saturation, which really requires an eyedropper/image sampling selection to get started.

In the following example, the consensus in the suite is that the red poster that's reflecting in the window behind the woman in the green shirt is too distracting (**Figure 5.25**). We'll take a look at how to quickly isolate the offending object and use the resulting matte to create the necessary correction to address this.

Figure 5.25 The image with a single primary correction.

HSL Qualification makes isolating the poster really easy.

NOTE

Some applications (Baselight and Resolve) put you into the mode for sampling color as soon as you enable the qualifier controls.

TIP

Assimilate Scratch ordinarily presents a "click to pick" method of color sampling, but holding down the Command key lets you drag a bounding box around a region in order to sample a larger area at once.

Figure 5.26 Using an eyedropper to sample the color from a subject for isolation.

1 If necessary, click your color correction application's eyedropper/color picker button to get into the mode for sampling a color from the image, either in your application's canvas/viewer or on your broadcast display.

2 Using whatever tool appears (an eyedropper cursor, crosshairs, or a bounding box), sample values from the image by doing one of the following:

- Click once to sample the initial value with which to create the key. Then, using a second tool or button, click elsewhere to expand the sampled region that contributes to the matte (**Figure 5.26**).

- In many applications, you can simply click and drag to immediately sample a wide range of values with which to create a matte. Applications such as Baselight present a bounding box as you drag to show you the region you're sampling.

When you release the mouse button, a few things happen. First, the matte you've just created should become visible. For example, in DaVinci Resolve, the icon of the node containing the new qualifier settings updates to show the new matte.

In other applications, dedicated matte preview areas may display the new matte, or the canvas/viewer may update with a preview display of the matte so you can judge how successful your sample was (**Figure 5.27**).

Figure 5.27 A preview display of the matte.

Finally, the individual qualifier control parameters update to reflect the range of values you've sampled (**Figure 5.28**).

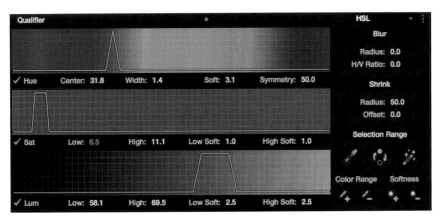

Figure 5.28 The updated individual qualifier control parameters in DaVinci Resolve.

CHAPTER 5

3 To prepare for the next stage, switch your color correction application to display the matte, if it hasn't already done so automatically.

WHICH IS SAMPLED, THE ORIGINAL OR THE ADJUSTED IMAGE?

It's important to know what state of the image the HSL Qualifiers are sampling. Many grading applications give you a choice of sampling the original uncorrected media or sampling the media after it's been adjusted with one or more corrections. There are advantages to both options, which are covered in greater detail later in this chapter.

REFINE THE KEY

With any key you pull, you'll rarely get it perfect with the very first drag of the eyedropper. In the best cases, there may be a bit of fringe around the edges that you don't want, as in the current example. In less ideal circumstances, you'll be attempting to isolate a difficult range of color (isolating swimsuit skin tones when the actors are surrounded by beige sand can be challenging) or working with video that has limited chroma information, making clean edges difficult.

1 You can sample another part of the image to add it to the matte. For example:

- DaVinci Resolve, Adobe SpeedGrade, and Autodesk Scratch present additional buttons, next to the other sampling buttons, that let you add to the currently selected range and softness of the key.

- In Baselight, holding down the Shift key while you drag a bounding box over another region of color adds to the selection in the Hue Angle keyer.

Trying this with our image lets us solidify the poster matte while at the same time adding other parts of the image that we don't necessarily want to include (**Figure 5.29**).

Figure 5.29 The matte after adding to the selection. More of the poster is included, but some of the woman's dress at the far left is included as well, which we don't want.

At this point, we're probably going to have to turn to the individual qualifier controls to make more specific adjustments to most successfully fine-tune the matte.

2 If your application's qualifiers work using the "center adjustment" model, a good tip for figuring out whether manipulations to any of the qualifiers will do you any good before you start manipulating them is to wiggle the center of each qualifier to the left and right while watching the matte. If the matte changes dramatically, then chances are that manipulating that qualifier will do you some real good. If the matte changes only slightly, then your initial sample probably got the range about right, and you can move on.

3 Once you've identified which qualifiers you need to adjust, carefully widen and/or re-center their inner range handles/parameter to highlight as much of the subject you're trying to isolate with white (or color, if you're viewing the matte in color/desaturate mode), while excluding as much of everything else as you can with black.

Adjusting the qualifiers one by one is a good policy, and I usually start with Hue, since that almost always does me the most good. For this example, I made the following adjustments:

- **Hue**: I increased the width of the isolated range of hue.

- **Saturation**: I increased the range of isolated saturation, shifting it asymmetrically to include less saturated values.

- **Luma**: No adjustment to luma was necessary to improve the key (**Figure 5.30**).

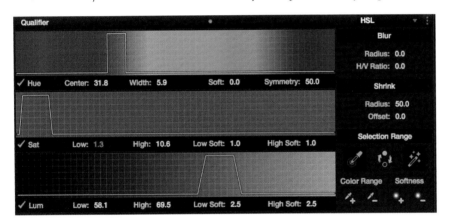

Figure 5.30 Adjustments to the individual qualifiers in DaVinci Resolve to solidify the matte.

This had the effect on the key shown in **Figure 5.31**.

Figure 5.31 The key after adjustments to the individual HSL Qualifiers.

At this point, several edge details of the woman at the left are being included in the matte. Fortunately, the unwanted details are far away from the poster we're trying to isolate, so we'll ignore all that for now to see what we can get away with.

MANIPULATE THE KEY

Once the general key has been defined and you think you've made it as good as you can using the individual qualifiers, it's time to refine the matte using some filtered postprocessing in the form of blur and edge processing.

The key created by any HSL keyer is simply a grayscale image, and these parameters apply a filter-style effect to this image to help you make difficult keys more usable by minimizing rough edges, eliminating small holes in the matte (if necessary), managing noise and grain, and subduing edge chatter.

At the least, every grading application has a blur parameter with which you can feather the matte, which can be a huge help in cases where fringe in the matte is hard to eliminate. It also comes in handy with highly compressed media that may exhibit blocky edges in the matte.

For this example, adding a small amount of blur helps to take the edge off the matte itself (**Figure 5.32**).

Don't overdo matte blurring or either you'll end up with a halo around the area you're keying once you start to make your correction or you'll unwittingly shrink the key so that original color will remain at the edge of the keyed subject after the correction.

Figure 5.32 The Blur parameter softens the matte just a little bit, to minimize aliasing.

ALWAYS WATCH YOUR KEY PLAY

Whenever you use the HSL Qualifiers, make sure you watch the shot play while you're looking at the matte in order to make sure it doesn't buzz or chatter visibly at the edges or in "thin" areas of the matte. If there is buzz or chatter, manipulate the matte until it becomes unnoticeable in the final effect.

USE A SHAPE/POWER WINDOW TO CROP UNWANTED FEATURES FROM THE MATTE

Often, unwanted portions of an image get included in a key you're trying to pull because the chroma or luma values are simply too close to the colors you're trying to isolate, with one of two results:

- You have good isolation but a crummy matte.

- You have a great matte but it's too loose, keying other parts of the frame that you don't want to include.

You can fiddle with the qualifiers all you want, but you just can't pull a completely clean key. In these situations, the best thing to do is to turn on whatever shape/Power Window control is available in your grading application and use it as a *garbage matte* (to use compositing terminology) to exclude the areas of the image you don't want to be included in the key.

Applications do this differently, but the general idea is that whenever you use both HSL Qualification *and* a mask/shape/vignette/Power Window within a single secondary/scaffold/strip/grade, the two will be combined so that the only keyed areas that are preserved are those appearing within the shape.

1 Turn on the type of shape that will best isolate the portion of the key you want to preserve (for more details on using shapes/Power Windows, see Chapter 5).

2 Make sure you feather the edge of the shape so there are no harsh edges should you need to crop the key really closely.

3 Reposition the shape to isolate the desired portion of the HSL key (**Figure 5.33**).

The resulting shape-limited matte is now suitable for making our correction. At this point, all we need to watch out for is whether it's necessary to animate or motion track the shape so that it follows the subject if it or the camera is moving (both of which are covered in Chapter 6).

So, if shapes are so handy, why not just use a shape all by itself? It's because, as you can see in Figure 5.33, shapes aren't nearly as specific and discriminating as a good key. In this example, the key conforms well to the red portion of the poster, while leaving the figures within alone.

If we were to try using a custom shape/Power Curve, it would require a lot of drawing, and we'd risk needing to rotoscope the resulting shape to match a moving camera.

It's much more detailed and faster to key the poster, even though we're including other parts of the image by accident, and then limit the key using this simple oval shape/Power Window, tracking it to generally follow the subject if there's motion.

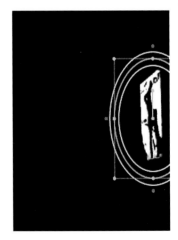

Figure 5.33 Cropping out unwanted portions of the key using a shape/Power Window.

MAKE YOUR CORRECTION

Now that we've refined the matte to our satisfaction, we're ready to make an adjustment. The spectacular example would be to change the red poster to another vivid color, but the whole point is to make the poster less noticeable, so we'll do the opposite of what we usually do, reducing contrast and fading the color to make it as much of an indistinguishable part of the background as we can. Here are the steps you need to take:

1 Turn off the matte preview so that you can see the actual image.

2 Eliminate the objectionable red by desaturating it until it's a muted, pale color, and then rebalance the Gamma color to be bluish rather than reddish.

3 Lastly, reduce contrast by raising the Lift contrast control, while lowering both the Gamma and Gain controls, doing your best to make the poster as unnoticeable as possible (**Figure 5.34**).

Figure 5.34 The final effect. The poster in the reflection is muted, no longer drawing attention to itself.

The correction is complete.

This is but one of the myriad uses of the HSL Qualifiers. In the next section, we'll look at what to do when you have a hard-to-key shot, for which HSL Qualification is your best bet.

TIPS FOR USING AND OPTIMIZING HSL QUALIFICATIONS

The quality of your secondary correction is going to be dictated by the quality of the key you can pull. As with ordinary keying, it can be tricky to pull the matte you need in every clip, especially if the clip isn't that great to begin with. This section discusses ways you can maximize the quality of your secondary corrections to keep noisiness and rough edges from standing in the way of a successful adjustment.

WHAT IS THE PERFECT KEY?

If you've spent any amount of time pulling bluescreen and greenscreen keys to create mattes for compositing, you know how time-consuming and imperfect a process chroma keying can be. Fortunately, one of the nice things about color correction is that it's not usually necessary to pull pixel-perfect keys in order to create a reasonably convincing and invisible secondary correction, although how true this is depends on how extreme a correction you're making.

- If you're making a subtle adjustment to a clip's saturation, you'll be able to get away with a pretty sketchy matte.

- If you're making a naturalistic adjustment to the highlights of the image when holes in a keyed matte correspond to shadows that are falling on the subject you're isolating, you probably don't want to include such shadowed areas in the correction, so there's no need to make further adjustments to the matte.

- If you're making relatively extreme corrections to color and especially to contrast, you'll want to pull a considerably tighter, denser key to avoid visible artifacts. At the end of the day, chroma keying for color correction is all about what you can get away with.

No matter how loose or tight a matte you're creating, the most important thing you need to watch out for is buzz and chatter in the key, both of which can be minimized by judicious use of blur and shrink filtering operations. Sometimes, it may be faster and just as good to create a decent key and just soften the edges to make sure the matte isn't too animated, while other times you'll need to work the qualifiers to improve the overall key. However, you want to make sure you don't soften the edge of the matte too much, or you'll end up with a halo around the correction.

In all cases, the best thing you can do to check any secondary key is to play it all the way through to make sure it's not buzzing and that the color isn't bleeding later in the clip. These sorts of problems aren't immediately visible while you're working on a clip with playback paused, and they're the very issues that ruin a perfectly good secondary.

USE HIGH-QUALITY DIGITAL MEDIA

There are abundant reasons for color correcting and otherwise finishing a program using the highest-quality source media possible. Aside from image quality considerations, secondary keying is one of the biggest beneficiaries of higher-quality media.

The best way to improve the quality of secondary color correction operations is to use the highest-quality video you can, ideally uncompressed or minimally compressed media with the highest chroma subsampling ratio possible. High-quality video formats such as Avid's DNxHD 220x, 220, and 145, as well as Apple ProRes 422 and ProRes 422 (HQ) encode video with 4:2:2 chroma subsampling. As a result, you'll get relatively clean keys and smooth edge detail in secondary keys when working with shots in these formats.

Other mastering codecs such as Apple ProRes 4444, as well as uncompressed image sequence formats such as DPX, allow for fully 4:4:4 RGB data streams with minimal to no compression. These media types will yield exceptionally good keys since they have a maximum amount of data with which to feed a chroma keyer's digital algorithms.

HSL QUALIFICATION WHEN YOU'RE FORCED TO USE HIGHLY COMPRESSED FOOTAGE

Because you're pulling a chroma key, highly compressed footage poses the same challenges for secondary color correction that it poses when you are keying to create visual effects. This is especially true when you are keying off of footage with limited color sampling.

Keys off of video formats using 4:1:1 and 4:2:0 chroma subsampling (including the DV-25, HDV, and H.264-based formats) will suffer from blockier edges and more compression artifacts exposed in the key (such as macro-blocking) than keying from 4:2:2 or, even more preferably, from 4:4:4 formats. You can see the difference in **Figure 5.35**.

If you're working with highly compressed source media, you'll find yourself frequently relying upon the Edge Thin and Softening sliders to smooth the edges of your key.

Another technique that works well when you are doing secondary color correction on highly compressed media is to create single-qualifier secondary keys using only the Luma controls. Because all video formats preserve the full quality of the luma component of a color signal (luma is the *4* in *4:1:1* and *4:2:0*), you'll find that this renders mattes with the best edge detail.

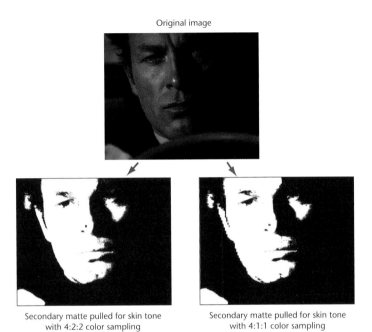

Original image

Secondary matte pulled for skin tone
with 4:2:2 color sampling

Secondary matte pulled for skin tone
with 4:1:1 color sampling

Figure 5.35 As you can see in this illustration, the key pulled from the 4:2:2 source media is much smoother at the edges than the key pulled from the 4:1:1 down-converted version of the same clip. The right matte's aliasing and blockiness makes it harder to make seamless corrections.

CHROMA SMOOTHING 4:1:1 OR 4:2:0 MEDIA

If you're correcting source material recorded with 4:1:1 or 4:2:0 chroma subsampling, you're left with as much color information as was captured, which is to say not very much. Although this isn't necessarily such a severe liability with simple primary corrections, blocky secondary keys can occur, depending on how much the chroma channel contributes to the key. In fact, even 4:2:2-encoded media displays some aliasing along the edges of keys. One way to smooth this out, and potentially to quiet some of the jitter inside of a noisy key, is to use some sort of chroma smoothing plug-in or control in your application.

Selectively blurring the Cr and Cb channels of video clips smooths the rough edges left by the blocks of missing color information from the original compression process, and in fact, if your color correction application allows selective filtering operations to specific color channels in the $Y'C_BC_R$ color space, you can do this yourself without the benefit of additional plug-ins. Slightly blurring the chroma component of a video signal slightly can in many cases improve the edges and lower the noise of a keyed matte.

CONTROL THE IMAGE PROCESSING PIPELINE

Another way you can optimize the keying process is by making adjustments to the image prior to keying it. Now, this is possible only if your application lets you control the image-processing pipeline that feeds the HSL Qualifier's keyer. Most do, some don't.

- In DaVinci Resolve, you can connect the input of the correction node containing the HSL Qualifier to the output of any node coming before it, choosing either the original state of the image or the state of the image as it's output from any other node, which lets you be very specific about which state of the image you want to sample for keying.

- In Assimilate Scratch, you have the option to key from the Source (the original media), the Primary, Recursive (the Primary and all scaffolds up to the one you're working on), or Texture Fill or Matte (for special effects).

- In FilmLight Baselight, a Reference strip appears along with the InsideOutside and HueAngle layer strips that are created when you add a keyer. The Reference strip controls whether you use the original or graded image as the basis for the key. The Baselight plug-in makes the Reference layer available as an operator on the Matte tab.

- In Autodesk Lustre, a Source Primary button determines whether to use the source, or the primary correction, as the basis for the key.

- If you're color correcting using an NLE, the filter interfaces of Apple Final Cut Pro, Adobe Premiere Pro, and Avid Media Composer are stack-based UIs, where the order of the filters determines the order of processing. When you insert a color correction filter at the bottom of a list of other filters, the keyer samples the output of all filters applied earlier in the stack.

When sampling values for a key, there are various reasons to choose either the original state of the media or a graded version of the shot.

In some instances, your grade may be so extreme (a low-saturation bleach-bypass effect, for example) that inserting an HSL Qualification at that point would result in a terrible key. This is a case where you'd want to sample the original image in order to get the best result.

On the other hand, if you're grading media that is inherently low contrast and low saturation (for example, a flat best light safety film transfer or media using a raw format such as RED), you'll probably get far better results by pulling a key from a color-corrected version of the image.

The following sections describe ways in which controlling the image-processing pipeline will improve your keys.

BOOST IMAGE OR COLOR CONTRAST

A key method that often helps improve keys is to boost the saturation and/or increase the contrast of the overall image, pulling a key off of the result. By increasing color contrast and luma contrast, you increase the distance between discrete values in the image, which can make it easier to manipulate the qualifier controls to isolate more specific slices of color. You can think of a saturation/contrast boost as widening the difference between the colors of the subject you're trying to isolate and the areas you're trying to exclude.

In **Figure 5.36**, the man's pale blue shirt in the uncorrected shot on the left is difficult to distinguish from the cool highlights overall, mainly because the initial contrast of the shot is so low. However, boosting contrast and raising saturation makes the shirt a much easier target for HSL Qualification.

Figure 5.36 The uncorrected image at the left will be difficult to key, owing to its low contrast and saturation. At right, the same image has had the contrast boosted, preparing it for keying.

Often, you'll be boosting contrast and saturation as part of your primary grade anyway. However, if your goal is ultimately a desaturated look, you'll need to boost contrast and saturation with one correction, add a secondary in another correction to create the isolated adjustment you need, and then reduce the contrast of the overall image using a third correction to get the overall look you require (**Figure 5.37**).

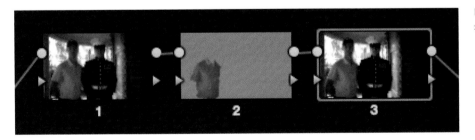

Figure 5.37 A three-correction sequence.

In Figure 5.37 we can see this process in action. The image is made ready for keying with node 1, the HSL Qualification to adjust the man's shirt happens in node 2, and a final correction in node 3 reduces overall saturation to create the final desired effect.

CHAPTER 5

MAKING A SECONDARY ADJUSTMENT BEFORE A PRIMARY

Another strategy is to make a secondary HSL Qualifier adjustment *before* making your primary correction. This is especially useful in instances where the primary correction you want will clip highlights or crush shadows to the point of impeding a high-quality key, preventing you from making an adjustment to retrieve necessary detail.

It should be noted that most contemporary grading applications have 32-bit floating-point image processing that's capable of preserving "out-of-bounds" image data for retrieval later, so if you're making minor adjustments, this problem shouldn't arise very often. However, there are always operations where you compress image detail substantially or where you may in fact end up deliberately clipping the image (using a LUT or other operation that specifically clips image detail in your application), for which this technique is still valuable.

In **Figure 5.38**, we can see that slight underexposure coupled with a white, reflective driveway, means that we can't simply boost the midtones to the level we want without clipping the driveway.

Figure 5.38 Adjusting contrast for a proper exposure results in the white driveway getting clipped, as shown in the image on the right.

To work around this, you can make a secondary adjustment as your *first* correction, which lets you key and manipulate the image using all of the detail found at the original signal levels. Then, in a second correction, you would use a primary adjustment to clip the highlights or crush the shadows as desired for the look you want (**Figure 5.39**).

Figure 5.39 Node 1 pulls a key on the road, allowing you to selectively control its contrast before the adjustment made by node 2, which raises contrast overall.

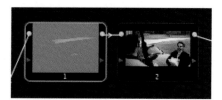

When you work this way, you can lower the exposure of the road in proportion to the amount you'll be raising exposure in the second corrections. In other words, if you know you'll be jacking up the highlights of an overall image and losing detail as a result, then isolate the detail you'll be losing and *lower it before it gets raised in the second correction*, so the final result is properly exposed all the way through (**Figure 5.40**).

Figure 5.40 The end result. By preemptively lowering the lightness of the road, you preserve detail even though you're still boosting the contrast of the entire shot.

This technique works equally well with saturation enhancements, enabling you to lower saturated elements before they get clipped later.

PREEMPTIVELY BLUR, NOISE REDUCE, OR OTHERWISE ADJUST THE IMAGE YOU'RE KEYING

In some cases, excessive noise or movement in an image makes it challenging to pull a smooth key, even if you're using a postkey blur. One thing you can try in such situations is to blur the image before you pull a key. There are several ways you can do this.

- Assimilate Scratch has a convenient Pre-Blur parameter that lets you blur the image before you pull a key. This doesn't affect the image visually; it simply softens a branch of image processing that's being fed to the keyer.

- In DaVinci Resolve, you can do the same thing by creating a node tree where a correction that blurs the image, applies aggressive noise reduction, or makes a radical color adjustment in an effort to improve the image for keying is connected to a second correction set up to pull the key. To avoid actually blurring the corrected image, you then insert that key into the mask input of another correction that takes the original state of the image as its image input (**Figure 5.41**).

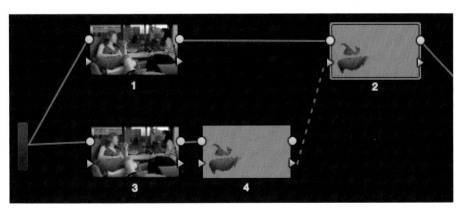

Figure 5.41 Blurring an image in order to improve a key, without blurring the final image in DaVinci Resolve. Node 3 blurs the image, and node 4 pulls a key from the result. Node 1 is the initial primary correction for the shot, while node 2 is a secondary correction that uses the matte that's fed to it from node 4 (via the key input at the bottom left).

However you employ this technique, keep in mind that you're modifying a version of the clip that is being used only for keying, with the key being fed to another operation that works upon the undisturbed version of the image data.

UNUSUAL QUALIFIER COMBINATIONS

One thing that's easy to overlook when you're trying to pull a tricky key is that you might be able to solve your isolation problem using an unusual combination of qualifier controls. I directed a movie that took place in the desert (and, being me, graded it as well), and I was endlessly vexed at how closely some of the character's costumes came to the hues of the earth that surrounded them.

However, I began to realize that I could pull a much more isolated key by limiting the qualifiers to one of the following combinations:

- **Hue and saturation:** I've had shots that were so equiluminant (the luma throughout the image was within a very narrow range) that it was tough to isolate the feature that I needed because the luma key kept polluting my matte in unwanted areas. Then I realized that those features were more saturated than the rest of the image. Keys pulled using only Hue and Saturation aren't necessarily going to be either pretty or smooth (especially with highly compressed media), but this combination can sometimes work in a pinch.

- **Luma and saturation:** The combination of luma and saturation can be a good way to isolate skies when there are other, less saturated blues in the image (water, costume).

DIFFERENT WAYS OF USING HSL QUALIFIERS

Image segmentation describes the process of divvying up an image into individually adjustable segments for the purposes of performing highly specific color corrections (**Figure 5.42**). The more you work, the more you'll spot easily segmented regions of the frame, and the faster you'll be able to deploy the most suitable secondary tools for the job at hand.

Figure 5.42 At left, the original image. At right, the image has been artificially color-quantized to show how the image is naturally segmented for the purposes of creating isolated corrections using HSL Qualification.

Segmented adjustments using secondary corrections is a key strategy, both for addressing specific problems and for stylizing an image. Although you can do a solid grade using only a single primary, it puts the burden upon the cinematographer to have anticipated and created the careful pools of light and dark and color and colorlessness by using a combination of lighting instruments, flags, and art department trickery and by working with the costume department to control the visuals' impact on the viewer.

This kind of control over the practical photography is not always feasible on lower-budget features with limited schedules or on documentary productions where you don't have a whole lot of control over where you shoot, when you get the shot, and what people are wearing. As a result, the colorist's job grows.

The following sections illustrate different ways of using the very same tool, HSL Qualification, to achieve very different creative goals.

ISOLATING AND ADJUSTING SPECIFIC ELEMENTS

This is the most basic use of HSL Qualification. In particular, I find the most common application of HSL Qualification in my work is to address problems with saturation.

As we saw earlier in this chapter, a common operation is dealing with subjects that are too distractingly saturated. For example, the image in **Figure 5.43** has had a primary correction to increase contrast and boost saturation. The result, unfortunately, is that the balloons in the background have become excessively bright. Using a qualifier, it's easy to isolate the balloons and make them more subdued.

Figure 5.43 The balloons and ribbons at left are distractingly saturated. Isolating them with a key lets us slightly reduce saturation so they don't draw our eyes away from the actor.

Another technique for dealing with the opposite issue, a lack of saturation, is to enhance the color contrast of an image by using "contrast of extension" (covered in Chapter 4) to create the illusion of higher saturation by using HSL Qualification to boost the saturation of specific subjects in the frame, rather than boosting the saturation of the entire image.

For example, **Figure 5.44** has plenty of saturation but not a lot of color contrast. An easy fix for this is to isolate the woman's sweater in the image and then increase the saturation. The resulting splash of color gives life to an otherwise blah image.

Figure 5.44 Isolating the woman's lackluster sweater lets us pump it up with a bit more color, bringing welcome color contrast into an otherwise monochromatic scene.

Using this strategy, you get to have your cake and eat it too: You can even desaturate an image yet by selectively boosting the color of one or two objects make it appear as if it's even more colorful.

CORRECTING TWO EXCLUSIVE AREAS

We've already seen how you can invert a key to leave one element alone when you want to correct everything else. Another segmentation strategy involves using an HSL Qualifier to key an easy-to-isolate region and then applying separate corrections to the inside and outside of the matte (**Figure 5.45**).

NOTE

Secondary keys in low-saturation shots tend to be tricky when you're trying to isolate small areas of specific color. As a result, this is one of the more time-intensive operations discussed here, and it's possibly not suitable if your client is in a hurry.

Figure 5.45 A basic correction is applied with node 1, and nodes 2 and 3 apply separate corrections to the inside and outside of a keyed subject, respectively.

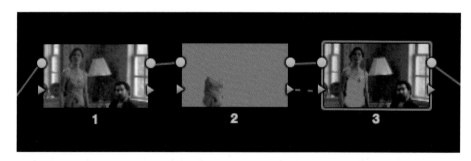

This is an especially useful strategy when you're trying to protect or uniquely grade a specific subject. For example, the woman's green dress in **Figure 5.46** is a deliberately specific shade that the client wants graded in a particular way, even though the environment is supposed to be graded very differently (in this case a very warm yellow).

Using HSL Qualification, it's an easy thing to key the dress to isolate it from the rest of the picture.

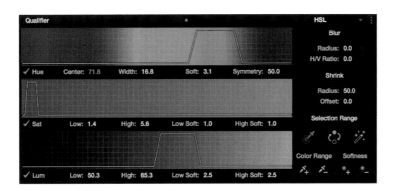

Figure 5.46 The green dress needs to be keyed to isolate it from the rest of the image in order to produce the grade the client wants.

Then, you can apply a correction to the inside (white) of the resulting matte, grade the dress however you need it to appear (in this case darker and more saturated), and apply a second grade to the outside (black) of the matte, grading the environment separately to blow out the highlights and add a burning warmth (**Figure 5.47**).

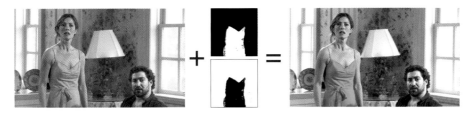

Figure 5.47 Grading a scene with two exclusive corrections, one applied to the inside of the keyed dress to boost its greens and darken the color and another applied to the outside of the dress to blow out the environment.

How you approach grading the inside and outside of a matte depends on your grading application:

- In DaVinci Resolve, create an "outside node" from the correction node with the dress qualification.

- In Adobe SpeedGrade, select a correction, and then assign either the inside or the outside of the mask to define what part of the image it affects.

- If you're using Autodesk Lustre, click the Inside button.

- In Assimilate Scratch, duplicate the scaffold that has your initial qualification, and invert the mask in this new scaffold.

- In FilmLight Baselight, select the layer with the qualification, and choose an appropriate grade type from the Inside column of the Inside/Outside table.

Many NLE filter-based secondary corrections handle this functionality by duplicating the filter doing the keying and inverting the filter to correct the outside region of the matte.

For a detailed example of using this technique to segment skin tone adjustments and environmental adjustments, see Chapter 8.

CHAPTER 5

GRADING LIGHT AND DARK REGIONS OF AN IMAGE SEPARATELY

In many instances, you may be dealing with an image that has areas of overexposure combined with areas of underexposure, such as when an underlit subject is standing next to a window or sitting in a car in front of a window. Backlit windows are notorious for being difficult to expose, and unless the crew was able to apply sheets of neutral density over the windows or bounce some fill light onto the subject in the scene to balance the exterior light with the interior, they're often deliberately overexposed.

If, in a situation such as this, the extremely bright region of the picture (the window) isn't overexposed to the point of losing all visible detail and the interior subject isn't too horribly underexposed, you should be able to use HSL Qualification to solve the problem. In particular, you can use the Luma qualifier all by itself to isolate either the highlights or the shadows—whichever portion of the image is more cohesive (**Figure 5.48**).

Figure 5.48 Luma-only key as created in DaVinci Resolve.

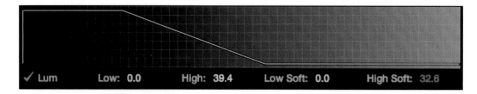

Then, you can use the resulting matte to grade the under- and overexposed areas of the image to bring them closer in line with one another (**Figure 5.49**).

Figure 5.49 Keying the darkest parts of the car exterior makes it possible to lighten the deeper shadows, adding detail to the man's face and the dashboard of the car.

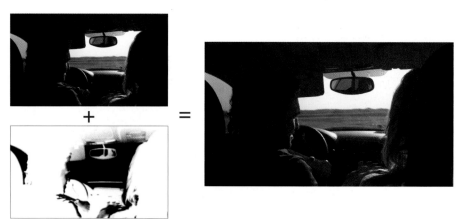

Aside from window shots, this technique is effective for any clip where you have to deal with two areas that are exposed very differently. However, be careful of how much the softened edge of the matte overlaps from the shadows into the highlights of the image; too much overlap can result in haloing that will look artificial.

CONTROLLING SHADOW CONTRAST

One of the hardest things to deal with is the adjustment of shadow ratios. For example, it's easy to generally lighten or darken a subject overall, although the result may appear a bit washed out. Unfortunately, if you're matching a shot from late in the day into a scene that was photographed at noon or if you're asked to change the apparent time of day of a scene, you're likely going to have a shadow ratio mismatch that you'll want to attempt to fix.

However, it's not that easy to alter the ratio of shadow to light that falls on someone's face. In the uncorrected image on the left in **Figure 5.50**, there's a distinct shadow on the woman's face, with a highlight on the other side, that indicates higher-key, dramatic, afternoon lighting.

One strategy would be to use a luma curve to lighten the midtone shadows, while keeping the deepest shadows to maintain a good sense of image detail. However, you might not be able to make a specific enough adjustment using just curves.

The other possibility is to use the previous technique, trying to carefully create a secondary key using the Luma qualifier to isolate the midtone shadows on the face that you want to lighten. Coupled with an adjustment to cool off the highlights, this does the trick, and we now have a lighter, less high-key shot, as shown on the right in Figure 5.50.

Figure 5.50 Keying the shadow regions of the image makes it possible to lighten them, gently, in an effort to reduce the shadow ratio for a more noonday look.

CHAPTER 5

When attempting to lighten the shadows on a subject's face, you need to pay particular attention to the transition between the unadjusted highlights and the adjusted shadows. If this middle point starts to reveal itself as a solarized border, you'll want to adjust the tolerance and/or feathering that you're applying to the Luma qualifier to try to minimize it. If that doesn't solve the problem, you may need to back off your correction a little bit.

When you create this sort of correction, make sure you don't overdo the shadow lightening or you'll *solarize* the image (create lighter areas where they should be darker, and vice versa, for an early-1980s music video look). The other possible consequence is that, if the feathering and brightening isn't done just right, the image could start looking like bad high dynamic range (HDR) photography.

ISOLATING A SUBJECT WITH DESATURATION

A commonly asked-about technique is that of isolating a color subject within an artificially created black-and-white environment, as used in the movie *Pleasantville*. From the techniques we've covered so far, this should now be an easy nut to crack, especially if the subject you're trying to isolate possesses a unique range of hue, saturation, or luma.

Basically, key on the subject you want to keep in full color, invert the matte, and then desaturate everything else (**Figure 5.51**).

Figure 5.51 Keying the woman's pink dress, inverting the key, and desaturating everything else.

DOING A BETTER JOB BY COMBINING MATTES

The previous example in Figure 5.51 is fine if we're happy with the one dress being in color and everything else being in black-and-white. However, things are rarely that simple. For example, what if we wanted both women to be in color? Fortunately, some applications let us combine mattes from different keys.

Figure 5.52 shows how, in DaVinci Resolve, we can use four separate corrections to isolate the pink dress, the red hair, both women's skin tones, *and* the other woman's green shirt, and then we can combine them using a Key Mixer node.

The resulting combination matte can be fed into the mask input of a correction (node 6), inverted, and used to desaturate everything we didn't key, all at once (**Figure 5.53**).

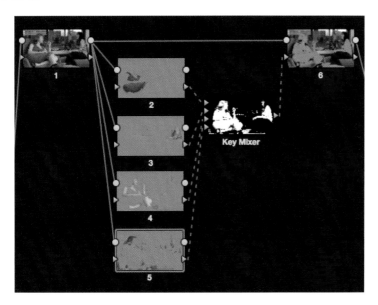

Figure 5.52 Using multiple nodes in DaVinci Resolve to combine four separate HSL keys to use as one. Each key can be optimized to isolate one subject well.

Figure 5.53 Desaturating everything outside of the combination key shown in Figure 5.51. I left the imperfections to illustrate just how difficult an operation this is and the importance of spotting these issues. I count 14. (You'll find a complete list at the end of the chapter.)

Now, the example in Figure 5.53 could obviously be further improved with some more aggressive keying combined with shape/Power Window garbage mattes, but hey, I have a book to finish.

When combining multiple mattes created with HSL Key nodes and shapes, you can use some time-honored compositing techniques to exercise more control over the process. Using whatever matte or image combining tool your application provides to apply the lighten and darken *composite modes* (sometimes called *blending* or *transfer modes*) lets you control how mattes interact. This is worth spending a bit of time on, as many grading, compositing, and editing applications have the facility to combine mattes using blending modes to create complex mattes, and you should be able to adapt these techniques to your own application if they're supported.

Figure 5.54 shows how you can combine two mattes using a *lighten* blending mode, with the result being that the white interiors of both mattes are merged together to become a single matte. This happens because the lighten blending mode compares both overlapping images and preserves the lightest pixels within each.

Figure 5.54 Combining two circular mattes created with GMask nodes using a Blend & Comp node's lighten blending mode in Autodesk Smoke.

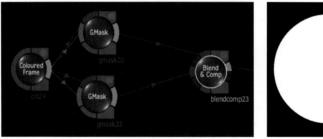 

Next, we can see in **Figure 5.55** how the *darken* transfer mode preserves the white interior *only* where both mattes overlap. This is, in fact, the very method that's used when combining HSL keys with shapes/Power Windows to limit the keyed matte to the interior of the shape (we'll see this combination later in Chapter 6). The opposite of the lighten blending mode, the darken mode compares two overlapping images and preserves the darkest pixels from each.

Figure 5.55 Combining shapes using the darken transfer mode.

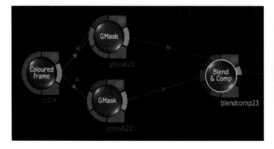 

Finally, **Figure 5.56** shows how you can use the darken blending mode in a different way, using an *inverted* matte to carve out the overlapping part of another matte. Since the darken blend mode compares two images and preserves the darkest pixels in each one, this means that you can use a black shape to surgically cut into a white shape.

 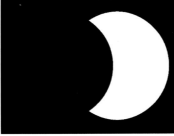

Figure 5.56 Inverting one of the GMask nodes prior to using the darken transfer mode lets you use the inverted circle to "carve a piece" out of the other circle.

Using intersecting mattes can be a great way of building ever more complex isolations. If you're having a tough time isolating every part of the subject you need to adjust with just a single matte, you might try using combinations of mattes instead.

ALTERING SATURATION WITHIN A SPECIFIC TONAL RANGE

Although some applications have specific controls for highlights and shadow saturation that let you adjust specific zones at the extremes of image tonality, if you lack these controls, there is a simple way to customize a tonal region for adjusting saturation.

All you have to do to use a Luma qualifier all by itself is to select a range of image lightness within which you will decrease or increase saturation (**Figure 5.57**).

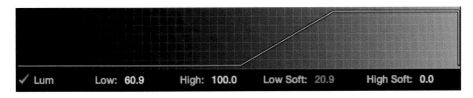

Figure 5.57 Using the L (luma) qualifier in DaVinci Resolve to isolate a range of image tonality within which you can adjust saturation.

Once you've defined the area of the image to adjust, it's a simple thing to lower or raise saturation to achieve the necessary result. In **Figure 5.58**, you can see that a much larger area of the highlights has been isolated for saturation adjustment than is typically possible using some applications' highlight saturation controls.

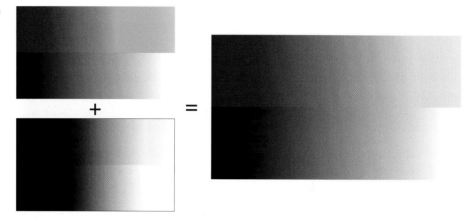

Figure 5.58 A custom tonal region of the image can be selected using the Luma qualifier for tailored saturation control, in this case desaturating a broad range of highlights.

Furthermore, you can make separate saturation adjustments to the inside and outside of the matte you've defined. This can be a good way of boosting midtone saturation without needing to subsequently lower saturation in the highlights and shadows for the purposes of video legalization.

This is also a good technique for isolating a limited range of highlights or shadows with an extremely soft falloff for subtle adjustments.

DESATURATING AN IMAGE AND SELECTIVELY RESATURATING IT USING HSL QUALIFICATION

This next technique is one that Chicago colorist Bob Sliga showed me. It's a bit more specialized, but it comes in handy for both creative looks and the occasional utilitarian adjustment. This technique is possible only on grading applications that let you pull keys off of the original source media, rather than the graded state of the image.

The trick is to desaturate an image completely and then pull a key based on the original colors in the source media, as shown in **Figure 5.59**.

Using that key, you can add artificial color back into the scene to "colorize" a subject you want to give a special look to (**Figure 5.60**). A node tree for creating this effect in DaVinci Resolve was shown in Figure 5.59.

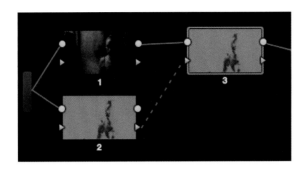

Figure 5.59 Pulling a key based on the original colors in the source media.

Figure 5.60 At left, the desaturated image with boosted contrast. At right, the portion of the image that was colorized using the key pulled from the original color in the source.

This technique is great for giving an otherworldly look to people in special situations. However, I've also used it for shot blowups that have excessive chroma noise in a brightly colored portion of the image. Desaturating the offending subject (an apron in the example I'm thinking of) eliminated the most objectionable noise pattern, and I could then make it red again by keying and colorizing. The final result was a vast improvement, and the effect was nearly indistinguishable.

HUE CURVE ADJUSTMENTS

Hue curves are powerful, fast-to-use controls that let you make gentle or sharp alterations to the color components of an image by placing control points along sections of the spectrum. Unlike RGB curves, which plot individual color channels versus image tonality, hue curves plot individual color components relative to user-defined ranges of hue (**Figure 5.61**).

TIP
Some applications, such as DaVinci Resolve, let you click, drag, and scrub to sample the image in the viewer in order to automatically place control points on the curves corresponding to the sampled color, making it easier to adjust specific elements.

Figure 5.61 The hue curves UI in SGO Mistika.

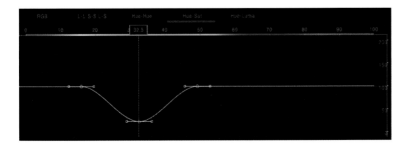

CHAPTER 5

NOTE

Even though you can make very specific adjustments by careful placement of control points to lock off certain parts of the curve while adjusting others, you may also find that HSL Qualifiers are able to isolate elements more tightly. With practice, you'll develop habits regarding when to use either type of control.

Their power lies in their ability to quickly make alterations to specific subjects in an image based on their hue alone, and the mathematics of curve operations make most adjustments really smooth and seamless, with none of the edge artifacts you can get when you're using HSL Qualifiers to pull a key. This is especially good when you're making huge targeted changes to image saturation (something I do quite a lot).

Most grading applications have, at minimum, three hue curves:

- *Hue vs. Hue*

- *Hue vs. Saturation*

- *Hue vs. Luma*

Some applications also have two more hue curve controls:

- Saturation vs. Luma, which provides curve-based control over saturation in targeted areas of image tonality that's quite powerful

- Saturation vs. Saturation, which allows for many kinds of targeted saturation adjustments, including the equivalent of a Vibrance operation to increase saturation in the least saturated areas of the image

However, the minimum hue curve controls correspond to the three essential color components of the video signal.

HUE CURVE CONTROLS COMPARED

Hue curves are available in many applications, including DaVinci Resolve, Assimilate Scratch, FilmLight Baselight, and Quantel Pablo (Quantel was the originator of these curves, and Quantel applications from Paintbox through Pablo have referred to this as the *Fettle* interface). **Figure 5.62** compares hue curves as represented in different color grading applications.

While we're on the subject, one of the standout features of the Colorista II color correction plug-in for NLEs is a pair of circular HSL controls, which essentially perform the same function (**Figure 5.63**).

These unique takes on the hue curve interface have efficiencies built into their UIs:

- The left control combines the functionality of the Hue vs. Hue and Hue vs. Saturation controls; changing the *angle* of a particular hue handle shifts hue, and changing its *distance from the center* adjusts saturation (similar, in fact, to the familiar use of color balance controls).

- The right control lets you alter Hue vs. Luma.

The only drawback of this system is that the number of hue handles is fixed, whereas curves let you add as many control points as you like. However, practically speaking, you can do just about anything with the Colorista interface that you can do with curves, except for perhaps a handful of extremely tight multihued adjustments.

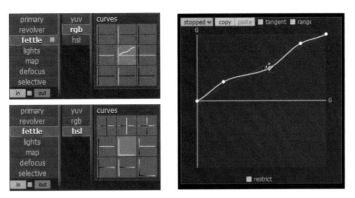

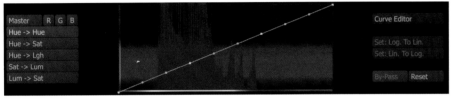

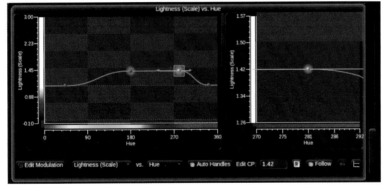

Figure 5.62 Images of hue curves in UIs compared, top to bottom: excerpts from Quantel's Fettle UI, Assimilate Scratch, and FilmLight Baselight.

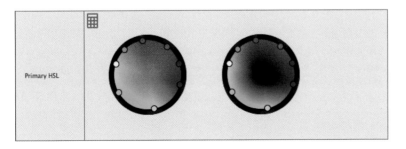

Figure 5.63 Circular HSL controls in Magic Bullet Colorista II.

Let's look at each of the three basic hue curve functions using a helpful hue-wheel test pattern to examine their effects.

USING HUE VS. HUE CURVES

Hue vs. Hue lets you isolate a range of hues that you want to change into other hues. The effect is similar to the hue parameter that most grading applications have, which rotates the hue of the entire image around a 360-degree axis (which causes a familiar "rainbow shift" if you animate it). However, using a curve interface, you limit hue shifts to specific portions of the spectrum.

In the following example, the blue portion of the spectrum is loosely isolated and raised on the curve (**Figure 5.64**).

The result is that the hue of the blue wedge of the color wheel is altered, in this case changed to green. Because the curve has a smooth falloff, you can see hue transitions from the altered green into the other original colors on the wheel. Although obvious on the test pattern, this isn't always obvious in a real-world image, but it shows that subtle hue shifts are usually more successful than huge ones.

Figure 5.64 The blue portion of the hue spectrum is isolated and raised on the curve.

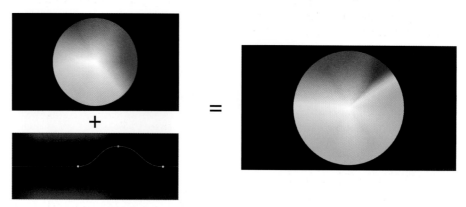

I use this control for making subtle adjustments to skin tone (taking advantage of the narrow range of hues that skin occupies), foliage, and skies (all techniques you'll see in subsequent chapters).

USING HUE VS. SATURATION CURVES

Hue vs. Saturation is the hue curve I use most frequently. It lets you isolate a range of hues within which to raise or lower saturation. Again, isolating the blue of the spectrum—in this case, lowering the curve—lets us desaturate that particular portion of the color wheel. Again, because this is a curve, the falloff is gentle, although a sharper curve results in a sharper transition from the desaturated to fully saturated areas of the image (**Figure 5.65**).

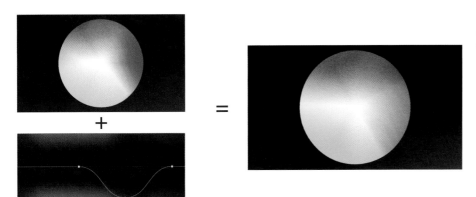

This is a powerful tool for stylistic adjustment (reducing the saturation of everything except the blue of the sky, for instance), addressing quality control violations (reducing the intensity of reds that are peaking too much), or shot matching (eliminating a subtle yellow cast that's otherwise hard to isolate).

USING HUE VS. LUMA CURVES

Hue vs. Luma lets you isolate a range of hues within which to lighten or darken corresponding features. Isolating the blue portion of the spectrum and lowering this control darkens the blue wedge of the test pattern (**Figure 5.66**).

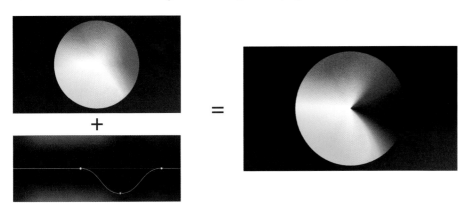

Figure 5.66 Isolating the blue portion of the spectrum.

This is a potentially powerful tool but also a really tricky one, the results of which depend highly on the quality of your application's image processing. Although it's possible to make smooth adjustments using nearly any type of application that uses Hue vs. Hue and Hue vs. Saturation curves, the Hue vs. Luma curve is at a disadvantage because it manipulates the most data-rich component of the signal (luma) relative to the most *data-poor* component (chroma). As a result, it can exhibit unpleasant artifacts such as macro-blocking and edge aliasing.

CHAPTER 5

These artifacts appear almost immediately (**Figure 5.67**), no matter how small a correction you're making, if you're working on media with 4:2:0 chroma subsampling (such as HDV or H.264-based formats). 4:2:2 chroma subsampled media has a bit more resiliency, allowing small adjustments before unpleasant artifacts appear; however, past a certain point, even 4:2:2 media will suffer.

Figure 5.67 At left, zoomed into our test pattern downsampled to the 4:2:0 Apple Intermediate Codec, showing harsh artifacts from use of the Hue vs. Luma curve. At right, the same image at its original ProRes 4444 encoding; an identical correction exhibits smoother transitions.

However, as you can see in Figure 5.67, this control comes into its own when you use 4:4:4 chroma-sampled media. With the full range of luma and chroma available to you, you'll be able to use the Hue vs. Luma curve to the best possible advantage.

CONTROLLING HUE CURVE ADJUSTMENTS

Some hue curve interfaces place a series of predefined control points on the curve, giving you a rapid starting point, while others present you with a blank slate.

The most important thing to know about controlling hue curve adjustments is that you should "lock off" parts of the curve you don't want to adjust using additional control points. For example, in the following curve, you might want to make a series of adjustments to alter the orange hues of the image, without affecting the neighboring yellows or reds.

Placing control points at the neutral center position at the border of the areas you don't want to affect limits the falloff of your adjustments, preventing your correction from spilling over into hues that you don't want to affect.

USING HUE CURVES TO FIX MIXED LIGHTING

Now that we've seen the theory of how hue curves work, let's look at some practical examples. One of the biggest bugaboos of many scenes is mixed-lighting scenarios, where you have light of two different color temperatures competing with one another. You might be able to overcome the problem with a creative use of color-balance adjustments, but more often the solution won't be that simple.

I've found that, especially for subtle mixed color shots, the Hue vs. Hue curve can make a quick fix that works really well. In the following shot, a subtle greenish/yellow cast from a practical fluorescent fixture that the production couldn't eliminate is polluting the cool blue sky-lighting of the scene (the spill is shown within the red circle of the original image in **Figure 5.68**).

The problem is too subtle for HSL Qualification (which is a mixed lighting solution I often use for window exteriors that are a lot more blue than the rest of an interior scene), and trying to fix this with color balance will only make the midtones more magenta than we want.

Figure 5.68 A Hue vs. Hue curve adjustment (shown in Assimilate Scratch) used to shift the green/yellow fluorescent spill toward the cool blue sunlight of the rest of the scene.

Another strategy could have been to desaturate the offending greens, but that would have leeched color from the scene; this way, the offending greenishness has been converted to a pleasing sunlight-emulating bluishness. The result is smooth, seamless, and quick.

USING HUE CURVES TO SELECTIVELY ALTER SATURATION

Here's a practical example of using the Hue vs. Saturation curve to make a stylistic alteration to a real-world image. In **Figure 5.69**, the original shot as graded has a saturated green pool table with an orange ball. The client wants to bring more attention to the ball, and one way of doing this in a creative way is to both raise the saturation of the narrow portion of oranges that correspond to the ball and lower the saturation of the green table to make it a subtler, darker shade.

Figure 5.69 A multipoint Hue vs. Saturation curve adjustment (shown in Assimilate Scratch), deemphasizing the green in the table and heightening the warmth of the orange ball and man's skin tone.

This serves to lend greater weight to the wood tones throughout the image, which are also picking up a bit more saturation because of the increased orange, which is additionally giving the man's skin tone a bit more warmth. More to the point, the orange ball really sticks out after this adjustment.

The Hue vs. Saturation curve is also great for quickly lowering the saturation of elements that are too distracting, such as an overly colorful blue shirt, a vividly painted red car, or an insanely reflective magenta life-jacket (all situations I've fought with).

Overall, it's a useful tool for enhancing color contrast, bringing out colorful elements that can't quite compete with the rest of the scene. For example, if the green grass of a summertime shot isn't grabbing you, you can pump it up using the Hue vs. Sat curve to give it more vibrancy.

USING HUE CURVES TO LIGHTLY EMPHASIZE CERTAIN COLORS

Another way you can achieve uniquely saturated looks is by using Hue vs. Saturation curves to consistently lower or boost the saturation of specific hues throughout an entire scene, creating a look based on the relative strength of certain colors.

This level of control has long been exercised by cinematographers through careful selection of film stocks. A frequently made generalization has been that Kodak color negative stocks yield excellent warm tones, with vivid reds and oranges, and Fujifilm color negative stocks are slightly cooler, with great sensitivity to greens and blues. These are generalizations—specific stocks vary—but they're useful nonetheless because many of the directors and cinematographers you'll be working with may have this as a frame of reference.

You may be thinking that with all this talk of warm and cool tones, why not just use the Color Balance control to warm or cool the images? Emphasizing more or less saturation in different parts of the spectrum is not the same thing as a color cast, because selective saturation adjustments won't have any effect on the neutral tones in your images. This is a wholly different technique for your bag of tricks.

OTHER TYPES OF HSL ADJUSTMENTS

Other tools are available in different grading applications for making similar types of targeted adjustments based on specific ranges of hue. Although the techniques found throughout this book focus on the use of hue curves where appropriate, it's useful to know that the following styles of correction may be substituted should you feel there is an advantage to doing so.

VECTOR/KILOVECTOR ADJUSTMENTS

Before HSL Qualification and hue curves, there were *vectors*, a means of isolating a wedge of color as represented by its distribution on a vectorscope for isolated adjustment. In 1982, VTA Technologies (the predecessor to DaVinci) introduced The Wiz, a telecine controller and color corrector built upon an Apple II computer, which featured 10-vector secondary correction. Later in 1989, the renamed DaVinci Systems introduced the more accurate subdegree Kilovector system to the Renaissance grading system.

Vector-style secondary correction is still in use and is now available in many different grading applications. Assimilate Scratch has a Vector interface, providing six customizable color ranges that you can use to shift the hue, saturation, and lightness of isolated ranges of color. Other applications with Vector-style adjustments include FilmLight Baselight and Quantel Pablo.

In the Assimilate Scratch interface, the Centre parameter specifies the angle of hue that's being isolated for adjustment, while the Width parameter specifies how much of a range of values to the left and right of the center hue to include within the adjustment (**Figure 5.70**).

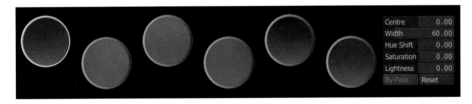

Figure 5.70 The Vector UI in Assimilate Scratch.

The six color pots of the UI show the default colors that can be immediately adjusted, namely, the primary and secondary colors of the RGB color space. Clicking a pot selects that range of hues for adjustment, and adjusting the Hue Shift, Saturation, and Lightness parameters allows them to be modified.

Other interesting implementations of vector controls include the following:

- Baselight has a *Six Vector* grade, using a UI similar to that of the Hue Angle keyer, that lets you choose one of six customizable hue ranges to adjust using either knobs on the control surface or sliders within the onscreen UI.

- Quantel's Pablo, iQ, and eQ systems have an interface called *Revolver* (**Figure 5.71**), which provides six customizable controls for altering color ranges. However, the adjustments are made using "color warping" algorithms that allow for a different quality of adjustment.

Figure 5.71 The Revolver UI in Quantel Rio.

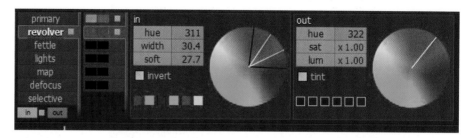

GRADING WITH HUE SHIFT IN FILMLIGHT BASELIGHT

FilmLight Baselight has another style of hue adjustment called the *Hue Shift* grade. Applying this adjustment opens a UI consisting of vertical sliders that correspond to each of the primary and secondary hues of the RGB color space.

To make an alteration to the image, simply manipulate the slider that corresponds to the hue you want to adjust. Two sets of sliders let you individually adjust the hue and saturation of each color range (**Figure 5.72**).

Figure 5.72 The Hue Shift UI in FilmLight Baselight.

ADVANCED KEYERS

The line dividing color grading and compositing grows fuzzier every year. In particular, compositing applications have long had a variety of keyers for pulling mattes to define transparency. However, keyers that are focused solely on blue or greenscreen compositing lack the necessary flexibility of being able to key any range of hue in preparation for color adjustments.

Still, HSL-based chroma keying isn't the only game in town when it comes to pulling keys to use as mattes for secondary color corrections. For example, many applications including DaVinci Resolve, Assimilate Scratch, Autodesk Lustre, and FilmLight Baselight also have RGB keyers (**Figure 5.73**).

While RGB keyers are a bit more difficult to use owing to the abstract nature of red, green, and blue additive color interactions, they can be handy for isolating ranges of color in different ways and, in conjunction with an RGB parade scope for reference, can give you an interesting alternative result in some instances.

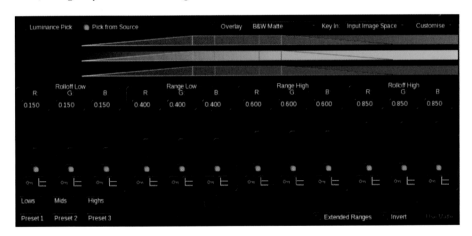

Figure 5.73 The RGB keyer found in FilmLight Baselight.

More sophisticated keyers, designed for color correction, use color models in different ways to organize the keying controls and even provide 3D color space interfaces with which to generate keys. The next two sections take a look at some of these other methods.

FILMLIGHT'S DKEY

FilmLight Baselight provides advanced keying in the form of the Dkey 3D keyer that lets you drag within the image to sample rectangular regions to create *volumes* within a 3D RGB cube (**Figure 5.74**).

Figure 5.74 Dragging a rectangle in the Baselight viewer to sample a region of color to key.

Once you've sampled to create a volume, you can adjust that volume's Start and End Offsets, Radius, and Softness settings in order to more precisely carve out the portion of the RGB cube that isolates that volume's range of color (**Figure 5.75**).

Figure 5.75 The DKey parameters for fine-tuning the shape of the region within the RGB cube that you're sampling in order to create a key.

As you work, you can middle-click and drag the RGB cube at the left to get a better look at the shape of the range of color you're isolating. You can sample as many additional volumes as you need, switching between each volume's parameters using the Selected Volume pop-up menu. They all combine to carve a region of the RGB cube that results in a key (**Figure 5.76**).

Figure 5.76 The final isolated scarf key.

AUTODESK'S DIAMOND KEYER

Autodesk Lustre incorporates the Diamond keyer found in other Autodesk compositing applications like Flame. But on the more affordable side of things, Smoke has a Colour Warper effect that, in addition to providing typical three-way primary correction controls and curve correction for gamma (in fact, the Gamma control is adjustable *only* via a curve), provides three *Selectives*, or secondary color isolations with separate color adjustment, all within the one interface. Choosing a selective from the Work On pop-up menu enables the controls for its Diamond Keyer (**Figure 5.77**).

Figure 5.77 The Selective controls Diamond Keyer found in Smoke's Colour Warper interface.

Clicking the Pick Custom button enables a sample mode where you can scrub over a region of the picture you want to isolate to define a range of color and saturation via a pair of diamond shapes on a flattened color cube (**Figure 5.78**).

These graphical shapes provide the means of fine-tuning your key. The inner light gray shape lets you define the range (Autodesk calls it Tolerance), and an outer shape lets you adjust tolerance (Softness). You adjust lightness using a separate, more conventional set of slider controls. As a region is defined, the isolated area appears in full color, while the excluded area remains grayscale (**Figure 5.79**). If you like, you can also choose Matte from the View pop-up menu to see a grayscale representation of the isolation.

Figure 5.78 Inner and outer shapes provide control over the tolerance and softness of the range of hue and saturation defining your key.

Figure 5.79 Dragging an eyedropper control over a region of the image to sample that range of color for keying using the Colour Warper Selective controls. The isolated region appears in color, while the excluded region appears in grayscale.

For *really* difficult isolations, you can use the ConnectFX interface in Smoke, in which the Action node provides the *Modular Keyer*, which is a node-based schematic designed for complex keying (**Figure 5.80**). Using the Modular Keyer, the process of creating multikey isolations with layered garbage mattes that feed other operations for postprocessing the resulting mattes is surprisingly streamlined.

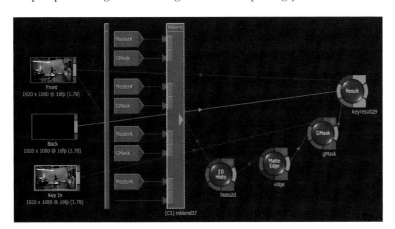

Figure 5.80 The node schematic of the Modular Keyer in Autodesk Smoke makes it convenient to combine multiple keys and post-process the resulting mattes in many different ways, according to the needs of the shot.

The Modular Keyer employs a variety of different keyers that can be used in combination (Luma, HLS, RGB, YUV), but the crown jewel is the *master keyer*. Within a single interface, the master keyer provides controls for a primary sample and three additional samples, called *patches*.

In addition, the master keyer provides excellent graphical matte manipulation where you can simply click a region of the matte to expose sliders that provide coarse and fine control over the translucency in that area. While the Modular Keyer is frequently used for greenscreen work, it's capable of keying any range of color and can be used to export a matte for use in limiting any other operation, including color correction.

NOTE
For more information on using Smoke and its Modular Keyer, you can consult my *Autodesk Smoke Essentials* (Sybex, 2013).

CHAPTER 5

THE PROBLEMS IN FIGURE 5.53

Let's see how good you were at spotting the issues in my first, rough pass at the saturated/desaturated grade in Figure 5.53.

1. There are holes in the pink dress woman's hair.

2. The pink dress woman's lipstick is desaturated.

3. The pink dress woman's elbow is desaturated.

4. The top edge of the pink dress woman's chair is still orange.

5. The arm rest by the pink dress woman's knee is still orange.

6. The edge of shadow along the pink dress woman's bottom is desaturated.

7. The shadow where the pink dress woman's legs are crossed is desaturated.

8. The pink dress woman's shoe bottom transition could be softer.

9. A flower is still saturated.

10. Some fruit is still saturated.

11. The book is saturated.

12. The cat's bottom is saturated.

13. The pillow behind the green shirt woman is saturated.

14. The green shirt woman's lips are a bit too desaturated.

CHAPTER 6

SHAPES

Like HSL Qualification, another way of isolating specific features for correction is the use of vignettes, which are also referred to as shapes, masks, Power Windows (DaVinci), or Spot Corrections (Avid). The idea is simple: You create a shape around the subject you want to adjust, usually a simple oval or rectangle, although most applications also let you draw Bezier shapes of any kind (**Figure 6.1**). The shape you draw creates a grayscale matte that is used to limit your correction to the areas either inside or outside of that shape.

> **TIP**
> As you'll see later, simpler shapes are generally going to be preferable to highly detailed shapes for introducing pools of light, shadow, and altered color temperature variations. Of course, there are always exceptions, but keeping things as simple as possible is usually a virtue.

Figure 6.1 At left, a simple oval shape used to isolate the man creates the matte in the center, which is used to isolate the lighting adjustment shown at right.

In many instances, shapes may be the best way of making such an isolated adjustment. For example, digital relighting typically works much better with shapes than with HSL Qualification, as it's easier to smoothly isolate large areas of light and shadow. It can also go faster if the area you need to isolate is clearly demarcated—for example, applying separate adjustments to the sky at the top of the frame and the forest below it (**Figure 6.2**).

Figure 6.2 Using a shape to separate a sky correction from a correction to the forest, fields, and road. A second shape protects the telephone pole on the left from being affected by the blue of this adjustment.

In other instances, you may find that HSL Qualification (as described in Chapter 5) is a better solution when the subject you need to isolate has chroma or luma components that are easily distinguishable from everything else in the frame and are highly detailed or move around a lot (for example, the illegally bright magenta shirt that somehow made it past wardrobe and the cinematographer).

Knowing when either shapes or qualifiers are going to be faster or better comes with experience, but it's not always an either/or scenario. As you saw in Chapter 5, qualifiers can be further limited using shapes to improve the final result, so colorists often use the two in tandem.

This chapter shows some of the most common ways you can use shapes to affect images. Additional examples elsewhere in this book will build on these techniques to show other things that you can do, but the examples in this chapter are the types of corrections you'll use every day.

SHAPE UI AND CONTROLS

The graphical user interface (GUI) provided for shapes varies widely from application to application, but the principles of geometry dictate that most shape controls work pretty much the same (**Figure 6.3**).

Figure 6.3 Onscreen controls and numerical parameters for shape manipulation, top to bottom: DaVinci Resolve, FilmLight Baselight, Adobe SpeedGrade, and Assimilate Scratch.

Let's take a look at the common controls that all shape UIs share, regardless of the application you're using.

SIMPLE SHAPES

In general you'll have at least two, sometimes three, choices of simple shapes (**Figure 6.4**):

- **Ovals** are the most ubiquitous shapes used for correction. They can be used to create vignetting effects, brighten faces, apply circular gradient effects, and—depending on whether you're applying a correction to the inside or outside of a large oval—make it possible to mask off the edge of an image with either a concave or convex curve.

- **Rectangles** are the second most common option. They're useful for any situation where you want the correction to take the form of a simple polygon, for ducking down detail in a window or doorway to the outside, and creating shadow falloffs along rectangular geometric surfaces. They also let you create a gradient when you lack a dedicated gradient control for doing things like sky corrections.

- **Gradients** are less common but extremely useful and quick when you need a simple linear falloff of some kind. They're great for creating sky grades or linear shadow falloff on any surface or region.

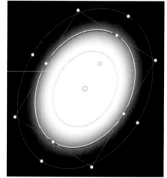

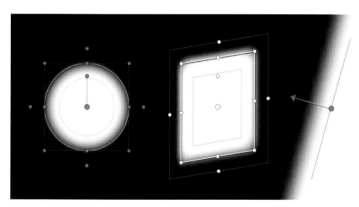

Figure 6.4 Oval, rectangle, and grad "Window" (shape) onscreen controls in DaVinci Resolve, compared.

An additional benefit of simple shape mattes is that they can be created and adjusted using the knobs, rings, and trackballs of a control surface. Typical shape adjustment parameters include size, aspect ratio, position, rotation, and softness. Some implementations let you position a shape using one of the trackballs on your control surface, with the outer ring controlling rotation. Others use two knobs—one for the x position and another for the y position (**Figure 6.5**).

Figure 6.5 Top, the onscreen shape controls you can use to graphically manipulate a vignette. Bottom, the corresponding numeric parameters in DaVinci Resolve.

However, there is usually an accompanying set of onscreen controls that let you manipulate shapes directly using your mouse or a graphics tablet. These UIs typically adopt common conventions from graphic design applications such as the following:

Figure 6.6 Adobe SpeedGrade has a multicontrol "widget" that provides control over eight shape adjustment parameters.

- A "transform" handle that allows you to reposition and rotate the shape (**Figure 6.6**).

- Corner handles for resizing a shape. Aspect ratio is sometimes locked, sometimes not. If aspect ratio is locked, side handles are often provided to squeeze the width or height of the shape.

- Holding down the Option key to adjust a shape around its center.

- Holding down the Shift key to constrain a shape's movement vertically or horizontally while moving it or to constrain the aspect ratio of a shape during resizing.

- A softness control for blurring the edges of the matte created by the shape, either as a separate edge control or as another interior "drag zone" associated with the transform handle.

Lastly, each shape parameter also has a set of numeric parameters that can be adjusted via sliders. Whether you adjust shapes with your control surface or the onscreen controls, these parameters store the data that defines each shape.

CUSTOM SHAPES

Custom shapes are typically found in dedicated color correction applications. Custom shapes are incredibly versatile in any situation where you need to isolate an irregular subject. Some colorists use them instead of ovals, finding it faster to draw a shape from scratch than to adjust ovals into place.

Generally, custom shapes have to be drawn using a mouse, pen and tablet, or trackball interface to place individual control points and to adjust them. However, once created, they usually have all the same adjustments for overall size, aspect, position, rotation, and feathering as the simpler oval or rectangle shapes (**Figure 6.7**).

Figure 6.7 A custom shape is used to darken a foreground element to help draw focus to the man's reflection.

Color correction applications usually try to make the shape-drawing process an easy one, on the premise that most of your shapes will probably be fairly loose (as with HSL Qualification, remember that you're usually thinking in terms of pools of light and shadow) and that you're in a hurry during a real-time session with a client looking over your shoulder.

Typically, you enter a shape drawing mode in which you click the image to add control points, "connecting the dots" around the subject you're trying to isolate. Control points come in one of two flavors:

- **B splines** are in many ways the simplest to operate. Control points are disconnected from the actual shape, exerting indirect influence by "pulling" the shape toward themselves. To create more complicated shapes, add more control points and arrange them closer together. Their simplicity can make them faster to use; however, you'll end up creating more points to create more complex shapes.

- **Bezier curves** (**Figure 6.8**) are the classic computer-drawing UI, used in applications such as Adobe Illustrator. Each control point has a pair of handles that controls the type and sharpness of the curve it defines.

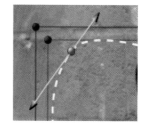

Figure 6.8 Bezier splines as they appear in FilmLight Baselight.

Typically, you'll also have the option of switching shape drawing between polygonal (hard-angled corners) and curve shapes.

TIP

Be sure to check your application's documentation to find out how easy it is to insert control points into an already-drawn shape; if it's not easy, try adding one or two extra points to areas of a shape corresponding to potentially complicated geometry.

As you're drawing your shape, it's a good idea to avoid adding an excessive number of control points—it can make later adjustments to that shape more cumbersome and may also complicate shape animation should that become necessary.

In most UIs, you can close a shape when you're finished drawing by clicking once on the first control point you created, although sometimes there's a Close Shape button you need to click.

FEATHERING AND SOFTNESS

The other critical means of adjustment for shapes is *feathering*, or softness. Simple shape softness controls consist of a single slider, which essentially blurs the edge of the resulting matte relative to the edge of the shape control.

More complex feathering controls, shown in **Figure 6.9**, provide custom shapes for adjusting the inside and outside of feathering. Typically there will be three control points for each adjustable segment of a shape:

- An inside control point defining the inner boundary of feathering
- An outside control point defining the outer boundary of feathering
- A "master" control point (the green control points in Figure 6.9) that moves both the inside and outside control points together

Figure 6.9 A custom shape with variable feathering (left) and the matte that results (right).

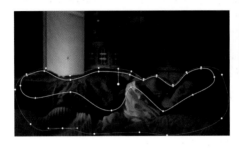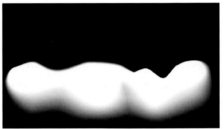

When using multishape feathering, moving the inner and outer shapes closer together reduces feathering, whereas moving them farther away from one another increases feathering.

Adobe SpeedGrade adds one other useful wrinkle to feathering control: A set of "contour" controls (**Figure 6.10**) lets you adjust how feathering falls off from the middle to the edge of feathering, with two parameters (Exponent and Weight) that adjust the falloff. Presets are available for common useful contour settings.

FilmLight Baselight provides control over softness falloff via a Matte Curve, which is available by clicking the Edit Matte Tool button (**Figure 6.11**). Using this curve, you can create whatever sort of custom contouring you like.

Figure 6.10
Contour controls available in Adobe SpeedGrade.

Figure 6.11 The Matte Curve in Baselight lets you customize the falloff of shape feathering.

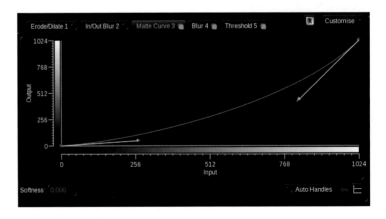

Whatever controls are available, shape-based feathering and contour controls are essential to creating subtle shape borders for operations where you need to tighten a shape in one area but feather it very lightly in another in order to create an invisible and seamless effect.

INVERTING AND COMBINING SHAPES

Most applications let you invert a shape in order to define whether a correction is applied inside or outside of it. On the other hand, many applications have the same ability to apply separate corrections to the inside and outside of a shape that they do when using HSL Qualification (for more information, see Chapter 5).

A more advanced use of shapes is to combine multiple shapes using Boolean operations (**Figure 6.12**). Typical operations include the ability to do the following:

Figure 6.12 The Boolean shape control in DaVinci Resolve lets you choose whether two shapes join or whether that shape subtracts from another shape, referred to as Mask (subtract from) or Matte (join to) modes.

- Combine two shapes to create one matte

- Subtract one shape from another

- Create a matte only where one shape intersects another

This ability is similar to the combining of multiple HSL mattes as shown in Chapter 5. Boolean matte blending is a valuable feature, particularly the ability to subtract one shape from another in instances where you need to isolate a large part of an image with one shape but protect another part of the image from the background correction.

Figure 6.13 shows a typical example of this. The rectangular shape used to darken the house in the background to draw more attention to the man at left is also throwing the man at right into shadow.

Figure 6.13 A custom shape is used to protect the man from the darkening effect caused by the rectangular shape.

Using a second shape, we can subtract a portion of the darkening matte to keep him in the light.

> ### MANUALLY MASKED CORRECTIONS IN OTHER APPLICATIONS
>
> If you're using an application that doesn't have shape-limited color corrections built in, you could turn to an add-on filter such as Magic Bullet Colorista II to provide this functionality. Alternately, you could use the built-in tools that came with your application to create these effects with a few extra steps.
>
> Creating shape-limited corrections in an application that only has the most simplistic layering tools available involves superimposing a duplicate of the shot you're correcting above itself and then drawing a mask to crop out the portion of the superimposed clip you want to make an additional adjustment to. After the mask is drawn, feather its edges, and then apply whatever filters you want to create the necessary correction.
>
> Another possibility is to use applications like After Effects that support Adjustment Layers. By applying a mask to an adjustment layer, you can limit the parts of the image that are affected by any effects applied to that layer.

HIGHLIGHTING SUBJECTS

When used to highlight a subject, shape corrections have traditionally gone by a different name—*vignettes*. Vignettes refer to twin optical and mechanical phenomena that are usually avoided while shooting: the appearance of a circular darkened region around the edges of a film or video image. However, such artificial darkening has been used to great effect for creative purposes. For example:

- A shadow surrounding a subject can call attention to it.

- A shape can be used as a virtual "flag," cutting down on the ambient light in a shot and salvaging clips that appear overlit.

- The introduction of a directional shadow gradient can add dimension to evenly lit images that appear somewhat flat.

- Artificial shapes can also deliberately mimic the effect of optical or mechanical lens vignetting, matching effects already present in other shots of a scene or creating a vintage film look.

Calling attention to a specific portion of the image through artificial vignettes is a technique that's been around since the days of silent film. Originally, filmmakers placed mattes in front of the lens to identify key subjects in longer shots or to highlight close-ups of actors, such as in this still from 1925's *The Lost World*, featuring Bessie Love (**Figure 6.14**).

Figure 6.14 Bessie Love in the 1925 silent film of *The Lost World*. A heavy vignette focuses viewer attention on the actor. Colorist Joe Owens points out that this technique also saw much use in D.W. Griffith's *Intolerance*.

This technique is still in use today, although the effect is usually accomplished with more subtlety in post. In the following example, the two women are competing with the background, which is uniformly well-lit. However, using a custom shape, the walls to the left and right, as well as the bottom of the woman's shoe in the foreground can be subdued and placed into shadow, bringing the women more into the foreground (**Figure 6.15**).

Figure 6.15 Calling attention to the women in the image through artificial vignettes

CHAPTER 6

Making the subject brighter than its surroundings draws the viewer's attention more readily. If you angle and construct the shape just right, the effect will have the appearance of deepening the shadows in the picture. The audience should never be able to detect the shape or presence of a shape, unless it's for deliberate effect.

TIP

To learn how to use vignetting to best effect, study the actual interplay of light and shadow in differently lit shots. An ideal shape has the effect of subtly cutting down the ambient light in parts of the frame you want to deemphasize, while hopefully masquerading as shadows that are justified by features in the frame.

As useful as this technique is, control of the lighting ratio between the subject and the background is best exercised by the director of photography during the shoot. Controlling the viewer's attention with lighting is a powerful technique, and the best vignetting is but an imitation of the cinematographer's art. Nonetheless, many projects with limited schedules or budgets benefit greatly from the additional light control that shapes afford.

Let's take a look as some practical examples of shape corrections used to direct viewer attention.

ADDING LIGHT TO FACES

Probably the most common shape correction I make when working on documentaries is to use an extremely soft oval to highlight a face and increase contrast, lightening it in the process. The effect is similar to using a bounce card on-set (which I always wish they'd have done anyway) in order to increase the contrast of the subject from the background.

The advantage of using a geometric mask is to isolate a portion of the image to correct; variances in saturation and luma don't matter as they might if you were to try to pull an HSL key. All you have to do is encircle the portion of the face you want to highlight.

In **Figure 6.16**, the man at the right doesn't really stand out within the scene relative to his importance within the moment. In this case, it's easy to use an oval shape to surround his face in preparation for lightening the midtones.

Figure 6.16 Lightening a face using a shape to create a soft matte.

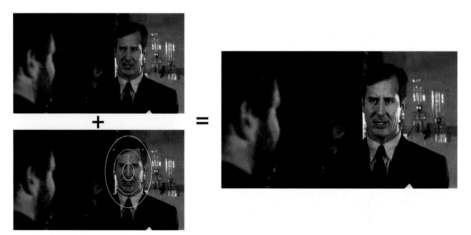

TIP

Another way to emphasize a vignetted subject is to switch to a correction that's applied to the outside of this shape and slightly desaturate the rest of the image.

Once isolated, it's a simple matter to expand contrast by raising the Gamma contrast control and lowering the Lift control. We're not just lightening his face; we're selectively *stretching the contrast* in the area where more light would plausibly be hitting him.

In a way, it's like we're adding our own bounce card to reflect more light on the actor in the scene. If you're careful about keeping the level of shadows where they were before, this helps to keep the vignette invisible, even though you're brightening the highlights.

The tricky thing about this technique is that you want to feather the isolating shape well enough so that it's hard to spot the effect but not so much that you end up adding a halo around the person's face; this is a surefire giveaway of a sloppy secondary operation, which spoils the magic of your operation (**Figure 6.17**).

Figure 6.17 The face correction to the left has a halo surrounding his head that's the result of a shape that's too large, with too little feathering and less-than-careful matching of the shadows inside and outside the adjustment. The face correction at right no longer has this problem after the shape and grade have been readjusted.

If you have problems with halos, adjust the size and feathering of the vignette to hide it. The amount of feathering will depend on what you're doing to the contrast of the isolated feature. If you can keep the shadow levels even on both the inside and outside of a shape, then very wide feathering and falloff will be appropriate. On the other hand, adjustments where you need to "open up the shadows" by lightening them require tighter edges to avoid haloing. If feathering alone doesn't eliminate the problem, you probably need to readjust your contrast settings to try to blend this secondary correction better with the background.

DEEPENING SHADOWS

Using shapes to isolate a subject to darken the surroundings, and in the process drawing the subject to the viewer's attention, is an especially valuable technique in situations where you're stuck with an *equiluminant* image, where the luma levels of the foreground subject are so close to those of the background that our vision system has a hard time differentiating between the two. If you don't know whether you're dealing with an equiluminant image, try completely desaturating it; if you have difficulty picking out the subject of the shot in grayscale, it's equiluminant.

TIP

Another good test of whether an image is equiluminant is to put your display into luma-only mode and then focus your eyes on a corner of the image. If you have a difficult time making out the subject of the image using your peripheral vision, it's probably equiluminant.

The shot in **Figure 6.18** is well graded for midday lighting, but the figures of the woman and boy are somewhat difficult to distinguish against a very busy background.

Figure 6.18 Desaturating an image reveals that the luma levels of the woman and the boy are very close to those of the background elements, making them difficult to easily distinguish.

Using a *very* soft shape to add some *very* subtle darkened vignetting around the outside of the subjects can be a good way of lowering the luma levels of the background, thereby providing a gentle visual cue that guides the eye toward the subject of the shot (**Figure 6.19**).

Figure 6.19 Using darkened vignetting to draw the viewer's eye toward the subject of the shot.

For this type of operation, ovals are often the most flexible and fast shape to use, with the exception of using a custom shape. However, it's been my experience that simple ovals often work *better* than a custom shape. When drawing a shape, it's tempting to find yourself tracing the contours of the subject you're isolating, rather than creating a pattern of light and shadow. The result can look artificial if you're not careful (**Figure 6.20**).

Figure 6.20 A custom shape with an inadequate amount of feathering gives itself away more than the simple oval in the previous example.

Ovals, on the other hand, are completely abstract and in fact end up looking a bit more similar to the effect of shining a practical light on the scene.

This isn't a hard and fast rule, of course, just a warning to keep your eyes open for the always-undesirable halo effect. *Whatever* type of shape you use, you'll want to feather its edges very well for two reasons: Typically, you don't want viewers to be able to discern the edge of the shape, and you don't usually want to have any solid black in the shape you're using.

This creates an extremely subtle darkening that is almost imperceptible to the viewer but that nonetheless draws attention to the brighter center of the image. If, at this point, you're unsure if the effect is really doing any good, toggle the Track Visibility control for track V2 off and on to compare the before (left) and after (right) shot. The results should now leap out at you.

ADDING SHADOWS BY COMPOSITING

If you're working with an application that doesn't have shape correction controls, you can easily add shadows and vignettes to your images using shape generators and composite modes, which most NLEs and compositing applications have.

1. Superimpose a shape layer or gradient generator over the shot to be affected. Use a shape type corresponding to the effect you want to achieve (oval, linear gradient, or rectangle usually).

2. Position and resize it so the darkest parts of the image overlap with the picture areas you want to obscure.

3. Feather the edge of the shape or gradient so that it's very, very soft.

4. Use the Multiply Composite/Transfer/Blending Mode to create the shadow effect.

Ideal layers to use are radial or linear gradients of black to white, which lend themselves to being multiplied, which combines your shape or gradient layer with the clip underneath such that generator areas of 100 percent white become transparent, increasingly dark gray areas become increasingly opaque, and black areas remaining black.

Another tip to this method of shadow creation is that if you alter the darkest shade in the generator being combined (for example, changing it from black to gray), you'll alter the transparency of the resulting effect without needing to change the opacity setting of the superimposed layer, which could result in slightly faster processing.

CREATING DEPTH

When using shapes to create depth, it's useful to be aware of how our vision system interprets various depth cues that have nothing to do with stereoscopic vision. In the documentary *Visions of Light*, cinematographer Vittorio Storaro talks about the ability of the cinematographer to add depth to the otherwise two-dimensional medium of nonstereoscopic film. We colorists can aid in this task using the tools at our disposal in ways that have nothing to do with 3D cinema.

UNDERSTANDING THE SIX DEPTH CUES

Painters and filmmakers share the necessity of creating depth within a two-dimensional canvas. Fortunately, it turns out that *stereopsis* (stereo vision) is only one of seven or more cues our vision systems use to distinguish depth. These other cues are of vital importance to the director, to the cinematographer, and, in a few cases, to the colorist concerned with presenting as expansive a visual experience as possible.

THREE DEPTH CUES YOU CAN'T DO MUCH ABOUT

The first three depth cues are important to know about, but they're also things you can't really manipulate in post unless you're planning on recompositing the shot using an application like Adobe After Effects or The Foundry's Nuke.

• **Perspective** is the sense that larger objects are closer and smaller objects are farther away. For example, a wide-angle shot with subjects occupying the foreground, middle ground, and background will do much to enhance the viewer's sense of depth. Perspective is controlled by a combination of shot composition and lens selection, and there's very little that we as colorists can do to alter it unless we use pan and scan transforms to reframe a shot.

• **Occlusion** refers to subjects that cover up other subjects within the frame. An occluded subject is always seen as being farther away, regardless of the relative size of the object in front.

• **Relative motion** also provides depth cues; for instance, if you think of the familiar sight of nearer objects passing by the window of a moving car faster than distant mountains or buildings. Filmmakers can capitalize on motion cues through creative blocking of actors and the camera (with the result being a lot of motion tracking and keyframing if you're using shapes in such a scene).

FOUR DEPTH CUES YOU CAN MANIPULATE

The following four depth cues are all image features you can manipulate to enhance and control viewer perceptions of depth.

• **Luma and color contrast** provide other distinct depth cues. Margaret Livingstone describes how luminance shading, specifically gradients from dark to light, trigger the brain's "where" system (as described in Chapter 3) to provide an illusion of depth.

• **Hue and saturation** are key but often underappreciated depth cues. Subjects with higher saturation generally appear to be closer to us then subjects with lower saturation. Meanwhile, warmer objects appear to be closer to us, whereas cooler objects appear to be farther away.

• **Haze and airlight** are atmospheric features that use hue and saturation to present depth cues that should be familiar to anyone who gets to take vacations in the mountains once in a while, as lower-contrast or bluer parts of a landscape shot indicate features that are farther away.

• **Texture and depth of field** provide other depth cues. Closer objects will have more perceptible fine detail, while objects that are farther away will have less because of the ocular limitations of our eyes. Think about standing next to a hedge; the leaves and branches closest to you appear with fine detail, but the farther away the hedge stretches, the more indistinct these details become.

Similarly, depth of field provides the dual cues of defocused parts of the image being closer *or* farther away than the features appearing in sharp focus.

- **Stereopsis**, lastly, describes the process of using two simultaneously captured images from lenses spaced apart similarly to our eyes (the *pupillary distance*) to create an illusion of depth. In conjunction with *convergence* (determining which parts of both images are in alignment) and *accommodation* (information derived by the visual cortex from the flexing of both eyes' intraocular muscles when they're focusing on a single object), this provides the stereoscopic effect. If you happen to be working on a stereoscopic program, most color correction applications provide some means to adjust the convergence of the left and right images.

NOTE
Mark Schubin has an excellent blog (http://schubincafe.com) in which he discusses stereoscopic film and television, among many other broadcast engineering–related topics.

CREATING DEPTH USING GRADIENT SHAPES

You can use shapes to create the perception of depth in an otherwise flat image. You can see how this works with a simple pair of gradients from black to white that meet at an imaginary horizon. These grayscale ramps alone give the impression of depth, without any other cues in the image (**Figure 6.21**).

You can exploit the same phenomenon using a shape. In the example in **Figure 6.22**, the image has been graded in a naturalistic but subdued manner. There's plenty of contrast, but the table that extends toward the foreground seems flat, and its lightness distracts from the seated trio.

Figure 6.21 The grayscale ramp creates an illusion of depth.

Figure 6.22 Using a rectangular feathered shape to darken a table, adding depth.

CHAPTER 6

In this instance, it's a simple thing to use a rectangular or polygonal shape, feathered *very softly* toward the seated actors, to isolate a darkening correction. Essentially, we're adding a gradient to the scene to achieve the same effect shown in Figure 6.21, adding depth via an artificial falloff of light.

SUBTLE DEPTH CONTROL VIA SATURATION ALONE

Since saturation itself is a depth cue, you can create an even more subtle sense of depth by combining creative shapes and saturation adjustments, playing up the colorfulness of subjects near the lens while selectively desaturating regions of the picture meant to fall into the distance. Productions with solid budgets for set dressing and wardrobe may exercise this kind of control via careful selection of paint, greenery, and attire, but if you're looking at a scene that lacks this kind of control, you can fake this sort of color interaction easily.

The example in **Figure 6.23** shows a couple on a city rooftop. The overall scene is warm, and there's a lot of color behind them. However, by isolating them with a *very* soft oval (a quick-and-dirty maneuver that could be done more precisely using multiple layers of HSL Qualification), you can subtly boost their color contrast with some selective saturation increases to red and blue and desaturate/cool off the background behind them to push it even farther into the background.

Figure 6.23 Using an extremely feathered shape to separate the couple in order to slightly enhance their reds and blues, while desaturating and cooling off the background of the image. The result is a subtle vignette (exaggerated for print) that brings the couple forward from the background.

Controlling saturation and hue in this way lets you create a sense of separation even in situations where alterations to contrast and lightness aren't appropriate.

CONTROLLING DEPTH PERCEPTION AND VIEWER FOCUS VIA LIGHTING CONTROL

Artful cinematographers tightly control the ambient light in a room in order to maximize depth cues and focus viewer attention at the same time (not to mention doing an overstretched art department a favor by hiding thin set dressing in the shadows).

Unfortunately, there's not always money or the time to accomplish detailed lighting setups for every scene. Fortunately, you have the tools to aid the harried cinematographer in post, flagging off light at the edges of each shot to emulate this type of classic light control.

In **Figure 6.24**, the shot has been graded with a subdued night look. However, there's still a lot of ambient light showing on the foreground wall to her right and the background wall to her left.

Figure 6.24 A shot graded with a subdued night look.

Using a simple feathered polygonal shape oriented along the angle of the natural light's falloff, it's easy to hit both walls. By inverting the matte, you can apply a darkening and desaturating correction to the outside of the shape, thereby bringing the woman into more immediate focus. This cuts down the light levels for a more convincing late-night look, all without touching the woman in the middle.

For this correction, the key is not to let the shadows get too crushed while you're darkening the midtones, since that could make the correction look artificial.

ARTIFICIAL CONTROL OF FOCUS

Another way of controlling viewer focus is to use your grading application's blur feature, along with a shape, to create an artificially shallow depth of field.

The image in **Figure 6.25** has been graded to throw the man into a near-silhouette, with a lightened background that's catching sunlight from the outside. The result is nicely understated; however, the director thinks the man doesn't have enough of the viewer's focus and is competing with the text on the side of the water heater. In this case, lightening the man using a shape would defeat the entire purpose of the grade, so instead we turn to the Blur/Softening control (**Figure 6.26**).

CHAPTER 6

Figure 6.25 A deliberately under-lit foreground figure contrasting unfavorably with the image detail in the background.

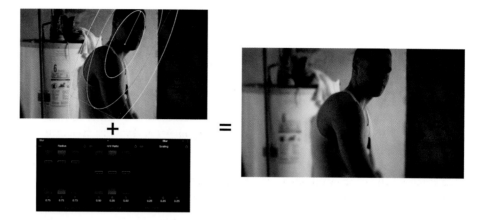

This result is easily remedied by using a soft oval shape to isolate the parts of the man that we want to keep in sharp focus, inverting it, and then using the resulting matte to selectively apply a blur effect to the background (Figure 6.26).

Figure 6.26 Using the Blur parameters in DaVinci Resolve to create artificially shallow depth of field.

The example in Figure 6.26 is shown using DaVinci Resolve, but this effect can be accomplished using any color correction application. Check your application's documentation for how to achieve a similarly controlled blur effect.

SHAPES + HSL QUALIFIERS

Shapes aren't useful only for contrast adjustment. You can also use them in conjunction with HSL Qualification to help isolate a hard-to-key element within a shot. This is a common, and in fact an essential, feature found in nearly every color correction application capable of both Qualification and Shape corrections.

This works similarly to the type of Boolean operations discussed earlier in this chapter. But when you turn on a shape and use a qualifier at the same time, the white parts of the matte that define where a correction is applied are preserved only where a key overlaps with a shape. This makes it easy for you to omit parts of a key that are too difficult to eliminate using the qualification controls because it would degrade the part of the matte you're trying most to preserve.

In a continuation of the example from Figure 6.9, the shadowy surroundings of the woman in bed are now perfect, but the woman herself fades into the background a little too much. We want to draw attention to her, but a simple shape wouldn't be the best solution because of the dappled, irregular shadows framing her that we've worked so hard to improve with a previous custom shape.

In this case, using an HSL Qualifier to isolate the skin of her face and shoulder makes for the best solution; however, when we sample pixels from her face, the cool lighting scheme of the room, combined with the bedspread's similarity in hue to her skin tone, makes it impossible to pull a clean key without including highlights of the bedspread (**Figure 6.27**).

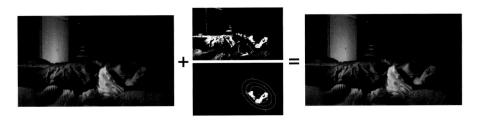

Figure 6.27 Using a shape to constrain the portion of an HSL key that we want to use to brighten and saturate the woman's face and shoulder.

The solution is to use a shape to isolate the portion of the key that we want to preserve. It's fast to do and gives us the best of both worlds: a highly detailed matte that only HSL Qualification can provide and the clean isolation that shapes make easy.

AGGRESSIVE DIGITAL RELIGHTING

When working on programs such as documentaries or indie narratives that rely heavily on fast lighting setups and available light, one of the challenges I regularly face is finding ways to add depth and visual interest to an otherwise flat-looking scene. Let's look at how to use custom shapes to control regions of light and shadow.

Now we need to ask ourselves about how well the lighting of the scene pictured in **Figure 6.28** supports its narrative composition. The initial grade creates a warmer, slightly lighter and less-saturated "American gothic" look for the scene.

Figure 6.28 Left, the ungraded scene. Right, a primary grade creating a warmer look.

If there was more time and budget, the lighting department might have waited for a different part of the day during which more light would fall on the house, or perhaps they would have used an off-camera silk to cut down the amount of light falling on the lawn in the foreground. On the other hand, there would have been no feasible method for silking the entire tree line behind the house, or doing other aggressive corrections.

Fortunately, digital grading provides other solutions.

DRAWING LIGHT AND SHADOW

The focus of the image is supposed to be a somewhat sinister house. Since it's naturally unsaturated, the best way to bring it closer to the viewer's attention is to lighten it a bit. This will also serve the dual purpose of making it a little more eerie, since this lightening will seem a bit unnatural relative to the natural lighting throughout the scene.

The house is easily isolated using a rectangular or polygonal shape (**Figure 6.29**). If we keep the edges soft enough, we can "bounce" light off of it without worrying about creating an incredibly detailed, house-hugging shape, which might give away the correction more readily if it's not done just right, especially if the scene is shot using a hand-held "wandercam."

Once the house is isolated, we can add some light to it by brightening the midtones and, to a lesser extent, the lighter shadows. Be careful not to boost any pixels that were originally at 0 percent/IRE absolute black, as that would give the house an unnaturally milky appearance relative to the rest of the scene.

Figure 6.29 Isolating the house and lightening it using a polygonal shape.

To help guide the viewer's eyes to the house, we'll next draw a custom shape around the grass in the foreground, feather it, and then apply a combination of darkening (gradient style, similar to what was done to the table example in Figure 6.22) and desaturation (**Figure 6.30**).

Figure 6.30 Isolating the foreground grass with a soft matte to darken, adding depth.

The result deemphasizes the grassy expanse and adds depth as we saw earlier.

The last thing we can do to keep the house at center screen is to darken the section of tree line to its left. Those trees catch some light, and the effect isn't as *spooky* as we want. Using another custom shape, we outline the contours of the lighting, soften the resulting shape, and then lower the Gamma in order to push the trees farther into the background (**Figure 6.31**).

Figure 6.31 Our last adjustment, isolating the tree line to the right of the house and darkening it to push it into the background.

Adjusting softness is key to getting a convincing effect for this last shot, especially where the trees meet the sky.

With this last correction, we're finished, and the result is a scene where our eyes go straight to the house, and the natural lighting has been altered to create the eerie ambience that the director wanted.

IMAGE SEGMENTATION AS A GRADING STRATEGY

The previous example is another great illustration of the idea of *image segmentation*. When making an initial evaluation of an image or scene, a good way to figure out how to create the desired effect is to break it up, mentally, into a series of discrete regions, each of which would best be manipulated using a particular correction. Once you learn to visualize a scene in this way, it becomes easier to see how to use secondary correction, whether it's HSL Qualification or shapes, to effect the change you need.

However, part of the trick of image segmentation is to also know when regions can be combined into the same correction for greater efficiency. Some colorists feel they're doing the best job when they use as many secondaries as they can to create a grade. Personally, I try to figure out how to use the *fewest* number of secondaries for a particular grade, on the premise that I'll work faster, the project will render more efficiently, and the result may ultimately be more naturalistic if I'm not worrying the shot to death.

However, the client's aesthetic and the type of project you're working on will ultimately determine the degree of image segmentation that's appropriate. It wouldn't do to over-grade a naturalistic documentary, but neither would it be good to under-grade an expensive commercial spot that's full of light and color and just begging for a hyper-real, stylized approach.

FLAGGING A SET

One of the most common lighting issues I find myself correcting is too much ambient light in a location. If you examine much of the cinematography in classics of cinema, and especially in black-and-white film (where shadow/light ratios are easier to spot), you'll begin to see how carefully skillful cinematographers keep our focus on the key subjects of the scene. They do this by manipulating the shadows falling within the background to cut down on unnecessary lighting that illuminates extraneous features in the scene.

In the primary correction that's applied to the initial image in **Figure 6.32**, the highlights have been adjusted to pop while keeping the shadows subdued and enhancing the excessively warm light of the interior. Unfortunately, this calls attention to the overhead lighting that is spilling onto the walls.

However, we can make the scene more intimate and tense by using a custom shape to darken the light bouncing off the ceiling, a simple correction that will make a dramatic difference (**Figure 6.33**).

Figure 6.32 The primary grade unfortunately boosts background lighting that we don't want to see.

Figure 6.33 Using a custom shape to flag the lighting falling against the far wall of a set to create a more focused lighting scheme.

Generally speaking, convincing lighting adjustments work *with* the lighting and shadows that are already in the scene, not against them. It's also good to keep in mind that you'll most likely be feathering the edge of the shape you're creating, so don't hug the outer boundary of the area you're isolating too closely; leave some space.

As with many of the other examples in this chapter, the fix is to drop the Gamma contrast to darken the upper wall, but keep a hand on the Lift control to make sure you don't overly crush the image.

The result makes the room appear much larger and more mysterious, both of which serve the narrative goals of the project.

CHAPTER 6

PRESERVING HIGHLIGHTS

Sometimes a shape you're using to create shadows in a clip overlaps with a practical light source or naturally reflective surface. The result is that the brightness level of those elements is artificially reduced. If the result looks noticeably bad, there's something you can do about it.

The image in **Figure 6.34** shows exactly this problem. The primary grade emphasizes cool lighting in the highlights (assuming illumination from the tube television), and a custom shape darkens the back wall, creating a greater sense of late night television watching. Unfortunately, the shape necessarily overlaps with the lamp, and when the wall is darkened, so is the lamp, which looks a bit odd.

Figure 6.34 Deepening the shadows behind the seated woman makes the lamp unnaturally dull, given that it's the light source in the room.

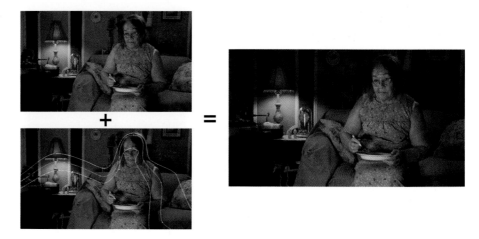

Depending on the application you're using, there are a couple ways of bringing those highlights back out of the shadows: by carefully controlling either the matte or your image-processing pipeline.

The easiest fix for this is to combine an HSL Qualifier to isolate the lamp with the shape that's been created such that the qualifier subtracts from the lamp.

To illustrate this example using DaVinci Resolve, you would select the node within which the shape correction is happening, enable HSL Qualification, and isolate the lamp (which is easy to do since it's both distinctly red and well lit). Once a solid matte has been created, invert it, and it will automatically subtract from the shape matte, as shown in **Figure 6.35**.

The result is that the lamp (along with some other reflective surfaces) returns to its original level of brightness, which gives the final grade the pop and contrast it so badly needs.

Figure 6.35 Isolating the lamp with HSL Qualification and subtracting the result from the shape matte puts the light back into the lamp.

In a more compositing-oriented application, the same thing can be done by duplicating the layer, keying the light sources you want to hold out, and superimposing them over the darkened grade in your initial layer.

WE'VE JUST SCRATCHED THE SURFACE

As you've seen, there are myriad uses for shapes. This section focused primarily on reinforcing and deepening shadows in the picture to focus viewer attention, but shapes can also be used to add or rebalance color, to lighten areas rather than darken them, and to split regions of the picture for more aggressive overall grading, depending on the capabilities of your grading application. Consult your documentation for more information.

SHAPES AND MOTION

Shape-based "digital relighting," as shown in the previous section, is a powerful technique for reinforcing (and occasionally overriding) pools of light and shadow in the original image, but camera and subject motion is a big factor in how you apply this technique.

It's important to begin this section by saying that often you can get away with stationary shapes applied to subjects that don't move that much, so long as the edges are feathered enough. In fact, it's not uncommon that such a soft shape ends up looking like a natural pool of light. Even if the subject moves into and out of it once or twice, as long as it doesn't call attention to itself, this might be a fine effect.

If you can get away with it, then you're finished and can move on. However, if the subject or camera's motion gives away the existence of your shape, then you're going to need to do something to match the shape to the movement that's happening. In the example in **Figure 6.36**, a rectangular shape successfully cuts down the amount of light falling on the tree. If this were a locked shot, then we'd be finished.

Figure 6.36 Camera and subject motion may foil the best laid plans.

However, the camera dollies in, and our cleverly placed matte ends up visibly moving past the tree and onto the woman's face, which is not helpful.

Fortunately, most grading applications provide two methods with which to address this. First, shapes can be keyframed in order to animate their position, rotation, and shape over time. Second, motion tracking lets you identify features within the image to be automatically followed by your program; you can use the automatically created motion path to match-move the shape matte relative to a moving camera and/or subject quickly and naturally.

TRACKING MASKS

Let's start by discussing motion tracking, since it's by far the preferable way to work. The premise of any motion tracker is that you choose a feature you want a shape to follow, and your program analyzes a range of frames (usually the entire shot) automatically creating a motion path that will animate the shape.

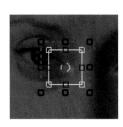

Figure 6.37 A one-point tracker tracking someone's eye. The image to the right shows, in red, the motion path that will be used to animate a shape.

A conventional point-based motion tracking system, available in Autodesk Smoke, uses a pair of boxes and a crosshair. Different applications use different terminology, but in general the inside box (the white box in **Figure 6.37**) is the *reference pattern*, which is centered upon the crosshairs, which defines the feature you want to track. The outside box (the red box) is the *analysis region* that defines how wide a range your application searches for the region (Figure 6.37).

Figure 6.38 shows a fairly typical operation, tracking someone's eye in preparation for making a shape follow the face. Smoke has one of the best one- and two-point motion trackers around. It's fast and accurate, which is great when you need to match a highly specific feature in an image. Additionally, when using the GMask tool in Smoke to create custom shapes, you can track each control point of the mask to follow a specific feature of a subject being isolated for even more specific match-moving.

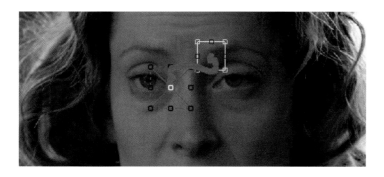

Figure 6.38 A single-point motion track in progress. The red line shows the motion path as it's defined by individual tracking points bunched together.

Usually trackers come in four varieties:

- One-point trackers track the position of a subject.

- Two-point trackers simultaneously track two features, providing both position and rotation tracking to a shape.

- Four-point tracking is less common, but it allows four-corner perspective distortion to be applied to a shape.

- Multipoint trackers allow you to track individual control points of a shape to conform to a subject that's moving and shifting around.

If you're using motion tracking for which you manually select the features to track, here are some general guidelines:

- Choose a feature to track that's both high contrast and angular. This makes it easier for your application to spot the feature from frame to frame.

- The larger you make the analysis region, the better your application will be able to track the feature, but the longer the track will take. Some applications are fast enough that this isn't a big deal, but others are slower and this can increase tracking times.

- If you make the analysis region too small, fast movement in the subject being tracked or the camera will cause the track to fail.

- If there's nothing to track on the subject you're applying a shape to, you can track something else that has the same motion. However, it's good to choose a feature to track that's at the same depth, relative to the scene, as the feature you're applying the shape to. For example, if the camera is moving and you're trying to apply a shape to an indistinct range of foliage, don't track the mountains in the distance; parallax makes the mountains move slower than the foreground foliage, and it won't look right.

- If you can track only a narrow range of frames, track what you can, and use manual keyframing to finish the job. This will still be faster than keyframing the entire shot manually, and most applications let you combine keyframing and motion tracking.

DaVinci Resolve uses a different type of motion tracker (**Figure 6.39**). Instead of manually choosing a feature to track, you simply create whatever shape you need for the effect you're creating, and then you use Resolve's tracker to automatically analyze the shot. A similar method of tracking has since been adopted by Adobe SpeedGrade and by FilmLight Baselight in their area tracker.

Figure 6.39 The top half of the DaVinci Resolve tracking controls, next to an image of the tracker in action, automatically choosing points to track based on the shape you create.

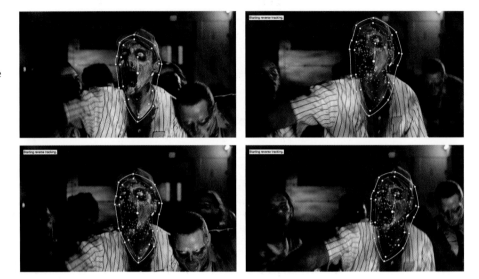

Resolve automatically chooses a cloud of trackable points and uses the resulting multipoint tracking information to transform your shape, using a user-selectable combination of Pan, Tilt, Zoom, and Rotation to make the shape follow along with the tracked subject and recording tracking data in a graph (**Figure 6.40**). If necessary, you can override any of these transformation methods to improve your result, as well as manually override which points are used for tracking in order to deal with occlusions (foreground objects blocking the subject being tracked).

Figure 6.40 The DaVinci Resolve tracking controls, showing the graph of analyzed tracking data that you can use to troubleshoot problems and override bad tracking data.

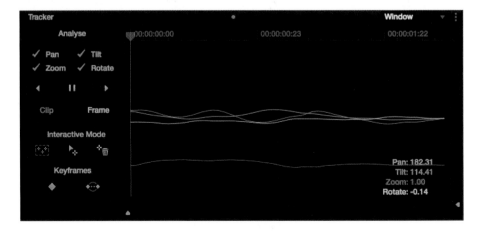

As you can see from Figure **6.41**, this type of tracker makes even complex movement with subject resizing and rotation relatively easy to deal with. Still, you can run into challenging situations, so here are some tips to overcoming common issues that come up when using area trackers:

- If tracking the entire subject results in unwanted motion or size/rotation transformations, you can usually shrink the shape in order to track a smaller feature that's restricted to the range of motion you're trying to achieve. For example, if someone's head is moving too erratically, you might be able to track an eye, ear, or nose to get the necessary type of motion. Once you've gotten the track you want, you can resize the shape as necessary, and it'll move with the shape.

- If your tracker lets you disable different types of transforms (Pan, Tilt, Zoom, Rotate), you can disable transformations that are unwanted. For example, if the position of your shape is tracking well but it's changing size too much because of some odd combination of motion in the image, then disabling Zoom could easily give you the track you want.

- Area trackers are still no help when the subject walks behind something else, like a tree, *occluding* the tracking points. This is what causes most trackers to fail. In this case, there's usually some kind of mechanism for tracking the first half of the motion before the subject walks behind that tree, then tracking the second half of motion after the subject comes out from behind the tree, and then *interpolating* the shape's motion from the last good track point to the next good one. As long as the subject is moving along a linear path, this can work well, but if the subject is moving erratically, you're probably looking at a manual keyframing job.

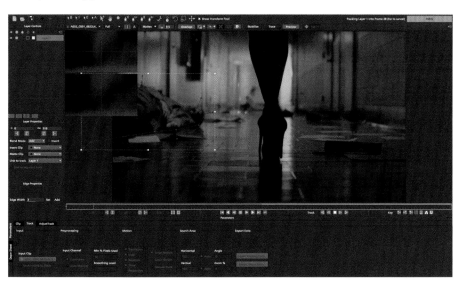

Figure 6.41 Imagineer Systems' Mocha does sophisticated tracking, rotoscoping, and object removal, solving many difficult problems that your grading application's built-in tracking and rotoscoping tools may not be able to handle.

If you're willing to learn yet another piece of software, Imagineer Systems' nearly ubiquitous Mocha (www.imagineersystems.com) takes an even more advanced approach to tracking. With sophisticated rotoscoping tools, planar tracking, and camera solving for 3D tracking, you can create detailed isolation mattes that stick to the subject in a variety of challenging tracking scenarios, which are easily exported for use in any grading application that's capable of importing external mattes. Furthermore, some applications including Assimilate Scratch and Quantel Rio let you import Mocha tracking data directly.

While your grading application may have faster tools that can take care of most simple issues quickly, advanced grading tools such as Mocha can come in quite handy when you have a difficult track for which you need a better result and you have the time to go out to another application.

Compositing applications are beginning to incorporate more sophisticated tracking as well. For example, Adobe After Effects has a built-in 3D tracker (**Figure 6.42**) that makes shape isolation in scenarios with a moving camera even more accessible.

Figure 6.42 Adobe After Effects has built-in 3D tracking capable of resolving camera moves, which lets you "stick" shapes and mattes into a scene as if they're actually in the room.

Continued developments in the realm of 2D and 3D tracking bode well for even easier use of shapes for grading shots with complicated motion. I used to warn new colorists against using too many shapes in their work, on the premise that the excessive keyframing you used to have to do would turn these operations into a time-sink. However, with the advent of fast and powerful tracking tools, I find my use of shapes has grown to the point where my only consideration is whether it's the appropriate tool for the issue I'm trying to resolve.

OTHER CAMERA TRACKING APPLICATIONS

If you're interested in learning more about camera tracking and how the intersection of tracking and compositing software may be able to aid your workflows, check out the following applications:

• The Pixel Farm's PFTrackX offers camera and object tracking intended for CG integration, while its PFMatchit is a node-based match-moving application that offers camera and object tracking with compositing in mind (www.thepixelfarm.co.uk).

• Vicon's Boujou also offers camera tracking and match-moving (www.metrics.co.uk/boujou).

• Andersson Technologies' Syntheyes offers camera tracking, match-moving, and image stabilization, and an After Effects plug-in lets you import tracking data (www.ssontech.com).

ANIMATING MASKS

As fantastic and time-saving as motion tracking is, it's not always a panacea. You may well run into the occasional shot where tracking doesn't give a satisfactory result and you need to resort to manual keyframing.

Chapter 6 will discuss the specifics of creating and manipulating keyframes to create different corrections. For now, it's enough to know that however your grading application handles keyframes for color corrections, keyframes for shapes are usually done in the same way. In fact, many grading applications provide a single track of keyframes for the entire shape. This simplifies the initial task of animation, but it can make later keyframe adjustment trickier.

For this and many other reasons, if you know you'll need to do some manual keyframing, you'll have a more successful result if you *keep your shapes simple*. Don't try to trace your subjects' every detail—it's probably unnecessary, and it'll be a nightmare to animate if you end up needing to do so. In fact, whether your shapes are still or in motion, you'll work more quickly if you get into the habit of keeping your shapes simple, organic, and focused on regions of light and shadow, rather than purely physical features.

If all you need to do is to animate the position of a shape, then it should be fairly easy to get a good result. My best advice for this is to choose a feature of the subject you'll be keyframing as a concrete reference point to follow (the nose, a button, a car handle) and then use a control point or crosshairs of your shape as a guide to follow the reference feature. In essence, you become the motion tracking computer.

However, with modern grading applications, it's rare that you'll find a simple position-matching situation where motion tracking won't do a better, faster job. You'll likely need to indulge in manual keyframing when forced by circumstance to partake of the horrors of *rotoscoping*, which is the process of manually manipulating a shape to follow the outline of a moving subject that is itself changing shape.

For example, the shot in **Figure 6.43** (shown previously in Figure 6.13) cleverly illustrates how the man can be isolated for correction using a custom shape. However, as seen in the two-image sequence, he moves, and the result is that the shape I've so cleverly created is good only for a single frame.

Figure 6.43 A shape that works well for a figure in the first frame is completely inappropriate if the figure moves. We need to rotoscope.

To fix this, we need to animate the control points of the shape so that it convincingly follows along with the moving figure (**Figure 6.44**).

Figure 6.44 Placing a keyframe and redrawing the shape to follow along with the moving man is the very definition of rotoscoping.

Animated intersecting shapes are a cornerstone of commercial grading when you need to precisely isolate product shots, cars, and actors you're applying aggressive looks or glamour treatments to, so it's a good idea to familiarize yourself with whatever shape and animation features your software provides when you're learning a new grading application.

TIPS FOR BETTER ROTOSCOPING

Lest I sound disrespectful, rotoscoping is an art, and it is difficult to do well and quickly. There are compositing artists who have become masters of this arcane task, and good rotoscoping is invaluable to a quality result in nearly any compositing workflow.

However, colorists are usually under the gun, and while a rotoscope artist may have days or even weeks to work on a shot getting it exactly right, a colorist working on the average program might have one to five minutes, so efficiency counts for a lot. Now, our computers do help a bit. Generally, a shape will be automatically interpolated in between each pair of keyframes that you create, so it's not like you need to keyframe *every single frame of the shot* to get a result. In fact, this is usually not desirable as it can result in stuttery motion that draws attention to itself.

Unfortunately, people seldom move in purely linear, predictable ways, and that's where the art comes in. Here are some tips:

- If you know you'll be rotoscoping, choose the position of the subject when it's at its most complicated, geometrically, and draw the initial state of your shape at this frame. You don't want to have to add control points midstream (if your application even allows this).

- When possible, save time by using a shape's position and geometry controls to move it along with the subject. In most applications, you can track a shape to match the motion of a subject first and then keyframe it to change form as necessary.

- Depending on the subject you're isolating, try breaking it up into smaller overlapping shapes that are individually easier to track and/or animate. In **Figure 6.45**, the man is being isolated by three different shapes that add to one another to create a single matte (or key, depending on your application's terminology). This makes problems that occur as you rotoscope and track much easier to correct without having to redo the whole job, and smaller shapes may more easily track to specific features, eliminating work when possible.

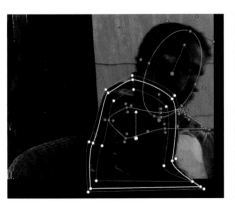 

Figure 6.45 If your grading application allows, combining multiple shapes to rotoscope a moving subject can make the job easier.

CHAPTER 6

- As you're rotoscoping, match the motion of a subject more successfully by paying close attention to when it slows down and speeds up in mid-move. These are the points where you'll be placing the most important keyframes.

- Once you've keyframed these major vectors of motion, then you can fine-tune the rotoscoping using the divide-by-half rule, scrubbing the playhead between each pair of keyframes, picking the frame where the shape is most off the mark, and adding only the keyframes you need.

- As always, watch out for the feathered edges of the shape. Haloing around the subject you're isolating is what you're trying to avoid.

So there you are. Keep in mind that motion tracking and rotoscope work are fairly new to the colorist's toolkit, relative to compositing applications that have indulged in these tasks for years. And while rotoscoping may be no fun, it's an important technique to get the hang of as it enables styles and grades that were unthinkable with previous generations of color grading workstations.

CHAPTER 7

ANIMATING GRADES

Most grading applications provide a facility for animating grades over time using *keyframes* (also called *dynamics*). Those of you familiar with compositing applications or with effects features in nonlinear editing applications (NLEs) know exactly what I'm talking about.

Which of a wide variety of grade animation features are implemented depends on the software you're using. However it's accomplished in your application, grade animation is an important technique that's essential for a well-rounded colorist's bag of tricks.

This chapter is designed primarily to get you thinking about different ways of using grade animation to solve different problems you'll encounter, as well as how it might be used for creative effect in programs that enjoy a daring sense of style.

GRADE ANIMATION CONTROLS COMPARED

In general, keyframing features in grading applications are far simpler than they are in the average compositing application. However, you have to keep in mind that for the grading artist, time is of the essence, and a typical keyframing interface for color correction has been designed for speed over features, favoring an approach that can be easily adapted to the buttons of a control surface.

In general, keyframing within grading user interfaces (UIs) takes one of three forms:

- **Place and adjust**, where you must first add a keyframe and then adjust the correction or parameter at that particular frame

- **After Effects–style**, where you turn on the parameters you want to keyframe, and then every adjustment you make to that particular parameter adds additional keyframes

- **Fully auto keyframing** wherein, once enabled, every single adjustment you make spawns a succession of keyframes to whichever correction or parameter you changed

Each of these methods of keyframing has advantages and disadvantages, and many grading applications let you switch among two or even all three of them, depending on the task at hand.

In addition, applications handle the scope of keyframing differently. Let's consider the nested hierarchy of color correction data within most grading applications, consisting of Grades > Corrections > Properties > Parameters. In other words, each grade consists of one or more corrections, each of which has a collection of properties (color properties, pan-and-scan properties, shape properties, and so on), each of which has individual parameters (shape properties include x position, y position, size, feathering, rotation, and so on). Your grading application may restrict the degree of detail at which you can set individual keyframes for an animated effect in one of the following ways:

- **Correction-wide keyframing** means that every aspect of a particular correction, including every parameter that correction contains, is animated using a single group of keyframes. This is fast, but it provides the least amount of individual control.

- **Parameter-level keyframing** lets you adjust the animation of each individual parameter within a correction, using separate sets of keyframes, one keyframe track for each parameter. This provides more detailed control at the expense of greater interaction with the graphical user interface (GUI), which can be time-consuming.

If you're lucky, your application provides the ability to switch the scope of keyframing between either method. Working with a single pool of keyframes for an entire correction's worth of parameters is fast and effective for the majority of simple adjustments you'll find yourself making. However, being able to open a correction in order to individually adjust or animate individual properties or parameters can also be a time-saver when you need to make a specific animated adjustment.

The following sections explore various ways that keyframing has been implemented in four grading applications. My apologies if yours isn't on the list (I had to finish the book sometime), but I hope this overview will give you a better idea of what to look for in your own application's documentation.

KEYFRAMING LIMITATIONS

Most grading applications have limitations on which parameters can and cannot be keyframed. For example, some applications don't allow for the animation of curves, and others may not allow animated HSL Qualifier controls. Check your user documentation for more information about your particular application.

DAVINCI RESOLVE

In DaVinci Resolve, all keyframes appear and are managed within the Keyframe Editor (**Figure 7.1**). The Keyframe Editor consists of multiple tracks, one for each correction node in the current grade, as well as an additional track for the sizing controls. Each Correction track can be opened to reveal multiple properties tracks corresponding to groups of parameters found within.

Figure 7.1 Dynamic and static keyframes as they appear in DaVinci Resolve. Notice separate keyframe tracks for corrections (each correction corresponds to a node) and for individual properties (groups of related parameters) within corrections.

Static keyframes appear as circles, and dynamic keyframes appear as pairs of diamonds connected by a long gray *x* (reminiscent of the lines you'd draw on a film work print using a grease pencil). Static keyframes create abrupt changes in the correction from one frame to the next; they're often used to alter a grade from one shot to another of a "baked master" if there's no actual edit point in the timeline.

Dynamic keyframes are used for animating the state of either an entire grade full of nodes, the state of individual nodes by themselves, or the state of a single group of controls from one set of adjustments to the next. You can adjust the actual transition by right-clicking either the outgoing or incoming dynamic keyframe and choosing Change Dissolve Type from the shortcut menu, after which point a window appears that lets you smooth or ease the transition start and/or end points.

Keyframes are used as transition devices so that you can park the playhead anywhere between two keyframes and make adjustments to that section of a clip. You don't have to place the playhead directly on top of a keyframe to make a static change as in other applications (unless you've enabled automatic keyframing for any of a node's properties, covered momentarily).

When animating corrections using keyframes, be aware that a shot's grade on each side of a set of keyframes must have the same number of nodes. If you need more nodes for a correction on one side of a keyframe than on the other, create the more complicated grade first, set your keyframes, and then reset the color and contrast adjustments of the nodes you don't need on the other side of the keyframes to achieve a smooth transition.

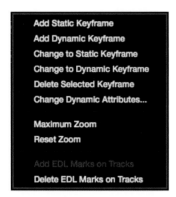

Figure 7.2 Keyframe editing commands in the contextual menu of the Keyframe Editor.

Figure 7.3 The Auto Keyframe button for a correction node.

Figure 7.4 The Keyframing Mode pop-up menu above the Keyframe Editor.

Figure 7.5 Keyframed corrections as they appear in Adobe SpeedGrade.

You can add keyframes to animate corrections in several ways, depending on the scope of your intended operation.

• Use the Add Static Keyframe and Add Dynamic Keyframe buttons of your control surface to easily make simultaneous animations of all properties within the currently selected node. This technique is good for making quick animated adjustments. These buttons add keyframes to every single property within all nodes at once.

• Right-click within the individual dynamics track you want to animate (the Quad Window track, for example) and choose Add Static Keyframe or Add Dynamic Keyframe from the shortcut menu (**Figure 7.2**) to animate individual node properties (for example, if you want to only add static keyframes to a Power Window, without adding keyframes to the color correction adjustment).

• Turn on automatic keyframing for any individual node property you adjust (color corrector, windows, defocus, and so on) by clicking the diamond "auto-keyframing" button to the left of the node property name (**Figure 7.3**). In this mode, any adjustment you make to the parameters associated with that property will be keyframed.

• Turn on automatic keyframing for all properties within a particular node by clicking the square auto-keyframing button for the Corrector track. In this mode, only the properties you specifically adjust will be keyframed, but any property within that node is enabled for keyframing.

• Use the All/Color/Sizing pop-up menu (**Figure 7.4**) or command to constrain keyframing using the buttons of your control surface. All enables all aspects of a node to be keyframed. Color restricts new keyframes to all of the Color Corrector tracks of the dynamics timeline for the selected node. PTZR restricts new keyframes to the pan/tilt/zoom/rotate track of the dynamics timeline.

Once you've created your keyframes, you can move them individually by dragging them left or right along the track in which they appear within the dynamics timeline display. You can move keyframes in groups by Shift-dragging to make a bounding-box selection and then Shift-dragging anywhere within the dynamics timeline to the left or right.

Keyframes can be individually deleted, or they can be deleted in groups by Shift-dragging the mouse to make a bounding-box selection of a group of keyframes, prior to pressing the Delete key of your keyboard.

ADOBE SPEEDGRADE

Keyframing within Adobe SpeedGrade is simple. A single set of keyframes is available for each clip's grade and for each adjustment layer you apply (**Figure 7.5**).

In the Color FX room, every node you add to the node tree to create an effect in that room has an individual set of keyframes governing its parameters. There are two types of keyframes: *hold* keyframes, which trigger abrupt one-frame changes to the grade; and *dissolve* keyframes, which create gradual interpolated changes from one keyframed state of the grade to the next.

SpeedGrade has both manual and automatic modes for keyframing. If you want to be on the safe side, you can do things manually. First you need to create a keyframe by clicking the Keyframe button (F2), and then you can adjust the state of the grade by positioning the playhead either on top of or to the right of that keyframe on the timeline and making whatever adjustment you need to.

When creating an interpolated change to a grade using dissolve keyframes, you need to click the keyframe button (or press F2) twice, once to place a second keyframe and a second time to turn it into a dissolve keyframe. The interpolation from the first keyframe to the second is shown by an arrow in the timeline, as you can see in Figure 7.5.

This sort of manual functionality prevents the accidental keyframing of parameters. (Believe me, it's easy to forget to disable auto keyframing in other applications and end up with a ton of unwanted keyframes for the last 20 tweaks you made.)

You can move a keyframe by dragging it within the timeline, and you can delete it by moving the playhead on top of it, using the Previous/Next Keyframe buttons (F3 and F4), and then using the Delete Keyframe button (Shift-F2). Alternately, you can drag within a keyframe track to select multiple keyframes to delete. To remove all keyframes, click the Delete All Keyframes button (**Figure 7.6**).

Figure 7.6 Keyframe controls found above the timeline in Adobe SpeedGrade.

If you want to have separate sets of keyframes triggering specific grading adjustments, you can use a separate adjustment layer for each keyframed adjustment you want to apply (**Figure 7.7**).

Figure 7.7 Multiple adjustment layers can be keyframed independently while affecting the same clip.

If you have excellent self-control, you can click the Auto Keyframing button to initiate automatic keyframing of all adjustments you make to any parameter or mask within a grade. Just be sure to turn this button off when you're done.

FILMLIGHT BASELIGHT

In Baselight—whether you're using the plug-in version or the workstation application—keyframes appear within the Keyframes display underneath the plug-in panel (**Figure 7.8**).

Figure 7.8 Keyframing in FilmLight Baselight.

Although each strip (or correction layer) within a grade has its own keyframes, all keyframes for all strips appear within a single track of the Keyframes display. To help manage a potentially dense thicket of keyframes, you can filter the Keyframes display (**Figure 7.9**) to show either a single type of interpolated keyframe or the keyframes for the currently selected control.

You can add and remove keyframes in the following ways:

Figure 7.9 The Keyframe Filtering menu lets you choose which parameter's keyframe appears in the strip.

Figure 7.10 The Set Key button and Keyframe Mode pop-up menu as they appear underneath the Offset color balance control.

- Clicking the Set Key button below any control manually adds keyframes for that operation to the corresponding strip (or correction layer) in the timeline. The Set Key button of a control turns blue when there's a keyframe at the position of the playhead.

- Clicking a blue Set Key button again disables that keyframe.

- Setting the keyframe editing pop-up menu to Auto Edit puts Baselight into a mode where any change you make to a control automatically adds another keyframe to the strip.

- Enabling Dynamic mode by clicking the Unset/Set button of the Blackboard control surface adds keyframes to every strip within the current grade.

The Stripe KFs button, if enabled, puts you into a mode where setting a keyframe for one control in a strip automatically sets keyframes for all controls in that strip at the same time.

The interpolation of each strip's keyframes depends on the setting of that strip's interpolation mode pop-up menu (**Figure 7.10**).

Keyframes corresponding to each control can be set and switched among the following modes using a pop-up menu to the right of each Set Key button:

- Switching to **Constant mode** removes of the current keyframe at the position of the playhead; the corresponding parameter remains at a constant value.

- **Linear keyframes** result in a steady transition from one animated state to the next.

- **S-curve keyframes** ease from the outgoing to the incoming value.

- **Smooth keyframes** introduce overshoot and undershoot where necessary to ensure a smooth transition from one value to the next.

Keyframe interpolation can be changed individually for all keyframes on a strip simultaneously.

When it comes time to edit a keyframe's value, there are three modes with which you can do so, selectable via either the keyframe editing pop-up menu (**Figure 7.11**) or buttons of the control surface.

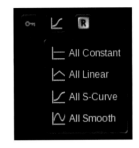

Figure 7.11 The Keyframe Editing pop-up menu.

- **Auto Edit mode** requires you to park the playhead right on top of a keyframe in order to edit it. Otherwise, making a change in Auto Edit mode while the keyframe is not on top of an existing keyframe results in the creation of a new keyframe.

- **Edit Left and Edit Right mode**s let you adjust either the next keyframe to the left or the next keyframe to the right of the playhead, which makes it easier to alter the values of existing keyframes while viewing a more useful frame of the image elsewhere in the shot.

You can copy and paste values among keyframes by moving the playhead to a keyframe and pressing Command-Shift-C to copy the value and then moving the playhead to another frame—with or without a keyframe—and pressing Command-V.

You can move keyframes by right-clicking one or more keyframes (one at a time) and choosing Add to Move Selection from the contextual menu and then pressing Command- [or Command-] to move the selected keyframes left or right (**Figure 7.12**).

Figure 7.12 Selected keyframes appear with arrows pointing to the left and right, ready to be moved using keyboard shortcuts or control surface buttons.

You can also move keyframes by parking the playhead over a particular keyframe and then simultaneously clicking the Control and Move buttons of the Blackboard control surface to select it (all keyframes in a strip can be selected by clicking Control, Shift, and Move together) and then clicking the Move button while using the jog/shuttle wheel to actually shift the keyframe's position.

To delete a keyframe, park the playhead on top of it and click the Unset/Set button. Alternatively, you can park the playhead between two keyframes and then click either the Delete Left or Delete Right button.

ASSIMILATE SCRATCH

Scratch displays keyframes in its mini-timeline as a series of vertical white lines. For simplicity, all keyframes appear here on one track; however, if you want to view and manipulate the keyframes that are applied to each correction and parameter individually, you can open the Curve window, which displays every keyframable setting in a hierarchical list (**Figure 7.13**).

Figure 7.13 Top, keyframes displayed in the mini-timeline in Assimilate Scratch; bottom, Scratch's Curve window.

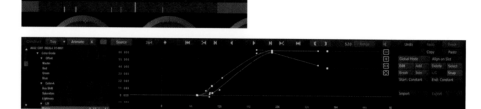

There are three modes with which you can enable or disable keyframing in Scratch (**Figure 7.14**):

Figure 7.14 The keyframing modes and controls in Assimilate Scratch.

- **Off** disables the ability to add new keyframes to a grade.

- **Manual** enables the various keyframing controls of the UI, which lets you manually place keyframes where you want them prior to making adjustments.

- **Auto** enables a mode where every single change you make to a parameter in Scratch generates a keyframe for that parameter. If you use Auto, don't forget to turn it off when you're done; otherwise, you'll have a ton of unwanted keyframes that you'll have to eliminate.

The Set Key button lets you add a keyframe at the current position of the playhead. First, you make an adjustment to the parameter you want to animate, and then you click the Set Key button, which stamps that adjustment as a keyframe. Adjust first, then set.

The Trim button lets you offset the value of the current keyframe by the amount with which you've adjusted a parameter. Again, you need to make the adjustment first and then click Trim to stamp that value into the previously existing keyframe. However, the Offset All button lets you offset the value of every keyframe in the currently selected parameter by that same amount.

The Curve window is quite powerful, letting you add, delete, move, and adjust keyframe position and value, as well as providing powerful Bezier curve control over custom keyframe interpolation. You can pan around and zoom into the Curve window for finer control of your adjustments.

CORRECTING CHANGES IN EXPOSURE

The animated correction I make most frequently is for shots where a camera's auto-exposure or auto-knee function causes brightness changes right in the middle of playback. Although this happens most often in documentaries, it also happens in narrative films when the cinematographer just can't keep their hands off of the iris or where the director is a fan of rolling takes and lighting adjustments are snuck in "between takes." It seems an increasingly inevitable fact of life that the very best take for a particular moment in a scene is one with an unwanted exposure change (**Figure 7.15**).

Figure 7.15 Two frames immediately before and after an unwanted exposure shift in the image. Keyframing will allow us to smooth it.

On the other hand, you will also run into situations, during longer takes, where the lighting changes subtly and unintentionally. You may wonder why the Waveform Monitor is rising and falling whenever you move the playhead, until you scrub the playhead quickly through the shot to notice it getting darker. In these cases, what you're seeing is the only cloud in an otherwise blue sky moving over the sun in the middle of the shot. Now, gradual cloud-cover changes may be allowable, but if they're noticeable enough, you may have to do something about them, too.

Whatever the source of the uneven exposure, you can usually minimize the problem (and occasionally fix it completely) by creating an animated correction to solve the issue.

Whenever possible, it's good to create these kinds of fixes using a separate correction from the underlying primary correction. By adding a second correction/node/layer/strip/scaffold that you'll use to create the animated fix, it's easy enough to reset it and start over without altering the original grade if you somehow paint yourself into a corner with a compensating adjustment that's not working (**Figure 7.16**).

Figure 7.16 Creating the animated adjustment in a second correction (in DaVinci Resolve) lets us make adjustments without altering the underlying grade.

The trick is to play through the clip to identify the start and end points of each change in exposure you need to take care of and to add two keyframes, one at the beginning and one at the end of each exposure change, with which you'll make your correction.

Assuming there's just one shift (lucky you), create an *unaltered* keyframe at the frame that dovetails with the ideal state of the image. In other words, this is the frame where the shot goes back to "normal" (**Figure 7.17**).

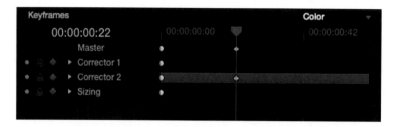

Figure 7.17 Adding a keyframe at the end of the exposure shift, where the exposure has reached the level that's normal for the rest of the shot.

To make your life easier in the next step, grab a still frame of the "end keyframe" image. You'll use this still for comparison when you adjust the beginning of the exposure adjustment.

Now, place a keyframe at the frame where the exposure shift has reached its maximum state of deviation from your grade, in this case the first frame where the image is at its darkest, and adjust the exposure (and possibly the saturation if it changes because you've either raised or lowered overall image contrast) so that the image at this second keyframe matches the image at the first keyframe you created (**Figure 7.18**).

Figure 7.18 Correcting the image at the first keyframe to match the appearance of the image after the exposure shift has occurred.

If you load the still you saved as a split screen, you can use the Waveform Monitor to help you make this adjustment. With the shifted frame split-screened against the grade as it should appear at the second keyframe, you can clearly see the difference between the highlights, midtones, and shadows. Better yet, in this example there's a thin trace that clearly shows exactly how much lower the highlights are (**Figure 7.19**).

 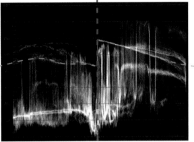

Figure 7.19 You can clearly see the difference between the exposure-shifted frame and the grade as it's supposed to look in the split screen. But the split screen, when analyzed by the Waveform Monitor, shows you exactly what the difference is: the speeding adjustment. Common features in each half of the split show the offset, as shown by the orange dotted line.

Depending on the clip, it can be difficult to get an exact match, but you should be able to eliminate most of the shift in brightness and, at the very least, make the problem less noticeable to the audience during a casual viewing (**Figure 7.20**).

Figure 7.20 The newly corrected sequence.

CORRECTING HUE SHIFTS

Another less common but equally problematic issue arises in one of two situations: Either a camera's auto white balance setting is triggered inappropriately in the middle of a shot, causing an unwanted color temperature shift throughout the shot, or a camera that's been set to manual white balance is panned, dollied, or Steadicam'd from one light source (outside) to another (inside). In either of these situations, you'll end up with a corresponding shift from neutral to orange (tungsten) lighting, or neutral to blue (daylight) lighting, *right in the middle of the shot* (**Figure 7.21**).

Figure 7.21 The one-shot sequence used to illustrate a common hue shift occurring as the result of panning from an exterior to an interior location.

TIP

Just like with the exposure shift example, you can grab a still of the ideal state of the image (somewhere the underlying grade is unaffected by the unwanted exposure shift) and use a split screen to help you match the keyframed correction you're trying to make with the clip's underlying grade.

This sort of transition is inevitable if you're working on a reality show or a documentary with a roaming camera that follows subjects as they go about their business, but it can also come up in a narrative program if the camera is focused on activities outside a window (for which there was no time to hang a color-temperature-correcting gel) and then pans to a bit of drama happening inside a tungsten-lit room.

Fortunately, this is another issue that we can solve, or at least minimize, by animating grades using keyframes. In fact, there are two ways we might go about this.

KEYFRAMING THE GRADE

The easiest way of correcting an unwanted color shift from one light's color temperature to another is to simply keyframe an animated color balance correction to compensate. Let's take a look at a practical example of correction the situation shown in **Figure 7.22**.

Figure 7.22 The beginning and end of the shot in Figure 7.21 shows a distinct shift from the neutral color temperature outside to a vivid orange color cast inside. We can fix this using animated corrections.

1 As with the solution to correcting changes in exposure, you want to start by parking the playhead on a section of the clip that has the correct color balance, then add a correction, and then grade the clip via a Primary adjustment with the look you want it to have.

2 Next, add a second correction (within which you'll create the animated fix for the color shift). Identify the range of frames during which the color temperature shift happens, and add keyframes at the beginning and end of this shift (**Figure 7.23**).

Figure 7.23 Keyframing the immediate range of frames over which the exposure shift occurs, shown with the frames of media occurring just before and just after the color shifts.

Although keyframing a compensating adjustment often works well when it matches the exact duration of the shift, sometimes the most seamless transition will be longer (such as sneaking a color transition in during a slow pan in darkness), while at other times a shorter transition might be preferable (such as shifting the color faster than the audience will notice during a whip-pan). There's no way to tell what will look right until you create the animation and see how it plays.

3 Now, move the playhead to the keyframe where the clip's color is at its most incorrect, and make a color balance adjustment within the second correction you added to make that part of the shot match the rest of the grade. If necessary, you can grab a still frame from the well-adjusted part of the clip and split-screen it with the keyframe you're adjusting to use as a reference for your correction (**Figure 7.24**).

Figure 7.24 Left, the original color cast. Right, the corrected image, graded after the second keyframe.

4 When you're finished, play through the clip to see how it looks and make any necessary alterations to achieve the closest match you can. If the color shift isn't perfectly linear, then perhaps adding a second or third keyframe will help if you can accurately spot the frames where the color is varying, but generally I find that two keyframes is enough for most situations.

The example clip works fine with a short dissolve, and while you can see a small change in color temperature as the camera pans across the corner of the doorway, it's subtle enough to ignore (**Figure 7.25**).

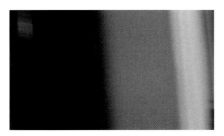

Figure 7.25 As the correction is animated during the camera pan, a small section of the wall turns blue just before going out of frame. If the transition is subtle enough and the problem disappears fast enough, this might be acceptable in the face of the larger fix.

However, there's one problem. As the camera passes by the window, the exterior light spilling through now appears a brilliant blue, because of the correction we've made to match the interior. Although this makes the example more complicated, it's actually a great excuse to show another strategy for dealing with unwanted mixed-lighting situations (**Figure 7.26**).

Figure 7.26 Another problem that can't be ignored: Our correction makes the light coming in from another window look terrible.

5 Fortunately, there's an easy fix: Add a third correction. Use an HSL Qualification to isolate the cool exterior highlights. The window light is blue enough to be easy to isolate, and using a well-softened key (using a combination of qualifier tolerance and key blur), you can then rebalance the window highlights to match the overall color temperature you're sticking with in the scene (**Figure 7.27**).

> **TIP**
>
> Using an HSL Qualifier to isolate and correct an instance of mixed lighting coming through a window is a great technique that's useful whenever you're confronted with a pool of light within a scene that's significantly different from the dominant color temperature of the rest of the environment.

Figure 7.27 An HSL Qualifier lets us isolate the radically different color temperature and make a fix.

With this accomplished, we're finished with the grade and can move on with a song in our hearts knowing there's no distracting color shift to kick the audience out of the scene (**Figure 7.28**).

Figure 7.28 The final sequence from outside to inside. Animated color balance let us make the correction.

CHAPTER 7

KEYFRAMING A SHAPE TO CONSTRAIN A GRADE

Although a simple animated grade often works well, there are other times—especially when you're dealing with a sharp border, like the one in this example—when it's impossible to cover the animated transition from one color temperature to another seamlessly. In these situations, you can try "wiping" the correction into the frame using an animated shape.

This is a trickier operation, as you have to make sure that the edge of your shape/ Power Window matches the moving edge of the border between the two color temperatures you're attempting to match. The following two examples will take you through two situations where this technique will be handy.

KEYFRAMED SHAPE EXAMPLE 1

In this first example, we'll take a look at how to correct a problem that bedevils documentaries, reality shows, and independent features alike: tinted car windows. The problem is that the window alters the exposure and color of the image, and if the camera has been balanced through the car window, the world as seen outside an open window can look strange indeed.

Because the window is a nicely defined geometric shape that naturally "wipes" onscreen, you can use a shape/Power Window to correspondingly wipe your correction onscreen as well, hiding the change you're making.

1 Scrubbing through the car clip, you can see that the camera pans from left to right, from the front window to the open side window, and it is this open side window that displays markedly different color (**Figure 7.29**).

Figure 7.29 In a continuous shot, the color as seen through the front window, and later through the open side window, is distractingly different.

2 First, with the image through the window shield visible, grade the shot to look as you would like it to. Assuming both sides of the shot have enough latitude to do what you want, it's quickest to grade the shot first and then grab a reference still to refer to later when you want to match the second half of the shot.

3 With this accomplished, add a second correction to deal with the change in color, again to provide you with the convenience of separating your animated effect from the base grade.

4 Now, move ahead to where the camera is pointing out the window. Load the still you saved in step 2 as a split screen, and make a correction to achieve a good match between the two halves of the shot. Because glass can affect light in interesting ways, it may be difficult to easily get an exact match, especially with skies that may be partially polarized, but in this shot you can get pretty close with a simple primary correction adjusting the Gain and Gamma color balance and contrast controls (**Figure 7.30**).

Figure 7.30 Before and after color correcting the side window view to match the color of the front window view using a split screen.

5 With a match accomplished, now it's time to animate a shape/window that will wipe the correction on. Move to the frame where the edge of the window bisects the viewer, and use a rectangular, polygonal, or custom shape/window to limit your correction to just the open window. Try as best you can to keep the edge between the corrected and uncorrected sides of the image running along the dark shadow of the car frame, and feather it to hide the transition. If the correction you made in step 4 is effective, the two windows should appear to be an approximate match, with allowances for the veiling glare on the glass of the front window (**Figure 7.31**).

Figure 7.31 The first placement of a window to limit the side window correction to the moving side window as the camera pans.

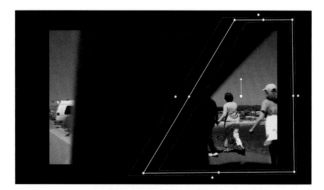

6 At this point, it's time to animate the shape to create the wipe. If your software allows you to keyframe the shape independently of the color correction, this is preferable, as it will allow you to make later tweaks to the color without having to ripple your change to every single keyframe that's necessary to create the wipe. In **Figure 7.32**, the Linear window was used in DaVinci Resolve to create the wipe, which can be independently animated using the Linear Win track

of the Corrector 2 node when exposed in the Keyframe Editor. Turning on the Linear Win track's auto keyframe control makes it easy to animate the window.

Figure 7.32 Keyframing the Linear Window separately from the color correction in DaVinci Resolve. Irregular movement may require several keyframes to achieve a seamless and hidden wipe. Automatic keyframing makes it easy to adjust the window as you scrub along the shot, animating as you go.

7 As you animate the window, make sure you keep the moving edge hidden in the shadows and aligned with the changing geometry of the area you're working to limit (**Figure 7.33**).

Figure 7.33 The animated window toward the beginning and toward the end of the section of the shot where the side window comes onscreen. It's important with a correction like this to keep the leading edge of the window hidden to hide the effect.

With the animation complete, scrub back and forth to make sure there are no visible artifacts, tightening the animation of the shape where necessary. Once you're happy with the final effect, you're finished.

KEYFRAMED SHAPE EXAMPLE 2

In this second example, you'll see how to use this same technique to wipe on a correction for the exterior to interior shot, in case a rapidly keyframed color balance operation proved too visible a manipulation.

1 Go back to the clip used in the previous example and play through the part of the camera pan from the outside, past the interior of the doorway. You can see in **Figure 7.34** that on one side of the wall, the light is cool, while on the other side, the light is warm. Darn that physics!

Figure 7.34 In mixed lighting, the color temperature on one side of the corner is a different color than that of the other.

CHAPTER 7

2   You need to add a second correction with which to address the color shift; once again, make a correction so that the interior matches the exterior lighting.

3   After making the correction, add a polygonal, rectangular, or custom shape/ Power Window (whichever is available) with a slightly feathered edge, offscreen at the left of the frame (**Figure 7.35**).

Figure 7.35 Setting up to use a shape as a wipe. The initial state of the shape is to the left of the frame, in preparation for wiping toward the right. Notice that the right edge of the shape is angled to match the edge of the wall that we'll be matching.

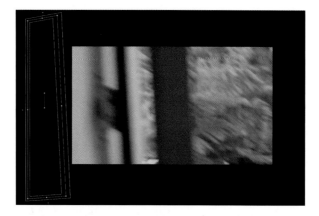

You want the initial state of the shape to be offscreen because you'll be animating it so that one side of the shape wipes from left to right along the corner of the wall that separates the two regions of differing color temperature.

4   Add a shape keyframe to the frame where the corner of the wall is just off of the left side of the frame. Then scrub the playhead to the frame where the corner just goes off of the right side, and place another shape keyframe there, adjusting the shape so that its left side is now off to the right of the frame and the shape envelopes the whole frame (**Figure 7.36**).

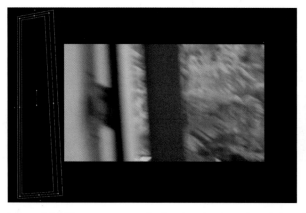 

Figure 7.36 The progression of animating the shape from left to right to follow the edge of the corner, masking the incoming color correction that makes the interior lighting less orange.

5   Playing through the shot, make any necessary adjustments to the timing of the shape animation so that the edge of the shape matches, as closely as possible, the motion of the corner.

When we're satisfied with the effect, we're finished, although we'll still have to apply the HSL-Qualified mixed lighting correction shown in the previous example to get rid of the color cast coming from the window the camera pans past.

GRADE TRANSITIONS USING THROUGH EDITS AND DISSOLVES

Another way of making transitions from one grade to another, which is more appropriate in situations where you're actually dissolving from one grade to a completely different grade, is by deliberately creating a *through edit* to cut the clip in two. Then you add a dissolve transition and grade the newly separated outgoing and incoming clips differently. Although it takes a bit of doing, this approach makes it easier to create smoother transitions between very different grades, and the result is often better looking.

This is an especially solid strategy for dealing with *tape-to-tape* style workflows that you're preparing ahead of time. Tape-to-tape describes the process of color-correcting a master tape of a program that was output by the editor. The tape is loaded on VTR A, controlled by and run through a color correction system designed to process the video relative to events synchronized via timecode cues, and ultimately recorded onto VTR B.

Nowadays, this workflow should more appropriately be called "baked master" color correction, since most modern grading systems are file-based (**Figure 7.37**). To save time and energy avoiding excessive and time-consuming project preparation, an entire program is exported (preferably textless) as a self-contained media file using whatever format is appropriate for the grading application being used, such as QuickTime, MXF, or a DPX image sequence.

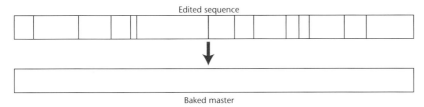

Figure 7.37 Turning an edited sequence into a single "baked master" media file.

This means that every transition, speed effect, image file, motion transform, filter, image generator, and superimposition is rendered and flattened into one big clip.

TIP

If you're stuck with a single flattened master file, some grading applications do provide you with tools to help. For example, DaVinci Resolve and Autodesk Lustre have automatic shot detection tools that you can use to notch a file you've been given, even if you weren't provided with an EDL. Although these automated tools usually require human intervention to massage the resulting data, it's still faster than finding all the cuts by hand.

The advantage of this (for the person doing the project preparation) is that a program doesn't have to be sifted through with a fine-toothed comb for individual clips using effects that aren't compatible with your grading application. The effects would need to be individually prepared, usually exported as a self-contained media file before being edited back into the main program to replace the original effect. From experience, I can say that this is indeed a time-consuming and laborious process, although it does create ideal projects for later grading.

Exporting the entire program essentially makes every single effect that's used compatible with your grading application by virtue of rendering it to the target format. However, now it's one giant file. If that's all you're given, then you're stuck having to manually keyframe grade changes at every single cut and dissolve in the program (using animated shapes/Power Windows to cover wipes and iris transitions). Speaking as a colorist, this sucks.

A better way to work is to have the editor who originally exported the baked master you're getting also export an EDL (most typical), AAF, or XML project file of the originally edited sequence, whichever your grading application is capable of ingesting. Using this edit list information, most grading applications can notch or preconform a single media file, adding cuts and dissolves to match the cuts and dissolves that are specified by the EDL and mimicking the original edited sequence (**Figure 7.38**).

Figure 7.38 Using baked master media with an EDL to create a notched, or preconformed, sequence in your grading application.

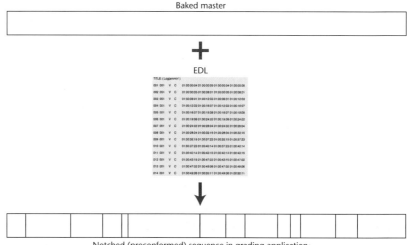

This makes your life easy because now each shot in the program appears as an individual clip in your grading timeline, even though the source media is one giant file. Even better, if there's a dissolve in the source material, then there's a dissolve transition in your grading timeline that creates a transition between the two shots it separates, eliminating the need for you to add keyframing to dissolve from one grade to another.

This is because, even though the original program dissolve is baked into the source media you've received, you still need to dissolve between the two different grades you'll be applying to each shot on either side of the transition, and the grades themselves also need dissolves (**Figure 7.39**).

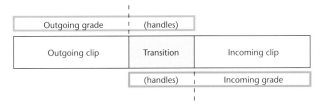

Figure 7.39 A transition in an EDL-notched grading sequence enables handles to be rendered for each pair of graded shots that overlap within that transition.

The dissolve essentially provides a cue to your grading application that it must render handles for each graded outgoing and incoming clip pair that is rendered, corresponding to the duration of each transition. You can then dissolve between these handles just like any other transition between two shots. This saves you work (no keyframing necessary), and it usually yields a cleaner result when you're dissolving between two extremely different grades.

PROBLEMS WITH BAKED TRANSITIONS AND HSL QUALIFICATION

Grading a notched baked master usually works identically to grading any other show, with one notable exception: HSL-Qualified corrections will shift at each baked-in dissolve.

This is because the $Y'C_BC_R$ or RGB levels of the media being keyed are changing because of the baked-in dissolves or fades to black. Since the media levels are changing, the keyed mask changes right along with the transition, sometimes disappearing altogether.

Sometimes the result is invisible, and sometimes not, but if it's a problem, you can try keyframing the HSL Qualifiers themselves in an effort to preserve as much of the key through the transition as you can (if your grading application allows it).

ARTIFICIAL LIGHTING CHANGES

Another animated correction you'll make frequently is to create a deliberate change in lighting. Often, practical effects for lights being turned on or off don't look quite as dramatic onscreen as the director thought they did while on location. Or, perhaps when the scene was originally shot there was no call for a change in lighting, but now one is needed because of changes in the edit. In either instance, you can solve the problem with an animated change to the contrast—and sometimes the color—of the image.

LIGHTING ANIMATION EXAMPLE 1

The following example shows how to alter the contrast of an image to intensify the effect of a practical light being turned off. This is primarily a contrast adjustment.

1 Play through the clip, and observe how the practical lighting looks (**Figure 7.40**).

Figure 7.40 With the initial grade, the practical lighting scheme when the switch is flicked off is unimpressive.

About halfway into the shot, the switch is turned off, but the resulting change in lighting accentuates a hot spot shining on the wall to the right of the light switch, and the overall lighting change is pretty weak. You should also notice that the change in lighting happens over two to three frames, depending on how picky you want to be.

NOTE

Another advantage of doing your initial grade using one correction and the animated effect with a second correction is that if you later decide to change the underlying correction, it has no impact on your animated effect, and you don't have to deal with making changes on either side of the animated transition as you would have if you did the grade and effect all with a single correction.

2 Apply your initial primary correction to the clip to give it a good overall look during the well-lit part of the shot (including giving it a bit of an orange tinge to indicate tungsten lighting). Then add a second correction, in which you'll create the animated effect.

3 Move the playhead to the first frame of the lighting change, where the finger is about to push down on the switch, and create a keyframe, although you need to refrain from making any kind of correction.

We're placing a keyframe here because this is the last frame with the original lighting scheme, and you want to lock it in place before creating the conclusion of the animated change that occurs over the next two frames.

4 Move the playhead forward to the frame where the lighting change is at its lowest level (two frames forward) and create a second keyframe (**Figure 7.41**).

Figure 7.41 The two keyframes used to set the beginning and end of the flicked-switch lighting change. Practical fixtures usually take a couple of frames to warm up or cool down.

5   At this second keyframe, manipulate the contrast sliders to create a darker look for the room when the light is off.

How dark you make the room depends on the situation. Is someone lowering the lighting in a restaurant or an auditorium, or is the light being switched off in a house at night with nothing but the moonlight streaming through a window?

For this example, create more of a night look by compressing the shadows (not too much or you'll lose detail) and then lowering the midtones and highlights to provide a dim environmental glow. Beware of making the highlights too dark; even though it's supposed to be lights out, the audience still needs to see what's going on.

Lastly, swing the highlights away from the orange you introduced earlier, to more of a cool neutral moonlight, and reduce the saturation until the image looks like a naturally subdued evening shot (**Figure 7.42**).

NOTE

When keyframing to animate a creative look, be aware of the limitations of your grading software. For example, some grading applications don't allow you to smoothly animate curve transitions. As a result, if you want to animate a contrast change, you should probably avoid using the luma curve.

CHAPTER 7

Figure 7.42 The new, animated adjustment, before and after flicking the switch.

6   As always, play back the clip to review the new animated effect, making any changes that are necessary to give you the effect you need.

Because the keyframed change is abrupt—over a mere two frames—the change appears to be fairly instantaneous. If you spaced out the keyframes more widely, however, the animated effect would happen more slowly, creating a more gradual change. Keep in mind that the distance between two keyframes determines the duration of the animated effect.

LIGHTING ANIMATION EXAMPLE 2

Changes to lighting don't just manifest themselves in image contrast; they can have an effect on the color of a scene as well, depending on the lighting scenario you're simulating. The next example shows how you can animate a grade to fake a timelapse change to the time of day—in particular, a shifting sunset effect. Granted, we can't make the shadow's lengthen as they should, but we'll do what we can.

1   Scrubbing through the shot of the back stairs, there's a strong delineation of shadow and light that can be used for this effect. Before beginning, it's important to create the initial grade, deepening the shadows a bit (but leaving room for them to go deeper without looking unnatural) and muting the highlights in order to convey a late afternoon look, in preparation for the final shift to sunset lighting (**Figure 7.43**).

Figure 7.43 Setting the initial look of the scene for a late afternoon lighting scheme.

2   With the initial primary grade completed, add two corrections. One will be used to add color to the highlights using HSL Qualification, and the other will be used to gradually darken the shadows of the shot with a simple animated change to master gamma. **Figure 7.44** shows the three nodes as they'll ultimately be used.

Figure 7.44 Setting up an additional two corrections for the two animated operations you'll use to create the timelapse effect.

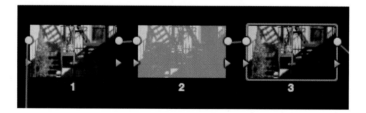

3   Use the second correction to isolate the highlights with HSL Qualification (**Figure 7.45**).

Figure 7.45 Isolating the highlights in preparation for making them golden.

4 With the highlights isolated, you can now set a pair of keyframes to gradually change the highlight color balance from the original neutral state of the image to a warmer, golden/orange hue. Once that's finished, add another pair of keyframes to the third correction to gradually change the gamma from neutral to a little bit lower (**Figure 7.46**).

Figure 7.46 Keyframing a simple animated transition from late noon to fake sunset, for both color balance and gamma exposure.

And that's it. Playing through the clip should show a smoothly gradual shift from the original neutral late-afternoon look to a more colorful, deeper lower sun look (**Figure 7.47**).

Figure 7.47 First and last frames of this animated lighting effect.

If you wanted to continue playing with this effect, you could try adding another, inverse key to the highlight qualification you pulled in order to animate a gradual (but *slight*) cooling off of the shadows while the highlights grow warmer, creating a more dynamic interplay of light and shadow.

CREATIVE GRADE ANIMATION

While animated corrections are often used for strictly utilitarian purposes, such as those shown earlier in this chapter, other possibilities remain, for the most part, unexplored by conventional cinema.

For this last example, we'll take a look at a more creative way of using animated grades, emulating an effect seen in fashion designer and director Tom Ford's *A Single Man* (Stephen Nakamura, Colorist: Company 3). In it, the saturation of people and places gently increases in specific POV shots, showing with no small impact the main character's state of mind.

It's a bold choice and not for the unimaginative. Let's take a look at one possible way of creating a similar effect.

1 Before you make any adjustments, evaluate the shot in order to come up with a game plan for what you're going to do (**Figure 7.48**).

Figure 7.48 The uncorrected shot.

For this image, you're going to create an initial grade with nice contrast, bright highlights, and a small bit of "misted blur" in her face. To create the effect of the woman's face "coming to life" just as she turns her head, you'll also start out the grade with an extremely muted color palette (not grayscale, just muted) that's pushed to a very cool tone for the woman in her initial state.

The goal is to increase the color in her face, but you'll do this with a two-part adjustment, first by increasing her overall saturation and second by boosting the rosy reds in her face and lips using an HSL correction.

2 Now that you've decided what you're going to do, create the initial correction (**Figure 7.49**).

Figure 7.49 The graded shot in its cool blue "muted" state, before we bring it to life during an animated grade.

3   Now, to create the animated effect, apply a second correction, adding two keyframes—one soon after the beginning of the shot and another about halfway through. At the second keyframe, boost the saturation back up by about 40 percent, and rebalance the color using the Gain control to slightly warm the image.

4   Now, to try being a bit more visually clever, add a third correction, using HSL Qualification to isolate just the reds of her face in the midtones. The resulting mask is a bit noisy, so you'll grow and blur the key by an exaggerated amount to minimize it (**Figure 7.50**).

Figure 7.50 Using HSL Qualification to isolate the rosy red tones of her face, for selectively increasing saturation as the last part of the animated effect.

5   To improve the quality of the red key, use the initial state of the image as your source, rather than the desaturated/resaturated image created by the earlier corrections.

As an example of this, notice how, in **Figure 7.51**, the key is pulled using a separate correction (node 4) that takes the initial state of the image as its source, feeding the resulting key into node 3, which is creating the red color boost. For more information on how to do this, see Chapter 5.

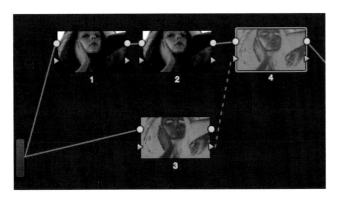

Figure 7.51 The order of operations used to create this effect, as shown in DaVinci Resolve. Node 1 is the base correction, node 2 is the animated saturation increase, and node 3 is the animated "rosy red" color boost.

6 To animate the additional increase in "rosy" saturation, add two more keyframes, beginning *during* the initial saturation boost and ending after the previous animated effect has finished (**Figure 7.52**). This will be the second stage of your "increased saturation" effect, and it will continue after the initial overall saturation boost has ended. In this example, I also animated the Hue vs. Sat curve to add more red specifically to her lips, accentuating her lipstick.

Figure 7.52 The two sets of keyframes used to create this effect, as shown in DaVinci Resolve.

7 At the second keyframe, boost the saturation of the woman's face by about 50 percent. Playing through the clip, the effect looks good, so *voilà* (**Figure 7.53**)!

Figure 7.53 The final animated sequence of corrections, going from cool muted (left) to rosy warm in two slow blooms of color (center and right).

Unfortunately, it's impossible to show the animated effect in print, but try it for yourself. Ideally, this sort of effect will coincide with a narrative event or emotional cue for which it makes sense, and the actual animation of the shift should be designed so that it's not too jarring or abrupt if you want it to seep into the viewer's awareness. We're all, at a subliminal level, accustomed to the chemical adjustments that the irises of our eyes make when adapting to different levels of lighting, and this kind of effect can feed into the same type of experience.

CHAPTER 8

MEMORY COLORS: SKIN TONE, SKIES, AND FOLIAGE

This chapter addresses the far-reaching topic of *viewer preferences*. One of our many tasks as colorists is to be aware of what the audience is expecting to see. If we're attempting to convey the most naturalistic rendering of a scene, it's tempting to think that our goal would be to photometrically reproduce the colors of that scene as they existed in reality.

More often, audience expectations reflect what each viewer would *like* to see. Apparently, we all view the world through rose-tinted glasses, or at least we expect to see the world depicted on the screen that way. This should be a comfort to the ambitious colorist. After all, if viewers want reality, they can get up off their couches and go outside. From the perspective of the visual stylist, people watch movies and television shows for a more beautiful, stylized, or interesting look at the world.

This is true even if you're working on the most serious-minded documentary. Although the reality might have been that a sallow-complexioned office worker was filmed in a fluorescent-lit conference room with flat white walls, a strictly accurate color rendition might well have the audience thinking that something is wrong with their televisions. Every viewer has an internal reference of what people "ought" to look like, and variation from these expectations will elicit a response, either positive or negative, that it's your job as a colorist to anticipate.

This is not to subject you to the familiar tyranny of "skin tone must fall on the I-bar" (the center point of the ideal range of skin tone—in fact, it can also fall *close* to the I-bar) and "water must be blue" (only if it's clean—rivers and ponds might also be brown or green). Natural variation in the subject being portrayed, as well as the nature of the scene's dominant light source (the *illuminant*), provide a perfectly good rationale for a wide variety of creative treatments.

That said, it's also useful to be aware of just what an audience's built-in preferences for certain things might be. You can use these expectations (or play against them), knowing how a typical audience will respond to your particular adjustment.

This section investigates a body of imaging and psychological research into how a viewer's color memory and color preference compare with strict photometric accuracy. As previous chapters have made clear, our experience of color is entirely perceptual; as a result, the majority of imaging research and experimentation involves studies examining the experiential overlap and variation of individuals evaluating collections of color swatches and images.

By comparing many subjects' perception of standardized test colors (usually Munsell color chips) under strictly controlled conditions, imaging specialists have long sought to quantify viewer preference, and the results of over 70 years of research are interesting to consider.

WHAT ARE MEMORY COLORS?

C. J. Bartleson of the Eastman Kodak Company presented some early data on the subject of memory colors in an article in the January 1960 issue of the *Journal of the Optical Society of* America, titled "Memory Colors of Familiar Objects." In it, Bartleson defines memory colors as "those colors that are recalled in association with familiar objects."

The goal of that study was to identify, based on 50 observers (combining "technical" and "nontechnical" viewers alike), which colors were most consistently associated with specific, highly familiar objects. Objects were named, and subjects were to identify which of an assorted collection of standardized Munsell color samples came closest to representing each one.

Ten visual objects were selected for which viewers exhibited consistent preferences across the entire group. These objects are listed in **Table 8.1**.

When all of the selections for each object were plotted as a close cloud of points on a hue vs. chroma graph, the results clearly showed clustered clouds of overlapping color preferences for each object, and that "two-thirds of the time the choices for hue were within 4.95 Munsell hue steps. Chroma was within 1.42 Munsell chroma steps, and value was within 0.83 Munsell value steps."

These results strongly indicate that we all have shared expectations of what certain commonly experienced colors should look like. These expectations aren't absolutely identical, but they're close enough to be statistically significant, and the deviations make sense given natural subject variation and differences in illumination.

Memory Color	X	Y	Z	x	y
Red Brick	2515	1834	1206	0.4527	0.3302
Green Grass	0660	1105	0898	0.2478	0.4149
Dry Grass	1637	1970	1247	0.3372	0.4059
Blue Sky	1876	2437	3778	0.2319	0.3012
Flesh	5877	5700	4988	0.3548	0.3441
Tan Flesh	2660	2757	1987	0.3593	0.3724
Green Foliage	0603	0833	0827	0.2665	0.3681
Evergreens	0498	0720	0716	0.2575	0.3723
Inland Soil	0644	0698	0382	0.3735	0.4049
Beach Sand	3771	4193	2906	0.3469	0.3857

Table 8.1 Chart of Observers' Mean Memory Color Choices

To make these results a bit more accessible to the colorist, Tom Lianza at X-Rite converted these preference means to Cb Cr so that I could superimpose the resulting plots relative to a vectorscope's graticule (**Figure 8.1**).

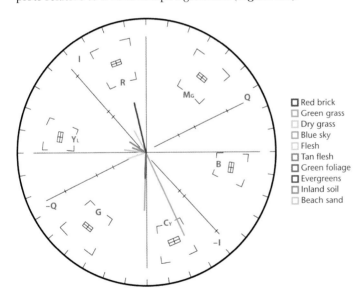

Red brick
Green grass
Dry grass
Blue sky
Flesh
Tan flesh
Green foliage
Evergreens
Inland soil
Beach sand

Figure 8.1 A mathematical CIE-to-Cb Cr translation from Bartleson's original data in order to see a vectorscope representation. I've deliberately exaggerated the excursions (saturation) for visibility.

CHAPTER 8

In my own experience, I've found that this list applies to compositional elements that I often isolate for secondary correction in various programs, before the client even makes their first comments. Having color corrected a feature that took place in the desert, I've spent lots of time obsessing about the ideal colors of earth and sand, and I've often found myself targeting the bricks on buildings to increase saturation just a touch.

MEMORY COLORS SIGNIFICANTLY INFLUENCE SECONDARY CORRECTIONS

Another illuminating article that was presented at the 2004 IS&T/SID Twelfth Color Imaging Conference (coauthored by Clotilde Boust and too many others to list here)—titled "Does an Expert Use Memory Colors to Adjust Images?"— addresses the correspondence between memory colors and the strategies used by Photoshop artists to segment an image when they are making targeted adjustments.

A series of experiments tracked which regions within a series of images were identi- fied by multiple expert Photoshop artists, in controlled environments, for making specific corrections. The direction in which each isolated region was adjusted was also measured. When data from each subject's work on four different images was correlated, it was found that the following elements were consistently isolated for targeted adjustment (secondary corrections, as shown in **Figure 8.2**):

- Skin tone

- Green grass

- Blue sky

Figure 8.2 Regions of U' V' into which expert Photoshop artists adjusted the color of grass, skin tone, and skies.

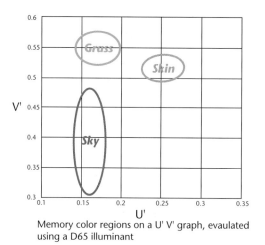

Memory color regions on a U' V' graph, evauated using a D65 illuminant

These three memory colors, in particular, come up repeatedly in numerous studies as the short list of memory colors for which most viewers exhibit a pronounced preference. From my own anecdotal experience I've found that these are the three elements clients most often want me to tweak in any given scene, whether it's a documentary, commercial spot, or narrative program.

As in Bartleson's study, the experts' ideals for these three colors were found to over- lap, and each test subject independently isolated and pushed those colors into the same directions when their individual adjustments were plotted with vectors on a U' V' graph.

Adjustments to a particular subject corresponding to a memory color fall within a tight enough region to be statistically significant, and the deviation within each region is large enough to leave room for individual preference, subject variation, and the influence of scenic lighting (a vital topic I'll address in a bit).

My interpretation is that the data supports the use of memory color ideals as general guidelines, rather than as hard rules.

IS MEMORY BETTER THAN THE REAL THING?

There's an abundance of data that supports the notion that there are certain things (skin, grass, skies, plants, sand) with which nearly everyone associates an ideal color. However, these same studies also indicate that our ideal colors don't necessarily mesh with reality.

Multiple studies confirm a general preference for increased saturation in scenic elements corresponding to memory colors, over the average actual measured saturation of the original subjects. Bodrogi and Tarczali's white paper "Investigation of Human Colour Memory" presents a succinct overview of the results of experiments performed by Newhall and Pugh in 1946:

> Brick appeared to be remembered as redder than the object, sand as more yellow, grass as greener, dry grass as more yellow, and pine trees as greener. Lightness of the memory colours, in all cases except brick, ran higher than in the object color perceptions; as a general average, 1.1 Munsell value steps extra value was required. An average 0.95 Munsell steps more chroma was required.

Bartleson calls out several specific examples of how memory colors deviated from measured instances of the same subjects in his study. The following paraphrases his results:

- The closest correspondence between a memory color and the measured color of the original subject is for human complexion.

- Although Caucasian human complexions do vary mostly in luminance, memory colors for skin tone are distinctly more yellow than photometrically measured averages for actual Caucasian skin tone. There is a preference for more yellow in the complexions of photographic and painted reproductions.

- Sand and soil are remembered as having greater purity, with more yellow.

- Grass and deciduous trees are remembered as being more blue-green than yellow-green.

- Blue sky is remembered as being more cyan and of higher purity than the measured blue of natural skies.

Figure 8.3 uses a butterfly split-screen to compare an original image (to the left) and a simulation of the "memory colored" equivalent (to the right).

> **NOTE**
>
> Butterfly splits are useful for comparing two versions of an image that may have a subtle change. They're often accomplished using two projectors that have been carefully aligned and masked to project two versions of a print or digital signal against one another.

Figure 8.3 Original and memory color (simulated) are compared "butterfly" style. The original image is on the left. On the right, two secondary corrections adjust the grass to be more saturated and yellow and adjust the sky to be more saturated and cyan.

In a later paper, Newhall compared the results of his and Bartleson's studies and found they were generally similar. Later studies by Bartleson and Bray reconfirmed these findings but added a twist.

COLOR PREFERENCE

It turns out that when they were asked to choose the *pre*ferred color when they were given a choice between a previously selected memory color and the measured natural color of a particular subject, viewers preferred the natural color for skies (more blue than cyan) and grass (more yellow-green than blue-green).

On the other hand, the same subjects continued to prefer the memory color for skin tone (a bit more yellow, or golden) over reality.

In his 1968 article "Color Perception and Color Television," Bartleson proposed that ideal color reproduction should "suggest the appearance of the original scene in such a way as to please the viewer." In other words, *pleasing* color rendition is more important than strict accuracy.

This proposition dovetails well with my personal philosophy for documentary grading. Although documentarians aren't necessarily interested in the sort of exaggerated stylization in which narrative programs often indulge, I've often commented to potential clients that another useful goal is to grade each scene to create, for the viewer, a sense of how the locations felt to the filmmaker at the time of the shoot, as opposed to neutrally and dispassionately reproducing the original quality of light (a sentiment I've also read expressed by photographer Ansel Adams). This is an admittedly emotional take on the goal of preferential vs. natural color rendition, but it's one that I've found resonates with many directors and cinematographers.

For commercial clients, a different take on the search for reproducible color preference is the holy grail of "what colors do people like best?" A study entitled "A System of Color-Preferences," by J. P. Guilford and Patricia C. Smith, from the December 1959 *American Journal of Psychology* sought to obtain data on pure color preference in the absence of object associations.

They tested 40 observers (20 men, 20 women) on their general color preferences, again using a series of standardized Munsell color chips. Subjects were instructed to rate each chip on a scale from 0 = "most unpleasant imaginable" to 10 = "most pleasant imaginable." The resulting preferences were collated as the "affective value" of various colors, with high affective values being liked and low affective values being disliked.

Although the locale of the tested subjects made this study somewhat region-specific (they all lived in Nebraska) and the age of the study might date the results if we assume that color preference is affected by a certain amount of trendiness, there is a fair amount of internal consistency in the findings that is still interesting.

In terms of pure hue, the most favorable responses in both men and women were for green-cyan-blues. The least favorable responses were a common dislike for greenish-yellows and magenta-purples (confirmed decades later by Patti Bellantoni's titular observation that *If It's Purple, Someone's Gonna Die* [Focal Press, 2005]). **Figure 8.4** shows an example of a Hue affective value chart.

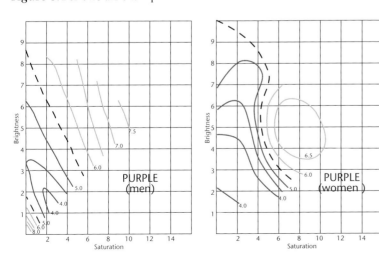

Figure 8.4 Example of an affective value chart from J. P. Guilford and Patricia C. Smith's paper "A System of Color Preferences." The dotted line represents indifference, the blue lines indicate positive responses, and the magenta lines represent negative responses. Men and women's preferences were separated in the study.

This study includes a series of isohedonic charts corresponding to each tested color group, of which I've redrawn a sample for illustration (**Figure 8.4**). The numeric value of each plotted line represents how favorable an impression that color made at the range of brightness and saturation indicated by that line's length and position relative to the axes of brightness and saturation.

Ultimately, it was found that specific hues were less significant as an indicator of viewer preference than were a given color's specific levels of lightness and saturation.

For example, reds, yellows, and violet-blues were preferred most at high saturation, while highly saturated greens and purples were preferred least. Meanwhile, yellows, greens, and blues were also most preferred at increased lightness.

An inspection of the saturation/brightness charts this study includes, which graph the viewer preferences for each family of hues, revealed the following basic generalizations:

- Reds and violet-blues were most preferred with either high saturation and medium lightness or medium saturation and high lightness, but not both.

- Yellows, including yellow-red and yellow-green, were most preferred with both high saturation and high lightness.

- Greens and blues were most preferred with medium to high lightness, but at medium saturation.

- Purples were most preferred in a restricted range of medium saturation and medium lightness.

Although subtle, this kind of data is still useful. Color correction tutorials often like to use the example of isolating someone's shirt to completely change its hue, but the truth is that it's much more common to make targeted alterations to saturation and contrast, with perhaps some subtle hue shifts. In other words, the experienced colorist is sensitive to viewer preferences for different colors at varying degrees of saturation and lightness and makes adjustments to optimize the rendition of the scene accordingly.

Incidentally, the Guilford and Smith study of all-Nebraska subjects also found that nearly all hues exhibited a high affective value at very low saturation and lightness. The authors chalked that up to a preference for physical texture in the observed samples, and I find that dovetails with many of my clients' preference for the preservation of fine detail within the shadows of an image. This also might be a cautionary tale; beware of overly desaturating the shadows.

From this study one can infer that a particular population will likely exhibit similar color preferences but that these relate more to preferred levels of brightness and saturation than to any particular hues.

CULTURAL VARIATION IN COLOR PREFERENCE

Another research paper addresses this issue in a more meaningful way for the colorist: Scot R. Fernandez and Mark D. Fairchild's "Observer Preferences and Cultural Differences in Color Reproduction of Scenic Images" (2005).

The authors present another series of experiments testing observer preferences in association with realistic scenes, this time sampling an international group of subjects (Chinese, Japanese, European, and American) to investigate whether there are consistent cultural preferences.

Although the results point to statistically significant preferences in different populations, the authors take pains to write, "[T]he cultural difference observed is most likely not of practical significance for most applications." Furthermore, the data showed that "images with faces have a much tighter range of preference in comparison to images without faces." This is consistent with findings that there's a shared worldwide preference for a fairly narrow range of color for skin tone (at least, relative to the spectrum). It's worth noting that, in this study, the image sets included a distinctly multiracial series of portraits.

However, subtle variations are still interesting given an occupation where you'll often find yourself making subtle 2 percent adjustments to give an image just the right look. With that in mind, the summarized results of the differences in cultural preference included in the paper are worth consideration. To paraphrase these results:

- Japanese subjects preferred a lighter image compared to the other groups.

- Chinese subjects preferred more contrast compared to the American and Japanese groups.

- Subjects from the eastern hemisphere preferred higher saturation than the American group.

- Japanese subjects preferred warmer images than the American group.

- Chinese subjects preferred cooler images than the American group.

Although this seems to indicate subtle cultural similarities in color preference, the authors sought to emphasize that the variations between subject groups was minor, and practical experience suggests that individual client preference will easily override these observations; however, it remains an interesting avenue of research.

On the other hand, certain colors carry different associative meanings across various cultures. This is an altogether separate issue from simple color preference, and it delves into the cultural semantics of color association. If you find yourself working on a cross-cultural program of some kind that you know will be distributed in a particular region of the world, it may be to your advantage to do a bit of regional art history research before you go into the session.

CHAPTER 8

THE "NATURALNESS CONSTRAINT"

There are clear expectations for color within a specific population, and we've seen that there's a subset of preferred rendition that relates to these subjects. Now, let's look at the issue from another angle, that of "naturalness."

Sergej N. Yendrikhovskij's 1998 paper, "Color Reproduction and the Naturalness Constraint," is a comprehensive document filled with a lot of valuable background on the search for a meaningful definition and means of measurement for color image quality in a world of incredibly different display devices and print technologies.

In a great example for colorists, Yendrikhovskij describes memory color within the context of a person looking for a banana at a grocery store. Taking for granted the various surround and illuminant phenomena affecting the eye's perception of color in that situation, the banana as perceived in the bin is compared with the viewer's internal mental memory color and preference for the color of an *ideal* banana.

This example reinforces these two key points:

- Memory colors are a basis of comparison for the appeal of a visual subject to the viewer.

- Someone's ideal color for a thing may have nothing to do with that thing's exact, measured color. This is when the client tells you, "I don't care if it's accurate, I want it to be yellower and more saturated!"

Yendrikhovskij hypothesizes that the appearance of image naturalness depends in part on a match between an element within a scene and the viewer's associated memory color. Furthermore, he suggests that naturalness also includes a requirement for how closely a subject's color matches that of the overall illuminant lighting the scene.

Lastly, he suggests that the perceived naturalness of a scene is also dependent on the naturalness of the color of *the most critical object in the scene*. This overlaps with much of the previously cited research on memory color. In other words, for a scene with prominent skin tone, foliage, or skies, if the memory colors are close to what the audience expects, they'll use those elements as a benchmark for how natural the color of the entire scene appears to be, with a tolerance for color variation so long as it's consistent with the overall color temperature of the scene's illuminant. This has clear ramifications for the importance of secondary corrections, and for the exercise of restraint in such secondary corrections if a naturalistic rendition is desired (i.e., don't overdo it).

Yendrikhovskij also takes pains to point out that the color of a given subject "is not a single point. Even homogeneously colored objects like bananas contain spots of different colors." Thus, were we as colorists to attempt to overly correct the natural color variation of a particular subject, the results would likely seem flat and unnatural.

A good example of this last observation is an experience I had color correcting a talking head shot in a documentary for broadcast. The woman being interviewed had a somewhat blotchy complexion (no budget for a make-up artist), with mottled red in her skin tone. I was asked to eliminate it, but when I made a hue curve adjustment to perfectly blend the red blotches with the rest of her complexion, the client balked. Despite the newly "ideal" color of her complexion, she looked *unnaturally* perfect. The solution was to slightly back off of the "perfect" match, the result being a happy medium between ideal skin tone and the natural color variation in her face.

A DEFINITION OF IMAGE QUALITY

Yendrikhovskij brings most of the research discussed in this section together in an attempt to create an algorithm to accurately predict what image "quality" actually means to an average viewer. This loosely summarizes his hypothesis:

Quality = Naturalness + Colorfulness + Discriminability

In other words, perceived quality is a balancing act between a viewer's tendency to favor a natural rendition, alongside the desire for an attractive amount of colorfulness and a need for maximum discriminability to make it easy to read an image and take in everything within the scene.

Yendrikhovskij cites findings that viewers exhibit a slight preference for more colorful images, even if the result is also rated as slightly unnatural. In other words, viewer definitions of "quality" may place a greater value on colorfulness than on the natural rendition of a scene.

WHAT IS COLORFULNESS?

Fedorovskaya, de Ridder, and Blommaert's paper "Chroma Variations and Perceived Quality of Color Images of Natural Scenes" also sought to establish a link between naturalness and the perceived quality of an image. After plotting viewers' ratings of various images, these researchers found that "naturalness is an important perceptual constraint in the color reproduction of images of natural scenes…[but] is not identical to image quality."

This study found that *colorfulness* has a significant effect on the perceived quality of images; viewers found images of increased colorfulness to be of higher quality but only up to a certain threshold, beyond which the images were judged to be of lower quality. This threshold, when graphed, is sharp enough and consistent enough to be statistically significant.

Colorfulness is an interesting concept, as it's not simply a reference to saturation. Colorfulness refers to a viewer's *perception* of how colorful a subject is, and that perception is affected by a variety of criteria.

CHAPTER 8

- Subjects that are lighter appear more colorful.

- Larger subjects with a dominant color appear more colorful than subjects that are smaller, even when they have identical color and saturation.

- Images with greater color contrast appear more colorful than images with lower color contrast, even at equal levels of saturation.

Interestingly, the authors found the plotted maximum threshold where subjects equated colorfulness with quality to be roughly the same regardless of the subject. In other words, the threshold was quite similar for tests involving images of fruit at a fruit stand, a woman against a portraitist's background, an exterior patio scene, and a sunlit interior seen through an exterior window. This suggests that a common threshold of acceptable colorfulness doesn't necessarily depend on the type of subject being viewed.

In a related observation, Edwin Land's "Recent advances in retinex theory and some implications for cortical computations: Color vision and the natural image" (presented at the annual meeting of the National Academy of Sciences, 1983) presented data indicating that viewers have greater tolerance for changes in saturation than for changes in hue. This indicates that when grading for a naturalistic look, you have more latitude for manipulating color components that relate to colorfulness then you do for altering hue when making creative adjustments.

WHAT IS DISCRIMINABILITY?

Discriminability describes the ease with which a viewer can discern the important details and subjects in an image. As Yendrikhovskij suggests, "A picture is unlikely to be judged of high quality if the items it contains are not distinguishable." From this point of view, image quality can be judged as a balance between naturalness and discrimination.

I suggest that discriminability is based on the interaction between three image characteristics that have been covered in previous chapters.

- As we learned in Chapter 3, increased contrast aids the perception of image sharpness and edge detail, which enhances subject boundaries, aiding legibility.

- In Chapter 4, we saw how color contrast further assists the separation of one subject within the frame from others. In fact, color contrast is also an important characteristic of colorfulness, which is another valuable aid for enhancing the perception of quality.

- Finally, Chapter 6 illustrated the use of artificial shadow enhancement using vignettes to reduce the effects of equiluminance, where the tonality of a subject is too close to that of its surroundings to be clearly discernible to the audience's luminance-sensitive "where" visual system.

Discriminability is discussed in Chapter 5 of Yendrikhovskij's paper, and he suggests that achieving acceptable image discriminability may require "exaggeration of certain features of the image (e.g., by means of increasing color contrast and colorfulness), resulting in a less natural but more optimal (from the information-processing point of view) appearance of images."

Thus, it's important to keep an eye on the legibility of the image as we make our corrections, using contrast adjustments, color balance, and careful control of artificially enhanced regions of light and shadow to make sure that the audience can easily see what they need to in any given scene.

From another point of view, the notion of discriminability has interesting consequences for some of the more aggressive stylistic treatments we might undertake. Particularly from the point of view of color contrast, we can use discriminability as a basis for judging just how extreme a grade might be for purposes of legibility. **Figure 8.5** shows three different levels of color bias applied to a graded image, from the intensity of a full-blown duotone at the left to the less aggressive yet still pronounced tint in the middle and the much more nuanced but still discernable color cast applied to the image at right.

Figure 8.5 A sliding scale of color contrast ranging from sepia tone (least contrast) to tint to neutral balance (most contrast).

Given the quasi-equiluminance of the image, it's clear that discriminability is affected by the intensity of the grade.

DON'T FORGET THE ILLUMINANT!

A crucial point to make amid all this information is that we shouldn't all be grading skies, grass, and skin tones identically in every project we work on. That would be dull, it ignores individual variation, and it also doesn't consider the important role that scenic color temperature plays in keeping all elements of the picture unified, rather than ripping an image apart to look like a poorly made composite.

Physics and human visual response dictate that the dominant light source in a naturalistic scene interacts with the color of everything it illuminates, and in a typical grade, I feel that subject highlights ought to reflect that. Edwin Land quotes Isaac Newton on this score (translating from the original Latin): "The colors of natural bodies are derived from the type of rays which they reflect to the greatest degree."

Land correctly points out that, because of the eye's now-understood adaptive nature (covered in greater detail in Chapter 4), this isn't strictly true. However,

CHAPTER 8

Yendrikhovskij's research clearly found that viewer preference is subject to variation based on the viewing environment, citing additional research showing that test subjects choices for preferred colors varied with the lighting.

Furthermore, in the 2006 paper "Color Enhancement of Digital Images by Experts and Preference Judgments by Observers" from the *Journal of Imaging Science and Technology,* the numerous authors state (the emphasis at the end of the quote is mine):

> *The expert also follows some rules: the corrections must be plausible inside each segment and for the whole image, in relation with the illuminant of the scene. The images are accepted by observers in relation with the presence of memory colors and when* the treatment of the whole image seems coherent.

Additionally, the "naïve observer" preference component of this study showed that "some rejected images have a high percentage of memory colors." This demonstrates that, even for images where skin, foliage, and skies have been color corrected to match "ideal" memory colors, the image is seen as artificial if the resulting corrected elements aren't compatible with the dominant color temperature of the overall image.

However, don't look at this as a limitation. When testing the effect of the illuminant on preferred object color, Yendrikhovskij found that people were more tolerant of variations along the warm/cool axis of daylight color temperatures than they were of variations due to reddish/greenish lighting (an observation that I can confirm from experience). This makes sense given our shared experience of light in the natural world, but it also gives us a valuable tool for affecting audience perceptions of ease and unease, even within a naturalistic series of colors, based solely on the adjusted color temperature of the illuminant within the scene.

Although it's perfectly possible to apply a multitude of secondary corrections to individually manipulate each significant element within a scene, it's also important to exercise primary correction as a tool for maintaining an overall consistency within the totality of the image.

DON'T GET CARRIED AWAY

So, is it really necessary for you, as a working colorist, to pore through all of this research? To paraphrase an email exchange I had with a colorist of considerable experience, much of the professional colorist's work is intuitive, based on years of experience grading many programs for lots of different clients. Any colorist who's been in the business for years is an individual treasure trove of this kind of information.

Having just presented a wealth of research that I genuinely believe is useful to the field of color grading, I also want to stress that it's a mistake to interpret memory color research too literally, holding your visual storytelling hostage to audience expectations of the way things ought to be.

Understand that an *awareness* of audience preferences doesn't require us to unthinkingly obey them. After all, centuries of painted masterpieces beg to differ, and it's valuable to search for a unique way of expressing the visual needs of whatever program you're working on.

Whatever the client and you decide to do from a creative perspective, you are at an advantage if you can keep in mind how you're either playing into, or against, these audience expectations, whether the audience is conscious of it or not.

That, to me, is the real fun of the job: finding the right tense scene in a thriller where pushing the greens of Central Park or the skin tone of the antagonist *very gently* against preference can give the audience just the right sense of unease. Or conversely, grading the scene of a kiss in a romantic comedy, knowing with full conviction the audience ideals for colorfulness, complexion, sky color, and naturalness of illumination that will put the shot right over the top.

IDEALS FOR SKIN TONE

Any colorist will tell you that half the job is grading skin tone. Generally speaking, if you want to sell a shot to the audience, you must strike a careful balance between the overall look of the environment in a scene and the skin tone of the subjects. In fact, colorists often rely on the skin tone of subjects within the frame as a benchmark for the color balance of the scene. Before looking at different approaches for judging and adjusting the skin tone of subjects in your grading application, you should understand a little more about what makes skin tones special.

Years of looking at one another have made us extremely sensitive to healthy skin tones, and even slight variations may create unwanted audience reactions. Too much yellow or green from a color cast may make someone look unintentionally sick; too much red may indicate the character spends more time getting sunburned (or in bars) than you want the audience to think.

One of the nice things about skin tone is that the complexion of everyone on earth falls within a fairly narrow range, which can be seen on a vectorscope. In instances when color casts may be difficult to spot, the distribution of hues that are plotted in the vectorscope graph may guide your correction by their relative distance from the I-bar which, because of the foresight of the video engineers who designed this system, indicates the center-point of the ideal range of skin tone.

To the casual observer, the uncorrected image in **Figure 8.6** may appear to have a relatively neutral color balance; nothing necessarily stands out as being blatantly incorrect, although the image may seem rather colorful.

Figure 8.6 An uncorrected image with a more or less subtle color cast (how subtle will vary depending on the differences between print and digital reproduction).

If we use a secondary correction to desaturate everything except for the skin tone, however, we'll see a much different image. Without the other colors to play off, the same skin tone appears much more red, and a look at the vectorscope shows that it's in fact stretching a little to the right of even the R target that signifies pure saturated red (**Figure 8.7**).

Figure 8.7 The same image, after desaturating everything but the skin. Now we see the actor's true colors.

Making a correction to the distribution of hues to rein in this redness results in more restrained, naturalistic skin tones that are a clear improvement over the original (**Figure 8.8**).

Figure 8.8 A simple primary correction results in a more naturalistic complexion for both actors.

In the following sections, we'll take a look at how and why people's complexions vary and explore ways that you can use this information to control your own corrections.

WHAT GIVES SKIN ITS COLOR?

Skin, as any 3-D modeler/texture artist will tell you, is an incredibly complex surface in terms of color, luminosity, and reflection. The more you understand its characteristics, the better you can see how people's complexions react to light, giving you more control over the look you want to create.

Skin is translucent, and our complexions are actually a combination of color absorption, light scattering, and reflection from several different layers of skin.

- *Melanin* is a biological polymer found in both light and dark complexioned people. This pigment adds color to the *epidermis* (upper layer of skin). There are two forms of melanin: *pheomelanin*, which ranges from red to yellow (also found in red hair); and *eumelanin*, which ranges from brown to black (also found in brown/black hair and eyes). Eumelanin is the pigment that primarily differentiates the complexions of people in different regions of the world. Although nearly everyone's skin has some amount of eumalanin, pheomelanin is a genetically distinct characteristic.

- Blood flowing through capillaries in the *dermis* (lower layer of skin) also contributes a significant amount of red to the overall hue of skin tone because of the oxygen-carrying cells *hemoglobin*. This hue is identical regardless of one's epidermal pigmentation, which accounts for the similarity in hue of people from all over the world. There is some variation in the color of blood, however, because of differing light absorption of oxygenated and deoxygenated hemoglobin (the former is more red, while the latter is more blue). Arteries contain more oxygenated blood (adding saturation to some parts of the body), while veins contain more deoxygenated blood (this doesn't turn people blue, it simply results in more average saturation).

- It has also been found that heavily pigmented skin (with increased melanin) absorbs more light, allowing less to reach the dermis and interact with hemoglobin. This also reduces the saturation of one's complexion (Elli Angelopoulou, "Understanding the Color of Human Skin," 2001).

- The dermis may also contain ß-carotene in large-enough amounts to lend a yellow or orange cast to the skin. ß-carotene is usually accumulated through diet (eating lots of carrots and other brightly colored vegetables).

- Lastly, the hypodermis is a subcutaneous layer of white fat cells that reflect any visible light that penetrates that far back up. In their article "A Study on Skin Optics" (2003), Aravind Krishnaswamy and Gladimir V.G. Baranoski point out that this reflectance, combined with a combination of surface and subsurface light-scattering, gives skin its luminous quality. In particular, the authors state that "collagen fibers are responsible for Mie scattering, while smaller fibers and other micro-structures are responsible for Rayleigh scattering." This scattering gives a diffuse quality to the internal light within skin (**Figure 8.9**).

Figure 8.9 The layers of human skin (epidermis, dermis, hypodermis).

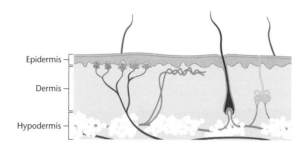

The combinations of melanin pigments, hemoglobin in the blood, ß-carotene, and scattering light that give skin its coloration and quality vary. However, we've seen this variation occurs only within a specific range (assuming an individual in good health). This is the reason that we'll later see that various skin tones fall within a specific wedge of the vectorscope, even though skin lightness varies widely.

MAKEUP

Makeup plays a vital role in narrative filmmaking, and it's interesting to note that makeup artists use tinted foundations to make color corrections to a subject's skin, similar to the way you might rebalance hues in the midtones of the video image to do the same thing. For example, applying yellow tones to fair-complexioned subjects or warm tones to dark-complexioned subjects gives the skin a healthy color that's tailored to the subject. Several layers of makeup contribute to the skin tones found in the face.

- Foundation is a layer of makeup applied to the overall face, and it performs the main "color correction" for the subject's complexion.

- Powder is added over the foundation to prevent shine, although some powders are formulated to create a subtle glow.

- Blush is added in the area of the cheeks both to accentuate (or deemphasize) the cheekbones and to add targeted warmth to the face. It simulates the natural blush response, and a common technique for choosing the appropriate blush is to pinch the cheeks and match to the resulting color. If you're sampling a hue from someone's face with an eyedropper tool, it's probably not a good idea to click an area with blush, as it will not be representative of the overall skin tone.

- Eyeliner, eye shadow, and lipstick are utilized for facial detailing, all of which will be accentuated with any contrast expansion you do.

Makeup, as with color grading, can also serve the narrative goals of a film. On the site Makeup.com, an interview with Richard Dean, who did Julia Roberts' makeup for the film *Eat, Pray, Love*, covered the role of varying facial color via makeup in different parts of the film:

In Italy, where Liz tries to rediscover simple passions, all the lines are softened. The blush moves from the outer cheekbone toward the apple of the cheek to create more of a natural, warm flush. Her soft rose lipstick is replaced with a more fleshy, nude color that's a bit more childlike.

In India, at the ashram, Liz's face is scrubbed. It's hot and she must work hard, so she's seeking a kind of purification. For this, her eye makeup is softened. The only time she seems to wear makeup is as a guest at a traditional Indian wedding, where her eye pencil mimics the lush kohl used by women in that country. Her lip color and blush are more golden here, and complexion is no longer matte but rather has a sunset glow.

In Bali, where Liz completes her journey, she has elements of all her earlier looks. Her eyes are lined again, but in a smoky, smudged manner. Blush has given way to a sun-kissed bronze across her cheeks and down the bridge of her nose. Her lips are moistened rather than lipstick-ed [sic]. A naturally sensual woman has emerged.

In general, there's nothing special you need to do when correcting a scene in which the actors are wearing makeup other than to try to stay true to the on-set color scheme (though I've had instances where I had to tone down bad actor-applied makeup on low-budget projects). However, you will notice some differences between people with and without makeup.

For example, subjects wearing makeup may have slightly different skin tones on their face than on other parts of their body (although this is also true of subjects who get a lot of sun). Depending on the makeup scheme, features such as cheekbones and the sides of the nose might be warmer, and possibly darker, than the rest of the face regardless of the lighting.

Furthermore, if you're doing an overall skin tone adjustment, rather than a slight modification to the base complexion (digital "foundation"), it might be a good idea to be sure you matte the entire face (except the eyes) in order to adjust the entire makeup scheme as a whole.

THE DIFFERENT CATEGORIES OF COMPLEXION

Everyone's complexion is different, and you're generally not going to want to park everyone's skin tone directly on the I-bar. To illustrate this, the collage in **Figure 8.10** shows skin patches sampled from 210 randomly selected swimsuit models. Each individual's skin patches were sampled from the arms, torsos, and thighs of each model in order to avoid facial makeup, and each swatch includes a gradient from moderate highlight through light shadow to include variation within each individual.

Figure 8.10 A collage of sampled skin patches from 210 variously color-corrected models demonstrates the variation of acceptable complexion values.

The sampled population includes self-identified Asian, African-American, Indian (Indian subcontinent), and Caucasian individuals, with additional sampling for pale/red-haired subjects and tanned members of each population. All images were previously color-corrected so they present a nonscientific survey of various photographers' ideals for appealing complexion.

When viewing this full range of sampled skin tones on a vectorscope, as in **Figure 8.11**, we can clearly see that while the overall range of possible hues for human skin is limited to a distinct cloud, there's plenty of room within that cloud for variation.

Figure 8.11 A vectorscope analysis of the overall image in Figure 8.10 shows the same range of sampled skin patches as a cloud of values on the vectorscope.

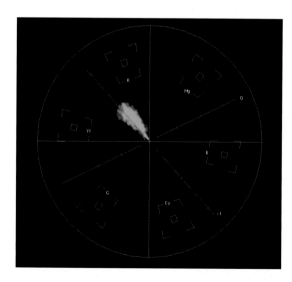

A similar range of color complexion has also been distilled into a set of four test patches on DSC Labs' ChromaDuMonde 12 + 4 test chart. These types of charts are widely used in the industry for camera calibration and are designed for accurate representation using ITU-R BT.709 colorimetry (**Figure 8.12**).

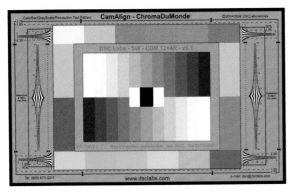 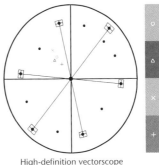

High-definition vectorscope targets at 2X magnification

Figure 8.12 DSC Labs' CamAlign ChromaDuMonde 12 + 4 test chart, with accompanying vector-scope plot showing the correct hue vector alignment for a vector-scope set to x2 magnification.

Speaking with DSC Labs president David Corley, he shared how his research teams have directly measured the spectral distribution of a wide sampling of ethnically varied individuals using spectrophotometers of extreme accuracy. Using this data, they settled on four test patches corresponding to "average" hue and saturation for ethnically African, Asian, Caucasian, and Indian complexions, which is shown in the chart in **Figure 8.12**. The accompanying vectorscope diagram shows the position on the scope that these targets should hit when a vectorscope is set to 2X magnification.

Another DSC Labs test chart shows the same general complexions within a more real-world image, starring four students from the Television Arts program at Ryerson University in Toronto. All four women were chosen for complexions that match the skin tone patches of the test chart in **Figure 8.13**.

Figure 8.13 DSC Labs CamBelles Summer test chart, intended as a reference for detailed camera evaluation after alignment. The skin tone hues match the skin patches in Figure 8.10.

CHAPTER 8

When accounting for or accentuating the variance among subjects in a scene, it's useful to know that complexions do fall into general categories. The following overview is based in part on categories derived from the cosmetics industry, including each category's corresponding rating on the Fitzpatrick scale, used by dermatologists to classify different complexions' response to UV light.

To aid our evaluation, these categories are presented in sequence by the angle at which they appear in the vectorscope, from golden/olive to ruddy/mahogany (**Figure 8.14**).

Figure 8.14 Hue of various complexions compared. Vectorscope analysis shows the subtle hue variation swinging from left (toward yellow/orange) to right (toward red) around the I-bar. For direct comparison, all models were lit identically.

As you can see, given neutral lighting, the visually varied complexions of the models in **Figure 8.14** translate into small angular differences on the vectorscope. Although subtle, these differences are hugely important because the audience is so sensitive to them. For this reason, skin tone adjustments benefit from a light touch and a sharp eye, as even small adjustments can significantly alter our perception of an individual's complexion. Here's a quick rundown of different skin types and how they react to light and sun exposure and what kinds of color adjustments they tend to require:

- **Pale/pink/fair-complexioned:** Type I skin doesn't tan but may freckle; burns easily. This includes redheads and very pale blondes (the same melanin that colors the skin also determines hair color). Generally fair-complexioned people tilt toward the red target (to the right of the I-bar), but because of reduced eumalanin levels, they can be quite desaturated. Some extremely fair-skinned people may even have a slight blue cast to their skin (which can be extremely confusing if you're trying to make a fast correction to the image based on skin tone).

- **Ruddy/mahogany-complexioned:** Type II skin tans lightly, burns easily. This complexion also tilts toward the red target (to the right of the I-bar) and tends to be much more saturated than the other complexion types. Both light and dark-complexioned people may fall into this category.

- **Medium/dark-complexioned:** Type III (tans gradually), also types IV, IV, and VI (tans with increasing ease). This is the average complexion for any individual not otherwise described in this list. In the absence of creative lighting, the hue falls right on the I-bar, and this complexion will be more or less saturated depending on the individual. It includes lighter to very dark complexions.

- **Olive-complexioned:** Type IV skin tans easily. These individuals typically appear just to the left of the I-bar. They have a tendency to stick out when they're in a two-shot with another subject that you're trying to correct, because they fall in between everyone else. A single midtones correction may have a significantly different effect on both subjects. If it's a real problem, you might have to do a secondary or masked correction on one of the subjects and create a separate correction.

- **Golden/Asian-complexioned:** Asian is a bit of a misnomer, as many different people may exhibit a golden complexion. As you would expect, these complexions can fall farthest to the left of the I-bar at the most extreme, although not always. If the complexion is due to a golden tan, then subjects will be more highly saturated; if the golden tones are due to a natural complexion, saturation may be more subdued.

- **Bad spray-on tans:** This is worth mentioning both because they're so horrible and also because spray-on tans are often a fast solution that's used to give an actor (or newsreader) some color. I've seen spray-on tans that make the wearer look like a carrot—they're that orange (although enough carrots will subtly alter the color of your skin, nobody eats that many bright vegetables). The problem is usually excessive saturation, and a good fix is often to isolate the skin with an HSL Qualification or narrow range of a Hue vs. Hue curve and simply desaturate it a bit.

The following section examines the specific characteristics of skin tone in terms of hue, saturation, and lightness.

COMPLEXION CHARACTERISTICS

Now that you know the elements responsible for creating skin tones, let's break these down even further into hue, saturation, and lightness characteristics for the purposes of analysis and correction.

HUE

When viewed on an RGB Parade Scope, all skin tones are weighted most heavily in favor of a strong red channel, a weaker green channel, and, with a few exceptions, a blue channel that is generally the weakest (**Figure 8.15**).

Figure 8.15 Skin tones represented on an RGB Parade Scope.

Zooming in on the face and examining the Parade Scope shows this much more clearly (**Figure 8.16**).

Figure 8.16 The Parade Scope limited to analyzing facial skin tone.

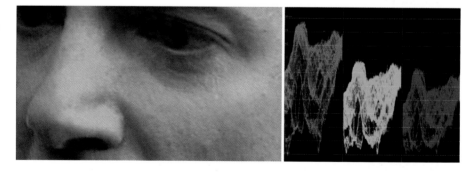

Also, hue will vary slightly even within a single subject's face. When examining the same zoomed-in face in the vectorscope, you can clearly see a wedge of values—hues in various parts of the face typically vary as much as 5 degrees (**Figure 8.17**).

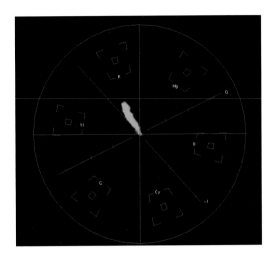

Figure 8.17 Vectorscope analysis of the zoomed-in face.

With clips of average exposure, skin tones usually fall solidly within the midtones. Since color casts are frequently correctable with a simple adjustment to the Whites color balance control, you can usually use the Midtones color balance control to fine-tune the skin tones, as we'll see in a later section.

I know I keep mentioning this, but it's crucial to understand that the appearance of skin tone is *highly* dependent on the quality of light and the color balance of the scene. Since skin is in part illuminated from within, it makes sense that the color temperature of light in the scene will interact with a subject's complexion to a certain extent.

The two shots in **Figure 8.18** have the same two actors and similar shot composition, but the environments are quite different. In one, warmer golden-hour lighting warms up the faces, lending more saturated and ruddy complexions. In the other, subdued neutral lighting leaves the faces less saturated and closer to the natural skin tones of the actors.

Figure 8.18 Same actors, same "over" framing, but different skin tones because of differing lighting within each environment.

The close interaction of skin and the illuminant is why, in nine out of ten shots (assuming competent lighting), a suitable primary correction made to the subject and background together yields terrific results and may be the only thing you need to do if you're working on a well-shot program with simple grading needs.

Another phenomenon that affects the appearance of skin tone, this time in a more troublesome way, is the interaction of the surrounding background on how we perceive complexion.

In the following example, two shots from the same scene appear side by side. As shown in the isolated split-screen excerpt in **Figure 8.19**, the skin tones are close to identical, but the pale green wall behind the marine results in a perceived difference that you'll need to account for, as it makes a difficult perceptual match to the audience in the backyard.

Figure 8.19 Although the skin tone of the faces match, the surrounding environment in each shot makes these two shots appear as if they're not well balanced.

This is an example of a situation in which you may well need to make a secondary correction to either the wall or the surrounding environment of the people in the yard (isolating everything *but* the skin tone) to make a slight correction that would create a more convincing perceptual match.

SATURATION

The ideal saturation of a subject's skin tone is *always* going to be relative to the rest of the scene. If the background is muted, then lower skin-tone saturation levels will appear to be more vibrant to the viewer. On the other hand, if the background is extremely colorful and highly saturated, it might take greater levels of skin-tone saturation to make an impression.

That said, skin tone saturation in an "ordinarily" lit scene will generally fall between 20 to 50 percent amplitude on the vectorscope. What amplitude is suitable depends on the type of complexion you want to convey. The following loose guidelines are based on my own experiences and my own nonscientific survey of fashion photography over the years:

• People whose complexions are considered to be fashionably *pale* are generally going to fall between 20 and 30 percent amplitude on a vectorscope (**Figure 8.20**, center). If you're adjusting for skin tone that measures less than 15 percent amplitude, you're likely grading either a porcelain-skinned actor with skin-lightening makeup, or a vampire.

- Extremely dark-complexioned people with high amounts of eumelanin in the epidermis absorb more light, reducing the light's interaction with the capillaries of the dermis that add color to skin tone. This doesn't necessarily alter hue by a huge amount since melanin has reds and browns, but it slightly reduces saturation, so that very dark-complexioned people may fall into the same range of saturation as pale light-complexioned people (**Figure 8.20**, left).

- People with average degrees of color in their complexions, whether darker or lighter complexioned, will more likely fall somewhere around 35 percent amplitude, with a spread of 25 to 40 percent amplitude (Figure 8.20, right).

- People with very colorful complexions, whether because of a golden suntan or a genetically ruddy skin tone, fall at the outer extreme of 35 to 50 percent amplitude, with 40 percent being a reasonably good limit if you don't want to overdo it.

Figure 8.20 Complexion saturation compared on the vectorscope. Gridlines have been overlaid on the vectorscope detail to provide a reference. From left to right, the models measure 30 percent amplitude, 32 percent amplitude, and 40 percent amplitude.

CHAPTER 8

LIGHTNESS (EXPOSURE)

Recommendations for exposure are *highly* subjective, but one generalization is probably safe to make: In every shot, the overall contrast and exposure should be optimized to keep the most important subject in the picture *clearly visible*.

If you think of exposure adjustments in the same terms as mixing sound, you want to set the levels of each element in the mix so that the most important subject, such as the vocals, is the clearest. In color correction, the skin tones of subjects in the frame are your vocals. If they're too similar in color and exposure to other elements in the background or foreground, your actors won't stand out (assuming you want them to). People in the shot need not be brighter or darker than everything else; they should simply be distinct.

The photographer Ansel Adams articulated this with his zone system, which is discussed in his book *The Negative* (published in the 1950s by Bulfinch Press and revised many times since; highly recommended reading). Dividing the tonal range of an image into ten zones (with zone 0 reserved for absolute black), Adams advocated exposing images so as to distribute detail throughout the available tonal range to maximize contrast. (The idea is similar to the contrast expansion discussed in Chapter 5.)

On this scale, Adams puts the shadows for Caucasian skin lit by sunlight into Zone 4, midtones for dark complexioned skin into Zone 5, average Caucasian skin into Zone 6, light Caucasian skin into Zone 7, and highlights on Caucasian skin into Zone 8 (**Figure 8.21**).

Figure 8.21 Skin-tone zones as defined by Ansel Adams in *The Negative.*

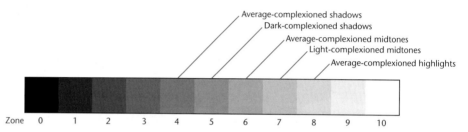

Adams' guidelines are suitable for programs such as documentaries where visibility of the subjects is of paramount importance. However, these guidelines may be a bit conservative if you're working on dramatic material shot by an ambitious cinematographer.

If you're considering an ideal set of overlapping luma ranges for the highlights, midtones, and shadows of a subject's skin tone, the following may be used as a starting point for idealized images of average exposure, with the higher portion of each range reserved for lighter complexions:

• Highlights from 60 to 90 percent, unless you're going for a deliberately blown-out look (typically used for rim or back-lighting). For beauty shots it's good to avoid hard clipping on the skin except for the occasional specular highlight—common on the nose, cheeks, and forehead if the complexion has shine. More naturalistic documentary treatments often tread softly with skin contrast ratios, keeping highlights low. On the other hand, dramatic photography often uses very high contrast ratios, with harder white highlights rimming the face.

• Average midtones usually range from 40 percent (dark complexions) to 70 percent (very light complexions). Appropriate midtone exposure depends entirely on the surrounding environment, since the reasonably light midtones of a subject in a brightly exposed scene would appear to be highlights in a much darker scene.

• Shadows range from 10 to 50 percent; make sure to avoid hard black clipping if it looks unflattering. Again, dramatic photography uses shadow to give form and shape to the face, and many cinematographers don't necessarily shy away from putting a large portion of the face into shadow, but there's generally at least a thin strip of light on the face that provides some midtones.

This admittedly general set of guidelines is illustrated in **Figure 8.22**. The contrast ratio of the entire image ranges from 10 to 85 percent/IRE, which is good given the depth of the shadows, the desire to preserve detail in the woman's face and jacket, and the lack of direct highlights (except for a few specular highlights and reflections) that spike up to 100 percent/IRE. However, it's difficult to make out the exposure of the skin tones alone among all the other detail in the shot.

 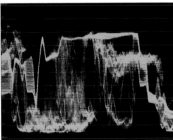

Figure 8.22 In spite of a good contrast range in this image overall, the exposure of the skin tones is tough to assess.

By masking out almost everything except for the highlights and shadows falling on the woman's face and the back of the man's head, you can get a good look at the contrast ratio of the skin tone itself, which falls from 12 to 80 percent/IRE. The contrast ratio is dramatic and nicely spread out relative to the tonality of the rest of the image. As predicted, both individuals fall squarely within the midtones (**Figure 8.23**).

 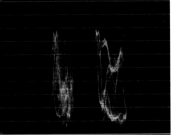

Figure 8.23 The same image as Figure 8.22, with skin tones isolated.

In any scene, people with darker complexions absorb more light and will be potentially 10 to 20 percent darker than lighter complexioned people within the same shot. This is normal and doesn't ordinarily require correction.

CHAPTER 8

In the following minimally corrected clip (**Figure 8.24**), the three men in the elevator are lit within a close environment, so they all catch the same lighting scheme to varying degrees.

Figure 8.24 Three different skin tones catch the same lighting scheme.

By masking the men's faces and examining them on the Waveform Monitor, you can see that the man in the middle falls lowest, with average luma levels approximately 10 percent below those of the other two men (**Figure 8.25**).

Figure 8.25 The same faces isolated to assess differing luma levels.

The recommendations within this section are simply guidelines to help get you started. Every program has its own look, requirements, exposures, and subjects, and it's difficult to generalize about every possible case. Furthermore, with experience (and a well-calibrated monitor) you'll find yourself relying more and more on your eyes to make accurate judgments about skin tone. When in doubt, however, know that you always have the scopes to fall back on.

ABOUT IN-PHASE, I-BARS, AND FLESH TONE INDICATORS

When Final Cut Pro 3 was in development many years ago, the color correction tools and video scopes that were added were new to the majority of desktop video editors. The engineering team was working to try to make this unfamiliar paradigm of Lift/Gamma/Gain-style controls and video scopes comprehensible to a new audience, and I was tasked with documenting these tools for folks who'd never been exposed to three-way color correction before. In Final Cut Pro's implementation of the vectorscope, it was a deliberate design decision to include one half of the in-phase axis line all by itself as an indicator of the average hue of skin tone, since the not-so-coincidental dual use of that indicator had been a documented rule of thumb of videoscope use for many years prior.

In an effort to make the purpose of this line more transparent, this indicator was named the "flesh tone line." This name made sense to new users, given that the purpose of this indicator had nothing to do with signal alignment and everything to do with providing a signpost of flesh tone to people new to reading scopes.

Later, when researching the documentation for the Color manual, I settled on the term *I-bar* (I for In-phase, and bar because it's a line), since the Color engineering team implemented all four in-phase and quadrature indicators, and I expected a more experienced audience would appreciate an acknowledgment of the original purpose of this line for standard-definition signal calibration.

I've discussed the history of the I- and Q-axes with many folks over the years, and while it's true that the engineering reasons behind these indicators have nothing strictly to do with flesh tones, my feeling is that the coincidental utility of the in-phase indicator's position has, over time, come to outweigh its original purpose.

TANNING

Tanned skin is a natural means of protection from excessive ultraviolet (UVA and UVB) exposure that, unchecked, can break down cellular DNA. When people tan, melanin at the top of the epidermis is oxidized by UV radiation, which turns it darker. Additionally, more melanin is produced and moved to the top of the epidermis, where it undergoes the same oxidation. The result is a darkening of the skin that serves as a protective barrier to the sun.

As popularly represented in fashion photography and film, tanned skin (excluding pale complexions) generally exhibits increased saturation of 30 percent or greater amplitude on the vectorscope, with below-average exposure (how dark is a matter of taste) and deep (not clipped) shadows.

Hue can range from golden to reddish, as tanning doesn't by itself significantly alter the natural complexion of an individual. This isn't true if tanning oils or other artificial products have been used to "enhance" the tan, but that strays from our focus on naturalistic rendition.

> **NOTE**
> The reddening of skin that appears as the first indication of sunburn is not, in fact, your skin being "cooked." It's the result of the body's reaction to UV radiation poisoning by sending extra blood to the dermis in order to speed healing. This is why sunburned areas go pale to the touch: You're squeezing out this extra blood, which returns as you release pressure.

THE COLOR OF EMOTION

If all this wasn't enough, it turns out that skin tone changes color, too.

Much is said about how color grading affects the emotions of a scene. However, I wanted to take a look at when emotions in a scene affect correction choices you make. This comes up most often for me in documentary productions, where the emotions are genuine and makeup on the interview subjects is generally light, but this topic applies equally to any situation where people—be they interview subjects or committed performers—become emotionally intense during a scene.

It's tempting to try to normalize human skin tones the same way audio mixers normalize dialogue levels, making a particular person's face identical in every shot, no matter what's going on. I think this is a poor approach, since there are lots of things that differentiate human complexion, including ambient illumination, position within the lighting scheme of an environment, deliberate differences in makeup from one scene to another, and so on.

However, a tricky variation is when people get upset. If it's genuine, then typically their faces will become flushed. Consider the two images in **Figure 8.26**.

Figure 8.26 Two photos of a pale-complexioned boy in a calm moment (left) and the same boy crying with blood flushing his skin (right).

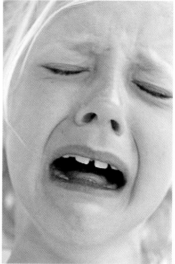

At left, the calm young man exhibits his ordinary pale complexion. At right, the upset young man is quite a bit ruddier, flushed as his face is with blood.

Here's the issue you'll face: As a scene progresses, the emotions in the room build, and people's complexions will shift as faces flush. What you do about it depends on you and your client's philosophical approach to skin tone. Here are some factors to consider, based on the type of scene (or what's happening in the scene) you're grading:

- **Narrative scene with actors**: Leave the color in. You're theoretically paying your actors for powerful performances, and if you color correct the performance away, what's the point? That said, there may be a challenge if, in the course of editing multiple takes together, the flush of an actor's face is more pronounced in some shots and less in others, so it may be necessary to add or remove redness to a person's face shot by shot to make sure their complexion matches the emotional build of the scene.

- **Documentary scene with interviewees**: This can be trickier. If you have talking head shots intercut with b-roll and you cut from an unflushed bit of interview to a landscape shot and then back to a flushed bit of interview from later, you risk an odd disconnect. In this case, I would be tempted to ease off on the flush to avoid too much discontinuity if the goal was a seamless transition. On the other hand, if the whole point of the interview excerpt being used is that the person is hugely upset, leave things be.

- **An already ruddy-complexioned person has turned beet-red**: This is the exception to any rule you might be following. If you have an actor or interview subject who's already got a reddish complexion, chances are they look like a grape once they get upset. In this case, I think you'd be absolutely right to ease off of the extent of their redness a bit, if only to ameliorate audience distraction. However, I'd still leave the actor somewhat flushed.

Obviously, at the end of the day you're going to do what your client asks. In the last documentary I graded where this came up, the client wanted me to even out all of the woman's headshots to ease off of the redness. However, if this comes up in your program, the previous considerations may add value to the conversation.

BUT WAIT, SKIN CAN BE OTHER COLORS TOO

It turns out there are other dynamic changes to people's skin tone that can occur. In the process of learning more about how we perceive skin and emotional cues in real life, we can learn even more about how the vision system works and in the process understand even better why skin tone is one of the most important aspects of any grade.

Mark Changizi, a cognitive scientist who's done a lot of research into the peculiarities of human vision, presents a compelling case in his book *The Vision Revolution* (BenBella Books, 2009) that the sensitivities of the three cones of our eyes to the wavelengths of light are especially tuned in to the varying color of human skin tone because of high or low oxygenation or even simple blood pressure (quantity of blood in the skin). Furthermore, he observes how these sensitivities enable us to detect the changes to another person's mood and health that are indicated by these subtle cues.

First, if you were to graph the spectral reflectance of human skin, you'll notice that no matter what the reflection, the graph has a certain shape, heavily influenced by the blood in the skin. The chart in **Figure 8.27** is adapted from Elli Angelopoulou's "The Reflectance Spectrum of Human Skin" (University of Pennsylvania, 1999) in which the skin reflectance (from the back of the hand) of 23 volunteers from 20 to 40 years of age, male and female, including subjects of various ethnicities, was measured using strictly controlled illumination, deploying an Oriel Multispec 77400 spectrograph to take readings of the spectral reflectance.

Figure 8.27 An excerpt of a study of the spectral reflectance of skin tone from Elli Angelopoulou's paper "The Reflectance Spectrum of Human Skin" (University of Pennsylvania, 1999).

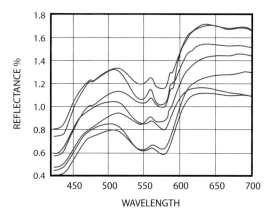

Unsurprisingly, the shape of each graph, which shows the distribution of hues, is more or less the same, even though the height of each graph (indicating lightness) varies. What's interesting is the *W* shape in the middle of each graph, which further measurements easily show corresponds to the oxygenation of hemoglobin in the blood.

If we look at a graph of the sensitivities of our three types of cone cells to the wavelengths of light (**Figure 8.28**), it's easy to see that the sensitivities of the short, medium, and long cones aren't evenly distributed, as one might expect, but that the medium and long cones are suspiciously close together.

Changizi's research found that the average sensitivities of the medium and long cones overlap with this *W*-shaped segment of skin tone color reflectance that coincides with variances in hemoglobin concentration in the blood. In short, our eyes are tuned to see these minute differences in oxygenation, which can be seen by overlaying the spectral sensitivity chart on the skin tone reflectance chart (**Figure 8.29**).

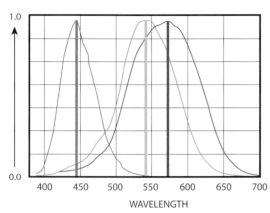

Figure 8.28 Graph showing simplified response curves of human cone cells with vertical lines showing the peak of each curve (source: Wikipedia visualization of data from "Spectral Sensitivities of the Human Cones," Andrew Stockman, Donald I.A. MacLeod, and Nancy E. Johnson, *Journal of the Optical Society of America*, 1993).

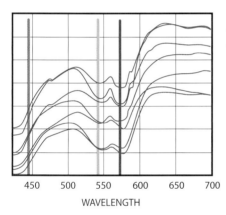

Figure 8.29 If we superimpose the skin tone spectral reflectance data over the maximum cone response spikes, we can see that human cone sensitivity aligns with hemoglobin reflectance.

In the first chapter of *The Vision Revolution*, Changizi makes an excellent case for this alignment resulting in the development of a baseline perception of skin tone, which makes us particularly sensitive to even minute changes because of mood or illness. As Changizi says, "We blush with embarrassment, redden with anger, and blanch or yellow with fear. If you are strangled or choking your face becomes purple… If you exercise your face reddens; if you are feeling faint, your face may yellow or whiten. If you watch a baby clenching to fill his diaper, you will notice that his face can, in an instant, acquire a reddish, purplish tint."

It's clear that all these colors—red, purple, and yellow—have distinct emotional associations. What's interesting is just how well we can see these colors in changes because of blood circulation.

- Quantity of blood provides either a bluer (excess blood) or yellower (low blood pressure) cast to the skin.

- Oxygenation of blood provides either a red to purple cast (high oxygen) or a greenish to blue (anemic)

If you look at these associations on a video-style color wheel (**Figure 8.30**), you can start to see how pushing around the hue of skin tone will alter audience impressions of what's going on with the people in your video.

Figure 8.30 Physiological responses of skin expressed as color with corresponding associations, adapted to the additive video color wheel from Figure 7 of *The Vision Revolution*.

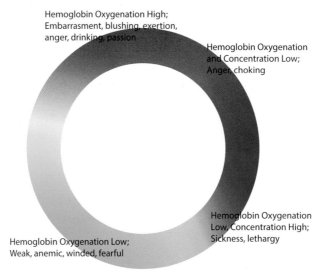

Hemoglobin Oxygenation High; Embarrasment, blushing, exertion, anger, drinking, passion

Hemoglobin Oxygenation and Concentration Low; Anger, choking

Hemoglobin Oxygenation Low, Concentration High; Sickness, lethargy

Hemoglobin Oxygenation Low; Weak, anemic, winded, fearful

The important thing to bear in mind is that, in life, these colors change dynamically according to our situation. With time and care, these types of *subtle* alterations in the hue and saturation of skin tone can become audience cues within the grading of a program, as well.

ARTISTIC LICENSE, FINE-ART PORTRAITURE, AND SKIN TONE

In the first edition of this book, I spent a lot of time researching the natural boundaries of human skin tone, trying to understand what is naturally possible, what audiences expect, and how those two axes intersect in the cinematic image. However, a question lingered at the back of my mind: Are there things the motion-picture and broadcast colorist could learn from the world of fine art, where there are theoretically no limits, and the process of starting with a white canvas means that it's *all* about preference?

Recently, during a Minneapolis "art crawl," I was lucky enough to meet Suzann Beck, a portrait artist who takes an exceptionally structured approach to practicing and teaching the fine art of portraiture. I was impressed both by her work and by the way in which she articulates her process, and she was generous enough to share in conversation how artists look at skin tone. Portrait artists, like colorists, work for commissioning clients, so there's a familiar amount of overlap between the combination of art and craft that's involved with this much more extensive means of manipulating the human image. I discovered a surprising amount of similarity between the portraitist's process and that of the digital colorist.

For this section, Beck was generous enough to share unfinished works-in-progress as well as quick studies to help illustrate the various topics of our conversation.

LIGHTING AND EVALUATION

It should come as no surprise that lighting is just as important to painters as to any cinematographer. Many artists paint in conditions that are as tightly controlled as the suites in which colorists work, choosing outdoor lighting or indoor bulbs very carefully. Interestingly, it's recommended that the light by which painters work should ideally match the lighting of the gallery in which the work will be viewed, a case of matching your working conditions to the audience's viewing conditions, as you read about in Chapter 2.

As has been discussed at length in previous chapters, the quality of light has huge effect on quality of the skin tone under observation. According to Beck, the classic color temperature for lighting is "north light," which is a slightly cooler quality of light that is the result of painters who rely upon natural lighting using windows facing north in order to minimize changes in lighting conditions as they work over the course of the day.

In her studio, Beck uses indirect natural light, supplemented by 5000K bulbs. This is clearly warmer than D65, and I find the correspondence with the 5300K of film projection an interesting coincidence. In terms of creating contrast in the lighting scheme, Beck typically aims for enough of a shadow ratio to create suitable dimensionality of the face. Generally speaking, I found that most of the portraits in her studio had healthy shadows, an indication of her leanings toward a classical, old-masters-informed style of painting (**Figure 8.31**).

Figure 8.31 Contrast in the lighting brings dimensionality to subjects.

Image courtesy Suzann Beck

I was particularly interested in the techniques painters employ for evaluating the image *without* digital tools. Since we colorists get to cheat by having five different graphical data analyses of our images (at least) to help us make our decisions, it was good to be reminded of how to just sit down, *look* at an image, and break it down into its constituent parts by eye.

Beck's primary advice was a heavy focus on learning how to analyze the shadows in an image and how to divide images into shapes of varying values (or luminances). Interestingly, Beck mentioned that most new students initially have a hard time actually "seeing" shadow and perceiving differences in value. Her tips for new students include the following:

- Squint to reduce light in the eyes to see value. This is identical to advice I got in a cinematography class back in film school, about cinematographers squinting or using darkened glass (used by painters as well) to cut light to the cones and trigger the rods of the eye to kick in, helping you evaluate the contrast between light and shadow in a scene.

- Compare elements of the image to a small 18 percent gray patch to see what parts of the image are lighter and darker than this "halfway" point for image luminance. Again, 10 percent gray as a reference should be familiar to anyone in photography or cinematography. In portraiture, as in the filmic process, holding up a white card to the canvas lets you see your color palette more objectively (**Figure 8.32**).

- Bringing things back around to color, when evaluating a skin tone mix on the canvas, comparing your hand to the skin tone of the painting lets you know how close you are to a naturalistic rendition (**Figure 8.33**). Keeping in mind that the hues of all complexions are similar, this is a fair test for many situations.

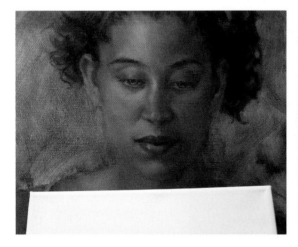

Figure 8.32 The white card helps you see your palette more objectively.
Image courtesy Suzann Beck

Figure 8.33 Comparing your hand to an image to evaluate skin tone.
Image courtesy Suzann Beck

THE IMPORTANCE OF VALUE

What colorists call luminance, painters call *value*, and in truth my conversation with Suzann Beck started with an in-depth discussion of the importance of value as the foundation of the image. Classically trained painters know the importance of value to providing clear recognition, shape, volume, and depth to an image even in the absence of hue, as shown in **Figure 8.34**.

Figure 8.34 Even without any color, the subject of the painting is clear, highlighting the importance of value, or luminance, as the bedrock of any image, whether painted or digitally displayed.

Image courtesy Suzann Beck

Beck raised the fascinating topic of different schools of painting treating value differently. For example, impressionist painters often use *color contrast* to differentiate light and shadow more than they do value, and the result is a more luminous image, despite its equiluminance.

On the other hand, "old masters" such as Rembrandt used value heavily to achieve a strong differentiation between pools of light and shadow. These two approaches to representing image tonality are analogous to high-contrast and low-contrast approaches to grading, where you can elect to let the luma or the hue and saturation of the image carry the burden of representing contrast.

Figure 8.35 Planes of value used to construct a three-dimensional appearance, first laid down very roughly in the underpainting.

Image courtesy Suzann Beck

Of particular note to me is how you treat transitions between different areas of tonality. Since value is the bedrock of the image, whether you want extremely soft transitions, greater ambient lighting, and softer shadows (a cinematic high-key or up-key approach) or hard transitions, starker lighting, and darker shadows (a cinematic low-key approach), it is critical to be able to create *smooth* transitions from one tonal zone to the next, which is something I've found myself focusing on in my own grading work. Harsh digital transitions from one region of tonality to the next come across as the kind of contouring artifacts you get from pushing a curve adjustment too hard, and they are generally unpleasant. It turns out that smooth contrast transitions are a preoccupation of the portrait artist as well. No matter how you treat the contrast of your image, viewers will subconsciously judge you on the quality of these transitions, so it's worth learning to see and manipulate them through deft handling of all the contrast controls at your disposal.

Another interesting aspect of how painters view value comes from the fact that the image is being constructed totally, from a blank canvas, so there's an explicit awareness of how the dimensionality of the face is built from "planes" of value. Chapter 6 discussed the notion of using graduated shapes or vignettes to lend a sense of depth to images, but painters build a three-dimensional appearance from scratch using these same principles, first in the underpainting, as shown in **Figure 8.35**.

Conducting a visual analysis of any image based on different planes of tonality is another great model for segmenting an image into individually adjustable regions. Furthermore, this is a good explanation for why some close-ups of interview subjects or actors appear flat and unappealing; without contrasting planes of value to provide depth, you end up missing the visual cues that give an image solidity. Teasing out this kind of contrast will help, but only if you know where to look for it.

Of course, portrait painting is concerned with manipulating reality even while representing it recognizably, a task shared with the colorist. Beck described the process of manipulating value to be favorable to the subject as that of emphasizing one highlight over another, referring to painting the "skin in the light," with careful highlights rendered for the forehead, the nose, the cheeks, and the top of the lips to give shape to the face and to direct the viewer's gaze (shown clearly in **Figure 8.36**). The goal is to emphasize the face while creatively reducing value levels elsewhere, all the while keeping the lighting scheme plausible by minding the direction of the illumination of the scene. A good parallel for the colorist to consider is the process of digital relighting, using windows in your grading application to reshape the light of the scene in various ways. Of course, you can do whatever you like with the lighting in your graded scene, but your adjustments will look more seamless if you respect the direction and quality of the lighting that was actually used to illuminate the scene, to make your adjustments to plausibly fit within that framework.

Figure 8.36 Note the way the highlights are rendered to emphasize the lips and face while keeping the lighting scheme plausible.

Image courtesy Suzann Beck

A small but important decision is the assignment of the brightest portions of the picture, a notion discussed previously as "peak highlights" or "sparkly bits," that Beck describes as "exceptional highlights." Pointing out that the highlights of the face are *not* at the top of the value scale, she says that small specular highlights provide a visual exclamation point within the image, giving it gloss and punch and serving as another tool to direct viewer focus even more specifically.

In portraiture, these exceptional highlights are the lightest points of paint on the nose, lips, and eyeballs that represent specular highlights. Even though these are technically "blown-out" bits of the image, portrait artists embrace them, since a few exceptional highlights lend clear sparkle to the image. However, as appealing as these highlights are, Beck recommends that her students add no more than three and encourages them to be careful about placing them only where they want the viewer to be looking. Even though the ears are frequently reflective enough to merit exceptional highlights of their own, you want to keep the viewers focused on the subject's face. Furthermore, too many exceptional highlights will diminish the impact of the ones you really care about.

COMBINING VALUE AND HUE

When it comes to adding color to the equation, it turns out that, in painting as in life, skin tone is not a color; it is a collection of layered pigments. Beck shared with me the challenge faced by all who represent life in a visual medium, which is the task of representing all the colors of the world with a limited palette.

With a strategy of overlapping coats of paint in mind, she begins by "painting in the middle," creating a base coat of midtones, and then building up lighter and darker planes on top of that. When it comes to mixing color for the highlight and shadow skin tones, Beck emphasizes the importance of using a hue for skin in the light that's subtly different from the hue you use for shadow skin tone, to create a vibrant visual differentiation. Along the same lines, she simplifies the range of tones, being careful not to put the "highlights hue" into the shadow zone, to maintain this clear distinction between light and shadow, as shown in **Figure 8.37**.

Figure 8.37 Note the clear distinction between light and shadow.

Image courtesy Suzann Beck

Here's a concept that really stood out for me. Beck mentioned that while there are many different ways to mix the paint used for face shadow, a simple desaturation achieved by mixing black into the hue used for skin in the light is often not flattering. Instead, mixing in a *complementary* color to create the shadow hue lets you build a differentiation between light and shadow that creates vibrance. At the same time, it's important to the portraitist to keep color in the shadow plane of skin tone.

Figure 8.38 shows two quick studies meant to illustrate this. On the left, the paints for the shadows of the face are created by mixing black with the hue used for skin in the light, basically darkening and desaturating them. On the right, the shadows are mixed by adding a complementary color instead, pulling the hue in another direction, rather than simply desaturating the color. The effect is hard to reproduce in print, but in person the difference was like night and day in terms of visual impact.

Figure 8.38 Two portraits illustrating the importance of keeping color in the shadow plane of skin tone.

Image courtesy Suzann Beck

This notion of handling the saturation of skin tone shadows with delicacy dovetails with my experience working on projects requiring vibrant color and popping skin-tone rendition. While I advocate selective saturation increases and reductions, keeping shadow saturation from getting too high and at times reducing it in order to make sure that shadow regions of the image don't start to look artificial, I have noticed over the years that desaturating the shadows of skin tone is a different story. A little is okay, and sometimes necessary, but past a certain point, desaturating the shadows of skin tone can make a complexion look gray and ashen, so you have to keep a sharp eye on this kind of adjustment. This also applies to the use of luma-only contrast expansion, which by reducing saturation as a secondary effect can inadvertently add the same dulling quality. Of course, if you need someone looking ashen, this bit of information will definitely help get you there.

To create more depth and color interaction when working with the mixes of pigment employed, techniques such as floating a layer of cool-hued oil paint over an undercoat of red to create an "optical cooling" of the shadows are used. Because oil paints are translucent themselves, this is a filtration of light that lets you actually perceive the color interactions at work.

In terms of which colors are used to build up skin tone, the fact of most complexions have a similar hue means that painters tend to rely on their own particular set of colors, ones they're familiar mixing with. For different complexions, simply mixing different proportions of their preferred skin palette is sufficient, with the exception of occasionally mixing in a particular "go-to" color in exceptional circumstances.

Beck uses a *prismatic palette* to organize her color selections, similar to that used by Frank Vincent DuMond (1865–1951), a painter and influential teacher who developed a method of laying out paints based on the light-splitting of the prism. Rows of reds, grays, blues, and greens in this palette are organized by value, lightest to darkest, with the color mix of each value based on the interactions of color in the atmosphere dictating how much yellow is mixed in. This is essentially setting up depth cues in the palette itself, with greens, blues, and reds that are close to the viewer having more yellow mixed in with them and with colors that are farther away having less yellow due, ostensibly, to the filtering of airlight. Pulling from this palette, Beck begins with mixes of cobalt blue, cadmium orange, cadmium red, yellow ochre, and titanium white to achieve pleasing skin tones (**Figure 8.39**).

Figure 8.39 Beck's use of a prismatic palette with skin tones used mixed for application.

Image courtesy Suzann Beck

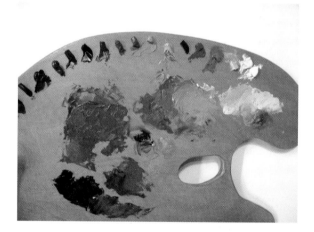

Aside from mixing pleasing colors that are recognizably human *and* flatter the subject, a secondary objective in portraiture, as with digital grading, is to differentiate the subject from the background. For this, some form of color contrast is often useful to play the skin tone off of the background, as shown in Figure 8.36 where Beck used contrast of hue and saturation, in addition to careful darkening, to separate the subject from the background.

When considering specific mixes of hue on the face, another interesting technique Beck brought up was that of the "traffic light"—using subtly differentiated regions of yellowish, reddish, and greenish hues to define regions on faces, which is a classical technique favored by generations of painters. The idea is that the middle third (vertically) of the face—the cheeks and nose—possess the most natural reddish blush, due both to the vascular blood in that part of the face and the amount of sun that stimulates color. In the top third of the face, there's not as much blood going through the skin of the forehead, which is also typically shielded from the sun by hair and hats, creating a yellowish tone. The bottom third of the face sees greenish hues on the chin (often corresponding to a man's 5 o'clock shadow), which are also a clever illusion, since green/blue/desaturated hues are known to provide the impression of a surface moving away from you. Especially when contrasted with red, a *slight* greenish tone on the bottom of the face lends a greater sense of dimension. All of these subtle interplays can be seen in **Figure 8.40**.

Figure 8.40 The "traffic-light" approach to skin hue of a yellowish forehead, reddish blushing cheeks and nose, and slight greenish chin can be seen in this painting.

Image courtesy Suzann Beck

Painters, like colorists, need to work quickly, in their case to rough in enough of an image to create the conditions where simultaneous contrast will kick in to reveal how the different hues work together. When putting colors together in a painting, you won't really *see* what they'll look like until you've put them next to one another. Consequently, painters block in a basic color scheme defining the various planes of the face to evaluate how their planned color scheme is working, afterward working more finely over the top of this base coat and making changes based on the actual color interactions on the canvas. It would seem that working in color is an iterative process no matter what the medium.

In painting as in cinematography, the illuminant is a crucial factor in the appearance of the painted scene. For example, in morning light, highlights employ more yellow, and this ambient light is reflected in the color of the face, with perhaps a bit of exaggeration for color preference.

With all this in mind, audience preference affects the portrait artist in the same way as the commercial colorist. Given that centuries' worth of paintings are available for reference, it's easy to see how the representation of skin tone has evolved with the fashions of the day. The powdered wigs and pale skin tones of women in the 17th century have given way to the current preference of tanned complexions and vivid skin tones in some parts of the world, while other cultures continue to favor lighter skin tones.

Nor is this all the fault of the client. Beck shared her impressions of an exhibit of the work of Nicolai Fechin, a Russian portraitist who worked from 1910–1955. Emigrating to New York, Fechin eventually moved to Taos, New Mexico, in 1923. The paintings he executed in Russia were, in Beck's estimation, considerably cooler in terms of color temperature than his later work. Despite the red and orange necessary in the underpainting to give life to the skin, he added an "optical cool" coat to give a pale luster to the skin tones of his portraits from this period. After moving to New Mexico, the skin tones he represented became warmer and more saturated. Whatever the specific reason, it wasn't that the skin tones of his subjects changed radically in the move; it was his response to working in a different region.

RENDERING DETAIL

One last vital characteristic of portraiture came up in my conversation with Beck: the notion of consciously rendering detail in a painting to control focus in the same way a colorist might selectively blur or remove contrast from parts of an image. Both of these digital techniques serve as powerful methods of directing the viewer's eye, and it's easy to find plenty of examples of painters controlling the level of detail in their work to lead the eye toward parts of the image they want you to focus on, while keeping you from getting lost in details elsewhere. As Beck put it, "The eye loves detail; the eye goes to detail," before continuing, "I'm a portrait painter, not a shirt painter."

Part of the process of exercising control over detail requires controlling contrast. You've seen that increasing contrast increases apparent sharpness; a potential problem is that too much of this contrasty sharpness can result in "over-rendered" parts of the image that you may not want. In the unfinished study shown in **Figure 8.41**, there's a clear difference between the detail rendered within the man's face and his hair. Where the face has fine details painted into the eyes, mouth, and beard, the hair is roughed in with considerably less detail, and less localized contrast defines the difference between the darkest and lightest strands of his dreadlocks.

This dovetails with the topic of crushing blacks. While viewing her more finished works, I found that, generally speaking, Beck always rendered *some* detail within the darkest shadows. This approach preserves a bit of picture information in the deep shadows of the face and hair that enhances the sense of dimensionality throughout the image, rather than flattening it out (**Figure 8.42**).

Figure 8.41 Regions of the face that are meant to draw the eye are highly rendered, whereas areas of the image that could potentially have detail that would distract the viewer, like hair, are rendered with much less detail.

Image courtesy Suzann Beck

Figure 8.42 Even the darkest parts of the face have some detail, while less important areas like the shirt have almost none.

STUDY REMBRANDT

One artist that came up repeatedly in our conversation was famed Dutch painter and printmaker Rembrandt Harmenszoon van Rijn. Anyone who has any desire to study the possibilities of exercising control over light and shadow using value should study his work carefully.

While working on the second edition, I had occasion to visit the Rijksmuseum in Amsterdam during a trip to the International Broadcast Convention (IBC), just after Beck and I spoke. Recently made available for public viewing after a lengthy restoration, the iconic "Night Watch" (http://en.wikipedia.org/wiki/The_Night_Watch), painted in 1692 (and actually named "The Company of captain Frans Banning Cocq and lieutenant Willem van Ruytenburch preparing to march out") is viewable in its new permanent home.

This one painting encapsulates everything covered in this section: a powerful use of value to create striking lighting, a careful use of color contrast, and specific control over the level of detail rendered into different subjects within the frame.

However, with the topic of depth effects, color, and rendering on my mind, I noticed something that's probably not apparent at small scale (here's your excuse for a business trip to Amsterdam). The hand of the leader of the company, Frans Banning Cocq (in black with the red sash), provides an astonishing experience of depth, appearing to reach straight out at you, bigger than life. While admiring this bravura effect, I noticed that his face was rendered with considerably less detail. Put bluntly, Rembrandt put the face of *the leader of the organization commissioning the painting* into soft focus, all so his hand would reach out toward the viewer with amazing clarity. It's an amazing and gutsy move to see.

SIMPLE TECHNIQUES FOR MODIFYING COMPLEXION

So, now that we've examined the natural variation that's possible for human complexion, let's take everything we've seen so far and put it together within the framework of making fast, controlled adjustments to the complexions of subjects within a scene.

When we use the vectorscope to judge naturalistically rendered skin tones, we've seen that average complexions within a neutrally balanced scene generally fall somewhere within 20 degrees of the I-bar. With experience, you'll begin learning to spot the clump of vectorscope values corresponding to people in a shot. Once you've spotted that clump, you can use various controls to push the hue and saturation of these values around.

Figure 8.43 provides a roadmap for where complexions typically fall relative to the previously described benchmarks.

Figure 8.43 General guidelines for complexion adjustments.

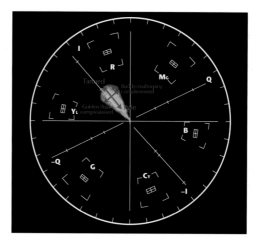

Bear in mind that these are only approximate guidelines; this is an art, not a science. Furthermore, it's unlikely you'll be grading scenes where skin tone is the only element of the scene, and since the vectorscope graph can sometimes make it difficult to pinpoint actors who are surrounded by similarly colored blonde wood furniture, beige walls or carpeting, and orange upholstery, it's important to also rely on your visual sense of the image as it appears on a properly calibrated display.

The following three examples should show that a general familiarity with the interactions of hue and saturation within skin tones gives you much more control over your ability to correct and manipulate them, no matter what techniques you use.

In each of these examples, the general strategy is to begin with corrections that are appropriate to achieving the desired look for the overall scene. Once that's done, additional adjustment to correct skin tone is performed using a variety of techniques.

COMPLEXION ADJUSTMENTS USING PRIMARY CORRECTION

When you're making adjustments to the color balance of an image, you can take advantage of the previously demonstrated quality of skin tones falling within the midtone range of an image. Since the hue variation of complexions in most well-exposed scenes is relatively subtle, you can get away with quite a bit of semi-targeted complexion adjustment using only a single primary correction.

The trick to controlling skin tone grades in primary corrections is to play the highlights against the midtones using your color balance controls. Whether you're correcting for an unwanted color cast or deliberately rebalancing an image to create a specific look, making your main adjustment to the overall image with the Gain color balance control first (assuming that's appropriate) makes it easier to control complexion using the Gamma control.

Of course, whether or not this is really a simple adjustment depends entirely on the tonal range of the image, but it's a good place to start. In the following example, the initial state of the image has already had some contrast adjustment, but the color of the image is fairly neutral, from the shadows through the highlights (**Figure 8.44**).

Pulling the Gain color balance control toward orange warms up the image, but the resulting correction is fairly aggressive, affecting most of the midtones as well and giving the image an obvious tint (Figure 8.44). We can fix this by making the opposite adjustment to the one we made earlier using the Gamma color balance control, pulling the midtones toward a blue/cyan split until her skin loses the excessive orange, but stopping before her highlights lose the color we've added (**Figure 8.45**).

Figure 8.44 Above, an example image with corrected contrast, but uncorrected color. Below, the image has a warming correction applied that has an excessive effect on the woman's skin tone.

Figure 8.45 The color balance corrections made to warm up the highlights and then cool down the midtones to keep the skin tone from being too orange. The small shadow adjustment toward orange corrects for over-compensation because of the midtone adjustment.

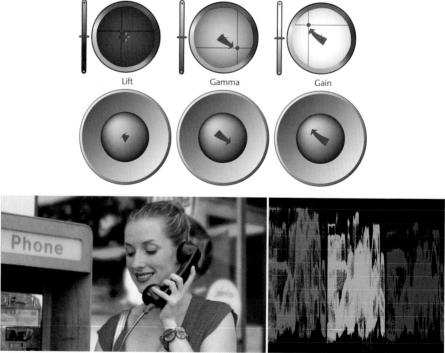

The resulting image (**Figure 8.46**) retains a reasonable amount of the warmth we introduced throughout the image, while dialing the skin tone back to a more acceptable, less orange treatment. The compensating midtone adjustment we made put a bit of blue into the shadows, but a small shadow adjustment toward orange fixed that (shown in Figure 8.46)—all with a single correction.

Before adjustment   After adjustment

Figure 8.46 Before and after excerpts showing the correction made.

It's a good habit to make sure you've exhausted the possibilities of the three color balance controls before you turn to secondary color correction to solve your skin tone problems. You'll work faster.

COMPLEXION ADJUSTMENT VIA CONTRAST

When it comes to making adjustments to alter the smoothness of a person's complexion, sometimes you can get a lot of mileage out of simple contrast alterations. For example, if you want to add just a bit of smoothness to someone with a few freckles or other facial detail, a tiny bit of overexposure can minimize this sort of detail in a pleasing way; just don't overdo it. For example, the following image is nice and neutral, but there's a bit of variation within the woman's complexion that you'd like to cover (**Figure 8.47**). This isn't something that will work for every shot, but when it does, it can be a simple thing to add.

Figure 8.47 The original graded image.

When employing this technique, it's best to limit your adjustment with a window/ shape (**Figure 8.48**) so you don't end up altering the contrast of the entire scene.

Figure 8.48 Using a circular window to limit your adjustment to the highlights of the woman's face.

Using your curves or other targeted contrast controls, you can boost the highlights of the face just enough to minimize the imperfections (**Figure 8.49**) but not so much as to make the image look clipped or unpleasant. If you don't have a luma-only adjustment, you'll need to follow up this correction with a targeted midtones desaturation to get rid of the overabundance of color that results, and you may possibly need to rebalance the color of the highlights of this operation.

Figure 8.49 Raising contrast using curves to boost the highlights of her face to minimize unwanted skin detail, while reducing midtone saturation to compensate for the unwanted saturation increase that results.

The result, if you're careful, can have a pleasing luminosity, but you have to be careful not to raise the highlights of the skin too much (**Figure 8.50**).

Figure 8.50 Be sure to keep skin tone highlights in check when you're boosting the highlights on the face to obscure unwanted detail.

On the opposite end of the scale, luma-only contrast can lend a more rugged look to skin tones when the need arises (**Figure 8.51**). Again, you want to limit this effect to only the regions of skin tone you need to "ruggedize" using a window.

Then, using your luma-only controls to boost contrast, you should easily be able to pull out every mole, freckle, and wrinkle on the subject's face (**Figure 8.52**).

This strategy can be effective in conjunction with a bit of sharpening when you're going for a high-contrast, low saturation sort of look when the narrative calls for a gritty, harsh atmosphere.

Figure 8.51 Isolating a man's skin tone in preparation for giving him a more rugged complexion.

Figure 8.52 Boosting contrast with the luma controls accentuates facial moles, freckles, and wrinkles for a grittier look.

CHAPTER 8

WHEN CONTRAST CRUSHES HAIR

When grading brunettes and people of color, it can often happen that the contrast adjustments that work well for a face as well as the rest of the scene end up making the hair look terrible, crushed, flattened, and chunky (**Figure 8.53**). In these situations, targeted isolations can often help you to make a fix by treating the hair differently from the rest of the scene. In the following example, a high-contrast treatment ends up crushing the man's hair unflatteringly.

To fix this, one effective strategy is to use the HSL qualifier within the problematic adjustment node or layer to key on the hair (**Figure 8.54**), which is typically the darkest, least saturated region of the image relative to skin tones and other colorful elements of the scene. Inverting the key now results in everything being affected by the initial adjustment but the hair and whatever other elements of the scene have a similar range of color.

Figure 8.53 A high-contrast adjustment ends up making the man's hair look bad.

Figure 8.54 Using HSL Qualification to isolate the hair. Usually there's some color to hair, so it's a mistake to use a luma-only qualifier in this case.

At this point, the image looks terrible, since the hair and other overlapping regions are washed out in such a way that you've introduced some faint solarizing of the image (**Figure 8.55**), stemming from regions of the image that are supposed to be darker being boosted above formerly lighter regions of the image.

However, now is the time to tell your client, "I'm not done yet!" Use whatever operation your grading software provides to add another contrast adjustment to the inverse of the key you used to exclude the hair, and use this operation to put some matching contrast back into the hair, just not as much as what was crushing the image before (**Figure 8.56**).

This sort of operation can be tricky, but it's a great way of maintaining a high-contrast look in scenes where the talent would otherwise end up looking awful.

Figure 8.55 Inverting the key now protects the hair from the contrast adjustment, but it's too much and doesn't look right.

Figure 8.56 Adding some contrast back to the hair using the inverted key lets you match the rest of the scene more closely, without crushing the hair this time.

COMPLEXION ADJUSTMENTS USING HUE CURVES

Now, if you wanted to make a different type of adjustment, perhaps a bit more extreme, another approach would be to use your color correction application's Hue vs. Hue and Hue vs. Saturation curves (if you have them) to adjust just the sliver of color that corresponds to the skin tone of the scene.

Hue curves are a great way to quickly and smoothly modify an adjustment you've already made with a primary correction when you just need to make a small alteration. They're especially useful when the skin tone of the subject is well-differentiated from the background.

For example, in Figure 8.46 we warmed up the image and slightly desaturated the initial image with a primary grade, while at the same time we boosted the blues of the robe back up to provide a bit of color contrast. The result is stylized, but the man's face, while acceptably within the range of possible complexions, has lost a bit of the vibrancy that it previously had, and the client doesn't like it.

Using a Hue vs. Hue curve, we can add a control point to define the range of orange through yellow that we want to modify (if necessary—some applications provide preexisting control points on the curves). Then, by adding another control point within the middle of the defined segment and dragging it up, we can shift the hue a bit more toward red (**Figure 8.57**). Remember, with curves, a little adjustment often goes a long way.

Figure 8.57 A hue curve adjustment to shift the range of orange through yellow a bit more toward red.

This adjustment ends up affecting a bit of the wall as well (since it's close to the hue the man's skin was), but that's fine because the adjustment is relative. The end result is that the man's skin tone now stands out from the surroundings a little more, and more importantly, he has a more robust look, which was important for the scene. In addition, the resulting modified complexion still integrates reasonably well with the illuminant and looks natural. Using curves, this wasn't that much more difficult an effect to create.

Hue curves are also great for toning down a mottled complexion. If you have a subject with an excess of facial capillaries that cause a reddish blotchiness on the cheeks and/or nose, you can make a very tight curve adjustment (using two control points that are very near one another) to adjust only the limited range of red that's objectionable in one of two ways.

- You could desaturate the excessive levels of red a little bit using the Hue vs. Saturation curve. This can be a subtle way of muting the problem as long as you don't desaturate too much, which would make the face look ashen.

- You could shift the hue of the redness toward the hue of the rest of the subject's face using the Hue vs. Hue curve, which would maintain the current level of saturation but make the blotchy areas blend in better. Again, a small shift is better than a large one. In this instance, creating a perfect match between the unwanted redness and the rest of the face can create a disturbingly uniform complexion that flattens facial detail and looks odd.

TIP

Some applications, like Film-Light Baselight, let you zoom in on the curves you're adjusting, which makes it easier to make extremely fine adjustments such as the one just described. Other applications, such as DaVinci Resolve, let you click in the image to automatically place control points on a hue curve that correspond to the sampled range of hues.

COMPLEXION ADJUSTMENTS USING HSL QUALIFICATION

If you can't get the look you want with the color balance controls or if the look you're creating is such an extreme grade that you *know* the skin tone will be affected, sometimes throwing on a secondary HSL Qualification is the best solution.

In particular, with tricky lighting setups, such as a mixed lighting scenario where one actor is illuminated by a fixture with a different color temperature than that of the rest of the room, it's sometimes faster to just adjust the skin tone separately. Whatever the reason, when making a complexion adjustment using HSL Qualification, be wary of straying too far from the color temperature of the principal scenic illuminant lest you introduce too much unreality to the shot. Unless, of course, unreality is what you're going for.

A somewhat more rare instance where skin tone is more easily adjusted using a secondary HSL Qualification is when you have two actors with very different complexions in the same shot. In the shot shown in **Figure 8.58**, making an over-all adjustment to benefit the overall environment, as well as the naturally paler woman, had the unpleasant effect of turning the man nearly purple. In this case, we were forced to attempt to pull a secondary key on one actor or the other to create an independent fix.

We were happy with the complexion of the woman; in fact, she was part of the reason for our original grade. Fortunately, the man's complexion is so extreme that it was relatively easy to key, and combining HSL Qualification with a limiting vignette/Power Window lets us isolate the purple highlights of his complexion nicely. If his face moves, motion tracking will help keep the mask centered on his face.

NOTE

This seems to happen most often when a scene combines actors with an olive complexion and a ruddy red complexion.

Figure 8.58 Combining HSL Qualification with a limiting mask/Power Window to isolate the man's face. The final correction got rid of the purple but left some variation in complexion between the two actors.

Once the man's complexion was isolated, it was a simple thing to pull the Gamma color balance control toward a yellow/green split to shift him to a more acceptable hue so that he's no longer at odds with either the woman or the rest of the scene.

In this instance, I made the decision to leave his saturation alone and focus on shifting his complexion away from purple, while leaving him a bit more red than the woman. My goal was not to make both actors look the same—it's natural that they would vary—but I wanted to keep them in the same ballpark so their different complexions wouldn't be distracting to the audience.

TIP

When keying skin tones, keep in mind that reds and oranges are fairly ubiquitous colors. As a result, pulling well-isolated secondary keys on skin tone can be tricky, especially with highly compressed video formats with low color-sampling ratios. It's likely that similarly colored furniture, wall coverings, or paints will necessitate you combining HSL Qualification with a limiting vignette/Power Window to isolate the skin tone you want to adjust.

CHAPTER 8

> ### DON'T GET IN THE HABIT OF OVERDOING SKIN TONE QUALIFICATIONS
>
> This last example is obviously extreme. Assuming well-shot footage and a good makeup artist, it's usually not necessary to perform isolated corrections to skin tone in every clip (unless you have a *lot* of time and/or money in the postproduction budget). Overdoing secondaries is a great way of losing time in your schedule, and if you're not careful, you also run the risk of creating more artificial-looking grades. The trick is to know when a primary correction will be faster and when a specific issue with the footage means you'll be faster moving on to a secondary; learning which is which simply takes time.

HOW MUCH OF A CORRECTION SHOULD I MAKE?

It's always a good idea to be aware of the original skin tones of the actors and subjects that were recorded so that you don't overcorrect them (when in doubt, ask the director or cinematographer). As long as skin tones look healthy and are recognizably human, however, the exact hues and saturation levels that may be considered ideal are fairly subjective. Some clients will want you to make adjustments toward more golden, kissed-by-the-sun skin tones, while others will prefer pinker, paler complexions.

Don't underestimate the effect that makeup has on an actor's complexion. On programs with an adequate budget, the desired skin tone of the actor may already have been decided, and the actor may have already been carefully made up to reflect the desired complexion. In this case, your job will be to preserve and balance the original skin tones in the shoot.

In lower-budgeted programs where less time was spent on makeup and lighting, you'll have considerably more leeway and may find yourself making substantial adjustments to balance groups of actors out and keep everyone looking their best (or worst, if a character is particularly put-upon in a scene).

As always, a client who was involved with the original shoot will be one of your best sources of information regarding what everyone's skin tone should be. If there are inconsistencies in the makeup or if an actor is more or less ruddy or tan from one shot to the next, you'll need to determine which is the preferred look for the program before balancing the individual clips in the scene.

ANECDOTAL AND SURVEYED PREFERENCES

I've heard numerous anecdotes about West Coast producers preferring tanned complexions and East Coast producers preferring paler complexions. Although I suspect this has as much to do with the complexions of the available performers as with specific director/cinematographer/producer preferences, these accounts always piqued my interest in just how different geographic preferences for complexion can be and whether they're significant.

There's an interesting body of academic research combining the subject of reproducing human skin tone in print and digital media with notions of attractiveness. For example, Katherine L. Smith, Piers L. Cornelissen, and Martin J. Tovée's 2007 study, "Color 3D Bodies and Judgments of Human Female Attractiveness," catalogued the reactions of 40 Caucasian Austrian observers, split equally between male and female, to a series of 43 videotaped Caucasian Austrian female volunteers with a range of tanned and untanned complexions.

As far as skin tone was concerned, Smith, Cornelissen, and Tovée found that, contrary to previous cross-cultural studies on the topic, the observers showed a marked preference for the darker-complexioned, tanned volunteers. Citing other research, the authors propose that a preference for tanning "seems to be largely specific to Caucasians in Western Cultures."

This agrees with findings by Benhard Fink, Karl Grammer, and Randy Thornhill in their 2001 paper, "Human (*Homo sapiens*) Facial Attractiveness in Relation to Skin Texture and Color." In this study, 20 female faces were judged for attractiveness by 54 male Caucasian observers (also in Austria, which seems to be a hotbed of attractiveness research). Again, a preference for tanned skin was found. Additionally, there was a clear preference for smooth complexions, which, while not surprising, accounts for the superabundance of "skin-smoothing" techniques in color correction for film, video, and magazines (which I find are sometimes taken to a regrettable extreme).

Lastly, in cases of skin variation by hue, the studies found that the only statistically significant hue that was negatively associated with attractiveness was an excess of blue. Considering that the blue channel of average skin tones is the typically the weakest and blue is quite nearly opposite the established range of hues found among the various complexion types, this makes perfect sense. Nobody wants to look like they've been drowned.

On the other end of the spectrum, various sociological studies have observed a preference for lighter skin in other regions of the world. Li, Min, Belk, Kimura, and Bahl investigate this in their paper "Skin Lightening and Beauty in Four Asian Cultures" (*Advances in Consumer Research*, Volume 35, 2008). By analyzing the messaging and complexion of models used by cosmetics advertisements in magazines within India, Hong Kong, Japan, and Korea, they clearly established that pale complexions appear prominently in the marketing of "cosmetics, skin care products, skin care services, foods and beverages claiming to improve skin quality, and other skin-related products and services." Although their paper describes this preference within the context of both positive and negative cultural associations, if you find yourself working on just such a commercial spot, this is good information to have.

Photographer Lee Varis, in his excellent book *Skin* (Wiley Publishing, 2006), relates some interesting anecdotes concerning unexpected regional preferences for skin tone that he's run into over the years. For example, it's typical in Chinese publications to favor very pale complexions. He also describes missteps where international clients wanted a lighter complexion in their final photographs than the initial color correction that he had based on the actual complexion of the subjects. Furthermore, since the first edition of this book, I've spoken with colorists around the world who've anecdotally confirmed a clear preference among clients in India and Japan for lighter complexions on behalf of the talent.

Now, I am by no means advocating any of this information as a set of rules for grading people in different parts of the world. Furthermore, because of centuries of emigration, the natural variation among members of most urban populations is going to be wide. It would be irresponsible to limit the possibilities of human complexion to regional boxes.

Still, high-end photographers, cinematographers, and colorists are an extremely international group, and it's clear that knowing the trends and visual preferences in your specific postproduction market is crucial. If you're working with an international client (or if you happen to be a visiting colorist in another country), it is to your advantage to get a feel for what unique visual expectations might exist among your audience, as opposed to making assumptions based on programs you've worked on back home.

TECHNIQUES FOR ADJUSTING COMPLEXION USING SECONDARIES

Much of the time, primary correction should be enough to do the job of creating pleasing skin tone while adjusting the environment to be the way you want it. However, there are plenty of times when you need to make targeted adjustments to push complexions into other directions in order to play the role of a "digital makeup artist."

The following techniques show different ways of using secondary color corrections to solve frequently seen problems. As you'll see, most of the techniques overlap heavily, relying on HSL Qualification to create targeted adjustments and vignettes/Power Windows to limit the key to only the subject you're trying to isolate, if necessary. The point is to get you thinking about the ways that secondary corrections can be used to solve these and other issues that you'll encounter.

IMPROVING COMPLEXION BY UNIFYING HUE

In some situations, uneven lighting conditions or lack of suitable makeup results the hues of a given skin tone being somewhat uneven. One simple fix is to use a qualifier to isolate the range of skin tone in need of improvement, desaturate it by about half (or so) to minimize the uneven hues, but not eliminate all color from the image, and then use the Gamma color-balance control to push the skin tone toward the value you want to emphasize (**Figure 8.59**).

Figure 8.59 From left to right: before, isolating the skin, desaturating the skin, rebalancing with a single stronger hue.

The less you desaturate before rebalancing, the more of the original variation of the skin tones you'll preserve, so this technique is extremely flexible. When done successfully, the effect is similar to using a gold-covered bounce card in the field to add a pleasing cast to the skin.

Beware of overdoing it, though. Part of what makes skin tone "alive" is its subtle variations in hue. Unifying the skin tone too much risks creating an artificial look that's similar to when people wear too much makeup. If the natural variation of skin tone is completely eliminated, the result can be fake-looking and listless.

PROTECTING SKIN TONES FROM EXCESSIVE ADJUSTMENTS

This technique is an important one for situations where you're creating extreme grades to the environment in which actors appear. Unless you do this carefully, you'll run into trouble when the people in the frame get sucked into your stylized correction, losing the very skin tone that we typically try so hard to get right.

For instances like these, a common solution is to create the stylized grade by using HSL Qualification to isolate the actor's skin tone. Then you split the operation into two secondary corrections, each using an inverted version of the same mask to grade the subject and background separately, making sure to keep the color of the isolated subject compatible with the new illuminant.

The following clip is a night shot that already has a primary correction: expanding the contrast, dropping the shadows (but retaining detail at 0 percent/IRE), and boosting the midtones subtly to enhance the visibility of the actress. The shot is naturally warm, with good skin tone. However, for various reasons, the client would like the environment to have a cool quality instead (**Figure 8.60**).

Figure 8.60 The initial image with its base primary correction.

With such a dark shot, the best effect will be accomplished by pushing the Gamma color balance control toward a blue/cyan split, since using the Shadows control will result in a huge blue shift in the blacks, which is ordinarily best avoided. Retention of the scene's pure blacks will provide a greater sense of colorfulness than a uniform blue shift throughout the image.

However, using the Gamma control will make the woman blue as well, given the extent of the probable correction to be made (**Figure 8.61**), so we need to do something to protect her from turning into an alien.

Figure 8.61 The blueberry-like complexion that would occur if we applied the client's desired stylistic correction indiscriminately to both the background and the actor.

Adding a second correction, we use HSL Qualification to pull a key off of the woman's skin tone, taking care to adjust the Hue, Saturation, and Luma qualifier controls to refine the mask, isolating as much of the woman's face and arms as possible, while minimizing the areas of the background that are included in the key (**Figure 8.62**). If necessary, we can use blur to minimize chatter in a challenging key. Then, after isolating the skin tones, we'll invert the mask using the appropriate control to limit our next adjustment to the outside of the isolated area.

NOTE

The resulting matte may not look very good from a compositing perspective, but keep in mind that you're keying to protect the midtones of the skin, not to create a blue- or greenscreen effect. There may be a bit of noise at the edges, but as long as any noise or irregularities aren't noticeable during playback, you can probably get away with a fairly ragged matte.

With the isolating matte in place, we'll use the Gamma color balance controls to push the scene toward blue, while simultaneously lowering the saturation so that the cool look we're giving the outside is muted, rather than vivid. To ensure the blacks stay black (I'm not a fan of color casts replacing 0 percent black), we'll also make a small opposite adjustment to the Lift color balance adjustment to balance the bottoms of the waveforms in the RGB Parade Scope.

Figure 8.62 An HSL Qualification will isolate the woman's skin tones by inverting the matte and using the result to grade everything but her skin.

The resulting correction appropriately protects the woman's highlights and mid-tones. However, even though we haven't done anything to change the woman's skin tone, the image now looks a bit ridiculous; reduced background saturation and complementary color contrast exaggerates the perceived colorfulness of the woman's face, making her pop out like orange soda. It's pretty obvious the woman isn't interacting with the new illuminant of the scene, and the result is clearly artificial-looking.

To fix this, we'll need to add a third correction, using an inverted version of the mask from the HSL Qualification we've already made. (For more information on how to invert a matte within your application, see Chapter 5.)

Once we've set up an inverted qualification as an additional correction, it's a simple thing to reduce the saturation of the woman's skin tone to make it fit in better with the color level of the scene. It's also a good idea to use the Gain color balance control to push her highlights a bit toward blue so that it looks like she's catching a bit of the light from her surroundings (**Figure 8.63**).

Figure 8.63 Adding another correction to make the woman's complexion integrate more realistically with the background.

The result is still a bold correction but one that looks plausibly naturalistic. This technique is useful whenever you're making a bold environmental adjustment that you're afraid will make people within the scene look terrible. It's also a way to make an actor pop out at the viewer a bit better in a scene that doesn't have a lot of color contrast where they're blending too much into the background.

DON'T START EMAILING ME ABOUT ORANGE AND TEAL

I've gotten a kick out of a series of articles that made the Internet rounds years ago concerning the merits and demerits of accentuating flesh tones against cooler backgrounds, which has been labeled of "the orange and teal look." One outstanding overview (with images) is Stu Maschwitz's "Save Our Skins," (www.prolost.com); a pointed critique of the entire trend is blogger Todd Miro's more humorous take on the subject, "Teal and Orange—Hollywood, Please Stop the Madness" (www.theabyssgazes.blogspot.com).

Here's the thing; as I hope this book illustrates, modern color-correction technology makes it straightforward to achieve a high degree of color contrast by segmenting images and applying individual corrections to each element within, as seen in the previous example. This has nothing to do with particular color schemes (those are created by the art department), but it has everything to do with how you maintain color separation in the face of aggressive grading or lighting. I'd also like to point out that not every aggressive use of color is the fault of the colorist–cinematographers have been using colored gels to splash color around the set for decades (and I've had a few shows where I needed to tone down excessive colored light in the photography at the client's request).

As discussed in Chapter 4, the hues of naturalistic lighting range from the cool (bluish) to the very warm (tungsten and "golden hour" oranges); there aren't a lot of ordinary scenes where you'll be dealing with either magenta or green hues in the fill lighting.

(continues on next page)

DON'T START EMAILING ME ABOUT ORANGE AND TEAL *(continued)*

Exaggerated color treatments go wrong when the grades distract from the content of the program, calling attention to some particular quality other than the image as a visual and narrative whole (although if you're grading a music video or promo, that may be the point). Digital color treatments are usually distracting in one of two ways.

- **Oversaturated skin tones:** As stated earlier, the saturation of skin tone varies, but ordinary complexions have a relatively subdued upper limit, and the perception of color-fulness will vary with the saturation of the surrounding environment. If the environment is muted or dominated by a complementary color (bluishness), the perceived colorful-ness will be intensified, so a naturalistic treatment would demand less saturation in the skin tone to keep it from seeming exaggerated.

- **Overprotected skin tones:** Skin interacts with the color of the scene's dominant illumi-nant. If the environment is cool but the skin tone doesn't reflect that, the result looks like a greenscreen composite where the foreground layer wasn't color corrected to match the background.

At the end of the day, if it's a paid client session, I present various options and then go with the one they choose. My personal inclination is to try to keep even stylistic grades within the realm of visual plausibility, but if the client wants something really bold, the tools are there to create that. As many others have observed, excessively isolated skin tones will doubtless become a visual hallmark of the turn of the century, but don't blame the hues; it's not their fault.

ANOTHER TECHNIQUE: COPYING SKIN TONE FORWARD

When you're working on a program that calls for aggressive grading, it can be chal-lenging to keep the talent from disappearing inside of the look you're imposing on the scene. When you're building a carefully calibrated stack of operations and you realize that you need to bring a little realistic skin tone back into the image, many grading applications have the facility to steal a portion of the image from a previ-ous layer or node of your current series of operations and insert it later, where it's needed. In the following example, a long series of exploratory tweaks has led to the look shown in **Figure 8.64**.

The skin clearly needs some help, but the client likes the color treatment's effect everywhere else so much that you're hesitant to mess with the four operations that have gotten you here. If your grading application is able, you can sometimes isolate image data from a prior operation using a window or qualifier and then overlay it on top of an operation at the end of the grade. **Figure 8.65** shows this at work as it's done in DaVinci Resolve, where node 6, which isolates the skin tone via a qualifier, is pulling image data from node 1 at the very beginning of the grade and feeding it (via the Layer Mixer) over the top of the state of the grade at node 4.

Figure 8.64 An aggressive grade has had a not-so-appealing effect on the skin tones of the image.

Figure 8.65 Node 6 is used to take image data from node 1, isolate and alter the skin tones, and feed them over the top of the state of the image output by node 4.

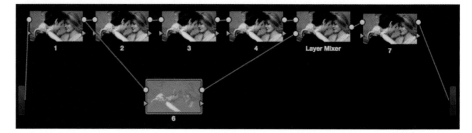

When you first do this, the skin tone will likely not match the scene at all, but a few adjustments to bring the average look of the isolated skin closer to that of the scene can have very pleasing results (**Figure 8.66**).

Figure 8.66 The final result of copying clean skin tone from earlier in the grade, and adapting it to match the look of the aggressive grade created several operations later.

CONTROLLING FIVE O'CLOCK SHADOW

For some men, a hirsute physiology makes it virtually impossible to go a full day without inevitable whisker growth resulting in some darkening in the mustache and beard area (I am reminded of an episode of *The Simpsons* where Homer's clean-shaven skin tone lasts about three seconds before his perennial 5 o'clock shadow literally bursts onto his face). When this happens, the result can be a bluish tint around the lips and jaw that may or may not be desirable.

Makeup artists typically overcome this by mixing a slightly warmer color into the foundation used by that actor, using the resulting color mix to airbrush out the shadow. In situations where this isn't possible, you can try a similar thing using secondary correction.

In the following example, we can see the man has some light whisker growth. The client would like to see what he'd look like a bit more clean-shaven, so we begin the correction.

Obviously, the darker the shadow, the easier it'll be to isolate. Keying a light five o'clock shadow is really, really tough. Despite the supposedly "bluish" cast, you'll actually be using your HSL Qualifier to target the darker portions of skin tone, and you'll inevitably catch other parts of the face in the process. Also, you'll likely want to use your qualifier's blur/smoothing control to feather out the resulting mask (**Figure 8.67**).

Figure 8.67 Isolating, as best as possible, the darker shadows of the face to try to target the whiskers. This is a tough key to pull.

Once you've made a reasonably targeted isolation, you'll use the Gamma color balance control to push this area of the face toward orange/yellow, whatever hue matches the complexion of the rest of the subject's face. After the whisker shadow has been counteracted with the appropriate skin tone adjustment, it might be worth one last Hue vs. Hue or Hue vs. Saturation curve adjustment to the skin tone hues if you need to readjust the overall result.

This technique is not going to be as good as a shave or makeup would have been, but it will help ameliorate a whisker problem in a pinch.

ADDING COLORFULNESS BY ACCENTUATING BLUSH

This next technique works best using Hue vs. Saturation curves (at least, it's fastest using these curves), although you can so something similar using an HSL Qualifier with only the Hue control enabled (to isolate a range of reds).

NOTE

Don't use this on a subject wearing a lot of makeup unless you want her (or him) to look a bit gaudy.

The idea is to punch up a limited portion of the most pure reds in a complexion to improve someone who appears somewhat plain after the primary correction has been accomplished. The result is going to increase saturation for most lipsticks and blush (if the subject is wearing it), and it'll also add color the more flushed parts of the subject's skin tone.

In the following example (**Figure 8.68**), a primary correction has made the woman's skin tone accurate, but since she's a bit pale and her makeup isn't particularly strong, the client indicated a desire for a bit more color.

Using the Hue vs. Saturation curve (shown in Figure 8.68), it's relatively easy to add control points to isolate a narrow portion of reds by "pinning down" the other areas of hue on the curve. Adjusting the falloff within the oranges is tricky: Too much orange and you over saturate the entire face; too little orange and the adjustment is barely visible.

Figure 8.68 Adjusting a hue curve (Hue vs. Saturation) to boost the reds in the actress's face.

You'll know you're on the right track if you can see a thin band of reds start to jut out from the vectorscope graph toward the R target, while the other values nearer the I-bar remain where they are. Visually, you should see the lipstick and blush areas of the woman's face become more vivid, and at that point you're simply adjusting saturation to taste. Most adjustments of this type are going to be pretty subtle (you don't want her to start looking like a clown).

The opposite of this technique can also be used to subdue the flushed skin of interview subjects in documentaries who've been crying or are otherwise upset. Some people turn beet red in these situations, and even though a bit of increased coloration is natural and should be allowed, too much might make viewers think something is wrong with their television.

In these situations, you'll make a similar isolation using either the Hue vs. Saturation curve, or the Hue control of an HSL Qualifier, and then reduce the amount of red, instead of increasing it.

CREATING GLOSSY SKIN HIGHLIGHTS

This next technique illustrates how to use HSL Qualification to add a deliberate glossy highlight to the contours of the body; it works equally well for men and women. This technique is especially useful for subjects in situations where glamour, fashion, or desirability is the goal.

An obvious example would be a swimsuit commercial, but this technique is useful for any scene where you want to accentuate the curve and shape of muscle and anatomy. Finally, this technique is a good "bust-enhancing" maneuver, since cleavage is defined by highlights and shadow.

The original shot in **Figure 8.69** reveals a lot of skin, which is ideal for this particular technique. In the original image, the highlights on the woman's torso are a bit flat, and there's not a lot of pop to her curves. This is easily corrected using HSL Qualification.

Figure 8.69 Adding a bit of gloss to the contours of the figure, subtly accentuating muscle tone and curves.

The general idea behind this technique is to do the following:

1. Pull an HSL key to isolate a fairly narrow portion of the highlights that affect the skin.

2. Adjust the Luma qualifier to further restrict the highlights to the specific parts of the body you want to highlight. The idea is to alter only the outlines of muscle tone.

3 Soften the edge of the mask by increasing the tolerance of the Luma control a bit, and then use the matte blur parameter to really soften it. You want the resulting matte to be diffuse so as not to call attention to itself.

4 Lastly, boost the midtones to add the desired amount of gloss, relative to the original exposure of the shot.

The end result is that the woman has more dimensionality and pop.

REDUCING UNWANTED SHINE

On an opposite tack, human skin, because of its texture and translucency, has a natural matte finish that's not ordinarily reflective. Skin shines when the presence of oils, sweat, or other cosmetics reflects light.

Shine is the result of specular highlights that are whiter and brighter than ordinary facial highlights. Shine occurs when reflected light at the very surface of the skin is bright enough to overpower the natural color of the subject's skin tone. In **Figure 8.70**, the white highlights on the woman's face are a clear example of shine.

Figure 8.70 A soft HSL matte (using the Saturation and Luma controls only) to isolate shine for correction.

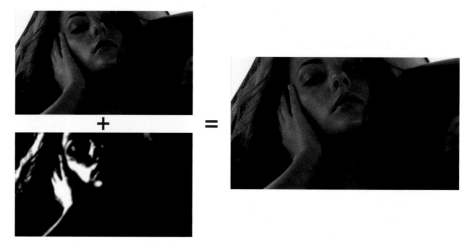

Ordinarily, makeup artists use powder to eliminate shine, but warm conditions, hot stage lighting, or stressful situations can create a challenge, and from time to time, you'll find yourself with a shiny actor. Of course, it's always good to inquire as to whether the subject is *supposed* to be shiny, because it could also be a deliberate makeup effect.

Much of the time, this kind of shine is not desirable. Although it's usually not possible to eliminate it altogether, you can take steps to minimize it. You can use the Luma and Sat controls in an HSL Qualification to sample the offending shine highlight on the subject and then softness or feathering to blur the resulting mask (as shown in Figure 8.70).

Which highlights you choose to isolate have a dramatic effect on the quality of this correction. You want to make sure that the secondary key includes a wide portion of shine, with a gradual falloff, that's centered on the specular highlights.

Once you have a good matte, lower the Gain of this secondary correction to reduce the brightness of the shine but not so far as to visibly discolor that area of her face (if you go too far, it'll look really unnatural). Adding a bit of color can also help to eliminate the shine (in this example, yellow); using the Gamma color balance control might help keep her complexion even.

If you're adjusting an image with particularly hard specular highlights, it's doubtful you'll be able to subdue the shine completely using a single correction. However, you can add another secondary correction after the first one, isolate the remaining specular highlights (making sure that the new HSL Qualifier mask is smaller than the first one), and use the Gain controls to further subdue the highlights.

Always be careful to avoid overdoing such targeted contrast adjustments because the results can be more unflattering than the original problem. This correction usually ends up being very subtle, and it won't always do the trick. Other times it can be highly effective; you may even want to remove the shine using two or even three secondary corrections, with each successive correction darkening a smaller region of slightly brighter shine. By suppressing highlights with multiple passes, you can sometimes avoid an inadvertent flattening of the image. You just have to be careful to soften the secondary keys enough to avoid posterization of the image.

SMOOTHING COMPLEXIONS

This next technique is also aimed at aiding troublesome complexions, and it also uses HSL Qualification, albeit in a different way. Using the same woman's close-up as in the previous example, we'll see how we can isolate an entirely different range of her face, using the resulting mask to selectively apply a light blur to give her a smoother complexion.

First, you want to examine the image to see what parts of the face exhibit the most blemishes. Generally, the most revealing issues will be seen in the highlights and midtones of the face, since shadows conceal quite a bit (**Figure 8.71**).

CHAPTER 8

Figure 8.71 The original shot with one primary correction.

We will again use an HSL Qualifier to create a mask for this skin, with one crucial feature—we want to omit as many fine details from the mask as we can. We're trying to blur the skin, but if we also blur the eyes, lips, and nostrils, we're just going to make a mess, so the mask must carefully target only the skin we're trying to smooth. If necessary, we can also combine the qualifier with a mask/Power Window in order to further limit this effect (**Figure 8.72**).

Figure 8.72 Using a qualifier to limit the Blur tab of DaVinci Resolve's Color page in order to smooth the woman's complexion (you can achieve a lighter effect using the Mist option).

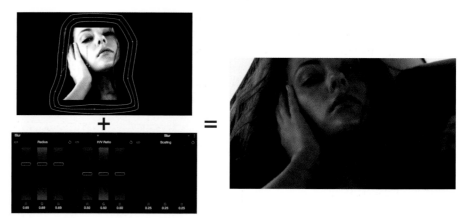

Once you've isolated the skin's highlights, you can use whatever features your grading application makes available to create the blur. For example, DaVinci Resolve has a dedicated Blur tab in the Color page, while Assimilate Scratch has blur options that are available within the texture menu, and FilmLight Baselight uses a Soften plug-in. All of these are blur/softening controls that can be limited using qualifiers and masks/Power Windows (Figure 8.72).

As an editorial aside, I have to observe that I've seen this technique woefully abused. People naturally have pores, and high-end photography has for years sought to pleasingly render the *texture* of faces in addition to color and contrast.

Assuming the subject doesn't have an acne problem or other significant blemishes that the client needs to have covered up, it's a shame to overly eliminate healthy skin texture, unless you're deliberately trying to create a sense of unreality.

REMOVING SPECIFIC BLEMISHES

Here's a technique you can apply in most grading applications to help you to minimize unwanted blemishes on the talent without needing to resort to digital paint. In this example, an eagle-eyed client spotted a freckle that they want you to eliminate (**Figure 8.73**).

The easy fix is to isolate it with a circular window or shape, feathering it well. If the subject moves, you should be able to use the tracker in your grading application to make the window move with them (**Figure 8.74**).

Now, all you need to do is to add a healthy amount of blur using whatever controls you have available. This will soften that tiny part of the image, but it shouldn't be noticeable, and the more blur you add, the more imperceptible the blemish will become as it's blended with the skin around it (**Figure 8.75**). This technique may or may not *eliminate* the blemish, but it will certainly make it less objectionable.

If you have the facility to add grain or noise back to the image, you can add texture back to the soft patch of the image using the same window, slowly adding the noise back in until it blends with the surrounding skin.

NOTE

If your application has other features for softening image texture, such as a "promist" style effect or noise reduction, these can provide other methods for softening skin tone using this same setup. Ideally, you should add the minimum amount of blur necessary to subdue the most egregious blemishes. The result in Figure 8.72 is softened by an appropriately subtle amount; you can see that there's a fair amount of detail kept sharp around the eyes, eyebrows, nostrils, and lips.

CHAPTER 8

Figure 8.73 A freckle in the talent needs to be removed.

Figure 8.74 Isolating the blemish using a circular window/shape.

Figure 8.75 Blending the blemish in with the surrounding skin tone using a blur operation until it's been minimized by a suitable amount.

FAKING VAMPIRISM, SUNBURN, ZOMBIES, AND OTHER EXTREME EFFECTS

And now, here's one last technique I present just for fun. Every once in a blue moon, you'll be called upon to create more extreme effects, such as the barely saturated complexion of a vampire or the bright red of sunburn. With significant alterations of this type, you really don't want the adjustment to affect the background if you can help it.

Although these kinds of effects are often done with practical makeup, the following examples will show how you can accentuate makeup to create an effect that goes even further. The clip in **Figure 8.76** shows the menacing glare of an actor who's already been made up to appear fairly disturbing. However, in this case, the client wanted a bit more oomph to the effect and wanted to see a more desaturated, "necrotic" look to the actor's face.

As with many of the other techniques shown in this section, doing this kind of complete skin tone isolation typically requires you to use HSL Qualification in conjunction with a mask/Power Window for a successful effect that doesn't include any of the background. If the actor moves around, you'll also want to use motion tracking or keyframing/dynamics to make the vignette follow the actor's movements.

Also, it's worth observing that there are holes in the mask that overlap the man's whiskers, facial shadows, and eyes. This is appropriate, since these regions either don't have a lot of saturation anyway or are elements (the eyes) that we don't want to affect.

Figure 8.76 An HSL Qualification limited with a vignette/Power Window.

Now, you already knew that keying the face would be the foundation of creating this effect, but the really interesting thing to discuss is the way we grade the face. Creating an appropriately creepy effect involves two types of adjustments. First, lowering the saturation by 10 percent starts giving him a seriously unhealthy look, but if you go much further, you'll simply start to make him look more and more grayscale.

Second, to really sell a dreadful look, turn to the Gamma and Gain color balance controls, shifting them both toward an appropriate blue/cyan split to not only rebalance the oranges to neutralize them but also add a bit of a cool cast to the skin, remembering the previously cited attractiveness research showing people's aversion to blue in skin tones (**Figure 8.77**). This is one time when we can gleefully do the opposite of what people expect.

Also, since a paler complexion would reflect more light, you'll boost the lightness of the man's face by manipulating the contrast controls, raising the Gamma a bit, raising the Gain a bit less, and lowering the Lift a little in order to lighten the face while keeping the shadows strong.

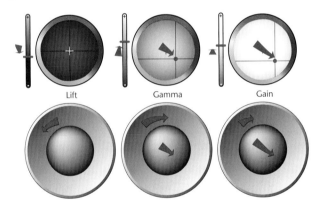

Lift   Gamma   Gain

Figure 8.77 These adjustments cool the man's face and lighten it.

CHAPTER 8

The resulting image is as disturbing as you could want. An alternate thing you could try would be to use a combination of control points on a Hue vs. Saturation curve to lower the orange but leave the red, which is especially effective if you want to preserve blood on the face in a horror movie.

In another example, a closely drawn custom window is motion-tracked to follow the face of a makeup-enhanced actor. By using a luma-only curve to jack up the contrast, bring the Gamma color balance toward a greenish-yellow pallor, reducing overall saturation. Then, by boosting the saturation of the darkest reds, you can give the zombie makeup a much more grotesque, sickly appearance (**Figure 8.78**).

Figure 8.78 A tracked window is used to isolate makeup in order to create a more grotesque appearance.

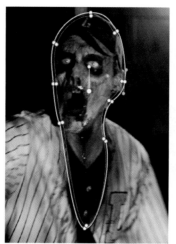 

Grading trickery can be a harried makeup artist's best friend.

IDEALS FOR SKIES

One of the most common corrections to nearly any exterior shot is to make the sky more blue. It's often difficult to capture the sky as we perceive it with either film or video because haze, overexposure, and uncooperative weather all conspire to rob filmmakers of the rich blue skies they desire. In these cases, you can employ a variety of techniques to put the color back in. To do so most realistically, however, it's useful to learn a few things about how color is distributed through the sky.

THE CLEAR BLUE SKY

Earth's atmosphere creates the sky's blue color by scattering a large proportion of the shorter blue wavelengths of light from the sun in all directions. This is referred to as *Rayleigh scattering*, after Lord John Rayleigh, an English physicist who described this phenomenon.

When making sky corrections of different kinds, bear in mind that skies are gradients, which in broad daylight are darkest at the top of the frame, lightening toward the horizon (**Figure 8.79**). This is because air doesn't just scatter the blue wavelengths; the other visible wavelengths of light are also scattered but in lower proportions. The farther light travels through the increasingly thicker atmosphere at the horizon, the more scattering takes place, and eventually enough of all wavelengths are scattered that the sky appears white.

What this means to you as you contemplate different strategies for grading a sky is that on a typical clear blue sky, the hue of the sky remains fairly consistent from the top of the frame to the bottom, but the saturation peaks at the top and gradually diminishes the closer to the horizon the sky gets. The brightness, on the other hand, is lowest at the top and highest at the horizon.

Rayleigh scattering also explains why mountains and other distant features of the landscape get bluer and then whiter the farther away they are, even in the absence of smog (**Figure 8.80**).

Figure 8.79 A clear blue sky as seen from Manhattan's Central Park, with an ideal blue and a clearly distinguishable gradient.

CHAPTER 8

Figure 8.80 Mountains turn bluer the farther they are from the viewer because of blue scattering of light in the atmosphere.

Light is scattered between a viewer and a mountain the same way it's scattered between a viewer and the outer atmosphere. This is referred to as *airlight* (which is a different phenomenon than haze).

THE SKY'S HUE

The average color of a blue sky varies widely in brightness, saturation, and hue, ranging from light cyan to dark blue, because of the following:

- The color of the sky is intensified at higher altitudes; a thinner amount of atmosphere makes for a darker, more saturated shade of blue.

- At lower altitudes, the overall color of the sky tends to be less saturated and considerably lighter.

- The height of the sun in the sky affects its color, depending on your latitude and the time of the year (**Figure 8.81**).

Figure 8.81 Different sky renditions, compared. Hues in each of these strips vary, but all are acceptable within the context of the images from which they originate.

Expressed in the HSB color space, the hue of an average uncorrected sky clip (without accounting for atmospheric effects such as pollution) ranges from about 200 (toward cyan) to 220 (toward primary blue). Examining this range (depicted in the previous image by multiple slices of sky gradients) on a vectorscope yields the wedge of hues shown in **Figure 8.82**.

Figure 8.82 The same range of sky hues and saturation levels shown in Figure 8.81 as depicted in the vectorscope.

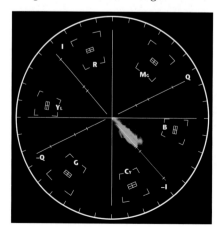

Because the saturation decreases as it nears the horizon, the light that's right at the horizon when the sun is high in the sky is generally white. However, it may be tinted by reflected light from the surface of Earth. In their excellent book *Color and Light in Nature* (Cambridge University Press, 2001), authors David K. Lynch and William Livingston make the following observations:

- Over water, the sky near the horizon is dark.
- Over lush vegetation, the sky near the horizon is slightly green.
- Over the desert, the sky near the horizon is a brownish-yellow.

This, along with other atmospheric effects such as sunrise and sunset lighting, weather conditions, and aerial particulate matter, account for the wide variation in hue that is seen at the horizon.

THE SKY'S SATURATION

The color component with the largest variation from the top to the bottom of any sky gradient is the saturation, which varies from perhaps 50 to 60 percent at the zenith, going down to as much as 0 at a level horizon that's unobstructed by buildings or mountains.

THE SKY'S BRIGHTNESS

Because of the nature of Rayleigh scattering, the variation in the brightness color component of the sky is the inverse of its saturation, with the lowest brightness at the top of the frame and the highest brightness at the horizon. You can see this in a waveform analysis of the sky gradient comparison, shown in the next section in Figure 8.84, which reveals the sky slices ranging as much as 35 percent from the zenith to the horizon, and possible more if the cinematographer was using a polarizing filter (**Figure 8.83**).

If a sky has a rich blue color, remember that its brightness is not going to be at the very top of the luma scale at 100 percent because the white point is normally reserved for desaturated highlights.

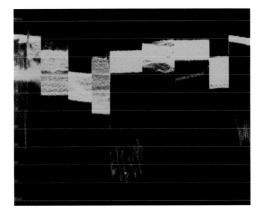

Figure 8.83 A waveform analysis of the sky gradient comparison in Figure 8.84, illustrating the range of possible luma that saturated skies may occupy.

THE ANGLE OF A SKY GRADIENT

The angle of a sky gradient depends on the position of the camera and of the sun. When the sun is high in the sky or when the camera is pointed directly away from the sun, the gradient of the sky is pretty much vertical. (Check in the sky gradient comparison, shown in Figure 8.81.)

However, when the camera is pointed in the direction of the sun, the gradient becomes more and more angled relative to the lower position of the sun, as shown in **Figure 8.84**.

Figure 8.84 The sky gradient varies based on the relative positions of the camera and the sun.

SKY COLOR RELATIVE TO CAMERA POSITION

When the sun is lower than its zenith, the darkest part of the sky is the portion that's farthest away from the position of the sun. In other words, when you turn your back to the sun, you're looking at the darkest and most saturated part of the sky. This can be a source of much consternation, depending on coverage of a scene with shot-reverse-shot sequences, because the sky in one direction looks very different from the sky in the other direction (**Figure 8.85**).

Figure 8.85 A shot–reverse shot sequence during late afternoon, when the sun's position affects the appearance of sky depending on the angle of the camera.

In these situations, your sensibility will dictate the treatment. Leaving the sky levels alone is technically realistic, but if it's too much of a distraction, you may need to adjust the sky in one angle of coverage or the other to create a greater sense of continuity.

OTHER SKY EFFECTS

Obviously, the sky isn't always blue. Given their cinematic value, here are some of the most common sky effects you'll see.

SUNSETS

As the sun gets lower in the sky, the increased atmospheric density between you and the sun filters out the blue and green light, leaving the longer red wavelengths.

When the air is very clear, the sunset sky is generally yellow, as shown in **Figure 8.86**.

Figure 8.86 A yellow sunset in clear air, with colorfully mottled cumulus cloud cover.

Particulate matter such as pollution, dust, and clouds catch and reflect the red wavelengths of light, resulting in the red/orange/peach sunrises and sunsets that photographers love (**Figure 8.87**).

Figure 8.87 A more peach-colored sunset caused by the particulate matter endemic to city life.

This is illuminated most dramatically if there are translucent clouds in the sky, causing striated sunsets, with multiple levels of reds, yellows, and oranges that vary with the density of the cloud cover (**Figure 8.88**).

Figure 8.88 An especially dramatic sunset comprising a range of colors, bouncing off the underneath of a cirrostratus cloud formation.

Brilliant reddish/orange skies over the ocean are because of salt particles, which scatter the longer red wavelengths in greater proportions (**Figure 8.89**).

Figure 8.89 A reddish-orange seascape sunset.

CLOUDS

Clouds appear white because water vapor and dust particles are significantly larger than molecules of air, so light is reflected off of these surfaces rather than scattered. This reflectivity explains the vivid desaturated white that clouds exhibit when they are catching the light (**Figure 8.90**).

Figure 8.90 The desaturated white of light cumulus clouds catching bright noontime light.

Clouds, despite their ethereal appearance, have volume that absorbs, reflects, and scatters light. This accounts for the silver and gray lining that clouds exhibit, which is simply the shadowed half of particularly dense clouds. In all cases, clouds are desaturated, and the shadow areas are generally lighter and darker shades of gray (**Figure 8.91**).

Figure 8.91 Cumulus congestus cloud cover showing areas of light and dark.

The exception is reflected sunrise or sunset lighting from below, which can also add a strong orange/red component (**Figure 8.92**).

Figure 8.92 Sunrise/sunset lighting reflected from below onto an eerie post-thunderstorm cloudscape, known as *cumulonimbus mamma.*

Clouds also filter light, and the ambient color temperature of an overcast day (approximately 8000K) is significantly cooler than the color temperature of average north sky daylight (6500K).

HAZE

Although Rayleigh scattering accounts for blue skies and airlight, *Mie scattering* is another phenomenon in which tiny particles scatter all wavelengths of light equally, resulting in a white glare and the absence of blue. This phenomenon accounts for the haze created by mist, fog, and the white glare that appears around the sun in certain atmospheric conditions. Mie scattering is also caused by aerosols—both natural (water vapor, smoke, dust, and salt) and man-made (pollution).

The effect is a diffusion and lightening of distant features of the landscape, which typically have low contrast and washed-out shadows as a result (**Figure 8.93**).

Figure 8.93 At left, Mie scattering resulting from smog hanging over a familiar skyline. At right, a contrast adjustment to minimize the effects of smog.

You can sometimes minimize haze by using either the primary contrast controls or curves to expand a shot's contrast, lowering the shadows and midtones, while maintaining the highlights where they originally were. You won't eliminate the haze, but you'll enhance the detail of the image, bringing out more color and depth.

PHOTOGRAPHIC MANIPULATION OF SKIES

Shooting skies can be tricky; depending on the overall exposure for the scene, it's easy to overexpose a bright sky. Furthermore, it's difficult to capture the rich blue colors that we perceive with unaided film and video.

In general, strong blues and distinct gradients are usually the goal when shooting exterior daylight scenes, unless specific weather conditions are called for. Two practical tools can help you enhance these aspects of the sky during shooting.

- **Polarizer filters:** Light from the sky is polarized, meaning that light waves traveling through the air are made to vibrate at one angle of orientation or another when scattered by the air. Light at the highest point in the sky is the most polarized. By rotating a polarizer filter, you can limit the light coming in through the lens to one orientation or another of polarization, which intensifies the color by darkening and saturating the sky. You can simulate this effect pretty well with secondary color correction (more on this in the next section). However, polarizing filters also mitigate the diffusing effect of haze and cut down on reflections from water and glass, and these effects are possible only at the time of shooting.

- **Graduated neutral density filters:** These filters have a neutral density (ND) coating on one half, and the other half is left clear, with a soft transition between both halves. By orienting the ND-coated half over the sky, you can lower its exposure to match that of the other subjects in the shot. This can sometimes result in a visible gradient in the sky (which will also cover the subject, depending on the shot composition). This is especially true when the shooter is using other kinds of graduated filters that actually apply color to the sky, adding blue or sunrise colors to an otherwise uninteresting sky. You can simulate this effect using vignettes.

Technical reasons for sky coloration aside, the color of the sky is ultimately a subjective decision. An awareness of natural phenomena provides a palette of choices that won't alienate the viewer, but how you choose to color the sky is subject to the requirements of the program and the look the client wants to achieve. There is plenty of room for variation.

TECHNIQUES FOR ADJUSTING SKIES

The fastest way of adjusting a sky to give it some extra flair is to use your application's hue curves, specifically the Hue vs. Hue and Hue vs. Saturation curves. Unless you're color correcting a Superman movie, chances are the blue of the sky is far

CHAPTER 8

enough away from the other hues in any given shot that this technique will be fast and successful.

1   The image in **Figure 8.94** already has a primary correction to deepen the shadows and to add some atmospheric color to the buildings. Unfortunately, the result is that the sky looks a bit too cyan for our client's tastes.

Figure 8.94 Nice, atmospheric color has been added here, but the client wanted less cyan.

2   To remedy this, we'll add a correction to the grade and use the Hue vs. Hue curve. We'll add three control points (if necessary): the outer two to isolate the range of cyan to blue, and the middle point to make the adjustment, dragging it up or down to shift the blue as seen in the vectorscope a bit closer to the blue target. As always when making curve adjustments, keep in mind that a little goes a long way—a little too much of an adjustment toward blue will result in an unnaturally purple-seeming sky (**Figure 8.95**).

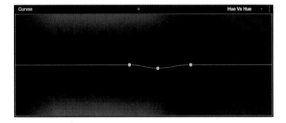

Figure 8.95 Subtle hue adjustments to the too-cyan sky.

We can see the successful result in **Figure 8.96**, with the vectorscope graph's arm extending a bit farther in the direction of blue.

Figure 8.96 The same image with the corrected hue.

However, we're not done yet. Now that the hue is right, we might be able to increase the saturation to make the sky more vivid without making it too distracting.

3   To try this, we similarly add three control points; the outer two to isolate the range of cyan to blue, and the middle point to adjust saturation, dragging it up to increase the saturation of the sky blue (**Figure 8.97**).

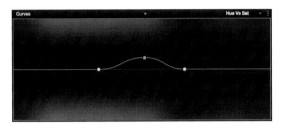

Figure 8.97 Increasing the saturation of the blue sky.

We can see the successful result in **Figure 8.98**, with the vectorscope graph's arm now stretching farther away from the center.

Figure 8.98 The same image with the corrected saturation.

The effect is successful, vivid yet still naturalistic, and the client is pleased. To more clearly see the adjustment's effect, let's see a before/after comparison (**Figure 8.99**).

Figure 8.99 Before (left) and after (right).

CHAPTER 8

When applying multiple consecutive hue curve adjustments in the same layer or node, different applications handle the correspondence between the curve and the hues in the image differently. In some applications, a change to a previous curve affects how you select hues in the next curve. In others, all curves sample the hues as they're input into that operation, such that even if you change a hue from red to orange using Hue vs. Hue, you still need to isolate the original red color using the Hue vs. Sat curve, even though you're now changing the saturation of the now-orange hue.

Be aware that although hue curves allow for very specific adjustments, their main strength—the gradual falloff that allows for smooth adjustments without the sometimes-jagged edges of an HSL-qualified key—is potentially a drawback if your curve adjustment ends up affecting other elements of the scene that are close in hue.

For example, in the previous example, light reflecting off some of the building windows is being included in the curve operation, but this is natural since those windows are most likely reflecting blue from the sky, so a boost relative to the sky is perfectly natural.

SKY ADJUSTMENTS USING HSL QUALIFICATION

If you don't have hue curves or there's some other blue feature that the hue curves can't quite avoid adjusting, the next simplest type of sky correction to make is a secondary correction, basing the key on the color of the sky. This is a fast and easy way to add or alter color in an uncooperative sky shot.

The original image shown in **Figure 8.100** already has a primary correction, increasing contrast and lightening the midtones to give our characters some visibility. The color treatment is fairly neutral, although a secondary correction has been added to boost the greens in the grass and tree line. The shot looks good, but it'd be nice to have more intense blue in the sky to play off the greens.

We'll use the HSL Qualifier to isolate the sky, using the eyedropper/color sampler to identify a range of blues in the sky that we want to enhance (Figure 8.100).

For the purposes of manual readjustment, bear in mind that because the range of luma throughout the sky is right in the midtones, the Luma control can be set to a fairly narrow band of midtone values and still isolate the entire sky.

Figure 8.100 This clip already has had primary and secondary corrections, but it could use additional grading to improve the sky color.

At this point, you have a creative choice. You can elect to apply a color correction to the *entire* sky by expanding the keyed mask to include the clouds, adding blue to the sky and clouds all together. Or, you can choose to carefully exclude the clouds as shown in Figure 8.100.

Before making the actual correction, take a look at the Waveform Monitor (**Figure 8.101**, left). You should notice that the sky consists of a distinct band of values that's solidly within the midtones. As mentioned in the previous section, this is pretty typical for a saturated blue sky. Since the sky is right in the middle of the midtones, drag the Gamma color balance control toward a cyan/blue split to intensify the sky's color. While you make this initial adjustment, drag back and forth from cyan to blue to see the difference a shift in hue makes (**Figure 8.101**, right).

TIP
Excluding the clouds from the correction is technically more correct (clouds are typically desaturated white). On the other hand, if the clouds are a dirty-looking gray, adding a bit of blue to the entire sky, clouds included, may look more attractive. The result will make them seem more diffuse and translucent. It all depends on look you're going for.

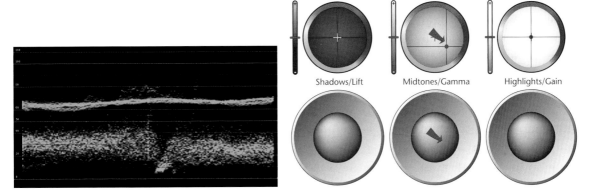

Shadows/Lift   Midtones/Gamma   Highlights/Gain

Figure 8.101 Sky values are grouped in the midtones in the Waveform Monitor at 60–70 percent/IRE. As a result, the corresponding sky adjustment will be most effectively made using the Gamma color balance control or the Hue control.

Skies ordinarily range in saturation from 0 to 50 percent amplitude, depending on the time of day. You could push it even further, but you'll quickly spot when the sky starts becoming unrealistically neon.

After making the color correction, if you're dissatisfied with the tone of the clouds—for example, they start to look like darkly hued storm clouds—relative to your newly juiced-up sky, you can readjust the Luma control to include the clouds in the correction.

This is a great technique to use when the sky already has a nice gradient, or shouldn't have one at all, because a single adjustment affects the entire sky uniformly. It's also useful when there is little color in the sky at all, such as when you're trying to turn an overcast or hazy day into a brilliantly clear blue sky; however, this works best when the light sky highlights are significantly differentiated from the foreground subjects and landscape. It's also the fastest technique when there's camera movement in the shot or people moving in between the sky and the camera.

CHAPTER 8

ENHANCING THE SKY USING VIGNETTES

Another type of sky correction is needed when there's plenty of blue in the sky but you think that it's a little flat. As covered in Chapter 3, gradients add a subtle depth cue that can help direct the eye toward the action, and sky gradients serve the same function.

Often, the cinematographer will add depth to a flat sky or add color to a white sky using graduated filters placed over the lens. This effect is easily created in post using colored vignettes. An added bonus of performing this step in software is that, unlike with optical filters, the color, brightness, softness, and width of vignettes added in post can be completely customized to suit the original color of the sky, the framing of the shot, and the grading needs of the program.

This technique is also useful in instances where intricate image detail prevents you from creating a successful secondary key. If there's not a lot of camera motion, your vignette's presence might go unnoticed; however, too much camera movement might be a little awkward unless you can make the vignette big enough to follow a motion tracked feature within the scene. Alternately, you could compensate for camera movement using keyframes/dynamics, but that can be tricky to do convincingly.

SIMPLE SKY GRADIENTS USING VIGNETTES

This next technique replicates the oft-used cinematographer's trick of using optical gradient filters to selectively add color to the sky. The effect is similar to the strip of blue or gray translucent film that some cars have at the top of their windshield: It's dark at the top and falls off to complete transparency at the bottom.

The goal is to replicate the natural gradients found in the sky and in the process darken an otherwise flat sky, adding dimensionality and color at the same time. Let's see how this is done.

The original image in **Figure 8.102** has a primary grade that is expanding the overall contrast ratio and lightening the tree line and has a secondary correction that is boosting the greens of the foliage to provide a bit of color contrast. The sky is somewhat lackluster, although there's a strip of faint orange because of the late hour that would be nice to preserve.

Since we're happy with the quality of the blue water, we can't just use hue curves to accomplish what we need. Furthermore, using an HSL Qualifier might be more trouble than it's worth because of the jagged tree line and the faint distinction between the blues that we want to enhance and the oranges we want to preserve.

Figure 8.102 In this example we need to punch up the lackluster blue in the sky without affecting the blue in the water.

The solution is to add a secondary correction and create any kind of shape/Power Window shape that you like. In this example, we'll use a rectangle that's been softened enough so that the bottom of the rectangle will serve as a soft gradient that tapers off at the orange part of the sky after we've positioned it appropriately.

You could also use an oval shape to create a rounded gradient or a custom shape that would follow whatever angle you wanted the sky enhancement to follow. In general, you'll get better results from following the natural angle of sky coloration, but if you're careful, you can reshape the angle of the sky if necessary.

Once the vignette is positioned, it's easy to use the Gamma color balance control to shift the top part of the sky to the precise hue and saturation of sky blue you want, readjusting the falloff as necessary so the resulting gradient mixes seamlessly with the existing color at the horizon.

You have a lot of leeway when it comes to enhancing the skies of your programs. Still, reality is often hard to beat. It may sound obvious, but one of the best ways to get new ideas for future corrections is to pay closer attention whenever you're outside. Depending on the time of day, the season of the year, and your location (desert, forest, city, or beach), you're bound to notice significantly different looks, some of which you may be able to use in your color correction sessions. Get a good photo app for your smartphone, or invest in a nice camera if you're the photographic type. You never know when a reference photo might come in handy.

One last thing: Beware of going overboard with your sky adjustments. It's easy to either make the sky too saturated or to swing the hue to be too blue or too cyan, both of which may result in a neon-looking sky—which might be fine if you're working on an episode of a popular crime procedural but problematic if you're working on a nuanced drama. A little correction goes a long way.

TIP

A little blue mixing in with the top of the tree line or someone's hair might be acceptable as long as it's not particularly noticeable. If it is, you should investigate your color correction application's ability to do Boolean combinations of multiple shapes, which would allow you to create another shape with which to "cut out" the part of the image that's being overlapped by the sky gradient vignette.

SUNSET AND MORNING LIGHTING

From time to time, you'll be confronted with scenes supposedly taking place during sunset and sunrise. Depending on the nature of the shoot, you may have to perform a lot of balancing to account for changing light or significant correction to simulate the unique qualities of the desired light, because the footage was shot at other times of day. Why?

Shooting during a sunset or sunrise is always a tricky proposition. Shooting any scene takes a lot of time, and anyone in production will tell you that the light fades fast. If a crew is efficient and things are set up well in advance, it's possible to shoot a variety of coverage, but the quality of light will change significantly from angle to angle as the sun moves along, and the resulting edited footage will inevitably need significant correction.

In other instances, the actual sunset will be used in an establishing shot only, with the rest of the scene shot at another time and with controlled lighting approximating the quality of light falling on the location.

Another reason that sunset and morning lighting are so tricky is that the camera (film or video) does not necessarily see what the eye sees. Sometimes, footage that was genuinely shot at these times in the day still isn't vivid enough, and it needs to be enhanced. An experienced DP can account for this during the shoot, but in other, less controlled circumstances, you'll be called upon as a colorist to make adjustments to fine-tune the unique qualities of light that are found at these times. To do an effective job, you must understand why the light behaves as it does.

THE SUN'S CHANGING QUALITY OF LIGHT

The warmth associated with both sunset and morning lighting is caused by the same phenomenon. As the sun falls lower in the sky, its light passes through progressively denser sections of atmosphere (**Figure 8.103**). The thicker atmosphere absorbs more of the blue and green wavelengths of the sunlight, producing an increasingly warmer light that at the moment of sunset may be around 1600 degrees Kelvin. (For comparison to other light sources, consult the color temperature chart in Chapter 4.)

The warmth of late-afternoon lighting begins with the so-called *golden hour*, which refers to the hour prior to sunset (which also includes the hour *after* sunrise) during which the color temperature of light from the sun changes from approximately 5000K for afternoon lighting to around 3000K at the peak of the golden hour, down to 1600K at the moment of sunset. (All of these values are subject to atmospheric conditions such as cloud cover.)

Because this quality of light is considered flattering to actors and outdoor settings alike, shooting schedules (when budget permits) are often tailored to take advantage of this time of day.

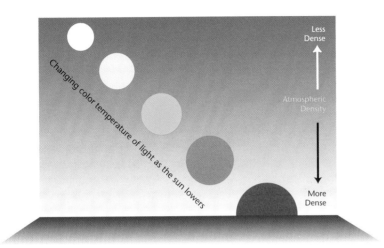

Figure 8.103 The color temperature of sunlight changes as the sun gets lower in the sky.

The warmth of sunset and sunrise lighting can also be intensified by particulate matter in the sky. Smog, smoke from forest fires and volcanoes, and dust carried on seasonal air currents all intensify the reddish/orange light coming from the sun.

Furthermore, the lower the sun falls in the sky, the less light falls on the scene. There are many ways of compensating for this with camera and lighting adjustments, and typically the most noticeable result in recorded footage is higher contrast, as the shadows become progressively deeper. Another byproduct of these reduced light levels may be increased noise or grain, depending on the camera or film stock being used.

So, that explains the overall quality of light falling on the subjects. This, however, is only part of the picture. An examination of a minimally corrected "golden-hour" shot from a narrative feature reveals other qualities that are just as important to creating a convincing sunset look. Study the image in **Figure 8.104**, and examine the quality of color in both the highlights and the shadows. A Parade Scope analysis is included for a more detailed examination.

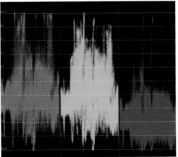

Figure 8.104 A minimally corrected "golden-hour" shot.

CHAPTER 8

A few things should leap out at you. In general, there are three important qualities to both sunset and sunrise lighting.

- An extremely warm color cast in the highlights from the direction of the sun, which is progressively warmer as the sun comes closer to actual sunset. This is the key light in the scene, and the color cast in the highlights can be quite intense, overwhelming the natural colors in the subject. (White-hot highlights will likely remain desaturated, however.)

- Warmer lighting in the midtones. However, the resulting color cast is not nearly as strong as in the highlights. This is the fill lighting that is still scattering in from other parts of the sky.

- Close to normal color in the shadows. Although the blue channel appears depressed, that's natural given all the green and brown in the shot. This is a key observation: The darker areas of the picture still have pure, fully saturated color that stands in stark contrast to the highlights.

In the following picture of late-morning light falling onto a city and park skyline (**Figure 8.105**), observe how neutral the greens in the shadows of the leaves are, as opposed to the more golden color in the highlights. The last of the golden sunlight affects the highlights much more than the shadows.

Figure 8.105 Late-morning sunlight creates warmly colored highlights but mostly neutral shadows.

These three observations provide a good start for analyzing sunset and sunrise scenes and adjusting them using a combination of primary and secondary corrections.

DIFFERENTIATING MORNING FROM EVENING

Although technically morning and evening lighting are identical, there are usually significant emotional differences between scenes meant to take place at the beginning and at the end of the day. For all the talk of degrees Kelvin and atmospheric conditions previously, the bottom line is this: How intense is the spirit of the scene supposed to be?

Although it's always dangerous to make generalizations, here are a couple of things to consider. Your options for close-to-the-horizon light fall from a golden yellow, through orange, to a dark reddish-orange. By the time most characters are awake, fed, and at whatever early-morning appointment has dragged them into the program you're working on, the highlights probably have a more golden/yellow color quality to them because the sun has risen higher in the sky, so I would suggest that golden light indicates morning really well. It doesn't hurt that this color is a brighter, more energetic, and optimistic sort of hue that usually fits well with scenes that take place in the morning.

On the other hand, people are accustomed to blazing red sunsets, so warmer orange/reddish highlights indicate evening quite nicely. And because these warmer hues are more romantic and/or intense, this may also play right into the director and cinematographer's themes for the program.

Ultimately, atmospheric accuracy shouldn't preempt the look that's necessary for the program, but it can be a guide to the different options that are available.

CREATING "EVENING" LIGHTING

With all of these observations in mind, it's time to apply them to correcting a clip. **Figure 8.106** was shot during mid-afternoon. The lighting-to-shadow ratio is appropriate for late in the day, but the sun isn't yet low enough in the sky to acquire the warmth of a true sunset. The director wants this scene to instantly read "sunset" to the audience, so it clearly requires some alteration.

1   Start with a well-exposed but otherwise ungraded clip. You can see it has strong highlights, which will be extremely useful in creating the look we need (**Figure 8.106** on the next page).

Figure 8.106 This ungraded clip has strong highlights.

2   Drop the Lift contrast control to deepen the shadows. This is supposed to be the end of day, and the picture should be slightly darker, but for this image it'd be a mistake to crush the shadows; there's a lot of nice shadow detail that it'd be a shame to lose.

3   Create the warm but muted color tones in the midtones by dragging the Gamma color balance control toward an orange/yellow split until you feel the image is warm, but not glowing. To retain pure blacks, also make an opposite adjustment to the Lift color balance control to even out the very bottoms of the graphs in the RGB Parade Scope.

The goal is not to create the super-warm highlights described in the previous section but to just warm up the overall image a bit to account for the slightly warmer fill.

4   Lastly, in preparation for adding a significant amount of color to the highlights, lower the Gain contrast control by about 10 percent (**Figure 8.107**).

Figure 8.107 Corrections applied to the image in Figure 8.106.

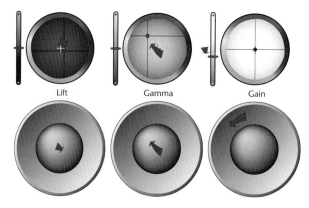

The resulting image is warmer, with deeper shadows, yet it retains detail within the shadows (**Figure 8.108**).

Figure 8.108 The corrected image.

The resulting RGB Parade Scope analysis (**Figure 8.109**) shows a slightly elevated red channel and shadows that are generally well-balanced, if leaning toward a bit of warmth (this is a case where you need to rely on your calibrated display to help determine what the most attractive shadow balance is).

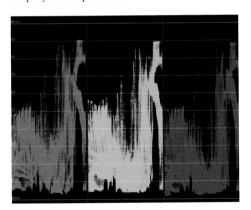

Figure 8.109 The resulting RGB Parade Scope analysis.

Now that you've established the general look for the clip, it's time to really sell the sunset by manipulating the highlights in the image to give it that warm key-lit look.

You could try to warm up the highlights by using the Whites color balance control of the filter you just applied, but because of the extent that the filters overlap, you may end up warming the entire image much more than you want. Using a secondary color correction operation allows you to restrict the correction to a much more specific portion of the image.

5   Add another correction to the shot, using the Luma control of the HSL Qualifier to isolate the brightest highlights within the image: those running along the woman's face, within the bag, and on the wall and background (**Figure 8.110**). By adjusting the range handles (usually the top handles in a qualifier control), you can isolate the brightest highlights and then adjust the tolerance handles (usually the bottom handles) to soften the edge of the resulting keyed mask to fall off smoothly into the shadows. Lastly, increase the soften or blue parameter to feather the key, blurring the edges to prevent buzz or chatter when the clip plays.

Figure 8.110 Isolating the brightest spots in the image using the Luma control of the HSL Qualifier.

6   Once you've successfully isolated the highlights, it's time to add the final touch and push the Gain color balance control toward an orange/yellow split to create the needed golden-hour highlights. While making this adjustment, keep an eye on the top of the graphs in the RGB Parade Scope to make sure you don't clip the red channel too severely (**Figure 8.111**).

Figure 8.111 Keep an eye on the RGB Parade Scope to make sure you don't clip the red channel.

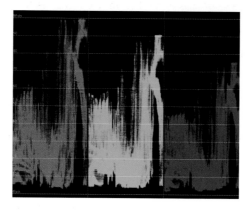

If you want to add more color to the highlights but the red channel is clipping too much, consider opening the primary correction and lowering the highlights a bit more in order to create more headroom for color in the shoulder of the signal.

You're finished when the image has light warmth in the midtones and healthy bright warmth within the highlights, as shown in **Figure 8.112**.

Figure 8.112 The corrected image, with simulated golden-hour lighting.

Keep in mind that the intensity of the color in the highlights is directly proportional to how low the sun is in the sky. If you're unsure about how to adjust the contrast and highlight color in a clip like this, ask the client what time it's supposed to be in the scene or how close it is to sunset.

ENHANCING AND CREATING SUNSET SKIES

The following procedure shows you how to put sunset-like colors into the sky to create sunset cloud color where before there was none. For our example, we'll use an establishing shot of a hypothetical horror movie, showing a small town with requisite church steeples looming in the foreground and distance. It's the perfect excuse for goosing up the image with something a little bold.

The initial shot in **Figure 8.113** on the next page has been color corrected to expand contrast and add some color to the buildings. To add a striated sunset look to the clouds, we'll add a secondary correction to the grade and use the HSL Qualifier eyedropper/color picker to isolate a portion of the lighter, lower-middle clouds in the sky. Using the Blur/Feather control to soften the mask gives us a relatively smooth result, given the noise in the image.

Unfortunately, the resulting key includes too much of the buildings, and no amount of fiddling will give us a mask that includes the clouds and excludes the steeple and other buildings. The solution is to use a custom shape/Power Curve to isolate the sky against the town and steeple.

Figure 8.113 Adding sunset lighting to a cloudy sky using HSL Qualification and shapes/Power Curves.

Fortunately, it's a locked shot, so we don't have to worry about animating or tracking the shape. Still, it's a fairly detailed mask to create, and we'll take advantage of our color correction application's ability to separately adjust the outer feathering of the shape via a separate set of control points to strike a good balance between keeping color off of architectural features where it doesn't belong and avoiding haloing around any of the buildings because of a lack of cloud color at the edge of the limiting shape (**Figure 8.114**).

Figure 8.114 Using a custom shape/Power Curve to omit the buildings from the sky key.

Once we're finished drawing the shape, combining it with the key has the desired effect of limiting the key's influence to the sky and smaller rooftops, as shown in Figure 8.114.

With a good matte, it becomes possible to push the Highlights/Gain color balance control toward a yellow/orange/pink color blend that looks vaguely plausible for the scene and integrates with the sky. As always, when adding bold colors to a scene, watch out for oversaturated colors in the highlights of the RGB Parade Scope that might clip unpleasantly; also keep an eye out for illegal color in the highlights of the image. When in doubt, turn on Saturation in the Waveform Monitor and check to see whether any saturated portions of the graph rise above 100 percent. The final result is a scene with suitably ominous color looming in the background.

Credible sunset and morning looks often involve targeted adjustments to the highlights. These techniques come in handy for many situations where you want to make extreme changes to one luminance zone of an image without affecting the others.

DRAMATIC CLOUD ADJUSTMENTS

Here's a way to pep up the clouds in a dramatic scene. One of my favorite tricks with curves is to make extremely selective stretches to the contrast in the highlights in order to bring out more cloud detail. The effect can add quite a bit of drama to an otherwise dreary gray expanse.

The shot in **Figure 8.115** has a single primary grade, deepening the shadows and cooling off the scene to give a cold, dreary look to the environment. The cloud cover is interesting, but it doesn't stand out as much as it could, so we decide to see whether boosting the cloud contrast would add some punch to the scene.

Figure 8.115 The uncorrected image, which would benefit from boosted cloud contrast for more drama.

To begin creating this look, we'll add a pair of control points to the upper half of the Luma curve (**Figure 8.116**). The first will lock down the darker areas of the image that we don't want to affect, while the second control point to the right will

---

TIP

Remember that performing secondary keying on the Luma component of a video clip is also a good way to get an extremely clean key, even with highly compressed media, because the Y channel of $Y'C_BC_R$ video always has the maximum amount of data.

affect the very top of the highlights that correspond to the highlights of the clouds, making the cloud tops more intensely bright. We need to make sure that, as we raise the cloud highlights, they don't begin to clip and lose valuable surface detail.

Now we add a third control point in between the two we just created, dragging it down to darken the shadows corresponding to the clouds and further exaggerating the cloud contrast to enhance edge detail and achieve maximum atmosphere for the scene. The trick to this correction is not to boost the contrast too much; you don't want the clouds to look artificial.

Figure 8.116 At left, adding control points to the upper half of the Luma curve to boost cloud highlights. At right, adding a third control point to darken cloud shadows.

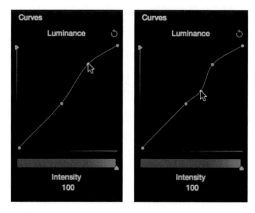

The result is exactly what we wanted, more dramatic-looking clouds, as shown in **Figure 8.117**.

Figure 8.117 The corrected image, with dramatically enhanced cloud cover; abnormally lightened highlights in the grass detract from the correction.

Unfortunately, the current correction also affects the lightest strands of grass in the field, which look odd. We could scale back the correction, or we could use a vignette/Power Curve to limit our correction to the upper half of the image, solving our problem while maintaining the current level of cloud contrast (**Figure 8.118**).

Figure 8.118 Limiting the effect of a Luma curve using a Power Curve in DaVinci Resolve.

This solves the problem brilliantly, and now our dramatic cloud cover effect is seamless and complete (**Figure 8.119**).

Figure 8.119 The corrected image, with the adjustment now properly limited to the clouds.

CHAPTER 8

For a closer look at the effect, **Figure 8.120** shows a before/after of a detail from the enhanced clouds.

Figure 8.120 The cloud cover enhancement, before (left) and after (right).

If you don't have a Luma curve in your particular color correction application, you can try to use an HSL Qualifier to isolate the clouds in the sky and then use the Gain and Gamma contrast controls to stretch the cloud contrast in a similar way.

IDEALS FOR FOLIAGE

Particular attention must be given to the color of foliage, especially when natural exteriors are intercut with exteriors filmed on a stage. There are many hues of green foliage, ranging from yellow-greens to very blue-greens. If the hue of the natural foliage is not faithfully reproduced on the stage, the difference will disturb the audience.
—SMPTE, Elements of Color in Professional Motion Pictures

Foliage is the last of the big-three memory colors that we'll examine, as it's another common feature of film and video images that audiences will be sensitive to. The green that most plants exhibit comes from the pigment of chlorophyll, which is generated within plant cells and is essential to the photosynthesis that provides energy to the plant, not to mention the oxygen that we breathe.

Chlorophyll absorbs violet-blue most strongly, and orange-red light to a lesser extent, reflecting the green hue that we instinctively recognize. For this section I spoke with Dr. Margaret Hurkman, PhD (no coincidence in the name—she's my mother), an ornamental plant breeder at Ball Floraplant, about the varieties of foliage, as well as the preferences in leaf pigmentation that influence which plant lines are chosen for distribution to greenhouses for consumer sales and landscaping, and which are discarded.

Chlorophyll breaks down in the presence of bright sunlight, so it must be regenerated by the plant. Different plants generate different levels of chlorophyll, with the result that the saturation and hue of different flora varieties will vary, albeit subtly in most cases.

Aside from chlorophyll, there are two other pigments that plants incorporate.

- Carotene absorbs blue-green and blue light, reflecting yellow. Carotene is more stable than chlorophyll, so it remains in leaves that are sickly with reduced levels of chlorophyll.

- Anthocyanins dissolved in cell sap absorb blue and green light, reflecting red. Anthocyanins are sensitive to PH levels of the soil in which a plant or tree grows. Acidic soil results in red pigmentation, while base soil results in purple pigmentation.

Despite the presence of these other pigments, the leaves of most healthy foliage (grasses, tree leaves, shrubbery) are a deep, rich green (**Figure 8.121**).

Figure 8.121 Healthy springtime greenery against the pinks of a cherry-blossom tree in full bloom.

Leaf hue also varies with age—younger leaves tend to be yellower but only briefly. Once in full leaf, leaves don't change color (except perhaps if they get dirty in a dusty, rain-free environment) until they die in fall. In **Figure 8.122**, you can easily see that leaves from the same plant vary from the yellow-green of the younger growth to the comparatively blue-green hue of the oldest leaves.

Figure 8.122 You can clearly see the difference between young and old leaf growth, where younger leaves are yellower and older leaves are a deeper green.

Based on commercial goals for popularly selling plants, here are Dr. Hurkman's tips for attractive foliage:

- Darker green leaves are generally better, with a greater appearance of health.

- Yellow adult leaves usually correspond to an appearance of sickness (possibly because of diminished chlorophyll or a viral or fungal infection).

- A minimum of variegation (yellow streaking) is preferred. You can use Hue vs. Hue curves to minimize this kind of variegation, if necessary (although variegated leaves are apparently highly prized in U.K. gardens).

- For flowering plants, high color and luma contrast between the leaf and the color of the flower is preferred, to accentuate the flowers.

- Leaf sheen (shine) is considered an attractive characteristic.

In the section on memory color and preference, studies showed that we remember foliage as being more yellow-green than blue-green; however, we *prefer* more blue-green than yellow-green. This would seem to indicate that we have latitude for acceptable ranges of green but that most people's preferences dovetail with the plant-breeder's selections for leaves that avoid yellowish-green hues. Given a naturalistic treatment, **Figure 8.123** shows an example of a range of green hues corresponding to different types of foliage.

Figure 8.123 A sampled range of foliage from a variety of scenes. The foliage was limited to create the accompanying vectorscope analysis, showing the average range of hue and saturation of typically graded plants.

 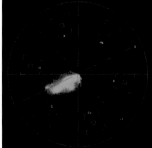

In my own experience working with clients on foliage-heavy scenes, deeper (richer) colors are more convincing than lighter, more vivid colors. Lighter greens tend to go neon pretty quickly unless you reduce their saturation, in which case you begin to lose the color contrast of the foliage. Of course, this is all relative to the type of look you're trying to give the scene, but if you want vivid greenery, darker leaves are generally better than lighter.

Despite the discussed aversion to yellow in foliage, leaves are thin enough to be translucent, and the highlights of foliage interact with golden-hour sunlight to turn yellowish (**Figure 8.124**).

Figure 8.124 Golden-hour and sunset lighting interacts with foliage to add yellow tones to the highlights of the greenery.

In these instances, it's good if within your correction it's not only the leaves that are receiving golden light, so it's clear that the golden color is because of the illuminant and not a viral infection.

ADJUSTING FOLIAGE GREENS

So, let's take a look at different adjustments we can make to quickly make selective adjustments to the natural greenery within a scene.

ADJUSTING FOLIAGE USING HUE CURVES

Hue curves are fantastic for adjusting foliage. In general, foliage has a lot of fine detail, and any small wind puts all of that detail into motion, the result being high-frequency detail that can make keying using HSL Qualification a nightmare—all that motion can appear to be noise or chatter at the fringes of your masks.

However, since the green of flora is usually pretty well separated from the other hues within most scenes (unless you're color correcting Martians), you have a fair bit of latitude to make the kind of smooth changes that hue curves allow, without affecting other elements within the shot.

In **Figure 8.125** on the next page, the primary correction to boost contrast and add more warmth to the initial state of the shot has resulted in green foliage that's a bit forward in how saturated and golden it is. The client finds that it distracts from the three characters in the scene and would like us to tone it down.

Figure 8.125 After the initial primary grade, the foliage is very colorful and might call too much attention to itself. Two simple hue curve adjustments let us subdue the foliage without affecting the actors.

The two hue curve adjustments shown are as follows:

- Using the Hue vs. Hue curve, it's easy to isolate the green portion of the spectrum using a pair of control points and then use a third point to shift the color of the leaves away from yellow and toward blue. This should not be a large adjustment or the leaves will start to look bizarre; yellow-blue is just a few degrees counterclockwise on the vectorscope.

- Another three points to adjust the green portion of the Hue vs. Saturation curve lets us reduce saturation, making the foliage more subdued relative to the people in the foreground.

In the final result, the greens are deeper and less distracting, and the scene retains the warmth of the primary grade without looking yellow (despite the best efforts of the man's polo shirt).

In general, I find that most hue curve adjustments to foliage greens are a very few percentage points clockwise or counterclockwise from where the greens start. More than that and foliage starts to look bizarre really quickly.

ADJUSTING FOLIAGE USING HSL QUALIFICATION

There are other instances when using HSL Qualification might be a better solution to greenery adjustment than hue curves. For one thing, some color correction applications don't have hue curves at all, so you're just out of luck. In other instances, the greens you need to correct are only a subset of the natural range of greens appearing throughout the entire picture.

In this latter case, HSL Qualification might be more selective than a hue curve, or it might be easier (or simply possible) to limit an HSL key using a vignette/Power Window to omit areas of green you don't want to affect.

In any case, remember that foliage is subject to having a lot of noisy detail. If your adjustments are subtle, this might not make a difference, but the following example will cover a couple of different ways you can pull a key, either of which might be more advantageous depending on the image you're working on.

1 In **Figure 8.126**, you want to alter the ivy color but leave the greens alone. This is a good reason to combine HSL Qualification with a vignette/Power Window in order to quickly limit the keyed range of greens. Apply a primary color correction to stretch contrast and lighten the midtones, as well as to rebalance the midtones toward a blue/cyan split to enhance the color of the stone building and lend a cool quality to the image. Add a secondary correction to the sky to push it away from cyan and closer to blue. Amid all of this correction, the ivy clinging to the side of the building appears too yellow, even though the grass and bushes are a fine, deep green.

Figure 8.126 In this image you want to adjust the color of the ivy but leave the other greens alone.

2 Next, it's time to add a correction, using HSL Qualification to key the ivy. Given the amount of color contrast there is between the greens of the image and all the other hues, you have two choices for how to pull a useful key:

   • Using an eyedropper/color sampling tool along with the Hue, Saturation, and Luma controls, you can make a very selective key using all three qualifiers, shown on the right in **Figure 8.127**.

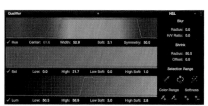

Figure 8.127 Adjusting the ivy colors using all three HSL qualifiers.

- Alternately, you can turn off the saturation and luma qualifiers and just use the hue qualifier by itself to try to capture a greater range of greens more quickly. The result may be a bit noisier, but it can sometimes be easier to create a denser matte this way, if necessary, as shown in **Figure 8.128**.

Figure 8.128 An alternate approach to the same correction using just the hue qualifier.

 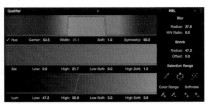

3 With an HSL Qualifier set up, you need to remember that we're dissatisfied only with the greens of the ivy—the rest of the foliage is fine. To protect the grass and bushes from the correction you're about to make, use a custom shape vignette/Power Shape to mask out the grass, setting the shape mask to exclude the encircled shrubbery (**Figure 8.129**).

Figure 8.129 Using a custom shape vignette/Power Shape to mask out the grass.

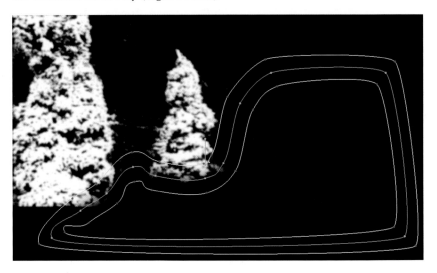

4 Now that the ivy is appropriately isolated, make the appropriate Gamma color balance adjustment to push the color of the ivy away from yellow and more toward a slight green-blue of our choice, with the results shown in **Figure** 8.130.

Figure 8.130 The final correction, with adjusted ivy clinging to the walls.

A more detailed before/after comparison appears in **Figure** 8.131.

Figure 8.131 Details of our final ivy correction, showing before (left) and after (right) renditions of the altered greens.

As you can see, variations in the greens of foliage, though subtle, can do much to enhance or detract from the appeal of a scene. Fortunately, necessary adjustments that have unfortunate consequences for the quality of greens in an image can be easily modified using hue curves or HSL Qualification, whichever tool is available and appropriate for the job at hand. Next, we'll look at another set of foliage issues entirely.

AUTUMN COLORS

In the fall, trees go through a process of abscission in order to shed leaves for the coming winter. A membrane forms between the tree branch and leaf, and chlorophyll production stops. As the chlorophyll fades, the pigmented anthocyanins and carotene show through, which is why leaves change their color just prior to dropping off (**Figure 8.132**).

Figure 8.132 The colors of fall, thanks to abscission, anthocyanins, and carotene.

When it comes to fall colors, here are three common problems that occur:

- The existing fall colors aren't vivid enough onscreen. This is a relatively easy fix using conventional color correction techniques.

- Insert shots or scenes with fall colors have been edited into programs taking place in the summer or spring. This is a difficult correction, but it can be done depending on the amount of color that needs to be subdued and the level of perfection required.

- Insert shots of green leaves have been edited into scenes taking place in the fall. This is the most difficult case of all as it involves inserting vivid color that was never in the image in the first place. This most likely requires a compositing application like Adobe After Effects or The Foundry's Nuke to create a convincing effect.

Fortunately, this is yet another case where secondary color is our friend, although there are limits to what can be practically accomplished.

ENHANCING AUTUMN COLORS

The following example shows one way of selectively drawing color out of a scene in which there is seemingly little color to enhance. Even though the image in **Figure 8.133** was shot at the beginning of fall, it doesn't initially seem as if there's much leaf color to bring out.

It turns out that there's more image data within the media (RED R3D source media) than is apparent to the eye, so we can enhance it using a combination of saturation and the Hue vs. Saturation curve.

If we simply turn up saturation to the point where we can see all of the colors within the scene, including the fall colors in the distant tree line, it brings out the fall colors brilliantly, but now the greens are incredibly oversaturated.

The trick is to use the saturation control to raise saturation to the point where we just begin to see good color in the tree line and then add a second correction, using a Hue vs. Saturation curve to selectively boost the reds and yellows, while lowering the greens to keep them at a subdued level given the shade in the scene.

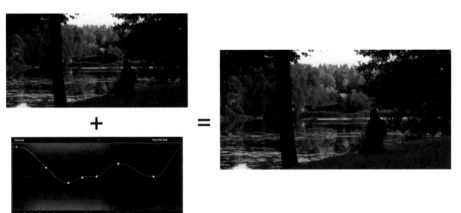

Figure 8.133 An early fall shot with little apparent leaf color. Combining overall raised saturation with selective hue curve desaturation to draw out the fall colors in the tree line.

The result is a nice dash of red and yellow color in the tree line and lake reflection and appropriately subdued greens in the grass.

Combining saturation and Hue vs. Saturation controls works well for drawing targeted combinations of color out of nearly any image with a seemingly subdued range of hues.

Keep in mind that if you're enhancing fall colors that are already vivid, red is one of the hues that's guaranteed to violate broadcast safe if you give it half a chance. Watch the red levels in both the highlights and shadows while you increase saturation to make sure that you're not doing anything you'll regret later.

HIDING AUTUMN COLORS

If you're trying to hide autumn colors in an effort to make an insert shot or scene match an otherwise verdant movie, you need to be realistic about what can be done with simple color correction. You have the tools for pushing color and contrast around, but most color correction applications aren't digital paint environments, and if the client wants a completely seamless effect, they might be better served by turning the shot or scene over to a VFX artist.

However, if they need a quick fix and are fine with a strategy of *subduing*, rather than eliminating the fall colors, then you can probably create a fairly convincing effect, at least to the casual observer.

This example shows the use of HSL Qualification to selectively key the reds, yellows, and purples, using the resulting mask to rebalance the foliage to match the greens found in the rest of the scene. Fairly aggressive keying will be required to isolate as much of the fallen leaves as possible, so this works best on establishing shots without a lot of people in the frame.

If there are people, you'll probably need to protect them from this effect using a custom shape vignette/Power Curve.

Examine **Figure 8.134**. It exhibits all the problems in a fall colors shot that you're trying to hide: vivid reds, yellows, and purples that occupy a wide range of hues, as well as leaves covering the grass and road that you may or may not be able to do anything about.

Figure 8.134 A fall foliage shot with a number of color issues to correct.

1   The first step, as I'm sure you've guessed by now, is to isolate the offending colors by adding a correction and using an HSL Qualifier to key on the brightest of the foliage.

It may be possible to use the Hue vs. Hue curves to shift the leaves toward green, but this is a pretty huge shift, and you'll also want to play with saturation and contrast to make the most convincing correction, so HSL may be your best bet.

You can elect to key all of the leaves with a single qualifier, or you can use multiple corrections to selectively key certain ranges of color: the reds with one, the yellows with another, the purples with a third. For now, since there's nothing else much in the frame to accidentally include, we'll use a single qualifier, since yellow, red, and purple occupy a continuous range of hues (**Figure 8.135**).

TIP
In some instances, you can also try using only the Hue control of the HSL Qualifier, isolating the red and yellow areas of the image, although this will result in a less discriminating key.

Figure 8.135 Keying the leaves with a single qualifier.

CHAPTER 8

2   Once you've created the key, it's time to shift the colors toward green. I like using the Gain and Gamma color balance controls to pull the keyed ranges of hue toward green; this leaves the rebalanced colors a bit offset from one another, relative to their original values. It also preserves a bit of variation, which I think is more realistic than shifting everything within the key to be the same identical hue of green.

3   Another good adjustment is to lower the Gamma contrast control, which deepens the green to match that of the other green trees in the scene (**Figure 8.136** on the next page).

Figure 8.136 Lowering the Gamma control to deepen the green.

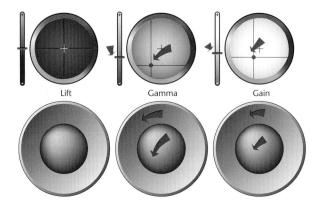

The result of this is green foliage, to be sure, but because the necessary adjustments are so large, the resulting Day-Glo green is way too vivid to be convincing (**Figure 8.137**).

Figure 8.137 The adjusted green is way too vivid.

4 The last step is to reduce the saturation of the adjustment and perhaps push the color balance around a little bit to see whether a yellow-green or blue-green would be preferable for the final color mix.

The vectorscope is a great tool to help you make this determination. **Figure 8.138** shows the vectorscope before correcting saturation (at left) and the vectorscope graph if you completely desaturate the keyed area so that it only analyzes the natural greens of the scene (middle). The trick is to use your color balance and saturation controls to move the keyed portion of the vectorscope graph to match the angle and distance from the center as the original greens shown in the graph.

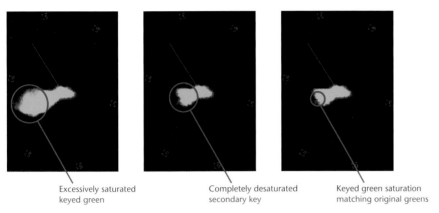

Excessively saturated
keyed green

Completely desaturated
secondary key

Keyed green saturation
matching original greens

Figure 8.138 Three vectorscope analyses: on the left, the oversaturated keyed and corrected greens; in the middle, original greens only; on the right, after saturation adjustment. A good match places the saturation of the adjusted greens at the same vectorscope levels as rest of the greenery.

Your final adjustment (shown in **Figure 8.139**) should appear to be a single cloud of unified green excursions so that your adjusted greens match the original greens in the image, as shown in the vectorscope all the way to the right of Figure 8.139.

Figure 8.139 The finished correction.

CHAPTER 8

The final result is not perfect—some leaves still stand out a bit against the grass, and there's a bit of purple fringing in the leaves against the sky. However, the correction was fast to do. It should be good enough to fool a casual audience, and it's saved our hypothetical client a trip to the compositor's office.

CHAPTER 9

SHOT MATCHING AND SCENE BALANCING

One of the most time-intensive tasks the colorist must perform is the process of matching the color, contrast, and visual quality of all shots within a scene so they look like they're all taking place at the same time, within the same location. Noticeable variations in color or exposure between two shots, such as one shot being a little brighter and another shot being a little dimmer, will accentuate the cut point joining them together, which can make the editing seem choppier than it really is. Also, in the worst cases, such variations appear as continuity errors, and you don't want that.

Careful cinematographers may make shot matching easier for you by balancing the lighting and exposure in each angle of coverage so that the lighting in a reverse angle shot matches, as well as possible, the lighting in the master shot. However, even the most carefully lit scenes can benefit from a bit of tweaking. All it takes is one small cloud to pass in front of the sun during a shoot for the lighting to change. Furthermore, if you're working on a project that was shot in a hurry or you are using available light, you'll have a lot more work to do balancing all the shots within a scene.

Big-budget narrative films and commercial spots can often be the easiest to work on when it comes to shot matching and scene balancing, as they have the time and budget to spend on finessing the lighting and can be carefully planned with deliberately lit angles of coverage that are designed to cut together.

On the opposite end of the spectrum, documentaries and reality television shows can be the most intensive to grade, as their low budgets often necessitate a combination of on-location available-light shooting and an aggressive schedule. One scene will often combine shots from a wide variety of locations and time periods.

COLOR TIMING

NOTE

An even older system of keeping track of color adjustments involved cutting a small notch into the edge of the conformed negative, which could be detected by the film printer. This is the origin of the term *notching,* which refers to breaking programs up into their constituent shots.

While we're on the subject, let's take a step back from the digital color correction methods we've been discussing so far and look at the traditional way that film grading has been done. In a purely photochemical process, this kind of scene-to-scene color correction is the principal activity of the *color timer.* The term *color timing* comes from the chemical film development process, in which the timed duration that film remains in the developer bath affects the exposure of the developed image. However, the process has evolved to use optical equipment.

Color timers are the artist/technicians who work for the film labs and take a conformed negative, color correct it, and make the graded internegative that's used to create all of the release prints that go to the theaters. Incidentally, color timing as a credit specifically relates to this photochemical process—if you're working digitally, you're not a color timer.

Figure 9.1 The Hazeltine 200H film analyzer.

Color timing involves hybrid analog/digital/optical systems, one of the most prominent of which was the Hazeltine, which was introduced in the 1960s (named for the inventor of the circuitry that made it possible, Alan Hazeltine). The actual device used to create the adjustments is called a *color analyzer,* and more recent models, such as the one in **Figure 9.1**, are available from companies such as Film Systems International (FSI). Precursor to the telecine, a color analyzer is essentially a video system that can monitor the film image while making and previewing adjustments to alter the color and exposure.

Figure 9.2 The control panel for the Filmlab Systems International Colormaster color analyzer.

Analyzer controls consist of three rotary dials that control the individual exposure of red, green, and blue. A fourth dial controls *density,* or image contrast. Classically, the adjustments for each shot were stored on 1" paper tapes, which kept a record of the frame count cue (FCC) and color settings for each corresponding adjustment. Later models of analyzers, such as the one shown in **Figure 9.2**, added such modern amenities as automated digital calibration (accomplished using the Kodak LAD chart), keycode readers for keeping track of film stock types, saved presets, floppy drive and hard drive storage of the data, frame-stores, and automatic color analysis.

Each rotary control makes adjustments in discrete increments called *printer points* (also referred to as *printer lights* or *c-lights*). Each point is a fraction of one *f*-stop (a doubling of light in the scale used to measure and adjust exposure). Various systems use different fractions, and each printer point can be anywhere from 1/7 to 1/12 of an *f*-stop, depending on how the analyzer is configured. Most systems use a range of 50 printer points for each color component and for density, with 25 being the neutral détente for each control.

Color adjustments are accomplished by using the paper tape or digital data output from the color timing session to control a *contact printer,* wherein the negative and the media being printed to are sandwiched, emulsion to emulsion, for a 1:1 duplicate of the frame size. The contact printer filters the light that exposes the duplicate through a series of optical filters (the combination of which is determined by the adjustments made with the color analyzer) in order to make a *proof print*, which is processed and projected in order to evaluate the corrections that were made. Typically, changes will be required to refine the color timing, done in additional passes, before printing the *answer print* that represents the final look of the film. As a side note, when creating an answer print, the lab will want you to specify whether you want the white balance of the print to be 3200K or 5400K. 3200K is appropriate for smaller, tungsten-illuminated projectors, while 5400K is necessary for larger venues using Xenon-illuminated projectors.

To preserve and protect the original conformed negative of the film, a duplicate is created by first contact-printing an *interpositive*. This interpositive print is then itself contact-printed, using the color timing data that was used to create the answer print, in order to create one or more *internegatives* that are used for striking the release prints that go to theaters. Since the internegatives have the color timing "baked in," they're easy to print using a wet-dry film printer such as the one shown in **Figure 9.3**. Because they're duplicates, it doesn't matter when they wear out (and they *will* eventually wear out through repeated printing)—new ones can be made, if necessary.

NOTE

There's an excellent overview of the color timing process by Leon Silverman in Chapter 2 of the book *Understanding Digital Cinema* (edited by Charles S. Swartz, Focal Press, 2004).

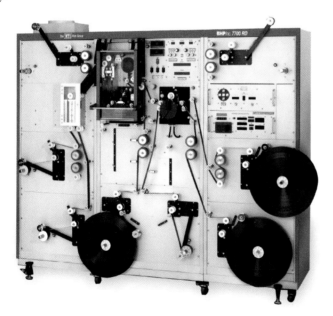

Figure 9.3 A wet/dry film printer used to color-time negative film in order to create a color corrected copy.

It's worth keeping in mind that, in this system, there are no individual controls for color in the highlights, midtones, and shadows. Nor are there secondary color corrections, vignettes/power windows, image processing filters, or curves. These controls all crossed over from analog and digital color correction systems developed for video and have been incorporated into the current generation of color correction applications for digital video, digital intermediate, and digital cinema workflows.

CHAPTER 9

It's sobering to realize that when working on competently shot footage, four controls should be all you really need to balance and grade an entire film. It's worked for talented color timers for decades, and these systems are still in use. It's for this reason that we often recommend that beginning colorists restrict themselves to making primary corrections *only* for a project or two. You'd be surprised what you can do with a single primary correction without resorting to secondaries for every problem you encounter, and it'll make you faster as you get more out of a primary correction before you turn to additional adjustments.

Also, know that there are many veteran cinematographers who prefer the simpler color analyzer/printer points system both for its direct relation to the optical method of exposure that is their bread and butter and for its simplicity and ubiquity. The printer points system was as close to a universal language for cinematographers working with the labs responsible for outputting the final image as seen by the audience as has ever been. It was also a far cry from the amount of variation in toolsets and grading control operation from all the different color correction applications available today. Furthermore, directors of photography (DoPs) who see their task as tightly controlling the image by painting with light and shadow on the set often take a dim view of the notion of colorists piling on secondary color corrections to make dramatic modifications of their own.

For these reasons, most color correction applications have actually implemented a set of printer points controls that you can use. If you're working in a DoP-supervised session and she asks for "two more points of red," it's not a bad idea to know where these controls are and how they work.

DIGITAL PRINTER POINTS AND LOG CONTROLS

As discussed in Chapters 3 and 4, many modern color grading applications provide a set of Log-style controls that seek to emulate, albeit with greater control, the red, green, blue, and density controls of the color analyzer.

- The Offset color balance control corresponds to the individual red, green, and blue controls that lift or drop each color component.
- Exposure (or Master Offset) corresponds to density, lifting, or dropping the entire signal.

For the purist, most color correction applications also have digital equivalents for the printer points interface, consisting of plus and minus buttons (or a single rotary control) for red, blue, and green, and sometimes an additional control for density.

These controls are usually customizable to take into account the fractional variations that define what a "point" corresponds to, owing to different equipment at different labs. If you're serious about using the printer points controls, it's worth checking your documentation for the formula used to customize your particular controls and also consulting with a lab to make sure the adjustments you're making correspond to the equipment they're used to.

STRATEGIES FOR WORKING WITH CLIENTS

Before diving into the nuts and bolts of shot matching and scene balancing, it's important to figure out how you're going to schedule the time you spend working with a client on a project.

If you're working on something short, such as a 30-second spot, music video, or narrative or documentary short subject, the whole project may be only an afternoon or daylong commitment, so you can simply dive in with the client supervising. However, if you're working on something long-form or feature-length, you need to decide, with your clients, just for how much time they need to be involved.

WORK SUPERVISED THE ENTIRE TIME

Personally, I like to have as much client participation during a project as they're willing to give. If I have a question about any shot, it's considerably more efficient if I can simply turn around and ask the DoP or director exactly what they want, instead of making my best guess and then possibly revising it later.

For a feature, if they want to sit there with me for five to ten continuous days, I'm very happy to have them. However, depending on the project, you may work with the director, the cinematographer, or a producer, together or separately. They may not always have the time to supervise the entire process.

WORK SUPERVISED FOR SAMPLE SHOTS ONLY

Another common way to work, if your client is on a tight schedule, is to schedule shorter supervised sessions, during which you'll focus on grading only two or three representative shots from each scene in the program. When I work this way, I try to start with the most representative shot for a given scene (a master shot, or the most prominent angle of coverage).

This way, you can focus the clients' time on working with you to set the tone for each scene (which is generally the most fun part of the process). Once that's done, they can go off to do something more interesting, while you move on, unsupervised, to balancing the rest of each scene to match the representative grades that you created.

THE FIRST DAY GOES SLOWLY

In my experience, the first day of a multiday project is typically the slowest, since this is the day that I spend learning the clients' aesthetic. It's also the day I figure out how to translate the clients' requests into actionable corrections—a not insignificant task since everyone tends to talk about color and image manipulation differently.

NOTE

If you're working on a commercial spot, promo, or corporate program, you may also have agency and company representatives present, making for a crowded and potentially contentious room indeed!

TIP

Colorist Dave Hussey (Company 3) has a great tip for workflows where you grade sample clips: Once you've graded one or two clips from every scene, save these to the still store. Then, sequentially display each still, "playing through" the grades you've set to see if the scenes all flow together. This can give you a game plan for future changes, and it relaxes the client by letting them see how the program is shaping up.

CHAPTER 9

In normal situations, it's wise to schedule your time to make allowances for a slower first day, because it's never a good idea to rush your clients while you're in the initial stages of setting the tone for the overall program. Also, this is the day when you build their trust that you're able to understand what the filmmaker or DoP was intending to do, visually, with the program.

My goal, by the afternoon of the first day, is to be in a position where I can make the first few adjustments to a new shot on my own and have it be pretty much what they wanted without them having to say anything.

DON'T FORGET TO SCHEDULE REVIEW AND REVISIONS

Professional colorists know that color correction is an iterative process. You would never assume that an editor would do a single edit and nail a scene, without revision. Similarly, while the goal of a color correction session should be to work as quickly and efficiently as possible to achieve the right look for every scene, clients will often sleep on a decision and come back the next morning having changed their minds about how aggressive they want to be. Furthermore, that scene that was giving you problems the previous day will usually come together within a minute when you look at it again the next morning.

For this reason, it's always a good idea to build a schedule that takes a certain amount of daily revision into consideration. In fact, colorist Bob Sliga once told me that he likes to do grades in two separate passes: one fast pass to achieve a quick balance and then a second pass for more detailed work.

Furthermore, once the individual scenes (sometimes divided into reels) have been separately graded, it's wise to have a review session where you watch the entire program with the client, noting any problems or changes that present themselves.

Finally, at the end of a session, I like to encourage clients to play their program in as wide a variety of venues as possible, on different televisions, and on digital projectors at various theaters if possible, noting any problems that leap out at them over the course of several different viewings. If a program is playing at film festivals, this can also be a great opportunity for the client to take notes about how the film held up over many different screenings.

The danger, of course, is that the program gets played on a terribly calibrated display and the client writes down lots of problems that don't actually exist. This is why I advise playback at *multiple* locations. Once the client sees that problems at one venue disappear at another venue, they can focus on issues that seem to be common at all venues, and these are the notes I encourage them to bring back for a final revision session later, making the program absolutely perfect prior to final theatrical, broadcast, or sales/rental distribution.

HOW TO BEGIN BALANCING A SCENE

The process of balancing all of the shots in the scene with one another starts with disciplined, strategic thinking. If you're not careful, you can end up chasing your tail as you match one shot to another and then start working on a third shot only to change your mind and end up regrading all three.

You want to begin the process of balancing a scene by watching it all the way through and then picking a single shot that you think is most representative of that scene. Grade this representative shot to define its look (be sure not to dwell on it for too long lest adaptation lure you into making the wrong change), and then use it as your basis for comparison as you match the adjacent shots to it, working your way out through each shot of the scene.

A word about choosing a representative shot: When you look through a scene, remember that master shots are often good because they usually have all the people who appear in that scene and provide you with a good look at the surrounding environment. However, there may be times when a two-shot or strategically framed close-up might be a better starting-off point. It all depends on the angles that are used.

The reason to choose a single representative shot is that this is the image you'll use to define the basic look of the scene, prior to digging into the rest of that scene's shots. Once you've decided what the basic color balance, exposure, and contrast ratio should be, you can use that shot as a single reference against which you'll evaluate all the other shots in that scene, as illustrated in **Figure 9.4**.

Use as master shot

Figure 9.4 It makes it easier if you choose a single master shot to compare to all other shots in a scene.

Choosing a single shot is the key. Ideally, you'll want to do all of your experimenting with this shot so that you can lock in the look and start working on the other shots in the sequence, comparing them to the first shot you worked on so that they all end up looking the same.

If you don't adjust each shot relative to a single reference and, instead, compare each shot in a scene to the one that came immediately before it, you can end up playing a game of "telephone," where the color balance and contrast of each shot in the scene subtly drifts. Even though each pair of shots matches well enough, the last shot in the scene will look quite different from the first.

NOTE

Realistically, it may take seeing two or three shots play together before you and the client are happy with the look of the scene. That's okay; the important thing is to eventually get to the point where you have one shot that looks right.

There may be times when this is exactly what you want. For instance, you might want to cheat a scene's balance when the first shots in the scene are so dramatically different from the last shots that you can't make a perfect match. However, with a typical scene, it'll make your life easier, from an organizational standpoint, to evenly balance the entire scene from beginning to end.

SOMETIMES YOU NEED TO SPLIT THE DIFFERENCE

Ideally, you can choose whichever shot you want to use as the master shot for the scene and make whatever adjustments you want to make it perfect. However, if the scene you're working on is a mishmash of well-exposed and poorly exposed shots, you may have to split the difference between the ideal adjustment for that scene's nicest shot and the best adjustment that's possible considering the limitations of the poorest shot in the scene. At the end of the process, consistency is often more important than beauty, unfortunately.

A good example of this principle is a car interior scene that's been shot on location. There will usually be many angles of coverage, each with potentially wide variations in lighting, including changing lighting conditions stemming from the moving position of the sun or unexpected shade coming from a building or highway overpass. Any combination of these potentially conflicting lighting variations might be edited together to match on the narrative flow of the scene and depending on which takes were combined to build the final performances. As colorist Joe Owens put it, "Editors cut for story, and it's up to somebody else to even it out." Good luck.

ORGANIZING YOUR ADJUSTMENTS

Keep in mind that once you've balanced a scene, you can fiddle with its creative or stylized "look" using additional corrections. This is especially true if you balanced the entire scene so that every single shot within is evenly matched with every other.

Most color correction applications let you apply multiple corrections to a shot, effectively layering several different adjustments together to create a final grade. Given the possibility of a multi-adjustment approach to color correction, there are two general approaches to organizing your corrections, each with pros and cons.

BALANCE AND STYLIZE ALL AT ONCE

If the grade you're creating is fairly naturalistic and/or relatively simple, you might opt to balance the scene and impose a style all within a single adjustment.

This approach is often the fastest and is completely appropriate for any project, especially when you're not doing much more than making a primary correction to most of the shots within a scene.

However, this "single-adjustment" approach can make later revisions a bit more challenging, especially if the parameters you manipulated to create a style are the same ones that accomplish the scene's balance, in which case significant stylistic alterations will require you to rebalance the scene. For example, if you originally created a high-contrast look for the scene—crushing the shadows and blowing out highlights—and the client later wants to go back to a lower-contrast version, you'll typically want to revise your initial grade for maximum image integrity.

On the other hand, if your relationship with the client and the nature of the project is such that you know later revisions will be light, this might not be a big deal. Additional corrections can be appended to every shot within a scene as long as they don't require image data that was discarded in previous operations.

BALANCE FIRST, STYLIZE LATER

This next approach is good when you have more time in your schedule and you're working on a project for which you know there will be frequent and ongoing revisions.

The idea is to approach the scene in two separate passes. In the first pass, you'll restrict your corrections to achieving a good, neutral balance that'll be conducive to the type of grade you'll eventually be creating. In this pass, it's best to avoid extreme contrast or color adjustments, since this will restrict what you can do later. The idea is to make sure that all the shots in the scene look good and that they all match one another according to their content.

Once that's done, you'll reapproach the scene in a second pass, creating the more stylized look that you want to achieve with an entirely separate set of corrections. In a perfect world, you'll be able to create a single set of "style" corrections that you can then apply to the entire scene. After all, since it's already balanced, these adjustments should apply to every shot equally, right?

Alas, it's also likely that one shot or another will have a unique feature that doesn't interact with your stylistic adjustments the way you'd planned. For example, a yellow shirt that's prominent in one angle of coverage but can't be seen in the four other angles in the scene might need special handling to accommodate your "muted cool look." Also, if your stylistic adjustment uses vignettes/Power Windows, then you'll likely need to readjust these to fit the framing of each new shot. Bottom line: You should always check to see whether your style adjustments need to be customized for any shots in the scene.

While this approach takes a bit more time, you'll get it all back if the scene requires ongoing revisions. For example, if the client originally wanted a high-saturation, warm look with orange skies and then later asks for a low-saturation variation with blue skies, you can easily redo the style grades without having to revisit the underlying scene-balancing adjustments. If the client then asks to preview blown-out highlights, cyan skies, crushed shadows, a cool evening treatment, or any other variations, you can speed through these adjustments without having to revisit the base corrections.

CHAPTER 9

HOW TO MATCH ONE SHOT TO ANOTHER

Now that we've gone through the different ways you'll approach balancing a scene, it's time to get into the nitty-gritty: actually making adjustments to match one shot to another.

The truth is, the skill you'll need to cultivate most to do efficient shot matching is image evaluation—learning to spot the differences between two shots that you need to even out through correction. Once you've learned to find the differences between two shots, making the actual adjustments is fairly simple.

There are a variety of tools available for comparing one image with another. To summarize, the three most common methods of comparing shots are as follows:

- Looking at one shot and then the other in succession
- Using a split-screen function to simultaneously compare two images
- Comparing the video scope analysis of both shots

Let's look at each one of these methods in depth.

COMPARING SHOTS VISUALLY

I find that one of the methods I use most frequently to compare two shots is also the least sophisticated. Sometimes I simply use the appropriate controls to jump forward and backward, from edit point to edit point, to compare one shot to the previous one.

Alternately, I might click or scrub in the timeline to jump from one shot to another if the shots I want to compare aren't right next to one another. It sounds kludgy, but I don't always want to grab a still frame just to see how two shots match, especially if they're right next to one another.

When working to balance two shots that are right next to each other, I also like to play through the edit that joins them together to see how smooth the match is. If it's a really thorny match, I might also constrain playback to include a second before and after the edit and enable looped playback, to let the cut cycle a few times while I try to make up our mind about what's wrong with it.

COMPARING SHOTS USING A STILL STORE

Another approach—especially useful when I'm evaluating every other shot in a scene relative to the master shot that we graded first—is to use the *still store, image gallery, storyboard, memories,* or *reference image* mechanism in a color correction application to grab a reference frame of a representative image in the "master" shot, which I can compare to subsequent shots in the program. Every modern color correction application has a still store (or gallery), which is an essential tool for shot matching.

Grabbing a reference still is usually a one-button operation. Most applications let you store as many stills as you like within a bin where they're typically visualized using thumbnails or poster frames (though you can often sort them as a text list as well). Many applications store only one set of stills per project, but some let you store or export separate sets of stills that you can access from any project, which can be useful for series work or multireel programs.

Loading a still is usually a matter of double-clicking a thumbnail in the gallery bin (**Figure 9.5**) or using buttons on a control surface to browse through the bin (usually a pair of buttons labeled previous/next).

Once a still is loaded, toggling it on and off is a one-button affair using either your control surface or a keyboard command.

NOTE

Usually there is an onscreen gallery interface that lets you visually browse the thumbnails representing each still. Quantel's Neo control surface actually displays the currently browsed reference images on small OLED displays that correspond to the image reference navigation and recall controls.

Figure 9.5 A gallery tab in DaVinci Resolve. Each thumbnail represents both a reference still and the saved grade of the shot it came from.

Both FilmLight Baselight (via its Gallery interface) and Quantel Pablo (via the storyboard) take a different approach to saving reference images. Instead of storing a single frame, they store a reference to the entire shot. This means that at any time, you can change the reference image to another frame within the same shot without having to grab another still.

Some implementations, including DaVinci Resolve, FilmLight Baselight, and Quantel Pablo, also store the grade that was applied to the shot you took a reference of. This makes it easy to copy the grade from a reference still to another shot in the program to which you're comparing it, using it as is (if you're lucky) or more likely as a starting point for further modification to create a match.

NOTE

Autodesk Lustre is an example of an application that takes the opposite approach, letting you load reference stills from saved grades in its Grade bin. It's the same functionality, just a different way of looking at it.

CHAPTER 9

TOGGLING A FULL FRAME STILL OFF AND ON

If you change the wipe setting of your reference still to 100 percent, you can toggle the entire image off and on to compare it with another shot in the timeline.

The purpose of doing this (instead of constantly using a split screen) is to outrace your eye's adaptation response. You'll find that if you look at any image long enough, your eye adapts to its overall color temperature, and you essentially "stop seeing the differences." This makes it extremely difficult to evaluate the picture and doubly difficult to create the adjustments necessary to match it to another shot.

Flipping quickly back and forth between two images doesn't give your eyes the chance to "rebalance" to the subtle color cast found in either image, and this is often the best way to get an overall, at-a-glance comparison of the essential differences between two shots.

ADAPTATION IN ACTION

If you don't believe me about the problem that color adaptation poses during color correction sessions, try the following experiment. Load a relatively neutral scene and warm it up by rebalancing the highlights toward orange. Push it up until the point you think to yourself, "That's pretty warm but not overbearing." Now, sit there and look at it for a good long time. Loop the clip, or better yet, apply this warm look to the rest of a scene, watch the scene for a couple of minutes, and then write down how warm you think your correction is.

Now, get up and leave your color correction room. Go outside and get some sunlight or have a cup of tea next to the window. Afterward, go back into your color correction suite, sit down, and take another look at the image you had been looking at before. I'm guessing that your impression of its color balance after the break is probably somewhat different from the impression that you wrote down on your piece of paper. With fresh eyes, you're no longer duped by the adaptation your eyes made when you were watching the clip earlier.

Adaptation is a fact of life and is one of the reasons some color correction suites have a "white spot"—an illuminated neutral white area that you can look at to "wash out your eyes." Alternately, some colorists display a white still image on their monitors that they can look at when they feel like they're being mislead by adaptation during a session.

USING SPLIT-SCREEN COMPARISONS

Although flipping back and forth between a still store's reference image and the current shot is a great method of comparison, sometimes it's useful to see an actual onscreen comparison of two subjects right next to one another. For example, if you're trying to match the skin tone of an actress in one shot with the same actress's tone in another and the match is tricky, you can usually use a split screen to accomplish this.

Split-screen controls, at their simplest, consist of a wipe parameter that lets you move the division between the reference image and the current shot. By adjusting the split, you can frame a common element within each shot (a person's skin, the sand on a beach, the blue of the sky) in each half of the split so that you can compare them directly while making the necessary adjustments to match the current shot (**Figure 9.6**, right) to the reference still (Figure 9.6, left).

Figure 9.6 A reference still (left) compared with the current frame (right) using a split screen, providing direct side-by-side comparison.

Usually, split-screen controls have additional parameters for switching between a horizontal and vertical split screen (**Figure 9.7**), changing the orientation of wipes, and possibly panning the images on either side of the split to reframe how much of the image you can see.

Figure 9.7 Customizable split-screen parameters in Adobe SpeedGrade.

Additionally, some applications have more exotic comparative mechanisms, such as DaVinci Resolve's ability to key out a color in a still store image and composite it against the image at the playhead.

CHAPTER 9

USING MULTIPLE PLAYHEADS

Several applications also provide an interface for adding multiple playheads to the timeline you're working on (**Figure 9.8**). This method of comparison usually provides the ability to flip back and forth among the frames at each playhead's location and create split screens where each half of the split corresponds to a particular playhead. The advantage of this implementation is that you can scrub and play through as many frames as you like at each playhead, as opposed to viewing a reference still that's limited to only a single frame.

Figure 9.8 A multiple-playhead UI in FilmLight Baselight (top) and in Adobe SpeedGrade (bottom).

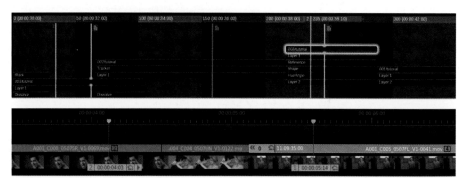

An additional option that's usually available to applications that support multiple playheads is the ability to simultaneously display multiple frames, either side by side or in a grid, *in their entirety*.

The effect is like a split screen on steroids, where you're actually comparing two or more whole images with one another. Some applications support this multiframe display sent via video output to your broadcast display, while other applications support multiframe display only on your computer's monitor.

Different applications support different numbers of playheads. For comparison, Autodesk Lustre lets you use two playheads, Adobe SpeedGrade lets you use two or three, and FilmLight Baselight lets you use as many as nine playheads at once in a timeline. Often, the playheads can be ganged together for simultaneous playback, if you want to see all of the shots play along with one another. See your application's documentation for more information on the available options.

MULTICLIP VIEWING

In yet another method of comparing shots, Autodesk Lustre lets you select up to
16 shots in the timeline in a "storyboard mode" to evaluate in a multiview layout.
DaVinci Resolve also has special split-screen settings that allow for different config-
urations of multiple-clip viewing, as shown in **Figure 9.9**.

Figure 9.9 Using the DaVinci
Resolve Split Screen feature's
Selected Clips mode to display a
full-screen grid of all selected clips
in the viewer.

These features do not require playhead management in the timeline; you need only
select a group of clips to set up a comparison.

STORYBOARD MODES

Lustre also has a timeline storyboard mode with powerful methods of sorting and
finding selections of shots based on different criteria. The result appears as a temporarily reorganized timeline, showing only the shots you want to work with.

Quantel Pablo also has a storyboard mode, but it's used more for grade management than for monitoring. You can assemble a selection of shots, or a series of
representative frames from every shot in the program, that you can save for later
recall. Using a storyboard, you can load a reference image for flipping or a split-
screen wipe, or you can use it for copying grades to paste to the current shot you're
working on.

CHAPTER 9

DaVinci Resolve has a Lightbox that takes the place of the viewer and lets you display the contents of the timeline within a grid of thumbnails of variable size (**Figure 9.10**).

Figure 9.10 The Lightbox in DaVinci Resolve, showing a thumbnail grid of all clips in the timeline.

These thumbnails can similarly be used to build groups, copy grades, or grade in context to the other thumbnails in the Lightbox, which can even be output to video for display on your hero monitor. The timeline and Lightbox can also both be filtered to temporarily display only a subset of clips matching various criteria.

WHAT YOU'RE LOOKING FOR

Once you've decided on how you're going to compare the two shots you're matching, it's time to examine them to look for what the difference are. This section goes over the process step-by-step, but with practice, it will become second nature. As with every craft, it takes a thousand shots to get to that point. However, a journey of a dozen movies starts with the first shot....

First we'll see how to compare shots just by eyeballing them. Although the video scopes can be a valuable tool for making precise matches, we've already discussed how a perceptual match is often more important than a numeric one, so it's an essential skill to be able to size up how two images match just by looking at them on your display.

COMPARING CONTRAST

A good starting point is to compare the contrast ratios of each shot. As mentioned earlier, the contrast ratio of a shot will affect how later color balance adjustments work, so it's ideal to make any necessary contrast adjustments first.

How do the black and white points line up? As you look back and forth between the reference image and the shot you're matching to it, how similar do the darkest and lightest parts of the image look? These comparisons will determine whether and how you make shadow and highlight contrast adjustments.

Looking into the midtones of each image, how does the average lightness of each image compare? This comparison determines whether a midtones contrast adjustment is necessary. **Figure 9.11** shows a graded reference shot on the left and an ungraded shot elsewhere in the same scene on the right.

Figure 9.11 A graded shot on the left compared with another ungraded angle from the same scene (right). The black point and average midtones of the second image require adjustment to match.

Just looking at the images, we can see pretty clearly that the black point of the ungraded shot is elevated by comparing the shadows of the woman's jacket in each shot. Furthermore, the second shot looks a lot brighter than the first. Since the sky in both images is really bright, this tells us that the midtones are most likely elevated in the ungraded shot. Based on this comparison, adjustments to the shadow and midtones contrast controls are likely the next step to balancing these two shots together.

COMPARING COLOR BALANCE

Once you have a reasonable contrast match, it's time to compare the color quality. Although contrast comparisons are fairly cut-and-dry, color comparison is trickier, as there are a host of perceptual illusions that we need to take into consideration. Fortunately, the criteria "if it looks like a match, then it is a match" is pretty much the rule of the day, so at a certain point you need to learn to let go and trust your eyes.

Flip back and forth between the reference image and the shot you're matching to it. Try to take in the color balance of the overall shot rather than focusing on any one particular element. While you're at it, see whether you can spot which tonal regions are the most different. Is the greatest color variation in the brightest portion of the image, the highlights, or is it in the midtones? This will guide you as to the most appropriate color balance.

A good tip is that most variations in color temperature result from differences in the lighting, so more likely than not you'll be making a lot of adjustments to the highlights, some adjustments to the midtones, and not that many adjustments to the shadows (unless the camera's original settings resulted in a shadows imbalance in every shot). On the other hand, if a shot is giving you a lot of trouble and you can't figure out why, check the color balance in the shadows. A small imbalance can lend an odd cast to the midtones that's difficult to put your finger on.

Figure 9.12 shows another graded reference shot on the left and an ungraded shot elsewhere in the same scene on the right.

Figure 9.12 A graded reference still on the left and an ungraded reverse shot that follows on the right.

The difference is subtle, but we can see by comparing the overall quality of light between the two shots that the ungraded shot is a bit warmer (more orange) than the reference still. In particular, if you look at the highlights of the man's face, you can compare them to the facial highlights of the reference shot to better isolate the quality of this warmth.

This shot is also a good example of the contribution of dominant colors to the general perception of the scene's color temperature. For instance, the man's orange shirt is definitely enhancing the warmth of the scene, as is the dry grass in the background. However, in this case a better match would indeed be made by making the overall color temperature of the scene a bit cooler. This can be done simply by pushing the highlight color balance control toward a blue/cyan split. However, if a highlight color balance adjustment ends up turning the white van door blue, then substituting a midtone color balance adjustment toward blue/cyan might be more appropriate.

COMPARING SATURATION

Even though saturation is a characteristic of the color component, I mention it separately because it's important to learn to evaluate it separately. This is because it's easy to confuse color balance and saturation intensity when you're trying to figure out what adjustments to make.

Beware of instances where the color balance is correct but the image is simply not saturated enough. It's tempting to keep pushing the color balance further and further to create a match, since this *does* increase saturation. However, you'll end up with an image with a mismatched color cast, however subtle. Easing off of your color balance adjustment and instead turning up the overall saturation will give the right result. The pair of images in **Figure 9.13** shows this principle in action.

Figure 9.13 Two shots where the color balance and contrast are well matched but the saturation is unmatched.

In Figure 9.13, the saturation in the image on the right is lower than that in the image on the left. It's not necessarily obvious, but if you look at the red piping on the man's uniform and the skin of the man's face, you can start to see that the color is definitely duller in the second image. Another element to compare would be the patchy green grass in the second image and the defocused trees in the background of the first. It's a subtle but important difference but one that's easily fixed with an adjustment to overall image saturation.

Now, spotting and quantifying differences in saturation is easy when you're using the vectorscope, but the point I'm trying to make is that learning to spot these subtle differences visually will speed you up, letting you know when to flick your eyes over to your video scope to check the measurements.

CHECK FOR EXCEPTIONS

Once you're generally happy with the overall match, take one last look. Is there any single element that's sticking out and throwing things off? One good example is an unusually vivid scenic element that appears in one angle but not in another (saturated red, yellow, and magenta objects often cause this). When confronted with this situation, ask yourself (or the client), is it supposed to stick out, or is this something you need to deal with using a separate correction so it doesn't distract the audience? Often, this is a prime case where a secondary correction will be useful to "hammer the nail that sticks out."

WASH, RINSE, REPEAT

Depending on the interactivity of the contrast and color controls in your application, image balancing may be an iterative process. Don't be afraid to go back and forth between your contrast and color adjustments, since changes to one often have a subtle effect on the other. Just be sure to work quickly to avoid falling into the trap of letting your eyes adapt to the shot you're adjusting.

CHAPTER 9

Also, it's important to know when to stop. Because of your eyes' adaptation, working on any pair of shots for too long will cause you to completely lose your objectivity, and you'll simply find it more and more difficult to see what it is you're doing. If you've worked on a pair of shots for more than a few minutes and you're beginning to feel frustrated, go ahead and move on to another shot.

I also have a "next-day rule." If there's a scene that's been giving me trouble, I wrap it up and move on to a new scene. I'll take another look at it first thing in the morning. More often than not, I'll immediately spot what my problem was and end up fixing it in a couple of minutes.

Don't think that you need to get everything perfect the first time through a scene. Often, it's best to go over a scene a couple of times in different passes before putting it to rest. This is another reason that the review session is so important. It's a good time to take one last look at each scene to see whether you catch any small things that eluded you earlier.

COMPARING SHOTS USING VIDEO SCOPES

Now that we've gone over how to evaluate shot differences visually, let's take a look at how to use video scopes to aid in this effort. Although a perceptual match is critical, there are many instances where using your scope's analysis to find the difference between two shots will identify a problem that you've been having a hard time working out visually. Also, if you're in a situation where you need to make precise adjustments to match a product color or interview backdrop, this can be the fastest way to consistently and reliably hit a particular target.

THE WAVEFORM MONITOR

As you can probably guess, matching contrast is best accomplished using the Waveform Monitor set to Low Pass (LP) or using a parade scope set to YRGB that displays the luma channel next to the red, green, and blue analyses. This is almost trivially easy, since comparing the black and white points is a matter of comparing the bottoms and tops of the Waveform graphs. Furthermore, the average midtones that usually manifest themselves as a dense cluster of the graph somewhere in the middle and the height of this midtones cluster is a great way to compare the average perceived lightness of two images.

When comparing images with the Waveform Monitor, you can flip back and forth between two full frames to compare each graph in its entirety. However, an alternate way of using the Waveform Monitor for shot comparison is to turn on a split-screen display, which when output to your video scope will show itself as a split in the actual Waveform Monitor analysis (**Figure 9.14**).

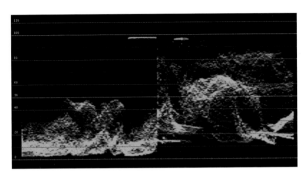

Figure 9.14 A split-screen comparison output to a Waveform Monitor analysis. The sharp line in the middle shows the center point between each half.

This gives you a direct comparison between each waveform on your scope, making it incredibly easy to make shadow, midtones, and highlight adjustments to align the bottom, top, and middle of the graphs as closely as you can.

THE VECTORSCOPE

Comparing and matching color is a different story. The vectorscope is your best tool for comparing the chroma component of two shots. Ordinarily, the best way to compare two images is to flip between full-frame versions, comparing the resulting graphs. In **Figure 9.15**, the vectorscope graphs for the cool and warm shots shown in Figure 9.12 are presented side by side.

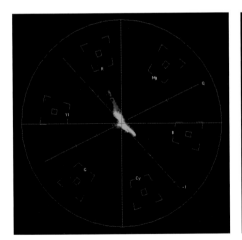
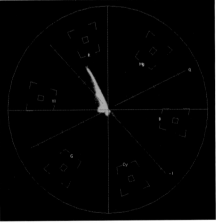

Figure 9.15 The vectorscope analyses of the images from Figure 9.12.

Flipping between these two graphs, it's easy to see that the graph to the left is nicely balanced because it's centered on the crosshairs, and likewise you'll note an abundance of cool blue in the image corresponding to the arm of the graph that extends toward the blue target. The graph to the right, on the other hand, leans significantly toward the yellow/red targets, with virtually no blue seen in the graph at all. If you had any doubt about the difference in overall color balance between these shots before, there is no doubt now.

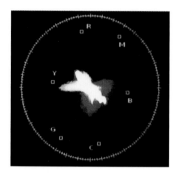

Figure 9.16 The Harris VTM series video scopes have the ability to superimpose a freeze frame of the analysis from another shot over the analysis of the current shot. In this image, the reference graph is shown in red, and the current analysis appears in green.

When evaluating a vectorscope, a split-screen evaluation makes little sense unless you wiggle one of the color balance controls around; the moving part of the vectorscope graph will appear as an overlay over the still part of the vectorscope graph, which represents the reference portion of the split screen. However, this can be a subtle method of evaluation.

Some outboard video scopes have options for grabbing a freeze frame of the analysis of one frame and superimposing it underneath the currently analyzed video signal (**Figure 9.16**).

When making vectorscope comparisons, keep the following in mind:

- Color balance comparison is fairly easy, revealing itself as the offset between the overall graph and the center point of the vectorscope (usually identified with crosshairs). Matched shots are generally offset in the same direction at about the same distance. However, this is not always easy to see.

- Comparisons between the hue consistencies of individual elements are a bit more nebulous, revealing themselves as the angles of each excursion within the vectorscope graph. For example, if a particular excursion stretches toward the red target in one shot and a similar excursion stretches to the left of the red target, that may be a sign that a particular element isn't matching.

- Comparing the saturation of two images is the easiest thing of all. Since saturation reveals itself as the overall diameter of the vectorscope graph, you simply need to compare the overall size of two vectorscope graphs to figure out whether a saturation adjustment is necessary.

Lastly, comparing color balance in the highlights and shadows is fairly easy to do using the RGB or YRGB parade scope. Similar to the Waveform Monitor, you can see differences either in full-screen or split-screen comparisons (**Figure 9.17**).

Figure 9.17 The RGB parade scope analysis of the images from Figure 9.12.

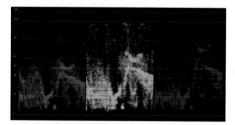 

When comparing RGB graphs, you want to see how the tops, middles, and bottoms of the red, green, and blue channels align with one another. Even if an image's three channels are offset, in an ideal match, the offset channels of one image should be similar to the channel offsets in the other.

In Figure 9.17, you can see a distinct difference from the tops to the midtones of the two sets of graphs. In the scope on the left, the blue channel is higher (stronger) while at the right, the blue channel is lower (weaker).

HOW CLOSELY MUST TWO SHOTS MATCH?

When you're balancing the need to work quickly with the desire to do a good job, a good question to ask is, how close of a match is good enough?

Although the answer is certainly influenced by how much time you've been given to work through the show, your ultimate goal is to create a *convincing* match from shot to shot so that no single shot sticks out during a casual viewing of the scene.

You don't need to match every single similarly colored item in every single shot with absolute precision. Although this is an ideal to aim for, as a practical approach to scene evaluation it may end up taking you significantly more time than you have. However, you must match all the elements in each scene closely enough to *appear* as if they're the same, as one shot plays into another.

Now, this advice is not meant to excuse poor scene balancing. Creating a convincing match isn't trivial, and it takes practice to do it quickly. My main point is that you don't want to find yourself obsessing over every single feature in every pair of shots that you're correcting, adding adjustment after adjustment, and piling on secondary corrections in order to make each element match with floating-point precision. Unless there's a specific reason for doing so, such painful attention to detail may be counterproductive, and it'll certainly add hours (possibly days) to your schedule as you make small adjustments to balance elements that nobody would ever have noticed.

At the beginning of this chapter, we mentioned the importance of avoiding shot imbalances that appear as continuity errors. This is key, but it's also valuable to keep in mind that most audiences have a surprising ability to overlook minor continuity errors so long as they're subtle (for example, longer shadows in one shot, and shorter shadows in another).

That said, it's also important to be sensitive to specific client requests. It's often the case that there's a particular element within a scene that the producer, director, or cinematographer is sensitive to that you had considered unimportant, and it's important to take that into consideration when you're asked to revisit a scene that you consider to be well-balanced.

Along these lines, keep the following in mind:

- Get into the habit of evaluating the image as a whole. Even though the subject of a medium shot might be a woman at center frame, the surrounding environment has an impact on how the image looks. Always remember that you're grading the whole frame.

- There'll likely be some desirable variation in lighting as the camera frames different portions of the environment in subsequent angles of coverage; for example, a high-contrast master shot where an actor is in a highlight with a pool of darkness behind him might cut to an extreme close-up of the actor's face within the highlight. There'll certainly be a difference in overall exposure when one cuts to the other, but it's deliberate. That said, you might make a small adjustment to subdue the close-up so that the difference doesn't blind the audience.

- In general, a perceived match is much more important than an actual numeric match, when you're taking into account how our eyes handle the influence of strong surrounding colors on subjects within. This is usually the case when you painstakingly match each aspect of the shot using video scopes only to hear the client say, "I don't know, they still don't quite look the same...." This happens much more frequently than you'd guess and is another reason why comparing two frames in their entirety, flipping back and forth from one to another, will reveal inconsistencies that a split screen may not.

- Beware of regrading different actors' skin tones in close-ups to match one another too closely. This may sound obvious, but actors' complexions vary, and it's easy to get so caught up in the shot-matching process that you end up making every single person's skin tone look the same (which is both unrealistic and boring). To help avoid this, it's sometimes valuable to keep a series of reference stills in the still store or gallery that represents the ideal complexion of each prominent person in the program you're grading.

The trick to efficient scene balancing is to be aware of the threshold of diminishing returns. Learn to know when to keep working and when to walk away.

WHEN TO BREAK DOWN AND USE A SECONDARY

As important as a well-adjusted primary correction is, if there are fundamental differences between two shots that are completely irreconcilable, you may need to make secondary corrections in order to accomplish a good match. For example, if you're balancing an insert shot that was recorded months after the principal photography and the insert shot has a white, hazy sky while the rest of the scene has a bright blue sky, the only way to reconcile the difference is to make a secondary correction to isolate the white sky and add some color to it (not an easy operation!). This is a great example of modern technology addressing an issue that once would have incurred a continuity error or necessitated a full-blown reshoot.

Another important exception is a show where a white, black, or gray background needs to match in every shot in which it appears or where a specific element (such as a shirt or a product of some kind) must match precisely from one shot to the next. In such cases, precision evaluation using your video scopes is critical, both for you to be able to make a precise match *and* for you to be able to prove to the client that the match is, in fact, accurate.

NOISE AND GRAIN—WHEN MATCHING COLOR ISN'T ENOUGH

There will be times when, no matter how closely you've matched the contrast and color between two images, you still can't get the match quite right. Many times, it may be differences in video noise or film grain that's causing the problem.

Sometimes, the best solution may be to use noise reduction to try to minimize objectionable video noise that's distracting to the viewer. However, other times, you'll need to replicate video noise or film grain to match a clip that's just too clean to a noisier series of clips.

There are many instances when you need to match a clip that's extremely well-exposed and clean to a noisy scene. This happens all the time with insert shots that were recorded much later than the original scene or when editors get creative and mix clips from completely different scenes in unexpected ways.

You'll also find many instances of video noise increasing in subsequent angles of coverage as the daylight slipped away from the filmmakers, at which point you'll be forced to add noise to pristine footage shot at 4 p.m. so that it matches extremely grainy footage shot at 6:30 p.m.

RECYCLING GRADES

Keeping in mind that shots are frequently repeated, it's often the case that you can apply a grade you've created for one shot to many other instances of similar shots in a program. This will save you time and effort by keeping you from reinventing the wheel with every single shot. Grade recycling is usually most effective in the following situations:

- It's effective when you're grading a scene that was carefully shot using multiple angles of coverage (usually narrative filmmaking), such as a master 2-shot (A), an over-the-shoulder reverse angle (B), and a close-up (C), as in **Figure 9.18**. As long as the lighting doesn't change within any particular angle of coverage, you can freely copy a grade from angle A to all the other shots corresponding to angle A. In the following illustration, all five shots can be graded using only three corrections.

A   B   C   A   C

Figure 9.18 Angles of coverage are represented by repeating letters. Both A shots share the same grade, as do both C shots. Shot B needs its own grade.

- If a narrative scene has been carefully lit, the color and exposure of each angle of coverage ought to be fairly close to one another. If this is the case, the grade you created for angle A may well be a good starting point for angles B and C. I like to call this the "do I get lucky?" approach. If I get lucky, the grade from one angle will work great for the next angle too, and I can move on. However, it's more likely that each angle will need unique tweaks. Still, starting with a generally close grade can sometimes save you time—unless the grade is not as close as you think. The trick is not to spend too much time tweaking a copied grade; at a certain point, it may be faster to just start from scratch.

CHAPTER 9

- In documentary filmmaking that uses "talking heads," you can often use a single grade for all talking head shots that correspond to a particular subject that were shot in a single interview session. Beware: Some directors of photography just can't keep their hands off the camera and lights, and I've had shows where one subject's talking-head shots required seven different grades, one for each time the lighting got tweaked. (Tip for DoPs: Please don't do that unless the ambient lighting is changing on you.)

- Many shows of different kinds recycle exterior establishing shots, so it's not a bad idea to keep a stash of grades for exterior locations that you've made to bring back whenever the same location reappears.

- This is doubly true for reality television, where 15 minutes of unique visuals can sometimes get stretched into 23 minutes of programming by creatively recycling re-creations, location shots, and stills. When working on a program of this nature, I typically save a lot of grades for future use. The trick here is not to overdo it, or pretty soon finding the grade you need will be like spotting the proverbial needle in a haystack. After working on a show for a couple of hours, you begin to get a sense of the type of shots that get used again.

So, with these comparisons of different reasons to recycle grades behind us, let's take a look at how some different applications let you do this.

CORRECTIONS VS. GRADES

Nearly every color correction application mentioned in this book has the ability to combine multiple *corrections* to create overall *grades*. It follows, then, that an individual correction is a single primary or secondary adjustment made to an image, while a grade is an entire collection of adjustments all working together to create an overall look. This relationship is expressed in various ways:

- FilmLight Baselight employs a series of bars appearing underneath clips in the timeline that represent the corrections that are applied (in Baselight they're called *strips*). Adobe SpeedGrade shows corrections as full-sized clips that appear beneath and above clips in the timeline, but they serve the same function.

- DaVinci Resolve represents individual adjustments as *nodes* that connect together to create overall grades.

- Autodesk Lustre organizes additional secondary corrections as numbered layers accessible from a keypad in the main user interface, organized in four banks of twelve corrections.

Check your product documentation for more information about how your application works with this process. For reference, the following sections discuss, in general terms, the different methods that are used to copy grades from one shot to another and otherwise manage saved corrections in order to recycle grades.

COPY AND PASTE

In most instances, the simplest way of applying a grade from one shot to the next is to copy and paste. Every color correction application has the facility to copy a grade into a buffer and paste it to another shot that's either selected or at the position of the playhead in the timeline.

Usually this functionality corresponds to a series of buttons on a control surface, but it's also something you can access using keyboard shortcuts, if that's how your application was designed. For example, DaVinci Resolve has "memories" that can be saved and applied using either control surface buttons or keyboard shortcuts. DaVinci Resolve also has numerous other functions for copying grades from other shots to the one you're working on, including the ability to copy and paste grades between any two clips, and controls to copy from two previous clips or copy from one previous clip.

DRAG AND DROP IS PRETTY MUCH THE SAME THING

Some applications also have a drag-and-drop version of copy and paste. For example, FilmLight Baselight employs a series of bars (called *clips*) that are associated with clips in the timeline and indicate which clips have what corrections applied to them. These strips can be dragged and dropped to other shots in the timeline if you're a hands-on type of colorist.

SAVING GRADES INTO BINS OR GALLERIES

All professional color correction applications have a mechanism for saving grades into some kind of bin for future use. The names differ (*bin*, *gallery*, *tray*), but the idea is to have a central repository for corrections and grades that you'll want to use again later.

Most gallery and bin interfaces are flatly organized areas containing thumbnails of every correction you're making. Others allow the use of folders to organize your corrections. Autodesk Lustre takes a more complex approach, providing a hierarchy of grade bins where grades can be organized by user, scene, project, or custom bins of your own creation, depending on how you want to be organized.

TIP

In DaVinci Resolve, you can copy grades on the Color page by selecting a thumbnail to copy to and then middle-clicking the thumbnail of the shot you want to copy from.

CHAPTER 9

Additionally, some applications have a "fast retrieval" interface for storing a series of grades that can be instantly recalled using buttons on a control surface. Examples of this functionality include the following:

- DaVinci Resolve has a Gallery page with a memory bank running along the bottom that you can use to associate a particular reference image and grade with an alpha character (a–z) used for recall.

- FilmLight Baselight has a "Scratchpad" capable of storing 20 grades (recalled via the numeric keypad).

- Shots in Assimilate Scratch can be added to a "Tray," which can be used for navigation and also for applying the grades of those shots to other shots in the timeline.

- Quantel Pablo lets you create and save "storyboards," either from selected shots or by encapsulating every single shot in a project.

Many applications also allow you to save grades that can be used in other projects. For example, Adobe SpeedGrade has a "look browser" into which you can save and retrieve grades for later use. Assimilate Scratch lets you save grades to disk for future recall in any project. DaVinci Resolve has a PowerGrade tab where you can save reference stills and their accompanying grades for use in any project you have open. Quantel Pablo lets you recall storyboards from any other project. Lastly, Autodesk Lustre has a Global grade bin for sharing grades among multiple users and projects.

GETTING A JUMP ON THE NEXT GIG USING SAVED GRADES

A lot of professional colorists save their own set of frequently used operations and "secret sauce" grades for future use. If you have repeatable methods that you use to get started with a clip or to address common issues with footage, it makes no sense to reinvent the wheel every time you need to add an S curve, medium-sized vignette, or red-, green-, and blue-channel highlight rolloff curves. Instead, build a set of your own presets that start with the adjustments, curve control points, or shapes that you use most often so you can apply and customize them more quickly and easily than starting from scratch.

Another tack is to create your own library of creative grades and effects that address common client requests to have on hand when someone wants to see "how would a bleach bypass look on this shot?" Again, there are many types of looks that come up often, and it can be faster to have these on hand as presets so that you can quickly apply them to see what the client thinks. If they hate it, you can blow it away and it took you no time. If it's close, then you have a good starting point, and you can further customize it to meet the needs of the new show.

CREATING GROUPS OF SHOTS

Another tactic you can employ, if your application supports it, is to link a series of shots together in a group for organizational purposes. For example, you could do any of the following:

- Group all the talking head shots corresponding to a particular interview subject in a documentary

- Group every shot from a particular angle of coverage within a scene (all the A shots would be one group, the B shots another, and the C shots yet another)

- Group all the instances of a particular establishing shot that reappears constantly in a program

Once you've created a group, this makes it easier to either automatically or manually apply a grade or make a change to all the shots in that group at once.

Shot grouping generally works by letting you select a series of shots (either automatically as a sort or find operation, or manually) and creating a group representation of some kind. There are several methods of working with groups, depending on the implementation in your application:

- DaVinci Resolve groups automatically ripple changed corrections among all other shots in the group. When trimming grades, you have the option to trim by the exact value you're changing, by a percentage of change to the value, by a numerical offset, or by overwriting the entire grade.

- FilmLight Baselight groups automatically ripple changes to all the other shots in the group. Grouped shots with identical corrections are altered, while grouped shots with different corrections are *trimmed* by adding additional corrections reflecting the adjustment you've just made.

- Quantel Pablo clip groups provide options to ripple changes to "all" of the grade, add changes to the "top," or just change the "base" of the grade. Options for rippling methods include "trim" to alter existing parameters, "add" to add corrections to what's already there, and "replace" to overwrite the grades in the rest of the group with the new grade.

- Adobe SpeedGrade doesn't have groups; it has adjustment layers.

Since implementations vary so widely, I encourage you to check the documentation for your application for more detailed information about using groups.

MANAGING STYLE SEPARATELY

Many applications provide a way of applying multiple sets of adjustments to an image, whether as multiple layers, nodes, adjustment layers on a timeline, or additional scene or track-wide grades that can be applied on top of each clip's individual grades. Whatever the method, some colorists working on highly styled shows like to apply two sets of grades: an underlying set of grades for balancing each shot and an overall grade to set a look for the entire scene.

This is a professional workflow that offers a great deal of flexibility in situations where the client may decide to change their minds five times as you're working your way up to delivering the show. Balancing clips neutrally in a first pass and then applying a stylistic adjustment on top of that, using whatever grouping or adjustment layer mechanism your software provides, can make changing up your style grade a snap. The client doesn't like the hard blue undertones they asked for on Monday? Fine, adjust a single grade to change the entire scene to a pale blue wash with protected dark shadows instead, with no need to readjust every single shot. **Figure 9.19** shows how you can set this up using an adjustment layer in Adobe SpeedGrade.

Figure 9.19 In Adobe SpeedGrade, a superimposed adjustment layer (named Romantic Fade grade) over the last four clips in the timeline applies a stylistic look to the cutaway scene.

You may find, however, that a two-pass approach can be more time-consuming than simply shot matching and styling within a single grade, and it can be unrealistic for projects with parsimonious clients. This is especially true if the client's definition of a "look" is a touch more warmth in the diffuse highlights or a bit more blue in the midtones—simply a different way of balancing the scene, easily accomplished by continuing your adjustment in the primary grade.

In fact, the difference between a neutral grade and a "style" grade for something like a documentary project, where the client doesn't want anything too exotic, can be subtle to the point of invisibility (**Figure 9.20**). In this case, doing everything in your main grade is a simple convenience.

The bottom line is *time*. If you're working on a well-budgeted program and your client's initial availability is limited, you can take advantage of downtime by preemptively balancing each scene in advance. Once the client rolls in, you can work with them to apply stylization to the whole scene and modify the look within two or three versions as necessary to get the client's buy-in. When following this approach, bear in mind that shots that seemed perfectly balanced with a neutral grade might go out of balance once you start pushing the contrast or the color balance of the overall scene in a different direction, so even when you've pre-graded, you may still need to continue tweaking the odd shot to maintain good balance.

Figure 9.20 Three progressive treatments of the image (clockwise): The first grade is a simple primary correction that's easily accomplished with a single grade; the second is more stylized and could be done as a second set of adjustments or not; and the third is highly stylized and a good candidate for management via a separate set of adjustments.

For example, DaVinci Resolve offers a *track grade* feature that lets you apply a single grade to every clip in the timeline at once. In the previous scenario, if you're working on a commercial spot, you can work unsupervised to balance all of the shots via their individual clip grades. Then, when the client arrives, you can use the track grade to apply an additional correction for style on top of everything else, focusing all of your energy on revisions to a single set of adjustments (**Figure 9.21**). Other applications enable similar functionality using groups, compound or nested clips, or adjustment layers.

Shots balanced with individual clip grade

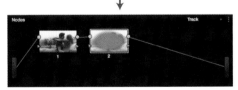

Creating a "look" with a single track grade

The track grade affects every clip in the timeline

Figure 9.21 Balancing clips in a music video with individual grades but then using a track grade in DaVinci Resolve to apply a set of style adjustments to the entire program at once.

CHAPTER 9

Another thing to consider is that grading workflows are not always either/or. If the main look the client wants is a subtly warm, slightly higher contrast treatment that you've decided to simply build into the primary grade, then doing an all-in-one grade makes a lot of sense. However, when they change their minds and say they want to cool down the overall look and lift the bottom blacks up, it's perfectly acceptable to add this adjustment on top of what you did previously so long as you didn't clip or over-compress valuable image detail in the initial grade. If you did, then you'll need to go back and change your primary adjustments to accommodate the new look or apply the modification as a layer or node *before* your primary adjustment.

SCENE MATCHING IN ACTION

In this last section, we'll take a look at a practical example of scene balancing using all the concepts we've covered in this chapter. To do so, we'll look at this five-shot sequence from Lauren Wolkstein's *Cigarette Candy* short:

1 To begin, choose a master shot that you'll grade first, looking through all of the shots of the sequence, as shown in **Figure 9.22**.

Figure 9.22 The uncorrected shot sequence.

| Shot 1 | Shot 2 | Shot 3 | Shot 4 | Shot 5 |

2 In this sequence, you'll start with Shot 1, the wide two-shot with the marine and the blonde woman (**Figure 9.23**). It has the advantage of showing both of the main characters and a lot of the surrounding environment.

Figure 9.23 Shot 1 in its uncorrected state.

3 Now, grade this shot. It's a narrow-contrast safety conversion of RED R3D media to DPX images, and the person who did the transfer elected to do so with elevated shadows and reduced highlights to avoid clipping, so the first thing you'll do is expand the contrast, dropping the shadows to just above 2–3 percent and boosting the blown-out sky to close to 100 percent to get some density back into the shadows and some energy in the highlights.

4 The DoP tells you that the shot was meant to take place in the late afternoon, but lowering the shadows ended up making the image look closer to evening, so you'll also boost the midtones, while adjusting the shadows to keep them where you put them initially.

5 In the process, you'll get some color back in the image, but you'll need to raise the saturation even more to get the rich tones you're looking for in his uniform and in the foliage of the yard.

6 You'll add some "golden hour" warmth to the scene by pushing the Highlights color balance control very slightly toward orange, as shown in **Figure 9.24**.

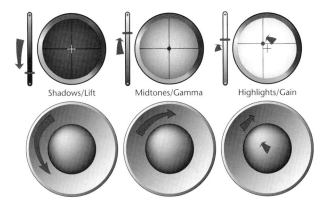

Shadows/Lift   Midtones/Gamma   Highlights/Gain

Figure 9.24 The adjustments used to create the initial grade for Shot 1.

The resulting shot (**Figure 9.25**) looks a lot more vibrant.

Figure 9.25 Shot 1 after being graded.

CHAPTER 9

Figure 9.26 Shot 1 saved as a reference still.

Figure 9.27 Evaluating Shot 2.

7 With that done, grab a reference still that you'll use to compare it to the next shot (**Figure 9.26**).

8 The next shot is a reverse angle, over the marine's shoulder and toward the blonde woman. Without even using the reference still it's easy to see that this reverse angle is darker (**Figure 9.27**).

One reason it's so dark is that the sky isn't in the shot, so it's not going to have the bright highlights of the previous shot no matter what you do, but that's not all. The midtones are significantly darker, and it's apparent that this scene was shot later in the day.

9 To match the contrast, you could flip back and forth between the reference and the current shot to compare the visuals and the waveform, but for purposes of print we'll use a split screen and compare the luma waveforms of both images directly (**Figure 9.28**). Adjusting the split screen, you can actually frame it so that the marine appears on each half of the split, both corrected and uncorrected. This makes it really easy to quickly create an accurate balance.

Figure 9.28 A split screen comparing Shot 1 and Shot 2, both visually and in the Waveform Monitor.

 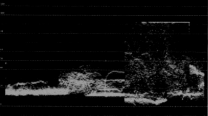

10 With that done, it's easy to see how you should adjust the contrast, lowering the shadows, boosting the midtones, and slightly raising the highlights of the uncorrected half so that the image and waveform match the corrected reference still (**Figure 9.29**).

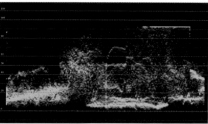

Figure 9.29 Shot 2 after matching its contrast to Shot 1. Notice how the split-screen waveform appears to be a single, continuous graph.

11 Next, compare the vectorscope graphs corresponding to both images. This time you'll set the reference still to be full frame, flipping back and forth to see how the images compare both visually and in the vectorscope (**Figure 9.30**).

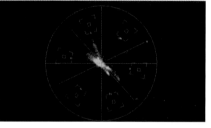

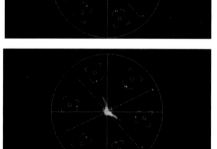

Figure 9.30 Comparing the vectorscope graphs for Shot 1 (top) and Shot 2 (bottom).

12 From this comparison, you can see the margin by which you'll need to increase saturation so that the uncorrected image's vectorscope graph matches the size of the corrected reference still.

You'll also get a good idea of how much to push the midtones toward orange to get a convincing match, judging from the offset of the vectorscope graph relative to the crosshairs (**Figure 9.31**).

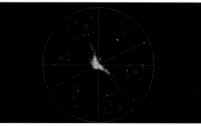

Figure 9.31 Shot 2 after matching its color to Shot 1.

CHAPTER 9

13 Look at the next shot in the sequence; you might get the notion that, in its uncorrected state, it looks awfully close to how the first shot appeared when you corrected it. To see whether you get lucky, try copying the grade from the first shot, and then compare the result to your reference still (**Figure 9.32**).

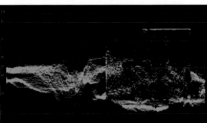

Figure 9.32 A split-screen comparison of Shot 3 (left) and Shot 1 (right), both visually and in the Waveform Monitor.

14 Judging from the waveform comparison, it's very close but not quite perfect. You'll need to raise the midtones a bit to make the contrast match. Also, a visual comparison of the color temperature of the woman's sweater on either side of the split screen reveals that the new shot is just a little bit too red, so ease back on the warming adjustment applied to the Highlights color balance control, and then the match is good (**Figure 9.33**).

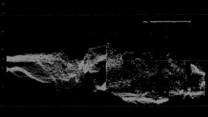

Figure 9.33 Shot 3 after being adjusted to match the color and contrast of Shot 1.

15 At this point, take a look at the next two shots in the sequence to see whether there's any more copying and pasting you can do.

The fourth shot in the sequence is from the same angle of coverage as the first shot, so copying the grade directly gives you an exact match. Don't get too cocky, though. Even though a shot is from the same angle of coverage, a passing cloud or bumped reflector board could easily introduce a difference. Fortunately, that's not the case in this scene, as you can see in **Figure 9.34**.

16 The fifth and last shot of the sequence is itself from the same angle of coverage as the third—in fact, it's a direct continuation of the same shot (**Figure 9.35**). Consequently, you'll copy the third shot's grade to the fifth shot, resulting in another perfect match.

Figure 9.34 Copying the grade from Shot 1 to Shot 4, which is from the same angle of coverage.

Figure 9.35 The end of Shot 3 compared with Shot 5. Shot 5 is a continuation of Shot 3, so you can use the same grade, saving time.

This shot is a great example of an instance where the thumbnail corresponding to that shot in the timeline didn't tell the entire story. Even though the two shots focus on completely different subjects at their Out point, the In point of each shot appears to be the blonde woman. This is the reason it's important to play or scrub through an entire shot before you start working on it, to make sure you're making the right decisions based on the overall content and not just the first frame.

17 Now that you've graded all the shots, it's a good idea to play through the entire sequence once or twice to see how the edits flow. **Figure 9.36** shows the shot sequence before and after your color grades.

Before

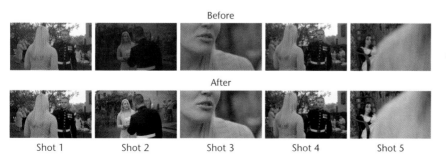

After

Shot 1   Shot 2   Shot 3   Shot 4   Shot 5

Figure 9.36 Your 5-shot sequence, before (top) and after (below) color grading.

CHAPTER 9

NOTE
Shots that look like perfect
matches when paused can
sometimes reveal subtle inconsistencies during playback,
so playing the entire scene is
always a good step. If you spot
any differences, go ahead and
make a change. It's these small
tweaks that put the final polish
on any program.

One last point: With a relatively neutral balancing job like this one (you haven't crushed or clipped the luma or chroma components of anything in your grade), subsequent revisions can be very simple.

Shots 1 and 4 contain a good example of an element that would trigger this kind of scene-wide revision. Now that the contrast has been expanded and the saturation increased, the reds and blues are just a little too distracting from the characters who are the focus of the scene. Since the scene is already balanced, it's an easy thing to add a secondary correction to Shot 1 to isolate these balloons and desaturate them a bit—just enough to take the edge off. This correction is then easily copied and appended to Shot 4, and you're finished.

However, don't simply assume things will always be this easy. Whenever you make a global change like this, it's always a good idea to watch the scene one more time, just to make sure your adjustment didn't inadvertently boost something else you didn't want to call attention to.

SOME FINAL TIPS FOR ADHERING TO A SCHEDULE

If you're going to be working on your own project, feel free to take as long as you want. However, if you're planning on working with clients, you'll need to learn to keep one eye on the clock. You can easily spend an hour making any particular shot look gorgeous, but your client won't necessarily be happy paying the bill. Here are some friendly tips.

Clients will happily ignore how much time is passing because the color correction process is so fun. Left to their own devices, some folks would spend their entire budget on the first scene of their movie. All I can say here is that it's good to learn to work quickly, and communication is absolutely key. Learn to interpret and anticipate what a particular client likes so that you can more efficiently cut to the chase. Also, there's an art to gently and diplomatically reminding clients of the scheduling constraints they've imposed upon you.

Get used to working at a steady pace. If you find yourself getting hung up on any one shot, make a note of it and move on. You'll have better luck later—trust me.

Lastly, bear in mind that there will always be changes during the final review session. Don't sweat it, but you can minimize them by keeping your eyes open as you initially work back and forth through the scenes, and don't be afraid to re-tweak any shots that stick out at you whenever you see them.

CHAPTER 10

QUALITY CONTROL AND BROADCAST SAFE

"Broadcast safe" is mentioned in many, many chapters of this book, on the assumption that most video professionals have at least a peripheral awareness of the importance of video signal standards. However, this chapter is intended to delve deeply into the subject of what broadcast safe means, to present a more complete picture of what you need to look for, and to show how you can deal with noncompliant video images in the most graceful way possible.

Digital $Y'C_BC_R$ video signals have defined ranges for signal overshoots and undershoots, which are those parts of the signal that go over and under the normally allowable limits based on how analog video was once recorded. Admittedly, it's easy to think that, since this signal range is defined by BT.709, you should be able to use the full range of digital code values to achieve even wider contrast ratios. Unfortunately, the truth for now is that you'll be constrained by current network standards whenever you grade for broadcast distribution.

For the uninitiated, a video signal is considered to be *broadcast safe*, or *broadcast legal*, if the measured luma and chroma of the signal fall within a prescribed range between *reference black* and *reference white*. Digital video signals can be measured in generic *units*, as a *percentage*, in analog form via *IRE* or *millivolts* (mV), or as an 8- or 10-bit numeric code value (64 through 940 is a common broadcast legal range within the 0–1023 code values of 10-bit video).

It's tempting—especially if you're not used to working in a broadcast environment—to wonder what all the fuss is about with all these broadcast legal issues. After all, nearly all consumer and professional video cameras are capable of recording video with super-white levels and extremely saturated color, and nothing prevents you from capturing, editing, and outputting such levels to tape or as digitally mastered files or discs. Furthermore, most, if not all, modern consumer Blu-ray, DVD, and tape devices record are capable of playing such levels without issue, while consumer monitors are capable of displaying these levels, assuming you've selected the correct menu settings (a sometimes difficult proposition).

Despite this rampant permissiveness on the production side of things, keeping your program broadcast legal—as of this writing—continues to be of paramount importance when handing off mastered programs for broadcast. Not respecting these levels will earn you the ire (as opposed to IRE) of the broadcast engineering team responsible for a particular network and will increase the likelihood of your program being rejected in their quality control (QC) process and sent back to you for further adjustments. This is not something you want to risk, especially if you're on a deadline, at least not if you want the client to continue working with you.

Even if you're not handing your program off for broadcast, keeping your video signal within legal levels guarantees a certain level of predictability with regards to how bright and saturated areas of the picture will look on the widest variety of displays. There are as many display technologies available to consumers as there are to professionals—including LCD, DLP, plasma, and OLED—and each has different menu options letting you choose how the upper and lower boundaries of a video input's signals are scaled to fit the reference black and reference white of the display. Given the fantastically diverse amount of consumer video equipment available, the concern is that there's no telling how any particular combination of excessively high-signal components will be handled or displayed.

For those of you dealing with archival analog tape-based formats such as Beta SP, illegal values pose a significant problem for other reasons. If your luma and chroma levels are too "hot" (high), you run the risk of interference with the timing signal on the tape, which, at its worst, can cause a complete loss of video sync, resulting in a garbled signal.

Before you begin color correcting any program that's destined for broadcast, it's crucial that you obtain the technical requirements from the specific broadcaster you'll be submitting to. After you've finished with the program and submitted it to the broadcaster, a video engineer will put your submitted program through a final QC process, checking to see whether your program's video signal contains any deviations from the network's standards.

A network's technical requirements are typically wide-ranging, covering aspects of the submitted program that include but are not limited to these:

- Approved source media formats, including what percentage of "low-quality" media formats is acceptable relative to a program's run time

- Approved mastering tape formats

- Approved methods for multiple-reel submissions

- Approved video formats, aspect ratios, and letterbox coverage

- Approved bars, tone, slate, timecode, and countdown requirements

- Closed captioning and audio requirements, including specific audio track assignments for stereo and surround sound channels

- Video signal requirements

Even the labeling of the tape and tape case may have specific requirements, and woe to the production company that hands off their media incorrectly. While all these rules sound draconian, they exist to make sure that the stressful and time-critical process of submitting your program to the network goes as smoothly as possible.

To avoid a possible rejection of your program by the broadcaster, it's in your best interest to take the time to make sure you're adhering to the requirements as closely as possible.

THE FUTURE OF BROADCAST SAFE AND HDR VIDEO

While the standards described in this chapter are a lowest-common denominator summary of the kinds of quality control guidelines you'll be required to adhere to from network to network *today*, the advent of emerging display technologies (mainly OLED and laser projectors), and specifically the promise of high-dynamic-range video, is causing some to question the necessity, and even the desirability, of clipping out-of-bounds signal excursions. Video imaging authority and author Charles Poynton has pointed out in conversation that it's perfectly possible to distribute and display full-range signals (should one choose the correct television menu settings) with digital code values from 4 to 1019 (as explained in following sections), which would provide additional headroom for exceptional highlights in the video signal rather than clipping video at the digital code values of 64 to 940.

This is not to say that, should full-range video signals become allowable for broadcast, the digital code value of 1094 would become the new ideal level for all of your highlights, but it would allow the "sparkly bits" of the image some extra room to shine. Furthermore, making the footroom of the signal available for broadcast would provide additional signal for retaining shadow detail that would otherwise be crushed. The overall result would be expanded dynamic range for viewing, but more importantly, not clipping the headroom and footroom of a digital video signal in the mastering process would, in Poynton's words, "make the future safe for high-dynamic-range video."

I am persuaded that increased contrast with brighter highlights is a desirable goal for our industry to move toward, and I would truly welcome the ability to let the highlights of my projects shine a little more brightly. However, as of the time of this writing, we're living in a broadcast-legal world, and the guidelines throughout the rest of this chapter still apply.

GRADING FOR FILM OUTPUT

When outputting an image sequence for film printing, you also need to observe the allowable minimum and maximum signal boundaries, so you know what parts of the image will be clipped as you make adjustments to color and contrast. The DPX and Kodak Cineon image sequence formats are RGB encoded and specify two values that define the minimum and maximum values allowable in an image destined for film output. These values are referred to as Dmin (the black point) and Dmax (the white point).

Typically these values are set to 96 Dmin and 685 Dmax for film output (assuming 10-bit images), unless the facility doing your film recording says differently. It's critical to check with the facility or lab in advance to find out what their specific requirements are. It might well save you a regrade and will definitely improve quality by giving you some guidance as to the allowable boundaries of image data so that you don't unknowingly clip the image.

If you're wondering how your color correction software's video scope analysis corresponds to Dmin and Dmax values, generally 0 percent is mapped to the Dmin value of 96, while 100 percent is mapped to the Dmax value of 685, with all other image values scaled linearly to fall between Dmin and Dmax. As always, check your color correction software's documentation for more details about this issue.

VIDEO SIGNAL STANDARDS AND LIMITS

NOTE

If you're interested in more detailed information, two good sources are the PBS Technical Operating Specifications (available at www.pbs.org/producers/) and the BBC DQ (Delivering Quality) TV Delivery for BBC Worldwide document (available at www.bbc.co.uk/guidelines/dq/contents/television.shtml).

This section examines the various ways in which video signals can be out of range and presents correction strategies. Individual broadcasters' standards vary, and it's always recommended that you check ahead for the specific QC standards that a particular program's broadcaster or distributor requires. Many broadcasters require that producers sign a "Deliverables" contract that stipulates how a program needs to be delivered; this often includes technical information about what levels are acceptable in the finished program.

This section points out what to look for and describes a set of general (and conservative) guidelines that are fairly common throughout the industry.

MEASURING Y'C$_B$C$_R$ ON A DIGITAL SCALE

Even though most video scopes and color correction tools default to using percentages, IRE, or millivolts, it's also good to understand the numeric encoding standards that are used for 8-bit, 10-bit, and RGB-encoded video for the increasing number of systems that support this analysis. For example, the DaVinci Resolve video scopes can be set to display the numeric code values to provide a direct evaluation of the digital signal levels in your media, which is valuable for understanding just how image data is encoded internally to your application.

The main point to remember is that Y'C$_B$C$_R$-encoded video is essentially an attempt to re-create an analog standard within the digital domain. As a result, portions of the overall digital numeric range are allocated to specific portions of the video signal as traditionally defined in analog video. RGB-encoded images have no such history to maintain, so they typically use the full digital numeric range that's available.

8-BIT PER CHANNEL Y'C$_B$C$_R$ NUMERIC ENCODING

The following values describe how 8-bit Y'C$_B$C$_R$ video clips are encoded:

- The overall 8-bit range is 0 to 255 (counting zero).
- The blacker-than-black range is 1 to 15 (unused, except for occasional camera noise).
- The Y' (luma) signal range is 16 to 235.
- The super-white range is 236 to 254.
- The range of each of the two color difference channels (Cb and Cr) is 16 to 240.
- No data is permissible at 0 and 255; these values are reserved for synchronization.

10-BIT PER CHANNEL Y'C$_B$C$_R$ NUMERIC ENCODING

The following values describe how 10-bit Y'C$_B$C$_R$ video clips are encoded:

- The overall 10-bit range is 0 to 1023 (counting zero).
- The blacker-than-black range is 4 to 63 (unused, except for occasional noise).
- 0 to 3 and 1020 to 1023 are restricted to timing reference.
- The Y' (luma) signal range is 64 to 940.
- The super-white signal range is 941 to 1019.
- The range of each of the two color difference channels (Cb and Cr) is 64 to 960.

12-BIT PER CHANNEL Y'C$_B$C$_R$ NUMERIC ENCODING

The following values describe how 12-bit Y'C$_B$C$_R$ video clips are encoded:

- The overall 12-bit range is 0 to 4095 (counting zero).
- The blacker-than-black range is 16 to 255 (unused, except for occasional noise).
- 0 to 16 and 4,080 to 4095 are restricted to timing reference.
- The Y' (luma) signal range is 256 to 3760.
- The super-white signal range is 3761 to 4079.
- The range of each of the two color difference channels (Cb and Cr) is 256 to 4079.

RGB NUMERIC ENCODING

There are three ways that 8-bit RGB color may be encoded.

- Full-range, 8-bit-per-channel RGB encodes color from 0 to 255. "White" is an RGB triplet of 255-255-255.

- Full-range, 16-bit-per-channel RGB encodes color from 0 to 65535.

- Studio-range, 8-bit RGB encodes color from 16 to 235 (this is not typical).

OTHER NUMERIC SCALES USED FOR IMAGE PROCESSING

Increasingly, digital cinema cameras capture 12-bit image data. Furthermore, most modern image processing applications are capable of 32-bit floating-point calculations, which are represented by many decimal places of precision within one's grading or compositing application. While 12-bit data and 32-bit image processing pipelines are fantastic for preserving image detail, these data ranges are not used for signal analysis as described in this chapter.

It's also interesting to note that image processing programs, such as compositing applications, often use image processing values in the 0–1 range to represent integer (8- or 10-bit) image signal values as adjusted by various parameters, where 0 represents the minimum value (black) and 1 represents the maximum value (white). So-called super-white values are preserved (if at all) via floating-point math as fractional values above 1.

REFERENCE WHITE

Reference white is the brightest white that's allowable in the luma component of a signal, typically corresponding to a digital code value of 940 for 10-bit video, 100 units if you're being generic, 100 percent on a digital scale, and 100 IRE or 700 mV on video scopes employing analog values.

> **NOTE**
> RGB source media generally won't have this problem, as the maximum 8-bit RGB levels of 255, 255, 255 are commonly scaled to the maximum video signal equivalent of 100 percent/IRE (700 mV).

The most frequent correction you'll find yourself making in most programs is to legalize the white level of every clip in a sequence by compensating for the super-white levels found in most camera original media.

When evaluating the white levels of clips in a program, you must understand the difference between reference white (shown in **Figure 10.1**, left), and super-white (also referred to as *headroom*), which is represented in the Waveform Monitor as the topmost section from 101 to 109 percent digital (Figure 10.1, right). Although most consumer and professional digital video cameras record overshoots above 100 percent and NLEs should happily preserve these super-white levels if they're present in an ingested clip, super-white isn't currently permitted in the majority of broadcast programming.

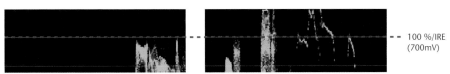

100 %/IRE
(700mV)

Maximum level at 100% white   Maximum levels in super-white range

Figure 10.1 Partial excerpts from the top of two Waveform graphs: 100 percent maximum white (left) and super-white (right).

Reference white is most effectively measured using a Waveform Monitor set to LOW PASS (LP), the commonly used name for the Waveform Monitor mode that filters out video signal chrominance and displays luma only. Alternately, a YRGB Parade Scope will give you the same analysis of the luma.

When mastering video, you must limit the maximum level of your signal to reference white, in part to avoid QC violations and in part because the network will probably be clipping this portion of the signal anyway. Even if you're simply creating a personal program to upload to a web video hosting service, you never know what combination of streaming devices and displays your video will make its way onto; even though web video, DVDs, and Blu-ray Discs are capable of containing super-white levels, you can't always be sure of every end user's setup.

REFERENCE WHITE VS. DIFFUSE WHITE

Given that reference white is the whitest thing allowable in an image, this absolute white level in a digital signal should be reserved for exceptional highlights, direct light sources, and things that should be self-illuminated or glowing. With that said, it's valuable to consider the notion of *diffuse white* when grading pictures that dally near the upper boundary of what's allowable. Diffuse white is the level of white on a bounce card held in front of the camera, which is the level of light reflecting off of soft clouds in the sky, and is generally considered to be 10 percent lower than reference white. Differentiation between diffuse white and reference white when you grade lets you maintain some contrast between the merely *bright* portions of an image and the portions of an image that you would consider *sparkly*.

BEING LESS CONSERVATIVE

Interestingly, European Broadcasting Union (EBU) Recommendation R103-2000 (used primarily by broadcasters using the PAL standard of video) recommends a luma signal range of –1 percent/IRE (6 mV) through 103 percent/IRE (735 mV). However, the extra 3 percent of latitude at the top of the scale is intended primarily for accidental overshoots, and I don't recommend making a habit of letting your video signal go that high if you're grading for broadcast.

> **NOTE**
>
> There continue to be regional differences in addition to those imposed by networks. While the 2013 PBS Technical Operating Specifications set reference white at 100 percent, the 2011 "Technical Standards for Delivery of Television Programmes to BBC Worldwide" specifies a slightly more permissive range for luma of –1 percent to 103 percent (–7 mV to 721 mV).

CHAPTER 10

BEING MORE CONSERVATIVE

On the other hand, some broadcasters are significantly more conservative with the maximum white levels they'll allow. If you know you'll be dealing with a stickler of an engineer who'll be QC'ing the daylights out of your project, you may want to consider maintaining an informal reference white level that's one or two percent lower than 100. This isn't too heartbreaking a compromise, and it will help ensure that any stray glints or highlights stay within the 100 percent if you're hand legalizing the picture (especially because software broadcast-safe filters aren't always perfect).

DIFFERING WHITE GUIDELINES FOR TITLES

Many broadcasters require that the peak luminance of electronically generated titles not exceed 90 percent/IRE (642 mV). The reasons for this will be covered later.

REFERENCE BLACK

Reference black is, correspondingly, the darkest black that's allowable in a signal. For all digital signals, reference black corresponds to a digital code value of 64 for 10-bit video, 0 units if you're being generic, 0 percent on a digital scale, and 0 IRE/mV on video scopes employing analog values.

While digital signals allow *footroom* (otherwise known as *undershoots* or blacker-than-black portions of the video signal that correspond to prior analog conventions), currently regions of black below reference black can trigger QC violations and are also generally clipped for broadcast.

There remains some confusion over what level reference black ought to be in different situations, mainly promulgated by industry veterans long used to analog conventions that no longer apply. I'll simplify this conversation by quoting the PBS Technical Operating Specifications for 2013, which are unambiguous: "Black level must be set to 0v on the Y' waveform. Black setup is not allowed in any digital submissions."

Interestingly, while you or your client may be fond of excessively crushed blacks in a program, not all broadcasters smile upon this particular stylization. To again quote the 2013 PBS TOC, "Objectionable black clipping must not be evident." It's worth repeating that excessively crushed blacks can average out poorly when digitally compressed at 8-bits-per-channel, with the result being unsightly macroblocking in the shadows of the broadcast image.

WHAT IS SETUP?

In the days of analog tape and $Y'P_BP_R$, *setup* was a deliberately elevated reference black setting of 7.5 IRE that allowed footroom in the video signal. However, this standard was used only for NTSC video in North America connected via analog $Y'C_BC_R$ using the Beta component standard (as when outputting to the analog Beta SP tape format). A black level of 7.5 IRE was also sometimes referred to as *pedestal*.

When outputting PAL (or NTSC in countries outside North America) via analog $Y'C_BC_R$ using the Beta component or SMPTE/N10 component standard, reference black was always 0 IRE/mV.

Today, this information is relevant only when accessing archival video on analog tape decks. When ingesting (or outputting) video to an analog deck, the driver software of your video interface usually controls the setup, whereas video decks may have either hardware switches or menu settings to accomplish this. However, for digital video, the notion of setup no longer exists and should be relegated to the dustbin of history.

CHROMA LEVELS

Although the guidelines for setting minimum and maximum luma levels in your program are black and white (sorry, I couldn't help myself), setting legal chroma levels is a considerably more complicated subject.

Digital and analog component video equipment is capable of recording and preserving extremely saturated color values, potentially up to or even exceeding 131 IRE.

> **NOTE**
> This ability to exceed 131 IRE is one reason why the graticules of many hardware scopes have room for excursions above white and below black of up to 40 additional units.

If present in a video signal, nonlinear editors (NLEs) will dutifully capture and preserve these excessively "hot" color values. Unfortunately, such high chroma values are rarely a good idea because they can cause unwanted artifacts such as loss of image detail and colors "bleeding" into one another at the border of oversaturated regions of the picture.

Even *more* problems occur when such hot chroma is encoded with the luma as an analog composite signal for purposes of broadcast. For all of these reasons, television broadcasters have strict requirements regarding acceptable chroma saturation.

Chroma can be measured using the vectorscope, by a Waveform Monitor set to its FLAT (FLT) monitoring mode, and by a variety of specialized gamut scopes. All of these will be covered in more detail later in this chapter.

RECOMMENDED CHROMA GUIDELINES

If you're providing a master tape for a particular broadcaster, always inquire as to their unique specifications. When in doubt, here are two recommendations:

- Peak Chrominance, which should be limited to temporary (also referred to as *transient*) highlights and spikes of color, should not exceed 110 percent digital/ IRE (785 mV). Some networks may allow transient peaks of up to 112 percent digital/IRE (800 mV), but don't ever take this for granted.

- Average Chrominance should be limited to 100 percent digital/IRE (700 mV) and under, depending on the lightness of the area in which it appears.

Unfortunately, oversaturated chroma is exceedingly easy to create (just think of your favorite glow operation), so you need to take care whenever you increase saturation or push one of the color balance controls toward a large correction.

WHAT CAUSES ILLEGAL CHROMA?

Chroma becomes illegal for three primary reasons.

- Any part of the chroma component of a signal exceeds the recommended maximum level. You can specifically monitor this in the vectorscope.

- A component RGB or YRGB Parade Scope measurement of each decoded color channel exceeds 100 percent/IRE (700 mV) or goes under 0 percent/IRE/mV.

- The composite of luma and chroma (seen in a gamut scope) exceeds the recommended maximum levels of 110 percent/IRE (785 mV) and the minimum level of –10 percent/IRE (–71 mV). You can monitor chroma at these highlight and shadow boundaries using a Waveform Monitor set to FLAT (FLT), where the luma and chroma are composited together for analysis.

These are the main causes of illegal chroma. However, they translate into the following predictable triggers of chroma illegality while evaluating and adjusting your clips:

- Certain hues are predisposed to becoming oversaturated. I find that high-energy reds and blues are the single biggest offender when it comes to undershoots (illegal saturation below 0), and yellows and deep blues seem to have an innate tendency to overshoot (illegal saturation above 100 percent [700 mV]), even when the other hues in the image are perfectly legal.

- The combination of high luma (bright highlights) and high saturation in the same part of the picture, especially in portions of the picture that appear above 85 to 90 percent in the Waveform Monitor, is a recipe for illegality. This is especially vexing because it's something you'll find yourself wanting to do (adding color to a bright sky, putting color into lighting highlights), and it's difficult to detect every stray pixel.

- Highly saturated values in really dark regions of the picture are also an unexpected source of illegal chroma levels. While it's technically possible to have saturation in portions of an image with low luma levels, absolute black is *supposed* to be completely desaturated. Even though subzero saturated regions will most likely be clipped to 0 by any display, most networks still consider this to be an illegal condition.

As you work, it's important to monitor your chroma levels with each adjustment you make.

RGB LEVELS

Most broadcasters have specific legalization requirements for the transformation of a $Y'C_BC_R$ video signal into component RGB, and any RGB-encoded color channel that goes above 100 percent/IRE (700 mV) or below 0 percent/IRE/mV is considered to be out of gamut. This standard is used by the 2013 PBS Technical Operating Specification document.

An acceptable tolerance for exceeding these minimum and maximum levels is defined by EBU Recommendation R103-2000, which states the following:

> When television signals are manipulated in YUV form, it is possible to produce "illegal" combinations that, when de-matrixed, would produce R, G, or B signals outside the range 0% to 100%. Ideally, there should be no illegal combinations in a television signal, but experience has shown that a certain tolerance can be allowed, based on similar tolerances allowed for RGB signals.

Accordingly, recommendation R103-2000 allows small RGB excursions between −5 percent/IRE (−35 mV) and 105 percent/IRE (735 mV), with the resultant luma signal lying inside the range of −1 percent to 103 percent (−7 mV to 721 mV). These standards are cited by the 2011 "Technical Standards for Delivery of Television Programmes to BBC Worldwide."

That said, it's still good practice to limit your average levels to between 0 and 100 percent. You can use the RGB Parade Scope to monitor the RGB transformation of a $Y'C_BC_R$ video signal to check for such illegal RGB values. Many networks pose this as a strict requirement, while others are more permissive of minor transient excursions. You'll want to check ahead to see what the specific guidelines are.

Similarly to "blacker-than-black" luma levels, any RGB levels that fall below 0 percent will most likely be clipped by the display device, be it LCD, DLP, plasma, OLED, or whatever technology is employed.

RGB levels above 100, on the other hand, are less predictable in how they'll be displayed. Most contemporary display technologies are capable of displaying this kind of headroom, so long as they're set up with the appropriate menu settings. For predictability and your own peace of mind, you may find it best to adhere to the legally prescribed limits to avoid unexpected artifacts.

NOTE
A bigger problem with hot YRGB levels for older analog signals and recording formats is when modulated values overlap the guard bands in the chrominance and audio carriers, causing cross-luminance artifacts and buzzing in the audio. This is the primary reason for rigorous standards adherence when working on broadcast programming.

GAMUT CHECKING SCOPES CAN HELP

Video scope manufacturers such as Tektronix and Harris Corporation have developed a variety of specialized (and patented) video scope displays specifically for checking composite (luma+chroma) and component (RGB encoded) gamut violations.

Although many of the functions covered by these gamut scopes overlap with things you can check using more conventional video scope displays like the vectorscope, Waveform Monitor, and RGB Parade Scope, they can make it easier to identify specific trouble spots in the images you're color correcting. Some of these scopes will be covered later in this chapter.

QUALITY CONTROL ISSUES THAT AFFECT COLORISTS

The following is a list of QC violations that you as the colorist are directly responsible for avoiding:

- Video level (white level)
- Black level
- Chroma level
- Excessive shadow/highlight clipping
- Image clarity (is the image distinguishable to the viewer?)

These additional QC violations may arise from the video format itself:

- Tape dropouts
- Compression artifacts
- Aliasing
- Bad video edits (with one-frame gaps or interlacing errors)
- Image faults such as dropouts, color smear, or dust and scratches

On top of all that, there are some QC violations that come from the way the project was originally shot:

- Focus
- White balance
- Moiré

For all of these reasons, many large postproduction facilities have both incoming and outgoing QC processes of their own. All material coming into the facility is checked for focus, white balance, clipping, and other issues that might be rectified while the shoot is still happening. This also gives the editor and colorist a heads-up for things to keep an eye on when they start working. An editor might want to avoid a particular take, for example, or a colorist may need to allocate additional time for a particular scene that is known to be problematic.

Prior to the delivery of the final product, the post facility may also put the finished program through an outgoing QC process of its own, preemptively checking for problems that the broadcaster's own QC process would reveal before handing it off. Regardless, after handoff, broadcasters perform a QC of their own on the program, just to triple-check.

> **NOTE**
> In some cases, broadcasters charge a fee for programs that are kicked back, so it's best to catch problems before they go out the door.

Once upon a time, a QC technician had to sit and watch the entire program using a set of scopes with alarms that indicated every error as it came up. These days, a variety of hardware- and software-based digital video scopes have the means to do an automatic QC pass, scanning the entire program autonomously and logging any detectable QC violations in a list, along with the timecode at which they occurred.

Either way, once you're presented with a list of QC violations, you'll need to go through the finished program one more time, adjusting your corrections further so that the program passes muster.

SIX STRUCTURED STEPS TO LEGALIZING YOUR PICTURE

Although the responsible way to work is to legalize clips individually as you grade each shot in a program, the process of legalization for broadcast can also be done in several stages, depending on the nature of the program and on the type of color correction you're doing. The following workflow may help you to organize your adjustments more efficiently:

1 Use the broadcast legal settings (sometimes called *clippers*) or Soft Clip settings in your color correction software to clamp or clip whatever out-of-bounds signal excursions you don't want to be bothered with legalizing and to provide a margin of safety for whatever corrections you're making. Some colorists like to work with the clipper turned off and turn it on at the end. I prefer to work with the clipper turned on so I can see my grades within the context of the clipper's automatic adjustments.

2 Individually legalize the white level of each clip by adjusting the Highlights (Log controls) or Gain and the Shadows (Log controls) or Lift contrast controls, while keeping an eye on the Waveform Monitor and Histogram as your guides.

Luma excursions are a *significant* error for most QC examinations, so you might want to consider making these adjustments according to the most conservative standard employed by those to whom you'll be submitting the program.

3 Make whatever corrections and adjustments are necessary to the color of each clip to achieve the required look. As you make these adjustments, carefully monitor the resulting changes to the clip's saturation in the vectorscope to make sure you don't stray outside the recommended limits. The good news is that you don't have to turn the saturation down on everything to legalize your picture (although this is sometimes the fastest solution). If the chroma of a particular subject in the clip is illegal but the majority of the clip is within legal limits, you can make a more targeted adjustment in the next two steps.

4 Manually adjust the saturation of specific chroma values that spike beyond the legal limits in the vectorscope using secondary correction or hue curves. Reds, magentas, blues, and yellows tend to be particularly guilty of unwanted excursions, so keep an eye on them in particular.

5 Use the Waveform Monitor set to LUMA (FLAT), or a gamut scope of some kind, to check for oversaturated highlight and shadow areas that will cause problems in composite broadcast. If necessary, you can desaturate the highlights and shadows of each clip without desaturating the otherwise legal midtone regions using either Shadows/Highlights saturation controls, a secondary correction isolating the highlights, or a Saturation vs. Luma curve.

6 If you're in a round-trip workflow and you're sending the final graded program back to an NLE, you can apply whatever broadcast legal filter, effect, or setting your NLE provides to the overall program in order to catch any stray values that may have gotten by your color correction application's clipper (no clipper is perfect). If you're outputting to tape and you want an extra margin for safety, you can use a hardware legalizer connected inline to clamp any stray values that are output from your video interface.

MONITORING AND LEGALIZING SATURATION IN DETAIL

Although it's always important to keep the overall saturation of your image to safe-for-broadcast levels, it's particularly important to control how much saturation appears in the highlights and shadows of your image.

Just to warn you, a frequent response to the question of how much saturation in different parts of a video signal is allowable for broadcast is "It depends." Some broadcasters are fairly permissive, while others have a reputation for being really stringent. Because of this, it pays to communicate with the video engineers at whichever station you'll eventually be handing your program. They can warn you what to look out for and give you more specific guidelines about what levels are and are not allowable.

Before you can fix a potential problem, you have to know it's there, and as always, the video scopes are there to help you. Here are some different ways of analyzing saturation to identify and fix specific issues.

SPOTTING AND FIXING OVERSATURATION USING THE VECTORSCOPE

You typically monitor the overall saturation of your programs using the vectorscope. The distance of a plotted value from the center of the scope shows its degree of saturation as a digital percentage.

A conservative way of quickly spot-checking the legality of chroma is to imagine a boundary connecting the 75 percent R, Mg, B, Cy, G, and Yl color bar targets that appear within the vectorscope (**Figure 10.2**). As long as the vectorscope graph fits within this boundary, you can be fairly sure your levels are legal.

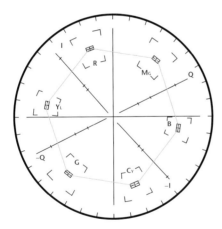

Figure 10.2 The blue line indicates the outer boundary that's used as a general rule of thumb for legalizing saturation in the vectorscope.

That's the simple rule of thumb. However, the truth is that the actual range of permissible levels of saturation is not quite so easily defined. In general, higher levels of saturation are permissible in the midtones of an image, while lower levels of saturation are permissible in highlights and shadows. On top of that, the extremes of permissible saturation vary with hue, and these extremes differ in the shadows and highlights, as illustrated in **Figure 10.3**.

Figure 10.3 Three different color-coded boundaries show different clipping thresholds for saturation depending on the overlapping luma intensity. Notice that different hues have different thresholds depending on the lightness of the image.

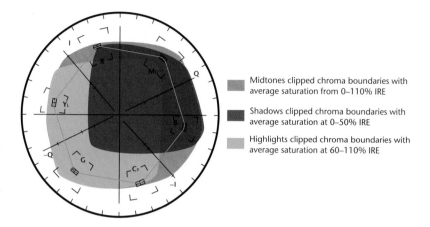

■ Midtones clipped chroma boundaries with average saturation from 0–110% IRE

■ Shadows clipped chroma boundaries with average saturation at 0–50% IRE

■ Highlights clipped chroma boundaries with average saturation at 60–110% IRE

The only limitation to using the vectorscope to monitor the legal chroma limits in your program is that you can't tell which highly saturated regions correspond to areas of high or low luma. Fortunately, there is another tool you can use to make this determination: a Waveform Monitor set to FLAT (FLT), covered later in this chapter.

If you have an image with excursions outside of this boundary in the vectorscope, there are a variety of possible solutions, depending on what the problem is.

TURN SATURATION DOWN

This may sound blindingly obvious, but before you get too tricky, see whether simply lowering the overall saturation of the image will fix your problem. It can be easy to overlook the simple (and fast) solution.

USE A SECONDARY TO ISOLATE THE OFFENDING HUE

Every once in a while, you'll have a clip or two with a particularly stubborn hue that insists on being oversaturated. The hue to blame is usually red, although yellow and magenta are also repeat offenders. If you try to lower the saturation of the overall clip to correct this, you'll end up with an unhappily desaturated image—not what you want.

In **Figure 10.4**, the saturation of the overall image is fine, but the light that's hitting the shoulder of the woman's sweater is causing a cyan highlight that's stretching beyond the inner box of the vectorscope's cyan target. Not only is this unlikely to pass any broadcaster's QC, it's probably going to be flattened by an automatic clipper.

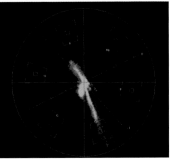

Figure 10.4 The original, uncorrected image.

Lowering the overall saturation would bring the cyan highlight into line but at the expense of reducing overall color intensity of the shot, changing its look. You don't always want to desaturate an entire image to fix just one illegal element.

In situations like this, one of the easiest solutions is to make a secondary correction using your program's HSL Qualifiers to isolate the range of values that are egregiously high (**Figure 10.5**). Often, using your application's eyedropper tool to scrub the offending area will suffice. Make sure your qualification is fairly soft so that your correction blends in with the image.

Figure 10.5 Isolating the illegally saturated subject using the Limit Effect controls. Once they are isolated, it's easy to reduce the saturation of only the offending hues.

Then, it's a simple thing to lower the Saturation parameter to bring the offending subject back to a reasonable level (**Figure 10.6**).

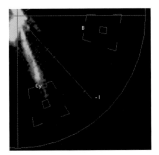

Figure 10.6 Lowering the saturation within your HSL Qualification reduces the targeted cyan highlight on the woman's shoulder.

CHAPTER 10

If you compare the manually and automatically legalized images, you can see the advantage to taking care of this yourself. The top image in **Figure 10.7**, which was manually legalized, has much more image detail; you can clearly see the weave of the shirt, and there's no artificial flattening. In the automatically clipped version on the bottom, all fine detail is flattened by the clipper's aggressive legalization. Because of this kind of clipping, oversaturated chroma can overwhelm fine detail in the same way that overexposed highlights do.

Figure 10.7 At top, the woman's shoulder has been manually legalized with HSL Qualification. At bottom, the woman's shoulder has been automatically legalized with a broadcast-safe filter, or clipper.

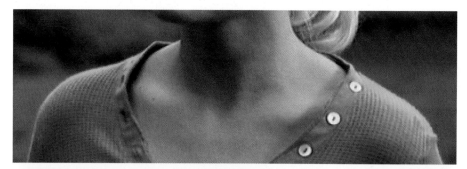

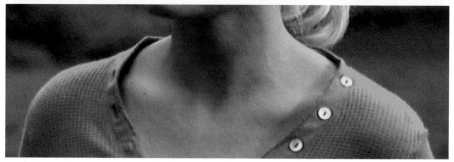

This is a great technique to use in situations where there's a specific hue that's causing problems.

KEY ALL OVERSATURATED, OVERLY BRIGHT HUES

If there's an entire range of hues that are going out of bounds, you can still use HSL Qualification to make the fix. In this case, though, you need to turn off the Hue qualifier and use only the Saturation and Luma controls to isolate all hues that fall above a particular range.

For example, the following shot of a police car has alternating red and blue lights that go way off the recommended vectorscope targets for broadcast legality (**Figure 10.8**).

 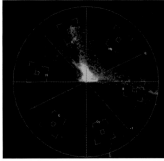

Figure 10.8 The saturated strobe lights of the police car are definitely not legal for broadcast.

To catch all the illegal values, no matter what the hue, you can set up a qualification that ignores hue and is focused on the most saturated colors found within the brightest highlights; just turn off the Hue qualifier and manually adjust the Saturation and Luma qualifiers (**Figure 10.9**, left) to isolate the offending regions of the picture (**Figure 10.9**, right).

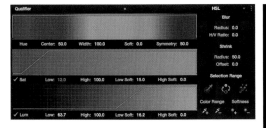 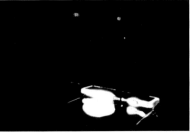

Figure 10.9 At left is a qualifier set up to isolate the brightest and most saturated pixels, shown in DaVinci Resolve. At right is the resulting matte with which you can desaturate these values to legalize all of the lights without affecting anything else.

This is a great technique to use with any shot that contains rapid and unpredictably changing lighting, such as a concert stage show or a nighttime establishing shot of Las Vegas with an abundance of neon lighting (all of which is illegal for broadcast, I guarantee you).

USE A HUE CURVE OR VECTOR CONTROL TO LOWER A SPECIFIC OVERSATURATED HUE

This next technique is limited to color correction applications that have hue curves used for adjusting hue, saturation, and luma within specific ranges of hue (**Figure 10.10**). These curves are covered in more detail in Chapter 5.

Figure 10.10 The Hue vs. Sat curve in DaVinci Resolve (found in the Curves palette).

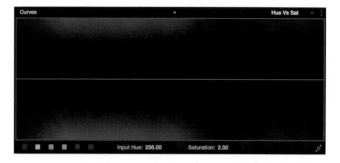

Using a Hue vs. Saturation curve, you can add control points to sections of the curve that correspond to the range of hues that needs legalizing (**Figure 10.11**).

Figure 10.11 The Hue vs. Sat curve adjusted to selectively lower the red color in the car. Notice how control points are placed to isolate the red portion of the curve, which is then dragged down to desaturate only the reds in the image.

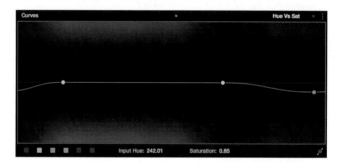

> **NOTE**
>
> Quantel Pablo (in its Fettle curves interface) provides means for sampling colors in an image to provide a guide showing the segment of the curve that corresponds to the sample pixel.

This technique can be extremely fast. Also, because the adjustment is made using a curve, rather than a mask, Hue vs. Saturation curves work wonderfully in situations where the offending subject may be difficult to key using the HSL Qualifiers or when the HSL Qualifiers result in jagged edges or artifacts in the resulting mask.

However, when you're aggressively legalizing a narrow range of hue, there's a danger that the gentle falloff between the affected and unaffected areas, which is the hue curve's greatest advantage, results in desaturating parts of the image that you didn't want to be affected by the hue adjustment. A common example is where you're trying to desaturate an aggressive red element but you end up desaturating human skin tone as well, since those values are right next to red. In these instances, you may be better off using HSL Qualification instead.

SPOTTING AND FIXING HIGHLIGHT AND SHADOW OVERSATURATION

The Waveform Monitor is an invaluable tool for monitoring the saturation of your images at the outer boundaries of the highlights and the shadows when set to FLAT (FLT). In this mode, the Waveform Monitor looks very different—image saturation is superimposed over the luma graph in such a way that you can see how highly saturated the highlights, midtones, and shadows are by the thickness of the graph at different heights on the scale.

Compare the following Waveform Monitor displays: the top image (**Figure 10.12**, top) is the Waveform Monitor set to LOW PASS (LP) that shows only the luma of the signal, while the image below it is the same image analyzed with the Waveform Monitor set to FLAT (FLT), which composites the chroma and luma together.

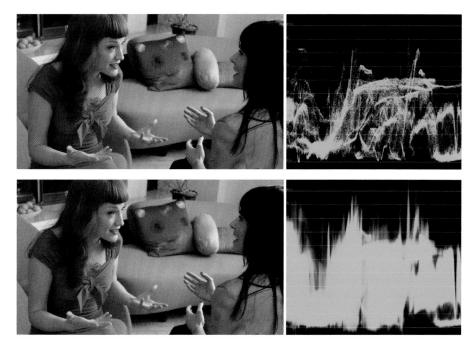

Figure 10.12 At top, the Waveform Monitor set to display luma only (LOW PASS). At bottom, the same image on the Waveform Monitor set to composite luma and chroma in FLAT (FLT) mode.

When in FLAT (FLT) mode, a thicker graph indicates higher saturation in that zone of image tonality (as shown in Figure 10.12), while a thinner graph indicates lower saturation (**Figure 10.13**).

Figure 10.13 An image with lower saturation has a thinner graph when analyzed by a Waveform Monitor set to FLAT (FLT).

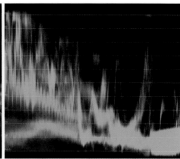

Why is this important? It turns out that greater levels of saturation are allowable in the midtones of an image than in the highlights and shadows. Although you can always legalize an image by turning down the *overall* saturation, it may be overkill and will limit your ability to deliver dazzling imagery. If you want to work your magic with highly saturated clips, it's important to know how to monitor and lower saturation where you don't want it so that you can raise saturation where you do want it.

It's important to pay attention to the saturation analysis in the Waveform Monitor (and also in the RGB Parade Scope, as you'll see next). For example, **Figure 10.14** has saturation levels that look perfectly innocent in the vectorscope.

Figure 10.14 This image appears to have legal saturation according to the vectorscope.

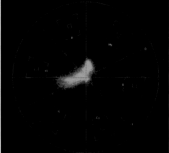

In fact, this image has problematically high saturation in the highlights that can be seen only by viewing the Waveform Monitor in FLAT (FLT) mode (**Figure 10.15**).

If you're working on a program with strict standards, be sure to look for excessive saturation excursions rising above reference white or falling below reference black on the Waveform Monitor's graph when Saturation is turned on.

Since the particular quality control standard to which you're adhering defines what "excessive" really means, you'll need to check with your specific broadcaster's recommendations. Extremely strict broadcasters may not allow any excursions at all, while a more reasonable broadcaster following EBU Technical Recommendation R103-2000 may allow excursions of up to –5 and 105 percent, respectively.

Figure 10.15 Looking at the Waveform Monitor with Saturation turned on reveals that there's excessive saturation in the highlights.

If you have so much saturation in your highlights and/or shadows that you need to reduce, here are some solutions.

LOWER YOUR HIGHLIGHTS TO PRESERVE SATURATION

An area of a picture that commonly suffers from the intersection of highlights and saturation is skin highlights. Because the skin is translucent, bright highlights often result in pools of hot orange. This may be a deliberate mechanization of the cinematographer, or it might simply be happenstance, but if you elect to preserve this effect as the look for your image, you'll have to do something to make sure these areas don't get clipped by a legalizer.

The image in **Figure 10.16** is a perfect example. The saturation of the highlight on the woman's face, when seen in the vectorscope, seems fine.

 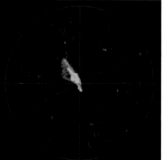

Figure 10.16 The original image seems to have perfectly legal saturation.

However, when you view it in the Waveform Monitor when it is set to FLAT (FLT), you can see that there's a saturation excursion rising well above 100 percent/IRE (**Figure 10.17**).

Figure 10.17 A waveform set to FLAT (FLT) reveals saturation excursions above 100 percent/IRE (700 mV).

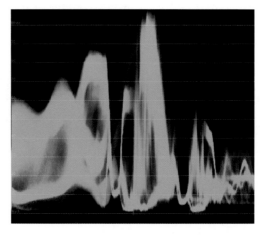

The simple fix, to preserve saturation within these highlights and maintain the "golden glow" look is to simply lower the Highlights contrast control. You may need to increase overall saturation to compensate for the minor reduction in overall saturation that this will cause (if you're using an RGB processing operation), and you might need to boost midtone contrast as well to prevent unwanted darkening of the image (**Figure 10.18**).

Figure 10.18 Lowering the white point, and slightly raising the midtone contrast and overall image saturation to compensate, also brings the highlight saturation down to an acceptable level, with only minor alterations to the image.

 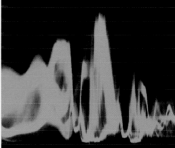

The result is an image that retains all the color within the highlights (in fact, with the highlights no longer being clipped by a legalizer, there may be even more color), at the expense of a few percentage points of lightness that nobody will miss.

USE HIGHLIGHTS AND SHADOWS SATURATION CONTROLS

Oftentimes, the simplest and easiest solution for oversaturation in the highlights and/or shadows is to eliminate it. This provides the added bonus of producing clean white highlights and neutral, black shadows, if that's the look you're going for. For this reason, some color correction let you modify the effect of a saturation control by a selectable tonal range (**Figure 10.19**).

Check your documentation to learn more about the functionality of your particular system.

Figure 10.19 In Adobe SpeedGrade, the tonal range buttons at the top of the Look tab modify the functionality of the saturation slider, letting you make simple saturation adjustments to specific tonal regions of the image.

USE AN HSL QUALIFIER TO DESATURATE SPECIFIC REGIONS OF HIGHLIGHT OR SHADOW

Some color correction applications lack dedicated Highlights/Shadows saturation controls. Another way of doing the same thing—and a more flexible technique—is to employ a secondary correction using your application's HSL Qualifiers, with the Hue and Saturation controls turned off, to pull a luma key of whatever range of highlights or shadows you need to desaturate.

For example, the image in **Figure 10.20** has illegal saturation within a broad portion of the highlights.

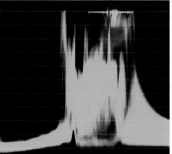

Figure 10.20 The original image, with saturation excursions in the highlights.

Using an HSL Qualifier, you can isolate the upper highlights using only the Luma control (**Figure 10.21**, left). This creates a mask that isolates only the likely areas that need to be desaturated (Figure 10.21, right).

Figure 10.21 To the left, an HSL Qualifier set to key luma only. To the right, the resulting matte that isolates the brightest highlights, ready to be desaturated.

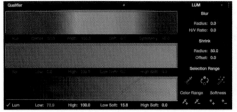

Now, you can simply lower the saturation control to legalize the image. Usually, you'll lower saturation by somewhere around half and then readjust the qualifier controls to encompass a wider or narrower range of values, as necessary, to bring most (if not all) the saturation excursions to within 100 percent/IRE.

In this example, we needed to reduce saturation to nearly 0 percent to eliminate saturation excursions in the highlights (**Figure 10.22**).

Figure 10.22 Desaturated high-lights in the window to legalize the signal.

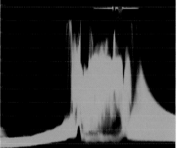

This technique is not just useful for legalization but any time you want to exert custom control over the saturation in different tonal zones of an image.

By the way, you win a gold star if you observed that, in Figure 10.22, there is satura-tion in the shadows that falls below 0 percent (an undershoot) that also needs to be eliminated for this image to be completely broadcast legal.

One way to kill two birds with one stone would be to isolate the midtones using an HSL Qualifier and then desaturate both the lightest highlights and the darkest shadows by applying the correction to an inverted matte or to the outside of the qualifier, whichever method your color correction system employs. If you're going to desaturate the shadows, *be gentle*. It's easy to inadvertently desaturate too much of the shadows, robbing your image of richness. Pay particular attention to skin tones to make sure you don't drain the color from people's faces.

USING SATURATION VS. LUMA CURVES

One last possibility, if your application supports it, is to use a saturation vs. luma curve to desaturate parts of the image that go out of bounds (**Figure 10.23**).

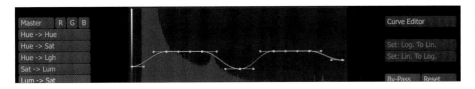

Figure 10.23 A Saturation vs. Luma curve, as shown in Assimilate Scratch, lets you precisely control saturation throughout the tonal range of your image.

This is an extremely flexible approach, with the added advantage that it can desaturate both the shadows and highlights in a single operation, as well as selectively boost saturation elsewhere in the image.

RGB COLOR SPACE LEGALITY AND THE RGB PARADE SCOPE

This last saturation issue is similar to the problem of unwanted saturation in the highlights and shadows, but it manifests itself in a different way. You need to watch for any portions of the Red, Green, or Blue waveforms in the Parade Scope that extend above 100 percent/IRE (700 mV) or below 0 percent/IRE/mV. Again, whether any excursions are allowable in the RGB Parade Scope depends on the quality control standard you need to adhere to.

If you're not legalizing to strict standards, keep in mind that while in many cases limited RGB excursions will be fine, overly strong spikes in one or more color channels can result in unwanted artifacts or loss of image detail (**Figure 10.24**).

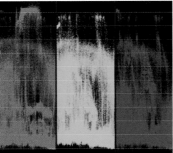

Figure 10.24 The RGB parade analysis shows unwanted saturation in the highlights of the red and blue color channels, extending above 100 percent.

Some color correction applications, and most NLEs, include RGB limiting as part of the functionality of their broadcast-legal filters or settings, which basically clip any color information above and below the legal boundaries in the RGB Parade Scope. Although effective, relying on a software or hardware limiter to clip your levels can also result in unwanted artifacts in the region of the picture where the clipping is happening. As always, it's in your interest to manually correct these areas of the image as much or as little as is necessary to make sure you're getting the results you want.

If a clip shows RGB Parade Scope excursions above 100 or below 0 percent, a variety of solutions follow.

VIDEO SCOPE SIGNAL FILTERING TO ELIMINATE SPURIOUS TRANSIENTS

It turns out that the mathematical process of converting $Y'C_BC_R$ into RGB signals for monitoring with a video scope can result in small out-of-bounds transients that, although a nonissue for actual broadcast and transmission, are good at triggering errors in video scopes. These transient errors make it difficult to do colorfully creative grades because they're always warning you to back off, when really it's not at all necessary. For this reason, EBU R103-2000 specifies "…the use of appropriate filters in all measurement channels… A suitable filter is specified in IEEE-205."

Furthermore, Tektronix has acknowledged this issue, boasting a proprietary low-pass filter in their gamut scopes to eliminate what they refer to as "false alarms." For more information, see Tektronix's various application notes for the Diamond and Lightning displays.

NEUTRALIZE COLOR CASTS IN SHADOWS AND HIGHLIGHTS

This one is in the "so simple it's easy to forget" category. Areas of the image that correspond to 100 percent are special in that they're generally reserved for actual, pure white. It follows that areas of the image that correspond to 0 percent are reserved for solid black. Given these two generalizations, an easy way of correcting unwanted spikes at the upper and lower boundaries of the Parade Scope is to eliminate any color casts that occur within the highlights or shadows by balancing all three channels using either the color balance controls or your application's RGB curves.

LOWER THE HIGHLIGHTS IN ORDER TO RETAIN SATURATION

If you're color correcting a sunrise or sunset image or some other bit of vivid imagery that you want to be as colorful as possible but the lightness is making your image's color illegal, a simple way to solve the problem is to lower the highlights.

I realize that you want the image to be bright, but keep in mind that lowering the highlights will allow you to retain greater saturation throughout the image, which will make it more energetic even though you're making it a bit less light. Done correctly, this is an excellent trade-off.

DESATURATE THE HIGHLIGHTS AND SHADOWS

This is the same advice given in the previous section. Since RGB spikes are attributable to colorations at the outer boundaries of the highlights and shadows, simply desaturating the highlights and shadows as discussed in the previous section will help you fix the problem. You can do this with Shadows and Highlights saturation controls, if present, or you can use an HSL qualifier to isolate a range of illegal saturation within the highlights and shadows to desaturate.

LEGALIZING RGB USING CURVES

I've saved the best for last. One of the easiest fixes for out-of-gamut RGB excursions is to add a control point or two near the top of the red, green, or blue curve controls that correspond to the color channels that are out of bounds in the RGB Parade Scope, make sure the RGB curves aren't ganged together, and then drag the topmost control point down until the tops of the offending color channel waveforms dip just underneath 100 percent/IRE (**Figure 10.25**).

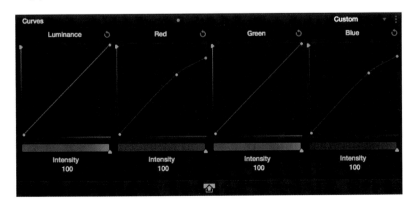

Figure 10.25 The tops of the out-of-bounds red and blue channels have been brought back down to under 100 percent by creating downward curves at the very top of the Red curve control. Some applications refer to this sort of an adjustment as *knee* or *soft clipping*, which describes the gentle roll-off this technique provides.

The result might noticeably alter the color in the highlights (just barely), but the image will be legal (**Figure 10.26**), and you can use this as a starting point for further adjustments, if necessary.

Figure 10.26 The correction smoothly limits the red and blue channels, while having little to no effect on the rest of the image.

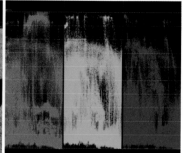

Learning to control image saturation with the precision that curves provide will give you the ability to craft more creative looks in the programs you correct, while maintaining a video signal that's safe for broadcast. The resulting images will display predictably on the widest variety of monitoring devices.

SOFT CLIPPING FOR LUMA AND RGB

DaVinci Resolve has a soft clip feature that, while not a full-blown legalizer (it does nothing to legalize gamut violations), does have the virtue of allowing you to retrieve detail from blown-out highlights and crushed shadows by compressing the very top and bottom of the signal, letting you push your levels harder to achieve a more intense grade while rolling off the portions of the signal being clipped at the top and bottom of the image more softly.

In **Figure 10.27**, the contrast has been stretched by a significant margin, giving pop and vibrance to the image. However, the highlights and shadows are sharply clipped as a result.

Figure 10.27 A high-contrast grade clips the boundaries of image detail.

By raising the Low Soft and High Soft parameters in the Soft Clip mode of the Curves palette, image detail can be retrieved from the top highlights and the bottom shadows, all the while keeping the majority of your contrast boost intact (**Figure 10.28**). The effect is similar to rolling off the tops and bottoms of the RGB curves, except that the result extends beyond the range of the top and bottom curve control points.

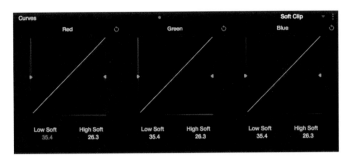

Using Soft Clip can provide a result that appears to all the world as more of a halated glow, rather than an aliased edge. Using Soft Clip can also allow you to get away with having a bit more saturation near the edges of your highlights and shadows.

Figure 10.28 Using Soft Clip to retrieve image detail and control the levels of your signal, while keeping the contrast and saturation high overall.

OTHER VIDEO SCOPE OPTIONS FOR BROADCAST GAMUT MONITORING

Other types of displays and out-of-gamut warnings are available in outboard scopes from various manufacturers. Although traditionally colorists haven't used these types of displays during sessions (gamut checking was once the province of the video engineer), nowadays most modern color correction suites have video scopes with one or another type of gamut monitoring, and they make rigorous legalization of your video signals that much easier if you're a colorist who works on a lot of broadcast programming.

Gamut scopes are concerned with monitoring the levels of composite signals, where luma and chroma are encoded together for distribution, and with RGB conversion, where a $Y'C_BC_R$ signal is mathematically changed to RGB.

THE TEKTRONIX GAMUT DISPLAYS

Tektronix has three proprietary, patented video scope displays that make it easier to identify and troubleshoot specific gamut conversion errors.

THE DIAMOND DISPLAY

This display shows two diamond outlines arranged vertically, one over the other. An alternate version of this scope, called the Split Diamond display, offsets the top and bottom diamonds to make it easier to see the center point, where both diamonds touch (**Figure 10.29**). This makes it easy to evaluate neutral black in an image, similar to the center point of a vectorscope.

Figure 10.29 Tektronix Split Diamond display, which shows an analysis of the RGB conversion of a signal in order to identify out-of-gamut excursions. Blue is plotted against green, while red is plotted against minus green.

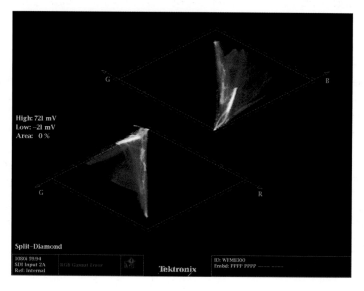

The red, green, and blue components of the image are represented by a graph in the center with the following characteristics:

- Black is represented by the center point where the top and bottom diamonds meet, although they don't actually connect in the Split Diamond display. If the bottom of the graph in the top diamond and the top of the graph in the bottom diamond don't touch this central area, it's not pure black.

- White is represented by the top of the diamond above and the bottom of the diamond below. If the top of the top graph and the bottom of the bottom graph don't touch these points, they're not pure white.

- The entire range of desaturated grays is represented by the center connecting the top and bottom of each diamond. A completely desaturated image with a range of dark to light grays will be perfectly centered in the top and bottom graphs. This makes it easy to spot color casts if the signal veers off to the left or right.

- The strength of the red channel is represented by excursions in the graph stretching toward the lower-right border of the bottom diamond (labeled "R").

- The strength of the blue channel is represented by excursions in the graph stretching toward the lower-right border of the top diamond (labeled "B").

- The strength of the green channel is represented by excursions in the graph stretching toward the lower-left border of the top diamond *and* by excursions toward the upper-left border of the bottom diamond (labeled "G" and "–G").

With this graph, the borders of each diamond indicate the outer legal boundaries of each color channel. All legal color values fall within the diamonds, and illegal color values cross the border to fall outside of the diamonds. The specific border that the illegal values cross indicates exactly which colors are illegal, guiding you to a suitable correction.

NOTE

Tektronix application note 25W-15609, Preventing Illegal Colors (www.tek.com/Measurement/App_Notes/25_15609/25W_15609_0.pdf), has detailed information about the Diamond display and its use.

THE ARROWHEAD DISPLAY

The scope in **Figure 10.30** displays a graph that's flat on the left and pointed to the right (similar to its namesake), with a scale indicating the strength that each outer border indicates. This graph displays the composite combination of luma and chroma in order to indicate out-of-gamut saturation in the highlights and shadows of an image.

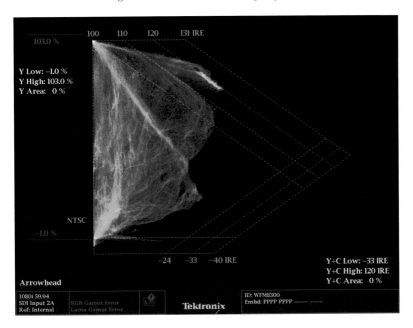

Figure 10.30 The Tektronix Arrowhead display, which displays a composite analysis of the signal used for spotting out-of-gamut saturation in the highlights and shadows.

The flat left side of the graph plots luma vertically, with black falling at the bottom-left corner and white at the top-left corner. Chroma is plotted horizontally, with 0 percent chroma at the left of the graph and the various targets at the right diagonal edge showing various levels of maximum chroma, letting you choose the boundary that corresponds to your particular QC standard.

NOTE

Tektronix application note 25W-15609, Preventing Illegal Colors, has detailed information about the Arrowhead display and its use.

If any part of the graph crosses the upper-right diagonal edge corresponding to the allowable signal strength for your QC standard (110 IRE is a common standard for NTSC video), it indicates an illegal amount of chroma, while the vertical height at which the excursion appears indicates the corresponding lightness level (or range of image tonality) where the oversaturation is occurring.

THE SPEARHEAD DISPLAY

The triangular Spearhead display shown in **Figure 10.31** does a lightness, saturation, and value (LSV) analysis of the image. It's similar to the Arrowhead display but is intended to combine analysis of RGB errors and oversaturation at various levels of signal value in order to correct out-of-gamut errors.

Figure 10.31 Tektronix Spearhead display.

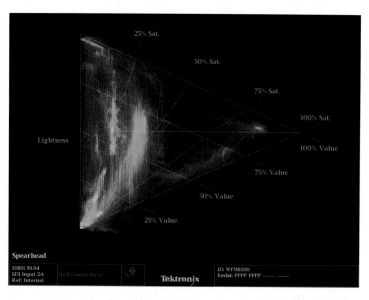

Lightness is represented by the vertical left side of the triangle (black at the bottom, white at the top). Saturation is represented by the diagonal upper-right side (0 percent at the top left, 100 percent at the bottom right). The bottom-right diagonal side of the triangle represents the value

For more information about these displays, see the Tektronix website (www.tek.com).

THE HARRIS DIGITAL GAMUT IRIS DISPLAY

Harris Videotek has a different patented gamut display for checking RGB or Composite gamut errors, called the Digital Gamut Iris display (**Figure 10.32**).

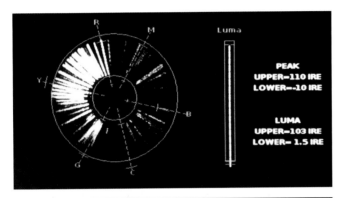

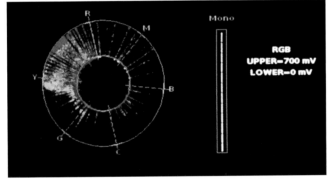

Figure 10.32 The Harris Digital Gamut Iris display for either Composite (top) or RGB (bottom) signal monitoring uses the same layout.

The Iris display can be set for either RGB or Composite monitoring, but it uses the same layout in either mode. Shaped like the iris of an eye, the inner boundary corresponds to legal minimum signal strength, and the outer boundary corresponds to legal maximum signal strength.

The graph consists of a series of excursions that stretch between the inner and outer circles. Similar to the vectorscope display, the angle around the circumference of this display indicates the hue of the analyzed signal. This way, the hue of illegal excursions stretching past the outside of the outer or the inside of the inner boundaries is easily identified, and you can take steps to legalize the problem.

CREATING GRAPHICS AND ANIMATION WITH LEGAL VALUES

As you color correct programs, remember that video clips aren't the only source of possible illegal video levels. Whenever you're dealing with a title card or a graphic created in another application for use in an NLE's project or whether you're creating title cards of graphics within your NLE or finishing system, you need to make sure you choose the colors carefully.

Typical 24-bit RGB images employ 8 bits per channel; in other words, there are 256 levels of color for each channel (0–255). When you import an image into an Apple Final Cut Pro sequence that's set to a $Y'C_BC_R$ codec, the color values are converted into the $Y'C_BC_R$ color space (for 8-bit video, this range is 16–235, with higher and lower values reserved for other image data). When this happens, the RGB colors may be too bright and saturated, and they may translate into luma and chroma levels that are too hot for broadcast, especially when used as titles.

WHAT'S SO SPECIAL ABOUT TITLES?

It's natural to wonder, why do the luma and saturation of titles need to be so much more conservative than other portions of your video signal? The reason is that titles consist of pure regions of color with sharp, contrasting borders between each letter of text and the surrounding background color. These high-contrast borders translate into sudden changes in brightness when RGB is converted to $Y'C_BC_R$, and if these sudden changes are too high, they can cause problems for broadcasters. **Figure 10.33** shows an example of this problem.

Figure 10.33 Excursions resulting from a high-contrast title graphic, as shown on the RGB Parade of an outboard video scope. The bright flat region at the top of each color channel graph indicates the maximum level of the graphic (attenuated to .65 mV for legalization); the small excursions above it indicate the spikes that can result when encoding this signal.

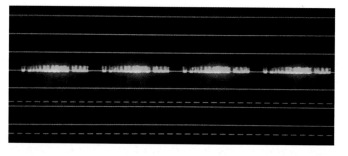

Such high-contrast borders result in small, fuzzy excursions at the top of the luma graph in a Waveform Monitor or the red, green, and blue graphs of the Parade Scope that can go much higher than the image itself. This issue isn't limited to designer-created graphics, either. High-contrast black-and-white photography or a scanned image of a newspaper headline or photograph (black text on near white with half-tone aliasing) can cause the same problems.

Although the results may look perfectly fine on your broadcast monitor, they won't necessarily be broadcast legal. For this reason, you must be even *more* careful when choosing colors for titles and graphics than for other color-correction adjustments you might make. For this reason, the maximum preferred white value for most broadcasters is 235, 235, 235, which sits at about 93 percent/IRE when analyzed using a Waveform Monitor. This is the brightest white you should use in your titles in order to be on the safe side when you are handing off your finished master to the client. However, some broadcasters are stricter, preferring that no title exceed 90 IRE. To most easily accommodate these requirements, RGB color values of 224, 224, 224 create a white level that sits right at 90 percent digital on a Waveform Monitor.

Now, before you start working in your favorite image editing application and worrying that your whites are going to look gray, remember that the viewer's perception of white is entirely relative to the brightness of the colors surrounding your titles. To prove this to you, the text at the top in **Figure 10.34** is exactly the same level of brightness as the text at the bottom.

WHITE WHEN IMPORTING GRAPHICS

When you transcode any RGB image or digital media file to a $Y'C_BC_R$ format, all of the RGB color values are scaled to corresponding $Y'C_BC_R$ color values. Ideally, your application will remap the white values in the imported image (255, 255, 255) to 100 percent digital/IRE (700 mV), the maximum broadcast legal signal. Black (0,0,0) should be mapped to 0 percent digital/IRE/mV, with all of the values in between smoothly scaled to fit the appropriate range.

CHOOSING COLORS IN ANOTHER APPLICATION FOR USE IN BROADCAST

Choosing colors is a more complicated subject. When you're designing still or motion graphics for use in a broadcast program, remember that colors that look vivid when output to video can look dull when viewed on your computer's display.

Many image editing applications have a video color-safe filter of some kind. For example, Photoshop has the Video > NTSC Colors filter, which automatically adjusts the colors in your graphics to create safe levels. See what happens when this filter is applied to the previous image: The modified color values are noted on each swatch.

In general, when you create titles and illustrations in RGB-based image editing and broadcast-design applications to be used in projects destined for broadcast video, keep in mind that you want to avoid very bright, very saturated colors and that primary and secondary colors (red, yellow) should be muted more than others. Lastly,

Figure 10.34 The level of the characters spelling "safe" is identical in both parts of the image. Relative contrast makes this light gray color appear white when placed against a black background.

although tools are available to help you manage the legality of your colors, you'll get better results if you yourself choose your palette carefully.

If you've been given a stack of graphics for your program and you don't have the time to reprocess them all, don't worry, you can always adjust them later in your color correction application. Just be aware that some darkening or desaturation of illegal colors may occur if you have to legalize a graphic or title after the fact.

BROADCAST-SAFE SETTINGS IN GRADING APPLICATIONS

In the event your grading application lacks a project-wide broadcast-safe or clipper setting, it may be desirable to apply a single set of legalizing adjustments to an entire sequence of clips in order to prevent unwanted excursions.

Applications that allow you to apply a single grade to an entire timeline make it possible to apply the kinds of adjustments described previously in order to add soft-clipping to compress excursions in the signal, highlight and shadow desaturation operations to tame chroma, or any other adjustment you think might be necessary to keep your program broadcast legal. Here are three examples of how this is handled in different applications:

- DaVinci Resolve has a Track Grade mode that lets you apply a single grade to an entire timeline. Within this grade, you can use the Soft Clip mode of the Curves palette to compress the highlights and shadows of the image to preserve more detail while clipping the upper and lower boundaries of the signal, as well as whatever other operations you think are necessary.

- Adobe SpeedGrade lets you add a superimposed *adjustment layer* to the timeline that affects as much of the timeline as you like. This adjustment layer can be graded using all of the tools that are available (including the fxLegalizeNTSC and fxLegalizePAL look layers) in order to legalize all clips in a program.

- FilmLight Baselight lets you stretch individual *grading strips* to cover an entire timeline (**Figure 10.35**), which you can use to apply grading operations, and legalizing LUTs that come bundled with Baselight.

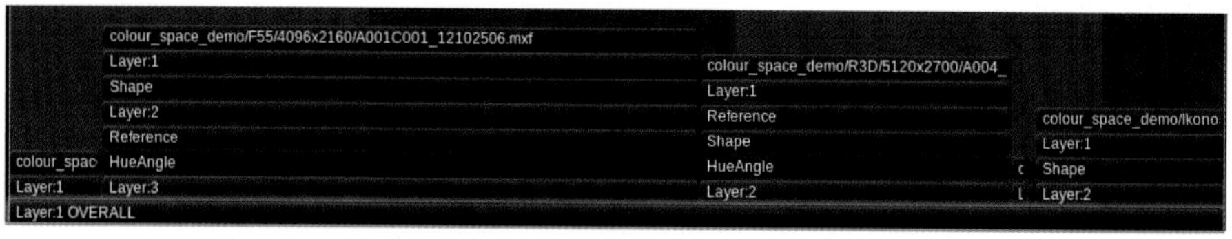

Figure 10.35 Stretching a grading strip in Baselight to cover the full duration of a spot to apply adjustments for broadcast legalization to the end of each grade in the program.

However you apply a broadcast-legalizing grade, you want to always make sure that it's the last operation that's applied to the image processing pipeline of the program.

LEGALIZING LUTS

Specialized lookup tables can also be applied as tools for legalizing video signals, clipping and compressing image data at the outer boundaries of what's allowable. For example, Baselight comes with three LUTs that can be used to legalize video being output as digital files or to tape.

- Full to Legal Scale
- Clip to Legal (HardClip in Baselight Editions)
- Soft Clip to Legal (SoftClip in Baselight Editions)

BROADCAST-SAFE SETTINGS IN EDITING APPLICATIONS

The majority of high-end color correction applications have traditionally not had broadcast legal settings built in. Although some have a simple clipper designed to limit maximum levels, reliably limiting RGB and Composite gamut and chroma components requires more sophisticated means of automatically manipulating the signal.

Although the responsible colorist heeds the issues presented earlier in this chapter and makes manual adjustments to exert the maximum control over the quality of the signal, broadcast-safe settings or clippers are a necessary safety net for automatically catching odd pixels that go out of bounds, as well as for forcing the clipping of parts of the signal that you want to deliberately blow out (in the highlights) or crush (in the shadows).

If your color correction application doesn't have clipping controls, then either you'll need to rely on a hardware legalizer capable of clipping the final video signal as it's output to a video deck for output or you'll need to send the corrected program media back to your NLE of choice for limiting there.

Most NLEs have one or more broadcast-safe filters or effects, which are designed to make automatic adjustments to the picture in order to limit illegal luma and chroma values.

Broadcast legalization is not an easy process, and although most broadcast-safe filters try their best, they're not meant to be used as across-the-board legalizers for uncorrected clips. In fact, most filters work best when they're applied to clips or sequences that have already been corrected via other means, and they're meant to be used as a precaution against stray values that might have gotten missed.

HARDWARE LEGALIZERS

If your work is usually output to tape, you may benefit more from a hardware legalizer (such as the Harris/Leitch DL-860) inserted between your video output interface and your recording deck. The advantage is that you gain real-time luma, chroma, and RGB limiting, and you don't have to worry too much about dealing with stray illegal pixels in your day-to-day color correction.

However, using a hardware legalizer does not excuse you from manually adjusting the individual clips in a program to enhance and bring out image detail and minimize color bleed and highlight blow-outs, all of which will most likely get rudely clipped by a hardware legalizer.

Also, not even hardware legalizers are foolproof all the time. You should get better results if you do at least a basic pass of legalization along with your other adjustments.

HOW TO APPLY BROADCAST-SAFE FILTERS IN EDITING APPLICATIONS

Ideally, you'll have corrected your program shot-by-shot first. Then, if you're pursuing a file-based finishing strategy, you'll typically send the rendered output from your color correction application back to your NLE, where you can apply the necessary broadcast-safe filters (along with any titles, animations, or other effects necessary for the finishing of your program) prior to rendering or otherwise outputting your final program file.

Most editing applications require you to apply broadcast-safe filters in one of two ways. You can apply one broadcast-safe filter to each clip that needs it in order to fix just individual clip issues using a variety of settings. Alternately, you can *nest* an entire program worth of clips inside another sequence (or create a *compound clip* of your entire timeline) and apply the broadcast-safe filter to the entire program so that a single group of settings affects everything all at once.

AVID MEDIA COMPOSER AND SYMPHONY BROADCAST-SAFE SETTINGS

For purposes of broadcast-legal monitoring, Avid has a group of Safe Color settings, a visual warning indicator, and a Safe Color effect that can be applied to clips or sequences for broadcast-legal limiting. Additionally, Avid's software is a capable color correction environment as well, with dedicated color correction effects and a set of built-in video scopes.

SAFE COLOR SETTINGS

The Avid Safe Color dialog contains three pairs of parameters, used by the Safe Color Warnings option for displaying a visible error icon when a clip goes out of bounds and also by the Safe Color Limiter effect as the default settings whenever a new instance of the effect is added to a clip or sequence.

- **Composite** (Low and High) lets you set lower and upper boundaries for the composite combination of luma and chroma. A pop-up menu lets you set whether to specify units in IRE or digital values (8- or 10-bit ranges are available).

- **Luminance** (Low and High) lets you set lower and upper boundaries for the luma component of the signal. A pop-up menu lets you set whether to specify units in IRE or digital values (8- or 10-bit ranges are available).

- **RGB Gamut** (Low and High) lets you set lower and upper boundaries for the RGB conversion of the signal. A pop-up menu lets you set whether to specify units in IRE or digital values (8- or 10-bit ranges are available).

Two pop-up menus to the right of the three sets of parameters described here let you either toggle Composite/Luma and RGB Gamut to be ignored or display Safe Color Warnings superimposed over the image in the source monitor.

SAFE COLOR WARNINGS

When the warning pop-up option is selected in the Safe Color settings, a color-coded icon appears superimposed over the program picture to indicate frames with out-of-bounds errors (**Figure 10.36**).

Figure 10.36 Safe color warning indicators in Avid Media Composer and Symphony.

Up to five indicators appear to show warnings for components that are out of bounds. Each indicator has three possible positions. The middle position indicates legal values for that component. The upper and lower positions indicate values that are either too high or too low. The indicators are color coded as follows:

- Yellow = Composite

- White = Luma

- Red = Red channel

- Green = Green channel

- Blue = Blue channel

SAFE COLOR LIMITER EFFECT

This effect uses the Safe Color settings as its defaults whenever it's applied. You can apply this effect directly to a segment within a sequence, or you can edit it into a superimposed video track in order to apply it over the entire range of your sequence, legalizing the entire program using one group of settings.

422 SAFE

This checkbox lets you choose between accuracy and speed by determining the precision of signal-limiting and chroma-subsampling calculations. Disabling this option speeds processing, giving you better real-time performance, but it may allow minor transients to escape legalization.

SOURCE MONITOR ANALYSIS

The Safe Color Limiter effect can display false colors in the source monitor to indicate what pixels are being clipped. Red, green, and blue indicate areas of the image affected by RGB gamut clipping. Yellow indicates composite errors that are being clipped, while white indicates luma excursions that are being clipped. This can be disabled if you like.

COMPOSITE/LUMA LEVELS

- **Composite L** and **H** let you set lower and upper boundaries for the composite combination of luma and chroma. A pop-up menu lets you set whether to specify units in IRE or digital values (8- or 10-bit ranges are available).
- **Luma L** and **H** let you set lower and upper boundaries for the RGB conversion of the signal. A pop-up menu lets you set whether to specify units in IRE or digital values (8- or 10-bit ranges are available).

RGB LEVELS

- **RGB Gamut L** and **H** let you set lower and upper boundaries for the RGB conversion of the signal. A pop-up menu lets you set whether to specify units in IRE or digital values (8- or 10-bit ranges are available).

ADOBE PREMIERE PRO BROADCAST-SAFE SETTINGS

Adobe Premiere Pro has two video filters for broadcast legal limiting, as well as a complement of built-in video scopes and a set of very capable color correction filters.

BROADCAST COLORS

The Broadcast Colors effect is simple, with three parameters for legalizing video clips.

- **Broadcast Locale** is a pop-up menu with options for the video standard of your media. Options include NTSC and PAL.

- **How to Make Color Safe** is a pop-up menu with options for two different ways of attenuating an out-of-bounds video signal and two ways of indicating out-of-bounds portions of the signal. Reduce Luminance darkens out-of-gamut pixels to legalize composite errors, while Reduce Saturation desaturates composite errors. Key Out Unsafe and Key Out Safe show you which parts of the image require correction and which do not so you can take steps manually.

- **Maximum Signal Amplitude (IRE)** lets you specify the maximum level of the video signal, in IRE. The range is 90–120 IRE.

VIDEO LIMITER

This effect provides more detailed controls for limiting out-of-bounds video signals.

- **Show Split View** gives you the option of displaying a split-screen of the corrected and uncorrected versions of the clip, which lets you evaluate the effect of limiting the signal on the picture.

- **Layout** is a pop-up menu that lets you determine the orientation of the corrected/uncorrected split-screen. The options are Horizontal or Vertical.

- **Split View Percent** lets you adjust the width of the corrected/uncorrected split-screen, defaulting to 50 percent.

- **Reduction Axis** is a pop-up menu that lets you select which signal components to legalize. The options are Luma, Chroma, Luma and Chroma, or Smart Limit, which legalizes the entire signal. The next two parameters' names will change based on the setting you choose.

- **Luma/Chroma/Signal Min** lets you set the minimum allowable video signal, depending on the setting of the Reduction Axis setting.

- **Luma/Chroma/Signal Max** lets you set the maximum allowable video signal, depending on the setting of the Reduction Axis setting.

- **Reduction Method** is a pop-up menu with options that let you define specific tonal ranges of the video signal in order to compress, rather than clip, the video signal. The options are Highlights Compression, Midtones Compression, Shadows Compression, Highlights and Shadows Compression, and Compress All (the default).

FINAL CUT PRO X BROADCAST-SAFE SETTINGS

Final Cut Pro X has a single effect for legalizing colors, named—creatively enough—Broadcast Safe. To make it work, you need to apply it in a specific way. As of version 10.0.9, all effects (or filters) that you apply to clips are applied *before* the color controls, according to the Final Cut Pro X image processing pipeline. That means there's no way you can apply a Broadcast Safe filter that will protect you from changes made to that clip via its Color parameters. You must first create a compound clip of the clips you want to legalize and apply the Broadcast Safe effect to the compound clip in order to legalize clips based on every adjustment that's applied to them.

The Broadcast Safe effect has three parameters.

- **Amount:** Specifies the maximum signal value, in percent, above which the signal will be legalized.

- **Video Type:** Lets you choose NTSC or PAL, depending on the standard of your program.

- **Fix Method:** Determines the way in which the signal will be reduced in order to legalize detected problems. There are two choices: Reduce Luminance, and Reduce Saturation.

FINAL CUT PRO 7 BROADCAST-SAFE SETTINGS

While this software has been abandoned by Apple in favor of Final Cut Pro X, as of this writing it's still in widespread use. In addition to a group of dedicated color correction filters suitable for high-quality color correction, Apple Final Cut Pro has a number of features for monitoring broadcast signal legality, including built-in video scopes, range checking options for giving you a simple warning when luma or chroma go out of bounds, and two filters that can be either individually applied to clips you want to legalized or applied to an entire nested sequence in order to legalize an entire program with one group of settings.

WHITE PROCESSING OF GRAPHICS IN FINAL CUT PRO 7

When legalizing projects using imported RGB graphics, Final Cut Pro 7 has a specific setting for determining how the maximum values of these media files are scaled, called Process Maximum White As, found in the sequence settings.

- **White (the default setting):** Final Cut Pro 7 remaps the white values in the imported image (255, 255, 255) to 100 percent digital, typically the maximum broadcast legal signal. This is the recommended setting for most projects.

- **Super-White:** Final Cut Pro 7 maps white (255, 255, 255) to 109 percent digital, scaling the color values to extend up into the super-white values supported by the $Y'C_BC_R$ color space. This setting is recommended only if you're trying to match super-white levels that already exist in other clips in that sequence and you have no intention of making the program broadcast legal.

Keep in mind that you can change this setting at any time, and all of the RGB clips and Final Cut Pro generators (including Title generators) in the sequence will be automatically updated to fit into the new luminance range.

RANGE CHECKING

Final Cut Pro 7 has two options, selectable from the View menu, for displaying warnings in the Viewer and Canvas to indicate values that are out-of-bounds. The thresholds for these warnings are not user-selectable.

- Range Check > Excess Luma displays a yellow exclamation point warning for frames with excessive luma over 100 percent. A green icon with an arrow pointed up indicates frames with luma values of 90 to 100 percent, while a green icon with a check mark indicates frames with legal chroma.

- Range Check > Excess Chroma displays a yellow exclamation point warning for frames with illegal chroma levels. A green icon with a check mark indicates frames with legal chroma. This option takes into account composite interactions between luma and chroma.

When either of these options is enabled, zebra stripes appear in the Viewer and/or Canvas to indicate which pixels have illegal values. Red zebra stripes correspond to values that are illegal, while green zebra stripes indicate pixels with close-to-illegal values.

If you're creating titles or graphics using one of Final Cut Pro 7's title generators, readjusting your colors for legal chroma is quite a bit easier, because you can change the colors used by a generator interactively while watching the range-checking zebra stripes and the vectorscope. Simply open the Text generator clip into the Viewer, click the Controls tab, and open the Start and End color control parameters to reveal the HSB sliders. From these sliders, you can interactively change the color values while watching the zebra stripes and vectorscope to make the colors legal.

When manually altering colors for broadcast legality, for any given color with illegal chroma, you can either lower its saturation or lower its brightness. As with video legal signals in general, you get into trouble when a portion of the image is both too bright and too saturated. How much you'll have to adjust each color depends on its hue. As you've seen, some hues become illegal more easily than others. Let your scopes be your guide, and remember to be *more* conservative with titles than you'd be with other images.

BROADCAST SAFE FILTER

The Broadcast Safe filter is a bit tricky in how it tries to keep values in your program legal. Instead of simply clamping oversaturated and overly bright values in your image, the filter attempts to make a series of different adjustments to preserve as much detail and saturation as possible, while limiting only what it needs.

- It compresses, rather than clamps, luma values above 100 percent when you are using one of the automatic modes, in an effort to preserve as much detail as possible. The resulting adjustment has a falloff from 100 to 95 percent.

- It gives you the option to darken regions of high saturation that appear above 50 percent in the Waveform Monitor, in an effort to minimize the amount of desaturation that's necessary to legalize portions of the image that are both oversaturated and bright.

- It attempts to desaturate images as little as possible, based on the brightness of the oversaturated pixels. It desaturates less in the midtones than in the highlights.

- It *does not* automatically reduce oversaturated blacks. You must do this yourself, if necessary, using the Desaturate Highlights/Lows filter.

- It *does no*t do a particularly good job of limiting illegal chroma values within the midtones of an image.

The Broadcast Safe filter has five groups of parameters, described in the next sections.

MODE

The Mode pop-up menu offers six options. Each setting is labeled with the maximum percentage of chroma that it allows.

Whenever you choose one of the bottom five presets from this pop-up menu, the custom sliders in the Luminance Limiting and Saturation Limiting sections are disabled, *except* for Reduce Chroma/Luma.

Although the amount of saturation limiting varies with the selected setting, each of these options limits luma to a maximum of 100 percent:

- **In-house** allows chroma saturation of up to 130 percent. For most broadcasters, this would allow unacceptably illegal values.

- **Normal** allows chroma saturation of up to 120 percent. For most broadcasters, this would allow unacceptably illegal values.

- **Conservative** allows chroma saturation of up to 115 percent. For most broadcasters, this would allow unacceptably illegal values.

- **Very Conservative** allows chroma saturation of up to 110 percent. This is probably an acceptable limit for more permissive broadcasters.

- **Extremely Conservative** allows chroma saturation of up to 100 percent only. In most cases, this is a good, conservative setting.

- **The Custom—Use Controls Below [may be unsafe] option** lets you use the sliders in the Luminance Limiting and Saturation Limiting sections to create custom limiting settings. These sliders are disabled if you choose any of the automatic settings from the Mode menu.

NOTE
Be aware that even though the sliders are disabled, they don't look disabled.

CHAPTER 10

LUMINANCE LIMITING

The parameters in the Luminance Limiting section let you customize how the luma component of the video signal is legalized.

- **Enable (Luminance Limiting)** turns on the three sliders in this group.

- **Clamp Above** determines two behaviors. All luma values between Start (Threshold) and Clamp Above are compressed down to the Max. Output value. Any luma value above this setting is clamped to the value specified by the Max. Output slider, in order to limit luma values that are so bright they would prevent smooth compression. In general, compressing preserves more detail than clamping, but it affects more of the image.

- **Max. Output** specifies the maximum luma value allowed by this filter. Any luma values that are higher are either compressed or clamped, according to the value of the Clamp Above slider.

- **Start (Threshold)** specifies the percentage at which to begin compressing illegal luma. Lowering this value results in a softer falloff between the legalized and nonlegalized portions of the image, but the resulting adjustment affects more of the image as a result.

SATURATION LIMITING

The parameters in the Saturation Limiting section let you customize how oversaturated values are compressed or limited.

- **Enable (Saturation Limiting)** turns on the first three sliders in this group.

- As with the luma controls, **Clamp Above** determines two behaviors. All chroma values between Start (Threshold) and Clamp Above are compressed, with the maximum value determined by Max. Output. Any chroma value above this setting is clamped to the value specified by the Max. Output slider.

- **Max. Output** specifies the maximum chroma value allowed by this filter. Any chroma values that are higher are either compressed or clamped, according to the value of the Clamp Above slider.

- **Start (Threshold)** specifies the percentage at which to begin compressing illegal chroma. Lowering this value results in a softer falloff between the legalized and nonlegalized portions of the image, but the resulting adjustment affects more of the image as a result.

REDUCE CHROMA/LUMA

Although part of the Saturation Limiting section of controls, the Reduce Chroma/Luma slider is always available, regardless of the Mode pop-up menu's setting.

Legalizing any image is going to alter it one way or another, but this slider lets you control the manner in which oversaturated portions of the image are legalized.

- Lowering this value desaturates illegal values more than darkening them.

- Raising this value darkens illegal values more than desaturating them.

For more control, there's also a dedicated RGB Limit filter (found in the Color Correction bin of the Video Filters), which provides options for clamping levels below a specific threshold, as well as for adjusting the method used for legalizing these areas of the signal (a sliding scale between desaturating the image or adjusting its luma levels).

RGB LIMITING

The parameters in this section allow for limiting of the RGB conversion.

- **Enable** turns on the one parameter in this group.

- **Max RGB Output Level** specifies the maximum allowable RGB signal components.

RGB LIMIT FILTER

There's also a dedicated RGB Limit filter with additional controls for RGB limiting. Each parameter can be individually enabled.

- **Clamp Levels Below** lets you specify a minimum RGB level.

- **Clamp Levels Above** lets you specify a maximum RGB level.

- **Desaturate** or **Darken Levels Above** works identically to the Reduce Chroma/ Luma slider in the Broadcast Safe filter, described earlier.

COLOR CORRECTION LOOK BOOK

Once you've digested the contents of *Color Correction Handbook*, *Color Correction Look Book* (www.peachpit.com/cclookbook) is the next step in learning about color grading. This follow-up volume focuses on how to create looks, walking you through a wide variety of creative grading techniques to give you an arsenal of stylizations you can pull out of your hat when the client asks for something special, unexpected, and unique.

The alphabetically organized techniques are the types of adjustments you'd make for music videos, advertising spots, and even re-creations and dream sequences within more conventionally graded programs, all of which will benefit from your ability to create something a little more wild. Each technique is highly customizable and can be tailored to suit your particular purposes. Most importantly, they're designed to be mixed and matched in order to create your own unique effects.

This preview presents three of the styles that are discussed in *Color Correction Look Book*, in their entirety. If you find them interesting, there's lots more that awaits you. In it, you'll learn about the following: bleach bypass looks, blue-green swap, blurred and colored vignettes, cross-processing simulation, day-for-night treatments, duotones and tritons, emulating film stocks, film looks other than grading flat looks and film flashing, flattened cartoon color, glows, blooms, and gauze looks, grain, noise, and texture, greenscreen compositing workflows, lens flaring and veiling glare, light leaks and color bleeds, monitor and screen glos, monochrome looks, sharpening, tints and color washes, undertones, vibrance and targeted saturation, and vintage film looks.

TINTS AND COLOR WASHES

Colours are light's suffering and joy.
Johann Wolfgang von Goethe (1749–1832)

One of the most basic stylizations in the colorist's repetoire is the tint, or color wash, when you just need to add *more*. The distinction between a tint or color wash and a color cast is a fine one, because both are caused by the same thing: the asymmetrical strengthening and weakening of an image's color channels above or below their original levels. Where digital grading is concerned, a tint is simply a deliberately severe color cast.

HOW DO CHROMATIC LENS FILTERS WORK?

Before we start looking at creating artificial tints, let's consider the original optical phenomena we're emulating. For years, cinematographers (and to a lesser extent, videographers) have been using optical filters to add a bit of color to images as they're recorded. To successfully re-create the effect of photographic filters in your grading application, it's helpful to understand how these filters—either chromatic or absorptive—affect the image.

- *Chromatic* filters warm or cool the color temperature of the image. With these filters, you can either correct for or create the quality of light as it appears at different times of the day.

- *Absorptive* filters increase the saturation of specific colors in the image; use them to emphasize a tone, such as the greens of foliage or the blues in the sky. When placed in front of the lens, absorptive filters block selected wavelengths of light while allowing others to pass. The result is a weakening of the color channels corresponding to the wavelengths being blocked, which introduces a deliberate color cast that affects the overall image as it's being recorded.

Seeing the effect is easier than describing it. **Figure 11.1** shows three versions of the same image. The top image was shot in afternoon daylight. Although the white balance of the video camera was manually set for daylight, the overall image is still warm given the quality of light.

NOTE
Wratten filters are named for Frederick Wratten, the English inventor who developed this system for optical filtration and sold his company to Eastman Kodak in 1912.

The middle image was shot using the same white balance setting but with a Wratten 85C filter placed over the lens. The Wratten 85C is a "warming" filter, because it blocks blues to emphasize a combination of reds and greens that provide an orange cast, similar to the light produced by lower tungsten color temperatures.

The lower image was shot with the same white balance and a cooling Wratten 80D filter, which emphasizes blues, similar to higher daylight color temperatures. The light blue cast neutralizes the warm tones in the image and renders "whiter" whites.

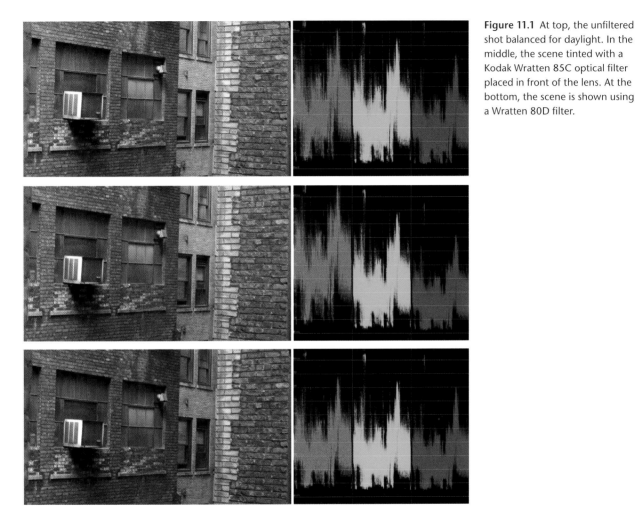

Figure 11.1 At top, the unfiltered shot balanced for daylight. In the middle, the scene tinted with a Kodak Wratten 85C optical filter placed in front of the lens. At the bottom, the scene is shown using a Wratten 80D filter.

HOW OPTICAL FILTERS AFFECT COLOR

There's more to optical filtration than color temperature. For example, the strength of an optical tint is nonlinearly applied across the tonal range of the image. This means that lighter portions of the image are more affected by the filter, while darker portions of the image are less affected. Regions of pure black are affected least of all.

To see this, compare an unfiltered and filtered chip chart side by side in the Parade Scope. In **Figure 11.2**, a standard broadcast chip chart was shot twice, once with a neutral white balance (left) and once with a Wratten 85 lens filter over the lens (right). Each chart was then positioned side by side for simultaneous analysis by an RGB Parade Scope.

Figure 11.2 A standard white balance chart shot with a neutral white balance (left) and a Wratten 85 lens filter (right).

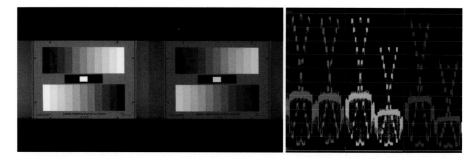

Looking closely at the pairs of bars at the top of the graph (which represent the brightest parts of the chip chart), you'll note several things.

- The left (unfiltered) and right (filtered) bars in the blue channel (the channel that is filtered the most) diverge quite widely, by approximately 29 percent.

- The bottom pairs of bars don't diverge nearly as much, with a maximum difference of about 4 percent in the blacks of the blue channel.

- You also can see that although the green channel is also filtered substantially, the red channel is virtually untouched.

Clearly, the filter is causing a strong color-channel imbalance in the highlights of the image that diminishes through the midtones, with almost no effect in the darkest shadows of the image.

HOW OPTICAL FILTERS AFFECT CONTRAST

Since optical filters block light, they affect an image's contrast as well; how much depends on the severity of the tint and the quality of the optics involved. As with color, this darkening is nonlinear, affecting the whites differently than the blacks.

Examine the resulting graph in the Waveform Monitor (**Figure 11.3**, right), and you'll see that the white points of each image differ by approximately 18 percent. The midpoint (represented by the gray bar appearing all the way to the right of each series) differs by approximately 13 percent, and the black points differ by only 3 to 4 percent. Typically, however, exposure is increased to compensate for this effect.

Figure 11.3 Unfiltered and filtered chip charts compared in the Waveform Monitor; notice how filtration reduces the overall amount of exposed light.

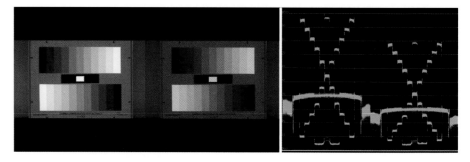

COLORED LIGHTING USING GELS

Instead of applying a filter to the camera lens, you can tint subjects indirectly by placing colored gelatin filters (called *gels*) directly in front of the scene's lighting instruments. The result is a more limited color cast that affects only the portions of the image being lit by the filtered instrument. As with lens filters, filtration done with gels is a subtractive process. In simple lighting situations—all lights are filtered with the same color of gel to create a uniform color temperature—the effect on the scene is similar to that of lens filtration.

You can simulate mixed lighting, with different color casts in various parts of an image resulting from different lighting fixtures, using HSL Qualification to isolate various regions of image tonality for discrete adjustment.

TINTING AND TONING FOR FILM

To the film preservationist, tinting and toning mean something quite different when applied to early methods for adding color to black-and-white motion picture photography. This will be covered in *Color Correction Look Book* in the chapter on vintage film looks, but for now know that these terms stem from specific film-colorization techniques. *Tinting and Toning of Eastman Positive Motion Picture Film* (Eastman Kodak, 1922) defines these terms very specifically:

- *Toning* is defined as "wholly or partially replacing the silver image of the positive film by some colored compound, so that the clear portions or highlights of the image, which consist of plain gelatine remains unaffected and colorless."

- *Tinting* is defined as "immersing the film in a solution of dye which colors the gelatine, causing the whole picture to have a uniform veil of color on the screen."

The digital colorist no longer needs to tone the blacks of an image using silver sulphide (for a sepia tone), or uranium ferrocyanide (for a red-orange tone), nor tint film highlights via immersion in an aniline dye solution. Today these processes can be achieved using image math and compositing modes.

ARTIFICIAL TINTS AND COLOR WASHES

When you want to tint an image, ask yourself how much of the image you want to affect and how extreme a tint you need. There's no wrong answer, just what's appropriate to the scene and the client's expectations. However, these questions will help you sort out which tinting method is best for the scene at hand:

- **To quickly wash color through the overall tonal range of the image:** Push the Offset control toward the color you want to wash into the image. Note that this operation will contaminate the blacks and whites, but you will achieve a mix of the color you're introducing with the original colors of the scene.

- **To create an extreme tint that still retains some of the original color:** Use a combination of the Midtones and/or Highlights color balance controls; or, take a version of the shot that's been monochromatically tinted, or a color generator or matte consisting of the tint color, and mix it into your shot using Hard Light or Add composite modes.

- **To replace all of the original color in the image with a monochromatic tint:** Desaturate the image with an initial correction, and then add color back in using the color balance controls (similar to the duotone technique demonstrated elsewhere in *Color Correction Look Book*). Using the Gain color balance control will tint the highlights, while using the Shadow color balance control will tone the shadows. Note that toning the shadows will invariably lighten them as the color mix will lift some of the color channels.

- **To tint a specific portion of the tonal range of the image:** Use the Luma control of an HSL Qualifier to isolate the tonal region of the image that you want to add the color cast to, and then use the appropriate color balance control to add as much or as little of the tint as you need. Or, use your application's Log controls (with customized control over the width of the shadow and highlight zones) or controls for customizing the tonal range of the Lift/Gamma/Gain controls. All these techniques are similar to the Undertones techniques shown previously in this chapter.

- **To tint only the highlights and midtones:** If your application supports Multiply, Overlay, or Soft Light composite modes, you can mix a color matte with the original with varying degrees of severity.

- **To tone only the shadows and midtones:** Use the Screen or Lighten composite modes to mix a color matte with the original image.

NOTE

This section covers tints and color washes as they're used in more modern contexts. For an understanding of how tinting and toning has been used historically, see the *Look Book's* chapter on vintage film looks.

BEWARE OF ILLEGAL LEVELS

Many of the composite modes covered in the next section easily create illegal luma or chroma levels. If broadcast legality is a priority, keep an eye on your scopes. If you're deliberately trying to create a bold look, do what you need to do and then compress and/or desaturate the highlights in a subsequent correction to make sure the final signal doesn't burden you with QC violations after you've delivered the show.

TINTING WITH COMPOSITE MODES

If you're not getting the results you're after using your application's color balance controls, you can try adding a color tint to your image using *composite modes* (also called *blending* or *transfer* modes). Composite modes work best when you're mixing a pure color generator, color matte, or color layer with the original image. The tint created using a composite mode can be moderated by either lowering the saturation or raising the brightness of the color being used or by using an opacity setting to render the superimposed color matte more transparent so that it contributes less to the final effect.

Some commonly used composite modes are shown in **Figure 11.4** (on the following page) affecting an image with an accompanying red color generator.

Your results will be vastly different depending on which composite mode you choose. The math each mode uses to combine the images determines how the tint applies and to which portions of your image it is limited. You don't need to understand this underlying math, but it's good to learn the effects some of the more common modes produce. Of the twelve commonly implemented composite modes, seven—Multiply, Screen, Overlay, Hard Light, Soft Light, Darken, and Lighten—are useful for tinting effects.

For more information about compositing or blending modes, including the mathematics behind their use, consult *The VES Handbook of Visual Effects* (Focal Press, 2010), which provides a list of "industry standard" formulas for each mode, referenced from the excellent www.dunnbypaul.net/blends/ page.

NOTE

Bear in mind that some composite modes are processor-intensive operations, so you may take a performance hit in using them. However, you can achieve unique color blends with this method that would be difficult to attain using other techniques.

PREVIEW

Figure 11.4 At top, the original image and color generator are shown. With the color generator superimposed over the image (my dog, Penny), the Multiply, Screen, Overlay, Soft Light, Darken, and Lighten composite modes are shown.

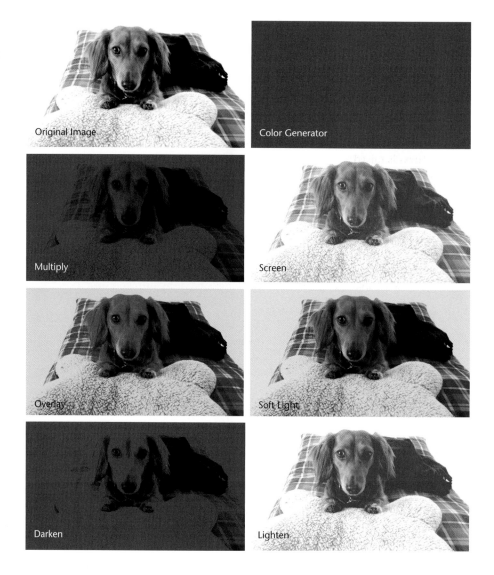

MULTIPLY

The Multiply composite mode is useful when you want a superimposed color matte to have the greatest effect on the whites of the image, with a diminished effect on the darker parts of the image and no effect at all on the black point. The white point literally becomes the tint color, and the midtones all become mixes of the original colors and the tint color. Absolute black is unaffected.

The Multiply composite mode multiplies the pairs of pixels from each image together. Any overlapping black areas remain black, and progressively darker areas of the clips darken the image. Overlapping white areas expose 100 percent of the opposing image.

This has a significant effect on the contrast of the image, with a tendency to darken that varies with the saturation and brightness of the color being superimposed. Unless your intention is to darken the image, the Multiply composite mode produces less extreme results when the superimposed color's saturation is reduced, and its brightness is raised.

SCREEN

The Screen composite mode is nearly the opposite of Multiply; it's useful when you want a superimposed color matte to have the greatest effect on the blacks of the image, with a diminished effect on the lighter parts of the image. The black point becomes the tint color, and the midtones become mixes of the original colors and the tint colors. Absolute white is slightly affected.

Screen is essentially the opposite of Multiply. Overlapping white areas remain white, and progressively lighter areas lighten the image. Overlapping black areas expose 100 percent of the opposing image. Like Multiply, Screen also has a significant effect on the contrast of the image, with a tendency to lighten that varies with the saturation and brightness of the color being superimposed. Reducing the brightness of the superimposed color is the best way to minimize this effect.

OVERLAY

The Overlay composite mode is one of the cleanest and most useful composite modes available for tinting an image. It combines the effects of the Multiply and Screen composite modes in an interesting way, screening portions of the image that are above 50 percent brightness and multiplying portions of the image that are below 50 percent brightness. The result is that the midtones of the image are affected the most, the white point is only slightly affected, and the black point remains unaffected.

An added benefit is that the Overlay composite mode's effect on the contrast of the underlying image is largely limited to the midtones and, to a lesser extent, the white point.

Lowering the saturation and/or raising the brightness of the superimposed color generator boosts the midtones and whites, and raising the saturation and/or lowering the brightness lowers the midtones and whites. Making these changes results in a nonlinear change to the distribution of the midtones.

NOTE

Because of the way it works, using Overlay with a superimposed color generator with a neutral gray color (0 percent saturation, 50 percent brightness) results in a minimal change to the image.

PREVIEW

HARD LIGHT

The Hard Light composite mode creates a more evenly distributed tint than the other composite modes, in that the tint has a significant effect on the whites, mids, and blacks of the image. It's most useful when you want to create an extreme tint. Unlike the Sepia or Tint filters, however, the tint color still interacts with the original colors from the underlying image.

The saturation and brightness of the superimposed color generator determine the degree to which different portions of the image are affected. Colors with higher saturation have a greater effect on the whites, and colors with higher brightness have a greater effect on the blacks.

The Hard Light composite mode also affects the contrast of the image, both lowering the white point and boosting the black point, as you can see in the Waveform Monitor. How the whites and blacks are affected by the superimposed color depends on the intensity of the color.

SOFT LIGHT

The Soft Light composite mode is a milder version of the Hard Light composite mode, with a significant difference—it has no effect on absolute black. It's useful when you want a more even wash of color over the whites and mids, and down into the blacks, but you want the absolute blacks of your image to remain unaffected.

The Soft Light composite mode's effect on the contrast of your image is similar to that of the Overlay composite mode.

DARKEN

Only the darkest of each overlapping pair of pixels contributes to the final image. The result is often more of a graphic effect than a tint, although the Darken composite mode can be used as a tool for creating other unusual looks, as seen in the "Flattened Cartoon Color" chapter of *The Look Book*.

LIGHTEN

The lightest of each overlapping pair of pixels contributes to the final image so that the brightest parts of each image are preserved. For tinting with a solid matte, this has the practical effect of flattening all of the shadow values darker than the superimposed matte to the overlapping color.

CREATING A COLOR MATTE FOR TINTING IF YOUR APPLICATION DOESN'T HAVE ONE

While tinting using a colored matte and composite modes is one of the oldest tricks in the book for NLEs and compositing applications, some grading applications lack the ability to create a colored matte, or at least to create a colored matte where you want one. If this is the case, don't fret; there's an easy bit of grading trickery you can pull to create one, without needing to import a colored still to use as a matte.

In the following example, you'll create a colored matte in DaVinci Resolve's node tree, for use in tinting. However, you can use this technique in any application.

1 As always, grade the application as needed prior to applying the tint.

2 To create the setup for this tint, you need to "superimpose" another correction in such a way as to use a composite mode to combine it with the previous corrections. In DaVinci Resolve, this is done using a Layer Mixer to combine two input nodes.

3 With the nodes (adjustments) set up, select the bottommost node (node 3 in **Figure 11.5**) and use any of the contrast controls to crush the entire video signal to clip at black.

4 Next—and this is important—use whatever controls are available to keep that data clipped. Most modern grading applications have a 32-bit floating-point image processing pipeline, which means data that gets clipped is preserved from operation to operation. You actually don't want this, since it will potentially ruin your nice flat matte, so in Resolve you can make a small adjustment to the Soft Clip curves, any adjustment really, to keep the crushed data clipped.

5 Add another adjustment after the one in which you clip the image (node 4 in Figure 11.5). This is where you'll turn the flat black field created in step 3 into a colored matte. Within this correction, use the Offset Master and Color Balance controls to turn the black image into any color you like.

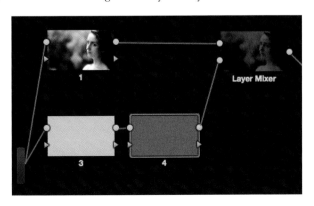

Figure 11.5 The node setup for creating a flat field of color and then combining it with the original image.

6 Finally, right-click the Layer Mixer node and choose a composite mode you want to use to apply the tint (Figure 11.5). In this example, the Multiply mode coupled with a deep red matte creates a vivid, graphic effect.

TINTING IN ADOBE SPEEDGRADE

Adobe SpeedGrade has a variety of look layers that employ these techniques without the need for a dedicated color matte. fxSepiaTone, fxTinting, and fxNight all provide different methods of tinting.

UNDERTONES

In visual perception a color is almost never seen as it really is—as it physically is. This fact makes color the most relative medium in art.
—Joseph Albers (1888–1976)

Undertones is the name I use for a particular commercial look that's especially popular with promos and that has, by its use in features, become associated with big-budget filmmaking.

A *tint* or *color wash* is a color cast that you apply to the overall image, even though it may deliberately not affect the highlights or shadows of an image. An undertone differs in that it's a color cast that you apply *very specifically* to a wedge of image tonality, often somewhere within the upper shadows of an image.

There are several different approaches you can take to creating undertones, each with different advantages.

UNDERTONES THROUGH CAREFUL GRADING

The easiest way to insert a limited zone of tinting into an image is to start by adding color throughout, using an indiscriminate tool such as the Offset color-balance control. Then you use neighboring color balance controls to eliminate unwanted color contamination from the shadows and highlights. The following example shows this in action within FilmLight Baselight (**Figure 11.6**).

Using the Film Grade's Offset control, a warm cast is added to the overall image, which adds color to the shadows and highlights as well. Switching to the ShadsMidsHighs tab, the Shadows and Highlights controls are then used to rebalance the tonal extremes of the image, limiting the tint to the middle.

Figure 11.6 Broad undertones achieved by adding color with the Offset color balance control and then neutralizing the shadows and highlights.

This isn't perhaps the most specific way to make this adjustment, but it's fast and easy to do with most applications and is useful when you want to add a broader undertone to the midtones of the image.

SPECIFIC UNDERTONES USING CURVES

The trick to creating undertones is to use a group of control points to add a tightly controlled boost or drop in a particular color channel of the image. For a more sophisticated look, try keeping the darker shadows in the image untinted so that there's some contrast between the tinted and untinted regions of shadow.

In **Figure 11.7**, you can see a fairly narrow boost to the green and blue channels created with three control points.

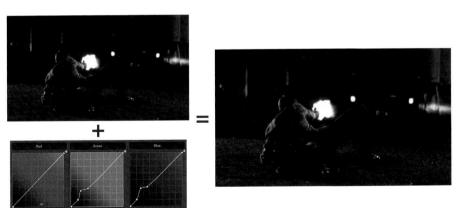

Figure 11.7 Using curves to create colored undertones in the upper shadows of the image, providing an extra splash of color.

Keep in mind that a curve is at its neutral position when it crosses the middle intersecting gridlines. When creating undertones, you want the majority of the curves to be at this neutral détente position.

The result of this selective boost is a blue-green undertone throughout the image that contrasts well with the natural color and lighting from the original scene. Also, by leaving the bottom blacks and upper midtones and highlights untouched, we give the image a clean vibrancy that it wouldn't otherwise have if we'd gone with a more aggressive tint.

This technique is useful for creating a bit of color contrast to spice up an otherwise chromatically uninteresting scene, assuming the situation and the client's tastes merit it.

This is a good way of creating undertones because of the smooth mathematical rolloff that the curves provide; you're unlikely to easily spot crunchy or chattering edges where your color undertones meet the untouched neutrality of the rest of the image.

SPECIFIC UNDERTONES USING LOG CONTROLS OR FIVE- AND NINE-WAY COLOR CONTROLS

Log-style controls, described in Chapter 4 of *Color Correction Handbook*, can be used with normalized image data to insert color into very specific tonal zones. They're useful for this technique as well, should your grading application have them. For example, **Figure 11.8** has a dark, high-contrast grade that the client would like to give a greenish-blue tinge to, in the shadows.

Figure 11.8 The original grade, before adding undertones.

Adding a layer after these initial grades and using the Film Grade operator lets you use the Shadows, Contrast, and Highlights pivot controls to limit the tonal zone that will be affected by the Midtones control-balance control so you can add a bit of color to tint just the light shadows of the image (**Figure 11.9**).

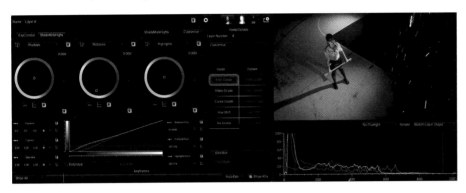

Figure 11.9 Using the Film Grade in Baselight to add undertones to the light shadows of the image. Notice how the LUT graph shows you what zone of image tonality you're affecting based on the settings of the pivot controls.

Similarly, if your application has five-way grading such as the "Bands" in SGO Mistika (**Figure 11.10**, top), or selectable nine-way controls as used in Autodesk Lustre and Adobe SpeedGrade (Figure 11.10, bottom), you can use their customizability to accomplish the same thing. For example, when you switch to the Shadows, Midtones, or Highlights tonal ranges in the Look tab of SpeedGrade, M/H (Midtones/Highlights) and S/M (Shadows/Midtones) sliders let you redefine the border of overlap between each of the three tonal regions of the image.

Using these sliders, you can limit all of the primary controls of the Look tab to a narrow zone of image tonality.

Figure 11.10 Shadows, Midtones, and Highlights controls used in Adobe SpeedGrade (top), and Bands controls used in SGO Mistika (bottom), for making color adjustments in limited regions of image tonality.

PREVIEW

EXCLUDING SKIN TONE FROM SINGLE-OPERATION UNDERTONES GRADES

A common technique—especially when you're using an aggressive color for your undertones that might not necessarily be flattering when overlaid onto the people within the frame—is to deliberately exclude all skin tones from the affected area where you're applying undertones.

How you accomplish this depends on the functionality of your grading application, but if you're creating undertones within a single-operation adjustment, an extremely simple way of fixing this is to use your HSL qualifier to isolate the skin tones of the image as best you can and then invert the resulting key (**Figure 11.11**). This assumes that your grading application is capable of limiting whichever controls you used to create the undertones. However, using your qualifier to omit part of the picture from being affected by the undertone operation is a quick way of dealing with this issue.

Figure 11.11 Using the HSL qualifier within the same operation used to created colored undertones to omit skin tone from the adjustment.

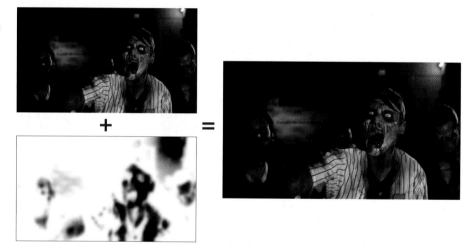

As has been said many times before, you do not need a perfect key when isolating skin tone for this type of adjustment. What you care most about are the visible midtones and highlights of skin, so those parts of your key should be solid. However, shadows would be plausibly affected by the undertone, so omitting them isn't the worst thing in the world. Furthermore, feathering the skin isolation using your HSL qualifier's soft and/or blur controls helps keep colored contouring and jagged edge artifacts from creeping into the image.

THE HAZARDS OF SKIN TONE OMISSION

Keep in mind that when you indulge in this type of skin tone holdout, you're increasing the visibility of your image segmentation. Overdoing the difference between the undertone and the untouched skin tone of the image will look increasingly artificial, so you might consider adding a little bit of the undertone to the actors in frame just to keep them "in the scene."

SPECIFIC UNDERTONES USING HSL QUALIFICATION

A different strategy is to use a Luma qualifier to isolate a range of darker midtones or lighter shadows to which to add your colored undertone (**Figure 11.12**).

Figure 11.12 Isolating a thin wedge of image tonality using HSL Qualification in order to create a color undertone.

When using HSL Qualification to create undertones, it's a good idea to feather the matte well using the tolerance or softening handles of the Luma qualifier. This gives a nice smooth transition from the tinted to the untinted portion of the image, without the haloing that excessive blurring of the matte might cause. Even so, adding a bit of blur afterward to smooth out the remaining rough patches of your key is usually a good idea.

This method allows you to use the three-way color balance controls, which make it easier to get the range of color you want. However, these controls work best when you're able to pull a clean key.

EXCLUDING SKIN TONE FROM
MULTI-OPERATION UNDERTONES

If you're creating undertones using HSL Qualification, then you'll need to combine a second HSL Qualification operation with a Boolean operation to subtract the skin tone key from the undertone key. Different applications handle this in different ways, but here's a look at how to accomplish this using the Key Mixer in DaVinci Resolve.

First, you need to set up a node tree that will allow you to pull two keys off of your initial correction, combine them using a Key Mixer node, and then feed the resulting mask into the Key input of the final node you'll be using to actually perform the undertone adjustment. (Note that the Key input is the small triangular input at the bottom-left of each node.) **Figure 11.13** shows this setup.

Figure 11.13 One possible node setup for subtracting a key of the woman's face from the undertones key we'd created earlier, using the Key Mixer.

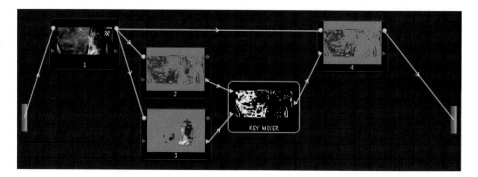

Figure 11.14 provides a closer look at this process. The top-left key is the original undertone mask. The bottom-left key is a key pulled off of the woman's face.

Figure 11.14 Subtracting the face matte from the undertone matte.

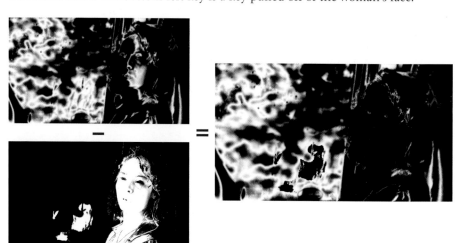

To actually perform the subtraction, you need to select the connection line running from node 3 to the Key Mixer node (highlighted yellow in Figure 11.13) and then open the Key tab (found within the Color page) so the controls are labeled "Input Link 2." Click the Invert checkbox, and then click the Mask radio button (**Figure 11.15**); the second mask will be subtracted from the first, as shown in the right image of Figure 11.14.

Figure 11.15 Inverting and setting the second key to Mask in Resolve's Key tab to subtract the second key from the first using the Key Mixer node.

This results in clean, untouched skin tones, even as the background of the van and the image outside the window are still affected by the bluish undertones (**Figure 11.16**).

Figure 11.16 The final effect: undertones throughout the background, excluding the foreground actor from the effect.

PREVIEW

UNDERTONES NEED NOT ONLY BE GREEN

While the "promo" look very often involves throwing an olive green undertone into an image, this technique is more versatile than that. For example, if you're trying to do a blue-tinged day-for-night look, this is a good way to introduce a bit of blue to the image without tinting it massively.

VIBRANCE AND TARGETED SATURATION

Full, saturated colours have an emotional significance I want to avoid.
—Lucian Freud (1922–2011)

A simple linear increase in saturation throughout the entire image doesn't always produce the most attractive result. However, an increase in saturation in a specific region of saturation intensity can create much more interesting and lively effects, so long as you target the right parts of the image.

VIBRANCE

Photographic applications such as Adobe Lightroom have a saturation control that's targeted at low-saturation color in an image. This control is referred to as *vibrance*, which typically excludes highly saturated areas of the image, as well as skin tones, letting you subtly enrich an image without oversaturating it.

If your application doesn't have a vibrance control, there are other ways of achieving the same result. For example, SGO Mistika has a Saturation vs. Saturation curve that lets you make targeted saturation adjustments based on the saturation within the image (**Figure 11.17**). This is an extremely flexible control that lets you make many other kinds of adjustments.

Figure 11.17 The Sat vs. Sat curve in SGO Mistika.

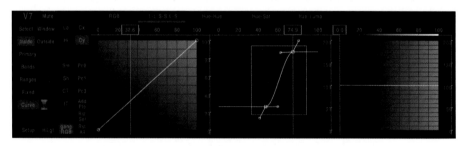

Lacking that, the HSL qualifier of your application can be used to create a custom vibrance effect. Simply turning off the Hue and Luma controls leaves you with a Saturation qualifier that you can use to target areas of middle-to-low saturation in your image.

When you do this operation, the actual range of saturation in your image may seem quite narrow, depending on how saturation is mapped onto the qualifier controls. In **Figure 11.18**, the middling saturation is isolated, with the band of saturation appearing far to the left of the qualifier.

Figure 11.18 Isolated saturation, far to the left of the HSL qualifier.

It's important, in order to avoid introducing contouring artifacts, to keep the edges of the qualified range of saturation feathered using the qualifier softness controls and possibly with a bit of blur applied to the key as well. Also, be careful not to contaminate the shadows of the image with an undue amount of saturation; the idea is to saturate only the lower and middle regions of saturation in order to give a colorful boost without overdoing areas of the image that shouldn't be more saturated than they already are (**Figure 11.19**).

Figure 11.19 Left to right: the original image, the image with a "vibrance" operation applied to increase the saturation of only a narrow range of low-saturation values, and the same saturation increase applied to the entire image.

Another caveat is that this operation can sometimes have an overbearing effect on skin tones. This can be remedied, but omitting skin tone from this operation depends on your grading application's ability to subtract one key from another. For example, you can subtract one key from another in DaVinci Resolve via the Key Mixer (**Figure 11.20**). When you do this, be sure that you've omitted skin tone shadows from the operation, since any fringing could end up oversaturated, looking problematic.

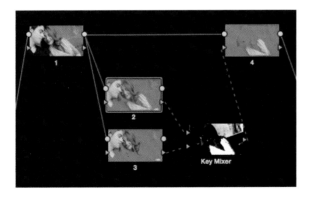

Figure 11.20 Omitting skin tone using the Key Mixer in DaVinci Resolve.

A vibrance operation, especially when used in conjunction with images that have darker colors, can be a great way to get beautiful deep colors that don't feel exaggerated.

TARGETING HIGH SATURATION

On the other hand, Giles Livesey, colorist of *Lara Croft: Tomb Raider, Shaun of the Dead*, and commercial spots too numerous to count, shared another technique for specific saturation adjustment: targeting regions of high saturation and intensifying the saturation of these areas even more to achieve a commercial look.

This is done in the same way as creating your own vibrance effect, by doing a Saturation-only qualification and isolating only the highest-saturated regions of the image, being sure to use the softening of the qualifier to keep the edges nicely feathered. With this done, you can now pump up the saturation, as shown in **Figure 11.21**).

Figure 11.21 Before and after a saturation boost to only the high-saturation parts of the image.

This seems to be particularly effective with glossy product shots, giving the images an almost "lickable" quality, if I can draw upon some old Apple marketing for adjectives. However, it can also be a good way to add a sheen of saturation to other types of shots when you're looking for a little something extra but you don't want to make the image look plastic all over (Figure 11.19).

Keep in mind when you use this technique that you can easily exceed the boundaries of broadcast safe, so be sure to keep your hand on the clipper if this is important.

INDEX

THE ESSENTIAL COMPANION TO
COLOR CORRECTION HANDBOOK

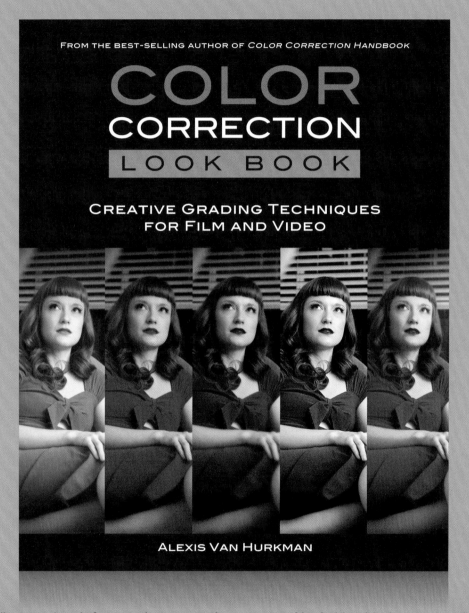

In this follow-up book from color correction master Alexis Van Hurkman, you'll learn to create jaw-dropping film looks with a wide variety of inspiring grading techniques.

COLOR CORRECTION LOOK BOOK:
CREATIVE GRADING TECHNIQUES FOR FILM AND VIDEO

by Alexis Van Hurkman

Peachpit Press, ISBN: 0321988183